ROUTLEDGE INTERNATIONAL HANDBOOK OF RESEARCH METHODS IN DIGITAL HUMANITIES

This book draws on both traditional and emerging fields of study to consider what a grounded definition of quantitative and qualitative research in the Digital Humanities (DH) might mean; which areas DH can fruitfully draw on in order to foster and develop that understanding; where we can see those methods applied; and what the future directions of research methods in Digital Humanities might look like.

Schuster and Dunn map a wide-ranging DH research methodology by drawing on both 'traditional' fields of DH study such as text, historical sources, museums and manuscripts, and innovative areas in research production, such as knowledge and technology, digital culture and society and history of network technologies. Featuring global contributions from scholars in the United Kingdom, the United States, Europe and Australia, this book draws together a range of disciplinary perspectives to explore the exciting developments offered by this fast-evolving field.

Routledge International Handbook of Research Methods in Digital Humanities is essential reading for anyone who teaches, researches or studies Digital Humanities or related subjects.

Kristen Schuster is Lecturer in Digital Humanities, King's College London.

Stuart Dunn is Senior Lecturer in Digital Humanities at King's College London. He is also a Visiting Scholar in Stanford University's Center for Spatial and Textual Analysis's Spatial History project.

ROUTLEDGE INTERNATIONAL HANDBOOKS

Routledge Handbook of Counter-Narratives
Edited by Klarissa Lueg and Marianne Wolff Lundholt

Routledge Handbook of Art, Science, and Technology Studies
Edited by Hannah Star Rogers, Megan K. Halpern, Kathryn de Ridder-Vignone, and Dehlia Hannah

Routledge Handbook of Bounded Rationality
Edited by Riccardo Viale

Routledge International Handbook of Charisma
Edited by José Pedro Zúquete

Routledge International Handbook of Working-Class Studies
Edited by Michele Fazio, Christie Launius, and Tim Strangleman

Routledge Handbook of Digital Media and Communication
Edited by Leah A. Lievrouw and Brian D. Loader

Routledge International Handbook of Religion in Global Society
Edited by Jayeel Cornelio, François Gauthier, Tuomas Martikainen and Linda Woodhead

The Routledge Handbook on the International Dimension of Brexit
Edited by Juan Santos Vara and Ramses A. Wessel; Assistant Editor, and Polly R. Polak

Routledge Handbook of Critical Finance Studies
Edited by Christian Borch and Robert Wosnitzer

For more information about this series, please visit: www.routledge.com/Routledge-International-Handbooks/book-series/RIHAND

ROUTLEDGE INTERNATIONAL HANDBOOK OF RESEARCH METHODS IN DIGITAL HUMANITIES

Edited by
Kristen Schuster and Stuart Dunn

LONDON AND NEW YORK

First published 2021
by Routledge
2 Park Square, Milton Park, Abingdon, Oxon OX14 4RN

and by Routledge
52 Vanderbilt Avenue, New York, NY 10017

Routledge is an imprint of the Taylor & Francis Group, an informa business

© 2021 selection and editorial matter, Kristen Schuster and Stuart Dunn
individual chapters, the contributors

The right of Kristen Schuster and Stuart Dunn to be identified as the authors of the
editorial material, and of the authors for their individual chapters, has been asserted in
accordance with sections 77 and 78 of the Copyright, Designs and Patents Act 1988.

All rights reserved. No part of this book may be reprinted or reproduced or utilised
in any form or by any electronic, mechanical, or other means, now known or
hereafter invented, including photocopying and recording, or in any information
storage or retrieval system, without permission in writing from the publishers.

Trademark notice: Product or corporate names may be trademarks or registered trademarks,
and are used only for identification and explanation without intent to infringe.

British Library Cataloguing-in-Publication Data
A catalogue record for this book is available from the British Library

Library of Congress Cataloging-in-Publication Data
A catalog record has been requested for this book

ISBN: 978-1-138-36302-1 (hbk)
ISBN: 978-0-429-77702-8 (ebk)

Typeset in Bembo
by Cenveo® Publisher Services

CONTENTS

Acknowledgements	viii
Research methods in the digital humanities: General introduction *Stuart Dunn and Kristen Schuster*	1

SECTION I
Computation and connection

11

1	Get some perspective: Using physical objects in the Glucksman Gallery to capture interdisciplinary stories of online teaching and learning *Briony Supple*	13
2	Digital aptitude: Finding the right questions for dance studies *Hetty Blades and Scott deLahunta*	31
3	(Critical) artistic research and DH *Sally-Jane Norman*	46
4	"A picture paints a thousand words": Hand-drawn network maps as a means to elicit data on digitally mediated social relations *Cornelia Reyes Acosta*	62
5	Multi-sited ethnography and digital migration research: Methods and challenges *Sara Marino*	76
6	Modelling and networks in digital humanities *Øyvind Eide*	91

Contents

7 Charting cultural history through historical bibliometric research:
Methods; concepts; challenges; results 109
Simon Burrows and Terhi Nurmikko-Fuller

8 Manage your data: Information management strategies for DH practitioners 125
Kristen Schuster and Vanessa Reyes

9 The library in digital humanities: Interdisciplinary approaches to digital materials 137
Paul Gooding

SECTION II
Convergence and collaboration 153

10 Humans in the loop: Epistemology and method in King's Digital Lab 155
James Smithies and Arianna Ciula

11 The Warburg Iconographic Database: From relational tables
to interoperable metadata 173
Richard Gartner

12 Information communication technologies, infrastructure and research
methods in the Digital Humanities 190
A.J. Million

13 Mapping socio-ecological landscapes: Geovisualization as method 203
Foka Anna, Cocq Coppélie, Buckland Phillip I. and Gelfgren Stefan

14 GIS for language study 218
William A. Kretzschmar, Jr. and Alexandra Petrulevich

SECTION III
Remediation and transmission 237

15 (Digital) research practices and research data: Case studies in communities
of sociolinguistics and environmental humanities scholars 239
Vicky Garnett and Eliza Papaki

16 Computational methods for semantic analysis of historical texts 261
Barbara McGillivray

17 Encoding and analysis, and encoding as analysis, in textual editing 275
Christopher Ohge and Charlotte Tupman

Contents

18 Opening the 'black box' of digital cultural heritage processes:
Feminist digital humanities and critical heritage studies   295
Hannah Smyth, Julianne Nyhan and Andrew Flinn

19 How to use Scalar in the classroom   309
Christopher Gilman, Jacob Alden Sargent and Craig Dietrich

20 Discovering digital humanities methods through pedagogy   331
Kristen Mapes

21 Course design in the digital humanities   353
Benjamin Wiggins

22 Crowdsourcing in cultural heritage: A practical guide to designing
and running successful projects   363
Mia Ridge

23 E-Learning in the digital humanities: Leveraging the Internet
for scholarship, teaching and learning   384
Rebecca A. Croxton

24 Eye tracking for the evaluation of digital tools and environments:
New avenues for research and practice   399
Dinara Saparova

25 What ethics can offer the digital humanities and what the digital
humanities can offer ethics   416
Nicholas Proferes

26 Intellectual property guidelines for the digital humanities   428
Kenneth Haggerty

27 Practicing goodwill ethics within digital research methods   441
Brit Kelley

Index   455

ACKNOWLEDGEMENTS

We would like to thank the authors who contributed their time and expertise so generously to this volume. We are also very grateful to Hannah Shakespeare and her team at Routledge, who have been a constant source of patient support.

RESEARCH METHODS IN THE DIGITAL HUMANITIES
General introduction
Stuart Dunn and Kristen Schuster

Introduction

In his 1965 classic satire of sex, Catholicism and the PhD, *The British Museum is Falling Down*, David Lodge describes an evening sherry party in the Comparative Literature department of an unnamed central London university. At the event, the Head of the Department sits in a corner, drinking with the two technicians who look after his pride and joy—a computer which generates concordances of texts. Only very senior members of academic staff dare to approach this coterie; most would never be admitted.

This literary depiction paints a picture of a conventional (humanities) research environment with its own rules, power structures and modi operandi; in which those who can work a computer— the "technicians"— are afforded a special, privileged access to the environment's intellectual and social apex. Yet admission is granted on restricted terms: they provide support and assistance, acting as accelerators and amplifiers of the Professor's achievements, which are in turn embedded in (and reinforced by) the social structures on display. Their reward is a purely transactional one for services rendered, *services* being the operative term. And they would certainly never be drawn on the meanings and interpretations of concordances they produced for the field of Comparative Literature.

In contrast, at the same time as this book was written, researchers, practitioners and scholars were beginning to ask questions about the impact of nascent computational networks of communication on the knowledge they enabled; and how these might drive, enable, or even determine human decision making, and indeed human thought itself. In 1960, five years before the publication of *The British Museum is Falling Down*, the US scientist and administrator J. C. R. Licklider, published his revolutionary paper, *Man Computer Symbiosis*, a vision of how automation would shape thinking in the future:

> *In one sense of course, any man-made system is intended to help man, to help a man or men outside the system. If we focus upon the human operator(s) within the system, however, we see that, in some areas of technology, a fantastic change has taken place during, the last few years. "Mechanical extension" has given way to replacement of men, to automation, and the men who remain are there more to helped than to be helped.*
>
> (Licklider 1960: 4)

Several chapters in the volume that follows address the techno-historical context highlighted by Licklider's heavily gender-biased use of language, and place it in a more twenty-first century context; but for the volume's more immediate purposes it describes a systemic process of knowledge creation in which human cognition and reasoning, and the fully automated processes that were once carried out by machines, came together as mutually interdependent parts of the same knowledge process, rather than being methodologically separated (as was the work of the Head of the Department and his technicians). We would argue that much the same description applies to today's DH. DH is a coming together of "the Digital", a field comprised of its own traditions of new media, science and technology studies, information science and so on; and "the Humanities", a collective intellectual term with all its problematic epistemological complexity.

Like many who have gone before us, we choose not to directly tackle the question "what is DH". There is a plethora of differing schools of thought that would take issue with any definition we might venture; however approaching the question in the framework of a methodological handbook—rather than a research anthology—allows us to consider it as one of *method* and *methodology* (more on the distinction between those two words below), rather than one of abstract nomenclature. This allows us to particularize based on what scholars across both "the Digital" and "the Humanities" actually <u>do</u> in their day-to-day practice, and how that practice combines the role of both humans and machines (and media). Articulating the ways in which the symbiotic knowledge systems which result are formed enables us to characterize the concept of a research method as a formalized way of doing things, drawing on multiple perspectives, but expressed in a shared language.

Collaboration: Problems and opportunities (or a problematic opportunity)

The argument that DH has a particular methodology or research method is not new. There is a plethora of conference proceedings (e.g. ACM Symposium on Document Engineering) , edited volumes and special journal issues, such as *Debates in the Digital Humanities*, and email lists like SHARP-L, Cambridge Digital Humanities and the Humanist that explain, debate and analyse what DH is, and what DH methods are (or should be). Among all of these opinions and projects, there is a consensus that DH is interdisciplinary and collaborative. However, something is missing from this deluge of opinions, arguments and theories. What are missing are efforts to describe what exactly interdisciplinary, collaborative and cooperative work does to the ways which academics explain their research methods and methodologies. What is more, there is an almost wilful lack of nuance in differentiating between disciplines within DH. Failing to acknowledge disciplinary differences at the very least foreshortens conversations about the particular approaches scholars from say history, literature, philosophy or art history use to organize and carry out digital research; and what is more, this lack of differentiation foreshortens or overlooks why and how scholars use "the Digital" to create and interrogate digital media.

Why the lack of nuance, one might ask? We argue that it is partly due to a fascination with, and need to explain how, digital technologies and digital media came to be, and how these have taken over 'modern' life. There are a plethora of texts, articles, conference proceedings (etc.) that explore the shift from analogue to digital (or what some might call the digital turn) (Anderson & McPherson, 2011; Haugen & Apollon, 2014 and McGill, 2016); and an equal amount of work discussing why this turn continues to cause widespread scholastic and popular anxieties (see Gailey, 2012; Apollon & Belisle, 2014 and Flanders & Munoz, 2014).

It is of course also possible to discuss the evolution and present state of research methods in the humanities without ever discussing "the digital". However, it is impossible to discuss *DH* of any disciplinary flavour without considering "the digital" in its own right. Considering DH research methods in this way constitutes a logical endpoint (or perhaps waypoint) in the trajectory that those methods have taken since Licklider's famous intervention in 1960 (which, incidentally, is also regarded as a key milestone in the chain of research and development which led, eventually to the early Internet itself). We argue that such a critical perspective on "the digital" allows us to explore the question of whom humanists collaborate with and why. This new diversity conveys an interesting challenge: we do not need to just be interdisciplinary amongst other humanists. We need to become interdisciplinary with people who have radically different perspectives, experiences, training and skills. Thus, this volume approaches DH by seeking perspectives on method both from inside and outside its conventional hinterland.

The differences we perceive across these traditions are real, but perhaps they aren't as substantial—or as intellectually divisive—as we imagine. The fact that there are differences offers an opportunity for learning and sharing, and this is one of the foundational goals of this volume. Thus, we do not seek to simply present DH projects or a humanistic interpretation of the digital. We want to promote an interdisciplinary perspective on humanistic forms of inquiry, and to bring the humanities, social sciences and computer sciences into conversation. And, to reach a bit further while making another bold claim: this sort of proximity and interaction might present an opportunity for building a *methodology grounded in negotiation*—but not necessarily the reconciliation—of very different syntactical and semantic schemes for producing research.

The remainder of this general introduction is dedicated to describing the scope and structure of the volume. We will discuss the themes we used to collect and then organise contributions and discuss terminology we perceive as problematic but useful for characterizing DH practice, research and teaching. DH has a long history, but beyond the context provided above, the volume does not seek to penetrate deeply into this history. There are plenty of volumes already that cover this ground, and share research about the evolution of DH (see Dalbello, 2011; Kirschenbaum, 2012; Robinson, 2013 and Sayers, 2016), and, as we have already mentioned, there are email lists aplenty to subscribe to for up-to-date debates and opinions there are also regular conferences (e.g. DH Benelux, the annual international Digital Humanities Conference, New Directions in the Digital Humanities) that provide a fora for discussions and debates about DH. Instead, we intend to explore and contextualize the different research methods and methodologies present in DH work and research. This exploration will, we hope, contextualize strategies practitioners, teachers and researchers can use to engage with DH.

Research methods or research methodologies?

First, however, we set out our perspective on how research methodologies are constructed across different approaches. The distinction between a method and a methodology is a well-rehearsed theme in the social sciences, where the former is seen as a tool for accomplishing research and the latter the rationale for using that tool. We do not depart from this view. However, we would refine it by arguing that a research *methodology* in DH is conceptually similar to metadata, the descriptive formats and frameworks that librarians and data curators use to structure and organize digital collections and formalize their rationale. In the same way that metadata provides a formal structure for datasets, defining their attributes according to existing standards, vocabularies or practices, methodology provides a prescribed structure for research methods. Etymologically this is the effect of the suffix λόγος, "-logos", a description which conforms to a logical pattern and applies it to an individual method. Methods are thus the structure we create for our research, which gives it shape. To be more precise, this structure is not the semantics of a project (which do not have to conform to formal standards), it is instead the syntax (which do).

Semantics, one could argue, are the underlying principles and concepts we use to determine *why* something needs structuring and *why* this structure will help us convey meaning to a wider audience. In the context of this particular metaphor (unorganized) semantics represent the <u>need</u> for research methodologies. In this case, to belabour the metaphor, semantics help us express the philosophical or ontological point of view we are drawing on to validate the steps we take (the research methods we use) to identify populations, cultivate a sample and organize any data we might collect.

Situating the question in the context of this distinction between semantics and method, how do research methods (as opposed to semantics) in DH emerge? One answer is repetition. If something works with the analysis of a particular type of research material, then it gains traction in the research community, it is repeated, and the cycle continues. Furthermore, repetition for the sake of revisiting to check understanding, repetition for the sake of clarifying, repetition for the sake of synthesizing and representing points of view, all enable semantic clarification and, possibly, rhetorical inclusion and expansion. This is a drawn out way of saying that repetition can help us notice details that can clarify and establish our point of view, communicate this point of view and (if we are very persistent) convince people we have a good point and persuade them to agree with us.

Shared methodological understandings, derived by communities through processes of negotiation, alignment and, yes, disagreement are essential for the development of disciplinary identity. Shared practices help us build disciplinary identities because they allow us to synthesize, but not conflate, the two processes. Synthesis here implies that there are differences that create friction. Any practitioner will pause here and roll their eyes about pedantic researchers, and researchers will pause and give an exasperated sigh about the lack of philosophical rigor in practice. This tension creates a unique space to reflect on identities, and we would like to encourage readers to use research methods to start considering why these identities matter, and to start discussing them more regularly and openly.

Computation, convergence, remediation

In order to construct a narrative about DH without explaining what DH 'is', we employ three themes to organize our narrative: *computation*, *convergence* and *remediation*. These are subdivided into further categories, with varying levels of epistemological definition. We chose these themes because they are relevant to multiple disciplines that contribute to DH, and despite their appearance across these disciplines these concepts do not seem to have a fixed or agreed upon meaning. Broadly speaking, they cover respectively the creation of knowledge, the alignment of knowledge, and the transmission of knowledge from one mode, platform, language or format to another. This, we argue, allows us to elaborate a picture of DH as a means of *doing*, rather than basing it on abstract boundaries separating what is and what is not DH. While we continue to look at projects and discuss their evolution, we examine how these projects define media and the ways technology facilitate their creation, preservation and re-use. Or, in a more succinct statement: how technology facilitates curation.

The fact that each concept illustrates a matter of *process* rather than *output* from different perspectives is, we argue, telling of how badly we need to discuss research methods at large instead of research outputs. Considering research as a process, rather than an amorphous mass of activity behind a scholarly output, makes room for identifying crosscurrents in theories, platforms, infrastructures and media used by academics and practitioners – both in and beyond the humanities. Pointing out that the humanities co-exist amidst a range of academic practices is important, as we argue above in relation to "the digital" in contemporary society. Equally important is to point out that humanities are a plural concept, term and discipline. It is not always fully acknowledged that the humanities are not a monolithic thing, but a diverse set of disciplines brought together based on historical ontological and cultural narratives about knowledge); and that the humanities and sciences cannot always be seen as the "Two Cultures" famously argued by C. P. Snow. Rather they are thousands of multivocal cultures, all connected by links of various kinds, some visible and obvious, some much less tangible.

Structuring and ordering the chapters in a manner which even obliquely reflects these cultures is a task which inevitably requires compromise. Some chapters could easily fit in to one or more sections, but we repeat that our aim here is not to categorise or suborn DH, and its constituent parts, with further abstraction and labelling. Rather, our aim is to construct a narrative flow which illustrates the observations we make above about the discursive formation of methodology.

Computation and connection

The first section deals with the ideas of computation and connection. We employ both terms very broadly, understanding their scope to extend well beyond coding, programming, or the employment of computational methods. Rather, we understand it to encompass the processes (and of course the methodologies) by which DH scholars approach one or more datasets and generate (or pass on through teaching, learning and training) new knowledge, and/or new types of knowledge, in the context of the connective affordances of the Internet.

Our broad definition of computation and connection reflects the stance taken by historians, sociologists, and those from other academic disciplines who have crafted histories of computation and media (see for example Ensmenger, 2012 and De Mol et al., 2018). This explicitly situates connectivity in research in the context of the emergence of networked (computational) devices, which in turn facilitate the creation of digital content. In turn, as computational technologies evolve, the types of content we engage with have become more complex. It is worth pointing out here that we are not attempting to provide a history of connective content, media and technology (there are texts and projects that accomplish this brilliantly, for instance McLuhan's *Understanding Media* is an early, but seminal work in this cannon); however, acknowledging that this scholarship exists offers an opportunity for to leverage these insights into interdisciplinary and collaborative efforts in DH.

The first part of this section therefore deals with computation and artistic practice, and with Briony Supple's discussion of integrating of teaching and learning within gallery spaces (Chp 1). This is followed by Hetty Blades and Scott deLahunta's (Chp 2) discussion of choreographic practice, and Sally Jane Norman's chapter (Chp 3) on the discursive properties of creative practice. The volume then moves on to themes of networking as a form of computational thinking. Cornelia Reyes Acosta (Chp 4) situates her research on networking in the context of creative design, and Sara Marino (Chp 5) explores connectivity across multiple sites in ethnographic research. Then Øyvind Eide (Chp 6) provides an overview of networks as tools for modelling and understanding data. The section concludes with a triptych of chapters on the organization of information and knowledge to *enable* connectivity. Simon Burrows and Terhi Nurmikko-Fuller (Chp 7) discuss the importance of bibliometrics and library-oriented uses of Linked Open Data. Then, Kristen Schuster and Vanessa Reyes (Chp 8) open a discussion, that is picked up later on, on library and metadata practices in DH. Finally, Paul Gooding (Chp 9) describes approaches to digital materials within libraries.

Convergence and collaboration

The execution of formal research methods in scholarship is a process which both implies and requires convergence: that is modes of doing based on shared understandings from potentially differing perspectives. In the social sciences, the process of convergence is supported and enabled by formalized, and often peer-reviewed frameworks that define what is, and is not a method, reinforced by grounded, shared understandings of terms such as "qualitative" and "quantitative", and what kind of research situation is appropriate for each. Most social scientists, for example, would agree that there are right and wrong ways to ensure a sample of a population is statistically significant, or that the transcript of an interview is correctly coded for qualitative analysis. In DH, the idea of the method—while still core to ensuring that research, and the knowledge it produces, is rigorous and able to withstand peer review —is undoubtedly present, but less converged.

Linking this argument about convergence to our point above about the importance of "the digital" in contemporary society, and the possibilities engendered by viewing more "classic" DH research problems through its lens. Such research had a heavy emphasis on the creation of content (for the digital humanities), and we wish to explore how the digital commodification of research content can be approached afresh. For example, Henry Jenkins' description of convergence asserts that the "… flow of content across multiple media platforms, the cooperation between multiple media industries, and the migratory behaviour of media audiences who will go almost anywhere in search of the kinds of entertainment experiences they want" (Jenkins Convergence Culture, p. 2). Jenkins' definition requires two things. First, he requires we pause and consider the implications of consumption and entertainment. Second, he requires we think about resource sharing and the implications this has for participation—participation from whom being the key issue he explores in his research. We choose this approach on purpose. The idea that information is a commodity is not new; however, it has gained significant traction recently, for example in popular media analyses of adolescent and young adult behaviour. In the meantime, scholars from the humanities and social sciences have invested time, effort and resources to tease out nuance and diversity in the media habits and practices of different social groups and cultural institutions like museums and libraries. In both cases, these efforts have transformed the ways academics think about how their scholarship converges through processes of collaboration and engagement, for the better in many cases.

Beyond providing a framework for an exploration of pop-media, Jenkins' description also gives us an opportunity to explore semantics and to promote conversations about practice and the reasons practices are valid and useful for research (see also Shirley Brice Heath and Brian Street). In fan studies and pop culture studies for example, convergence might mean the mixing, matching, mashing up of genres and plots and/ or reimagining an entire universe (see Matt Hills, *Fan cultures* (2002) and Scodari & Felder, 2009). In digital asset and media management (or just digital asset management) and digital curation, it might mean the reuse or migration of content from one project to another (see Higgins, 2008 and Regli, 2016). In the humanities it might mean the historical interaction between schools of thought or social and political networks (see Liu, 2016 and Robertson, 2016). In the social sciences convergence might mean a synthesis of phenomenon through interactions and negotiations between actors (see Castells, *Communication power* (2013).

Using the term convergence in this multifaceted way requires that we collaborate to consider our methods for evaluating the integrity and provenance of media. We borrow these terms from library and archives, but we also argue that this strategic borrowing points to the role(s) collaboration play in building a shared language for encouraging an opening up and remixing of content so that its value remains relevant, even if our modes for interpreting it change. Again, and unsurprisingly, there is a long history of debating and discussing these terms, both outside DH and within DH.

The first subset of three chapters deals with the significance of infrastructure for convergence. Concepts of the idea of physical and virtual space acting as containers of convergence and collaboration is provided by James Smithies and Arianna Ciula's chapter (Chp 10) on the King's Digital Lab at King's College London. Then, Richard Gartner (Chp 11) picks up this theme in a more applied way with his use of metadata for enabling convergence in photographic collections. Finally, in this subsection, A. J. Million (Chp 12) provides an overview of research infrastructures and DH. The next three chapters take up the theme of convergence of datasets by aligning and analysing their geographic and linguistic attributes. Anna Foka, Coppélie Cocq, Phillip I. Buckland and Stefan Gelfgren's (Chp 13) describe the use of geovisualization to map the ecologies of landscapes, and Alexandra Petrulevich and William Kretzschmar (Chp 14) follow this by exploring the use of Geographic Information Systems (GIS) in linguistic studies. Collectively, these two chapters provide an example of how similar methodologies (such as those supported by GIS). Vicky Garnett and Eliza Papaki (Chp 15) then return to the broader infrastructural theme, but situated firmly within the scope of methodological convergence, with their chapter on communities in DH. In the following chapters, authors explore different aspects of convergence: when data, practices, methods, methodologies and institutions converge, there is always a question of ethics, and of who is included and excluded when those practices come together. Kenneth Haggerty (Chp 16) sets this critical scene with a discussion of the inevitable matter of intellectual property rights (IPR) in DH research, after which Nick Proferes offers a broader perspective on what ethics can offer DH. Again moving to a more applied case, Brit Kelley (Chp 18) concludes this section with an exploration of the ethical implications of involvement in communities that one is researching.

Remediation and transmission

There is an inherent risk in discussing convergence and remediation in such close proximity. Remediation, like convergence, deals with the re-use of media (Bolter & Grusin, 2002); yet whereas the former suggests a process of compromise, negotiation and alignment; the latter involves reinterpretation and reimagination of content. From a methodological point of view, these are very different concepts.

Research methods in the digital humanities

Like other forms of media in use since the Renaissance—in particular, perspective painting, photography, film, and television—new digital media oscillate between immediacy and hypermediacy, between transparency and opacity. This oscillation is the key to understanding how a particular instance of media is fashioned by both its predecessors and by other contemporary media. Although each medium promises to reform its predecessors by offering a more immediate or authentic experience, the promise of reform inevitably leads us to become conscious of the new medium. Thus, in the case of digital media, immediacy leads to hypermediacy. The process of remediation makes us aware that all media are at one level a "play of signs," which is a lesson that we take from poststructuralist literary theory. At the same time, this process insists on the real, effective presence of media in our culture. Media have the same claim to reality as more tangible cultural artefacts; photographs, films, and computer applications are as real as airplanes and buildings. Furthermore, media technologies constitute networks or hybrids that can be expressed in physical, social, aesthetic, and economic terms. Introducing a new media technology does not mean simply inventing new hardware and software, but rather fashioning (or refashioning) such a network (Bolter & Grusin, *Theories of New Media*, 22).

Bolter and Grusin do not quite define remediation so much as explore the ways technology have transformed our relationships to media, and methods for interpreting and consuming the contents represented by media. Their theory requires more than a few historical digressions, but the overall point they make is something humanists and social scientists alike might do well to remember: Media do not have to be digital to be remediated. However, technology does change our expectations of what media do—and how we can communicate with (or more perhaps via) media.

Like convergence, remediation is more than simply re-using media, or combining different types of media. However, remediation and convergence part ways where the subject of analysis scholars take up differ. While convergence makes space to consider cycles of production, consumption and adaptation, remediation engages in a history of the relationship between media and technology. So, while both convergence and remediation explore audiences and forms of communication, they do so from different points of view which, we think, highlights the need for semantic differentiations between complex practices so that scholars and practitioners are clear while describing their practices and sharing their outputs. What is more, it creates space to discuss, debate and innovate the ways we think about technology and use technology to carry out, share and preserve our research. Wondering how (or whether) media effects technology (or vice versa) is, at its core, remediation through the digital sphere. In DH, this offers a space that is slightly different from convergence to think about media, representation and knowledge. . . and how, simultaneously, decisions effect practices and strategies for representing (and/or communicating) knowledge.

Chapters in the following sections address the subject of remediating text using semantic analysis, mark-up. Barbara MacGillivray (Chp 19) highlights recent advances in semantic analysis for historical text, following which Christopher Ohge and Charlotte Tupman (Chp 20) assess methodologies for semantically encoding text. Then, recalling and linking to the previous section on ethics, Hannah Smyth, Julianne Nyhan and Andrew Flinn (Chp 21) deliver a powerful critique of what happened to DH when it moved *beyond* consideration of text, and the exclusionary practices that non-textual DH highlight. Most would argue that the most effective counterweight to such practices is inclusive teaching and learning; and both remediation and transmission (especially transmission) relate to practices of pedagogy. The next tchapters therefore discuss pedagogical themes. Christopher Gilman, Jacob Alden Sargent and Craig Dietrich (Chp 22) begin this with a discussion of the Scalar tool in the classroom. Kristen Mapes (Chp 23) then broadens this discussion, with a review of DH pedagogy seen through the syllabus of core DH module. Benjamin Wiggins concludes this subtheme with his chapter on how instructors can effectively teach DH in an era in which the power and potential of the digital grows and evolves at such pace. Mia Ridge (Chp 25) presents a project management perspective on how crowdsourcing can be employed to remediate and enhance data from museum collections. Rebecca Croxton (Chp 26) then expands this to broader themes of using the Internet for scholarship, teaching, and learning more broadly. And finally, Dinara Saparova (Chp 24) discusses a more specific instance, of the use of eye tracking technology as a means of enhancing research and pedagogy approaches.

Conclusion

One of us (KS) is an art historian turned librarian, and the other (SD) is an archaeologist turned spatial humanities scholar. This volume is therefore a product of our own collaboration, between the work of a metadata expert (in the most generic and enthusiastic way), and that of an expert in GIS and geospatial data, with a particularly humanities-driven "slant". Aligning our perspectives entailed a process of negotiation, discourse and, and times, disagreement. So, for us, the production of knowledge has evolved out of particular disciplinary practices and culminated in a shared perspective on the processes we use to structure research.

We are incredibly pleased with the range of disciplinary perspectives we brought into this book, but we simultaneously acknowledge that there remains a European and North American centric point of view. Diversity is a gradual process, and it is a process we hope we can contribute to through a process of critical engagement and inclusion, and are excited to see in future volumes about DH and DH work.

As we (and others) have made clear, DH is a sprawling term that does not just apply to humanists who use computers, or get others to do so for them—like Lodge's satirical Head of Department and his technicians—and because of the expansive potential the term allows, there is an equally wide range of people who *do* DH for research, people who *practice* DH for work, and people who *learn* about DH as they broaden their skillsets and knowledge bases. While these verbs are not exhaustive, they do reflect the diverse ways and reasons people conceptualize and discuss DH. This raises the question: Are digital methods for DH different from DH research methods?

Asking this question now, practically at the end of this introduction, is a strategic choice. We are asking readers to reflect on *what* they do, not just *why* they do it. In part this is because we are both teachers and research practitioners, and we are both interested in developing a deeper understanding of research methodology which enables practices of technology which are robust, helpful, interesting and effective.

With this framing in mind, when we started sketching out our plans for this volume, we had four audiences in mind: practitioners, students, teachers and researchers. Undoubtedly, there is overlap between these audiences—researchers can practice DH and students can teach DH. We think identifying areas of overlap and blurred boundaries between practice, research, teaching and learning is important because it enables simultaneous conversations about the humanities and digital content from multiple perspectives. Our goal is to provide readers with insights into how they can frame their work and interests to communities of practice, colleagues and students.

Acknowledgements

We would like to thank the authors who contributed their time and expertise so generously to this volume. We are also very grateful to Hannah Shakespeare and her team at Routledge, who have been a constant source of patient support.

References

Anderson, S., & Mcpherson, T. (2011). Engaging digital scholarship: Thoughts on evaluating multimedia scholarship. *Profession by the Modern Language Association*, (2011), 136–151.

Apollon, Daniel; Belisle, C. (2014). The Digital Fate of the Critical Apparatus. In C. Bélisle, P. Régnier, D. Apollon, & C. Bélisle (Eds.), *Digital Critical Editions* (pp. 81–113). University of Illinois Press.

Research methods in the digital humanities

Bolter, J & Grusin, R. (1999). *Remediation: Understanding new media.* Cambridge, MA: MIT Press.

Brice Heath, S. (1983). *Ways with words: Language, life and work in communities and classrooms.* Cambridge, UK: Cambridge University Press.

Castells, M. (2013). *Communication power.* Oxford, UK: Oxford University Press.

Dalbello, M. (2011). A genealogy of digital humanities. *Journal of Documentation, 67*(3), 480–506. https://doi.org/10.1108/00220411111124550

De Mol, L., Maarten, B., & Daylight, E. G. (2018). Less is more in the fifties: Encounters between logical minimalism and computer design during the 1950s. *IEEE Annals of the History of Computing, 40*(1), 19–45. https://doi.org/10.1109/MAHC.2018.012171265

Ensmenger, N. (2012). The digital construction of technology: Rethinking the history of computers in society. *Technology and Culture, 53*(4), 753–776. https://doi.org/10.1353/tech.2012.0126

Flanders, Julia; Munoz, T. (2014). An Introduction to Humanities Data Curation. *Digital Humanities Data Curation,* 1–9. Retrieved from http://guide.dhcuration.org/contents/intro/

Gailey, A. (2012). Historical perspectives on digital editing. *Textual Cultures, 7*(1), 3–4.

Haugen, Odd Einar; Apollon, D. (2014). The digital turn in textual scholarship: Historical and typological perspectives. In P. Apollon, Daniel; Belisle, Claire; Regnier (Ed.), *Digital Critical Editions* (pp. 35–57). University of Illinois Press.

Higgins, S. (2008). The DCC curation lifecycle model-abstract.pdf. *International Journal of Digital Curation, 3*(1), 134–140.

Hills, M. (2002). *Fan cultures.* London, UK: Routledge.

Jenkins, H. (2006). *Convergence culture: Where old and new media collide.* New York, NY: New York University Press.

Kirschenbaum, M. G. (2012). Digital Humanities As/Is Tactical Term. In M. K. Gold (Ed.), *Debates in the Digital Human ties* (pp. 415–428). University of Minnesota Press. Retrieved from http://www.jstor.org/stable/10.5749/j.ctttv8h1.26%0AJSTOR

Licklider, J. (1960). Man–computer symbiosis. *IRE Transactions on Human Factors in Electronics, 1*(March), 4–11.

Liu, A. (2016) N+1: A Plea for cross-domain data in the digital humanities. In L. Gold, Matthew; Klein (Ed.), *Debates in the digital humanities 2016* (pp. 559–568) University of Minnesota Press.

McGill, M. L. (2016). Literary history, book history and media studies. In H. Blum (Ed.), *Turns of Events* (pp. 23–39). University of Pennsylvania Press.

McLuhan, M. (2002). *Understanding media.* London, UK: Routledge.

Robertson, S. (2016). The differences between digital humanities and digital history. In L. F. Gold, Matthew K.; Klein (Ed.), *Debates in the digital humanities* (pp. 289–307). MInneapolis.

Robinson, P. (2013). Towards a theory of digital editions. *Variants, 10,* 105–131.

Sayers, J. (2016). Dropping the digital. *Debates in the Digital Humanities,* (May 2018), 475–492. Retrieved from http://dhdebates.gc.cuny.edu/debates/text/88

Scodari, C., & Felder, J. L. (2000). Creating a pocket universe: "Shippers," fan fiction, and the X-Files online. *Communication Studies, 51*(3), 238–257. https://doi.org/10.1080/10510970009388522

Street, B.V. (2005). *Literacies across educational contexts: Mediating learning and teaching.* Philadelphia, PA: Caslon.

Regli, T. (2016). *Digital marketing and asset management: The real story about DAM technology and practice.* Brooklyn, NY: Rosenfeld Media, LLC.

SECTION I

Computation and connection

1

GET SOME PERSPECTIVE

Using physical objects in the Glucksman Gallery to capture interdisciplinary stories of online teaching and learning

Briony Supple

1.1 Introduction

This chapter will present the key findings from a focus group which was undertaken with teaching staff at University College Cork (UCC). The focus group was located at the Glucksman Gallery, a campus-based modern art museum, with a cross-disciplinary team of teaching staff who used the works of art within the Glucksman to talk about their experiences of transitioning from face-to-face to online teaching.

The chapter is organized as follows: a brief context for the study outlines how this work is situated within institutional learning and teaching approaches and describes the physical learning and teaching spaces within the Glucksman Gallery. A section covering a brief history of arts in education approaches at UCC navigates the reader in terms of the current application of arts-based approaches, and their influence on this research piece. The contextual elements also serve to underscore 1) the relevance of engaging participants in the process of slow looking in an art gallery to make sense of teaching and learning online and 2) the reasoning for using this methodological approach.

1.2 Context for this study

The Centre for the Integration of Research, Teaching and Learning (CIRTL), University College Cork (UCC), delivers the only fully online qualifications in Teaching and Learning in Higher Education in Ireland. These qualifications—the Certificate and Diploma in Teaching and Learning in Higher Education, have a rich history of face-to-face delivery. In 2015 these qualifications transitioned from fully face-to-face delivery to fully online.

The Certificate and Diploma are undertaken by staff members with active teaching timetables in Higher Education settings. The move to online learning has meant that these programs can now be accessed by teaching staff who are external to UCC and to Ireland. Each year since this transition to online teaching there have been up to 100 enrolments in the Certificate. In general, around 40% of those who undertake the Certificate then go on to complete the Diploma. The programs are delivered by a multi-disciplinary team of academics—known as teaching fellows—lead by a program coordinator from CIRTL. At the time this research was undertaken, there were ten teaching fellows facilitating the Certificate and four facilitating the Diploma. These fellows are full time academics in their own disciplines and are drawn from the four colleges of the university—the College of Arts, Social Sciences and Celtic Studies; the College of Medicine and Health; the College of Law and Business Studies and the College of Science, Engineering and Food Science.

All of the teaching fellows have significant experience in teaching and in their own discipline and have completed a Masters in Teaching and Learning in Higher Education. Yet the transition to online teaching has been an interesting journey: we frequently have had to consider competing notions of what constitutes 'teaching' online: Is there a difference (and should there be) between teaching, administration and content creation in an online setting? Articulating the complexities of online teaching became problematic; concepts were alien and hard to explain or explore. We found that the importance, intensity and demands of online teaching were sometimes being downplayed as 'second best' compared to face-to-face. As a teaching team we began to wonder: how do we underscore the importance of teaching online and helping ourselves and others in illuminating what constitutes online teaching and learning? How do we tell these stories in a way that makes sense to ourselves as teachers and to our students, who are also teachers? Arts in education approaches at UCC have been used in both physical and virtual settings for a number of years as a way of exploring elements of the Scholarship of Teaching and Learning (SoTL). Participants working within an arts education lens engage in a process of 'slow looking', which requires "patient, immersive attention" to artworks, providing "scope and space for meaning-making and critical thinking that may not be possible through high-speed means of information delivery…addressing multi-disciplinary applications…" (Tishman, 2017:24). As the coordinator of these programs and point of support and contact for the teaching fellows, the author was curious to see what tools an arts in education focus might provide the teaching team in exploring complexities around teaching and learning online.

1.3 The Glucksman Gallery at UCC

The Glucksman Gallery is a modern art gallery based on the university campus; the gallery building was designed by award-winning architects O'Donnell and Tuomey. Opened in October 2004, the gallery prides itself in fostering "creative connections between people and disciplines…enabling public understanding of the visionary research undertaken in all four colleges, and welcoming students, staff and visitors to explore, enjoy and learn about art right in the heart of the UCC campus" (Glucksman Gallery: A History, n.d.) The Glucksman Gallery space is discipline agnostic (in other words, not associated with a particular discipline). It provides a playful and creative space away from 'traditional' learning spaces on campus. Many from the university community may have only visited for pleasure rather than as part of an interdisciplinary learning experience. The constantly changing artworks and the gallery space itself has served as a rich and dynamic place to explore facets of teaching and learning through an arts in education lens. Inspired by thoughts from De Botton and Armstrong in their book "Art as Therapy" in utilising art as a way to explore the elements of our minds and emotions "we have trouble with" (De Botton & Armstrong, 2013:5), the author was interested to see whether using the artworks in the gallery might serve somehow as a way for the teaching fellows to talk about the complexities, tensions, and challenges of teaching online, but also defining the potential inclusivity, empowerment and transformation afforded by online teaching and learning.

What followed was a research piece: teaching fellows attended the Glucksman Gallery as part of pre-semester training and were set a simple task: to look closely at the works in the gallery (engaging in a process known as 'slow looking' or 'seeing slowly') and think about what the artworks might be 'saying' about teaching and learning in an online context. After this exercise the group came together and were joined by the Glucksman Gallery art director for a conversation and reflections, which were audio recorded.

For this research, the artworks within gallery as part of two exhibitions: 'Please Touch: Tactile Encounters' and 'Josef and Anni Albers: Voyage Inside a Blind Experience' became the framework for talking about complexities of teaching and learning in an online space. It became apparent that the artworks served as a powerful tool to help the teaching fellows articulate stories of their teaching and learning which had previously been difficult to articulate and conceptualize. The data unveiled meaningful and enlightening ideas about 'what is lost and what is gained' through teaching in a digital setting; how one form does not replace or supersede the other. The depths of these conversations had not previously come to light prior to using art in this way.

1.3.1 Site of investigation: Art and the Glucksman Gallery—Why?

Using artworks to facilitate deeper learning moments can be thought of in a broader umbrella of Object Based Learning Approaches (OBL); an approach which utilizes 'material culture' (documents, works of art, specimens, artefacts, everyday objects) in order to "enhance critical thinking and the acquisition of key skills" (Kador, Chatterjee & Hannan, 2017:61).

There has been a proliferation of arts in education approaches emerging in the United Kingdom and the United States in recent years through OBL. (Geismar, 2018; Kador, Chatterjee & Hannan, 2017). Discussing difficult or challenging concepts that might be hard to articulate can be "brought into being by things" (Geismar, 2018: xv); this is at the heart of arts-based approaches to teaching and learning. These "things" whether they be paintings, sculptures, or multi-media installations, invite "audiences to fill in the blanks with their own experiences." (Geismar, 2018: xv); Engaging in these processes then "helps to set emotional connections, which are deeper than intellectual understanding" (Pujol et al., 2013:4). Essentially, the process is about engaging with material cultures in a process of slow looking, observing closely, paying attention to detail and asking questions such as 'how does this make me feel'? (Elkins, 2009; Findlay, 2017; Tishman, 2017).

Working within the context of staff development means establishing and building relationships and a shared language between different disciplines. This can often be difficult to establish. However, arts in education approaches have been proven as an enabler to finding common ground and developing a shared language of teaching and learning across disciplines (McCarthy, 2010; Kador, Chatterjee & Hannan, 2017).

The very location of a gallery suggests a space "set apart from our everyday lives" (Geismar, 2018). The Glucksman Gallery on UCC's campus provides a rich and dynamic discipline neutral space for learning; a perfect backdrop for the coming together of interdisciplinary knowledge communities such as the teaching fellows. The constantly changing exhibitions provide ongoing means for interaction and engagement. The Glucksman is a democratic space—a welcome contrast to traditional campus architecture where the divide between lecturer and student is often maintained through lecture theatres (Kador, Chatterjee & Hannan, 2017). The Glucksman's open spaces do not assume one person as the 'knower' who stands at the top of the room; and, therefore, invites flexible, inclusive dialogue between participants.

1.4 Arts in education pedagogies at UCC: A history

The exposure to artworks in both real and virtual formats have enabled individuals engaging in teaching and learning qualifications at UCC from across different disciplines to learn from each other, encouraged higher order thinking, helped participants make connections between previously disparate concepts and encouraged a diversity of perspectives (McCarthy, 2010).

UCC has a rich history in terms of the development of various arts in education practices across the university; these developments are punctuated via specific movements and leaders as follows. From 2001–2007 was the establishment of identifying visual practices across the university as Professor Alistair Rowan established the History of Art as an academic discipline at UCC in 2001. James Elkins was then appointed by UCC from the School of the Art Institute of Chicago in 2004 as the second professor in History of Art. James Elkins' period coincided with the establishment of Cork as a European City of Culture in 2005 and the 2004 opening of the Glucksman Gallery. Elkins was educated as a studio artist and art historian. Therefore, he was interested in the role of teaching and learning within studio practices. His book, *Visual Practices Across the University* (Elkins, 2007), highlights his interest in the visual arts as a means to communicate disciplinary ways of seeing and perceiving domains of knowledge. Creative Art, Culture and Inclusion (Disability Studies) was also introduced as a program offered through UCC's Adult and Continuing Education Centre.

1.4.1 2006 (embedding Project Zero at UCC)

In 2006, as a natural development, *Ionad Bairre*, The Teaching and Learning Centre, was established. The approach of the Centre for almost a decade has been one of scholarly enquiry into teaching and learning practice. The National Academy for the Integration of Research Teaching and Learning (NAIRTL) was funded by the Higher Education Authority (Ireland) between 2006 and 2012, with UCC as the lead partner in this national collaborative project. The goal of NAIRTL was to enact a series of activities and initiatives to support students, researchers and staff to implement and advance effective research-informed teaching and learning practices throughout the Irish higher education sector. This was achieved through staff development initiatives such as national conferences, small grants, and teaching excellence awards. NAIRTL is currently transitioning from an academy to a national network, linked through contact points in each partner institution.

1.4.2 2008 (establishing visual thinking strategies at UCC)

The Jennings Gallery was established through the leadership of Siobhan Murphy and supported by the then President of UCC, Michael Murphy, to promote and support visual literacy and creative growth among the staff, students and graduates of the College of Medicine and Health.

1.4.3 2009 (visual practices as metacognitive approaches to learning and teaching)

UCC academics Cronin, McMahon and Waldron's (2009) publication about making explicit the processes of looking in art history, adult and community education and was later critically reviewed in Woolard's (2011) *Psychology for the Classroom: E-Learning*.

1.4.4 2010–12 (documenting uses of Project Zero in higher education)

CIRTL's promotion of visual literacies and application of the Project Zero Classroom across UCC is documented in Blackshields, et al. eds.), *Integrative Learning International Research and Practice*.

Research undertaken at UCC by McCarthy (2010) focused on investigating how an arts in education lens could work as a catalyst to inform processes and facilitate integrative learning. For this study, participants from different cohorts undertaking the Certificate and Diploma in Teaching and Learning in Higher Education attended a workshop where they engaged in an exercise involving approaches from project MUSE.

McCarthy's study collected data from reflections during the session, blog responses and reflective evaluation questions. Her results pointed to the following themes regarding learning in the Glucksman Gallery: how the space itself served as a catalyst for integrative learning, how engaging with artworks fostered making connections between cross-disciplinary concepts (the views of staff members who were engineers contrasting those from anatomy, the realization that 'we bring our conceptions and background to the problem' (McCarthy, 2010:121). Allowing for multiple perspectives of an artwork highlighted to staff members how students learn in different ways, that each perspective on an artwork might be different but is equally valid (and how this is relevant to students). Imagining a scenario behind an artwork also highlighted higher order thinking and analytical skills.

Get some perspective

1.4.5 2013–2014 (VTS as a tool for professional enhancement)

Professor Tony Ryan was one of the first graduates of the Masters in Teaching and Higher Education at UCC. His awards include the President's Award for Excellence in Teaching and Learning (2002) and two Irish Health Awards (2009 and 2017) for International Development and Health Systems improvement (Omdurman Maternity Hospital, Sudan) and the Cork-Sudan Helping Babies Breathe Partnership). In 2012, he was awarded a National Teacher Award from the National Academy for the Integration of Research in Teaching and Learning (NAIRTL). In 2013 his TedEx talk: "Using art education to make better doctors" was recorded.

1.4.6 2015–2017: Award-winning art and medicine linkages

In 2015 the School of Pharmacy team received an award at the European conference on the Scholarship of Teaching and Learning for their study on the use of art-based teaching strategies. The prize was awarded to an interdisciplinary team of experts from the School of Pharmacy for their work on embedding arts-based teaching strategies in the Pharmacy curriculum. ("School of Pharmacy Team Wins Award", 2015).

2017 then saw the exhibition of 'Art and Medicine' at the Jennings Gallery, UCC. The exhibition, entitled 'Just What the Doctor Ordered: Arts & Creative Expressions by Medical Graduates', ran from 1st November 2017–18th January 2018 and showcased the work of six Cork-based medical graduates from psychiatry, oncology, anaesthesia, and cardiology. ("Medical Graduates Exhibition", n.d.)

1.4.7 2018 (taking Project Zero into non-traditional learning communities)

Making Thinking Visible: drawing lessons from the Project Zero Classroom for prison education (James Cronin, UCC, Thérèse Cooper and Edel Cunningham, Education Unit, Cork Prison)

A learning partnership between Adult Continuing Education, UCC, and Education Unit, Cork Prison drawing on the Project Zero Classroom to scaffold studio education. The resulting exhibition, "Inside-Out" on Spike Island, was a community partnership promoting learner autonomy through the visual arts as means of reflecting on experiences of incarceration.

"A Learning Journey: UCC's Cork Prison students celebrate ACE art course achievement" *Independent Thinking* [Online] https://www.ucc.ie/en/mandc/ezine/ [accessed 15th August 2018]

Utilising the Glucksman Gallery with pharmacy students in creating poster presentations: Masters in Teaching and Learning in Higher Education thesis by Dr JJ Keating from the School of Pharmacy, UCC.

1.4.8 2019: Administrators vs. educators: the tensions, dilemmas and challenges in online teaching

This historical backdrop and context underscores the rich history informing arts-based approaches to teaching and learning at UCC.

The transition from face-to-face to online facilitation in 2015 was challenging for the teaching team. Meetings were often fraught with the tension of trying to encourage participation as well as the tension of facilitating the learning of students who are also staff and peers. The onus within these discussions was often focused on the weaknesses of the students (e.g. their inability to engage being the main issue) as well as the weaknesses of the Virtual Learning Environment. Teaching felt very 'top down' and hierarchical rather than allowing for democratic facilitation, . There was also an increase in administration and frustration with the lack of learner engagement.

The prevailing discourse seemed to be presenting digital learning and learning technologies as "either firmly utopian or despairingly dystopian" (Geismar, 2018:9). The author was keen to explore how teaching online was being conceptualized as administration and as second best to face-to-face. Meetings with teaching fellows were constantly focused on the negative aspects and putting out fires related to technical issues. The author wanted to introduce a new way of thinking about online teaching and learning and inject some new perspectives about online teaching for both herself and the wider team.

Given the rich history of the arts in education approaches at UCC and the depth and breadth of interdisciplinary applications, the author decided to pursue the Glucksman Gallery as a site for investigating these challenges with the team. Furthermore, many of the teaching fellows were new to the role in Semester 1 2018, and so it was seen as a promising way for people to get to know each other via a different means that simply meet and greet; encounters with objects often serve as a catalyst for social interaction (Kador, Chatterjee & Hannan, 2017). On an even deeper level: "We are hard to get to know: we are mysterious to ourselves and therefore no good at explaining who we are to others" (Botton & Armstrong, 2013:58). And yet, as Botton and Armstrong argue, engaging in conversations around art has been found as a useful medium for getting to know others as well as ourselves.

As the discussion and results section outlines, staff were able to articulate ideas about their teaching, their students learning and the nuances of the online and physical spaces, all through the medium of chosen objects at the Glucksman Gallery's 'Please Touch: Tactile Encounters' (featuring work by artists Rhona Byrne, Maud Cotter, Richard Forrest, Katie Watchorn) and 'Josef and Anni Albers: Voyage Inside a Blind Experience' exhibition.

The storytelling metaphor was important to the author as being at the heart of the investigation: Stories put us in touch with ourselves and others, allowing for shared experience, for building a community, encouraging and developing empathy, trust and connection. Stories are cross-disciplinary, cross-cultural, multi-sensory and constructivist (Springer et al., 2004, p. 2); perfectly aligned to the needs and aims of a wide team of teachers from across the university in coming together for the first time. Storytelling is also interactive and requires attention (an audience/listeners) who will incite empathy; the common thread here being the complexities and challenges of facilitating online learning for students who are also staff members. It was also felt that storytelling was an important lens in bringing in personal elements of the storytellers themselves; when teaching online can feel so disembodied and distant, a personal story brings in a personal element which can be lost online.

Engagement in the real space The study was concerned primarily with questions around how engaging in 'slow looking' using physical objects in an art gallery help to capture interdisciplinary stories of online teaching and learning and parallels these teachers draw between their learning and teaching in a physical vs. a virtual space

Teaching staff from the following disciplines were present for the workshop: Applied Psychology, Education, Irish Language, Alternative Therapies, Disability Support Services, Microbiology, Neuroscience and Anatomy, Medicine and Dentistry, Learning and Teaching, as well as the exhibition curator. Participants were given information via a research information statement about the context of the research and consent forms before the workshop. A briefing about the exhibition took place by the Gallery curator and author of this chapter. Participants were then given approximately 40 minutes to interact with the various works on display—this being an exhibition which allowed for tactile interaction as well as simply visually observing pieces.

Participants were asked to think about this question as they engaged in slow looking with the artworks:

What story can this piece tell about teaching and learning in online and face-to-face settings? The focus group was audio recorded and audio files were transcribed by a third party. The author analysed these by through thematic analysis through a narrative inquiry lens. Our resulting themes and sub-themes were found as follows:

- Theme 1: Embodiment
  - a) Flexibility and inclusion in online learning
  - b) What is lost and what is gained: multi-sensory experiences and virtual learning
- Theme 2: Creativity as a gateway for disciplinary and interdisciplinary connections

Get some perspective

Theme 1:

Embodiment. Embodiment as a theme was an interesting parallel to explore regarding the real gallery experience, face-to-face teaching and online teaching. Both experience in a physical gallery setting as well as a face-to-face teaching scenario bring with them the concept of 'embodiment'—a live and physical moment of synchronous interaction.

> The real presence tends to be invested in the face to face. But the thing is, it was almost an act of sacrilege, literally and metaphorically, if you were to kind of think of the online as predicating that and as going – giving more. But in a way, in some ways, the online does give you more. (Participant M).

Art gallery enthusiasts (such as Findlay, 2017) point to the lived experience of an artwork:

> "Staring at a painting (and having it stare back at you) is a real-life, real time experience. Energy is exchanged. Looking at a digital image, only information is exchanged, no energy." (Findlay, 2017, p. 277).

This was echoed by one participant:

> So you bring all your experience and your thoughts and words to the world of the artwork. And the artwork will resist. So it's strong. It's not going to be overtaken by you. (Participant F)

This energy is an inherent part of the Glucksman Gallery space as one participant said:

> There is an amazing power in this building. It operates on so many levels… culturally, aesthetically, artistically, politically. You know, so much is I think powerful. The Glucksman Gallery is the finest teaching space in the university for that reason. (Participant M).

The Gallery space also forced participants out of their comfort zone: The Glucksman has many open spaces for exploration of artworks, which can be challenging and confronting. There was a useful parallel drawn here between the gallery space as 'unsafe' or 'challenging' and the virtual space as being the same:

> I think the space … The openness of the [Glucksman] space alone does contribute to that feeling of being a very unsafe space. There's always an element of safety in traditional classrooms - desks and chairs and four narrow walls….[being out of that traditional space] it's challenging. Particularly, I always think, for students…which is also relevant for online learning contexts. (Participant G).
> Students going in [online], asking how do I write this? How do I navigate this? Am I writing the right thing? Is this what I'm supposed to do? That really speaks to that idea of space as well, in terms of how do I operate within this space. I'm not familiar with this. And I think if we think of our students who are lecturers, who may not have experienced the online space as a student, they're navigating those kind of dilemmas. (Participant BJ).

We can also forget how being in a physical space also includes all of the senses:

> I think the acoustics of galleries are extraordinary. It really shifts how you relate in your own body to the work that you're looking at (Participant F)

This is also true of teaching online and face-to-face - the challenge is in how we recreate that lost energy: educators can often mourn the physicality of face-to-face teaching moments, citing lack of atmosphere and difficulty in creating relationships as main barriers (Oldale & Knightley, 2018). Educators can feel a sense of being 'disembodied' and invisible in the online teaching context (Rehn, Maor, & McConney, 2016), articulated here by Participant J:

> We pick up a lot, not only what the person is saying, but maybe whether they like the look of someone or the feel of them, or the way they're dressed or whatever. And these are the things you get in that face to face classroom context that creates security, because you naturally think oh, when you just see a person across the room, I think I'll go and pair up with them. And you know, the challenge is to figure out how to pick up on that in the online environment. I don't know what the answer is. But that can be some of the lack of security or safety for people to come forward and…there's certain dimensions present but there's the dimensions that are missing [online]. And that's strange for us, because we're social beings. (Participant J).

However, the conversation began to reflect how conceptualising teaching and learning in fully online or fully face-to-face contexts as two polar opposites and trying to work out 'which is better' was flawed.

> I think the point about the thing technology gives you…it always amazes me that people view technology as being in competition. But like a colleague of mine researching virtual reality and what you can do in virtual reality. And all the talk with virtual reality is how it's complementary as opposed to in competition with traditional teaching and learning. (Participant O).

The discussion turned to thinking about what the artworks might do in helping us tell our stories about the puzzlement of online teaching as a 'space', much like a classroom. For example, the anonymity and asynchronous elements of contributing in an online space had been viewed previously as something negative, where that interaction and 'energy exchange' in the moment had been lost. However, thinking about interactions with art, the gallery and tactile objects help to re-calibrate some of those perceptions:

> With an artwork you like to observe it, then walk away, then think about it. Think about what your reaction is to it. And that's how some people also operate online. They like to kind of go in, read the conversation, reflect on it, and then kind of go in again…so they might just need more time. (Participant BJ)

Observing and taking time to reflect on a work of art also drew some other interesting parallels in terms of the practice of teaching:

> The other thing was the tapestry….I looked at it. And I guess until I closed my eyes and touched the representation of it, next to it, that I realised I was looking at something but not quite seeing it… And I don't think you'll ever be finished looking at your teaching. And going back to it… And sometimes you can just glaze over a little bit and you've been doing things for a while and doing them in a particular way. (Participant N)

This particular orientation of the tactile artworks, visual pieces and the windows (see Figure 1.1 below) prompted participant R to think about the layout of the online as a 'space' and how behaviour and participation might be influenced by its architecture, just like in the gallery.

The image above shows the visual representations on the wall, with tactile representations on the wooden stands below each image.

> Because my usual thing is don't touch in the gallery, when I saw the things that were tactile, I didn't – until I saw other people doing it – go and touch. And I wondered about [online] being

Get some perspective

Figure 1.1 Josef Albers, Homages to the Square, Gallery 2.
Image from: http://www.glucksman.org/exhibitions/josef-anni-albers

different learning space….So I think even though it seems very logical that you would click on things and interact, the students are probably like me where I was more focused on the window, and the not touching, than I was about actually engaging. (Participant R).

A similar response was echoed by Participant N, but in the context of a different artefact (Figure 1.2):

The very first day I walked up to the 'Hive'. And I know if you paint something dark it's supposed to highlight the front and foreground and background. But I just walked up to it, and I just didn't see it until I touched it. And it just kind of gave me the idea that what you might believe you

Figure 1.2 Richard Forrest, Hive, Gallery 1.
Image from: http://www.glucksman.org/exhibitions/please-touch-tactile-encounters

have prominent and foreground when you are teaching your class or an online space, may not be what the person experiencing that sees straight away. And you have to think about maybe how you get that going. (Participant N)

Participant J's response to this same artwork was:

What we look at is, we don't see everything when we see one little snippet…Because [teaching online] it's not as simple as this versus that, and get an answer. You really need to look at it much more deeply. And the deeper we go, the more we're going to get. (Participant J).

1.4.9 a) Flexibility and inclusion in online learning

Embodiment was an overarching theme from which other themes emerged; for example, in thinking about the flexibility afforded by learning online. Participants articulated how entering a gallery space can feel intimidating for some people, and that this might dissuade some from visiting an art gallery or inhibit enjoyment of art. "Anni and Josef wanted their art to bring pleasure and new experiences into the lives of as many human beings as possible" (Weber, 2018:20). This resonated with the accessibility and inclusion theme of learning in an online context which the group discussed: the availability of artworks online was seen as a way of people being able to dip their toe in the water; to experience an unfamiliar medium in a 'safe space'. As Participant M stated: "Far better for them to have a virtual experience of an exhibition than to have none at all." This related then to a similar feeling students might have in engaging in learning online and feeling safer in a space where they can feel anonymous:

Some people may actually find it safe because people are – they can't see the people behind who they're writing to. And I hadn't actually thought of it in that way. I'd always thought people felt a bit isolated. But some people might actually like that because they can be more honest. (Participant BJ).
   I think anonymity could help people who want to share something about their teaching, but are embarrassed by the social situation…Or think that they would be too exposed if they'd been teaching in a certain way for 20 years and nobody's ever been at their classroom…They might suddenly feel actually, no, I'm much too self-conscious about this. But if I do this online thing, I can hear, I can connect with other people a little bit facelessly, but I still have a connection…And I think that's part of the gallery experience for me is sometimes…I actually just sit and see how people interact with the art, rather than actually interacting myself. (Participant R). The online space was also highlighted as something which could add value to real objects:
   But also something you can do with the online experience of art, is that you can actually analyse the painting in a way that you can't do in a museum. For example, I'm interested in manuscripts. And if you're faced with a page of a manuscript – so the Book of Kells is something everybody would be familiar with – in the museum context or in an art gallery context, you're just standing – you can barely see. You can barely read anything through the glass. Whereas when you're looking at it online, you can zoom right it and you can see every word. It's something really marvellous. (Participant I).

Participant R also agreed, stating online artworks "might be a way in which that you would open the opportunity up to somebody who would feel self-conscious in a new artistic space". She highlighted this point by talking about her husband as an example:

I love going to concerts. While my husband isn't interested in music hugely and wasn't keen to go to concerts with me and he'd say, oh no, I listen to the piece of music with you at home. And I said, why? And he said well, I don't know how I would want to behave in that situation. I haven't been to a concert before. Can I tap my foot? Can I tap my finger? Can I bop along? Can I not? So he said he'd be much more comfortable in a virtual space listening to the thing. And then watching a concert on the television or something. And then he'd be willing to go. (Participant R).

Botton and Armstong (2013) argue that engagement with art is useful because it "presents us with powerful examples of the kind of alien material that provokes defensive boredom and fear, and allows us time and privacy to learn to deal more strategically with it" (Botton & Armstrong, 2013: 45). This was echoed by Participant G's reflection:

Yeah, well I mean, an interesting thing about being here is, for me at least, and I would imagine I'm not alone in this, that's it's a very unsafe space in a way. It really does challenge you to put yourself out there. Especially if you're coming from a background that's much more, say like scientific or – you know, for me. So I think it's also very challenging. But in a very good way. (Participant G).

1.4.9 b) What is lost and what is gained: multi-sensory experiences and virtual learning

This particular exhibition was unusual in that we were able to see as well as touch the artworks; this provided an added layer of engagement and thought around how this tactile engagement is something that is lost online.

This exhibition is quite extraordinary because the artists here were really one of the pioneers of modernism….you could have the virtual display of this [current exhibition]…but the tactile element would be lost (Participant F).

Battistoni (2018) in writing about the Anni and Josef Albers artworks in the exhibition says the "multi-sensory approach that uses touch and hearing, allows us to enlarge the experience and suspend judgement giving rise to a more detailed study" (p.11), giving opportunities for all gallery visitors to explore and consider the pieces in different ways and from multiple perspectives.

Physical objects. "The first creative decision an artist makes is the choice of materials, and no great artist ever takes this for granted." (Findlay, 2017, p. 112). Participant F prompted the group to think about this:

Think about a newspaper, how different that is to a thick piece of drawing paper, how different that is to a tablet of stone, how different it is to vellum. It's a challenge for an artist – because it's going to create a different set of mark-marking. Whether the paper absorbs the ink, whether it resists ink… do you have to cut into it, or do you have to chisel your mark? (Participant F).

Findlay (2017) also emphasises the power of texture and physical objects, stating that "even when we are not actually touching an object, our eyes can sense its texture, and we can be shocked by the novelty of the material or we can enjoy the physical 'feel' of it" (p. 119). This was of particular relevance to us—a colleague we had in attendance has a vision impairment and, as such, had previously been excluded from discussions around art. The tactile physicality available in these objects meant that:

I enjoyed being around and experiencing [the exhibition]. It's not, I suppose, usual for me to be able to experience a museum in the way in which this exhibition makes available. (Participant B).

The tactile elements of the exhibition helped to underscore how it is predominantly the visual out of all of the senses, which is privileged within the online learning space. As stated by Participant F: "the digital does tend to flatten everything" and as a result "things that you're touching and using and feeling" is not captured online, and therefore a "loss occurs".

> And to be able to touch the tapestry itself, it was a nice experience. And it just gives a whole glimpse into what these people were thinking. (Participant B).

The engagement with tactile elements also helped participants realize aspects of their own disciplines:

> I realised that the tactile things [in the exhibition] that are there helped me to see things in the art that I wouldn't have seen otherwise….this helped me think about teaching students how to look down a microscope. It's not just the physical act of using the microscope. Students know that cells are tiny. But when they look down the microscope they don't know what they're looking for. (Participant RS).

This experience was heightened for RS in terms of these particular artefacts: the image of squares accompanied with the tactile representation. This is reflected in Figure 1.1 above but is easier to see the relationship between the wall image and the tactile representation in Figure 1.3.

> What we see is steeped in our past experience. So for me, I looked at those three squares inside each other. And I didn't see any kind of perspective at all. And then I saw the tactile thing and I saw okay, one is going out, one is going in. And when I looked at it again I was able to see it. So the two different kind of modes of it helped me to understand it better. (Participant RS).

Figure 1.3 Anni Albers, Red Meander II and tactile model, Gallery 2.
Image from: http://www.glucksman.org/exhibitions/josef-anni-albers

Get some perspective

This echoes Battistoni's summation of the purpose of the Anni and Josef Albers exhibition in that "sight in fact immediately clarifies an image, but implies a purely aesthetic judgement…Therefore the [exhibition] increases fruition for the visually disabled but also, opens up the possibility of a new explorative path accessible to everyone" (Battistoni, 2018, p. 11).

The use and experience of different mediums also highlighted the flexibility of the artist in order to create, and be creative:

> What I liked especially too, was the way in which Annie Albers changed her style of artwork to suit her stability as her hands began to shake in later life. And instead of feeling that she had to turn away from her creativity and her artwork, she just adapted it. And she created a whole new way of addressing her artwork and demonstrating her talent. I thought that was very important. (Participant B).

Auditory. Being within the gallery space reminded the group of "how much of the world is available to you through other senses" (Participant F). The auditory element in terms of a gallery space was highlighted:

> In the real space, it's just a different atmosphere completely. Like the minute you come in, the atmosphere changes and the sounds are different. (Participant B)
>
> I think the acoustics of galleries are extraordinary. It really shifts how you relate in your own body to the work that you're looking at, if you can hear lots of things… sometimes it's not really that great if you keep hearing the lift pinging on, and if you're looking at a work quietly to study a work, you maybe don't want that. But then sometimes it can be really joyous, because it's lovely to hear other sounds or other things. (Participant F)

Again, this is a profound learning moment for the team, in considering which senses are privileged in the online environment (arguably mainly visual although with some auditory). This realization of imbalance is also being recognised by certain academics in the way they structure assessment tasks and provide feedback to students – e.g. they are allowing oral and aural options. (Oldale & Knightley, 2018; Sinclair, 2018).

Olfactory. The Glucksman Gallery has hosted some very innovative and provocative works, as this comment from Participant F highlights in particular:

> We did an exhibition…with our colleagues in the microbiome institute. And we had an eight meter wall of Nutella….we opened the show at the beginning of December. It was kind of magical for the month of December when we were all thinking chocolate and Christmas. But coming in in January when we all kind of feeling really different…And then in February, and then in March. I thought there was going to be a mutiny. I don't think anyone here will ever eat Nutella again. You know, it was interesting, if you can describe that to [students online]. Because Nutella is one of those almost like global smells, I just think that people can extrapolate to it almost being that [overwhelming], but it's to remember that if you're looking at just an image of that space in a virtual gallery, you will not have the same experience of being in the space. But you can conjure it. (Participant F).

Findlay argues that "The choice of materials is obviously based on culture, but artists who break with historical precedent and use unconventional materials are challenging themselves to create the equivalent of new alphabets and challenging us to engage them as potent vehicles of expression." (Findlay 2017, p. 112). Participant F's description of the 'wall of Nutella' is multi-faceted and links here with Finday's ideas of materials choice being cultural, one could also argue, political (given the global concern over palm oil and

Figure 1.4 Richard Forest 'Cube' (far left) and 'Hive' (right).

Image from: http://www.glucksman.org/exhibitions/please-touch-tactile-encounters

Nutella). Whilst the real impact of the smell of the Nutella wall would not be felt in an online context, as participant F states, 'you can conjure it' due to its universality. Again, when we view the virtual teaching context as a continuum rather than being all good or all bad, we can see how this makes sense: Leaving students to fill in the blanks with their own learning.

> And the last thing I saw was Richard Forest's cube [Figure 1.4]. And I'm looking at it like, I'm kind of feeling it. It was the spaces in between that really made the cube be the cube. So I was just thinking again, it's not about filling the script for people or whatnot. You have a lot of time when [students online] need to be in a space on their own, thinking, and figuring out and squaring up their own cubes for themselves…and what we need to do is just to be positive, say it's your space and your think, and share whatever comes out of that. (Participant N).

Participant N's comment echoes the ethos at the heart of object-based learning: "If…we open up the opportunity to students asking their own questions, thus risking that we the 'experts' might not have the answers, we can begin to collaboratively explore much more fundamental issues" (Kador, Chatterjee & Hannan, 2017:60).

Thinking about the various sensory aspects of the exhibition underlined some important insights for the teaching team, as Participant RS outlines below:

> I was thinking how [the different sensory elements] translated to the online space. If you're dealing with text to get ideas across, but like what other modes might there be? You could use sound, maybe, to explain something…so the methods used does kind of impact how you understand something. The extra kind of resources and modes that are available to interpret it are really important. (Participant RS).

Emotional. "Growth occurs when we discover how to remain authentically ourselves in the presence of potentially threatening things" (De Botton & Armstrong, 2013:52). This emotional element was an

Get some perspective

Figure 1.5 Anni Albers, Line Involvement VI and tactile model, Gallery 2.
Image from: http://www.glucksman.org/exhibitions/josef-anni-albers

important throughline for participants in reflecting on their own learning, as Participant G's comment regarding Figure 1.5 indicates:

> So in this unsafe space…standing for me in front of the line – the arrangement of lines, being able to stand there a only a couple of inches away and looking closely at that is fantastic, because for me, what I take from that is…we work on brain wiring and how cells grow together and so on. And that's what I see. But somebody else could equally see a Celtic knot, for example…and students being in that space, I think is extremely challenging. But that's not necessarily a bad thing… To make connections between where you're coming from, and how what you're looking at makes you feel. (Participant G).

This is indeed the refrain echoed by Findlay (2017): we should be asking when we look at a work of art, not 'what does it mean' but rather 'how do I feel?' This changes the experience and encounter with the object into something transformational.

Theme 2: Creativity as a gateway for disciplinary and interdisciplinary connections

Creativity surrounds us on all sides: from composers to chemists, cartoonists to choreographers. But creativity is a puzzle, a paradox, some say a mystery" (Boden, 1994:519).

Being creative is integral to all disciplines, yet it is not often mentioned as an explicit skill for development in higher educational contexts, such as syallabi or course outlines (Jackson & Shaw, 2006; Kleiman, 2008; Marquis et al., 2017; Marquis, Radan, & Liu, 2017). However, the modern 'super-complex' world is likely to require qualities and dispositions that beyond capture within a language of skills and outcomes (Barnett & Coat, 2005, in Jackson & Shaw, 2006).

For this installation (Figure 1.6) 'Colour Threshold #3', gallery visitors are invited to wear a cloak provided and walk between the screens. This piece prompted discussion participants to think of concepts such as play and creativity.

> That piece [Colour Threshold] also really reminds me of the ease of play that children have. It is so important to try and recoup into our teaching our learning. And you know, they are so uninhibited in how they engage with that. Because just naturally they build worlds around it, and

Figure 1.6 Rhona Byrne, Colour Threshold #3, Gallery 1.
Image from: http://www.glucksman.org/exhibitions/please-touch-tactile-encounters

> they'll be telling you whole narratives…they're exploring their world. And they're pushing their boundaries of thinking. And to me, that kind of creative work that we all need to do as scientists and researchers is really linked play. Because it lets us kind of have this unburdened exploration. And hopefully the museum space and the online space can share that. Because those are values that we can equally have online or offline, is a little bit of play. (Participant F).

Participant F's comments reflect the notions of creativity in higher education: the definition of which can be distilled down as the ability to "imagine, explore, synthesize, connect, discover, invent and adapt" (Jackson & Shaw, 2006:90), which works across multiple disciplines.

It also reminded the group of the competing narratives around whether technology is inhibiting or encouraging creativity and imagination. However, as Participant O's comments highlight with the example of virtual reality, one could also argue that the tenets of imagination, exploration, synthesis, connection, discovery, invention and adaptation could be applied to this context:

> So in virtual reality you can take get students to lift their chemical elements off the page, and you can have them two molecules of hydrogen, or you can have them hold molecules of oxygen, and you can put them together. And water appear in front of them. Things that you just can't do in a traditional teaching environment. And so they're really working on how you facilitate and engage a child's imagination. And really engage a child's imagination. And when you experience that stuff yourself, you see it's absolutely amazing, and it evokes your creative side, definitely (Participant O).

This is a useful concept to tie the thoughts together: the artworks became a way of tying in multidisciplinary aspects together in a similar way to how the idea of creativity is a connection across disciplines and modes of delivery.

Conclusion

Although some artwork may seem odd, confusing, or boring, "there is likely to be an aspect of [an artists'] ambitions that we can, with sufficient self-exploration, relate to in a personal way." (Botton & Armstrong, 2013:49). This is why art works so well across disciplines, because the fear of vulnerability and opening up personally in relation to a work of art can be ameliorated by looking at it through a disciplinary lens. Staff in this workshop were not asked to give their personal perspectives on the art per se. but look at it through the lenses of a teaching and learning context.

This experience of engaging in slow looking provided a space which was out of the ordinary for the usual feedback and professional development workshops for staff which usually would be focused on complaining about the limitations of the technology and inhibitions in terms of teaching. The artworks provided a further means and depth for exploration of issues which as a result became less like 'whinging and moaning' and consisted more of reflection and in-depth consideration of the nuances of online teaching. Engaging with artworks prompted language and thought around processes and concepts arguably would not have otherwise been articulated with such clarity.

Being forced out of their comfort zone or space was a transformational moment for teaching staff in helping them to realize the complexities and challenges their students face, and possible emotions they feel, when interacting in an unfamiliar environment. It enabled thinking about different patterns and 'energy', of observational and reflective learning timelines of their students. Even the consideration of an online platform as an architectural space was a useful framework for discussion, when considering the layout of the gallery and the artworks within it.

The implications are wide-reaching in terms of further development of this practice for teaching fellows. The author intends to further explore these teaching and learning stories in order to help these inform curriculum development of the online Certificate and Diploma in Teaching and Learning in Higher Education. For example, there is huge scope for the consideration of how to encompass more alternative sensory elements into the programs, and offering choice to students in seeking these out. Further development for the teaching fellows will be developing scope for expression of values and intersection with their teaching—to what extent can teachers be their "real selves" online? (Oldale & Knightley, 2018) and what are the implications for the virtual space being perceived as 'unsafe' for the teaching fellows? The author plans to repeat these workshops twice— at the start and end of each academic year—so that the teaching fellows can reflect on their experiences before and after engaging in their online teaching. The great advantage of the Glucksman Gallery exhibitions is that they are constantly changing, allowing for fresh perspectives to emerge at different points in time.

The implications for further development of the practice of slow looking extends beyond the context of this research and into other realms of digital humanities work as it is multi-faceted and applicable across all disciplines and expertise levels, can involve staff as well as students, and can be fully inclusive such as the 'Please Touch' and 'Voyage inside a blind experience' exhibitions.

References

Adult and Continuing Education, Creative Art, Culture and Inclusion (Disability Studies) https://www.ucc.ie/en/modules/ace/ad5847.html

Anonymous. *School of Pharmacy Team Wins Award* (2015). Retrieved from: https://www.ucc.ie/en/pharmacy/events/news/school-of-pharmacy-team-receives-award-for-their-study-on-the-use-of-art-based-teaching-strategies.html

Battistoni, G. (2018). Feeling the experience. In A. Sarteanesi, V. Maggini and Atlante Servizi Culturali (Eds.), *Josef and Anni Albers: Voyage inside a blind experience*. Perugia: Atlante Magonza.

Blackshields, D., Cronin, J., Higgs, B., Kilcommins, S., McCarthy, M., & Ryan, A. (Eds.). (2014). *Integrative learning: International research and practice*. London: Routledge.

Boden, M.A. (1994). Précis of the creative mind: myths and mechanisms. *Brain and Behavioural Science*, 17: 519–531.

Cronin, J.G.R., McMahon, J.P., & Waldron, M. (2009). Critical survey of information technology use in higher education – blended classrooms. In Carla R. Payne (Ed.), *Information technology and constructivism in higher education: Progressive learning frameworks* (203–215). New York: Information Science Reference. http://www.igi-global.com/chapter/critical-survey-information-technology-use/23497

De Botton, A., & Armstrong, J. (2013). *Art as therapy*. London: Phaidon Press.

Elkins, J. (Ed.). (2007). *Visual practices across the university*. Munich: Wilhelm Fink Verlag.

Elkins, J. (2009). *How to use your eyes*. Oxon: Routledge.

Findlay. M. (2017). *Seeing slowly: Looking at modern art*. New York: Prestel.

Geismar, H. (2018). *Museum object lessons for the digital age*. London: UCL Press.

Glucksman Gallery: A History. Retrieved from http://www.glucksman.org/about/information/history

Hyland, A. (2018). The Contribution of Project Zero to our Understanding of Teaching and Learning: CIRTL Seminar Presentation, 23rd January, 2018. https://www.ucc.ie/en/media/support/cirtl/HylandA_PZ.pdf

Jackson, N., & Shaw, M. (2006). Subject perspectives on creativity. In N. Jackson, M. Oliver, M. Shaw & J. Wisdom (Eds.), *Developing creativity in higher education* (89–108). New York: Routledge.

Kador, T., Chatterjee, H., & Hannan, L. (2017). The materials of life: Making meaning through object-based learning in twenty-first century higher education. In B. Carnell and D. Fung (Eds.), *Developing the higher education curriculum: Research-based education in practice* (60–74). UCL Press: London.

Kleiman, P. (2008). Towards transformation: Conceptions of creativity in higher education. *Innovations in Education and Teaching International*, *45*(3), 209–217.

Jennings Gallery: https://www.ucc.ie/en/jennings-gallery/gallerymissionpolicy/

Marquis, E., Haqqee, Z., Kirby, S., Liu, A., Puri, V., Cockroft, R. et al. (2017). Connecting students and staff for teaching and learning enquiry. In B. Carnell and D. Fung (Eds.), *Developing the higher education curriculum: Research-based education in practice* (203–216). UCL Press: London.

Marquis, E., Radan, K., & Liu, A. (2017). A present absence: undergraduate course outlines and the development of student creativity across disciplines. *Teaching in Higher Education*, *22*(2), 222–238.

McCarthy, M. (2010). The arts in education as an integrative learning approach. In Higgs, Kilcommins & Ryan (Eds.), *Making connections: Intentional teaching for integrative learning* (115–127). Published by NAIRTL, Ireland. Retrieved from http://www.nairtl.ie

Medical Graduates Exhibition: Just What the Doctor Ordered. (2017). Retrieved from: https://www.ucc.ie/en/jennings-gallery/past/current/

Oldale, M., & Knightley, M. (2018). Values, identity and successful online teaching relationships. In J. Baxter, G. Callaghan and J. McAvoy (Eds.), *Creativity and critique in online learning* (219–239). Cham: Palgrave Macmillan.

Pujol L., Roussou M., Poulou S., Balet O., Vayanou M., & Ioannidis Y. (2013). Personalizing interactive digital story-telling in archaeological museums: The CHESS project. In G. Earl, T. Sly, A. Chrysanthi, P. Murrieta-Flores, C. Papadopoulos, I. Romanows- ka, D. Wheatley (Eds.), *Archaeology in the digital era. Papers from the 40th Annual Conference of Computer Applications and Quantitative Methods in Archaeology (CAA)*. Amsterdam.

Rehn, N., Maor, D., & McConney, A. (2016). Investigating teacher presence in courses using synchronous videocon-ferencing. *Distance Education*, *37*(3), 302–316.

Sinclair, S. (2018). Creativity, criticality and engaging the senses in higher education: Creating online opportunities for multi-sensory learning and assessment. In J. Baxter, G. Callaghan and J. McAvoy (Eds). *Creativity and critique in online learning* (103–122). Cham: Palgrave Macmillan.

Springer, J., Kajder, S., & Brazas, J.B. (2004). Digital Storytelling at the National Gallery of Art, presented at Museums and the Web Conference, Arlington, Virginia, 2004. Washington DC / Arlington VA, USA: Archives & Museum Informatics.

Tishman, S. (2017). *Slow looking: The art and practice of learning through observation*. London: Routledge.

Weber, N.F. (2018). New ways of seeing. In A. Sarteanesi, V. Maggini and Atlante Servizi Culturali (Eds). *Josef and Anni Albers: Voyage inside a blind experience*. Perugia: Atlante Magonza.

2
DIGITAL APTITUDE
Finding the right questions for dance studies
Hetty Blades and Scott deLahunta

2.1 Introduction

2. 1.1 Trajectories from the intersection between dance and digital

Dance research has evolved significantly over the past four decades, during which dance studies has been established as an academic discipline with its own university departments, courses, publications, conferences and networks. The scope of the discipline has widened significantly during this time. As Janet O'Shea, co-editor of The Routledge Dance Studies Reader points out:

> The period from the late 1980s to the early 2000s was one of intense activity in dance scholarship, characterized by fundamental shifts in the field. Dance writers no longer concerned themselves only with the dance work and the artist's biography but also with how dances engage with their social, historical, political and economic contexts. (2010: 1)

Scholars in dance studies now often draw on thinking from disciplines such as literature, anthropology, history, cultural studies, gender studies, critical race studies and philosophy, among others. This broadening of the field has called for the adaptation and development of various research methods drawn from the different disciplines, and the field of dance studies, like performance studies before it, has demonstrated how adept it can be at this. Therefore, given the rapid growth of the field of research, new theories, methods and tools, referred to as the digital humanities, one might imagine dance scholars would have begun to integrate new digital methods of study into their research. Especially since the early 1990s, when 'digital dance', sometimes referred to as 'dance and technology', established itself as a sub-field within creative dance practice (see Birringer 1998; deLahunta 2002; Dixon 2007; Salter 2010).[1] However, based on a general lack of evidence from the field, e.g. indicative panels and papers at prominent dance studies conferences, this is arguably not the case to date.[2] The proposal we wish to make here draws attention to the role of digital aptitude in the development of digital methods for dance studies. Crucial to digital aptitude is understanding how to combine the right research questions and frameworks with the appropriate digital tools. To do this we will firstly focus on a narrower field of research emerging from practice and tightly connected to the development of 'digital dance'. Secondly, we will consider projects which demonstrate the combined approach we envision required for dance studies to make advances in digital methods for research.

The term 'digital dance' refers to dance making processes and performances that include digital technologies as an integral feature. Starting in the early to mid-1990s, dance and technology artists used the early Internet for distributed performances, explored the multimedia potential of the CD-ROM and experimented with sensor technologies to map movement and gesture to other media (e.g. sound and video) in real-time. Importantly, these projects often involved close collaboration between dance artists and technology specialists, usually artists themselves; composers, filmmakers, designers, with expertise in computer hardware and software. Many of these same basic ideas and kinds of collaborations have continued since the end of the twentieth century with more emphasis on 3D motion capture, developments such as 'wearable technologies' and more recently robotics, Artificial Intelligence and Virtual Reality applications have been incorporated into dance making.[3] Whereas dance scholar Harmony Bench (2015), proposes a distinction between these practice-based developments and dance studies research using digital methods, we wish to point towards a continuum between the two areas and consider how research and thinking about dance and digital technology has arisen from practice, in particular where 'digital dance' has evolved alongside the documentation turn in contemporary dance practice.

Over the past two decades, there has been a shift in the ways that the documentation of dance takes place as well as a re-thinking of its value and potential contribution both to the development of the art form and its communicative potential. This documentation turn signals not only an examination of how and why dance might be inscribed, preserved and shared, but also a change from thinking about documentation as 'other' to artistic practice to considering it is as an integral part of the form. The ephemerality which is often understood to be fundamental to what dance 'is' makes the nature of its documents particularly interesting, and a number of scholars have explored this new thinking around the relationship between performance and its record (see Boxberger and Wittmann 2013; Reason 2006; Sant 2017; Whatley 2008). The increased presence of practice-as-research within the academy, as well as the growth of digital technologies and their effect on the recording, analysis, representation and distribution of artistic practice are factors that have contributed to this rethinking of the role and value of documentation. Practice-as-research opened the way to questions regarding the epistemic yield of embodied practices including dance, aligning these practices with other disciplinary fields. This has interesting implications for dance documentation, shifting it away from the domain of historical preservation[4] toward a means of knowledge transmission. Furthermore, the advent of digital recording technologies and their subsequent widespread availability, particularly video, significantly altered the conversation about the documentation of dance, with many scholars examining how technology impacts on the nature of dance and its records (see Bleeker 2016; Dixon 2007; deLahunta and Shaw 2006 & 2008). In the field of contemporary dance, documentation is now often viewed as an integral part of the creative process and/or the work itself (see Khan 2018).[5] In research contexts which are often interdisciplinary, as will be discussed below, documentation is increasingly examined as part of contemporary dance and integral to our understanding of the form.

The evolution of 'digital dance' practices alongside this shift in dance documentation can be seen in a small number of ambitious interdisciplinary choreographer-led research projects that sought to bring choreographic ideas and processes into new exchanges with general audiences and other specialist knowledge areas. The projects were developed primarily in the first decade of the twenty-first century and grew from artist-led experiments with technology. This collection of projects, sometimes referred to as 'choreographic objects'[6] (Leach, deLahunta and Whatley 2008) involved various collaborations between dance artists, interaction designers, filmmakers, programmers and scientists. They drew on a range of digital approaches to analyse and visualise choreographic principles and became the focus of diverse scholarly study for the first time in Maaike Bleeker's edited collection *Transmission in Motion: The Technologizing of Dance* (2016).

> Each in their own way, these projects explore the potential of various technologies (from the old technology of writing to the latest possibilities for motion tracking and movement steered interfaces) to become how we create, make sense, and share. Together these projects offer a

Digital aptitude

complex image of knowledge cultures in transformation. The ways in which they explore the potential of various media from the perspective of dance reflects broader transformations in practices of knowledge transmission" (Bleeker 2016: xx–xxi)

In this chapter, we discuss some of these projects and examine what they meant for the development of dance research and practice, before turning our attention specifically to the role of annotation within the field. We go on to discuss *Movement on the Move*,[7] a project which does not belong to the field of 'choreographic objects' and has different aims in as much as it arises not from dance practice, but from the needs of dance scholarship, in particular the historical study of dance touring. This project, led by dance scholars Kate Elswit and Harmony Bench demonstrates how digital methods might enhance knowledge about dance, using map visualisations to highlight the circulation of dance through different cultural contexts. The term digital methods can be misleading as many of the procedures used are already standard and "not unique to the digital realm" (Berry and Fagerjord 2017: 107). However, we will use it following Bench and Elswit (2015) to describe some of the ways that technology has been adopted and collaboratively developed by dance practitioners and researchers to enhance understanding of dance. More precisely, we propose that digital methods rely on the development of specific questions and frameworks and a certain level of aptitude with digital technologies to be used effectively. By putting both the 'choreographic objects' projects and *Movement on the Move* into dialogue, we aim to draw attention to these key aspects.

2.1.2 Choreographic objects

A pivotal moment in the development of 'digital dance' practice and research was the publication of choreographer William Forsythe's CD-Rom *Improvisation Technologies: A Tool for the Analytic Dance Eye* in 1999, which he created in collaboration with the ZKM/Center for Art and Media beginning in the mid-1990s (Forsythe 1999). The distinctive component of *Improvisation Technologies* are lines drawn on top of digital video to demonstrate some of the key principles of Forsythe's approach to improvisation and make potential connections between body parts visible. Former Forsythe dramaturg, Rebecca Groves suggests that the CD-Rom "offered a new pedagogical tool for professional and student dancers. It provided audiences with a set of analytical skills to become better readers of dance performances" (2007: 92). In the mid-1990s, multi-media was seen to be the leading edge in digital development (see Gansing 2016), and Forsythe's *Improvisation Technologies* was considered the exemplar of what could be done using digital technologies to communicate or transmit dance knowledge. As such, the CD-Rom was an early and significant contributor to the documentation turn in dance. In 2005, Forsythe followed up the collaboration with ZKM through a close research partnership with the Advanced Computing Center for the Arts and Design, The Ohio State University, to create the website *Synchronous Objects for One Flat Thing, reproduced* (Forsythe, Shaw & Palazzi 2009). This project involved a large interdisciplinary team including geographers, mathematicians, designers and architects, working alongside dance practitioners, researchers and programmers. During a four-year period, they examined the abstract choreography of Forsythe's *One Flat Thing, reproduced* (2000) from a range of different perspectives and used a variety of digital approaches to demonstrate its principles. The resulting visualisations, interactive tools and explanatory graphs and presentations are outcomes of the team's attention to the structuring principles of the work such as the cuing system, which Forsythe created as "an intricate network of dependency between the dancers by embedding the piece with hundreds of cues." (Shaw 2014: 111). [Figure 2.1].

The term 'choreographic objects' was first proposed by James Leach, Sarah Whatley and Scott deLahunta in their AHRC-funded project 'Choreographic Objects: Traces and Artifacts of Physical Intelligence' (2008–2009).[8] This project drew Forsythe's projects into dialogue with three other choreographers and companies working on related digital outputs. The other 'choreographic objects' involved were *Siobhan Davies Replay* (2009), an online archive of choreographer Siobhan Davies' work developed in collaboration

Figure 2.1 Cueing System. Still from annotated video illustrating the complex system of cueing in One Flat Thing, reproduced

Source: Synchronous Objects Project, The Ohio State University and The Forsythe Company

with researchers at Coventry University, Italian/Dutch choreographer Emio Greco | PC (Pieter C. Scholten)'s *Double Skin/Double Mind*, (2007) an interactive installation developed in collaboration with the Amsterdam School of the Arts and the *Choreographic Language Agent*, a project emerging from the Choreography and Cognition dance-science research collaborations of London-based dance maker Wayne McGregor (2008). There are three key characteristics these 'choreographic objects' projects share: 1.) The aim to make explicit aspects of choreographic practice for others to access and study often via a form of publication; 2.) the varying (from simple to complex) use of digital technology; and 3.) their collaborative nature gathering together designers, editors, filmmakers, artists, programmers and other specialists. These characteristics are shared by other projects, therefore the concept of 'choreographic objects' assumes a more substantial connection to the documentation turn dance has taken in the past twenty years and have contributed significantly to the impact digital technologies have had on this. From this perspective, 'choreographic objects' can be seen to include Steve Paxton's multimedia DVD-Rom project *Material for the Spine: A Movement Study* (2008), developed in collaboration with researchers, filmmakers and designers working for the Brussels-based Contradanse dance resource centre[9], and the series of book and DVD-Rom publications by Anne Teresa de Keersmaeker and Bojana Cvejić beginning with *A Choreographer's Score: Fase, Rosas danst Rosas, Elena's Aria, Bartók* (2012). While using low-end technology, mainly films of de Keersmaeker demonstrating and drawing choreographic principles on a blackboard while being interviewing from off camera, these publications explicitly aim to connect with the 'choreographic objects' projects of Forsythe and Greco.[10]

With diverse artistic approaches as starting points, these 'choreographic objects' projects achieved the required levels of digital aptitude and expertise through forms of collaboration, cooperation and commission. The methods used drew on key research questions arising from practice, (e.g one of the questions Forsythe was asking was "what else might physical thinking look like?"), clear research frameworks involving iterative processes and the use of digital tools. These projects continued to bring dance artists and technology specialists together, working collaboratively and carrying on this relationship established in the 'digital dance' and 'dance and technology' projects of the 1990s. A very high level of digital aptitude, with perhaps the exception of de Keersmaeker and Cvejić's publication, was integral to these projects, and in this regard they had resources for designers and programmers not easily available to others. This sometimes meant that software developed specifically for the project was not easily shared and entering or picking up where the project left off required equivalent levels of software expertise. Even these relatively high levels of resource could not assure long term sustainability with the result that components and platforms no longer run on current operating systems. Some of the research trajectories emerging from these projects, such as that involving annotation as we will discuss, take into consideration these core issues regarding technology development in relation to future digital methods for dance research.

2.1.3 Movement on the Move

Movement on the Move arises from a different perspective to 'choreographic objects'. Bench and Elswit are motivated by their scholarly interest in the history of touring and how digital methods might enhance knowledge in this area. *Movement on the Move* comprises three research projects: *Mapping Touring, Dance in Transit* and *Dunham's Data*. Each of these combines archival research, data analysis and visualisation using digital tools to track the geographical movement of dance such as Tableau Public, a free service for publishing interactive data visualizations on-line,[11] and Palladio, a data-driven set of tools for analyzing relationships across time developed by Stanford University.[12] *Mapping Touring* is the primary focus of this chapter. This project focused on the touring of ballet and modern dance companies in the first half of the twentieth century and resulted in three components: A Database, Map Visualisation and Route Visualisation.[13] The development of the database itself was a critical step in the 柔 research process as it relied on existing archival dance material, mainly written records. Later in this chapter, we closely examine these three outputs, describing how they were enabled through digital aptitude which drew on methods comprising the right tools and strong research questions. We also discuss the nature of the unique insights offered to the study of dance history.

Despite arising from different motivations, 'choreographic objects' projects and *Movement on the Move* both share a concern with dance documents as diverse as customised recordings, existing films, written records, photographs, press cuttings and programmes. To develop both the 'choreographic objects' results and the maps and databases produced in *Mapping Touring,* these documents are processed to generate data, which is then structured and analysed. Their research frameworks make use of iterative processes, involving several stages during which the information from the document is extracted, ordered, analysed and re-presented, with results often folded recursively back into the next research phase. Although motivated by artistic and scholarly research concerns rather than dance preservation, both 'choreographic objects' and *Movement on the Move* highlight aspects of the documentation turn. The way that documents are processed, generated and (re)contextualised sheds light on their value for the understanding of dance and implies that dance cannot be disentangled from its record, thus demonstrating this new paradigm for dance documentation. To add another perspective, performance scholar Toni Sant has published an edited volume titled *Documenting Performance: The Context and Processes of Digital Curation and Archiving* (2017) in which documentation refers to "the process of storing documents and preserving them in a systematic way for long-term access through an archive" (1). For Sant the distinction between documentation and document is critical as it draws attention to "what happens and needs to happen when a document is created." (1) While the examples we discuss in this chapter are not archives in the conventional sense of the word, the projects are aligned with Sant's concept of documentation due to the way that they work with and re-organise documents to shed new light on their meaning and relevance. This understanding of documentation as part of a process, rather than an individual record, also draws attention to the labour and skills involved in these projects, which are motivated by pertinent questions about the potentials of technology in relation to dance and involve skills in gathering and organising data, the kinds of skills that constitute what we are referring to here as 'digital aptitude'.

2.2 Annotation: Collecting dance data from practice

The 'choreographic objects' projects described already emphasised the idea that choreographic principles could be made more "visible as explicit traces" (deLahunta 2013: 176) using computer-aided design. Some of this was achieved through graphic visualisation, drawing dynamic lines and curves on top of digital video recordings to demonstrate improvisational ideas or indicate structural relationships in the choreography [Figure 2.1].[14] To achieve this in the *Synchronous Objects* web-based project of William Forsythe, data was extracted manually by asking the performers to comment on the video recordings they were themselves in. They were asked to explain certain dance units, naming them, identifying where they started and stopped (Forsythe and Shaw 2009). Once this information was collected and converted into machine readable data, software such as *Processing*[15] was used to generate new visual forms that reflected the underlying choreographic structure, recalling Forsythe's original question regarding "what else can physical thinking look like". In another high-profile example from the *Motion Bank* project with American choreographer Deborah Hay,[16] Amin Weber, a digital artist using tools for 3D digital cinema created a high-resolution film animation based on Hay's written score *No Time to Fly* [Figure 2.2] (see Vincent et al 2018). In the final on-line presentation of the results of this research, the animation is linked to the relevant parts of the written score, which plays alongside the film. In another example of linking the time of one "digital object" (see Hui 2016) to another, small interactive animations are triggered by the figure of the performer (Jonathan Burrows or Matteo Fargion) recorded on video, or other sources from YouTube, offering an insight into how they work with patterns in a particular way in their performances.[17] In each of these are examples of annotation of time-based media, the unitisation of the Forsythe recording, linking between Deborah Hay's written score and the film animation and playback of one digital object triggered by another. For each, the aim was to use computer-aided design to reveal something about the unique artistic approach, not possible without the use of digital technology.

Figure 2.2 Still from animation by Amin Weber based on Deborah Hay's written score corresponding to the Mend the Road section of the performance

Source: Motion Bank

Digital aptitude

Crucial to our discussion of digital methods in relation to dance studies, the annotation processes for these projects involved human observation and decision taking (what to mark and how) which further demonstrates how digital methods require more than just the adoption of digital tools. As part of an iterative design framework, the annotation generated new data recorded in a corresponding form; e.g. an Excel sheet, or using a custom-built software for recording the annotations directly to the playtime of the digital video. The machine-based linking from one digital object to another relies on standards and data models (see deLahunta & Jenett 2016), but the manual annotation of dance recordings as described above resists the application of standards. These manual annotations made as a part of these projects corresponded to particular perspectives and approaches, for example, Deborah Hay's annotations marked the start of each part of the written score sequence.[18] The annotations for *Synchronous Objects* corresponded to the three different parts of the overall choreographic system (Forsythe and Shaw 2009). In both cases, performers in the video made or validated the annotations. General annotation approaches have yet to materialise in dance practice and research. While digital video recording devices have become ubiquitous in dance creation and rehearsal contexts, the practice of video annotation currently has no such foothold in the professional field. Dance focussed software development to date only goes so far as to speculate about the possible benefits of video annotation.[19] In the sciences, a field like cognitive linguistics has been using video annotation for behavioural analysis (see Elan and Anvil[20]), but this kind of systematic research involving video analysis is not integrated into the culture of dance practice and scholarship, although there are exceptions.[21] Several dance education institutions, such as Trinity Laban in London, have expressed interest in annotation due to the integration of commercial streaming media services such as Planet eStream[22] into their IT systems. These video services provide annotation tools, but the lack of extant methods of annotation practice means the schools are not using them.[23]

The only professional dance company to date to regularly use video annotation has been The Forsythe Company (TFC). The tool they used was called 'Piecemaker' a web-based application originally developed by company performer/collaborator David Kern for annotating video recordings of the creation process of new works of TFC from 2008 to 2014. Piecemaker was used for recording video and dramaturgic notes simultaneously, live, during rehearsals and automatically linking the two (Vass-Rhee 2019). In 2010, the *Motion Bank* project took over the development of this software application (applying it to the previously described 'choreographic objects' with Deborah Hay and Jonathan Burrows & Matteo Fargion) and continues to develop it today. It was the application used to support the creation of the on-line digital scores already mentioned, e.g. for annotating Deborah Hay's *No Time To Fly* (2010). Following the end of this first phase of *Motion Bank* in 2014, the aim shifted toward a full rewrite of the software to be low-threshold (easy to use), standard-compliant and open source designed for use in a variety of contexts, including dance education, creation, research and archiving. Standard compliant refers to the new W3C annotation standard published in February 2017, which offers insight into longer-term goals for the accumulation of annotations as dance data. Complying with the W3C standard will facilitate future digital pattern searching and discovery, support code sharing and enhancement, and contribute to the long-term sustainability of the software.[24]

In addition to the design and development of these systems, *Motion Bank* is engaged in on-going methodological research into the practice of annotation. There has been no empirical research undertaken specifically regarding the lack of extant methods for annotation in dance practice and research, but it may have different causes. One reason might be the position it imposes on the viewer to assume an analytical perspective and position fixed visual reference points relative to the experience of continuous flow valued in dance. It may also relate to tensions regarding an assumed difficulty in using verbal language to describe movement. In this regard, what is emerging is a new concern with the concept of dance vocabularies alongside these annotation forms. This has a very practical basis: the aim is to enhance a recording of dance by naming, tagging and/or describing events taking place at the precise time they happen. Dance vocabularies themselves are not new. They are already part of practice. They exist or emerge as an augmentation or aid to the dance experience, for example terminology used in training or rehearsal situations.[25] Vocabularies can constitute a shared conceptual framework the dance takes place 'inside of'. These vocabularies often, but not always, make use of metaphor. They can be descriptive or associative, "as a trigger for the imagination" (deLahunta 2015: 253). Other disciplinary lexicons might infiltrate and influence how these vocabularies evolve. These are not so-called 'movement' vocabularies, but are words, expressed explicitly in verbal or written form. They intersect with tacit understandings in unique ways and can be associated with the transmission of embodied knowledge. A key question now is to what extent these vocabularies might be used in annotation. What forms do they take, how much more classification structure or consistency is required? How do these vocabularies change when harnessed (as data) to mediated versions of the live experience?

There are currently more questions than answers, but here we wish to draw attention to the potential of digital methods for the study of dance emerging from the field of practice, with clear overlap with scholarship. This has much to do with the digital technology underpinning a major increase in the amount of on-line streaming video of dance.[26] In March 2012, the renowned French choreographer Jérôme Bel took part in an interview for Tate Live: Performance Room during which time he made the following statement "YouTube is very important for the performing arts because it's our first library, it's our first data (…) it's a new world for the performing arts."[27] That was 2012 and now it is 2019. Streaming video numbers are simply staggering, the current Google answer to the question of 'how many videos are uploaded per minute' is 300 hours (60 hours per minute in 2012[28]), with 5 billion videos watched every day. Services like YouTube and Vimeo are used increasingly by choreographers world-wide to distribute and communicate recordings of their works. Bel's unstudied comment is a reflection on this new information distribution space for dance, one that is more accessible to a greater number of artists than many of the approaches used to publish the high-profile interdisciplinary research projects already discussed. What is required is an annotation tool for dancers that is sustainable, open source, interoperable, persistent and free. This then needs to be adopted by the professional and scholarly dance community, who are willing and interested to explore the kind of 'manual' vocabulary creation required to generate annotations than can link to other annotations, that are searchable and discoverable.

Motion Bank aims to continue the development of Piecemaker (now in its third version) to use in documenting and transmitting tacit, collaborative and embodied forms of knowledge and bringing these this into alignment with research into linked data, semantics and ontologies from information science. The view of some researchers (including *Motion Bank* but also other efforts in Athens, Lisbon, Zurich[29]) is that there is a link between dance vocabulary, annotation of time-based dance recordings (2D and 3D) that someday may generate the kinds of dance data that can be probed computationally, that can be scanned for unseen patterns and connections. However, now we don't know if or when this development from within the professional and scholarly dance community might happen, or if even such a collective effort involving the digitisation of practice is appropriate given other socio-political questions regarding data privacy, regulation and usage. Individual, unique collaborative projects continue to evolve, e.g. the recent *Motion Bank* collaboration with Finnish choreographer Taneli Törmä[30], but the software development challenges are significant and not well understood by non-developer communities, which includes most cultural and research funding organisations. And a lack of resources remains a challenge for other on-line dance publication projects, even when developed to be sustainable such as Oral Site[31] running on an open source and free software called Olga. These challenges make the following reflections on the *Movement on the Move* research especially interesting, as the scholars involved were less restricted by issues of software development but could build their questions because of their ability to manage the software aspects themselves.

2.3 Mapping touring

Movement on the Move is a collaborative project between Bench and Elswit, which arose from a recognition that they were individually exploring how digital methods could provide insight into the nature of dance touring (2016: 577). Elswit's previous work was concerned with considering how digital methods might "tackle the particular historical problem of tracing dance's complex global networks and infrastructures"

Digital aptitude

(Bench and Elswit 2016: 577) and she had been experimenting with how visualisations might enable better understanding of dance's circulation. Bench, on the other hand, had started to look at touring as a way to "historicize dance's screen-based transmission", building a series of datasets to track touring activities (Bench and Elswit 2016: 577). Both scholars therefore had digital aptitude before they began their joint venture. Together they aim to develop:

A broad account of how, why, and by what means dances travel requires that scholars attend to the lived, day-to-day experiences of multiple bodies, together with the financial, technical, and political infrastructures that support such movement moving. (2016: 577)

In order to do this, they created a database about the touring activities of Anna Pavlova's company during World War One and American Ballet Caravan's tour during World War Two by cataloguing archival data.[32] The cataloguing of this data allowed easier and more in-depth analysis than was possible working with archival material alone. Bench and Elswit suggest that, "The power of the digital database lies in the standardization of data, which facilitates access and usability, and its ability to manage datasets of whatever size." (2016: 583). The process of extracting information from the archival records and organizing it into the database links to Sant's point about documentation as a process, rather than merely a record. While the documents are likely to have been organized in a conventional archive when Bench and Elswit accessed them, their process of re-organization or 'documentation' allowed for new insights into the records, thus reiterating the idea that it is through the process of organisation that the record becomes part of the documentation of dance (Sant 2017:1).

Bench and Elswit describe how the process of organising the data and developing the visualisations in their shared work allowed scholarly insight into the cultural and political contexts of the tours. They suggest, "Digital research methods can work in tandem with more traditional scholarly ones to manage the scale of data truly necessary to model traveling dance in terms of what we call "dynamic spatial histories of movement" (2016: 575). These outputs are not intended solely to share information with other scholars, but the process of making them is itself research. For example, Bench and Elswit draw on Richard White to describe the visualising spatial history as a means of doing research (2016: 582). In this way, *Movement on the Move* aligns with *Motion Bank's* annotation processes in that both projects are driven by curiosity about what digital methods can offer our knowledge of dance. While *Motion Bank* and other 'choreographic objects' have been primarily motivated by questions arising from dance practice, *Movement on the Move* is motivated by the scholarly concerns of researchers. In both cases, key research questions and iterative frameworks support the specific digital tools being deployed.

Mapping Touring, was the first in the series of projects that comprise *Movement on the Move*. It was led by Bench, who used data about the touring activities of nine ballet and modern dance artists and their companies to develop a searchable database and two visualisations; one static Map Visualisation map and a Route Visualisation which traces the routes the companies travelled. All three of these outputs are available on the *Movement on the Move* website. Bench and Elswit suggest, "In the case of dance touring, the scale of digital analysis, particularly organized as a database and represented as a map, expands our capacity to trace real and potential networks of relation" (2016: 582). How then might the visualisation of spatial histories inform the thinking of other scholars? Bench and Elswit's acknowledgment of the tracing of 'potential' networks seems particularly relevant when encountering the *Mapping Touring* maps without prior knowledge of the touring activities of the company or access to detailed records of their experiences. Viewers can draw on their individual knowledge of the cultural and historical context of the period to imagine why the companies might have visiting the places they did as well as those places missing from the tours. This hypothetical analysis offers a form of insight which is based partially in historical facts about the places and dates of performances, represented in the visualisations and partially in the imagined logic motivating these decisions. This type of analysis might stay at the level of hypothesising or else become the starting point for

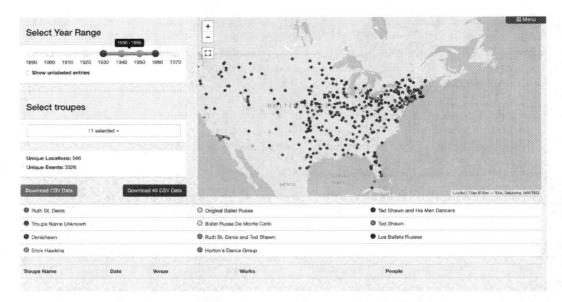

Figure 2.3 Screengrab from Map Visualisation. https://mappingtouring.osu.edu/visualization/map
Source: Harmony Bench & Chris Britt

more in-depth historical enquiry. Either way, the space for imagining potential networks and motivations offers a way in to thinking about the topic that might generate new research.

The way that the geographic movement of the companies is represented on the visualisations raises questions about the relationship between bodies, space, place and movement. The Map Visualisation [Figure 2.3] offers a static representation, indicating the positioning of people. Viewers can select the time period they wish to study (between 1890 and 1970) using a sliding scale on the left of the screen. Moving between different time periods allows viewers to see the emergence of clusters, where companies converged in states and cities during the same year. For example, selecting 1920 one can see how Ted Shawn and Ruth St Denis's companies moved around each other as they travelled the United States, almost converging on the Californian coast. Zooming out allows us to see how companies travelled beyond the United States, to South America, Europe, India, Asia and Australasia. Notably, during the entire period mapped, not a single company performed anywhere in Africa, Russia, the Middle East or Scandinavia. The ability to visualise which geographic regions were and were not included in touring activities sheds light on the potential political and diplomatic relations at play during the period.

While the act of touring is necessarily transient, the static nature of the representations created through the Map Visualisation draws attention to the situatedness of performance events within specific times and places. One can start to imagine the experiences of the performers arriving and performing in each town or city. On the other hand, the Route Visualisation [Figure 2.4] offers animated renderings of the routes of each company. Reading the history through moving lines, with dots representing each performance draws attention not to specific places but to the way that bodies move through space. Viewers can select the time period, from the same range as the Map Visualisation, and which companies they want to track. As the animation plays, a counter indicates the date of the performance being represented by the dot and whether it was an evening performance or a matinee. The visualisation and counter move quickly, but viewers can pause the action using a button on the left of the screen. As with the Map Visualisation, one can zoom into a country, continent or region, or zoom out to watch the way that the companies toured the world.

Digital aptitude

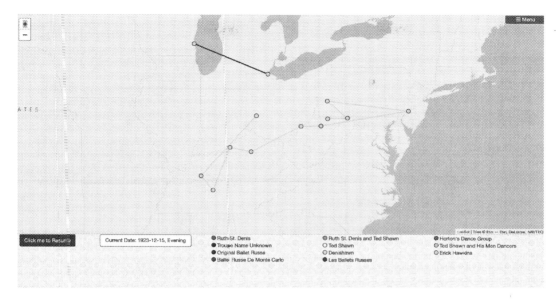

Figure 2.4 Screengrab from Route Visualisation. https://mappingtouring.osu.edu/visualization/route
Source: Bench & Elswit

The Route Visualisation offers another reading of the body's relationship to space through the abstraction of the movement of the body. It is the body's mobility through transportation that is inscribed, as opposed to the specific movement of the body. The renderings used in these maps simultaneously foreground and abstract place. They draw attention to the sites of performances, but the renderings are abstract and the visualisations detail countries and states or regions but not specific towns or cities. Zooming in to each site of performance the dot which represents the visit is partially situated in a specific place and partially suspended in digital 'no place' (Bench 2008). Human geographers draw a distinction between space and place, with space considered abstract and place understood as lived in, meaningful and "shaped by the activities and perceptions of its users" (Isomaa et al 2013: ix). In creating 'spatial histories' through digital media, place is rendered abstractly and therefore replaced by space.

In relation to the ways that bodies travel through digital 'no-place' Bench writes, "In digital media, no-place lubricates the transition among places by erasing the act of 'getting there'" (2008: 43). The Route Visualisation is a reversal of this erasure, by foregrounding the act of travel, yet the abstraction of the body and geographical markers do not render the body in relation to places. This part of the enquiry, to situate the specific bodies of the performers in places full of cultural and historical markers is down to those engaging with the maps.[33] Returning to Bench and Elswit's articulation of 'imagined networks', we can see how the role of the imagination might play a significant part in the viewers' engagement with the visualisations and their ability to gain insight into the maps.

Although these visualisations are offered as ways to conduct historical enquiry and are based in factual evidence derived from archival materials, they offer more than simply historical data. They also provide a way into thinking about the particularities of these bodies as they travelled through and performed within geographical places. This thinking depends on the imagination and knowledge of the person using the map, combined with the data that situates the dancers. This imaginative and intellectual work required on the behalf of the viewer is shared with the 'choreographic object' annotations. For example, the lines drawn on top of the *Synchronous Objects* video [see Figure 2.1] are derived from specific data about the cues passing between the dancers. However, the shapes generated through the visualisations do not immediately offer deeper insights into the knowledge that is meant to be transmitted here. The viewer needs to go through their own process of analysis, deconstruction and study of additional contextual information included on the website in order to understand the relevance of the annotations. Both of these projects therefore demonstrate how outcomes of the documentation turn which treat documentation as a process and intrinsic part of our understanding of dance offer ways of articulating aspects of dance that move beyond didactic forms of articulation, in turn provoking processes of analysis and imagination in the viewer/researcher.

Conclusion

We have discussed so far two areas of enquiry which share some features but began very differently and had very different planned outputs. One has emerged from the artistic field, has a relatively long trajectory and often involved large interdisciplinary teams, the other a smaller scale, but clear effort emerging from dance studies undertaken by two academics. However, despite these differences, the 'choreographic object' projects and *Movement on the Move* arise from similar questions regarding the exploration of digital technologies to understand more about dance. They also both undertake similar processes of generating, re-structuring and recontextualising data pertaining to the documentation of dance, demonstrating key aspects of the documentation turn. Considering them alongside, we can see how there is a continuum between artistic practice and scholarly research. Whichever service, tool or platform is used, whether Piecemaker, Tableau or Palladio, they clearly do not offer digital methods in and of themselves. It is up to the individual scholar to develop good research questions and an analytic framework that iterates rigorously through various stages, creating data from data with which to think through and with. Digital methods for the study of dance arise through the drawing together and combining of these different aspects. While there were dance analysis models and approaches developed in the 1980s (Foster 1986, Adshead et al 1988), these are no longer widely used, with scholars and practitioners often drawing on their own individual frameworks to analyse works and practices, echoing the idiosyncrasy we see in approaches to documentation. The outputs of these projects we have been describing here certainly appear different to non-digital forms of documentation, but the enquiries and ways of looking that underpin the outputs are only partially digital.

Movement on the Move demonstrates an experimental approach that can be adopted and adapted by other researchers and their datasets can be used to generate new visualisations. The potential of *Movement on the Move* to shape new thinking in the field echoes the development of annotation tools, which help practitioners and scholars to develop skills and experience in the digital annotation of movement, opening new ways of working with dance. From the perspective of the annotation efforts being undertaken by *Motion Bank* and others, there is clear interest in and motivation to aggregate annotation data that is structured so that it might be available to forms of computational analysis. However, in the context of dance studies or scholarship, there are no effective examples to date demonstrating the value of such an approach. This may be in part because the field has not the same kinds of born digital resources that much of digital humanities focuses on, collecting and analysing data from computer networks or accessing already digitised archives and collections through their APIs. This is one of the reasons we have combined the two areas of enquiry, both involved with data creation. However, as we have emphasized from the start, digital methods for dance study involves more than just access to more data. The work of Bench and Elswit demonstrates that a very tight connection between clear questions, research design frameworks, available resources, manual labour, aptitude for and willingness to learn specific digital tools and a vision that sees the potential is essential. Their example shows there is no need to wait for more data sources. And in the future, as *Motion Bank* and other annotation platforms seek to stabilise and find resources for a sustainable development, we look forward to dance scholars who have instinct, rigour, openness, digital aptitude and curiosity availing themselves of the research opportunity presented by annotation data.

Digital aptitude

Notes

1 The 1990s in particular saw a number of organised labs and workshops e.g., Terry Braun's annual *Digital Dancing* workshops 1994–1998 in the UK and a series of *Dance and Technology* conferences hosted by the University of Wisconsin (1992), Simon Fraser University (1993), York University (1995), and Arizona State University (1999).

2 For example, since 2015, the International Federation for Theatre Research has convened a Digital Humanities and Theatre Research working group. There is nothing equivalent for dance.

3 Eg. The work of Gibson/ Martelli: https://gibsonmartelli.com/, William Forsythe's Black Flags robot choreography: https://www.youtube.com/watch?v=6XVrrmm9jno and Wayne McGregor's work with AI: https://www.wired.co.uk/article/google-ai-wayne-mcgregor-dance-choreography

4 As described in Johnson, C. J. & Snyder, A. F (1999). *Securing our Dance Heritage: Issues in the Documentation and Preservation of Dance.*

5 As described in the Introduction to: Blades and Meehan (eds.) *Performing Process: Sharing Dance and Choreographic Practice.* And see for example, 'What's the Score? On Scores and Notations in Dance' http://olga0.oralsite.be/oralsite/pages/What's_the_Score_Publication/

6 The use of the term 'Choreographic Objects' throughout this article is distinct from use of the term by William Forsythe to refer to a series of artworks he has been developing for several years. https://www.williamforsythe.com/

7 Movement on the Move website: http://movementonthemove.osu.edu/

8 Choreographic Objects Beyond Text documentation: http://projects.beyondtext.ac.uk/choreographicobjects/

9 Contredanse website: https://www.contredanse.org/contredanseV4/templates/index.php

10 As the "keen interest in developing modes of documenting, arching and transmitting contemporary dance" emerging in Europe (de Keersmaeker and Cvejić 2012: 7).

11 Tableau software: https://public.tableau.com/

12 Palladio software: https://hdlab.stanford.edu/palladio/

13 See Movement on the Move: http://movementonthemove.osu.edu/project-mapping-touring

14 Eg. *Improvisation Technologies* & *Synchronous Objects.*

15 Processing website: https://processing.org/

16 Motion Bank Phase One (2010–2013) was a research project of The Forsythe Company focused on creating unique on line digital dance scores with guest choreographers including Deborah Hay. http://scores.motionbank.org/dh/. The three dance artists involved were Jeanine Durning, Ros Warby, Juliette Mapp.

17 Motion Bank Scores: http://scores.motionbank.org/jbmf/#/set/sets

18 To read about this annotation process: http://www.perfomap.de/map6/medien-und-verfahren-des-aufzeichnens/a-conversation-on-motion-bank. (deLahunta and Jenett and Cramer 2015).

19 An early project Video Traces developed for dance education in the early 2000s (https://web.archive.org/web/20080321182857/http://depts.washington.edu/pettt/projects/videotraces.html), and Rotosketch (https://web.archive.org/web/20070429232234/http://thesystemis.com/rotosketch/index.html) and more recently DancePro (https://www.europeana-space.eu/dancepro/) continues this line of developing a tool for drawing on top of video. But the fact that tools have been developed does not mean they are taken up in practice more generally.

20 Elan: https://tla.mpi.nl/tools/tla-tools/elan/ and Michael Kipp (2014) ANVIL: The Video Annotation Research Tool. *The Oxford Handbook of Corpus Phonology.* Eds. Jacques Durand, Ulrike Gut, and Gjert Kristoffersen

21 Including dance unitisation for *Synchronous Objects* facilitated quantitative analysis, e.g. https://synchronousobjects.osu.edu/content.html#/StatisticalCounterpoint; Carla Fernandes' BlackBox http://blackbox.fcsh.unl.pt/. Elizabeth Waterhouse PhD 'Dancing Together' http://dancingtogether.ch/.

22 Trinity Laban offers guest access to selected videos via Planet eStream: https://estream.trinitylaban.ac.uk/

23 For a report on annotation research with Codarts, a dance education school in Rotterdam see: https://medium.com/motion-bank/developing-vocabularies-for-dance-education-e4c4584950a8

24 https://www.w3.org/blog/news/archives/6156. 'It will allow anyone to annotate anything anywhere, be it a web page, an ebook, a video, an image, an audio stream, or data in raw or visualized form. Web annotations can be linked, shared between services, tracked back to their origins, searched and discovered, and stored wherever the author wishes; the vision is for a decentralized and open annotation infrastructure.'

25 Pre-choreographics Emio Greco | PC, an exemplar for vocabulary development: https://pre-choreographicelements.net/

26 A recently funded and one of the only 'digital humanities' and dance projects by the National Endowment of Humanities explicitly makes this point: https://www.ua.edu/news/2018/12/professor-to-strengthen-digital-dynamics-of-dance-via-neh-grant/

27 Jérôme Bel – BMW Tate Live: Performance Room (22 March 2012): https://www.youtube.com/watch?v=lCTmUQmKpDg

28 According to Wikipedia: https://en.wikipedia.org/wiki/History_of_YouTube

29 WholoDance Movement repository, educational platform and data curation tools (Athens) http://www.wholodance.eu/movement-repository-and-data-curation-tools/; Europeana Space, Best Practice Network, Dancepro (Lisbon) https://www.europeana-space.eu/dancepro/; Research Video Zurich University of the Arts https://process.studio/works/zhdk-research-video/.
30 Between Us is a cooperation between Motion Bank, a research project of the University of Applied Sciences Mainz, the Kunsthalle and the Staatstheater Mainz: https://betweenus.motionbank.org/#/
31 Oral Site is a platform that exists as a project space to support digital artist publications: http://oralsite.be/pages/Index
32 Obtained from collections at the Jerome Robbins Dance Division at the New York Public Library, the Jerome Lawrence and Robert E. Lee Theatre Research Institute at Ohio State University, the New York City Ballet Archives, and the Rockefeller Archive Center (see Bench and Elswit 2016: 577).
33 The ways that historical embodiment can be foregrounded in visualisations and datasets is an area that Bench and Elswit are continuing to explore in their current project Dunham's Data: https://www.dunhamsdata.org/

References

Adshead, J. Huxley, M., Hodgens, P. and Briginshaw, V. (1988). *Dance Analysis: Theory and Practice*. London: Dance Books
Bench, H., & Elswit, K. (2016). Mapping Movement on the Move: Dance Touring and Digital Methods. *Theatre Journal*, 68(4), 575–596
Bench, H. (2015). Digital Research in Dance Studies: Emerging Trends in a Still-Emerging Field. *Humanities Futures: Franklin Humanities Institute*. https://humanitiesfutures.org/papers/digital-research-in-dance-studies-emerging-trends-in-a-still-emerging-field-2/
Bench, H. (2008). Media and the No-Place of Dance. *Forum Modernes Theater*, 23(1), 37–47
Berry, D. M., & Fagerjord, A. (2017). *Digital Humanities: Knowledge and Critique in a Digital Age*. Cambridge: Polity
Birringer, J. (1998). *Media and Performance: Along the Border*. Baltimore and London: The John Hopkins University Press
Blades, H. and Meehan, E. (Eds.) (2018). *Performing Process: Sharing Dance and Choreographic Practice*. Bristol: Intellect
Bleeker, M. (Ed.). (2016). *Transmission in Motion: The Technologizing of Dance*. London and New York: Routledge
Boxberger, E. and Wittmann, G. (Eds.). (2013). *pARTnering documentation: approaching dance, heritage, culture. 3rd Dance Education Biennale 2012*. Frankfurt am Main. epodium Verlag: Müchen
Davies, S. (2009). Siobhan Davies RePlay. http://www.siobhandaviesreplay.com/
de Keersmaeker, T. and Cvejić, B. (2012). *A Choreographer's Score: Fase, Rosas Danst Rosas, Elena's Aria, Bartók*. Brussels: Mercatorfonds
deLahunta, S. (2015). The Utility of Words (the poet's Technique). In Haffner, N. & Quast, H. (Eds.). *Research Environments: Reflections on the Value of Artistic Processes Berlin*. Universitaet der Kunste Berlin, pp. 245–254
deLahunta, S. (2013). Publishing Choreographic Ideas: Discourse from Practice. In Wilson, M. and van Ruiten, S. (Eds.). *SHARE. Handbook for Artistic Research* Amsterdam: ELIA, pp. 170–177
deLahunta, S. and Shaw, N. Z. (2006). Constructing Memories: Creation of the Choreographic Resource. *Performance Research*, 11(4), 53–62
deLahunta, S. and Shaw, N. Z. (2008). Choreographic Resources Agents, Archives, Scores and Installations. *Performance Research*, 13 (1), 131–133
deLahunta, S. (2002). Periodic Convergences: Dance and Computers. In *Tanz und Technologie/Dance and Technology*. Berlin: Alexander Verlag, pp. 66–84
deLahunta, S. and Jenett, F. (2016). Making Digital Choreographic Objects Interrelate: A Focus on Coding Practices. In Beyes, T., Leeker, M. and Schipper, I. (Eds.). *Performing the Digital Performance Studies and Performances in Digital Cultures*. Bielfeld: Transcript-Verlag, pp. 63–79
deLahunta, S., Jenett, F., and Cramer, F.A. (2015). 'A Conversation on Motion Bank'. In Cramer, F.A., Buscher, B (Eds.). MAP (media archive performance) nr. 6. Published online
Dixon, S. (2007). *Digital Performance: A History of New Media in Theater, Dance, Performance Art, and Installation*. Massachusetts: MIT Press
Foster, S. L. (1986). *Reading Dancing: Bodies and Subjects in Contemporary American Dance*. California: University of California Press
Forsythe, W. and Shaw, N. Z. (2009). The Dance The Data The Objects. *Synchronous Objects*. https://synchronousobjects.osu.edu/assets/objects/introduction/danceDataObjectEssays.pdf
Forsythe, W., Shaw, N.Z. and Palazzi, M. (2009). Synchronous Objects for One Flat Thing, reproduced. The Ohio University/The Forsythe Company (http://synchronousobjects.osu.edu/)
Forsythe, W. (2000). *One Flat Thing, reproduced* [dance work], premiere Frankfurt
Forsythe, W. (1999). *Improvisation Technologies: A Tool for the Analytical Dance Eye*. ZKM, Karlsruhe & Hatje Cantz Verlag.

Digital aptitude

Gansing, K. (2016). *1995: The Year the Future Began, or Mulitmedia as the Vanishing Point of the Net*. https://transmediale.de/content/1995-the-year-the-future-began-or-multimedia-as-the-vanishing-point-of-the-net

Greco, E. and Scholten, P. (2007). Double Skin/Double Mind. https://www.ickamsterdam.com/en/academy/education/ick/double-skin-double-mind-20

Groves, R. et al (2007). Talking about Scores: William Forsythe's Vision for a New Form of" Dance Literature. In Gehm, S., Husemann, P. and von Wilke, K. (Eds.) *Knowledge in Motion: Perspective of Artistic and Scientific Research in Dance*. New Brunswick and London: Transaction Publishers

Hay, D. Using the Sky. (2013). Motion Bank/The Forsythe Company (http://motionbank.org)

Hay, D. (2010). *No Time to Fly* [dance work], premiere St Mark's Church in-the-Bowery, New York, 25 March

Hui, Y. (2016). *On the Existence of Digital Objects*. London: University of Minnesota Press

Isomaa, S., Lyytikäinen, P., Saarikangas, K., and Suominen – Kokkonen, R. (2013). *Imagining Spaces and Places*. Newcastle: Cambridge Scholars Publishing

Johnson, C. J. and Snyder, A. F. & Council on Library and Information Resources (1999). *Securing our Dance Heritage: Issues in the Documentation and Preservation of Dance*. Council on Library and Information Resources, Washington, D.C.

Khan, A. (2018). Akram Khan: Digital has Revolutionised Dance but We Mustn't Abandon Tradition. *The Stage*. https://www.thestage.co.uk/opinion/2018/akram-khan-digital-has-revolutionised-dance-but-we-mustnt-abandon-tradition/

Kipp, M. (2014). ANVIL: The Video Annotation Research Tool. In Durand, J. Gut, U. and Kristoffersen, G. (Eds.). *The Oxford Handbook of Corpus Phonology*. Oxford: Oxford University Press, pp. 420–436

Leach, J., de Lahunta, S. and Whatley, S. (2008). Choreographic Objects: Traces and Artifacts of Physical Intelligence [research project] http://projects.beyondtext.ac.uk/choreographicobjects/

McGregor, W. (2008). Choreographic Language Agent. https://waynemcgregor.com/research/choreographic-language-agent/

O'Shea, J. (2010). Roots/Routes of Dance Studies. In Carter, A. and O'Shea, J. (Eds.) *The Routledge Dance Studies Reader*. London: Routledge, pp. 19–34

Paxton, S. (2008). *Material for the Spine: A Movement Study*. Brussels: Contredanse.

Reason, M. (2006). *Documentation, Disappearance and the Representation of Live Performance*. Hampshire: Palgrave Macmillan

Salter, C. (2010). *Entangled: Technology and the Transformation of Performance*. Massachusetts: MIT Press

Sant, T. (Ed.). (2017). *Documenting Performance: The Context and Processes of Digital Curation and Archiving*. London and New York: Bloomsbury

Shaw, N. Z. (2014). Animate Inscriptions, Articulate Data and Algorithmic Expressions of Choreographic Thinking. *Choreographic Practices* 5 (1), 95–119

Vass-Rhee, F. (2019). Haunted by Hamlet: William Forsythe's Sider. In McCulloch, L. and Shaw, B. (Eds.) *The Oxford Handbook of Shakespeare and Dance*, London and New York: Oxford University Press, pp. 455–475

Vincent, J.B., Vincent, C., Vincs, K., deLahunta, S., and McCormick, J. (2018). Artworks-Spawning-Artworks: Trans-disciplinary Approaches to Artistic Spin-offs and Evolution in the Dance and Digital Context. In Whatley, S., Cisneros, R., Sabiescu, A. (Eds.). *Digital Echoes: Spaces for Intangible and Performance-based Cultural Heritage* London: Palgrave Macmillan, pp. 283–299

Whatley, S. (2008). Archives of the Dance (21): Siobhan Davies Dance Online. *Dance Research*, 26(2), 244–257

3
(CRITICAL) ARTISTIC RESEARCH AND DH

Sally-Jane Norman

Preface

This text is written from a vantage point gained within and largely outside academia. My first university post, in Newcastle, began during the 2004 DRH conference.[1] Then European Commissioner and Newcastle University Chancellor Chris Patten's keynote speech Digital Europe: a key to the competitiveness of the European Union *was exciting to me as a committed European engaged since the 1980s with digital platforms—via industrial Research and Development (R&D) translation, European projects focussed on Computer Supported Cooperative Work at the Zentrum für Kunst und Medientechnologie in Karlsruhe, performance technology innovation at the Studio for Electro-Instrumental Music in Amsterdam, and media experimentation at a French arts cooperative, then as director of an art school. It was exciting and challenging to tune to the predominantly literary, linguistic, library/archival, and museological thrust that characterised the Newcastle conference on Digital Resources for the Humanities (DRH). Yet debates at that time and ever since, about the place of creative practice in the Digital Humanities, and about how and even whether to link DH scholarship to other sectors, feel oddly remote. Input of creative critical practice to digital technology-related activities is urgent: it allows us to share and imaginatively question our relations to the technologies that shape us as we shape them. But for many theorists, unless such practice clearly and transmissibly espouses specific pursuits such as data encoding and mark-up, mining and visualisation/sonification, semantic indexing, topic modelling, or network and link analysis, it is viewed as an ad hoc contributor to, rather than integral constituent of, the growing digital humanities field. As a result, much of the work referenced below—whose artistic integrity depends on wilfully idiosyncratic, ludic, irreproducible qualities—is expediently dismissed from DH scholarship. The value of disciplinary creep—or undisciplined creep—across research types and sectors is however precisely what this chapter seeks to emphasise, to hopefully widen digital humanities discussion.*

3.1 Introduction

Digital Humanities (DH) as a more-or-less formally identified field[2] that builds on decades—if not centuries—of research has been the stage of confrontation between defenders of "hack" versus "yack",[3] makers versus observers, and advocates of representational versus performative systems.[4] For scholars who, like Richard Grusin, see such confrontation as obfuscating the growing instrumentalisation of higher education, focus on commodifiable content delivery that undermines humanistic inquiry drives an "invidious distinction between making things and merely critiquing them (which) has come to be one of the generally accepted differences that marks DH off from the humanities in general" Grusin, 2013). These differences continue to fuel debate in DH, still construed as essentially text-based, albeit a construal widened to include "all material cultural forms, such as images, books, articles, sound, film, video, etc." (Berry and Fajerjord, 2017, 60). But in material cultural forms arising from artistic practices, manifestations of shaping work and articulating critical reflection are inextricably combined, making these differences hard to discern. Indeed, much artistic work comments on its own modes of mediation as part of creatively crafted, sometimes subversively ambivalent self-reflection.

While the humanities are devoted to the study of human culture and its forms of expression, the arts in universities have tended to be dominated by studies of cultural theory and history, with practice-informed artistic research being admitted only recently as a legitimate higher education pursuit.[5] As a result, arts practitioners tend to work in contexts different from those of humanities scholars apprehensive of neo-liberal education's insidious techno-economic drivers. The story of these differences outstrips the scope of this paper, but their influence on humanities uptake of computational tools is significant. Some digital practitioners prefer to support their experimental work through transparent commercial activity rather than to engage with the opaque hype that can accompany institutional 'digital media' trends.[6] Practitioners may steer clear of being treated as mere technical apprentices of academics ill-equipped to lead digital media projects that suddenly run into major skills gaps (Rockwell, 2013, 249). Conversely, previously sidelined practitioners may be drawn to experimental opportunities promoted by DH, and their skills may be welcomed by scholars hungry for competence they knowingly lack to devise computational resources and methods that can invigorate their fields. When diversity of profiles and inputs—thus potential synergies—are upheld, collaborative projects can indeed inspire novel approaches to DH.

In an environment marked as much by serendipitous encounters of motivated individuals as by top-down institutional strategies, DH attracts creative energies at times attributable to ground-breaking arts initiatives hosted by visionary individuals in sympathetic university contexts,[7] at others to work undertaken by arts practitioners long before they were eventually admitted as researchers to institutions of higher learning.[8] The situation is compounded by academic calls for scholars to strengthen relations with practitioners, stemming from thematic interests such as the 'practice turn' (Schatzki, Knorr Cetina, von Savigny, 2001), the 'performative idiom' (Pickering, 1995), 'non-representational theory' (Thrift, 2008), and the cultural, organizational, and technological manifestations of performance (McKenzie, 2001). In this unsystematic, messily asymmetric context, the examples that follow correspond to three kinds of contributions digital arts practice have made or are making to the digital humanities:

1. Works that have already garnered documented DH recognition and that are here re-contextualised to emphasise the history of their emergence within broader technology development processes.
2. Works that predate and/or sit outside DH as recognised from humanities or computing science perspectives, yet that appear as determinant vectors for ongoing and emerging creative DH. To limit the study of DH to intra-institutional humanities computing perspectives—however cross-disciplinary—is to risk ignoring some of the multiply-stranded legacies needed to develop this field. Arts practices harbour many such potentially productive legacies by virtue of their ad hoc extra-institutional modes and sites of operation.
3. Works that are absent from DH literature because subversive critique of their own and wider digital mediation processes runs uneasily counter to often positivistic DH claims. Artistic work is under-represented in current scholarly DH reflection, whereas art's radical modes of enquiry can spark the self-reflexive cultural criticism needed for DH's sustained development. Beyond work "complacently rooted in past verities" (Hayles, 2015, 505) or jaded art-science debates, art's critical engagement with the technological systems that increasingly determine our post-human nature offers means to explore these systems, through freely imaginative, shareable constructs.

3.2 Multiply stranded genealogies

Digital archives and databases that form the core of DH projects have featured in interactive, generative art for decades. Specifically, with respect to performance/performing arts, theatre scholar Debra Caplan asserts that "the ephemerality of the performance event, the significance of its live presentation, the multisensory output produced, the need for an audience" make theatre particularly amenable to digital humanities methodologies. Consequently, the "tools and theoretical vocabulary that we have developed for thinking about mediation, liveness, spectatorship, and collaboration in performance may be more relevant to the concerns of the academy at large than ever before." (Caplan, 2015, 348–349).

Performance and dance scholar Sarah Bay-Cheng, in considering "the effects of emerging technologies on the writing of history, specifically, the intersection of digital history with contemporary performance practices", notes that DH methods have "significantly altered the relations of theatre, performance, and history" (Bay-Cheng, 2016, 509). Without disputing its accuracy or the historical sensibility that appreciably characterises Bay-Cheng's work, one can turn her statement around, given the number of digital humanities archive projects that are anchored in pre-DH performance technology initiatives. To recall the complexity of these relations is not to steal DH's thunder, but to foreground its intertwined origins to inspire new approaches: in a post-archival context,[9] it would be ironic if the field of digital humanities were to hubristically overlook its own history.

Harmony Bench and Kate Elswit's study of wartime touring dance companies (Anna Pavlova, WWI; the American Ballet Caravan, WWII), demonstrates reciprocal benefits that strengthen relations between DH and the fields of theatre and dance, "which can not only draw from the digital humanities, but also propose new means to consider embodied experience in terms of dynamic spatial histories of movement" (Bench and Elswit, 2016, 576). Their project is an informative relational mapping of archive materials including programmes, diaries, performance previews and reviews, international transportation records, financial documents, theatre records, and customs and border-related documents, as well as evidence of local traditions taken into account for programming purposes, or to inspire new creative works. The project amply bears out Bench's and Elswit's claim that DH enables "discovery and display at a scale not available in analog media" (ibid).

The importance of DH's often tangled roots in longstanding artistic practice is exemplified by the history of Motion Bank. In its current form under the co-direction of Florian Jenett and Scott deLahunta, this project has been housed since 2016 at the Hochschule Mainz - University of Applied Sciences. Funded by the German Federal Ministry of Education and Research, Motion Bank addresses the relations between embodied and machine-based knowledge forms:

> "developing low-threshold, standard-compliant open source and free systems designed for use in a variety of contexts, including dance education, creation, research, and archiving. In addition to the design and development of these systems, Motion Bank is engaged in ongoing methodological research into the practice of annotation, the documentation and presentation of processes involving tacit, collaborative and embodied forms of knowledge and bringing these into alignment with research into linked data, semantics and ontologies from information science"(Jenett, 2018).

Although this declaration resonates nicely with DH terms and goals, the story behind Motion Bank shows how a simple practical imperative for a community of performing artists has gradually become an acclaimed digital humanities milestone. During the 1980s, as Frankfurt Ballet director, Forsythe used video to record his constantly evolving choreography, equipping dancers with portable players to monitor collective work; the footage was digitised as a company archive, *The Loss of Small Detail* (1994). Video lectures, movement demonstration materials and excerpts of the staged performance *Self Meant to Govern* were then edited to form a CD-ROM teaching tool in 1995. The first publicly available digital dance CD-ROM, published by the Zentrum für Kunst und Medientechnologie in Karlsruhe, was entitled *William Forsythe: Improvisation Technologies. A Tool for the Analytical Eye* (1999) (Ziegler, 2017). Forsythe's creation of *One Flat Thing, reproduced* the following year led to the online choreographic visualisation *Synchronous Objects for One Flat Thing, reproduced* (2009), developed by Forsythe and project co-directors Norah Zuniga Shaw and Maria Palazzi from Ohio State University, heading researchers from architecture, statistics, cognitive psychology, philosophy, visual arts, design, animation, geography, dance, and computer science (http://synchronousobjects.osu.edu). Far from pursuing an etymological, archaeological, or historical rationale to conjoin the performance and its archival residue, Forsythe's intention was to imagine "what else this dance might look like". (Zuniga-Shaw, 2017, 100). Digital documentation of the choreography thematically organised from multiple disciplinary, technological and aesthetic perspectives yielded a set of interactive digital "objects".[10] Computational imagery of these 20 *Synchronous Objects*, linked to video footage of Forsythe's 15 minute creation for 17 dancers, produces constructs that acquire autonomy as dynamic digital forms, offering otherwise inconceivable renderings of physical movement patterns. The choreography's organisational structures are thus given novel readings, as noted on the project website, by "translating and transforming them into new objects".

One Flat Thing, reproduced in turn gave rise to the initially four-year Motion Bank project (2010-13), where Forsythe, together with project leader deLahunta et al., sought to establish the "first library of digital dance scores"[11]: computer-aided design enables "the ideas incumbent in choreography to be graphically displayed as the work itself plays before the viewer" (Forsythe cited by deLahunta, 2017, 130). Alongside Forsythe's work at the Frankfurt Motion Bank spaces,[12] online digital dance scores were developed by five resident choreographers. By combining techniques from dance with those of computational archiving systems, Motion Bank has inspired and linked to cognate collaborations across international networks as an evolving marker of digital archiving in the performing arts (documented examples of related initiatives feature in Beeker, 2017, Salazar Sutil and Popat, 2015).

Digital performance history counts significant instances where transpositions and recreations of works have produced similarly unforeseeable, creatively stimulating findings. For example, computerised segmentation of dancers' motions ensured by LifeForms software developers in collaboration with Merce Cunningham revealed gestural syntax possibilities that, while biomechanically feasible, were inconceivable for the choreographer, blinkered by his habits — however exceptionally trained — as a humanly embodied cognitive system.[13] It is perhaps this gap between the discretisation inherent to computational systems, and the continuity of sensed, embodied experience, that makes performance such a uniquely productive area for digital humanities experimentation.

3.3 Remediations as generators of aesthetics

Relations between artworks and their documentation, notably as catalogues and archives, are imbued with the intangible cultural values and intricate contextual factors borne by such works. Recent waves of artist reconstructions and reinterpretations of historic performances,[14] and the spread of digitisation, have intensified efforts to fathom the temporal dynamics that distinguish live from archived performance (Ostoff, 2009; Jones and Heathfield, 2012; Giannachi, 2016; Clarke et al., 2018). Those of interactive, realtime digital media which resist conventional genres because of their experientially grounded qualities, raise their own archiving challenges, aggravated by the swift obsolescence of digital tools and platforms. Bolter and Grusin's concept of remediation (1999), where emerging media secures recognition of its specificities by refashioning, thus demarcating itself from existing media, has contributed to attempts to preserve and transmit digital artworks, as has the expansion of media archaeology studies (Zielinski 2002, Friedberg 2006, Huhtamo 2011, Parikka 2012, Ernst 2013). Much critical theory dealing with born-digital artworks in past decade addresses DH-relevant concerns such as human relations with data and automated processes, contextualisation demands, cultural and machine-driven temporal frameworks, and modes of intervention in and interaction with databases. Imperatives to uphold otherwise fleeting legacies of experimental digital art, often designed — like performance art — to exploit the immediacy of real-time encounters, have prompted the creation of means to disseminate and somehow preserve traces of these experiments.

In 1994, the Zentrum für Kunst und Medientechnologie in Karlsruhe launched *artintact*, an 'Artist's Interactive CD-ROMagazine', producing five volumes each containing three unique works of interactive electronic media accompanied by a substantial printed publication (https://zkm.de/en/publication/the-complete-artintact-artintact-komplett).[15] The CDROMs are structured to highlight the respective authors' often critical if not dystopian preoccupations: Ken Feingold's *JCJ-Junkman* (1995), features a ventriloquist dummy head set amidst a swarm of recalcitrant command buttons that trigger the dummy's speech if only one manages to click on them. George Legrady's *Slippery Traces* (1996) takes us through a maze of 200 thematically diverse postcards, each containing hotspots that allow a new image to be called up in a decidedly disruptive narrative trajectory. Marina Grzinic and Aina Smid's *Troubles with Sex, Theory and History* (1997) is a game where exploration of the artists' film and video work is subject to hidden rules and disturbing questions that control the user's freedom to proceed. Masaki Fujihata's *Impalpability* (1998) displays a hyper-realistic human-skin coated ball that is rotated by manipulating the mouse, generating a troubling tactile relation with the screen image. *Artintact* proposes original, provocative approaches to interactive digital media, elsewhere chiefly developed as predictably responsive, 'intuitive', and streamlined for mainstream consumer markets.

The *Anarchive* series founded and led since 1995 by Anne-Marie Duguet consists of monograph-oriented digital arts databases (www.anarchive.net/). So far comprised of publications by and dedicated to Antoni Muntadas (1999), Michael Snow (2002), Thierry Kuntzel (2006), Jean Otth (2007), Fujiko Nakaya (2012), Masaki Fujihata (2016), and Peter Campus (2017), the series presents the corpus of each artist's works as an archive crafted to constitute a full-fledged new work. Far from a static catalogue, the '*Anarchive*' reveals a wealth of perspectives as the artists weave historical, social, and economic links across their works. The resultant synthesis is articulated as a unique database accessed via a custom-built interface whose modes of interactive consultation are dictated by the artist's aesthetic. Over its two decades, *Anarchive* has integrated major technical developments: Muntadas's 'Interom' title designated its combined CD-ROM/Internet format, while Fujihata's ring binder edition — the archetypal archive file — holds 17 booklets incorporating iOS-activated augmented reality functionalities to access video and 3D simulation materials. Fujihata planned his 'anarchive' as a growable and remixable book: readers provided with his artistic works as raw materials and corresponding code, can freely perform their own creative remixes.

Publications by *Artintact, Anarchive, Voyager Company*[16] and other platforms dedicated to experimental digital media promote vital debate amongst scholars, developers and artists about making aesthetically meaningful works in a densely computational world. Macro— and micro—processual logics corresponding to successive generations of technologies used by artists must be made inter-operational within overarching timeframes, without bulldozing the distinctive markers of historicity that determine their holistic fabric. The Preservation & Art - Media Archaeology Lab PAMAL (http://esaavignon.eu/Pamal/), an interdisciplinary team of artist-designers, curators, and developers at the Ecole supérieure d'Art d'Avignon led by Emmanuel Guez and Lionel Broye, is working on digital archive preservation and restoration, networked exhibitions, and the effects of blockchains on networked digital arts.[17] In collaboration with Dominique Cunin and Gilles Rouffineau at the Ecole Supérieure d'Art et Design de Valence, and inspired by their 'Media Platform Synochronoptic' (a time-referenced visualisation of computational systems employed for the *Anarchive* series), PAMAL is building a database of timelines representing key digital arts tools. These endeavours are fired by the need for critical space where, as humans and humanists, we can engage in creative dialogue on our fast changing relations with technologies. In their capacity as speculative yet adamantly material works, such endeavours provide the DH community with novel methodological insights and paths for critical reflection.

(Critical) artistic research and DH

3.4 Hands-on artistry and digital shadows

Practitioners of live or performing arts, whose work makes use of real-time embodied expression, have been swift to recognise opportunities opened up by interactive, multimodal deployments of digital data, necessary for devising DH methods that more informatively address massively scalable datasets than those imported from traditional 'close reading' and 'long form' scholarship. An example is the project developed by artist researcher Dan Norton, who notes that DJs provide a model of information interaction that is creative and capable of managing large bodies of material, reusing digital content and authoring links and connections by selecting and mixing. Norton's residency with British Library Labs used DJ-inspired interface approaches to inform new ways of exploiting data representations offered by the British Library's digital collections (https://www.bl.uk/projects/british-library-labs).

As an inherently interface-based skill, puppetry employs diverse techniques to manipulate multiple materials at multiple scales: gloves, strings, sticks, masks, electronics and animatronics feature among the numerous handling systems that together form a platform for research into gesture and use of physical interfaces. Additionally, entertainment industry uptake of motion capture — driven as much by the imperative to lower animation costs, as by the quest for compelling visual effects — has tuned production studios to human animators able to artistically impart symbolic life to objects. This recognition has reinforced film industry use of motion capture, which increasingly calls on creative movement specialists as doubles for 'talking head' filmstars to optimise use of this technique, hiring dedicated motion capture acting studios established to meet sector needs (e.g. MoCap Vaults: https://www.themocapvaults.com/).

Parallel to industrial and commercial developments, digital artist practitioners engaging puppetry skills and interests in academic contexts are developing initiatives that, like earlier cited examples from dance, may be rooted in longstanding histories and players operating beyond the confines of scholarly institutions. Such is the work undertaken by artist, programmer, and puppeteer Ian Grant, who combines professional experience in puppetry and real-time computer graphics with scholarship in performance history and interdisciplinary practice methodologies, to bring together traditional shadow puppetry skills and touch-based, interactive, multi-user computer technologies. Grant's focus is on the distinctive movement qualities obtained by remediating longstanding puppeteering forms to integrate digital haptic resources and collaborative interfaces, whence the "media archaeological approach" subtitle to his thesis on *Shadows, Touch and Digital Puppeteering* (Grant, 2018). His taxonomy of shadow puppetry techniques of diverse origins is offset by descriptions of interactive devices offering surface-based single— and multi-user touch and finger level control, and whose pressure, acceleration and orientation affordances provide proprioceptive sensing cues of interest for DH interface developments.

Grant's practical experimentation seeks to expand traditional forms of shadow puppetry by creating and implementing "a software system which enables touch control, gestural and a variety of other forms of input, to be mapped onto a range of digital shadow figures: characters and props of varying complexity from various world shadow traditions… (enabling) a level of cinematic and scenographic control that presents a collaborative space for digital storytelling" (Grant, 2018). Familiarity with traditional puppetry techniques, and with physics and interactive control programming functions implemented with Open Sound Control (OSC) protocols, underpins a series of projects collectively named the *ShadowEngine*. Works digitally reconstructed with the *ShadowEngine* include traditional Turkish Karagöz materials, a *Digital Hand* animation inspired by German film-maker Lotte Reiniger's 1920s fastidiously fashioned silhouettes, and a piece based on mid-nineteenth century British Galanty Show woodcut ephemera telling the story of *Billy Waters: The London Fiddler*. Proficiency with multiple manipulation techniques, with physics modeling and haptics, and interest in collaborative control processes, are brought together in Grant's *ShadowEngine* to demonstrate how historic artistic materials and techniques can open up otherwise untapped possibilities of emerging performance technologies.

Exploration of the Karagöz shadow puppet collection at the International Institute of Puppetry in Charleville-Mézières, France, aligns with historiographic remediation aspects of the digital humanities. For this work, Grant photographed and digitised the 222 shadow figures, props and sets commissioned by the Institute's founding Director, Margareta Niculescu, and made by puppeteer Çelebi for a touring exhibition in 1982. These stock Karagöz items range from simple two-part to complex multi-jointed elements whose adaptation to interactive digital animation requires careful translation of their rigging dynamics, i.e. control rod emplacements, to provide equivalents for parameters puppeteers typically deal with (e.g. balance, weight, and related movement constraints). Where evidence was available, Grant's Karagöz portfolio specifies character type, number of parts used to form the figure, joint and control points (i.e. rod attachment points), and kinetic qualities, such as use of rods to accentuate the movement of clothing or accoutrements. Some items feature multiple figures made of large numbers of parts; the collection includes animals, supernatural characters, sets of buildings and landscapes, and props. The portfolio reproduces summary descriptions of standard scenes and skits, with references for scholars and practitioners seeking further detail. The digital images are edited into atlases to constitute animatable game assets for collective storytelling: Grant is developing his *ShadowEngine* to enable engagement of a broad user base via personal devices, and/or large screen displays for collective entertainment.

This research has encountered inevitable but unforeseeable shortcomings due to issues such as physics-based animation limits, simulation failures, and software obsolescence to weigh up against the no less formidable constraints of physical puppetry. At the same time, Grant's production of a tool-kit to generate what he calls elegant, nuanced multi-touch shadow puppetry has yielded serendipitous discoveries on which he continues to build, for example, by integrating parameters related to gaze and eye direction, as well as touch, to enrich collaborative animation activities. As a so-called 'minor art', puppetry can inject unique gestural and proprioceptive know-how into digital humanities projects seeking new ways to engage with multimodal affordances, welding communities and highlighting the relevance of often overlooked historic cultural forms.

3.5 From individual virtuosity to wider platforms—and back

By leveraging artistic performance and technical skills to invent a resource with potential for wider creative community uptake, the *ShadowEngine* belongs to a lineage of artists' experiments that have driven the development of new instruments and techniques—a lineage that includes such diverse endeavours as Marie Taglioni's promotion of pointe technique in Romantic ballet, and Willie Kizart's electric guitar distortion experiments of the 1950s, subsequently honed by Jimi Hendrix. Such developments have mushroomed in recent decades, as artists concerned to maintain individualised alternatives to massively normative systems and dependencies have reacted to the surge in distribution of commercial electronic and digital instruments. This reaction prompted the founding of the Studio for Electro-Instrumental Music (STEIM) in the late 1960s, to develop contemporary electronics for experimental music performers. These resources were first and foremost geared to individual needs, and only thereafter, and where relevant, developed as soft- and hardware tools for the wider performance community.

STEIM considers the virtuosic knowledge of the fingers or lips to be musically as important as 'brain-knowledge', adamantly instating idiosyncratic, virtuosic behaviours as drivers rather than consumers of emerging performance technologies.[18] These behaviours increasingly involve circuit-bending, hacking, or hijacking the expanding panoply of off-the-shelf resources, while maintaining a defining focus on individualised expressive possibilities (in an ironic parallel movement, commercial developers increasingly need creative user feedback to demarcate market-geared products). Like their academic counterparts, performing artists often form groups and networks to ensure critical feedback amongst professionally grounded peers, and to share resources, challenges and responses.[19] But unlike cliques of scholars, such groups emphatically set corporeal intelligence and physical engagement on a par or tightly intertwined with intellectual skills. Their valuing of cooperation and practical competence constitutes a behavioural asset for cross-sector digital humanities in search of novel collaborations and audiences. In a context where machine learning and its ubiquitous artificial agents are reinforcing our status as inextricably computed and embodied beings, critical creative experimentation can reach beyond functional, market-bound exploitation of our datafied shadows, enhancing our ability to discern the ways computational systems allow — or require — us to link with our surroundings and with our fellow humans.

Artistic practitioners producing original location sensing and gesture-related experiments are developing affordances that tightly tie our sense of physical being-in-the-world to its computational representations: we literally get our bearings from personal digital devices on which we are ever more dependent, as multi-modal actuators weave them inextricably into our everyday activities.[20] Design of tools and platforms to promote artistic experimentation and digital literacy feeds — and frequently blurs — into digital humanities. Computing specialist Rebecca Fiebrink (Goldsmiths), affiliated with the Embodied AudioVisual Interaction (EAVI) group, combines human-computer interaction, machine learning, and signal processing techniques, to develop interactive technologies for digital humanities scholarship and machine learning education that promote expression, creativity, and embodied interaction. Fiebrink's *Wekinator* audio analysis, machine-learning based software allows anyone to build "new musical instruments, gestural game controllers, computer vision or computer listening systems, and more" (www.wekinator.org), using real-time feature extraction to create datasets for tasks such as music information retrieval and gesture classification for live performance. A comparable ethos drives the *Gesture Recognition Toolkit*, authored by creative technologist Nicholas Gillian in collaboration with pianist Sarah Nicolls, whose experimental performances master an impressive range of sensors. This "cross-platform, open-source C++ library (is) designed to make real-time machine learning and gesture recognition more accessible for non-specialists" (Gillian and Paradiso, 2014, 204).

Real-time processing tools launched by IRCAM[21] have proved determinant for ongoing creative DH endeavours: IRCAM-hosted breakthroughs include the late eighties invention of the widely used Max/MSP graphical programming environment (and related Pure Data software) by Miller Puckette. Diemo Schwarz's concatenative synthesis CataRT software (2006), a content-based extension to granular synthesis implemented in Max/MSP that ensures direct access to specific sound characteristics, provides a visual descriptor space for exploring a sound database. Source sounds are segmented into units, and a unit selection algorithm finds the sequence of units best matched to a target sound or phrase. Applications include "high level instrument synthesis, resynthesis of audio (…), texture and ambience synthesis, artistic speech synthesis, and interactive explorative synthesis in different variants" (Schwarz et al., 2006). Amongst other possibilities, CataRT's interactive sound browsing enables identification of speech content types such as transition points and turn-taking, gender-based conversation dynamics, and vowels versus fricatives, while ensuring availability of provenance data (file origin, time within file, etc). Versatile feature-surfing affordances make programmes like this, informed by a combination of deep artistic and technical skills, potentially relevant for DH projects seeking means to generate more compelling models than those generally obtainable with prosaic topic-modeling type resources.[22]

3.6 Invisible powers: Making sense of data

The poetic, critical work of art — work here being synonymous with labour, rather than product — is uniquely equipped to address Hayles's provocation to the digital humanities community: "How are our engagements with technologies affecting human purposes?"(Hayles, 2015, 504). While SIRI, Alexa and other ubiquitous agents might be the latest avatars of Mark Weiser's 'disappearing computers' (1991),[23] our need for ways to reckon with these transformational technologies is a need to which the humanities can, must, and to a certain extent do respond. Critical reflection through the lens of disciplines such as cognitive science, cultural and media studies, philosophy, social anthropology, and communication studies, expressed as scholarly theory in keeping with rigorous academic requirements, is however not always conducive to sorely needed wider public dialogue. Artistic work, which values subjective interpretation over authoritative closure, and playful ambivalence over affirmative analysis, offers more accessible means to trigger shareable discussion and reflection.

The ways hidden flows of power can be reconfigured by aesthetics are the subject of Graham Harwood's art, which he considers as a mode of enquiry into technical objects and their interconnections. YoHa - Harwood and his partner Matsuko Yokokoji - have engaged since 1994 with diverse media, collaborators and publics, testing art's means of expression, challenging power relations on which media systems depend, and prioritising art's public function as instigator of imaginative, inclusive social processes and dialogue. As a producer of social software,[24] Harwood does "not have any problem with creating media systems that have utility from my art methods", but this utility "must reveal something about the nature of power in which its mediation is taking place" (quoted in Iles, 2010). Beyond the introduction of electricity,

> "software/computational culture is the largest media system that humans have known. Yet very little work has been done analysing the agency of algorithms, semiconductors or database management systems. We have very few cultural spaces, critical tools that allow us to understand multifarious ways in which these systems are unfolding into the present" (Harwood, cited in Iles, 2010).

This lack of analytical or critical resources is aggravated by the fact that "most people working within database or software construction have no critical training", whereas, in Harwood's experience, "any introduction of art methodologies, or art as action research into these spaces is met with a huge sigh of relief" (ibid).

YoHa works addressing databases and related media systems include *Invisible Air,* created in 2011 with the assistance of Stephen Fortune. This consists of a series of contraptions, where a contraption is defined as "the unruly exuberant machine of experiment" (http://yoha.co.uk/taxonomy/term/6), applied to "what seem to us as illogical barbaric, redundant, violent uses of machines, and assemblages of machines and their energies." (http://yoha.co.uk/invisibletalk). The contraptions are here designed to reveal the power of databases as "transducers of knowledge and power rapidly moving through us, separating us, reforming us, folding us up into their parts"(ibid). Power is physically manifest as bursts of pneumatic energy relayed by theatrically instantiated interactive contraptions: The Open Data Book Stabber, Public Expenditure Riding Machine, Expenditure Filled Spud Gun, and Older People Pneumatic Brusher.

The energy animating these Heath Robinson-type machines, to the delight of publics in Bristol where the works were presented, is driven by actuators connected to open data lists of Bristol City Council expenditure items exceeding £500. For example, a violent impulsion felt by someone sitting on the Riding Machine indicates a high expenditure item for the city and its taxpayers, which can be traced back to the publicly accessible database. The pneumatic control references tube systems used to "push data around 1850's telegraphic bottlenecks, sucking and blowing messages between The Central Telegraph Office and the Stock Exchange, between Fleet Street, where newspapers were written, and the nearby City of London" (ibid). It is also, as YoHA points out, a principle we viscerally relate to, as organisms whose lungs vitally compress and exhale an invisible, shared resource. *Invisible Airs* creates physically memorable social experience from data usually kept abstract, thus somewhat meaningless, for the public it in fact deeply concerns. In a mode that is ambivalently playful and deadly serious, the work challenges open data governance initiatives that sometimes seem to be surreptitiously crafted to redeem "gaze as a technology of power" (Harwood, 2011).

Hidden flows of power that control our wireless networks are creatively sonified in Wes Goatley's *Wireless Fidelity* (2014). Goatley used OFCOM statistics to identify corporate network market shares, giving them sonic profiles as elements of a generative sound composition experienced by a listener wandering through the city of Brighton. The listener equipped with headphones and a Raspberry Pi computer in a small black box encounters sounds mapped to the presence of ambient Internet Service Providers. Materials are composed to facilitate appreciation of distinctive sonic identities, and their dynamic overlays and morphing as providers move in and out of dominant positions in the invisible wireless landscape. Multiple signals of the same ISP are panned to different positions in the headphones to reflect and allow one to "listen to" actual distribution. What are physically busy crossroads or quiet residential streets, urban malls or secluded parks, take on a very different guise as hotspots for contested market influence.

ISP profiles and sounds to which the deambulations are mapped are BT (30.5% market share) manifest as a low bass drone, Sky (22%) granular piano sound, Virgin (20.1%) female vocal samples, TalkTalk (18.3%) high frequency distortion drones, and EE (3.2%) piano loops. Unreadable ISP data is rendered as binaural shoreline recordings—a familiar 'white noise' in the Brighton seaside environment. Deambulation is both pleasurable and resonant with darker undertones: turning one's head or modulating one's pace and direction to enhance a given sonic mix, or merely stopping to enjoy a given inadvertent 'composition', is literally to nod to the provider/s. Goatley crafts his elegantly simple initial concept to give listeners immediate, embodied experience of the normally imperceptible realm of data that innervates our everyday living space. By individually interacting with these sonic materials, we physically and literally navigate systems of power and access that govern our networked lives.

Invisible Airs and *Wireless Fidelity* mine digital databases, using custom soft- and hardware to precipitate physical, communicable artefacts and experiential situations that could not have been previously imagined, and that directly reveal some of the intangible yet highly significant socio-economic pressures inherent to digital networks. By transposing categories or streams of data into sensible, shareable experience, YoHa and Goatley extend possibilities for discussion about how engagements with technologies are affecting our human purposes.

3.7 Critical thinking as 'grit in the machine'[25]

For Alan Liu, DH has a unique role to play in enriching cultural criticism: "Beyond acting in an instrumental role, the digital humanities can most profoundly advocate for the humanities by helping to broaden the very idea of instrumentalism, technological, and otherwise. This could be its unique contribution to cultural criticism" (Liu, 2012). Critical engagement with our computational turn earlier this century led to social scientist and designer pleas for seamful ubiquity (Chalmers and MacColl, 2002) and ambiguity as a resource for design (Gaver et al., 2003), to counter unrealistic ideals of sleekly convergent ubiquitous computing systems. In parallel, art works ranging from teasingly playful to fiercely dystopian have challenged the instrumentalised impact of digital technologies for decades[26], leaving historical legacies that make them largely comparable to technical initiatives heralded as decisive DH precursors.[27]

A key question driving artistic engagement with databases and machine learning is how we can relate to automated data processing and machine learning whose scales and modes of operation massively outstrip our all-too-human cognitive capacities. Victor Liu's *Turn All Things* (2013) employs image analysis, random media access, and logical iteration processes to ascribe formal rules to a flow of film footage (video recordings that follow traditional still life, portraiture, and landscape art conventions), to see how computational techniques might imbue images with a different sort of life to that wrought by human intention.[28] Liu's algorithm for recombining image flows is based on propagator matrices governing the system's probabilistic evolution, generated by computing "energy differences" based on composition of the visual field (position, colour, and light of formal aspects within the image), image trajectory (using Markov chain technique), and beat frequency (that of specific periodic phenomena identified within each set of rushes). While the resultant computationally edited sequences of flying gulls, bobbing lobster pots, changing interior daylight conditions, or a portrait subject's facial expressions, reflect an undeniable formal coherence, this coherence feels — and is — eerily non-human. Yet we are fascinated by and absorb this foreign aesthetic into our own imaginative resources, as we learn to tune to the machine learning behaviours we have initiated.

The 'Happy Valley Band' (HVB), created in 2011 and defined by its creator, musician David Kant, as pop music heard by a computer algorithm and (re-)performed by humans, is based on a machine learning system's notations of pop songs, the resultant scores being performed by a group of musicians (https://happyvalleyband.bandcamp.com/album/organvm-perceptvs). Like Victor Liu's quest to learn to see differently through machine intelligence, Kant's question in creating this system is how machines can help us to hear differently. Again here, results are both disconcertingly familiar and alien: because the model cannot fully capture the complexities of acoustically mixed sound, it makes what might be written off as simple errors except that, as Kant points out, "the artifacts often find structures in the sounds that I have never heard before and now cannot unhear", such that "Composing HVB music is like building hypothetical worlds and listening through them" (Kant, 2017, 5). Given our increasing reliance on technology to think, listen and feel for us, Kant suggests that we need to be more responsible with it, i.e. irreverent: "We should use machines to hear differently, not to reinforce our expectations - because whose expectations are they anyway?" (Kant, 2017, 22).

Machine listening is at the core of John Bowers' and Owen Green's "Hijacking Listening Machines for Performative Research" (2018). The artist/authors query how far the functionally-oriented approaches that characterise much machine listening research, inherited from engineering domains, are "suited to the exploratory, divergent, boundary-stretching, uncertainty-seeking, playful and irreverent orientations of many artists" (Bowers and Green, 2018, 114). To address this question in practice, they implemented a range of listening algorithms, presenting them with "input which challenged their customary range of application and the implicit norms of musicality" (ibid), and created a 3D spatialised multichannel environment allowing exploration of the algorithms in a performative/performance mode.

Listening algorithms thus produced — designated "makes" by their authors — include an 'AntiGate: Amplitude Version' where input signal is amplitude envelope-followed and let through the gate when it drops below a given threshold (i.e. the opposite function of a classic noise gate), an 'Eternal Resonance Machine' that converts any input into a sustained noise texture, and 'Re-De-Reverberation' where a de-reverberation plugin and reverberation pedal construct a controllable feedback loop. 'Schlechtmusik' subjects a recording of Mozart's *Eine kleine Nachtmusik* to tonal component extraction, sinusoidal analysis, and degradation by playback and re-recording in a noisy, reverberant space, then mixes five of the resultant outputs together with the original using a good-to-bad ("Nacht- to Schlecht-musik") crossfader, calibrated to rate as "good" materials the Shazam application recognises as Mozart's, and as "bad" unrecognisable materials.

According to Bowers and Green,

> "Our makes walk a narrow line between, on the one hand, being sincere attempts to work with established research in machine listening and genuine attempts to construct processes which embody well-engineered principles, and, on the other, somewhat tongue-in-cheek responses which willfully push techniques in a direction they were not intended to take and which have an eye for absurdity and a little humour. (…) we are not mocking existing research so much as to explore the field's boundaries and limitations. Similarly, we are exploring the utility of available machine listening techniques never mind their limitations, provided a rich enough experimental context is given for them…" (Bowers and Green, 2018, 118).

The authors emphasise the creative and intellectual importance of a genuinely open experimental context that is not sanitised or idealised in preparation for research, and is not exclusively organised along functional-engineering paradigms likely to over-determine outputs. They note that relatively conventional musical forms dominate music information retrieval and machine listening, which, as a state-of-the-art research field, is thus left paradoxically inept at dealing with contemporaneous experimental practice.[29]

Conclusion: An appeal for the arts in DH as providers of deep diversity

In the networked, standardised world of computational culture, "economies of scale and scope are producing many strong drives toward shallow diversity" (Agre, 2002, 282).[30] As a counterweight, creative digital practices linked with digital humanities can be a vital vector for deep diversity, defined by Agre as "a diversity that arises from independent evolution in unrelated and completely incommensurable institutional cultural, and technical contexts" (ibid).

The race to stay perceptively and cognitively abreast of the expansion of storable digital media and processing techniques gives rise to paradoxical tensions: how do we deal with the recursive dynamic linking us to things computational, as human learnings gleaned from unforeseeable machine learnings in turn transform human capabilities? While yielding intellectual breakthroughs, couplings of humanities projects and computational technologies have also won ambivalent traction in knowledge markets where interactivity and multimodality are viewed as mere added value for commodified, commercialised intellectual products. This is an odd context for involving arts practices, whose idiosyncratic modes of operation are totally out of kilter with the modularisation and economies of scale that determine the spread of humanities computing. Then again, if digital humanities is to get beyond text and image inherited literacies to invent new forms of humanities experience, these same arts practices are exceptionally equipped to explore our extended sensorimotor capacities, and the intersubjective interaction which is "the cognition and affectively charged experience of self and other" (Thompson, 2005, 408) that deeply defines us as human. Instead of the authoritative closure of purportedly expert solutions, digital arts critically problematise normative visions to elicit fresh perspectives, and drive the widely shareable discussion needed to address pressing socio-technological transformations.

Acknowledgements

Alice Eldridge and the Humanising Algorithmic Listening community, Wes Goatley, Ian Grant, Victor Liu, Paul Stapleton, Norah Zuniga-Shaw.

Notes

1 The UK 'Digital Resources in the Humanities' conference became, from 2008, 'Digital Resources in the Humanities and the Arts' to encourage artistic engagement with DH.
2 "Over the past years, the field that we now refer to as digital humanities has been known by many terms: humanities computing, humanist informatics, literary and linguistic computing and digital resources in the humanities, to name but a few." (Terras, Nyhan, and Vanhoutte, 2013, 2). Blackwell's *Companion to the Digital Humanities* (2004) and the 2005 founding of the Alliance of Digital Humanities Organizations (http://adho.org/about) are early users of this term.
3 Digital Humanities scholars' emphasis on, and tensions around, the "more hack, less yack" slogan, are described by Bethany Nowviskie ("On the Origin of 'Hack' and 'Yack'", 2014).
4 John Unsworth's statement that "Humanities computing is a practice of representation, a form of modeling" (Terras et al, 2013, 36) has complex implications: modeling varies as a function of its relation to the reality it is intended to model, including abstract computational realities unmoored from physical events and materials (cf. Morgan and Morrison, 1999). Experiential performative research that prototypes data scaled beyond human cognition, thus predictability, challenges the nature and function of both models and representational practices.
5 The legacy of artistic practice teaching in academies and conservatories, largely initiated and operated in Europe by royal or state authorities, continues to influence contemporary debates on artistic research and academia. See Borgdorff, 2012.
6 Fuelled by opportunist views of the creative industries filling gaps in budgets and job markets, these trends have evolved since the nineteen-sixties when, in prospection for new computing products and markets, "key players like Remington Rand and IBM teamed up with humanities scholars and funded conferences and projects that explored new applications of computing" (Vanhoutte 128). This movement was further boosted by the 1980 implementation of the Baye-Dohl act, allowing US universities to patent publicly financed findings (Norman, 2002, 289).

7 An example is the productive collaboration between choreographers and computer scientists established in the late 1980s at Simon Fraser University, Vancouver, led by dancer and computer scientist Thecla Schiphorst, and biomedical engineering and computing scientist Tom Calvert. See Schiphorst and Calvert, 2015.

8 Harwood worked as an independent artist from the 1980s, creating the UK's first computer generated graphic novel in 1990 and the acclaimed 'Rehearsal of Memory' collaborative digital media work in 1995, before integrating Goldsmiths as a lecturer in Interactive Media in the 2000s.

9 For cinema and media scholar Tara McPherson, the "post-archival" seeks to retrieve the best of the archive and the digital for new modes of practice. See McPherson, 2015.

10 Videos with animations, standalone animations or slideshows of geographic, architectural, textual, and statistical interpretations, and interactive applications allowing further analysis and development of the dance ideas.

11 Computerised notation programmes have developed steadily, notably since Lucy Venable's Mac-based *Laban Writer* in 1987 exploited notation principles developed by Rudolf van Laban.

12 Funding was kickstarted by the German Federal Cultural Foundation, with institutional match funding secured from the Advanced Computing Center for the Arts and Design Department of Dance at Ohio State University, Fraunhofer Institute for Computer Graphics Research, Hochschule Darmstadt-University of Applied Sciences, and Hochschule für Gestaltung Offenbach. Local match funding and corporate sponsorship (Volkswagen Foundation) were provided by further education and cultural bodies. See deLahunta, 2017.

13 "One can *make* things with it (Life Forms), one doesn't have to put things in one already knows... one can make *discoveries*, and that interested me from the beginning." Cunningham (1991), quoted in Schiphorst, Calvert, 2015.

14 For example, the 2004 Guggenheim *'Seeing Double. Emulation in Theory and Practice'* exhibition of original and emulated versions of works by Cory Arcangel, Mary Flanagan, Jodi, Robert Morris, Nam June Paik, John F. Simon, Jr., Weinbren and Friedman; Marina Abramović's 2005 *Seven Easy Pieces* (reworkings of performances by Bruce Nauman, Vito Acconci, Valie Export, Gina Pane, Joseph Beuys, and two of Abramović's own earlier works); André Lepecki's 2006 reconstruction of Allan Kaprow's 1959 *18 Happenings in Six Parts*.

15 The volumes were bound as a consolidated DVD in 2002 (Artintact production ceased in 1999).

16 Bob Stein's Voyager works for CD-ROM include Morton Subotnick's Max Ernst-inspired *All My Humming Birds Have Alibis* (1993), Laurie Anderson's *Puppet Motel* (1994), and the Residents' *Freak Show* (1994). See Geoffrey Brown, 2012.

17 The '(BLOCK)CHAIN OF LOVE' studies how the blockchain influences and/or might influence the creation and preservation of digital artworks, through the following provocative questions: 1) Since all blockchain content identifies its author via an identification key and encryption date, might we have come full circle from the infinite reproducibility of digital works, to a renewed concept of the "original"? 2) Despite its logic of anonymity and sharing, manifest with Bitcoin, the blockchain allows identification of owners—though as this is the prerogative of machines, is the network thus to be seen as the "author of the author"? 3) What imaginary productions are arising from the blockchain, influencing our material world and other technical media?

18 STEIM's artist-developer guest directors, engaged for decades alongside managing director Michel Waisvisz (1949-2008), include Netochka Nezvanova, author(s) of the Max-based nato.0+55+3d experimental software packages that significantly influenced digital arts as one of the first applications to allow realtime, modular video and multimedia manipulation and display (1999).

19 "There are undoubtedly cliques of scholars in the community, unofficial discussion groups, friendships, scholarly support networks, mentoring programmes, and many other relationships associated with academic communities and disciplines active within Humanities Computing." Terras, 2013, 75.

20 Actuators include gyroscopes to monitor and control device positions, direction, angular motion and rotation, accelerometers to automatically change screen orientation, and pulse and vibration systems to provide tactile feedback

21 Institut de Recherche et Coordination Acoustique/ Musique), inaugurated in 1977 under the leadership of Pierre Boulez, to promote experimental music, sound research, and related technologies. www.ircam.fr

22 For example, Tim Hitchcock's project, *Hearing voices in an 18th century coutrtroom: Sound, space and experience at the Old Bailey*, seeks to remediate the 'voices' of the dead—i.e. textually recorded speech archives of the Old Bailey proceedings—through analysis of texts, acoustics, synchronic linguistics, architecture and proxemics to design a dynamic, accurately rendered digital environment for consultable 'voices'.

23 As Weiser's text famously begins: "The most profound technologies are those that disappear. They weave themselves into the fabric of everyday life until they are indistinguishable from it."

24 Social software invented by Harwood and his previous group, Mongrel, began with *Linker* in 1999 and culminated with *Nine(9)* in 2003; these are early examples of multimedia authoring software designed by artists for running collaborative arts projects sensitive to the cultural expressions of marginalised social groups. http://yoha.co.uk/node/642

25 This heading borrows from Berry and Fagerjord (2017) to align with their affirmation that "introducing critical approaches into digital humanities projects often slows them down. (...) Critical thinking can act as 'grit in the machine'... However, we think that critical work offers a productive slowdown, forcing a project to reflect on its approach, method and goals..." (p.143). Berry and Fagerjord cite work by artists Zach Blas, Adam Harvey, and Julian Oliver, as well as poet Edouart Glissant's claim to the right to difference, and to opacity, that does not boil down to "enclosure within an irreducible singularity". (p.148)

26 Lynn Hershman Leeson's work has explored emerging tools and platforms since the 1970s to focus on relations between humans and digital technology; Perry Hoberman's *Bar Code Hotel* (1994) recycles product barcodes to create a multi-user interface to an unruly virtual environment; Natalie Jeremijenko's *Live Wire (Dangling String)* (1995) installation is formed of suspended LED cables that respond to internet traffic volumes.

27 For example, widely recognised pre-DH initiatives include Busa's Lexical Text Analysis-based *Index Thomisticus* of the 1950s; productions of the Literary and Linguistic Computing Centre founded at Cambridge in 1964; the International Conference on Computers in the Humanities launched in 1973; the Text Encoding Initiative Guidelines published in 1990 (Vanhoutte, 2013).

28 Information on this work kindly forwarded by Victor Liu.

29 A situation commonly encountered in humanities computing: the SLAVs (stations de lecture audiovisuelle) created by the French Institut National de l'Audiovisuel to explore its radio and television archives, have been endowed since the nineties with analytical tools for 'expert consultation'. Yet many affordances designed to explore conventional audiovisual materials (e.g. identifying chrominance and luminance patterns across massive image bases), cannot cope with the non-normative visual languages of artists. While it is understandable for technologies to be largely geared towards wider user bases, overlooking emerging forms of expression when deploying such powerful tools is tantamount to refusing or pre-determining cultural evolution.

30 Agre defines shallow diversity as "diversity that is generated from within a shared framework, such as a grammar, a set of modules, or the settings of parameters".

References

Agre, Philip E. 2002. The Market Logic of Information. pp.275–283 in Hartmut Böhme, Christina von Braun, Martin Burckhardt, Wolfgang Coy, Friedrich Kittler, Hans Ulrich Reck (eds.). *Die Politik der Maschine*, Hamburg, Hans-Bredow Institut

Bay-Cheng, Sarah. 2016. Digital Historiography and Performance. *Theatre Journal*, Vol. 68, n°4, December, pp.507–527

Bench, Harmony, Elswit, Kate. 2016. Mapping Movement on the Move: Dance Touring and Digital Methods. *Theatre Journal*, Vol.68, N°4, December, pp.575–596

Berry, David, and Fajerjord, Anders. 2017. *Digital Humanities*, Cambridge - UK, Polity Press

Bleeker, M. (ed.). 2017. Transmission in Motion. *The Technologizing of Dance*. Oxon, Routledge

Bolter, Jay David, and Grusin, Richard. 1999. *Remediation: Understanding New Media*, MIT Press

Borgdorff, Henk. 2012. *The conflict of the faculties: perspectives on artistic research and academia*, Amsterdam, Leiden University Press https://openaccess.leidenuniv.nl/handle/1887/18704

Bowers, John, and Green, Owen. 2018. *All the Noises: Hijacking Listening Machines for Performative Research*. NIME Proceedings, pp.114–119

Brown, Geoffrey. 2012. Developing Virtual CD-ROM Collections: The Voyager Company Publications, *The International Journal of Digital Curation*, Vol.7, Issue 2, pp.3–20

Campus, Peter. 2017. Anarchive n°7. Peter Campus. 3 volumes: 2 exhibition catalogues, Augmented Reality monograph (IoS and Android devices). Paris, Editions Anarchive

Caplan, Debra. 2015. Notes from the Frontier: Digital Scholarship and the Future of Theatre Studies. *Theatre Journal*, Vol. 67, n°2, May, pp.347–359

Chalmers, Matthew, and MacColl, Ian. 2002. Seamful and Seamless Design in Ubiquitous Computing. https://www.researchgate.net/publication/228551086_Seamful_and_seamless_design_in_ubiquitous_computing

Clarke, Paul, Jones, Simon, Kaye, Nick, Linsley, Johanna (eds.). 2018. Artists in the Archive. *Creative and Curatorial Engagements with Documents of Art and Performance*. Routledge

deLahunta, Scott. 2017. Motion Bank, pp.128–137 in Bleeker, Maaike (ed.), *Transmission in Motion. The Technologizing of Dance*. Oxon, Routledge

Ernst, Wolfgang. 2013. *Digital Memory and the Archive*. Minneapolis, University of Minnesota Press

Friedberg, Anne. 2006. The Virtual Window. *From Alberti to Microsoft*. Cambridge, Mass, MIT Press

Fujihata, Masaki. 2016. Anarchive n°6. Masaki Fujihata. Ring binder publication incorporating Augmented Reality access to videos and 3D simulations (IoS devices). Paris, Editions Anarchive

Gaver, William W., Beaver, Jacob, Benford, Steve. 2003. Ambiguity as a resource for design. Proceedings of the SIGCHI Conference on Human Factors in Computing Systems. pp.233–240

Giannachi, Gabriella. 2016. *Archive Everything: Mapping the Everyday*. Cambridge, Mass, MIT Press

Gillian, Nicholas, and Paradiso, Joe. 2014. The gesture recognition toolkit. *Journal of Machine Learning Research* 15, pp.3483–3487

Goatley, Wes. 2014. *Wireless Fidelity*. http://www.wesleygoatley.com/wireless-fidelity/

Grant, Ian. 2018. Shadows, Touch and Digital Puppeteering. PhD thesis, University of Sussex

Grusin, Richard, 2013. The Dark Side of the Digital Humanities - Part 2, Thinking C21 https://www.c21uwm. com/2013/01/09/dark-side-of-the-digital-humanities-part-2/

Harwood, Graham. 2011. Steam Powered Census. https://www.academia.edu/563634/Steam_Powered_Census)

Hayles, Katherine. 2015. Final Commentary: A Provocation. pp.503–506 in Svensson, Patrik, Goldberg, David Theo (eds.). *Between Humanities and the Digital*. Cambridge, Mass., MIT Press

Huhtamo, Erkki. 2011. *Media Archaeology: Approaches, Applications, and Implications*. Cambridge Mass., MIT Press

Iles, Anthony. 2010. In the Mud and Blood of Networks: An Interview with Graham Harwood. Mute magazine, October. (http://yoha.co.uk/mud_blood_networks)

Jenett, Florian. 2018. Motion Bank at Hochschule Mainz. https://medium.com/motion-bank/motion-bank-at-hochschule-mainz-c89ef4a61643

Jones, Amelia, Heathfield, Adrian (eds.). 2012. *Perform, Repeat, Record: Live Art in History*. Bristol, Intellect

Kant, David. 2017. Organum Perceptus. *The Long Answer*. Santa Cruz, Indexical

Kuntzel, Thierry. 2006. Anarchive n°3. Title TK. DVD-Rom directed by Thierry Kuntzel. Paris, Editions du Centre Pompidou

Liu, Alan. 2012. "Where is Cultural Criticism in the Digital Humanities?" http://dhdebates.gc.cuny.edu/debates/text/20

McKenzie, Jon. 2001. *Perform Or Else: From Discipline to Performance*. Routledge

McPherson, Tara. 2015. Post-Archive: The Humanities, the Archive, and the Database. pp.483–502 in Svensson, P., and Goldberg, David Theo (eds.). *Between Humanities and the Digital*. Cambridge, Mass., MIT

Morgan, Mary, and Morrison, Margaret (eds.). 1999. *Models as Mediators: Perspectives on Natural and Social Science*. Cambridge, UK, Cambridge University Press

Muntadas, Antoni. 1999. Anarchive n°1. Muntadas Media Architecture Installations. Interom directed by Antoni Muntadas with the collaboration of Anne-Marie Duguet. Paris, Editions du Centre Pompidou

Nakaya, Fujiko. 2012. Anarchive n°5. Fog/ 霧/ Brouillard. Monograph, DVD-Rom, DVD-Video. Paris, Editions Anarchive

Norman, Sally Jane. 2002. Information as a Prime and Primarily Relational Value. pp.284–294 in Hartmut Böhme, Christina von Braun, Martin Burckhardt, Wolfgang Coy, Friedrich Kittler, Hans Ulrich Reck (eds.). *Die Politik der Maschine*, Hamburg, Hans-Bredow Institut

Noviskie, Bethany. 2014. "On the Origin of 'Hack' and 'Yack'", http://nowviskie.org/2014/on-the-origin-of-hack-and-yack/

Ostoff, Simone. 2009. *Performing the Archive: The Transformation of the Archive in Contemporary Art from Repository Documents to Art Medium*. New York, Atropos Press

Otth, Jean. 2007. Anarchive n°4. ...Autour du Concile de Nicée. DVD-Video, DVD-Rom directed by Jean Otth; editorial and scientific direction, Anne-Parie Duguet. Paris, Editions Anarchive

Parikka, Jussi. 2012. *What is Media Archaeology?* Cambridge, Polity

Pickering, Andrew. 1995. The Mangle of Practice: *Time, Agency, and Science*. Chicago, University of Chicago Press

Rockwell, Geoffrey. 2013. Inclusion in the Digital Humanities. pp.247–253 in Terras et al.

Salazar Sutil, Nicolás, Popat, Sita (eds.) 2015. *Digital Movement: Essays in Motion Technology and Performance*. Palgrave

Schiphorst, Thecla, Calvert, Thomas, text in Salazar Sutil, Nicolás, Popat, Sita (eds). 2015. *Digital Movement: Essays in Motion Technology and Performance*. Palgrave

Schwarz, Diemo, Beller, Grégory, Verbrugghe, Bruno, Britton, Sam. 2006. Real-time corpus-based concatenative synthesis with CataRT. 9th International Conference on Digital Audio Effects (DAFx), pp.279–282

Snow, Michael. 2002. Anarchive n°2. Digital Snow. DVD-Rom directed by Michael Snow. Paris, Editions du Centre Pompidou

Terras, Melissan, Nyhan, Julianne, Vanhoutte, Edward (eds.). 2013. *Defining Digital Humanities. A Reader*, Farnham, Surrey, Ashgate

Thompson, Evan. 2005. Sensorimotor subjectivity and the enactive approach to experience. *Phenomenology and the Cognitive Sciences*, 4 (4):407–427.

Thrift, Nigel. 2008. *Non-Representational Theory: Space, Politics, Affect*. Routledge

(Critical) artistic research and DH

Vanhoutte, Edward. 2013. The Gates of Hell: History and Definition of Digital Humanities Computing. pp.119–156 in Terras, Melissan, Nyhan, Julianne, Vanhoutte, Edward (eds.) 2013. *Defining Digital Humanities.* A Reader, Farnham, Ashgate

Schatzki, Theodore R, Knorr Cetina, Karin, von Savigny, Eike. (eds.). 2001. *The Practice Turn in Contemporary Theory.* Routledge, London

Weiser, Mark. 1991. The Computer for the Twenty-First Century. *Scientific American*, pp.66–75 (https://www.ics.uci.edu/~corps/phaseii/Weiser-Computer21stCentury-SciAm.pdf)

YoHa. 2012. Invisible Airs. yoha.co.uk/invisible

Ziegler, Chris. 2017. William Forsythe's Improvisation Technologies and beyond: a short design history of digital dance transmission projects on CD-ROM and DVD-ROM, 1994–2011. pp.41–51 in Bleeker, Maaike (ed.). *Transmission in Motion. The Technologizing of Dance.* Oxon, Routledge

Zielinski, Siegfried. 2002. Archäologie der Medien: Zur Tiefenzeit des technischen Hörens und Sehens. Reinbek, Rowohlt Taschenbuch. Translated by Custance, Gloria. 2006. *Deep Time of the Media:* Toward an Archeology of Hearing and Seeing by Technical Means. Cambridge, Mass, MIT Press

Zuniga Shaw, Norah. 2017. What else might this dance look like? pp.99–107 in Bleeker, Maaike (ed.). *Transmission in Motion. The Technologizing of Dance.* Oxon, Routledge

4

"A PICTURE PAINTS A THOUSAND WORDS"

Hand-drawn network maps as a means to elicit data on digitally mediated social relations

Cornelia Reyes Acosta

4.1 Introduction

Digital platforms have fostered a social environment that creates spaces for new forms and qualities of social interaction (e.g. Baym, 2015; Willson, 2006). The individuals' use of online social networking platforms is assumed to create an "extended and disembodied sociality" (Willson, 2006, p. 49) to such an extent that digitally mediated social interaction challenges our traditional conceptual understanding of social relatedness. This is because digital environments and the properties of online platforms facilitate a way of engaging in an ampler bandwidth of communicative practices that impact the dynamics of relationship building (e.g. Baym, 2015, Lambert, 2013, Haythornthwaite, 2002). In practice this means that we see individuals form social ties with perfect strangers – previously unacquainted individuals – by for example connecting with others on the basis of shared interests through online communities formed in comment sections for example. As a result of this, traditional factors conducive to forming social bonds such as geographical closeness or a shared biographical timeline (e.g. sharing time together at school) become less relevant.

The impact of digital social spaces on the individuals' experience of social engagement prompts a number of questions: What does it mean to the individual user to connect with others online? What aspects of digitally mediated social engagement do individuals highlight? And how do individuals make sense of these new social spaces? Wittel (2001) portrayed digitally mediated social spaces as consisting "of fleeting and transient, yet iterative social relations" (p. 51). The concept of "network sociality", which describes this phenomenon, challenges the traditional 'narrational' character of social relations, as individuals seem to perceive of these momentary social encounters as an indispensable means to relate with others.

Platforms like Facebook, Twitter and Instagram have assumed great significance for building valuable social ties with previously unacquainted individuals; one important aspect to characterise these ties is that these are often ephemeral, fleeting forms of social interaction (see for example Wittel, 2001). A common trait of this type of tie is that respondents may not be able to recall data (e.g. concrete names and social roles) of individuals they are connected to. Nonetheless, research has shown that these ties may often take on crucial importance for individuals by providing emotional support and fostering social inclusion (e.g. Bayer, et al., 2016).

A growing amount of scholarship evidences the impact of digital sociality and its various effects on social phenomena (e.g. Boyd, Golder and Lotan, 2010, Donath and Boyd, 2004). Relatively little attention has been paid though to conceptualising the actual nature of digitally mediated social interaction. Conceptualising digitally mediated sociality, as Wittel (2001) argued, requires understanding "what kind of sociality is at stake in the information age" (p. 52). To achieve this, digital methods (e.g. Rogers, 2013) and its applications is a promising point of reference for researchers aiming to unpack the impact of digital technology. One example is the analysis of online social networks, which are increasingly analysed utilising automated procedures of data harvesting (e.g. Rieder, 2013), analysis and visualisation (e.g. Jacomy et al., 2014).

Whereas these methods are useful to analyse structural aspects of online social networks and models of social relations, they rarely deliver data on the individuals' perception of "the making of networks [and] networking as a practice" (Wittel, 2001, p. 52). I argue that instead of looking at digital sociality from a macro-perspective, more attention should be given to tackle online relations as a phenomenon of practice, by unpacking individuals' *experience* of connecting with others online. This chapter discusses a new method for the digital, looking at the micro-perspective of online relationship building by tracing individuals' motivations of using digital tools and an interpretation of their respective properties.

4.2 Hand-drawn network maps: Tapping into arts-based research techniques to uncover the quality of digitally mediated social ties

The hand-drawn network maps I present in this chapter resulted from interviews with creative professionals (fine artists, photographers and sculptors) as part of my research on the significance of digitally mediated social ties in attaining recognition in the cultural and creative field (see Reyes, 2016). I realised that even though the use of online social networking platforms has become a central element of these individuals' day-to-day social activities, verbalising their perception of the social relations they build online is challenging. I suspected that this is to do with the relatively intangible nature of digitally mediated social relations, owed to their ephemeral, fleeting nature.

Wittel (2001) holds that social relations in the digital age "are not 'narrational' but 'informational'; they are not based on mutual experience or common history, but primarily on an exchange of data and on 'catching up'" (p. 51). This fragmented form of social exchange is mirrored in respondents' inefficacy to produce a coherent narrative of digitally mediated sociality. I argue that this lacking narrative of online social engagement is key to understanding why respondents struggle to produce concrete evidence of their experiences in the field, which motivated me to provide respondents with an alternative tool – the hand-drawn network map.

The value of utilising these maps in the field emerges from its capacity to elicit data in a creative and unconventional way, which unlike interviews or surveys bypasses "language as the privileged medium for the creation and communication of knowledge" (Bagnoli, 2009, p. 547). Whereas the value of traditional research methods is undeniable, research can benefit from a more intuitive approach by engaging respondents in a cognitively stimulating way. Drawings and diagrams are a central element to achieve this: Commonly referred to as arts-based research techniques (e.g. Finley, 2008), drawings rely on visual artefacts and symbols to create a communicative platform between researcher and respondent (Crilly, Blackwell and Clarkson, 2006). Specifically, when dealing with abstract or novel phenomena, visual elements assume particular importance as they can serve as memory aids (Scott, 2008) that bridge potential verbal barriers. In other words, the drawings might help respondents to establish knowledge in spite of lacking the verbal means to express the conceptual richness underlying the data they provide.

In the social sciences and beyond, drawings and diagrams are particularly useful for incentivising rapport with respondents and for their capacity to serve as an icebreaker (Morrow, 1998). Most importantly, not only the drawing itself is vital to the research process; rather its value lies in the communicative space enacted by the creative process, which provides an environment that encourages respondents to express their own meaning without the constraint of responding and adhering to existing conceptual knowledge (Morrow, 1998). Drawings rely on visual artefacts and symbols (e.g. CohenMiller, 2018, van der Vaart, van

Hoven and Huigen, 2018, Den Besten, 2010) to create a communicative platform between researcher and respondent (Crilly, Blackwell and Clarkson, 2006).

Analysing visual cues (e.g. pictorial representations, sketches, illustrations and symbols) is central to this method and their function can be summarised as follows: Visual cues used in drawings act as stimuli that help respondents re-engage with moments of social interaction. They act as triggers to evoke data on fleeting moments of social interaction which may have been only superficially retained as memory and are thereby difficult to access through targeted recall (see Tolia-Kelly, 2004). Equally, these cues act as "concrete indicators of abstract values" (Firth, 1973, p. 54) and enable respondents to establish data through means other than language (e.g. Crozier, 1997). I conclude that leveraging attributes of visual cues, such as colours and shapes facilitates the elicitation of information that may have remained hidden using traditional, structured forms of analysis. Thereby, visual symbols anchor the respondents' thought process and allow them to "explain the concrete by reference to the abstract […] and to extract from the concrete its hidden meaning for an understanding of the abstract." (Firth, 1973, p. 55).

4.3 Data collection procedure

In my research project I focused on the relevance of digitally mediated social ties in fostering access to social capital resources, such as professional mentorship, provision of tangible financial support and access to professional work contracts. I was interested in tracing the relevance of digitally mediated social ties compared to more traditional forms of social engagement. While I was keen to utilise established analytic techniques, I speculated that the conceptual baggage inherent in standardised surveys for example would coerce individuals to recall information on social ties in accordance with predefined triggers (i.e. names of actors and/or indicators of status, alongside measures of social proximity). While recalling traditional social contacts is often logically connected to a person's name, this rationale is ineffective when it comes to digitally mediated social relations; rather than associating social proximity to particular individuals via their name, digitally mediated social bonds were better remembered in conjunction with concrete experiences, contexts and circumstances (see Reyes, 2016).

Researching social capital resources through tracing the meaning of social relations is one area of research where network maps can be useful. However, this method can be valuable for any researcher trying to unpack the individual perception of social ties such as in management research, social interaction in the classroom or in marketing research. The key to making this method work is to adapt the trigger question which incentivises the drawing process to mirror the respective research interest. Equally, the material provided can be adapted to match respondents' preferences. For example, working with children might benefit using colourful pencils and stamps, whereas management practitioners might prefer working with flip charts and highlighters or markers.

Working with hand-drawn network maps I sought to enable respondents to provide recall data by illustrating particular moments of social interaction that emerged out of their day-to-day socialising practices. This resonates with White & Godart's (2007) concept of stories, whereby

> "[a] relationship gets interpreted in stories both by its participants and by observers. How does this process come about? Identities perceive and invoke the likelihood of impacts from other identities, which are seen to do the same. These relations get coded from raw reports into various shorthands of discourse and deportment. Then sets of signals, communications on topics, get transposed from one situation to another. Eventually these sets can settle down into stories or other conventions." (White & Godart, 2007, p. 6)

The aim of utilising hand-drawn network maps was to elicit exactly such stories in order to uncover social acts that constitute social ties alongside respondents' interpretation of their relevance. Drawing seemed particularly apt in this instance as the respondents all had a background in creative practice, ranging from photography to fine arts. As a result, respondents were familiar and at ease with forms of creative expression which is considered a pre-requisite for the successful use of arts-based research approaches (e.g. Walker, Caine-Bish and Wait, 2009, Bagnoli, 2009). The drawing process was considered a co-constructive effort resonating with action-research approaches (see Marcu, 2016) and "researching 'with' participant" techniques (see Cook, 2012), whereby the visualisation of data emerged out of a collaboration between researcher and respondent. This entails that verbal statements throughout the drawing process are a considerable aid to guiding the subsequent analytical process, drawing on a "talk and draw" rationale (Prosser, 2007, p. 22).

My field work was comprised of five case studies including fine artists, photographers and sculptors active in different parts of England who were all using online social networking platforms as part of their professional practice. I recruited respondents through both convenience sampling and snowball sampling procedures, whereby initially established contacts referred me on to colleagues in the field.

I provided respondents with a blank sheet of A3 paper, sticky notes, felt tips and colour markers (Emmel, 2008). I then asked them to think about their creative practice and bring onto paper the relationships that they thought mattered in that context. To facilitate this process, I prepared the following trigger question as a prompt: "Who are the people that you consider to be important, so that you can produce successful work as a creative professional?" I provided no instructions as to how and when to use these resources. Instead it was respondents' choice whether or not to use these and how to integrate these into the procedure. I refrained from intervening during the initial drawing period and I did not set a time limit for producing the network map. Once respondents had finished their hand-drawn network map, I invited the respondent to reflect on their map and share with me ideas and thoughts that emerged. After respondents had finished their reflection, I noted down some of my own observations on specific parts and visual cues used in the map. I then invited the respondent to tell me more about specific visual cues featured in the map and to explain their rationale of using a specific colour, a specific shape or specific symbol. I also asked respondents to reflect and elaborate on parts in the network map which they thought were crucial. This was important to grant respondents ownership of the data and to ensure that the representation of their network was interpreted in accordance with their views – an important measure to ensure the credibility of the produced evidence (see Schwandt, 2001).

One particularly rich example of a network map above (Figure 4.1) is based on respondent Fiona's case: Fiona is a self-taught photographer in her mid 30s. She has previously worked as a social media and

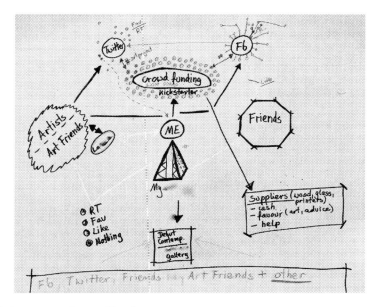

Figure 4.1 Hand-drawn network map (Fiona)

marketing manager in the UK and abroad. While Fiona is still trying to establish in the field, she has previously presented her work in several smaller exhibitions, primarily in London, and has been featured as an emerging artist on Saatchi's digital screen. Aside from that, Fiona is presenting her work on her business Facebook page and on the websites of several online galleries, where she has already been able to sell several of her works. Above all, Fiona is an avid social media user frequently active on Facebook, Twitter and Pinterest. I chose Fiona's network map as an example given the attention to detail that has been given to expressing different types of social ties whereby the visual language underlying the network map offers multiple leverage points for analysis.

Acknowledging the limitations of this unstructured approach, I would like to highlight that working with creative professionals afforded me a significant advantage. The task of drawing their social network from scratch required a significant amount of imagination on the part of the respondent, along with an openness to create data under minimal guidance. While respondents enjoyed this exercise and were happy to engage with an experimental technique, it has to be noted that this may not be always the case and it is the responsibility of the researcher to identify whether using an unstructured method suits the background of targeted individuals. Equally, the co-constitutive nature of such a data collection procedure obligates the researcher to exercise caution in guiding the respondent through the process and avoid compromising the integrity of the data.

4.4 Analytical approach

Facilitating the analysis of visual cues, I draw on features of the documentary method. The documentary method places emphasis on the analysis of data that circumvents limitations of "physical sources, most commonly written documents" (Payne and Payne, 2004, p. 61). The use of this method has been described as providing a "methodical access to pictures" (Bohnsack, 2009, p. 296) that aims to establish knowledge "through pictures" instead of "about pictures" (Bohnsack, 2008, p. 3). Rather than relying on visual cues as facilitators of knowledge, the documentary method tackles images as an autonomous unit of analysis. The novelty of applying this method lies in the specific status it ascribes to network maps as a data source: Traditionally, visualisations like network drawings and diagrams are considered cognitive aids that allow a communication about the visualisation, ultimately resulting in recording written text; here the visual language inherent in network maps is considered the main source of information and is initially independent of verbal statements.

Using this method incorporates tacit and atheoretical knowledge into the analytical procedure (see Froggett, Manley and Roy, 2015; Boehm, 1978), which can be an advantage when tracing socialising processes that lack distinct theoretical understanding. This analytical approach avoids integrating existing conceptual knowledge such as established network data into the analysis, precisely to give voice to the "action-guiding practical knowledge" (Baltruschat, 2010, p. 312) that may conflict with prevailing conceptual traditions. Giving full credit to the respondent as the author of the drawing and letting their language set the standard opens up a possibility to unlock the characteristic meaning (see Panofsky, 1955) of the drawing and allows them to visualise perceptions of the distinct quality of various social ties. At the same time, they provide information on the functions that social ties hold in terms of providing access to resources.

The documentary method relies on two analytical steps: the "formulating interpretation" and the "reflecting interpretation" (Bohnsack, 2009). The "formulating interpretation" describes the formulation of an outline, i.e. reproducing and summarising the content of the drawing without interpreting or evaluating it. This portrays the sequential progression of how the visual language in the drawing unfolded. The subsequent "reflecting interpretation" traces how specific elements in the drawing are being defined, "how they are represented and how they are substantiated" (Baltruschat, 2010, p. 315). In the "reflecting interpretation" I explore how visual cues are defined, represented and substantiated (Bohnsack, 2003) through statements of the respondent. I first interpret the highlighted symbol and then corroborate this with verbal

Hand-drawn network maps

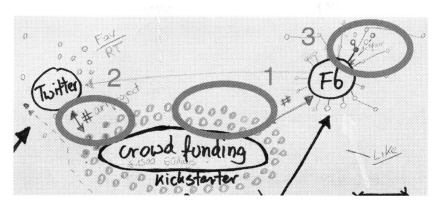

Figure 4.2 Highlighted visual cues – Hand-drawn network map (Fiona)

data from the respondents' interview. This highlights the importance of analysing the drawings in conjunction with the respondent (Rose, 2007), as it attributes legitimacy to respondents' perception of social relations resulting from their networking activities. Strictly speaking the integration of verbal data into the analytic process deviates from the guidelines of the documentary method. Nonetheless, I maintain that merging the interpretation of a symbol with verbal statements of the respondent should be encouraged as it adds substance and clarifies meaning.

For demonstrative purposes I apply this method to pre-selected parts of the network map as deemed relevant to the research question (see Figure 4.2): the significance of digitally mediated social interaction. This however does not suggest that the remainder of the drawing is irrelevant and not worthy of analysis but was simply a necessary measure to stay within the scope of this chapter. Relevant visual components in the network maps were accessed by identifying key features that included visually prominent cues (Bland, 2012) that stood out because of particular properties (e.g. its colour, shape and location in the drawing) or aspects of the drawing that were highlighted by the respondent as specifically relevant. These key features (Figure 2, segments highlighted in red) can be summarised as follows:

1. Shapes: Visual cues that stand out because of their specific shape.
2. Symbols: Areas that stand out because of use of symbolic artefacts.
3. Colours: Areas in the network map that draw on use of colours or colour combinations.

4.5 Analysis of the Hand-drawn network map

Accessing indicated segments of the network map displayed in Figure 4.2, I now move on to illustrating the sequential flow of analysis for each of these segments. I proceed from Section 1 through to Section 3, which I have structured in accordance with key features detailed above. Sections 5.1 to 5.3 are organised as discussion sections in which I illustrate key findings in response to analysed visual cues (see Figure 4.3). Equally, I use these sections to harmonise key data elicited with relevant conceptual knowledge around social relatedness. For researchers intending to use this method, these sections are therefore understood as examples in view of organising and communicating findings and insight.

4.5.1 Shapes: The "Bubble"

Drafting a formulating interpretation of highlighted Section 1 in Figure 4.2 I observed a densely knit network of blue coloured bubbles arranged around a central element (black ellipse labelled "Kickstarter"), which represents Fiona's use of "Kickstarter", a popular crowd funding platform.

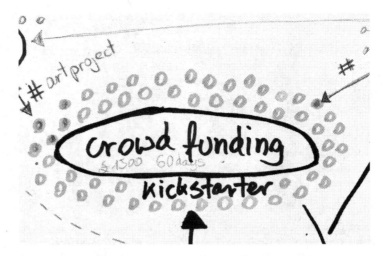

Figure 4.3 Highlighted visual cues – Sequence 1: Shapes

The fact that these bubbles were used repeatedly and consistently is the most visually striking aspect of this segment of the map. I noticed that both the shape and colour of these bubbles remain uniform in most cases and facilitate a "crowd-like" appearance. Equally, I observed that none of the bubbles exhibited any visually manifest connection to the shape labelled "crowdfunding", other areas in the map or among one another. Thereby, these bubbles remain disjointed in their overall appearance. Nonetheless, the proximity of the blue bubbles to the central shape gives an impression of one coherent item. I noted that five of the initially blue bubbles on the left-hand side had been filled in purple colour; another single bubble on the right was filled in grey colour. The purple coloured bubbles seem connected to an arrow tagged with a "#" symbol, which features the same purple colour. The same connection is repeated for the single grey bubble on the right-hand side, which is also connected to a grey/purple coloured arrow.

Moving on to the reflecting interpretation on the use of these blue coloured bubbles suggests the assumption that these addressed a uniform, unspecified crowd of actors. This assumption is supported by two aspects: First, the bubbles exhibited no specification of an identity (e.g. names, function, relation); second, the bubbles do not change in their appearance and are all of similar size and form. Interpreting the missing connections of these bubbles to any other elements in the map, I assumed that the bubbles represent actors that are disjointed and disconnected to any specific actors or actions represented in the map. Nonetheless, the proximity of these bubbles to the central "crowdfunding" shape suggests that these bubbles are relevant for illustrating actions established or facilitated through use of the platform. Equally, the fact that some of the initially blue bubbles have been filled in purple/grey colour suggest (see Figure 4.4, discussed in the next sequence) that actors represented with these bubbles changed their status/role and are related to processes illustrated in other segments of the drawing). I then used Fiona's verbal statement to corroborate my reflecting interpretation and to unpack the symbolic meaning of the "bubble":

> *Fiona: So around that "crowdfunding" to give you a better idea, is just … I did those little bubbles. And those little bubbles are anonymous people out there – in the web – who may be interested in supporting my project.*
> *IV: Is there a reason that you chose blue for these circles around the crowdfunding section?*
> *Fiona: No, but all those dots mean anonymous people […] And here, the only thing which I can do here put these little bubbles to represent them all because, to be honest with you, I interact with those people but because they are not close in any way, shape or form, I don't even remember their names. So I have 719*

Hand-drawn network maps

Figure 4.4 Highlighted visual cues – Sequence 2: Symbols

strangers who are supporting my art, send me some comments but I'm completely detached from them [...] I really cannot tell you their names. [...] And it's quite... it may sound quite weird but they are important only in a way that they are not even faces."

Note that Fiona said that inserting various little bubbles was "the only thing" she could do in this instance to give these "random people" a place in the network map. This leads to an interesting observation: Fiona's use of the bubble subsumes several individuals who remain "faceless" at the time of the drawing. This suggests that loose online connections are processed in a different way when compared to established social relations: It is not the specific individual identified by a name that respondents recall; rather, it is an image of a crowd of seemingly anonymous individuals that are perceived relevant only in terms of the function they take on.

Fiona's claim prompts the assumption that the relation she maintains with social actors addressed through bubbles is anchored around notions of anonymity and potentiality, which is supported by the fact that Fiona did not connect these bubbles to one another through inserting a line. Interestingly, the anonymity and perceived emotional distance does not necessarily render these social contacts irrelevant. On the contrary, Fiona asserted that to her these connections are vital, because "as a group, they are the most important people for me, because out of that group you always find somebody who can help you or who will forward your content and that's what you want." (Fiona).

4.5.2 Symbols: "Hashtags" as facilitators of interaction

Proceeding with the formulating interpretation of the Section 2 (Figure 4.4), I observe five of the blue bubbles that are coloured in purple, which distinguishes them from the rest of the bubbles. The purple colour matches the colour of a straight arrow labelled with the symbol "#".

The arrow points in both directions establishing a connection between the purple bubbles and the Twitter circle. This arrow therefore seems to connect the purple bubbles to a black circle labelled "Twitter". In addition, the "#" symbol is followed by the annotation "artproject" written in red colour. The colour of the word "artproject" is matched with nine smaller bubbles in the vicinity of the Twitter circle.

I focus my reflective interpretation of this section around the symbol of the "#" which seems central to understand the connection between the area located around the Twitter circle and the purple coloured bubbles. The fact that only five of the blue bubbles are highlighted in purple colour suggests a change of status and/or significance of actors represented by these bubbles. This might suggest that those previously unidentified actors may exhibit a more concrete status, which seems to be in context with the purple arrow labelled with a hashtag symbol. On the basis of the matching colour, we may assume that perhaps the hashtag symbol plays a specific role in transforming the status of the purple bubbles. This led me to assume that hashtags mediated the perceived connection between Fiona's followers on Kickstarter and her Twitter account. In the following excerpt, Fiona explains this mediation process as follows:

> Fiona: So, sometimes what happens is ... one of this [Fiona is pointing to one of the blue bubbles in the network map] is becoming your fan and that's how you make a new connection. [...] If somebody is really happy about what they see they will follow you further ... so they will have a look at your Facebook account then they will have a look on your Twitter account. [...] that is the power of the hashtag [...] if you use one hashtag for the project then your visibility in the ... in the social media will be constant, because of that hashtag, because people will note it, people will favourite ... some people will even start to use your hashtag.
> IV: What does the hashtag represent in terms of the connection it portrays with the users on Twitter?"
> Fiona: [...] basically it means like that, so that is the power of the hashtag, but needs to go both ways, because not only people will be coming to you from the platform ... let's say these people are interested in the project, yeah ... they are randomly ... getting on your platform, because they are browsing kickstarter, because some people are browsing kickstarter, you have some search options so if somebody is interested in something they can actually find the category, so on and so forth. So let's say these people came from here, they are going this way (coming from kickstarter to Twitter), but on the other hand you have a hashtag and hashtag brings people from Twitter to crowdfunding.
> IV: How do you interpret this connection?
> Fiona: [...] let's say I am posting something about social media, so I am usually doing the hashtag social media or art or photography. In this case let's say "hashtag art project" or something like that yeah and in the moment I'm posting on Twitter within that time people around the world are looking for something. In that moment they will see my tweet, they will read it look at the link if they like what they see they can favourite it they can retweet it or they can follow me, but this is very random, you never know who, you never know how sometimes and I get followers, which are not connected at all to art or IT or anything, they are just interested in the fact that I posted something about hashtag "art project".

Fiona's statement allows a number of insights into the formation of connection on online platforms. As illustrated in Section 5.1, connections in this specific scenario are maintained with a crowd of individuals that remain unspecified and distant. We observe a relation to a crowd of individuals that seem relevant only in terms of their instrumental function of offering support to Fiona's work – either by providing financial aid through donations to the Kickstarter project or by promoting visibility of the project through activities on Twitter. It is indeed challenging to interpret these relations alongside traditional notions of social interaction. Nonetheless, it offers insight into digitally mediated forms of connections that are perceived as vital to the respondent. Interestingly, these connections do not exhibit characteristics of traditional relations where notions of emotional affect play a role. Instead these ties manifest on the basis of mutual interest in a specific type of content, which is devoid of any form of relational investment. Thereby the distinct criteria that allows these ties to assume relevance is personal interest in subject specific content. Hashtags assume an important mediating role in establishing these ties and making them visible to other potential actors. The function of the hashtag is described as forming a relational bridge between previously unacquainted individuals and offers the potential to facilitate a communal spirit around a certain (shared) piece of information.

Hand-drawn network maps

Boyd (2010) refers to this phenomenon as "networked publics", which describes an "imagined collective that emerges as a result of the intersection of people, technology, and practice" (p. 39). This space constitutes a social arena that draws together individuals who "share a common understanding of the world, a shared identity, […] a consensus regarding the collective interest" (Livingstone, 2005, p. 9). Fiona's statement characterises the relational affordance of the "hashtag" feature as facilitating the emergence of a (virtual) collective. Engaging with an audience through hashtags is understood as an extended form of already existing yet disjointed offline communities and facilitates a connection in spite of lack of traditional relational practices common to face-to-face encounters. This observation adds an additional dimension to tracing phenomena that constitute a social tie and deviate from traditional tie concepts that are established around notions of affect, time, mode and frequency of interaction.

4.5.3 Colours: Activating digitally mediated social ties

Highlighted Section 3 (Figure 4.5) exhibits a number of small red bubbles arranged around a central circle labelled "Fb" (for Facebook). I observed that all of the red bubbles are connected to the "Fb" circle with a straight red line.

Five of the red bubbles are connected through other bubbles and are more distant to the central circle. In the upper right quadrant of this section one of an initially red bubble is filled in blue colour. Connected to this blue bubble are four other bubbles highlighted in green. The connecting line of these bubbles is also in blue colour. In addition, the blue bubble is tagged with the label "artfair", which is also connected to the central circle with a blue dashed arrow pointing towards the circle.

What is striking about this section is that Fiona decided to use three different colours for the bubbles. Unlike the blue bubbles in Section 1 all bubbles are connected to the central "Fb" circle, which evokes the assumption that Fiona perceived ties with these actors as more manifest and tangible. The blue bubble connected with a blue line seems to indicate a different type of tie. Given that the label "artfair" is written in the same colour suggests that a specific event related to an artfair might have contributed to establishing this tie. The green bubble that is directly connected to the blue bubble is circled in blue. This may suggest that this blue bubble played a role in facilitating the connection to the green bubble. However, it is unclear

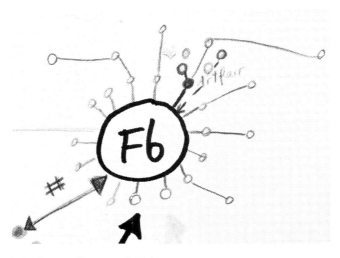

Figure 4.5 Highlighted visual cues – Sequence 3: Colours

whether or not the actor signified through the blue bubble is relevant in understanding the significance of the remaining green bubbles. Given the adjacency of the red, blue and green bubbles to the "Fb" circle suggests that Fiona's use of the platform played a role in facilitating these ties. Equally though we may assume that the "artfair" event may have played a role in facilitating another, perhaps different type of tie. Fiona later disclosed that the blue bubble represented an encounter with a fellow artist that she had met at an art fair in London. I thus assumed that the specific event of the "artfair" led to the formation of a very specific tie that seemed to be particularly relevant in terms of influencing Fiona's work. Fiona's decision to use two different colours to distinguish a small number of bubbles from the otherwise homogenous (unspecified) group of red bubbles sparked my interest in understanding the events that characterised this tie. In the following excerpt of the interview, Fiona describes how an offline event (i.e. an encounter at an art fair) led to the formation of a connection with a fellow artist and was later mediated and sustained through engagement on Facebook:

> Fiona: [...] on Facebook, what I would actually do is this also [starts drawing around the Facebook circle, scattered red bubbles that are connected back to another red bubble] Facebook works like that, so you can have somebody random here, but that random person is never random it is more or less always somehow connected to you or let's say your friends ... it is working like that.
>
> IV: And are there any Facebook contacts that became supportive of your work?
>
> Fiona: OK yes, because you meet somebody let's say ... you meet somebody at the art fair [blue bubble around the FB circle] any art fair... you meet that person and I am putting that person very close [in the drawing] because s/he will become your "like" yeah ... so they are connected to you ... but that person has friends [small green bubbles] ... so what happens is that somebody close to that person sees "Oh this person added a friend" ok so let's see what's gonna happen and you have other people who are starting to look at your profile, some of them will like you through that person, they will request either a friendship or they will just like your page. Some of them will have a look and connect straight away to you and you will have another direct and some of them will just become not interested at all and they will drift as green circles.
>
> IV: And these green bubbles, what are they?
>
> Fiona: [...] well, I don't know how to classify him [i.e. artist whose work she admired] because I never met him. That's the truth. But I'm really inspired by his creations. He draws with ink and alcohol and he's doing mostly portraits but, in a way, which is nothing I have ever seen before and he creates plenty of them. [...] We talked through Facebook, we talked through email, but I never met the guy so I'm not sure where I should put him, to be honest with you.
>
> IV: And how did this happen, you looked him up on Facebook?
>
> Fiona: Oh, how did this happen? He was part of the same gallery I was and at some point, you know, I just looked at the list of the artists. I've seen their work in the gallery and I think I contacted him [on Facebook] just to ask how he's doing and, you know, what are his plans for the future, what he actually wants to create. Despite the fact I don't know him personally, I mean I know how he looks like and because of the talks we had, he already influenced me enough to actually make friends. It sounds weird because I don't know him personally, you know, face-to-face but, still, I feel connected to him more than I feel connected to those 700 people [i.e. other contacts on Facebook] let's say. [...] so, these green ones ... I would see them more as connections for growth, either personally or to reflect upon or for my practice for me to learn from.

Even though we may only speculate what exactly the colour green represents for Fiona personally, it is interesting that the colour green was consistently used to indicate relationships that Fiona characterised as opportunities for growth in the sense of suggestions, feedback and advice. Notice also that Fiona referred to these relationships in green as "interactions" and "connections", which points to the instrumental character of these relationships. Conceptually this is interesting insofar as it echoes previously formulated theoretical notions on the nature of social relatedness in the digital age:

> [R]ather than report their experience and prospects in terms of 'relating' and 'relationships', people speak ever more often (aided and abetted by the learned advisers) of connections, of 'connecting' and 'being connected'. [...] Connections are 'virtual relations'. Unlike old-fashioned relationships, [...] they seem to be made to the measure of a liquid modern life setting (Bauman, 2007, p. xii).

Interpreting this section of the network map also allows drawing conclusions in reference to the significance of digital platforms and their role in sustaining social ties. It shows that the platform is attributed central relevance in managing social ties established during offline encounters. Equally it demonstrates that these ties then lead to the formation of related ties (i.e. the artists' Facebook friends). Thereby, the platform assumes a relevant bridging function to other relevant ties. In spite of the fact that Fiona does not seem to maintain a tangible relation with these individuals, they are perceived as relevant given their association with the artist.

Conclusions

This chapter discussed hand-drawn network maps a suitable method to trace the relevance and meaning of digitally mediated social ties in the day-to-day practice of creative professionals. The main aim of using these network maps was to trace how respondents perceived the nature of social ties created in the digital realm and what significance they assumed as a tool for social interaction. The element of drawing was essential to this process as it allowed respondents to verbalise information that may have remained undisclosed using traditional interviewing techniques, not to mention using traditional computer-based network analysis techniques.

The significance of visual cues and symbols established throughout the drawing process is particularly relevant here: This is because symbols and other visual artefacts serve as anchors that help respondents to "go beyond a verbal mode of thinking" (Bagnoli, 2009, p. 566); one aspect that is particularly relevant when tracing social phenomena that are novel and remain poorly conceptualised. The use of standardised interviewing techniques may thus obliterate important data, simply because respondents are discouraged from expressing a more intuitive understanding of a phenomenon. In this regard, respondents appreciated being able to make sense of their drawings "on-the-go", bringing something onto paper that may have been challenging to verbalise in absence of visual incentives.

This is not to say that symbols in themselves may not be equally standardised, holding a potentially misleading connotation. Nonetheless, I argue that they were essential in facilitating the elicitation of data, by encouraging new perspectives. In addition, drawings are appreciated for their capacity to serve as an icebreaker, facilitating instant rapport between researcher and respondent. Utilising this method, researchers benefit from their capacity to turn the research process into a mutual effort, which holds obvious advantages in terms of steering the research process in accordance with continuously emerging areas of insight. In this regard, visual cues assume striking relevance: Once being established, symbols serve as anchors that allow the research and respondent to re-engage continuously throughout the research process. This is important, because it reinforces an organic data elicitation process during which information is revealed gradually by unpacking the wealth of information that visual cues hold as the interview progresses.

Throughout this chapter I have tried to contextualise data that emerged from the drawings with relevant debates in the literature. This was meant to highlight conceptual aspects that I deemed particularly relevant. It is important to note that these examples of insight were meant to illustrate the relevance of projective, arts-based techniques, as I evaluated the significance of visual cues in the drawings as particularly relevant in these instances.

Applying network maps in my research, I made an effort to remain as open and flexible as possible in my approach. As a result, aside from providing respondents with a trigger question, I took minimal intervention throughout the initial stages of the drawing process, intending to leave ample space for structuring the process according to the respondents estimate. Whereas the respondents primarily responded in a positive way to this approach, appreciating the freedom for expressing their subjective view on the subject, this approach may not always resonate with respondents' preferences. It is most likely the case that working with creative professionals was a central element that contributed to the success of using this method. To them, drawings and creative expression are a central element of their day-to-day practice, which resulted in a readiness to produce something with limited instruction. Other respondents, however, may feel slightly ambushed by the prospect of having to visually establish their interpretation of a specific phenomenon. Thus, in these cases, more structured, traditional techniques may be better suited.

References

Bagnoli, A., 2009. Beyond the standard interview: The use of graphic elicitation and arts-based methods. *Qualitative Research*, *9*(5), pp.547–570.

Baltruschat, A., 2010. Film interpretation according to the documentary method. *2010): Qualitative Analysis and Documentary Method in International Educational Research*, pp.311–342.

Bauman, Z., 2007. On being light and liquid. *The Contemporary Bauman*, Routledge pp. 29–34.

Bayer, J.B., Ellison, N.B., Schoenebeck, S.Y. and Falk, E.B., 2016. Sharing the small moments: ephemeral social interaction on Snapchat. *Information, Communication & Society*, *19*(7), pp.956–977.

Baym, N.K., 2015. *Personal Connections in the DigitalAage.* John Wiley & Sons.: Cambrige, UK

Bland, D., 2012. Analysing children's drawings: applied imagination. *International Journal of Research & Method in Education*, *35*(3), pp.235–242.

Boehm, G., 1978. Zu einer Hermeneutik des Bildes. In: Ehrenspeck,Y. /Schäffer, B. (Eds.): *Film- und Fotoanalyse in der Erziehungswissenschaft. Ein Handbuch.* Opladen: Leske + Budrich

Bohnsack, R., 2008. The interpretation of pictures and the documentary method. In *Forum: Qualitative Social Research* (Vol. 9, No. 3, pp. Art-26). Forum Qualitative Sozialforschung.

Bohnsack, R., 2009. The interpretation of pictures and the documentary method. *Historical Social Research/Historische Sozialforschung*, pp.296–321.

Boyd, D., 2010. Social network sites as networked publics: Affordances, dynamics, and implications. In Papacharissi Z (ed) *Networked Self: Identity, Community, and Culture on Social Network Sites*. Routledge, pp. 39–58.

Boyd, D., Golder, S. and Lotan, G., 2010, January. Tweet, tweet, retweet: Conversational aspects of retweeting on twitter. In *2010 43rd Hawaii International Conference on System Sciences* (pp. 1–10). IEEE.

CohenMiller, A.S., 2018. Visual arts as a tool for phenomenology. In *Forum Qualitative Sozialforschung/Forum: Qualitative Social Research* (Vol. 19, No. 1, p. 22).

Cook, T., 2012. Where participatory approaches meet pragmatism in funded (health) research: The challenge of finding meaningful spaces. In *Forum: Qualitative Social Research* (Vol. 13, No. 1, pp. Art-18). Forum Qualitative Sozialforschung.

Crilly, N., Blackwell, A.F. and Clarkson, P.J., 2006. Graphic elicitation: using research diagrams as interview stimuli. *Qualitative Research*, *6*(3), pp.341–366.

Crozier, W.R., 1997. The psychology of colour preferences. *Surface Coatings International Part B: Coatings Transactions*, *80*(12), pp.577–585.

Den Besten, O., 2010. Local belonging and 'geographies of emotions': Immigrant children's experience of their neighbourhoods in Paris and Berlin. *Childhood*, *17*(2), pp.181–195.

Donath, J. and Boyd, D., 2004. Public displays of connection. *bt Technology Journal*, *22*(4), pp.71–82.

Emmel, N., 2008. Participatory Mapping: An innovative sociological approach. *Real Life Methods, ESRC National Centre for Social Research*.

Finley, S., 2008. Arts-based research. *Handbook of the Arts in Qualitative Research*, pp.71–81.

Firth, R.S., 1975. *Public and Private.* Ithaca: Cornell University Press.

Froggett, L., Manley, J. and Roy, A.N., 2015, September. The visual matrix method: Imagery and affect in a group-based research setting. In *Forum Qualitative Sozialforschung/Forum: Qualitative Social Research* (Vol. 16, No. 3). Forum: Qualitative Social Research.

Haythornthwaite, C., 2002. Strong, weak, and latent ties and the impact of new media. *The Information Society*, *18*(5), pp.385–401.

Jacomy, M., Venturini, T., Heymann, S. and Bastian, M., 2014. ForceAtlas2, a continuous graph layout algorithm for handy network visualization designed for the Gephi software. *PloSOone*, *9*(6).

Lambert, A., 2013. *Intimacy and Friendship on Facebook*. Springer: London.

Livingstone, S., 2005. On the relation between audiences and publics. In Livingstone S (ed) *Audiences andPpublics:W hen Cultural Eengagement Matters for the Public Sphere*. Changing media – changing Europe series (2). Intellect Books, Bristol, UK, pp. 17–41.

Marcu, O., 2016. Using participatory, visual and biographical methods with Roma youth. In *Forum: Qualitative Social Research*, 17(1), pp. 1–30.

Morrow, V. 1998. If you were a teacher, it would be harder to talk to you: reflections on qualitative research with children in school. *International Journal of Social Research Methodology*, 1(4), pp.297–313.

Panofsky, E., 1955. Iconography and iconology: An introduction to the study of Renaissance art. *In Erwin Panofsky, Meaning in the Visual Arts (pp. 51–81)*. Harmondsworth, Middlesex: Penguin Books.

Payne, G. and Payne, J., 2004. *Key Concepts in Social Research*. Sage: London.

Prosser, J., 2007. Visual methods and the visual culture of schools. *Visual Studies*, *22*(1), pp.13–30.

Reyes, C., 2016. Eliciting data on social relationships: The use of hand-drawn network maps in tracing the perception of digitally mediated social ties. *International Review of Social Research*, *6*(4), pp.256–268.

Rieder, B., 2013, May. Studying Facebook via data extraction: the Netvizz application. In *Proceedings of the 5th annual ACM web science conference* (pp. 346–355). ACM.

Rogers, R., 2013. *Digital Methods*. MIT press: Cambridge, MA.

Rose, G. 2007. Researching visual materials: Towards a critical visual methodology. In *Visual Methodologies. An Introduction to Interpreting Visual Materials*. London: Sage (2007): 1–32.

Schwandt, T.A., 2001. *Dictionary of Qualitative Inquiry*. Sage Publications: London.

Scott, J., 2008. Children as respondents: The challenge for quantitative methods. In *Research with Children* (pp. 103–124). Routledge.

Tolia-Kelly, D., 2004. Locating processes of identification: studying the precipitates of re-memory through artefacts in the British Asian home. *Transactions of the Institute of British Geographers*, *29*(3), pp.314–329.

Van der Vaart, G.V.D., van Hoven, B.V. and Huigen, P.P., 2018. Creative and Arts-Based Research Methods in Academic Research: Lessons from a Participatory Research Project in the Netherlands. In *Forum Qualitative Sozialforschung/ Forum Qualitative Social Research* (Vol. 19, No. 2, p. 30). DEU.

Walker, K., Caine-Bish, N. and Wait, S., 2009. "I like to jump on my trampoline": An analysis of drawings from 8-to 12-year-old children beginning a weight-management program. *Qualitative Health Research*, *19*(7), pp.907–917.

White, H.C. and Godart, F., 2007. Stories from identity and control. *Sociologica*, *1*(3), pp.1–17.

Willson, M.A., 2006. *Technically Together: Re-thinking Community within Techno-society* (Vol. 28). Peter Lang.

Wittel, A., 2001. Toward a network sociality. *Theory, Culture & Society*, *18*(6), pp.51–76.

5

MULTI-SITED ETHNOGRAPHY AND DIGITAL MIGRATION RESEARCH

Methods and challenges

Sara Marino

5.1 Introduction

The article reflects on the implementation of multi-sited ethnography in migration research and discusses the application of a range of ethnographic methods to online and offline field-sites. Within the context of the digital humanities, ethnography represents a fertile field of research offering scholars the tools and approaches needed to explore the different roles of digital technologies in the everyday life of individuals and communities. In cultivating a profound interest in the multi-sited and mobile nature of contemporary phenomena, ethnography enriches the epistemological landscape of the humanities through its interpretive practices and processes. Both inter and trans-disciplinary, these two fields of research seem to similarly reclaim the materiality of digital cultures, while experimenting with new methods and modes of intervention. In saying this, I therefore intend to situate my work within the broader scope of the digital humanities, that is the interpretation of the digital not only as a subject but also as a method of research.

Theoretically, I first intend to review the premises of multi-sited ethnography within the transnational paradigm and with reference to digital migration research. Following this overview, the paper will address the research design, methodological approach and limitations of the author's long-term study of the community of Italians living in London.

The scope of this paper is not to discuss any research findings, which have been published elsewhere (Marino, 2015a; 2015b, 2017); rather, it reflects on the methodological framework used within my doctoral project and addresses how it progressed—or better adapted to—over time to reflect the *evolution* of the community being observed. In using the term 'adaptation' I want to make a preliminary point about the nature of multi-sited ethnography as an open and flexible tool that researchers need to adapt to the changing needs and practices of the population under study (see Pink et al., 2016; Robinson & Schulz, 2009). In my case, and without explicitly following the paradigms of multi-sited ethnography, the need to 'follow' my participants as they naturally moved from online to offline spaces as part of their daily 'media diet' combined with a need to understand the specificities and affordances of each medium I was observing from time to time. In fact, I very quickly learned that my participants used different media for different purposes and in different ways. Moving in-between interactive websites, web forums, and social networking sites (Facebook in particular), the digital reconfigurations of the Italian diaspora in London opened a range of research trajectories and interests that I could have not understood without a flexible approach.

Implementation of multi-sited ethnography

Broadly speaking, I was interested in observing how socio-cultural processes such as the development of inter and intrapersonal relationships among migrants are sustained through the creative use and consumption of media; to what extent media can improve migrants' quality of life by affecting their transnational experience; and finally, whether—and if so to what extent—digital media enhance the process of integration with the local community by affecting the development of offline relationships (see Marino, 2015a; 2015b; 2017).

Ethnographically speaking, this meant immersing myself into the technical and affective *uses* of each field-site in order to discover patterns, infrastructures, and processes of identity and community formation. Originally, the intention was to conduct an ethnography of online conversations as they unfolded in web forums; however, I quickly discovered that focusing on the digital only would have returned a very limited and limiting account of the complexity of diasporic groups. Therefore, a multi-sited ethnography comprising web forum analysis, online and offline participant observation, and interviews—both face-to-face and digitally mediated—was produced and will be here reviewed. As I will argue towards the end of this paper, the use of multiple methods of research allowed me to discover the social and connective functions of digital diasporic communication (Marino, 2015b), the meanings attributed to different sites of belonging and the unfolding of a sense of digital togetherness among migrants (Marino, 2015a).

Before I move on with the analysis, an overview of the content of this paper seems necessary. In reviewing my approach to the study of digital diasporas, I situate multi-sited ethnography within three considerations, which also represent the theoretical backbone of this paper.

The first theoretical consideration, which I will return to in the next section, sees the relationship between multi-sited ethnography and transnationalism as fundamental to an understanding of the complexity, hyper-connectivity and flexibility of contemporary migrations. Since anthropologist George Marcus initially devised the founding premises of multi-sited ethnography in 1995, an ongoing attempt at 'refunctioning ethnography' has taken place (Marcus, 2007). On the one hand, this process was considered necessary for mapping the structures and narratives of contemporaneity, where the somewhat coherent and stable structures of the past were being replaced by more fluid and fragmented spheres of life. On the other hand, it was clear that single-sited research was no longer able to grasp the complexities of a multifaceted world. In urging researchers to *follow people* as they move across spaces and sites of cultural production (Falzon, 2009; Marcus, 1995), multi-sited ethnography expanded the boundaries of ethnographic research and opened new spaces of enquiry and objects of study.

The second consideration builds from the one outlined above and considers the application of ethnography to the study of digital diasporas. In the last twenty years, the debate about the impact of the digital within ethnography has flourished. From Escobar's *cyber*-ethnography (1994) to Hine's seminal work on *virtual* ethnography (2000) and Murthy's overview of *digital* ethnography (2008), the relationship between ethnography and the digital has been identified with different labels. In discussing the peculiar challenges brought by the digital to the field of ethnographic practice, I consider the imperative of following people in conjunction with Rogers's invitation to *follow the medium* (2013), that is, to "consider the Internet not so much as an object of study, rather as a source of new methods and languages for understanding contemporary society" (Caliandro, 2017, p. 3). Here, I argue, 'to follow the medium' implies—at least for researchers—a broader consideration about how media, as well as people, evolve, mutate and expand over time. In the case study here discussed, what started as a doctoral project and as an intellectual curiosity quickly transformed into a much more intensive engagement with a community I kept following over the years as it moved into other digital spaces. To certain extents, I consider this practice of following a community not just across spaces but also across time and media a re-interpretation of traditional ethnography, where the process of learning a community's way of life usually took place over long periods of time and throughout the researcher's continuous engagement with that community.

The third and final consideration, which intends to bring the debate around multi-sited ethnography and migration research a step further, considers how multi-sited ethnography should not simply 'follow' but rather deeply engage with, and learn from, the contested meanings, appropriations and everyday uses of technologies by migrants as they evolve over time. In this, I am not suggesting that researchers should not explore different avenues of research over the course of their intellectual work; rather, I am simply reviewing my own journey with the hope of providing a set of useful considerations that other researchers can adapt to their own population of interest. As a deeply interpretative work, ethnography—and digital ethnography of course—is often challenged by critiques of its own validity and objectivity. This analysis does not want to provide a set of guidelines for analysing diasporas; rather, it describes a journey that other scholars might find useful and inspiring in their own way. Despite how much has been done in the field of online and multi-sited ethnography, more case studies are needed to shed light on the multiple underlying forces that are shaping today's world.

5.2 Multi-sited ethnography and migration research: Definition and approaches

Originally framed in 1995 by anthropologist George Marcus, multi-sited ethnography represented an attempt to adapt science to the new systems and practices of contemporaneity. Moving away from the stable and monolithic interpretations of modernity brought by single-sited research, the process of 'refunctioning ethnography' was meant to grasp the more fragmented and dynamic aspects of globalisation. In Marcus' words, multi-sited ethnography:

> "moves out from single sites and local situations of conventional ethnographic research designs to examine the circulation of cultural meanings, objects and identities in diffuse time space" (Marcus, 1995, p. 96).

In this brief statement, Marcus identified some of the key changes contemporary societies were witnessing as they moved towards a new postmodern stage characterised by growing interactivity, liquidity, and fragmentation (Falzon, 2009; Massey, 2005). Here, and to really capture the essence of what we now commonly refer to as globalisation, that is the interconnectedness of systems of production, flows of information (Castells, 1996) and global mobility (Appadurai, 1996), a new way of mapping the connections taking place on a global scale and faster pace was considered necessary. Interdisciplinary at heart, the scope of multi-sited ethnography was to follow the people, the thing, the metaphor, the story, the biography, or the conflict (Marcus, 1995). Similarly, and by encouraging openness, collaboration and experimentation across and within disciplines, the digital humanities field encourages us to think about how each mode of research can serve as an entry point to a better and more organic understanding of the relationship between technologies, people and environments as they unfold and evolve. In recognising the tension between the global and the local and the changing nature of political, cultural, social and economic systems, digital humanities scholars and ethnographers have soon recognised the need to re-focus their objects of study, the ways to approach them, and the type of fieldwork they wanted to conduct in order to make sense of such heightened complexity. This was recognised by Marcus in particular, who argued that multi-sited ethnography is "always constructed with a keen awareness of being within the landscape, and as the landscape changes across sites, the identity of the ethnographer requires negotiation" (Marcus, 1995, p. 112).

The word *negotiation* is key here, as it taps into broader conceptualisations of the flexibility and adaptability required to understand the fluidity of contemporary systems. In a nutshell, multi-sited ethnography has laid the foundations for a reconceptualization, in both theoretical and methodological praxis, of a) the site and fieldwork and b) the people, to which I now briefly turn.

Implementation of multi-sited ethnography

5.2.1 Sites and fieldworks

Starting with the site, Marcus pinpointed a crucial difference with more traditional sociological modes of research. In respect to traditional ethnography, usually bounded to a single site of research (a given community, a moment in time, a certain ritual etc.), multi-sited ethnography:

> "is designed around chains, paths, threads, conjunctions, or juxtapositions of locations in which the ethnographer establishes some form of literal, physical presence, with an explicit, posited logic of association or connection among sites that in fact defines the argument of the ethnography" (1995, p. 105).

Sites become contingent, continuously shifting, mobile and inherently fluid. This is also observed by Amit among others, who says that:

> "[I]n a world of infinite interconnections and overlapping contexts, the ethnographic field cannot simply exist, awaiting discovery. It has to be laboriously constructed, prised apart from all the other possibilities for contextualisation to which its constituent relationships and connections could also be referred" (2000, p. 6).

In other terms, as Candea (2007) recognises, it is the concept of site/field that has changed from being a tool to being an object of ethnography; something that has its own reality and breath, where "the ethnographer is increasingly understood to be working 'in' (and 'on') the sites which are meaningful to the people he or she works with" (Candea, 2007, p. 171). In practical terms, and connected to the concept of site, the fieldwork is also continuously questioned and designed throughout the study, rather than fixed a priori (Burrell, 2009), thus including every possible interaction, situation, form of communication that the observation returns. This openness brings several questions to the fore. Some of these questions are explored by Candea in relation to the delimitation of the field-site and the indeterminacy that is intrinsic to the principle of following (2007). Hannerz has argued that multi-sited research cannot have an "ethnographic grasp of the entire field" (2003, p. 207), which is probably why—according to Marcus (1995)—a research design evolves during the ethnographic process/discovery. In this respect, the connections between sites of research are just as important, and susceptible of further research, as the relationships taking place within a site (Hannerz, 2003, p. 206). This seems particularly relevant if we think about the complexity of online spaces and the fluidity of connections taking place regardless of time and geographical constraints. Drawing from Greschke (2009), this is also relevant to "ethnography's capability for understanding new cultural practices and techno-social realities, which have been emerging along with digital media usage in contemporary migration contexts" (3).

5.2.2 People

One of the founding premises of multi-sited ethnography is the principle of *following the people* (Marcus, 1995). For the purposes of this paper, and drawing upon Marcus' theory, migration and diaspora studies are identified as a fertile terrain where multi-sited ethnography can, and has in fact, flourished. The development of a transnational approach is discussed by Marcus (1995), Falzon (2009) and others as part of those new processes emerging in the 1980s that contributed to the methodological shift from single-sited research to multi-sited approaches. In thinking about these processes, I would like to refer to two key theoretical standpoints that will help the reader to frame the case study under discussion here: the first calls into question Glick Schiller, Basch and Szanton Blanc's transnational perspective on migration (1992; 1995); the second considers the application of mobile methods to the study of everyday mobilities (Büscher & Urry, 2009).

In its original formulation, transnationalism is described as a social phenomenon characterised by a growing interconnectedness and an expansion of cross-border relationships as a result of a technological development that since the late 1990s has made communication and travel across national borders much easier and faster than ever before. This process is described by Doreen Massey as characterised by a form of *time-space compression* (1994) whereby travels and communications between places shrink while social relationships stretch-out. A couple of years later, Castells (1996) developed his understanding of globalisation as characterised by simultaneity (*space of flows*) and time sharing (*timeless time*) as places become increasingly connected by networks of information powered up by individuals living increasingly *in-between* and *across* multiple spaces and time zones at a given time.

Similar to what Massey and Castells, among many others, have argued, Glick Schiller and her colleagues understood this phenomenon as a reflection of broader transformations affecting the unfolding of political relationships across nation states, the now larger-scale economies interconnecting cities regardless of time lags and geographical distances, and of course the complications taking place in the balance of power between countries.

Most importantly for the present discussion, anthropologists Nina Glick Schiller, Linda Basch and Christina Blanc-Szanton argued that the combination of social, political and economic processes stretching across borders had radically transformed the way people move, settle, and integrate in new countries. Compared to the past, where moving to another country meant leaving families and friends behind with no hope of coming back, contemporary migrants or *transmigrants* can maintain multiple linkages to their homeland, both physical as well as affective. This group of scholars was in fact among the first to recognise that:

> "Our earlier conceptions of immigrant and migrant no longer suffice. The word immigrant evokes images of permanent rupture, of the uprooted, the abandonment of old patterns and the painful learning of a new language and culture. Now, a new kind of migrating population is emerging, composed of those whose networks, activities and patterns of life encompass both their host and home societies. Their lives cut across national boundaries and bring two societies into a single social field" (1992, p. 1).

Within this context, and locating itself within a transnational paradigm, multi-sited ethnography seemed able to understand, capture and reflect on these in-between spaces and sites of communication among migrants, while embracing the complexity of 'geographical and non-geographical territories including networks, connections and cross-border formations' (Amelina, 2010, np) that are at the core of transnational processes and flows (Faist, 2000).

In addition to this, and while not explicitly discussed by Marcus, it is perhaps useful to contextualise the premises of multi-sited ethnography within the new mobility turn in the social sciences (Cresswell, 2006; Sheller & Urry, 2006). More specifically, it seems to me that by paying attention to the "investigations of movement, blocked movement, potential movement, and studies of immobility, dwelling and placemaking" (Büscher & Urry, 2009, p. 99) the mobilities paradigm embraces and further expands the commitment of multi-sited ethnography to follow not just the people, but also the stories, lives and conflicts inherent to movement.

It is within this transnational and mobile framework that the present paper evaluates future directions of research for those researchers who wish to develop the idea of multi-siting further. In the next section, I briefly consider the application of multi-sited methods to the study of digital diasporas. As Hallet and Barber note, it is "no longer imaginable to conduct ethnography without considering online spaces" (2014, p. 307). Especially in migration research, it is now clear that migrants live and breathe across online and offline spaces of communication where relationships, communities and aggregated interest take place. In referring to the contribution of multi-sited ethnography, Marcus talks about a "differently configured spatial canvas" (1995, p. 98) where researchers must move "beyond an initial site where situated knowledge is very literally probed in relationship to its referent elsewhere" (Marcus, 1999, p. 13). Haviland et al., (2013) call this type of research a mobile ethnography, where "researchers seek to capture the emerging global dimension by following individual actors, organisations, objects [..] as they move about in various interrelated transnational situations and locations" (52).

5.3 Multi-sited ethnography in digital migration research

A growing body of scholarship has recently explored the relationship between technology, migration and diaspora and suggested that the Internet has become the primary channel where transnational connections can be developed, maintained, and nurtured over time (Alonso & Oiarzabal, 2010; Hiller & Franz, 2004). Migrants are now always connected (Diminescu, 2008) in a web of relationships, modes of communications and ways of life that affect migrants' sense of identity, community formation and sense of belonging (Navarrete & Huerta, 2006). Over the last ten to fifteen years, scholars have approached the study of digital diasporas from various points of view: to explore political engagement in both home and host countries (Aouragh, 2011; Brinkerhoff, 2009); identity politics (Georgiou, 2006), youth participation (Leurs, 2015) and family relationships (Madianou & Miller, 2011) just to name a few contributions.

Increasingly, the need to observe how people, and migrants, use online spaces to form and maintain transnational relationships has occupied a pivotal role in the social science and humanities. Alongside the principle of following the people as they move from online to offline spaces, the need to follow the medium (Rogers, 2013) in its affordances, opportunities for access, and limitations of course, has provided further challenges for researchers. This has been true for ethnography as a discipline first and then as a methodological approach. The first challenge relates to the way traditional sociological concepts characterised by a certain degree of stability such as the notions of community and identity are reconfigured online (Caliandro, 2017). A second challenge, which this study has also encountered, relates to the tools and approaches used to make sense of the digital. Following Rogers' imperative to follow the medium, one of the main challenges associated with the study of digital spaces has always been the dichotomy made between online and offline, which have often been translated into a representation of the Internet (and of the life within it) as separated from the 'real' (see also Robinson & Schultz, 2009; Marres, 2012). In this respect, it is fundamental to acknowledge that the Internet must, first and foremost, be situated in the practices and processes it contributes to sustain; second of all, that the 'digital' should be better contextualised as a plurality of experiences, locations, infrastructures and modes of use that lead to different 'cultural manifestations' and histories (Abbate, 2017, p. 13).

Rogers (2013) among many has particularly advocated for the need to approach digital media not in their specificity, but in their ability to tell us something about the broader society—migration patterns in this case. This point is also made by Tsatsou in arguing that Internet research provides a more comprehensive understanding of the case study under investigation when it combines "multi-layered research designs in which both online and offline methodologies are utilised, and multiple sources and types of data inform and offer nuances to research" (2014, p. 212). Similarly, Murthy points out that the combination of online and offline ethnography can increase data validity (2008). More interestingly for the purposes of this study, recent contributions have emphasised how the combination of multiple methods of research proves particularly useful in providing a comprehensive account of phenomena that increasingly take place online *and* offline.

However, and not only in migration research, such combination has often been problematic. Although there is now widespread recognition that the boundaries between online and offline are not as clear-cut as previous understandings of the role of the Internet seemed to acknowledge (Markham, 1998), other concerns call into question the priority of one method over the other. At what stage of the research process do we need to move to offline contexts? Are offline data more reliable than information collected online?

Questions of 'authenticity' and reliability still seem to permeate current studies on the Internet. Walker, among others, recognises that

> "qualitative researchers interested in digitally-located social and cultural practices have struggled with ways in which to design studies that can account for the digital aspect of cultural practices while also taking into account that those digital practices do not exist as separate (or separable in terms of our research) from other social and cultural practices" (2010, p. 23).

The question is not how to simply combine online and offline data, but how to integrate them. How do we make sense of communities where relationships, behaviours, and encounters shift continuously from online to offline worlds and vice versa? This paper precisely tries to understand how the richness of online communities can be understood without compromising on the important contribution that offline observation can provide to the study of migrant groups.

The following sections will explore benefits and limitations of three qualitative methods of research utilised in both online and offline spaces: web forum analysis, participant observation, and interviews. More importantly, the paper will discuss the rationale behind the methodological framework utilised and reflect on how each method contributed to the overall understanding of what migrants do, how they do it, and why.

5.4 Research design

In what follows I provide a brief overview of the different steps involved in my research design. Far from being a linear and straightforward process, my engagement with the community of Italians living in London proved particularly challenging. First, circumscribing a field site was complicated by the very nature of the object under study. Theoretically and methodologically, I had to adapt to a population constantly moving from place to place but also likely to disappear from my research radar: return movements, difficulties in the integration process and other migration-related episodes threatened the 'stability' of my case study and were reflected in the research design. Second, each method (and each site of research) presented unique challenges and limitations that at times returned a sense of incompleteness and arbitrariness. Below, I expand on the seven steps of my research design before I turn to each method.

Step 1 - Identification of community of interest. The number of sites available to Italian migrants was higher than initially imagined. Seven online communities and related social networking sites providing information in Italian were identified: *Italians of London, Italians in London, The London Link, The London Web, Sognando Londra, Qui Londra*, and *Italiani a Londra*. At the time of writing, *The London Link* and *The London Web* communities still exist on Facebook but not as web fora.

Step 2 - The second step involved studying the field and taking notes. As in traditional ethnography, this activity implied 'spending time' with my community of interest online, observing the unfolding of users' activity (new topics being added to the forum, community growth, frequency of online interaction) but also analysing the type of information being provided online, and the targeted audience each community seemed to have in mind (tourists, Italians already living in London, or about to move).

Step 3 - Three sites were selected as main case study where a more focused digital ethnographic observation was going to take place. These sites (*Italians of London, The London Link*, and *Italiani a Londra*[1]) were selected by virtue of their popularity among users and relevance of posts for the key dimensions the research sought to explore. Compared to other sites, these three communities had a web forum. Since the original plan was to mainly focus on the online reconfigurations of the Italian diaspora, it was believed that web forums represented the ideal place where an ethnographic participant observation could have been conducted.

Step 4 - The fourth stage involved approaching gatekeepers to ensure field access. By gatekeeper, I mainly refer here to site and group administrators monitoring websites and discussion fora. This was deemed necessary in order to grant access to different fields of research (public and private) and in order to achieve a better understanding of the social dynamics taking place within each group.

Step 5 - The fifth stage was born out of a series of challenges encountered during the observation. First, it was clear that users' interactions were opening a series of fascinating narratives that I wanted to explore further in order to return a more comprehensive overview of my population. Second, it appeared—especially within the community *of Italians of London*—that users and administrators used the online space to organise *offline* meetings. Thus, it was decided to investigate these directions with two additional methods: interviews and offline participant observations.

Step 6 - The added complexity of the project returned a massive collection of data that needed to be examined in relation to my research questions and objectives. This stage mainly involved a cross-examination and analysis of data.

Step 7 - The final stage included a series of follow-ups with my respondents if deemed necessary.

5.5 Online forum analysis and online participant observation

As mentioned, Step 1 mainly consisted of identifying the field-site. Seven online communities were isolated as main case study. These were initially examined in relation to: the way information and links were displayed and their accessibility; the information provided; the targeted audience the site was addressing, and the space dedicated to users' interactions (forums, chat-lines, social networks). A more focused ethnographic observation was later conducted inside the web forums of three selected communities (*Italiens of London, The London Link*, and *Italiani a Londra*), in order to explore users' interactions, the nature of their conversations (and if recurrent patterns were emerging online) and the eventuality of *offline* meetings discussed within the forum. The qualitative corpus consisted of publicly viewable posts to the three forums between 2009 and 2012 with a follow-up in 2014. The analysis consisted of domain ontology and text-mining techniques, where transcripts of forum discussions were manually inserted into a dataset containing information about the user, the topic of the post, and the content included within. This dataset was then transferred and analysed using NVivo software, which allowed a more in-depth observation of content, frequency of words, and recurrent patterns. A total of 300 posts were collected and analysed (Marino, 2015a; 2015b). Initially, as my intention was not to quote these posts but only trace recurrent patterns of conversation (words, themes, topics), users were not directly approached. This analysis was mainly covert as I decided to approach these communities as a Lurker. Together with Greschke (2009; 2012) I disagree with those who consider lurking a form of non-participant observation (see Given, 2008). In the time I spent observing the communities of Italians chatting, sharing, discussing the difficulties of living abroad and the different steps of integration, I very much participated in their life, and understood a large part of what they were going through as a migrant myself. In this, I echo Silverman's point that those ethnographers practising lurking have access to 'naturally occurring' data (2007). Participation, in this respect, should not only be linked to direct engagement and interaction with a given population; in a context such as the online, the variety of interactions taking place does allow for different typologies of participant observation. The benefits and limitations of lurking in online spaces have been the object of several discussions in digitally mediated research (Hewson et al., 2016). More specifically, there are several ethical issues to be considered when doing unobtrusive IMR (Internet Mediated Research).

5.5.1 Informed consent

One of the most important ethical issues when using information that is already available online is that of informed consent. According to the British Psychological Society (2014) the only type of information that can be used without gaining informed consent is data that is openly and publicly available. However, as the Association of Internet Researchers also recognises, "users may operate in public spaces but still maintain strong perceptions of privacy", which researchers cannot of course predict or know in advance (Markham & Buchanan, 2012 p. 6). In some cases, as in discussion forums, the boundary between public and private is more ambiguous and users might not know whether their participation is public or not (Hewson et al., 2016). Bearing this in mind when I collected posts that were publicly available (that is, no registration was required in order to access the forum), I still avoided quoting or providing information that could have exposed the identity of my users. This is of course related to a second ethical issue, the anonymity of respondents and the confidentiality of data.

5.5.2 Anonymity and confidentiality of data

The issue of anonymity is explained within the AoIR 2012 ethical guidelines in the form of how texts and persons are being studied. In using online data, researchers should ask whether exact quoting is needed, and if so, what could be the consequences for the people involved (Markham & Buchanan, 2012). A key guiding principle behind this is that when making ethical decisions, researchers must balance the rights of subjects (the right not to be harmed, for example) with the social benefits of research. In my case, although the nature of the posts being available did not generally disclose any sensitive information that could have potentially harmed the person either in the short or long-terms, I decided to only focus on the textual elements of my online discussions (words, themes, topics). When explicit quotations were deemed necessary, users were approached and asked permission to be quoted. Similarly, the British Psychological Society invites researchers to paraphrase rather than using a direct quote; in other situations, one solution could be to not disclose the name or address of a website, which would lessen the risk of compromising participant confidentiality. In my case, and in order to gain access, I personally subscribed to the forum and disclosed myself as a researcher to the community administrators, who granted me access to observe the community without participating directly. This is of course not to say that every researcher should conform to these rules. In fact, researchers are responsible for ensuring that that research is ethical, transparent and accountable while considering the benefits associated with the study. As the field of internet-mediated research evolves constantly, so ethical guidelines should never be considered final. They should instead remain open to unforeseen implications and consequences.

Context is crucial, and it is related to a second set of limitations I encountered during the online participant observation. As Schrooten notes, "rather than information on people who are speaking and acting, an ethnography on the Internet provides mainly textual and visual material" (2012, p. 10). Who these migrants were and at what stage of the migration process they became actively involved with the community were questions that the online observation was unable to address. As a result, one of the limitations of online observation relates to the process of 'flattening' the natural differences existing among migrants. Surely, online conversations returned a sense of who these migrants were and how their needs changed accordingly to the different stage of migration they were living (pre-migration, settlement or other), but that was mainly a feeling, a work of personal interpretation, rather than evidence. A final limitation that the research observed was the presence of a grey zone between users' participation online, and the impact of these forms of online support on migrants' process of integration in the host country. In other words, the observation proved insufficient to explain whether online support was a one-off request or an easier path to long-lasting 'offline' friendships. It was precisely at this point that the urgency of putting together physical and online sites emerged as necessary step forward.

Implementation of multi-sited ethnography

Regardless of these limitations, online forum analysis still proved an effective method of analysis for the purposes of my research. On the one hand, it was useful in order to understand the ways in which the Internet is integrated into users' everyday life, and how processes of identity and community formation develop among people that are, at least at the beginning, stranger to each other. It also allowed me to gain a deeper understanding of the composition of the Italian contemporary diaspora. Of course, identifying what users talk about online allowed me to understand how each migration stage brings a set of peculiar challenges, difficulties, and questions that the community is invited to answer. In my case, it was clear that the formation of a sense of community among Italians—which comes through forms of material support and emotional closeness (see Marino, 2015a; 2015b)—starts online and only afterwards it moves into other spaces. Although data can only be interpreted as limited to the sample observed, they nonetheless returned a vivid and detailed picture of the role of digital technologies for Italians, while confirming important similarities with other diasporic groups (see Schrooten, 2012).

5.6 Interviews

Those users who agreed to be interviewed were given the opportunity to be approached either face-to-face or online. Following a stage of initial contacts via the web forums, eight out of the ten responders agreed to be interviewed online, which meant sending questions via PM (private messaging), via chat or on Skype. Two respondents agreed to be interviewed face to face. Interviews aimed at asking users

a. when they joined the community, and why;
b. how often did they visit the community and in what capacity;
c. what was the role of the community and the purposes of subscription;
d. whether the forum helped them to build a network of friends over time (and in other spaces).

Interviews also presented a series of challenges including gaining access to the sample and establishing trust. When doing online interviews, the lack of visual and social cues that would otherwise characterise the relationship between interviewers and interviewees bring a whole new set of considerations.

5.6.1 Access and informed consent

The first issue is, of course, access. Recruiting participants is always a difficult task (Bakardjieva, 2005) but even more so in anonymous settings (Hewson et al., 2016). If anonymity can lead to greater transparency due to "a reduction in the social cost of disclosure" (Hewson et al., 2016, p. 47), establishing a relationship with participants online is rarely easy. First, participants may agree and later disappear from the forum or any other social space. Second, attention should be paid to using technologies that can facilitate reliable exchanges and that participants can access in a comfortable manner. Third, the use of asynchronous (email, messaging system) or synchronous (chat) approaches should be carefully designed in relation to the research design. In my case, participants were invited to decide which platform was more convenient for them to use; needless to say, the type and length of questions I was able to ask largely depended on the platform used. While email and messaging-based interviews allow respondents to think about their responses and reply at a later time, chats did not provide the same level of *relax*: questions had to be straightforward, easy to digest and to the point. Skype, on the other hand, seems to be a hybrid between synchronous and asynchronous communication: while access is still an issue, as Skype requires a strong connection, the opportunity to see the participant partially filled the gaps deriving from a lack of visual and social cues. The interview appeared more relaxed, it could be recorded, and allowed me to establish an almost 'physical' relationship with respondents (see Lo Iacono et al., 2016 for a review of Skype as a tool for qualitative research interviews). Whatever platform was used, participants were given a participation sheet and an informed consent form to sign prior to the interview. The forms were sent either as attachments to Skype or via email.

5.6.2 Trust

The issue of trust is, of course, relevant as interviewers and interviewees do not often have time (nor the space) to establish a strong relationship. Here, some scholars have opted for using forms of personal disclosure in order to establish less detached forms of communication (Madge & O'Connor, 2002). However, as Hewson et al., (2016) argue, maintaining detachment can be beneficial in reducing biases, or forms of social desirability, that are usually present in face-to-face interactions. In my case study, sharing a common background, a language and, of course, the experience of being a migrant myself helped to reduce the sense of distance.

While considering these challenges, interviews filled the gap of missing out the essential meanings contributed by face-to-face encounters. How do migrants form relationships? What importance do they attribute to them? Do Italians attribute the same relevance to offline and online encounters? In this respect, interviews contributed to and expanded on what I observed during the preliminary online ethnographic participant observation. Italians confirmed the crucial role that online communities have had for them, especially during the settlement process. The community provided solidarity as well as material and psychological support in difficult moments, shared job vacancies and information about renting, thus helping migrants navigate the first stages of integration while providing a comfortable space where users could freely talk about their problems, anxieties and hopes for the future. More importantly, the community did so in a known language. Another important element stood out during the process of observing and interviewing migrants and especially within the community *Italians of London*. Here, more than in any other community, Italians found opportunities to meet *offline*, socialise and have fun together. The frequency and popularity of the events organised by the community administrator in some of the most popular Italian restaurants, cafes and clubs, was something I could not simply ignore: for this reason, I decided to move my ethnography 'offline': a final stage of participant observation and interviews was then organised.

5.7 Participant observation and offline interviews

Compared to the first stage of participant observation online, this one was completely overt. In this case, I decided to be introduced to the community by the *Italians of London* founder and main administrator Giancarlo Pelati. He first introduced me to a group of Italians who habitually participated at the events, and I then expanded my network to include friends of friends and newly arrived migrants. My intention was to complement the data gathered online by observing what kind of conversations took place outside the discussion forums. Did Italians share the same difficulties, or did they focus on the positive aspects of their diasporic experience to match the fun-based nature of these events? Why did they attend? What types of network were created? This stage of participant observation also allowed me to focus on a set of cues that I could have not grasped online: facial expressions, body language, conscious and unconscious behaviours. In order to dig deeper into the questions I mentioned earlier, in-depth interviews were conducted. Compared to other types of interview, in-depth or unstructured interviews allow

> "the interviewee to talk from their own perspective using their own frame of reference and ideas and meanings that are familiar to them. Flexibility is the key with the researcher able to respond to the interviewee, to trace the meaning that s/he attaches to the 'conversation with a purpose', to develop unexpected themes and adjust the content of interviews and possibly the emphasis of the research as a result of issues that emerge in any interview" (Edwards & Holland, 2013, p. 30).

Implementation of multi-sited ethnography

From a research point of view, this stage—which seemed to resemble more closely the way traditional ethnography and ethnographic interviewing are usually conducted—returned a body of rich information about the Italian community and their lifestyle (Marino, 2015a; 2015b). However, challenges should be also considered.

5.7.1 Limitations and later shift to Facebook

The first limitation worth noting is that the Italians who met offline (and I later interviewed) were not the same people encountered in the forums. As acknowledged by my respondents and by the community administrators I also interviewed to understand the motivations behind community building, the web forums were not participated in to the extent that they were in the early 2000s. Social media, and Facebook in particular, were more frequently visited. For this reason, subsequent studies of the Italian diaspora moved out of these initial field-sites to consider users' participation and engagement on Facebook. Later research has mainly focused on the Facebook community *Italian Gals in London* (Marino, 2017) and on the role of Skype in enabling conversations among transnational families (Marino, 2019). Here, I mostly used the community to post my activity as a researcher and to recruit respondents for my study. The reason why I decided to disclose myself here was mainly due to the nature of the community itself: by encouraging its members to communicate in a spirit of friendship and mutual help, the community represented a fertile and safe space where conversations could take place openly.

The second limitation relates to the setting of my interviews during the Italians of London's events. Here, the location of my interviews did not seem to facilitate long and in-depth conversations due to noise and of course the fact that the occasion was, in fact, a party to which people wanted to come back to quite soon. A follow-up round of interviews in different places was later held in order to expand on the first set of interviews.

These limitations were, however, balanced by the opportunity to meet my respondents face-to-face and to 'live' with them the experience of being a migrant in London. Undoubtedly, 'participating' meant sharing a comfortable, socialising environment. The joy and light heartedness we all together experienced certainly offset the bitter aspects of living in a foreign country but at the same time returned a vivid illustration of a close community. Here, issues of access, trust and accessibility were mitigated by the fact that I was a living person speaking, sharing and consuming the same experience, thus confirming that multi-siting strategies can indeed share a more comprehensive light on complex social phenomena such as migration.

Conclusions

As Sade-Beck points out, "ethnography solely based on online research [..] cannot be the sole source of data as it provides only a partial and limited picture without the link to the 'real world', and from which it is difficult to obtain an 'overflowing description'" (2004, p. 8). The evidence presented in this paper has hopefully demonstrated that a combination of methods, a multi-sited ethnography that follows people as they move from online to offline spaces, is probably the most useful way to approach phenomena such as digital diasporas. I have argued that this method needs to remain open and adapt to the research design in order to unfold the complexity of sites and fieldwork. In my case, this flexibility has meant 'adding' methodologies and field-sites during a process of continuous discovery. It also meant considering how my population of interest used each of these sites, the meanings and importance attributed to them, and the processes of negotiation. On the one hand, this open-ended research problem has brought a sort of 'fatigue' that Candea among others has explored in depth (2007). The "un-boundedness" of the research design can, according to the author, return a sense of arbitrariness in deciding what to explore and what to ignore. I resonate with this as I review some of the questions I have asked myself over the course of this project. Which community should I have observed more closely? How many people should I have interviewed?

Did I adopt the right strategy in hiding from my participants or should I have disclosed myself? How many Facebook group should I have explored? In retrospective, collecting and generating a huge amount of data has provided me with material I was able to use in subsequent analysis. Altogether, they returned a vivid picture of Italians' sense of digital togetherness, the variety of social and cultural capital circulating online and the social and connective functions of media. However, the sense of uncertainty I experienced while in the process of observing, interviewing, participating and analysing proved extremely unsettling. In conclusion, I would like to propose a few notes:

- Multi-sited ethnography applied to digital migration research should follow the principles of following the medium and the people from a non-digital-centric-ness point, that is the idea that "digital methods should always be developed and designed specifically in relation to the particular research questions being asked" (Pink et al., 2016, p. 10).
- Ethnography solely based on online research cannot not be the sole source of data as it ignores the multiple overlaps, mixes and matches taking places *across* sites. This is valid for migrants and, more broadly, for all media audiences. A pure offline ethnography would not have been able to grasp, on the other hand, the activities taking place online, where in my case the sense of community initially took place even before moving to other spaces of interaction.

Future research should consider approaching more case studies from a multi-sited point of view in order to provide researchers with a series of guidelines that would help them navigate a complex scenario that is constantly evolving and mutating. Data ethics should become of paramount importance in the discussion of how to approach these sites. As current developments in information and communication technologies are increasingly blurring the boundaries between public and private, ensuring that we act transparently and openly in respect to data privacy, anonymity, and accountability will prove more challenging but necessary. This is, I argue, the new task in front of contemporary researchers: a task never unbounded, always open, and always in flux.

Note

1 The *London Link* community does not exist anymore and *Italiani a Londra* closed its 'social network' section in 2018. The *Italians of London*'s webpage was not accessible at the time of writing.

References

Abbate, J. (2017). 'What and Where Is the Internet? (Re)defining Internet histories'. *Internet Histories. Digital Technology, Culture and Society*, 1(1–2), 8–14.

Alonso A., & Oiarzabal, P.J. (2010). The Immigrant Worlds' Digital Harbors: An Introduction. In A. Andoni & P. J. Oiarzabal (Eds.), *Diasporas in the New Media Age: Identity, Politics and Community* (1–15). Reno: University of Nevada Press.

Amelina, A. (2010). Searching for an Appropriate Research Strategy on Transnational Migration: The Logic of Multi-Sited Research and the Advantage of the Cultural Interferences Approach. *Forum: Qualitative Social Research*, 11(10).

Amit, V. (2000). *Constructing the Field: Ethnographic Fieldwork in the Contemporary World*. London: Routledge.

Aouragh, M. (2011). *Palestine Online: Transnationalism, the Internet and the Construction of Identity*. London: I.B Tauris.

Appadurai, A. (1996). *Modernity at Large: Cultural Dimensions of Globalization*. Minneapolis: University of Minnesota Press.

Bakardjieva, M. (2005). *Internet Society. The Internet in Everyday Life*. London: SAGE.

Brinkerhoff, J. (2009). *Digital Diasporas: Identity and Transnational Engagement*. Cambridge, UK: Cambridge University Press.

British Psychological Society (2014). *Code of Human Research Ethics*. Leicester: The British Psychological Society. Retrieved from https://www.bps.org.uk/sites/bps.org.uk/files/Policy/Policy%20-%20Files/BPS%20Code%20 of%20Human%20Research%20Ethics.pdf

Burrell, J. (2009). The Field Site as a Network: A Strategy for Locating Ethnographic Research. *Field Methods*, 21 (2), 181–199.

Büscher, M., & Urry, J. (2009). Mobile Methods and the Empirical. *European Journal of Social Theory*, 12 (1), 99–116.

Caliandro, A. (2017). Digital Methods for Ethnography: Analytical Concepts for Ethnographers Exploring Social Media Environments. *Journal of Contemporary Ethnography*, 1–28.

Candea, M. (2007). Arbitrary Locations: In Defence of the Bounded Field-Site. *Journal of the Royal Anthropological Institute*, 13 (1), 167–84.

Castells, M. (1996). *The Rise of The Network Society: The Information Age: Economy, Society and Culture, Volume 1.* Oxford: Wiley Blackwell.

Cresswell, T. (2006). *On the Move: Mobility in the Modern Western World.* New York: Routledge.

Diminescu, D. (2008). The Connected Migrant: an Epistemological Manifesto. *Social Science Information*, 47(4), 565–79.

Edwards, R., & Holland, J. (2013). *What is Qualitative Interviewing?* London and New York: Bloomsbury.

Escobar, A. (1994). Welcome to Cyberia: Notes on the Anthropology of Cyberculture. *Current Anthropology*, 35 (3), 211–231.

Faist, T. (2000). Transnationalization in International Migration: Implications for the Study of Citizenship and Culture. *Ethnic and Racial Studies*, 23 (2), 189–222.

Falzon, M. (2009). *Multi-sited ethnography: Theory, Praxis and Locality in Contemporary Research.* Surrey, England: Ashgate Publishing.

Georgiou, M. (2006). *Diaspora, identity and the media: diasporic transnationalism and mediated spatialities.* Cresskill, N.J., United States: Hampton Press.

Given, L. (2008). *The SAGE Encyclopedia of Qualitative Research Methods.* London: SAGE.

Greschke, M. (2009). Mediated Cultures of Mobility: The art of positioning ethnography in global landscapes. In T. Faist (Ed.), *Working Papers - Centre on Migration, Citizenship and Development* (1–17). Bielefeld, Germany.

Greschke, M. (2012). *Is There a Home in Cyberspace? The Internet in Migrants' Everyday Life and the Emergence of Global Communities.* New York: Routledge.

Hallett, R.E., & Barber, K. (2014). Ethnographic Research in a Cyber Era. *Journal of Contemporary Ethnography*, 43 (3), 306–330.

Hannerz, U. (2003). Being There… and There… and There!: Reflections on Multi-Site Ethnography. *Ethnography*, 4 (2), 201–216.

Haviland, W.A., Prins, H.E.L., McBride, B., & Walrath, D. (2013). *Cultural Anthropology: The Human Challenge.* Belmont, CA: Thomson/Wadsworth.

Hewson C., Vogel, C., & Laurent, D. (2016). *Internet Research Methods.* London: SAGE.

Hiller, H. H., & Franz T. M. (2004). New Ties, Old Ties and Lost Ties: the Use of the Internet in Diaspora. *New Media & Society*, 6(6), 731–752.

Hine, C. (2000). *Virtual Ethnography.* London: SAGE.

Lo Iacono, V., Symonds, P., & Brown, D.H.K. (2016). Skype as a Tool for Qualitative Research Interviews. *Sociological Research Online*, 21(2), 1–15.

Leurs, K. (2015). *Digital Passages: Migrant Youth 2.0: Diaspora, Gender and Youth Cultural Intersections.* Amsterdam: Amsterdam University Press.

Madge, C., & O'Connor, H. (2002). On-line with E-Mums: Exploring the Internet as a Medium for Research. *Royal Geographical Society*, 34 (1), 92–102.

Madianou, M., & Miller, D. (2011). *Migration and New Media: Transnational Families and Polymedia.* New York: Routledge.

Marcus, G. (1995). Ethnography in/of the World System: The Emergence of Multi-Sited Ethnography. *Annual Review of Anthropology*, 24, 95–117.

Marcus, G. (2007). Ethnography Two Decades after Writing Culture: From the Experimental to the Baroque. *Anthropological Quarterly*, 80 (4), 1127–1145.

Markham, A. (1998). *Life Online: Researching Real Experiences in Virtual Space.* Walnut Creek, CA: AltaMira Press.

Markham, A. & Buchanan, E. (2012). Ethical Decision-Making and Internet Research: Recommendations from the AoIR Ethics Working Committee (Version 2.0). Retrieved from https://aoir.org/reports/ethics2.pdf

Marino, S. (2015a). Making Space, Making Place: Digital Togetherness and the Redefinition of Migrant Identities Online. *Social Media + Society*, 1–9.

Marino, S. (2015b). Transnational Identities and Digital Media: The Digitalisation of Italian Diaspora in London. *JOMEC Journal* (7).

Marino, S. (2017). Digital Food and Foodways: How Online Food Practices and Narratives Shape the Italian Diaspora in London. *Journal of Material Culture*, 23 (3), 263–279.

Marino, S. (2019). Cook It, Eat It, Skype It: Mobile Media Use in Re-staging Intimate Culinary Practices among Transnational Families. *International Journal of Cultural Studies*, 22 (6), 788–803.

Marres, N. (2012). The Redistribution of Methods: On Intervention in Digital Social Research Broadly Conceived. *Sociological Review*, 60, 139–165.

Massey, D. (1994). *Space, Place and Gender*. Oxford: Polity Press.

Massey, D. (2005). *For Space*. London: SAGE.

Murthy, D. (2008). Digital Ethnography: An Examination of the Use of New Technologies for Social Research. *Sociology*, 42 (5), 837–855.

Navarrete, C., & Huerta, E. (2006). Building Virtual Bridges to Home: The Use of the Internet by Transnational Communities of Immigrants. *International Journal of Communications Law & Policy*, 11, 1–20.

Pink, S., Horst, H., Postill, J., Hjorth, L., Lewis, T., & Tacchi, J. (2016). *Digital Ethnography: Principles and Practices*. London: SAGE.

Robinson, L., & Schulz, J. (2009). New Avenues for Sociological Inquiry: Evolving Forms of Ethnographic Practice. *Sociology*, 43 (4), 685–698.

Rogers, R. (2013). *Digital Methods*. Massachusetts: MIT Press.

Sade-Beck, L. (2004). Internet ethnography: Online and offline. *International Journal of Qualitative Methods*, 3(2).

Schiller, N.G., Basch, L., & Blanc-Szanton, C. (1992). Transnationalism: A New Analytic Framework for Understanding Migration. *Annuals of the New York Academy of Sciences*.

Schiller, N.G., Basch, L., & Blanc-Szanton, C. (1995). From Immigrant to Transmigrant: Theorizing Transnational Migration. *Anthropological Quarterly*, 68 (1), 48–63.

Sheller, M., & Urry, J. (2006). The New Mobilities Paradigm. *Environment and Planning A: Economy and Space*, 38 (2), 207–226.

Schrooten, M. (2012). Moving Ethnography Online: Researching Brazilian Migrants' Online Togetherness. *Ethnic and Racial Studies*, 35 (10), 1794–1809.

Silverman, D. (2007). *Interpreting Qualitative Data. Methods for Analyzing Talk, Text and Interaction*. London: SAGE.

Tsatsou, P. (2014). *Internet Studies: Past, Present and Future Directions*. Surrey: Ashgate Publishing.

Walker, D.M. (2010). The Location of Digital Ethnography. *Cosmopolitan Civil Societies Journal,* 2 (3).

6

MODELLING AND NETWORKS IN DIGITAL HUMANITIES

Øyvind Eide

6.1 Modelling with networks

6.1.1 Models

Models are all around us. Climate models, economic models, and actor network theory, to name just a few, have been at the core of scholarly as well as political discussions for decades. Furthermore, 'model' is a concept used also in quite different senses, for example 'photo model'. While there are links also between these quite different model concepts (Fishwick 2017; Eide and Eide 2016), this chapter will focus on models as we know them from digital humanities, with some notes on the humanities in general and on the sciences. While the examples will mainly be different types of networks, the principles behind them are still applicable also to models in research more generally.

The ontological nature of models will not be discussed much in this chapter.[1] In line with recent research both in the sciences and in digital humanities, we will rather focus on the process of modelling as a pragmatic activity. After clarifying the basic concepts, we will proceed to an outline of the scholarly tradition behind networks, namely, graph theory. Then we will continue with a general section on networks, a discussion of trees as a special case, followed by some notes on the visual aspect of networks in modelling. Next follows a section that includes some examples of types of networks in use in the humanities, before we conclude by discussing some common practice-based patterns.

Modelling is here connected both to practices of production and to learning strategies. When we consider models as part of practices of production, the main focus of the modelling process is to develop a product—for instance a grammar documenting a certain dialect or an online digital photo archive as a computer system to be used for storing and accessing images. In modelling as a learning strategy, on the other hand, we work on the creation and use of models with the purpose of developing new understandings of the nature of the target being modelled, as well as of the modelling process itself. Thus, the focus is on the epistemological potential of modelling. The distinction between the production process and the epistemological aspects is important to consider for work on models, but the two sides are not strictly divided. Even if the goal is to make something, one will also learn from the process; and when the main goal is to learn, one will also make external representations as part of modelling processes as they are understood here.

The pragmatic aspects of modelling are linked to the nature of the relationship between a model and the objects or systems that are the targets of modelling. Although previously this relationship has been understood as representational and has largely been unquestioned, another view has emerged over the last two decades in which modelling is seen as a practice where someone with some purpose creates something (the model) to understand and work on the target of the modelling process (Gelfert 2016). This pragmatic view of modelling also forms the basis for how we currently see modelling in digital humanities (Marras and Ciula 2014). Thus the process of abstraction must be seen as part of the modelling process and the principles and practice behind the abstraction are parts of the model.[2] The focus on abstraction is especially important in the humanities, and we will return to it several times in this chapter.

This chapter will be based on a semiotic understanding of modelling established by, among others, Knuuttila (2010) and Kralemann and Lattmann (2013) and brought into digital humanities in the recent years.[3] In this view on models, they are seen as icons in the sense established in Peirce semiotics.[4] According to this tradition, there are three types of iconic relationships between the model and the modelled object: *image like, structural*, and *metaphorical*.

Let's use the example of the apple as a sign.[5] An image of an apple outside a grocery store may establish in the mind of a hungry tourist the understanding that apples are sold in the store. This is based on a rather direct, visual similarity between the image and a typical apple; thus, the relationship is *image like*. A botanical textbook, on the other hand, contains a structural drawing of the functional parts of an apple's reproductive system. This drawing has a *structural* relationship to real apples. And finally, an apple can represent a concept through a more complex metaphorical relationship. Based on the description in the Book of Genesis of how Eve gave Adam the fruit of knowledge, a link between the apple and sin has been established through many works of art over the centuries. This link is *metaphorical*.

What does this mean in practice? Consider a map where the travels of a character as we can read it from a novel is added as a thematic layer. Then, the lines from place to place have a structural iconic relationship to the relationships between places as they are expressed in the text of the novel. There will always already be a pragmatic aspect— in order to establish the understanding of the relationship between the places needed to make the visual representation, the text must be read and understood.[6] Thus, this representation is always made by someone for a purpose. Given a different interpretation of specific aspects of the text,[7] the map could be different. Thus, it is not a map of the text as such but a map of a specific interpretation of the text. This pragmatic aspect is often not explicit, but it is always there.

The semiotic understanding establishes a process-based pragmatic understanding of the relationship between the map and the novel. The process of creating the map can also be seen as a process of media transformations. Models as they are discussed in this chapter are material objects that can be shared in groups of people working together—they are shared conceptualisations expressed in the form of media products. As the targets of modelling in the humanities are often in themselves media products, the modelling process can fruitfully be understood as a process of media transformation, in line with, for example, adaptation. The theory used to understand such processes in intermedia studies can be used to understand the processes we perform in modelling. Useful theory includes the distinction between media representation and remediation taken from Elleström (2014) and discussed in the context of modelling in Eide (2015).

The forms models take is key to understanding their role in modelling and how they can be useful for our research, teaching, development, and outreach. A discussion of form, however, must go beyond visual appearance. In the following pages the forms of models will be discussed with a focus on network models, including both abstract mathematical forms (graphs, Section 6.1.2) and forms more readily connected to visual figures (networks, Section 6.1.3). The section will be concluded with a discussion on the use and function of visual forms in research.

Modelling and networks in DH

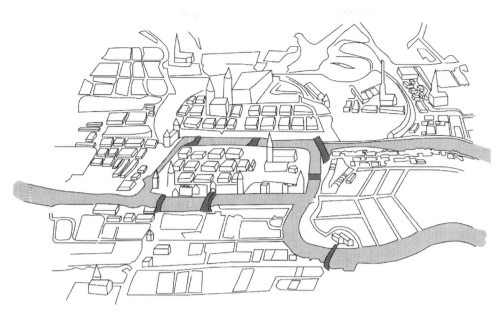

Figure 6.1 The Königsberg bridge problem (illustration: Julia Sorouri)

6.1.2 Graphs

In the city Königsberg, in East Prussia (today's Kaliningrad in Russia), there were seven bridges connecting the city, as shown in Figure 6.1. An old puzzle reads: Is there a way to cross all seven bridges without crossing any of them more than once?

There are several ways of attacking such a problem, including actually walking across bridges. If the problem is easily solved, then this strategy can work well. With two bridges, it would. But then again, such easy problems rarely become puzzles. With difficult problems, including the one discussed here, one can only find a solution either by being very clever, very persistent, or very lucky. Most of us are none of those most of the time. Furthermore, these strategies depend on the puzzle having a solution. Walking across the seven bridges and repeatedly failing to solve the puzzle in order to prove that no solution exists is hard. In general, showing that a problem does not have a solution calls for different methods.

Alternatively, one could try out different modelling strategies. Instead of walking over bridges in Königsberg one could create a small model city using dolls for the walking, or one could use pen and paper and make drawings of a different scenario. These scenarios can be seen as simulations; today a computer simulation would often be chosen, based on a model of the problem.

In the eighteenth century, it turned out that one specific type of model suited this problem especially well. If we see each land mass as an area and each bridge as a connector between these areas, we have an abstract model which is identical[8] to the concrete problem: if the puzzle is solvable for one of them it is by necessity solvable also for the other. Such a structure is shown in Figure 6.2. From that we can easily see that the size and form of the landmasses, and the exact location of the bridges, are not relevant for solving the puzzle. Thus, we arrive at the structure in Figure 6.3, which is also identical to the Königsberg bridge problem.

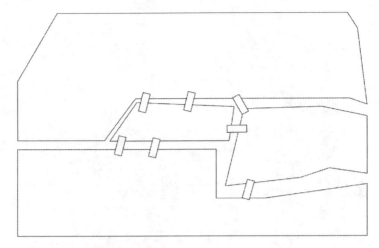

Figure 6.2 Abstraction of the Königsberg bridge problem (illustration: Julia Sorouri)

The structure in Figure 6.3 is known as a graph. More precisely, a graph is an abstract mathematical concept which can be visualised as in Figure 6.3.[9] It can also be expressed as in Figure 6.4, which is an adjacency matrix listing all the nodes and showing which are connected to which though how many edges: The first one is not connected to itself; it is connected to the second one via two edges, not to the third one, and to the fourth one via one edge. The following lines express the connections for the other nodes.

Leonhard Euler (1707–1783) was a Swiss scholar who made significant discoveries, not the least in mathematics. He defined a specific group of graphs which has been named after him, Eulerian circuits. He showed that crossing bridges as described in the Königsberg bridge problem is only possible for these graphs. The Eulerian circuits are identifiable by having an equal number of edges connected to each node. Thus, we can easily see that the graph in Figure 6.3 does not represent a Eulerian circuit; thus, the graph represents a structure for which the puzzle cannot be solved.

Whenever we plan to cross bridges it is convenient to know how to go, and for this Euler's work can be quite beneficial. However, and more importantly in this context, we see how graphs let us create abstract models of certain properties of a specific concrete problem and through this abstraction process we can find solutions to such problems through well known and proven solutions to abstract problems expressed in a formal language. Other examples of mechanisms for this type of problem solving include mathematical formulas such as Pythagoras' theorem.

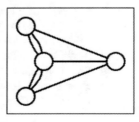

Figure 6.3 The Königsberg bridge problem expressed as a graph

$$\begin{bmatrix} 0 & 2 & 0 & 1 \\ 2 & 0 & 2 & 1 \\ 0 & 2 & 0 & 1 \\ 1 & 1 & 1 & 0 \end{bmatrix}$$

Figure 6.4 The Königsberg bridge problem graph shown as an adjacency matrix

6.1.3 Networks

'Network' can have a number of different senses in different contexts. In this chapter the term is used for graphs where the nodes and edges have attributes. For instance, nodes and edges can have a number or a name attached to them. In many cases, especially for trees, as we will see below, only the nodes have attributes. The labels can be complex, moving beyond what we usually understand as labels towards a data package attached to each node. The addition of attributes has a significant impact on the usability of graphs in the humanities.

Networks have a fairly long history in the social sciences and also in parts of the humanities.[10] An early use of network structures was the work of the teacher Johannes Delitsch, who documented social relationships between schoolboys in 1880–81. More systematic use of networks for analysing social relationships came in the 1930s through the work of, among others, Jacob L. Moreno. F.R. Pitts' work on Russian trade routes in the mid-1960s, where he introduced graph theory to historical geography, was followed by a significant amount of network-based work in history in the 1970s. From the 1990s network analysis has also been used in literary studies. While computers have been used for a long time, not the least in archaeology, there has been a boost in the use of networks in digital humanities over the last eight to ten years (Sack and Weingart forthcoming 2019).

When a network with carefully selected attributes connected to its nodes and edges is created based on a sound analysis of relevant source material it can represent many aspects of human culture, present as well as past. In the establishment of such networks, digital methods can be of significant importance but the process must still be run by knowledgeable researchers. If this is the case, the network has a potential to say relevant things about the target objects and phenomena. In this way, networks can meaningfully be used in model-based research.

There are many different types of networks in use in different disciplines. Although the sizes of networks in the humanities are usually moderate compared to those used in other areas, the use cases we find here tend to necessitate quite complex structures, including multi-layered and temporal networks. Furthermore, given the source situation in historically oriented research, biased, uncertain, and incomplete data is the norm and have to be taken into consideration in the methodologies we develop. Indeed, the concept of data is in itself disputed in the humanities (Drucker 2011).

Feedback mechanisms in the establishment of the data, combined with the focus on the scholarly process of abstraction as part of the modelling process we saw above, are necessary in the humanities. Indeed, the source situation means that we always have to base our work on an open world assumption, which means that we must assume there can always be more evidence we do not have access to. Thus, we cannot assume non-existence based on lack of data as one often can in, for instance, business applications. Additionally, much research in the humanities is focusing on the specific aspects of the particular rather than generalised and generalisable laws.

There are many problems in the real world which can be solved through abstraction to a form where proven mathematical relationships can give a solution and evidence for it. In humanities research, abstraction is typically domain specific; the concrete setting the situation exists within—its context—is vital. If one abstracts away too much of this context, the result will be that even if solutions can be found in the model world of the network, such solutions are too detached from the original problem to have any relevance. The original problem remains unsolved; the baby is thrown out with the bathwater.

With the right approach such analysis can be quite useful for problems we face in the humanities. In order to gain the benefit of networks, we must face the challenges of modelling in each use case. In order to differentiate and compare, we need to create common classes. The more we abstract, the easier it is to make comparisons and to structure the network in a useful way. However, too much abstraction risk taking away too much of what connects the networks to the object of study, so that the networks can be nice to look at and manipulate but irrelevant to real research questions.

Networks can be visualised by graphical representations of labelled nodes connected by edges. They can also be analysed using a variety of methods. Both visualisation and analysis of networks enable us to learn new things about the target for the network through interaction with and analysis of the network. Network visualisation has been more central in the humanities than network analysis. Networks as rhetorical tools, including time-based approaches and good mechanisms for leading the user through the network in meaningful ways, are still important areas of research and development. That said, and keeping the focus on the complex source situation, there is significant room for new and different uses of networks in the humanities. Indeed, network-based research is not one method, it represents a wide variety of research approaches, ranging from highly quantitative to highly qualitative (Brughmans et al. 2016, p. 6). In the following pages we will see a number of examples showing clearly how network-based modelling always operate in a fluid area where knowing how to create our abstractions is difficult.

6.1.4 Trees

A subset of networks fulfil certain additional criteria and are called trees.[11] In library science and information organisation, as well as in digital humanities, trees have filled a number of different roles. They have historically been important in the organisation of knowledge, to some extent based on an assumed tree structure existing in the external system being the target for the tree-based model. Examples include Linne's classification of species and trees of knowledge. In other cases this structure has been introduced for practical reasons, as in library classification systems such as the Dewey Decimal System[12] and for thesauri such as the Getty Thesaurus of Geographic Names and the Art & Architecture Thesaurus.[13]

Although trees are not always the best form in which to express our models there may still be other reasons for using them, conceptual as well as practical. We do inherit visual languages, and this partly steers what we can say and what visual languages we can consider. This was the case for tree structures in knowledge organisation for centuries, and we may also see something similar connected to how XML is used in areas such as scholarly editing and lexicography. Inherent limitations in tree structures have led the development into other structures for knowledge representation, usually more general graphs. For instance, ontologies such as CIDOC-CRM are represented by directed graphs; as they have multiple inheritance, they cannot be represented by tree structures. We will come back to ontologies in Section 6.2.5 below.

One of the most well known and discussed problems in digital humanities is the role of tree structures in the encoding of digital textual documents. Trees are convenient as they form the basis for widespread data standards that make formal validation of syntactical aspects of the documents possible. The short example poem in Figure 6.5 is shown as a fragment of a TEI document in Figure 6.6. The corresponding tree structure is shown graphically in Figure 6.7.

As water fall
we fall

As we fall
standards fall

Figure 6.5   An example poem

Modelling and networks in DH

```
<poem>
  <lg>
    <l>As water fall</l>
    <l>we fall</l>
  </lg>
  <lg>
    <l>As we fall</l>
    <l>standards fall</l>
  </lg>
</poem>
```

Figure 6.6 An example poem encoded in TEI (fragment) in which <poem> is used as a short form for <div type="poem">

It is also well established that many features of texts are hard to express in such a structure, including overlapping features. If we consider the version of the poem shown in Figure 6.8 and assume that the italics has a meaning as complete sequences of letters, we have a poem which cannot be encoded so easily in TEI. That is, if the assumption is that "fall we" and "fall standards" needs to be encoded as complete expressions for analytical purposes. The problem is that the encoding in Figure 6.9 breaks the tree structure because the **hi** element starts inside one **l** element but ends inside another one and thus introduce an overlap which is illegal in any XML-based formalism, including TEI.

There are several workarounds for this, as described in Chapter 20 of the TEI guidelines.[14] Although attempts have been made to develop encoding standards based on different principles,[15] most scholarly editors still live with the tree-based structure and use these workarounds to solve any problem introduced by overlap. However, the direct overlap problem is just a part of a more complex structural issue. XML is described as a formalism expressing a tree structure. This is not exactly precise. XML is a formalism which enables *validation* of a tree structure. Both XML and the earlier standard it was based on (SGML) allow us to encode graph structures, which goes beyond the tree. But the additional structures, the ones breaking the tree structure, cannot be validated.

Aggregation is one of the standard TEI solutions to the overlap problem. Such an encoding is found in Figure 6.10. In this example the parts in italics are fragmented to fall into the line elements so that the overlap is avoided. In order to keep the assumed integrity of the italicised segments each of the **hi** elements are given an **xml:id** value as a unique global identifier, in our case {i1, i2, i3, i4}. Then **prev**

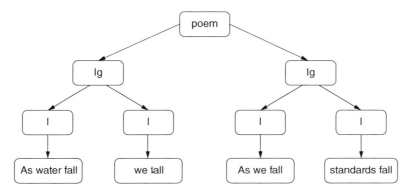

Figure 6.7 A visual representation of a TEI document

Øyvind Eide

As water *fall*
we fall

As we *fall*
standards fall

Figure 6.8   An example poem with possibly meaningful italics

```
<poem>
  <lg>
    <l>As water <hi rend="italics">fall</l>
    <l>we</hi> fall</l>
  </lg>
  <lg>
    <l>As we <hi rend="italics">fall</l>
    <l>standards</hi> fall</l>
  </lg>
</poem>
```

Figure 6.9   ★The italicised example poem encoded in incorrect TEI

```
<poem>
  <lg>
    <l>As water <hi rend="italics" xml:id="i1" next="i2">fall</hi></l>
    <l><hi rend="italics" xml:id="i2" prev="i1">we</hi> fall</l>
  </lg>
  <lg>
    <l>As we <hi rend="italics" xml:id="i3" next="i4">fall</hi></l>
    <l><hi rend="italics" xml:id="i4" prev="i3">standards</hi> fall</l>
  </lg>
</poem>
```

Figure 6.10   The italicised example poem encoded in correct TEI

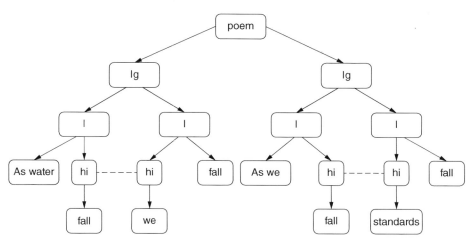

Figure 6.11 A visual representation of the fragmented TEI document

and **next** attributes are used to store the connections between the parts of the fragmented segments. This solution leads to a TEI document expressing a non-tree graph structure. However, the aggregation cannot be validated using the standard XML validation methods. Figure 6.11 makes this clear: the broken lines represent edges which are not part of the structure being validated in XML.

If the two pairs of **hi** elements had been combined into two unified elements we would have had a blatant break of the tree structure and the XML document would not have been well formed. By fragmentation and by the reconstruction using **xml:id** with **prev** and **next** links we can express the same meaning without breaking the tree structure. The cost of doing so is partly a more complex encoding (compare Figure 6.10 to Figure 6.9) and partly a structure that cannot be validated. But if we had rather chosen the solution in Figure 6.9 we could not have our encoding validated by standard tools anyway. Furthermore, as shown for MECS (Multi Element Code System), the rules would have had to be much more complex than in the case of XML if we were to enable meaningful and useful validation for a formalism allowing overlap.

The aim here is not to argue for one solution rather than the other. The aim is rather to show how the choices of formalism in our modelling processes are based on trade offs where no solution stands out as the best in all cases. We have to weight our different priorities against each other and find the best compromise.

6.1.5 Visualisation and visual thinking

In research articles networks are typically included as figures in order to assist the description of research and conclusions. These network visualisations are static in printed publications. The reader sees the network, reads the text, and at best she can establish a good understanding of the research process and the outcomes. Often, however, these visual networks only give a very limited understanding to the reader of an article. This can be hard to understand for the authors, for whom the illustrations carry deep layers of meaning which seems to be obvious and easily accessible to any knowledgeable reader.

While there may be many reasons for lack of comprehension and for communication problems, it is still the case that the solid understanding on the side of the researchers at least partially is established through active work with the data, often in interactive visual network systems where different layouts can be tried out together with different types of analysis made possible by the tools. Such interactivity is not available to the reader of static publications. Even in digital publications the network figures are often static, except for them enabling some basic zooming functionality.

Visualisations can present knowledge already established outside the context where the visualisation is found. As static presentations they do not really allow the reader to interact. In such cases the understanding of the network being visualised often remain limited. This aligns with a communicative setting where the reader is treated mainly as a consumer. But networks do not have to be static. Interactive digital publication systems where the reader can interact with the networks and other visualisations offer further possibilities. We already see many examples of systems enabling another level of visual thinking in online publications, as will be exemplified in Section 6.2 below.

Equally important in this context is the distinction between visualisation and analysis. Analysis here includes the traditional sense, looking into aspects such as centrality and weak connections. But it also includes analysis based on interacting with the visual language of the graph. In order to think visually with networks one must at least be able to change the form of the visualisations, that is, how the nodes and edges are lain out in space. Being able to deform the network by trying out changes of the network itself can be an additional way of coming to know through the use of visual network tools, enabling creative visual thinking and reasoning as part of a research process.

In the humanities it is vital for the analytical process, whatever form it takes, as well as for visualisation aimed at external users, that our tools include good mechanisms for working on and visualising uncertainty. This must be combined with flexible visual languages and solid and usable systems for interaction. Then we can avoid being steered too much as to what can be read out of the networks due to them being expressed in specific visual forms.

6.1.6 Network fixation

Manipulation of networks in the sense of changing their form without changing the underlying graph, that is, changing between different isomorphic forms, is indeed highly useful. Still, there are cases where it also makes sense to fix a network to another, spatially fixed, figure.

One example is a network of communication based on letter exchange, where nodes represent places and edges represent letters sent between two places—if a letter is sent from Paris to London an edge is added between the Paris node and the London node. While the flexibility of moving nodes around to see the network from different viewpoints and from different perspectives is indeed useful, it can be equally useful to fix each of these nodes to the representation of the place on a geographical map.

In such a network visualization, the figure becomes a merging of map and graph structure. One of the strengths of network visualisation is that this visualisation of the graph fixated to a map can be used alongside visualisations linked to other structures; for instance, a collection of family trees, as well as the traditional network visualisation where it is not connected to any fixating background structure.

6.2 Networks in use

Strictly speaking, there are no networks in the traces from previous cultures and cultural expressions we study. Networks as we represent them in computers are categorically different from historical structures and situations. We can still create networks in order to use them to study targets that have a strong image like or structural similarity to networks. For instance, in historical studies we can hypothesise past network-like structures such as road networks to have existed (Brughmans et al. 2016, p. 8).

In other cases, quite different aspects of human behaviour where the relationship is less straightforward can be translated into network concepts. Then the network can gain a stronger epistemological value. This is in line with modelling in general, where a greater conceptual distance between model and target can lead to models that tell us more about the target. An example of this is trade between cities, where the network of trading cities, e.g., in the Hansa network, can be represented by digital networks which can then be analysed and visualised in different ways. For both the road and the trade network there is a structural

Modelling and networks in DH

similarity between the assumed real world network-like phenomena and the digital network we make based on it: if two cities are recorded as connected by roads or in trade based on certain criteria, they will also be connected in the digital network model.

We can use network representations to model fictional as well as factual parts of a human culture under study. Indeed, network analysis of literature, TV series, and computer games are all growing fields, both of research in a traditional university-centred sense and of independent studies of popular culture in line with citizen science. Hypothesis testing and developing understandable visual expressions based on political and criminal events is a further area where networks play important roles, as seen in, e.g., Forensic Architecture.[16]

We can also use networks to analyse targets that are not usually seen as network in themselves. This can for instance be links between words representing specific concepts in texts.[17] In such use cases the relationship between the network used in the analysis and what can be read out of the sources has strong metaphorical aspects, in line with the use of metaphors in the natural sciences.[18]

6.2.1 Actor-oriented networks

An important area of network-based research in the social sciences the last decades is in the study of social networks, as mentioned briefly in Section 6.1.3. This is also highly relevant in many areas of the humanities, including history and the study of fictional networks of actors in literary and media studies. These networks can be based on different criteria for the establishment of connections. For instance, in the study of theatre and other dialogue-oriented media the addressing in dialogues can be stored as directed links between two or more fictional characters.

Initially seen as metaphorical, the perception of social networks changed over the years towards a view on them really existing in the social systems under study (Erickson 2012). This is especially interesting because of the later development of social networks. One can argue that networks between people did not exist before the twentieth century and that the established of such scientific models of society led to the creation of something new. The network as it was created as a formalism for understanding, based on for instance the fishing net, had metaphorical power.[19]

But the development of the network as a framework for understanding social interactions has not only taken place in research. Over the last decades, and intensified the last ten years, we have seen the establishment of concrete networks between humans, when individuals are linked tightly to nodes in digital networks of great societal significance, such as Facebook. Thus, what used to be a metaphor and a method used by researchers to understand society is now a core construction in the nature of society itself with significant political power—not just in the sense of computer systems such as Facebook and Twitter, but also in the thinking about political organisation, such as networks of female politicians across political parties. Thus the network has become a social reality in addition to and to some extent in replacement of systems based on other principles such as strict hierarchies and representational structures for decision making.

6.2.2 Networks in textual studies

Mikhail Bakhtin (1895–1975) was a Russian literary scholar and philosopher. His view on language use took the dialogue as a basic category. He also saw literature as fundamentally dialogical. This connects to the later concept of model readers (Eco 1981). Model readers can be multiple, and also linked to multiple author instances, creating a symphony which establishes the internal structure of a text as a network (Tønnesson 2004). But networks in literature are not confined to the interior of a single text. One of the key dialogical aspects is the link to previous works, where one text is addressing a multitude of texts, more or less explicitly, creating an intertextual network of works.

This network is usually implicit in fiction and is one of the aspects of texts that literary critics are interested in, establishing the place of the single text in the tradition, uncovering parts of the weave of influences between works. In non-fiction this network can be more explicit, put on the surface through footnotes, literary references, and bibliographies (Grafton 1997). This explicit layer will still exist in parallel with implicit networks of less outspoken intertextuality. All texts exist in traditions; all texts refer to other texts in a multitude of ways.

In specific traditions these networks have additional scholarly features, as in the study of pre-modern manuscripts. Through stemmatological studies of the sources for each extant copy the philologists can develop hypotheses about possible reconstructions of the manuscript tradition. This includes copies as well as translations and other adaptations. Due to the fact that manuscripts often have more than one source the stemmatological structure is a directed graph where the textual contents of lost manuscripts can be reconstructed, often with a significant level of accuracy. One of the aims is to reconstruct lost originals, but also understanding how information flowed across cultures and languages is an important aim of such studies. Given the use of such networks for research into the configuration of the networks themselves, systems to work on these relationships will necessarily have to cope with uncertainty and include the possibility of testing different possible situations in order to work well as research support systems.

A comparable phenomenon has been studied for newspapers in the United States in the nineteenth century. Given the small editorial staffs in many newspapers it was impossible to write a sufficient amount of original text for each edition. Thus, significant parts of the newspapers would consist of re-set articles where the text was copied from cuttings taken from other newspapers. Based on advanced fuzzy search algorithms working on un-corrected OCR, The Viral Texts Project has been able to establish the spread across the continent of a large number of newspaper articles copied from newspaper to newspaper, linked in time to other historical features, e.g., how the train and coach based communication networks functioned.[20]

6.2.3 Dictionaries and word-net

The tools we use when we work with a specific type of information will influence the way in which the structure of this information is perceived. Dictionaries have been a way to condense and express information about words in specific languages for hundreds of years. The source information has been organised in various types of archives, e.g., on index cards, for more than a hundred years.[21] The writing of the dictionary articles, however, was done sequentially by hand, typewriter, and later by word processor up to the late twentieth century.

The arrival of relational and later XML database-based production systems for dictionaries established the tree structure as the main organisational principle for a dictionary article. In the analysis of pre-existing dictionaries the tree structure was also clearly visible for the analyst developing the digital solutions. Thus, such a structure is readable also from pre-digital printed dictionaries. However, not everybody working with printed dictionaries saw it that way. With digital tools it has become the main, sometimes even the only possible, structure for dictionaries.

While the tree structure is indeed important for dictionaries and represent a natural way of organising production tools as well as online publication of dictionaries, there are several aspects that go beyond such structures, including cross references. The tree structure is more fitting for a dictionary than a linear form, but it too can become a straightjacket (Eide 2014). Indeed, based on the development of digital dictionaries another way to organise information about words in a language was developed: Wordnets.[22]

Wordnets have been developed as network of words, often based on dictionary information, since the 1980s. They organise information about words and relationships between them in a different way from

Modelling and networks in DH

what dictionaries do through combining hierarchical part-of relationships with sets of synonyms. They express a network structure of words related to each other in various ways. The relationships are different from what we know from dictionaries, which organises the relations based on grammatical information, etymology, hierarchies of meaning, etc.

Different ways of organising information connect to different forms of formal languages which afford different aspects of the target for the modelling, in this case language, based on the values of those who make the system and the views they want to convey. What we have discussed here are just two different structures, each with advantages and limitations. The choice between them is not based on a historical development with a move over to Wordnets leaving dictionaries aside as a tool of the past. To the contrary, dictionaries have made the transfer to digital formats without any significant loss of society level importance. Wordnets are rather additional formalisms that serve different purposes from those still served by dictionaries.

6.2.4 Networks and maps

As we saw in Section 6.1.6, networks can be spatially fixed to background images. Maps are important examples of the usefulness of this approach. There are numerous applications where networks are combined with geographical maps. One good example is communication networks, as seen in the Republic of Letters projects,[23] where networks of letter exchanges are lain out on geographical maps.

Based on the tradition of metro and rail network visualisations, and on route finding applications, the ORBIS project has developed an online route finding system for the Roman Empire with travel times based on route, means of transportation, time of year, etc.[24] This system establishes a flexible perspective based on where one chooses to locate oneself in the geographically connected network. While there are questions to be asked about the accuracy of such systems, the method for producing them includes interesting combinations between the strengths of geographical maps and the strengths of network-based formalisms, in this case a database of information establishing a basis for hypotheses about historical travel time between places.

Such map-network combinations can also be used for non-real worlds. This has been common in mapping of written fiction for quite some time, more recently we also see it for maps within computer games as well as external maps connected to games. The possibility of presenting networks both connected to background maps and as un-fixated networks which can be visualised in different ways gives a high level of flexibility in how to visualise data; thus, the different visualisations offer different epistemological possibilities based on the same base models.

6.2.5 Conceptual modelling and ontologies

The tradition of organising knowledge about the nature of the world in the form of trees dates back several hundred years. This was connected to a part of metaphysics known as ontology. As research directions known as knowledge management and knowledge organisation grew out of artificial intelligence in the 1980s, ontologies gained a new meaning as formal models for storing knowledge about the world based on a particular set of perspectives. A top-level ontology is focusing on general basic categories relevant for all systems of knowledge; a domain ontology organises a corner of the world and can in principle be plugged into a top level ontology. While ontology integration and ontology matching are important practices, no generally agreed upon top level ontology seems to be possible to make, at least not in the near future. Agreements within communities on how to develop and use domain ontologies, on the other hand, are often reachable.

In the 1990s, development towards ontologies in digital humanities and cultural heritage was initiated, leading up to what is now the CIDOC-CRM family of standards with museums as their point of departure, and IFLA-LRM[25] growing out of the library community. These ontologies represent meta-models based on a large number of information systems and standards for their respective domains, both computer-based and based on other technologies such as protocols and index card catalogues. These models are abstract constructions not based on specific implementations – they are not data standards. However, their purpose and organisation makes them well suited for the semantic web, and they are structured as networks. An important syntax for expressing practical implementations based on such ontologies is The Resource Description Framework (RDF).[26]

Again the difference between the abstract and the concrete is important. In a system developed, for instance, for a museum or a library, one must make concrete implementations based on data and process models meeting the specific needs of the institution or group of institutions the system is developed for. These concrete implementations are based on specific models and are implemented in specific programming languages, using specific database engines, etc.

But there are also general principles behind information systems in these areas. Such principles must have a longer life span than specific implementations, technologies, or development paradigms. For long term data integration we need systems which stay fairly stable. The choices of structures for such standards must be based on more abstract principles than implementation considerations. This is the role of ontologies such as CIDOC-CRM and IFLA-LRM. Current state of the art methodology for expressing such models is in the form of networks.

6.2.6 Neural networks

Neural networks as they are used in digital humanities play a different role from other networks described in this chapter. Although neural networks have been inspired by models of the human brain, they are now the core of deep learning system that uses complex computer based communication networks in order to solve problems, for instance, in classifications of text and images.

6.3 Common practice-based patterns

In this chapter a number of use cases for networks have been presented, through concrete examples as well as based on more general methods. Can we, from this small sample, see any patterns for the use of modelling in the digital humanities that are common across the field?

Such patterns do not have to be specific to the humanities. Furthermore, they may very well be overlapping, so that more than one pattern can be seen at work in any specific use case. The word 'pattern' is deliberately chosen. It is a less theory laden word than, for instance, methodology. Through the use of less scholarly laden language we try to identify commonalities, without connecting them to specific scholarly traditions—even basic concepts such as 'theory' and 'method' are used quite differently across disciplines. This helps us in developing a multi-disciplinary perspective.

Networks as we discuss them here are models. The *target* of the network-as-model is any set of objects and/or systems that the model seeks to represent in a meaningful way. In line with the brief establishment of the theory and practice of modelling in Section 6.1.1 we see these network models with a pragmatic perspective in the sense that each of the networks is created by somebody, an individual or a group, with some purpose and using some methodology and some tools. Furthermore, the relationship between the network model and its target is understood as a semiotic connection, deeply entangled with the purpose of the modelling. The network models are also media products usually established through a media transformation process. Thus we link the use of the network models to the active creative processes of representing the targets of the networks.

Modelling and networks in DH

So we aim at establishing some commonalities in the modelling processes among the networks and network types discussed above. This is based on our basic focus which is more on modelling as an activity than on the nature of the model itself—the epistemological process of learning through modelling is more important than the ontological nature of the models.

Abstraction was a key element in the solution to the Königsberg bridge problem described in Section 6.1.2. The ability to formalise the features of the problem—a city with bridges and instruction for a type of movement—in an abstract data structure is key to find solutions to many different problems through the use of modelling. The fact that the model in this case was a graph is not essential to this pattern: it has a much wider application than that.

Abstract data structures have a non-trivial connection to their visual versions. For the solution of the Königsberg bridge problem the relationship is quite clear: the solution is abstract in the sense that the spatial nature of the graph visualization—with circles and lines between the circles—is not relevant to the solution, which can equally well be read out of the matrix in Figure 6.4 by summing up the lines or the columns.

This is not so clear for other examples though. Network analysis as applied mathematics has a different epistemological way of working than what visual analysis based on interacting with a graphical representation of a network has. In visualisations of the Network of Letters, to take one example, the mathematical structure underlying the network cannot in itself express the importance of geography for the network. It is also difficult at this level to make the point that the target of the visualisation is the available and used archival material rather than the actual historical situation. It is easy to assume that the system represents the historical situation directly.

While the mathematical expression of a network is fundamental to the implementations we use to interact with it at one level, this is usually not how it is experienced by a digital humanities user. A researcher populating and interacting with the system may never see the network in anything else than its graphical form. Indeed, our practice can only function as epistemological processes if we have a certain visual representations of the material. The learning process cannot be disentangled from the human minds taking part in it. Following McGann (2003), the network is non-self-identical in the sense that its meaning can only be grasped when it interacts with an understanding mind.

The fragmentary nature of extant sources in the humanities goes together with a high level of complexity and fuzziness. While modelling will remove many aspects of particulars, it is also necessary to cater for their fuzzy nature. We must be able to shift between different layers, to zoom in and out. One must also be able to go back to sources on which the networks and the conclusions were based. This drilldown from the abstractions we use back to the messy concrete sources is necessary in order to establish a level of scholarly reproducibility.

In the modelling exercise of establishing a good formal structure for data in the humanities, for instance, when we create data models (Flanders and Jannidis 2018), we know that some of the aspects of our data will not fit into the structures we use. Furthermore, aspects that are missing are usually potentially important for the understanding and only in the technical perspective of the modelling process can they be seen as neglectable. The modelling process as a media-transformative intersemiotic translation will necessarily lead to changes in the meaning of the target. In a sense this is tautological: the whole point of modelling exercises is to remove and add aspects of the target in order to clarify certain aspects. But while this is a natural part of process it still highlights how we must be able to re-establish our abstractions based on a hermeneutical process of re-modelling. We must be able to try out new ways of doing the modelling process.

The trade-off we saw in the TEI encoding of the small poem is presenting a simple example of this point. We cannot both get the convenience of an XML structure that can be validated and the expressiveness of a human reading. Something must be sacrificed and in the case at hand the most meaningful sacrifice was the integrity and ease of processing the italic structure. Only an understanding of the use of the model can form the basis for establishing criteria for this solution as being the best one available. Thus, the evaluation must be based on a pragmatic view on modelling.

Modelling in this sense is necessarily connected to abstraction as a learning, problem solving, and development strategy. It is also a practical line of work where the concreteness of the tasks at hand – to develop a programme, to establish and clean the data set for a graph, to run an analysis in a process of tweaking parameters—is key to its epistemological power. Thus the use of modelling in digital humanities research, teaching, and development is a truly theoretical-practical activity where one part cannot work to its full potential without the other. Critical digital humanities practice must go hand in hand with a deeper theoretical understanding. The connections between problem solving in research and teaching, as they have been pointed out, e.g. for physics by Nersessian (2008), add interesting perspectives to this, perspectives it would be good to see further developed also in digital humanities.

Modelling is a complex but also highly rewarding process which must be further developed in digital humanities, as in other disciplines. Among the different forms we can express our models in we have seen a significant growth in the use of networks. Still, only the first parts of the full potential of networks in digital humanities have yet been seen. We need more practice, more theory, and better tools to develop better methodologies, for making as well as for understanding.

Notes

1 There is a significant bibliography on this. See for instance Stachowiak (1973) for a classical theoretical approach on modelling; Mahr (2009) for modelling in computer science; McCarty (2005, Chapter 1) and Flanders and Jannidis (2018) for digital humanities.
2 For a discussion of this aspect of modelling in the context of network science, see Brandes et al. (2013, esp. p. 4).
3 See e.g., Ciula and Marras (2018).
4 The usefulness of this model of models is currently being investigated; see e.g., Ciula and Eide (2017). It is already clear that it helps us to establish a basic relationship between model and modelled object. However, that is not in itself enough to establish how models are used in reasoning. Views on modelling based on richer semiotic systems might be useful tools for further theorising around such questions.
5 This example is taken from Ciula and Eide (2017) where also more developed examples taken from digital humanities research can be found.
6 Parts of this process can be automatised but the rules for the automatic system, doing e.g. part of speech tagging and geocoding, is established by one or more humans based on an understanding of the text being processed. The difference between a manual process and a process where one uses digital tools is significant but not important in the context of this discussion.
7 Or an adjustment or replacement of the algorithm used to established the mapping.
8 'Identical' is here to be taken in the context of problem solving: the two are identical in the sense that the problem can be solved in reality if and only if it can be solved for the representation.
9 For formal definitions and characteristics of graphs see, e.g., Kerren et al. (2014, Chapter 1).
10 As we will see below, trees have a much longer history than other graphs.
11 Trees are connected sense acyclic graphs with attributes connected to the nodes. Attributes can be connected to edges too but this is not common for the trees we will discuss here.
12 <https://www.oclc.org/en/dewey/resources/summaries.html>
13 <http://www.getty.edu/research/tools/vocabularies/>
14 Cf. <http://www.tei-c.org/release/doc/tei-p5-doc/en/html/NH.html>
15 An early example is The Multi Element Code System (MECS) (Sperberg-McQueen and Huitfeldt 1999). Other systems include LMNL (Piez 2015) and various annotation systems such as CATMA <http://catma.de>. In the social sciences such annotation systems have been known as CAQDAS systems <http://onlineqda.hud.ac.uk/Intro_CAQDAS/>.
16 URL: <https://www.forensic-architecture.org>.
17 See e.g., Weingart and Jorgensen (2013).
18 This links back to early modern natural philosophy, cf, Marras (2013) and Bod (2018).

Modelling and networks in DH

19 The link to other areas where network-based thinking was developed in the mid-twentieth century, such as neural network-based views on the brain, is highly relevant for the historical development but beyond the scope of this chapter.

20 URL: <https://viraltexts.org/team/>.

21 The slip archive of the Oxford English Dictionary was established in the latter part of the nineteenth century and represents an early example of such paper based archives later established also for many other dictionaries.

22 The first wordnet is just called WordNet and was initiated in 1985, see <https://wordnet.princeton.edu>. Wordnets have later been developed for several languages.

23 URLs: <http://republicofletters.stanford.edu>, <http://www.republicofletters.net>.

24 URL: <http://orbis.stanford.edu>

25 In the last years, what used to be known as the FRBR family of standards (FRBR, FRAD, and FRSAD) are being unified in the new model LRM, with a number of novel features.

26 RDF is a model for exchanging semantic web information. URL: https://www.w3.org/RDF/

References

Bod, R. (2018), 'Modelling in the humanities: Linking patterns to principles', *Historical Social Research/Historische Sozialforschung (HSR)* 43(4).

Brandes, U., Robins, G., McCranie, A. and Wasserman, S. (2013), 'What is network science?', *Network Science* 1(1), 1–15.

Brughmans, T., Collar, A. and Coward, F., eds (2016), *The Connected past: challenges to network studies in archaeology and history*, Oxford University, New York.

Ciula, A. and Eide, Ø. (2017), 'Modelling in digital humanities: Signs in context', *Digital Scholarship in the Humanities* 32(suppl 1), i33–i46.

Ciula, A. and Marras, C. (2018), Exploring a semiotic conceptualisation of modelling in digital humanities practices, *in* A. Olteanu, A. Stables and D. Borţun, eds, '*Meanings & Co.: the Interdisciplinarity of Communication, Semiotics and Multimodality*', Springer, Dordrecht, pp. 33–52.

Drucker, J. (2011), 'Humanities approaches to graphical display', *DHQ: Digital Humanities Quarterly* 5(1).

Eco, U. (1981), *The role of the reader: explorations in the semiotics of texts*, London: Hutchinson.

Eide, Ø. (2014), 'Sylviane Granger and Magali Paquot (eds). 2012. Electronic lexicography', *International Journal of Lexicography* 27(2), 180–191.

Eide, Ø. (2015), *Media Boundaries and Conceptual Modelling: Between Texts and Maps*, Palgrave Macmillan, Basingstoke.

Eide, Ø. and Eide, O. B. (2016), Modeller av mennesker, mennesket som modell [models of humans, the human as a model], *in* '*DHN 2016 – Digital Humanities in the Nordic Countries, Conference Abstracts*', Oslo, pp. 65–66.

Elleström, L. (2014), *Media transformation: the transfer of media characteristics among media*, Palgrave Macmillan, Houndsmill, Basingstoke, Hampshire.

Erickson, M. (2012), 'Network as metaphor', *International Journal of Criminology and Sociological Theory* 5, 912–21.

Fishwick, P. A. (2017), Modeling as the practice of representation, *in* '*2017 Winter Simulation Conference (WSC)*', pp. 4276–4287.

Flanders, J. and Jannidis, F., eds (2018), *The Shape of Data in Digital Humanities: Modeling Texts and Text-based Resources*, Digital Research in the Arts and Humanities, Routledge.

Gelfert, A. (2016), *How to do science with models: a philosophical primer*, Springer, Cham.

Grafton, A. (1997), *The footnote: a curious history*, Faber and Faber, London.

Kerren, A., Purchase, H. and Ward, M. O., eds (2014), *Multivariate network visualization: Dagstuhl Seminar #13201, Dagstuhl Castle, Germany, May 12-17, 2013: revised discussions*, Vol. 8380 of *Lecture notes in computer science*, Cham, Switzerland.

Knuuttila, T. (2010), Not Just Underlying Structures: Towards a Semiotic Approach to Scientific Representation and Modeling, *in* A.-V. P. Mats Bergman, Sami Paavola and H. Rydenfelt, eds, 'Proceedings of the Applying Peirce Conference'.

Kralemann, B. and Lattmann, C. (2013), 'Models as icons: modeling models in the semiotic framework of Peirce's theory of signs', *Synthese* 190(16), 3397–3420.

Mahr, B. (2009), 'Information science and the logic of models', *Software & Systems Modeling* 8(3), 365–383.

Marras, C. (2013), 'Structuring multidisciplinary knowledge: Aquatic and terrestrial metaphors', *Knowledge Organization* 40(6), 392–399.

Marras, C. and Ciula, A. (2014), Circling around texts and language: towards 'pragmatic modelling' in Digital Humanities, *in* 'Proceedings from Digital Humanities July 8–12, 2014', EPFL – UNIL, Lausanne, Switzerland, pp. 255–257.

McCarty, W. (2005), *Humanities computing*, Palgrave Macmillan, Basingstoke.

McGann, J. (2003), 'Texts in N-dimensions and interpretation in a new key [discourse and interpretation in N-dimensions]', *TEXT Technology: the journal of computer text processing* 12(2).

Nersessian, N. J. (2008), *Creating Scientific Concepts*, MIT Press, Cambridge, Mass.

Piez, W. (2015), 'Tei in lmnl: Implications for modeling', *Journal of the Text Encoding Initiative* (8).

Sack, G. and Weingart, S.B. (forthcoming 2019), Literary network analysis, in J. O'Sullivan, ed, *Digital Humanities for Literary Studies: Theories, Methods, and Practices*. Penn State Press, University Park, Pa.

Sperberg-McQueen, C. and Huitfeldt, C. (1999), 'Concurrent document hierarchies in MECS and SGML', *Literary and Linguistic Computing* 14(1), 29–42.

Stachowiak, H. (1973), '*Allgemeine Modelltheorie*'. Springer-Verlag, Wien/New York.

Tønnesson, J. L. (2004), Tekst som partitur, eller Historievitenskap som kommunikasjon: nærlesning av fire historietekster skrevet for ulike lesergrupper, PhD thesis, University of Oslo.

Weingart, S. and Jorgensen, J. (2013), 'Computational analysis of the body in European fairy tales', *Literary and Linguistic Computing* 28(3), 404–416.

7

CHARTING CULTURAL HISTORY THROUGH HISTORICAL BIBLIOMETRIC RESEARCH

Methods; concepts; challenges; results

Simon Burrows and Terhi Nurmikko-Fuller

7.1 Introduction

Historical bibliometrics—i.e. "bibliometric study of periodicals and books published in the framework of time and space" (Herubel, 1999, p. 382)—has long been a significant part of the book historian's toolkit: it also deserves a distinguished place in the history of digital humanities. From the 1970s, as cultural history came into vogue and the 'cliometric' statistical-historical approaches favoured by social and economic historians fell from fashion, practitioners of the new inter-disciplinary field of book history, among them luminaries such as Robert Darnton, François Furet and William St Clair, continued to make significant use of statistical methods (Darnton, 1996; Furet et al., 1965–1970; St Clair, 2004). Such methods allowed them to conduct large scale "quantitative analysis of publications for the purpose of ascertaining specific kinds of [cultural] phenomena" (Herubel, 1999, p. 380). Book history was thus ideally suited to computational methods of analysis, and to experimental approaches to combining digital data-sets. Hence some of the aforementioned scholars, notably Furet and Darnton, were digital pioneers,[1] though Darnton has remained curiously sceptical about the analytical value-add of computational techniques (Takats, 2020).

An enduring strength of historical bibliometric research—digital or otherwise—is that it is generally driven by strong research questions. The starting points are often relatively narrow. How did the subject matter of the stock in the widow Desaint's Paris printing shop change over time? What titles were borrowed most frequently from the Wigtown Library? Or how many times did the word 'virtue' appear in quarto editions on Samuel Johnson's bookshelves? By accumulating datasets and interrogating their wider representative value, it is possible to use distant reading techniques to explore wider questions such as 'What did the French read in the eighteenth century?' or 'Does the output of religious reading matter between 1700 and 1900 support the hypothesis that Western European society was becoming progressively more secular?' Recent research has shown that digitally-based historical bibliometric work can challenge or radically modify existing historical understandings. Moreover, since books can be used as a proxy for the ideas that they contain, such projects have the potential to revise and expand our vision of intellectual and cultural life across the print era.

In this chapter we will explore methods, concepts, challenges and best practice in digital historical bibliometric research and how well-constructed historical-bibliometric research can enrich cultural history and related fields, drawing on the authors' experience as researchers or collaborators on the Universal Short Title Catalogue (USTC), the French Book Trade in Enlightenment Europe (henceforth FBTEE) and MEDIATE projects, and other digital projects in library history and bibliography.

7.2 Types of historical bibliometric research

Essentially, any research activity which seeks to quantify books, or events involving books, from or in past societies, is a historical bibliometric project. Such projects generally fall into several broad categories.

Large-scale bibliographic cataloguing projects, aim to provide comprehensive data on about titles or editions of various types of book. They gather and make available for digital analysis information about the scale of production—at least in terms of titles or editions published—within geographically, linguistically, thematically or genre specific categories. Many such bibliographic projects target subject specialists. Smaller scale projects include the 'Biblos 18' database, which catalogues all books known to have been published in Lausanne in the eighteenth century, or published elsewhere under a false Lausanne imprint, or the 'New Zealand Law & Literature/Law & Visual Media Database.'[2] Owing to the small size of the country, the latter is one of the more comprehensive national resources arising from the Law and Literature movement. Angus Martin, Vivian Mylne and Richard Frautschi's soon-to-be-published database of the French novel is larger in scale and scope.[3] The successor to their analogue-era, printed *Bibliographie du genre Romanesque française, 1751–1800* (1977), it aims to catalogue every known edition of every novel published in the eighteenth century, supplementing bibliographic data with semi-structured information on genre, tone, principal characters, plot summaries and principal library holdings.

More ambitious still is the Austlit database of Australian Literature which presents itself as an important piece of the national research infrastructure and claims that 'No other country in the world has attempted to compile such a comprehensive record of a nation's creative writing and associated critical works'. Expanding by 600 records per week, it seeks to 'make database records that communicate and, when possible, link to authoritative bibliographical and production information for works of fiction and poetry, writing for the theatre, biographical and travel writing, writing for film and television, criticism and reviews'.[4] Other bibliographic resources have yet broader ambitions. Andrew Pettegree's 'Universal Short-Title Catalogue' is creating a record for every printed work and edition published in Europe before 1700; the "Global Historical Bibliometrics" project attempts to quantify the global output of print in different societies.[5] Using complex mathematical algorithms, Pettegree's team has also tried to quantify the number of editions which have not come down to us from the first centuries of European printing (Pettegree, 2016).

Other projects concentrate on the dissemination of books. One long-running project widely considered to be a game-changer is the French Book Trade in Enlightenment Europe (FBTEE) project. It traces the movement of books around the pan-European business network of a single Swiss publisher-wholesaler, the Société typographique de Neuchâtel (STN). The FBTEE database documents around 450,000 copies of 3,600 titles circulating among 2,900 correspondents based in over 500 settlements across Europe over a 25-year period. Its user interface, launched in 2012, allows researchers to create maps, bestseller lists, and sales charts for titles, individuals, places, authors, subject keywords and much more.[6] Studies based on the original FBTEE database offer original and challenging interpretations of the book trade, print culture and intellectual and cultural life of the later eighteenth century.[7] Further datasets now in production will deepen and extend these insights into the later enlightenment, particularly with regard to France.[8] As both authors of this chapter are investigators on this project, which is currently funded by the Australian Research Council grant 'Mapping Print, Charting Enlightenment', we shall return to it as an exemplar several times in what follows.

However, book trade sources reveal little about end users: the apparent '*pointilliste* precision' of FBTEE's maps conceals the fact that the booksellers who bought or sold the STN's books were not the end consumers. The maps' value therefore rests upon the assumption that most booksellers sold to a predominantly local clientele (Darnton, 2012). Hence other types of project attempt to trace the library holdings of private individuals or institutions. Radboud University's European Research Council-funded MEDIATE project, headed by Alicia Montoya, drawing inspiration from the analogue-era work of Daniel Mornet a century earlier, seeks to create a database of several thousand private library catalogues from the seventeenth and

Charting cultural history

eighteenth centuries, concentrating on smaller to medium sized libraries, in which the owners probably read most books that they owned.[9]

This search to find what was actually read—the real best-sellers of the past—rather than works revered as part of a retrospectively-created literary canon, is typical of much historical bibliometric research. the MEDIATE project focuses on discovering the forms of popular literature that 'mediated' between the pious popular literature consumed in huge quantities in the late eighteenth century and the works of the high enlightenment (Montoya, 2020).

Another sub-genre of bibliometric project focuses on sites of reading and reading communities, in particular public or community libraries. Libraries in particular have left a whole range of records ideal for bibliometric research. Catalogues, borrowing registers, acquisitions records, minute books, and in some cases the original collections, or remnants of them, survive. Moreover, library documentation often takes standard structured forms, facilitating comparative research (Burrows, 2015).

Still other types of projects seek to understand reader reception. Among the most ambitious and impressive are nationally-based reading experience database (RED) projects that cover Britain, the Netherlands, Australia, Canada and New Zealand. Using a mix of volunteer and funded labour, and elaborate data entry forms, these projects have accumulated information both on how readers discussed their reading experiences in writing, recorded conversation or other means, and how they read, including information on where, when and in what postures. The largest such project, UK RED, has drawn on the labour of over 100 volunteers to assemble a database of over 30,000 acts of reading across the years 1450–1945.[10] However, the RED approach to data capture is labour intensive, involving lengthy and complex forms to record a single act of reading. It also tends to be rather arbitrary and elitist in coverage, often mining sources connected to well-known (and therefore perhaps atypical) readers.

Alternative approaches to capturing reader reception, which may be more socially inclusive or more efficient, include the presentation of records of small town library borrowings and diaries as in the Australian Common Reader database,[11] or FBTEE's proposed link-ups to evidence of reading contained in the Electronic Enlightenment corpus of letters. The full realisation of this last ambition is linked to the development and implementation of linked open data techniques for joining datasets, an issue to which we will return.

Many of the most innovative and significant projects in historical bibliometrics—and indeed digital humanities more generally—also seek to map where books were produced, encountered, disseminated, consumed, or (in the case of fictional works) set over time and space. In their typology of historical bibliometric resources, Simon Burrows and his collaborators identify two main types of mapping projects (Burrows et al., 2016). First come projects seeking to 'map the production [or dissemination or consumption] of text over time and space, often incorporating Geographic Information System (GIS) techniques to capture, interpret and visualize spatial data'. Examples they cite include the "Atlas of Early Printing", the "Atlas of the Rhode Island Book Trade", the "Mapping Colonial Americas Publishing", and the "Geography of the London Ballad Trade, 1500–1700".[12] A second sort of project, literary mapping projects, exploits spatial data to create new or deeper understandings of fictional texts through the digital exploration of their locational settings. Examples include "A Literary Atlas of Europe" and "Mapping the Lakes: A Literary GIS".[13] While less directly orientated towards capturing historical bibliometric data, this type of project nevertheless provides quantitative as well as geo-temporal markers relating to fictional locations and the literary imaginations of authors and readers.

7.3 Data and data sources

The raw materials for historical bibliometric research are many and varied. They encompass any document which records numbers of books, or discrete instances of events involving books (or ideally both). Besides books themselves, this includes documents created in the production, publication, distribution, advertising, censoring, cataloguing, lending, reading, reviewing or policing of books or the regulation and administration of the printing and bookselling trades. Key primary sources include publishers and booksellers accounts, book listings and sales records; library catalogues, membership lists and borrowing records; censors' reports and confiscation records; registers of printers and booksellers; will inventories; indices of banned books; texts and imprints contained within books themselves, and many other sources.

Most such records typically offer formulaic, if not entirely standardised, records of one or more types of event involving books. Booksellers accounts record when (and often where) particular books were sold, in what quantities, and sometimes to whom. French *ancien régime* confiscation records include what titles were confiscated in what quantities, their provenance, who they belonged to, and what legal judgments followed their seizure. Library borrower records tell us who borrowed which books, when and for how long.

These events generally have common features that enable us both to count them, and to locate them geo-temporally, in the places where books were produced, distributed, controlled, consumed, or even impounded and destroyed. Typically, they reveal a book's title and sometimes its edition. They also usually reveal one or more human actors in the event. The police officer who confiscated a packet of books; the hapless pedlar caught with them on his cart; and, metaphorically or occasionally physically present, the author of the books and perhaps the publisher or wholesale supplier, too. In short, historical bibliometric projects gather data about events relating to people, places, time and texts, and the digital resources they create should be structured accordingly.

Generally, this data is gathered, stored and analysed in databases. These need not be grand-scale customised online tools like those produced by the highest-profile and most lavishly funded projects in the field; some of the best and most interesting historical bibliometric research has been done on a spreadsheet. A classic example is Cheryl Knott's work on the stock of six tiny American libraries from the early days of the Republic, three each from either side of the Potomac river (Knott, 2018).[14]

Once 'cleaned and standardised' (itself a labour-intensive time-consuming process the resource implications of which should not be under-estimated), data can be aggregated, enriched or annotated, empowering further analyses. Places can be grouped into larger political, economic, religious or cultural communities. Titles can be classified according to subject, genre, language or country of publication and several other variables. People can be classified by profession, social status, genre, nationality, religion and so forth. Sometimes this information can be derived from our primary sources. For example, many book catalogues come organised into pre-selected genre or subject categories. Other such data is the fruit of further research. Alternatively, it might be drawn digitally from third parties using APIs or other digital tools.

Because of their multiple common features, existing historical bibliometric datasets often use broadly similar database structures and fields to capture similar sorts of data about people, objects (books/texts) and places. Moreover, datasets produced by different projects often have overlaps in terms of authors, titles, places they describe. They are thus an ideal testbed for the development of common base data-structures, data standards and linked open data tools. Several leading projects on the early modern period, including USTC, MEDIATE and FBTEE are currently working together, and in combination with projects in cognate areas, such as Early Modern Letters Online (EMLO), to facilitate linked open data approaches and conceptual thinking around them.

7.4 Describing books: Bibliographic data models and taxonomic description

Describing books is central to historical bibliometric research. But the very notion of a 'book' is ambiguous and unstable. This can make counting books deeply problematic. The term 'book' might signify, among other things, a physical object encompassing a single copy of an edition of a particular text (or miscellaneous texts); a physical object comprising just part of a particular edition; several such objects united by a single title or as part of a distinct intellectual project or edition (e.g. Gibbon's multi-volume *Decline and Fall of the Roman Empire*; Voltaire's *Complete Works*); or an abstract 'work', in the sense of a unitary intellectual creation. Ambiguities and subtleties also surround many other aspects of books: the concept of authorship, for example, involves many roles (writer, co-writer, editor, translator, corrector, compiler, etc.).

To counter these difficulties, International Federation of Library Associations in the 1990s developed a descriptive schema for library bibliographic records, FRBR, or 'Functional Requirements of Bibliographic Records'. Although not to date incorporated in most library records, and controversial among librarians, FRBR is ideally suited to many, if not all, historical bibliometric projects. Simply put, FRBR offers a four level bibliographic structural model for describing 'books' (Tillett, 2005). These four levels, or FRBR 'group one entities'—*viz* the 'work', the 'expression', the 'manifestation' and the 'item'—describe the products of intellectual endeavours.

The top-level group one entity, the 'work', is the overarching intellectual creation, for example the marquis de Sade's *Justine*. The second level is the 'expression', that is to say the version of the text: over time Sade wrote three different versions of *Justine*. Each might be considered a separate expression. The third level is the precise 'manifestation' of a particular 'expression'— usually an individual edition. One such 'manifestation' of *Justine* is the 1973 *Livre de Poche* edition, which was published by *Librairie générale française*. It generally follows the second version (expression) of Sade's text. However, it also contains notes on textual variations between 'expressions', an editorial introduction, a unique cover illustration and other added features. In short, this manifestation differs from all others in numerous ways. The fourth and final level of FRBR is the individual physical copy or 'item'. Despite their general similarities, each item is also unique. For example, the copy of the *livre de poche* edition of *Justine* which graces the bookshelves of the author of this sentence has several distinctive features. It is, for instance, a little thumbed, contains a pencilled price (£1.50) left by a second-hand bookdealer, and has two deep creases running diagonally across the back cover.

According to the FRBR model, then, "the 'work' is 'realized' in the 'expression' which is 'embodied' in the 'manifestation' which is 'exemplified' by the 'item'" (see Figure 7.1). In order to count copies of works circulating in time and space, historical bibliometric data structures are likely to need to aggregate items into manifestations and manifestations into works. Many historical bibliometric projects will capture all three of these tiers of the FRBR model in their structural modelling, though some may only need or be able to capture one or two of them. For example, a comparative study of works appearing on Indices of Banned Books might only need, or be able, to record Works. Other projects may need to identify precise manifestations, in order, for example, to quantify partial sets of multi-volume editions or the provenance of items.

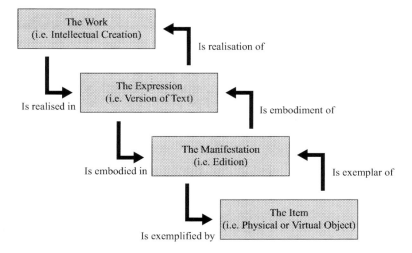

Figure 7.1 FRBR Group One Entities and Relationships between Them (after Barbara Tillett, *Functional Requirements for Bibliographic Records*)

Few projects will have the capacity to consistently identify the fourth and final tier of the FRBR group one entity model, the 'expression'. There are both philosophical and practical reasons for this. First, most source materials for historical bibliometric research do not systematically record the 'expression', though this is occasionally captured, for example, when a work is identified in the imprint as the 'new revised' or 'first folio' edition. Instead, identifying 'expressions' requires specialised scholarly knowledge of the authorial history of a text, and perhaps access to a physical copy: equally, isolating what constitutes a distinct 'expression' frequently involves subjective judgment. It should be noted here, too, that identifying precise editions or even works in primary sources is often an inexact science, particularly when source materials are in manuscript form. Individual projects will need to develop protocols to deal with ambiguous data on a case by case basis.

Further groups of FRBR entities describe (group two) the persons or corporate entities who created, produced or had custodianship over the group one entities, or (group three) are the subjects of group one entities: concepts, objects, events, places, or indeed persons or corporate entities or other books. These second and third groups of entities, and the relationships existing between entities, may also provide helpful ways of organising and thinking about data for some historical bibliometric projects, but it is the group one entities that are our main concern here.

However, FRBR is not the only useful structural or ontological model. Alternative or complementary models such as FRBRoo,[15] MODS[16] and MADS[17] RDF, Bibframe,[18] BiBO[19] and FaBiO[20] might also be appropriate, particularly for aligning larger projects with others, and facilitating the Linked Open Data approaches currently being developed and trialled by some of the larger and best resourced historical bibliometric projects globally (Burrows and Roe, 2020).

Of these, FRBRoo and FaBiO are FRBR-aligned models. FRBRoo is distinctive as an event-based model, designed to map on to the cultural heritage and GLAM-sector (galleries, libraries, archives, and museums) ontology CIDOC CRM.[21] This opens up possibilities for alignment between datasets of complementary if not directly overlapping information. Using the FRBRoo model would allow us, for example, to assert that a book was published during a historical event, or that multiple items were produced in a single publication event, whether or not the temporal specifics of date or year are known. This flexibility of the model comes at the cost of increasing internal complexity: of the bibliographical metadata ontologies summarised here, FRBRoo is not the largest based on number of Classes (of which it has 54) nor properties (74), but the event-centricity of the model adds an additional 'step' to each representation (Jett et al., 2016; Nurmikko-Fuller et al., 2015; Nurmikko-Fuller et al., 2016).[22] For example, whilst other models may readily assert a direct relationship between an author and a book, the FRBRoo model asserts that there is a creation event, in which both the author and the book take part.

FaBiO Classes and properties have similarly been designed to align to the FRBR schema's 'Work', 'Expression', 'Manifestation' and 'Item'.[23] FaBiO's creator, David Shotton, has extensively compared FaBiO to the BiBO (or Bibliographical Ontology),[24] accrediting the latter as the first of bibliographical metadata ontologies, and one which provides a representation of a high level of granularity. Where FaBiO supersedes BiBO is in its size, diversity, and interconnectedness to other ontologies, particularly those of the SPAR-family.[25]

No discussion of bibliographical metadata ontologies would be complete without mentioning the three models produced by the Library of Congress (LOC). The first two, the largely interconnected MOD and MADS RDF vocabularies provide a flat and descriptive approach to metadata description. The third LOC ontology, Bibframe, achieves the graph-structure representation of library metadata, providing greater opportunities for more complex research questions. The challenges and opportunities presented by the representation of information in a graph will be discussed in greater detail below, but what is important to recognise is that the structural design of a database (be it tabular, relational, or graph) has an effect on the ways in which information is recorded, retrieved, and analysed. Graph databases and Triplestores (the latter of which contains information represented as Linked Open Data, as RDF, in a graph structure rather than a

Charting cultural history

collection of tables or columns in a spreadsheet), by comparison, facilitate an investigation, which manifest as a navigation of the graph. In a Linked Data system, datasets that exist elsewhere on the Web can be used as a mechanism for the addition of complementary information from these external sources to contribute to the answer.

MODS and MADS RDF are closely aligned to the MARC[26] (MAchine-Readable Cataloguing) record, a standard for cataloguing library objects (such as books) in digital formats developed some half a century ago (and thus an already well-known and widely utilised method for capturing bibliographical data). Whilst this has undoubted uses and benefits, what these models risk is, to some extent, missing out on the opportunities presented by the reinterpretation of these information structures as a graph. These opportunities include the ability to start questions at any point within a decentralised structure (rather than moving down a hierarchical structure); the relative ease of capturing complex information through complex implementations; or indeed the possibility of inferring implicit knowledge from the relationships that connect explicitly declared facts. In recreating the strict hierarchies of information of the MARC standard, these models provide descriptive structures that answer traditional research questions based on combining and filtering of information categories. They are thus capable of answering questions based on Who, What, When, and Where (for example, to identify "Authors who wrote books banned in France in the eighteenth century")—questions, which relational databases are already well-suited to answer. An example of such a question might be to identify "Corporations, which have as members people living in France, who have authored works confiscated during French customs inspections, and whose works are predominantly ordered by booksellers in Paris". If an event-based model is used, we could feasibly expand this question to a query that incorporates historical events as one of the parameters. Where external data (from sources such as DBpedia, the Linked Open Data version of Wikipedia) could be consulted to enrich the question, it could become something along the lines of "Corporations, which have as their members people, who inhabit a place in France that today has three railway stations, who authored works that were confiscated by Parisian customs, and whose works were predominantly ordered by clients in locations that are currently départemental capitals".

Of the ontologies discussed above, FRBR group one entities are fully represented by FRBRoo and FaBiO. Neither the MODS and MADS RDF ontologies nor BiBO represent them in any way whatsoever—Bibframe contains only the 'Work'. Yet each ontology provides either potentially useful detail that can help capture object biographies of individual items, or—crucially— large numbers of subclasses, which bring in valuable specifications (Jett et al., 2016).

A further challenge in describing books revolves around genre and subject content. Many historical bibliometric projects will want to consider the benefits and costs of classifying books by subject and genre, and how this might be achieved. The lowest hanging fruit exist where all or most works being described are already classified in an existing and accessible dataset. British book historians working on eighteenth-century, for example, can draw on the existing eight metadata classification categories in Gale-Cengage's remarkable digital collection Eighteenth-Century Collections Online (ECCO), and confidently expect most titles they encounter to be present there. The main expense is to ensure time for classifying any new titles encountered and, outside of Britain —where JISC has subscribed to ECCO for the nation— acquiring access to ECCO or its metadata, which includes full text of the digitized works (the latter being available separately for researchers).

However, depending on the research questions asked, alternative or more detailed classification categories may be required, and implementing these can have significant resource implications. At the most lavish end of the scale, the FBTEE database incorporates two different subject taxonomies. The first is an iteration of the tree system of the Parisian booksellers, in which every work is assigned to a single category. Developed by Gabriel Martin and Prosper Marchand in the late seventeenth century, it was widely applied in eighteenth-century catalogues: its evolution and contours are superbly discussed by Edward Edwards in *Memoirs of Libraries* (Edwards, 1859, II, 772–82). The main limbs of this tree system are familiar to book historians through the works of Daniel Mornet; François Furet and his collaborators in the *Livre et Société* group; Robert Darnton; and more recently FBTEE research outputs by Mark Curran and Simon Burrows. They comprise five capacious categories capable, with a little intellectual gymnastics, of embracing all fields of human intellectual endeavour: 'Theology', 'History', '*Belles-Lettres*', 'Arts and Sciences', and 'Jurisprudence'. However, the system is flexible, with many sub-branches, and so, beyond these five basic categories, probably no two catalogues applied it quite alike. Anyone wishing to adopt the Parisian booksellers' system will need to settle a final iteration.

The second FBTEE classification system is bespoke, comprising over 1,000 carefully-defined, free-standing keywords developed for the project's needs. The keywords included a relatively limited set of over-arching terms—for example, Science, Literature, Geography, Military Affairs, History—and many narrower categories that often exist in hierarchical relationships within the over-arching categories, but in such a way as no relationship was invariable. For example, generally works tagged as 'Medicine' were also tagged as 'Science', but this was not always the case. A satirical play about Doctors would certainly be classified as being about 'Medicine' and the 'Medical Profession' and would also carry the tags 'Literature', 'Drama', 'Comedy' and 'Satirical Works'. However, it would not be considered a work of 'Science' on our definitions.

The purpose of these twin taxonomies was to capture both eighteenth century and twenty-first century modes of thinking about knowledge; to enable the creation of statistical tables where all books were weighted equally and each had only one place (via the Parisian booksellers' system); and at the same time to offer rich description (via keywords). In addition, the Parisian system facilitated direct comparison of FBTEE's findings with those of previous projects that had used its over-arching categories.

The cost of taking this approach was considerable. Even after developing and piloting the twin taxonomies, around a full year of investigator's time was spent classifying the 3,600 works in the database. This involved consulting content pages, prefaces and introductions of digitized copies available on line through Gallica, Google Books, Project Gutenberg, the Hathi Trust, RERO and miscellaneous other repositories; bibliographic sources such as Martin, Mylne and Frautschi's *Bibliographie du genre romanesque française* or the CESAR database of the French novel; online antiquarian bookseller catalogues; and contemporary book reviews in digitized eighteenth-century journals. Failing all else, keywords in online catalogues or the book titles themselves could be helpful.

Only 15–20 minutes was available to classify each work, mainly from online sources, on the basis of 'best available information'. For classifying works in subsequent datasets, FBTEE has adopted a simple numerical key to record on what basis each book was classified, together with a field to explain that decision. For certain genres, that has speeded work by empowering classifications based on title alone—for example, if its title indicates it is a 'book of hours', a work almost certainly belongs to a standard genre for which FBTEE applies standard keywords. Although titles can occasionally be misleading—for example, our putative book of hours might be an impious and scurrilous satirical work—in most cases we would expect title or imprint details to alert us to this possibility (since, to secure an audience, author and publisher would wish to advertise to readers the book's true nature).

Numerous off-the-peg classification systems might equally serve particular historical bibliometric projects. FBTEE's reasons for rejecting them were project-specific. For example, the Library of Congress (LoC) system seemed too complex and haphazard to apply consistently; Dewey seemed ill-adapted to the preoccupations of much eighteenth-century material. The taxonomic practices of many research libraries when applying LoC keywords to eighteenth-century material were also a consideration. Searches in the global collective library catalogues WorldCat and the Karlsruhe portal revealed that when digital catalogues do classify early modern books, which is relatively rarely, they are often described by the unhelpful catch-all term 'Early works to 1800'. Fortunately, this problem is distinctive to early modernists. Scholars working on the nineteenth century or later are likely to encounter much more precise keywords applied (sometimes inaccurately) to their primary sources in WorldCat and its component library catalogues. Those working

Charting cultural history

on the later twentieth century are likely to find more benefit in LoC keywords, which increasingly were attached to publications by authors and publishers.

Applying subject taxonomies in large projects is time-consuming and costly. However, experience suggests that classifications systems in which works are assigned to a single generic category are much more rapid to apply. When using the Parisian system, FBTEE classified most books in under five minutes, but required 10–15 more to apply its keyword system rigorously. A further possibility for FBTEE, now it possesses a large pre-prepared learning set, is to experiment with machine learning, at least to apply the five main branches of the Parisian booksellers' system.[27]

For some projects, subject classifications can be drawn primarily or entirely from primary source data. The private library catalogues used by the MEDIATE project often include contemporary classifications for the books listed within. By capturing this data, it may be possible to classify books without needing any researcher interventions or interpretations. Intriguingly, however, as the MEDIATE project has confirmed, classifications are frequently inconsistent between different catalogues, even where the same categories are employed. Moreover, the meaning of key categories and classificatory practices can shift over time—for example, local Saints' lives might be treated at different periods as theology, folklore, religious history, literature or biography. Thus where subject classifications are used as analytical tools, pilot studies should seek to verify in advance how far taxonomies are applied in a standard and consistent way across all the data. At the same time, the differing ways in which contemporaries applied taxonomic systems to bodies of literature is itself worthy of further research. A well-designed public-facing database might therefore offer a range of taxonomic systems. Alongside project specific systems, it might choose to record the classifications encountered in primary source material, and provide fields for user annotations. As these choices will have major resourcing and analytical implications, they merit serious reflection.

7.5 Actors, readers and networks

Typically, historical bibliometric projects capture data about a range of activities involving human and institutional actors. It thus pays to think in advance about the full range of activities revealed in the data, and whether and how to capture them all. Decisions taken at this early stage will have long-term implications. Consider, for example, the treatment of people in the original FBTEE database, which ostensibly measured the circulation of books by a single publisher around a network of almost 3,000 correspondents. The database had fields for correspondents' names and places of residence, and each correspondent was allocated a unique individual 'client' code. But some correspondents also appear in other database fields, where they had other codes or none at all. Some were authors of works and were therefore given a distinct author code. Others were named as publishers or booksellers in imprints recorded in our bibliographic data: these had no codes. Still others, among them Catherine the Great and Voltaire, appear in the database in the taxonomic 'keywords' in the database—i.e. they are themselves the subjects of books, and have unique identifier codes on that basis. The lack of a single controlled list of individuals (including institutional actors) limited the sorts of queries that could be run as well eventually as requiring costly and complex remedial action to remedy.

Data concerning people is typically quite limited in the primary sources used for historical bibliometric research. The name of an author or publisher in a catalogue; the name of a borrower in a library register; the name and residence of a client in a trade ledger; the owner of business premises raided by the police; the name of the holder of a publishing licence. Often the data is abbreviated or cryptic, perhaps a surname which cannot be deciphered with certainty, and lacking a Christian name. However, supplementary data in the data sources often provides further clues to aid identification: Parisian book confiscations registers from the 1770s and 1780s often give a title or profession for the owners of confiscated books, the names of their clerks or associate, or record postal marks derived from their initials: the Monsieur Didot owning a parcel marked 'M.D.J.' is almost certainly the publisher-bookseller Didot *le jeune* rather than his older brother (Didot *l'aîné*). Sometimes, too, researching the authorship of a confiscated title reveals that the owner of contraband books was the author himself. Often identifying titles, people and even places from manuscript sources is not an exact science, and relies on such inferences and educated guesswork. Hence the best that can be expected from much historical bibliometric data is what Dan Edelstein calls 'a fuzzy snapshot of reality.' Hence database design will ideally incorporate notes or tools to indicate the degree of certainty with which a given piece of information is known.

Once the people in a dataset have been identified there are, as with books, almost unlimited opportunities to enrich the metadata. Data about individuals' professions, social status, genders, and places of residence and activity is frequently available in the primary source documentation. Sometimes, too, it reveals intriguing glimpses of their associates: business partners, family members, employees, clients. Often, this data can be supplemented with (ideally, structured) data drawn from digital or secondary sources. Life dates, educational and professional trajectories, family names, date of marriage, names and dates of children and heirs, titles and official positions, setbacks, financial status, entanglements with the authorities, patronage or political allegiances, nationalities and more. In some cases, this data is available through supplementary sources in the archives, or through archival guides (the Bibliothèque publique et universitaire de Neuchâtel's magnificent geographically arranged type-list of STN clients, which provided FBTEE with professional data, gender and social status, is a good example). For persons who authored a book, much personal data is now available through VIAF (Virtual International Authority File) numbers, an initiative which 'combines multiple name authority files into a single OCLC-hosted name authority service'. VIAF files also exist for many books.[28] For individuals involved in publishing and the book trades in Europe before the mid-nineteenth century, CERL's online Thesaurus provides authority files, though its coverage is still far from comprehensive. (The CERL Thesaurus also has place data drawn from Geonames and a great deal of author information, too).[29] APIs make it possible to draw data from these resources efficiently. In due course, for the early modern period, it is to be hoped that a single data point, Early Modern People – which is currently being prepared by the EMLO project and its partners – will aggregate data on every significant individual in the cultural life of the period.[30]

The availability of such metadata opens new research vistas. In larger datasets containing enhanced metadata on many individuals, it will become possible to ask new sociologically based research questions. Drawing on FBTEE data, for example, it might become possible to discover and analyse the typical French dealer in clandestine works (*livres philosophiques*). Was he or she typically a new, younger bookseller breaking into the trade for the first time? Or were such dealers more likely to be established traders with regular, trusted clients and supply networks for 'under the cloak' literature, as well, in all likelihood, as powerful protectors and patrons among the local elite? Were women booksellers less likely than men to dabble in the illegal trade? And how did the profile of the average dealer change from August 1777 and June 1783, when—as our digital analyses were able to establish—new decrees led to more effective policing? (Burrows, 2018, pp. 134–5).

The process of identifying individuals typically draws on a range of supplementary primary source materials. From the late 1700s, many European cities began to have street directories, providing names and addresses of businesses, which may help for identifying or learning more about, say, the members of subscription libraries, reading rooms and other cultural institutions where books circulated. Professional directories and listings often provide details of people working in a given industry: the 1781 *Almanach de la Librairie* is a goldmine of information on which printers and booksellers operated in the various towns across Europe, as well as many details of laws and customs governing the trade. For high office holders, annual civil lists such as France's *Almanach Royal* are enlightening. For later historical periods these sorts of sources can often be supplemented or superseded by census data, voter records, tax or local government records, or telephone directories.

7.6 Dealing with incomplete, inconsistent and poor-quality data

Historical bibliometric data is often incomplete, inconsistent, 'messy' and relatively low grade. Historical manuscripts, printed catalogues of books, and even MARC records drawn from modern digital library catalogues generally offer data that is neither comprehensive nor internally consistent. For example, MARC records may lack the publisher, format and pagination data needed to identify precise editions. Contemporary printed catalogues are even more unreliable. Handwriting and signatures are often ambiguous: experience suggests that some researchers struggle to decode signatures and handwritten names even in their native languages, while others quickly become proficient even when dealing with foreign language material. This is a project variable to be borne in mind.

Interpreting title or imprint data can also be a drag on historical bibliometric projects. To minimise this problem, it is often more efficient to gather in advance data on titles and editions that are likely to be encountered, by consulting relevant catalogues or other booklists. For example, a library project looking at reader borrowing registers might use surviving library catalogues to load all known title holdings. This can result in significant cost savings. FBTEE timestamp evidence suggests that where pre-entered, well-structured book and edition metadata records already exists, researchers enter records in 5–10% the time required for records where titles needed to be identified through further research in online catalogues. It follows that, wherever possible, bibliometric research should work from a well-structured, and ideally (near) comprehensive set of bibliographic metadata relating to their topic. For the early modern period, Early English Books Online (EEBO) or ECCO for Britain and more broadly the USTC can serve this purpose, as well as national digital bibliographies where they exist (such as Austlit or the Dutch National Bibliography).

Sometimes, it is impossible to identify books or people even from high quality title, imprint and name data. In some genres, ephemeral editions—and even works—frequently do not survive in the global research collections mined by WorldCat or the Karlsruhe portal. These include cheaply-produced, flimsy, small format religious works, self-help manuals, and school textbooks, which were often reprinted and published in multiple editions with large print-runs. For example, Barrême's *Comptes faits*, an accounting manual containing mathematical tables was produced in such numbers in the eighteenth century that it was probably to be found besides the trade ledgers in most retail shops and artisanal workshops in France. Very few editions survive in library research collections.

For this reason, many bibliometric projects are faced with an interpretative problem. Should they record only what is certain, recording titles and names as they appear to the person entering the data. Or should they try also to interpret and present what they think the data means. The first approach has the disadvantage of making it hard to derive the precise answers and figures their research questions would seem to demand. The second has the problem of adding an extra interpretative layer, in which mistakes will inevitably be made, and there are dangers of circularity, presenting hypothesis as fact. Again, the best we can do is to accept that we can only ever aspire to create a 'fuzzy snapshot' of reality; and provide research notes and tools to explain and compensate for this uncertainty. This will allow other researchers to evaluate our data and claims. Such transparency, and the ability to compensate for weaknesses in the data, are among the cardinal virtues of digital humanities research, enhancing its credibility and robustness.

7.7 Short-cuts: OCR and machine learning

A much-touted partial solution to the data entry conundrum is the possibility that Optical Character Recognition (OCR) and machine learning might offer solutions to some data-entry tasks, particularly once OCR can be applied to handwriting. At time of writing (early 2019), such a vision is still some way from being fully realised. For example, the MEDIATE project briefly dreamed of relying on OCR for their work on catalogues, drawing on technological expertise being developed in the Netherlands and elsewhere. The rich range of typefaces in their printed sources (booksellers' catalogues), the poor quality of impression in some catalogues and more generally across the hand-press era, the rich range of languages in the source material, and shortness of the text in titles and some contextual material, all proved constraints for applying OCR technology effectively without significant human intervention. Most of these issues also apply to many manuscript sources for historical bibliometric research, as would the frequent changes of clerks' hand in many such documents. As a result, OCR-based approaches remain, for the moment, experimental and aspirational—any project hoping to use them continues to need a viable 'plan B'. Eventually MEDIATE opted to work with commercial teams in the Philippines who have long specialised in the preparation of large-scale digital archives of historical material (including ECCO) and whose methods include manually correcting OCRd text.

7.8 User interfaces: Publishing and presenting historical bibliometric data

Particularly for large publicly-supported historical bibliometric projects, in an age where funders increasingly seek to support projects with wide 'impact', the issue of user interfaces and what functionalities they contain is a pressing one. Significant projects may attract a large number of potential users—the FBTEE project web interface, for example, had well over 20,000 visitors in its first five years, despite the challenge presented by its combination of English language tools containing much French-language data (e.g. most titles are in French). Most of these users will be unfamiliar with the search-language for querying the downloadable my-SQL version of the database, so have needed to use FBTEE's online interface.

As a result, modelling and researching the range of queries users may wish to make is an important part of project design. So, too, is the question of how the data should be presented—for example, as a table, spreadsheet, map, graph/chart or potentially all four. FBTEE's path-breaking solution to these issues was to provide users with a large but finite range of controlled choices in user interface and mapping tools. They could for example browse books by title, author, or taxonomic terms associated with our keyword system or the Parisian booksellers' system. Clients can be browsed by name, profession or various groupings of professions. Places can be browsed—and mapped—at the level of individual towns, provinces and states, and supra-national geographic zones. Separate functions also allow users to map, rank, or make statistical comparisons between titles, people, places keywords etc. and these queries can be calibrated down to the individual day. Finally, searches can be filtered to restrict findings by client gender, profession or place of residence; language or (putative) place of origin of editions; or by degrees of illegality. Applied carefully, such search facilities have allowed users to investigate questions such as the impact of the decrees of August 1777 and June 1783 on the STN's illegal and pirate trades with France.

Of course, mapping and visualising data is a far from neutral activity. Scale, graphical and geographical representation, the taxonomic classifications into which we organise our data and even the calibration of time can all impact how we portray and perceive our results. If space here precludes an extended discussion of these issues, they have been treated elsewhere—including with regard to the FBTEE project (McDonough, 2020; Burrows, 2018, pp.77–89). Suffice it here to observe that any historical bibliometric researcher needs to be self-aware in approaching these issues, weigh their decisions, and be prepared to play extensively with existing data before deciding how best to present their research outputs or reaching firm conclusions. This endeavour, like so many other issues discussed in this chapter, will be assisted by the development of linked data approaches.

7.9 Linked open data, methods, models and conceptual possibilities

Humanities Linked Open Data has been described within the Digital Humanities community as rather like teenage sex.[31] Everyone talks about it, but no one seems to really know how to do it. Everyone thinks everyone else is doing it, so they claim they are doing it, too, even when they are not. People who are doing it, are probably doing it alone; the first attempts are quite clumsy, often with messy results; and those who have done it, even if successfully, may find themselves considering the whole affair to be a bit of an anticlimax.

Charting cultural history

So why the excitement? One answer might be found in the thought-experiments published by Simon Burrows and his various collaborators in *Library and Information History* and elsewhere (Burrows, 2015; Burrows et al., 2016; Burrows and Ensor, 2018). They offer a vision of interoperable Linked Open Datasets organised around precisely pinpointed and quantified geo-temporally located historical bibliometric events. Such data could offer precious insights into the circulation history of a text or idea through networks of users.

Another answer may emerge from the context of successful prototypes using Linked Open Data to combine and thus enrich existing digital libraries, facilitating a new kind of research question, such as the aggregator "ElEPHãT: Early English Print in HathiTrust, a Linked Semantic Workset Prototype", which was selected as a prototyping sub-project by the HathiTrust Research Centre as part of their overarching Workset Creation for Scholarly Analysis (and Andrew W. Mellon Foundation funded project) in 2014. This project brought to the foreground object biographies such as that of a copy of the *The Game and Playe of the Chesse* by Jacobus de Cessolis. According to Terhi Nurmikko-Fuller et al's analysis, this is a single item, held by the Bodleian Library and included in the Early English Books Online project, but which was, at some (unknown) point in time, used to produce a (microfilm) copy (Nurmikko-Fuller et al., 2015; Jett et al., 2016). This copy was then printed out, bound, and found its way to the collections at the University of California, where it was digitised and included into the HathiTrust Digital Library. None of the details of this biography are captured in the metadata, but idiosyncratic features of the book's first page prove without a doubt that the same physical object is in question, albeit at different parts of the digitization and collection acquisition workflow. The possibility of discovering similar object biographies in historical examples is tantalising.

Why then, when there is such potential for information discovery, and the discovery of previously unknown complementary data, are we all not embracing this information paradigm, and producing large quantities of high quality RDF? The answer no doubt lies in the inherent flexibilities and challenges of the Linked Open Data paradigm, as well as the relative newness of the technology, which manifests as the immaturity of many tools.

The Linked Data publication paradigm challenges the academic capturing their data in two distinct ways. Firstly, the heavy intellectual lifting of representing, explicitly, the knowledge of the domain, as well as tacit knowledge and new discoveries. Secondly, the graph structure, whilst more in line with the interconnected ways in which most humanities scholars make meaning, differs radically from the tabular and relational database structures that we have been trained and conditioned to use for information storage. In the worst case, scholars might feel that extensive data representation duplication is necessary in order to represent information as Linked Data. Thirdly, the tools and technologies, which have been developed for RDF and Linked Data have not yet had the benefit of being used and developed for decades, as have, for example, relational databases. This has and can lead to unreliably set up projects with no long-term maintenance, to SPARQL endpoints that crash, and datasets that become unavailable. In summary, there are two challenges: an intellectual one, and a technological one. Add to this the still relatively small numbers of domain experts in the humanities who also have experience of the Linked Data paradigm, and the challenges of this method become clear. As in so many other areas of historical bibliometric research, major conceptual, technical and logistical challenges still need to be overcome before utopian visions of seamlessly conjoined and interoperable datasets can be realised.

Notes

1 Results of Furet's teams computational work are presented in François Furet, et al, eds. *Livre et Société dans la France du XVIIe Siècle*, 2 vols (Paris, 1965–1970) Darnton's digital experiments include the literally all-singing digital version of American Historical Society presidential address, 'An Early Information Society: News and the Media in Eighteenth-century Paris', *American Historical Review* 105 (2000), 1–35, formerly available with links to songs on the American Historical Association website at http://www.indiana.edu/~ahr/darnton/texts/p01.html; the presentation of research data and commentaries on his website 'A Literary Tour de France' at Robertdarnton.org; and his involvement in project Gutenberg.

2 See https://db-prod-bcul.unil.ch/biblos/intro.php and https://www.victoria.ac.nz/lawlit/: both resources were last consulted on 14 January 2019.
3 A beta version of this database is currently being prepared for publication at Western Sydney University as part of the Australian Research Council-funded 'Mapping Print, Charting Enlightenment' project (project number DP160103488) which supported research towards the current chapter.
4 https://www.austlit.edu.au/austlit/page/5961893 on 5 December 2018.
5 See http://socialhistory.org/en/projects/global-historical-bibliometrics and http://www.ustc.ac.uk/, both last consulted 14 January 2019.
6 See http://fbtee.uws.edu.au/stn/interface/ last consulted 14 January 2019.
7 See *The French Book Trade in Enlightenment Europe*, 2 vols (London: Bloomsbury 2018) vol. 1, *Selling Enlightenment* by Mark Curran; vol. 2, *Enlightenment Bestsellers* by Simon Burrows.
8 See http://fbtee.uws.edu.au/mpce/ last consulted 14 January 2019.
9 See http://mediate18.nl/ last consulted 14 January 2019; Daniel Mornet, 'Les enseignements des bibliothèques privées (1750–1781)', *Revue d'histoire littéraire de la France* 17 (1910), 449–96.
10 See https://www.open.ac.uk/Arts/reading/UK/ last consulted 14 January 2019.
11 See http://www.australiancommonreader.com/. Links to the database of library borrowings and diary records (currently limited to just two diarists) were not working on the date of consultation, 17 December 2018.
12 *The Atlas of Early Printing* (http://atlas.lib.uiowa.ed), *Atlas of the Rhode Island Book Trade in the 18th Century* (http://www.rihs.org/atlas/), *Mapping Colonial Americas Publishing Project* (http://cds.library.brown.edu/mapping-genres/), and *Geography of the London Ballad Trade, 1500–1700* (http://ebba.english.ucsb.edu/balladprintersite/lbp_main.html), all consulted 17 January 2019. See also Eleanor Shevlin, 'Book History and Digital Humanities: SHARP at #MLA 14 #s738', *Early Modern Online Bibliography*: EEBO, ECCO, and *Burney Collection Online*, 29 January 2014 <http://earlymodernonlinebib.wordpress.com/2014/01/27/book-history-and-digital-humanities-sharp-at-mla-14-s738/> Accessed 27 October 2014.
13 *A Literary Atlas of Europe* (http://www.literaturatlas.eu/en/2012/03/23/ein-literarischer-atlas-europas-poster/), *Mapping the Lakes: A Literary GIS* (http://www.lancaster.ac.uk/mappingthelakes/), both last consulted on 17 January 2019.
14 Cheryl Knott, 'Uncommon Knowledge: Late Eighteenth-Century American Subscription Library Collections' in Mark Towsey and Kyle Roberts, eds., *Before the Public Library: Reading, Community, and Identity in the Atlantic World, 1650–1850* (Leiden: Brill, 2018), pp. 149–73.
15 http://www.cidoc-crm.org/frbroo/home-0
16 https://www.loc.gov/standards/mods/modsrdf/
17 http://www.loc.gov/standards/mads/rdf/
18 https://www.loc.gov/bibframe/
19 http://bibliontology.com/
20 https://sparontologies.github.io/fabio/current/fabio.html
21 http://www.cidoc-crm.org/
22 Here we adhere to the convention of referring to Classes (data type categories in ontologies) with capital letters, and properties (relationships between data categories, or instance level data entities) in the lower case.
23 Shotton and Peroni have provided extensive documentation of the FaBio ontology on https://sparontologies.github.io/fabio/current/fabio.html
24 Available at https://opencitations.wordpress.com/2011/06/29/comparison-of-bibo-and-fabio/
25 For details of the interconnected ontologies that form the SPAR family see http://www.sparontologies.net/ontologies.
26 Available at https://www.loc.gov/marc/.
27 As we write, this initiative is being led by FBTEE developer Dr Michael Falk.
28 See https://viaf.org/.
29 See https://data.cerl.org/thesaurus/_search last consulted 14 January 2019. On Geonames see http://www.geonames.org/.
30 For EMLO's homepage see http://emlo.bodleian.ox.ac.uk/.
31 Although the comparison has been known in the field of Data Science for a number of years, it was first applied to Linked Data in the Humanities was by Lief Isaksen at the Digital Humanities conference in Montreal, Canada in 2017. In his presentation for the paper "Social Semantic Annotation with Recogito 2", Isaksen stated: "everyone is talking about it, no one is really doing it; many more claim to do it than actually are" and "LOD is like sex, it's totally OK to do it by yourself, but it's much more productive if you do it with someone else". The analogy has subsequently been adapted by other members of the DH community (including Terhi Nurmikko-Fuller) in various ways.

Charting cultural history

References

Books and Articles

Burrows, S. (2018). The French Book Trade in Enlightenment Europe, vol. 2, *Enlightenment Bestsellers*. London: Bloomsbury.

Burrows, S. (2015). Locating the Minister's Looted Books: From Provenance and Library Histories to the Digital Reconstruction of Print Culture'. *Library and Information History*, *31*, 1–17.

Burrows, S., & Ensor, J. (2018). 'Afterword: The future of FBTEE – Towards a Digital History of the Book' in Burrows, *Enlightenment Bestsellers*, pp. 175–80.

Burrows, S., Ensor, J., Heningsgaard, P., and Hiribarren, V. (2016). 'Mapping Print, Connecting Cultures'. *Library and Information History*, *32*, 259–271.

Burrows, S. and Roe, G. (Eds.). (2020). *Digitizing Enlightenment*. Liverpool, Oxford Studies in Enlightenment.

Curran, M. (2018). *The French Book Trade in Enlightenment Europe*, 2 vols (London: Bloomsbury 2018) vol. 1, *Selling Enlightenment*.

Darnton, R. (2000). An Early Information Society: News and the Media in Eighteenth-century Paris. *American Historical Review*, *105*, 1–35.

Darnton, R. (1996). *The Forbidden Best-Sellers of Pre-Revolutionary France*. London and New York: Norton

Darnton, R. (2012). Review of 'The French Book Trade in Enlightenment Europe, 1769–1794'. '*Reviews in History*' at http://www.history.ac.uk/reviews/review/1355

Edwards, E. (1859). *Memoirs of Libraries: Including a Handbook of Library Economy*, 2 vols. London: Trübner.

François, F. et al. (Eds.). (1965–1970). *Livre et Société dans la France du XVIIIᵉ Siècle*, 2 vols. Paris.

Herubel, J.-P.V.M. (1999). Historical Bibliometrics: Its Purpose and Significance to the History of Disciplines. *Libraries & Culture*, *34*, 380–88.

Jett, J., Nurmikko-Fuller, T., Cole, T.W., Page, K.R., & Downie, J.S. (2016). 'Enhancing scholarly use of digital libraries: A comparative survey and review of bibliographic metadata ontologies'. *Proceedings of the 16th ACM/IEEE-CS on Joint Conference on Digital Libraries* (pp. 35–44). ACM.

Knott, C. (2018). Uncommon Knowledge: Late Eighteenth-Century American Subscription Library Collections. In Towsey, M. & Roberts, K. (Eds.), *Before the Public Library: Reading, Community, and Identity in the Atlantic World, 1650-1850* (pp. 149–73). Leiden: Brill.

McDonough, K. (2020). 'Putting the Eighteenth Century on the Map: French Geospatial Data for Digital Humanities Research'. pp. 277–303. In Burrows, S. and Roe, G., (Eds.), *Digitizing Enlightenment*. Liverpool: Oxford Studies in Enlightenment.

Montoya, A. (2020). "Shifting Perspectives and Moving Targets: From Conceptual Vistas to Bits of Data in the First Year of the MEDIATE Project' pp. 195-218. In Burrows, S. and Roe, G., (Eds.), *Digitizing Enlightenment*. Liverpool: Oxford Studies in Enlightenment.

Mornet, Daniel. (1910). 'Les enseignements des bibliothèques privées (1750–1781)'. *Revue d'histoire littéraire de la France* *17*, 449–96.

Nurmikko-Fuller, T., K. R. Page, P. Willcox, J Jett, C. Maden and T. Cole & J. S. Downie. (2015). Building complex research collections in digital libraries: A survey of ontology implications. *Proceedings of the 15th ACM/IEEE-CS Joint Conference on Digital Libraries*, pp. 169–72. ACM

Nurmikko-Fuller, T., J. Jett, T.W. Cole, C. Maden, K. R. Page & J. S. Downie. (2016). *A Comparative Analysis of Bibliographic Ontologies: Implications for Digital Humanities*, pp. 639–42. DH.

Pettegree, A. (2016). The Legion of the Lost. Recovering the Lost Books of Early Modern Europe. In Flavia Bruni and Andrew Pettegree, (Eds.), *Lost Books. Reconstructing the Print World of Pre-Industrial Europe* (pp.1–27). Leiden: Brill.

Shevlin, E. (2014). Book History and Digital Humanities: SHARP at #MLA 14 #s738'. *Early Modern Online Bibliography: EEBO, ECCO, and Burney Collection Online*, 29 January 2014 <http://earlymodernonlinebib. wordpress.com/2014/01/27/book-history-and-digital-humanities-sharp-at-mla-14-s738/>.

St Clair, W. (2004). *The Reading Nation in the Romantic Period*. Cambridge: C.U.P.

Takats, S. (2020). Beyond digitizing Enlightenment 375-83. In Burrows, S. & Roe, G. (Eds.), *Digitizing Enlightenment*. Liverpool: Oxford Studies in the Enlightenment.

Tillett, B. (2005). What is FRBR: A Conceptual Model for the Bibliographic Universe. *The Australian Library Journal*, *54*, 24–30.

Websites

http://atlas.lib.uiowa.edu
http://bibliontology.com/
http://cds.library.brown.edu/mapping-genres/

http://ebba.english.ucsb.edu/balladprintersite/lbp_main.html
http://emlo.bodleian.ox.ac.uk/
http://fbtee.uws.edu.au/mpce/
http://fbtee.uws.edu.au/stn/interface/
http://mediate18.nl/
http://robertdarnton.org/
http://socialhistory.org/en/projects/global-historical-bibliometrics
http://www.australiancommonreader.com/
http://www.cidoc-crm.org/
http://www.cidoc-crm.org/frbroo/home-0
http://www.geonames.org/
http://www.literaturatlas.eu/en/2012/03/23/ein-literarischer-atlas-europas-poster/   (http://www.lancaster.ac.uk/
    mappingthelakes/
http://www.loc.gov/standards/mads/rdf/
http://www.rihs.org/atlas/
http://www.sparontologies.net/ontologies
http://www.ustc.ac.uk/
https://data.cerl.org/thesaurus/_search
https://db-prod-bcul.unil.ch/biblos/intro.php
https://sparontologies.github.io/fabio/current/fabio.html
https://viaf.org/
https://www.austlit.edu.au/austlit/page/5961893
https://www.loc.gov/bibframe/
https://www.loc.gov/marc/
https://www.loc.gov/standards/mods/modsrdf/
https://www.open.ac.uk/Arts/reading/UK/
https://www.victoria.ac.nz/lawlit/

8

MANAGE YOUR DATA

Information management strategies for DH practitioners

Kristen Schuster and Vanessa Reyes

8.1 Introduction

Information is everything we deal with that informs us about events, problems, actions, and people (Etzel and Thomas, 1996). Information is essential if we are to perform effectively as individuals and as professionals. Management is the aspect of information that refers to the development of a strategy to handle that information. Without management, information just remains where it was created or last placed. Information management, therefore, is the practice of acquiring, creating, storing, organizing, maintaining and retrieving, information needed. Jan Aidemark (2009) states that knowledge management scholarship focuses on the organization of information in cognitive and theoretical ways.

Knowledge management involves the process of creating, sharing, using and managing the knowledge and information of an organization. In Information Organization research, studies are also conducted in the practical ways that can give insight into how information organization affects individual lives. The present glimpse into information management may offer insights into why information organization is necessary. If archivists, librarians, and curators understand how information is organized and stored, then perhaps they may be able to suggest strategies for the preservation of information for library and archives users.

To better understand the relationship between information management theory and practice, there needs to be an understanding of the history and rich nature of information organization. According to Vannevar Bush (1945):

> Science has provided the swiftest communication between individuals; it has provided a record of ideas and has enabled man to manipulate and to make extracts from that record so, that knowledge evolves and endures throughout the life of a race rather than that of an individual (p.1).

Bush's research suggested new ways of storing information. He considered a future device for users that would bring together private files stored in the way a library would store them. Of course, even Bush could not anticipate the extent to which information would continue to grow. In 1965 Gordon E. Moore's postulated exponential growth in the number of transistor and resistor elements on computer chips. They had been doubling roughly every year—and Moore expected that these increases would continue for the next ten years. According to Poeter (2015):

> It was a prediction that ended up extending far past its first decade. And what later became known as "Moore's Law" would prove to be perhaps the most reliable and enduring guide to the pace of technological advance in not just the semiconductor business, but in the computing industry. (p.12)

From the perspective of information management, Lansdale (1988) noted that these studies sparked an interest in concern for how information is created and kept. It is known that information intuitions have various organization processes for filing a document, storing a document, and disposing of it. This same ideal can be reflected upon information organizations that are making choices that fall into a pattern of organization such as Lansdale explains this process is one that information professionals understand as well and use regularly in their day-to-day activities while fulfilling user's information needs.

Just as technology has rapidly changed, so has research in the field of archival and information studies. There have been several advances in the technologies of information management, particularly those that include tools for managing information. The interest in information management research has expanded during the last three decades. Researchers have widened the focus of inquiry from management of software tools and information management and retrieval processes, to the digital curation of diverse types of information (Huvila, 2015, p.1). Forming relationships with the people who are constantly creating and managing information will initiate conversations and help gain awareness of the many issues that lead to the loss of digital heritage.

8.2 Terminology we can use while managing DH research

There are a myriad methods for organizing and curating information and, consequently, we can use many different terms we can use to describe our decisions and practices. So, instead of viewing these terms as neutral or universally applicable it is important to explore and contextualize disciplinary nuances in meaning. By exploring and contextualizing disciplinary nuances in meaning, researchers and practitioners can clarify and share their approaches to organizing and curating information. This is particularly important in interdisciplinary fields DH, where scholars share similar interests but design and conduct research from different perspectives, have different goals and produce diverse research outputs. So, although DH scholars might use or create similar types of digital objects and data, they have diverse approaches for arranging, describing, curating and managing digital objects and data. What follows is an introductory description of different terms and concepts researchers and practitioners can use describe their methods and strategies for collecting, organizational and curating data. As practising library and information science professionals our discussion does reflect a certain disciplinary bias; however, this bias is not without certain benefits. We draw on a range of well-established theories that bring together social science and humanities interests in the relationship(s) between information, knowledge and culture, which reflects the interdisciplinary and diverse technical processes involved in contemporary DH practice and research.

8.3 Terminology and context

Libraries, museums and archives endeavor to remain on the forefront of digitization initiatives (Sula, 2013; Green & Courtney, 2015, Sagner Buurma & Tione Levine, 2016), through these efforts librarians and archivists have developed particular disciplinary perspectives on methods for preserving, sharing and curating digital content (Sundt, 2013; Conway, 2015; Liu, 2016). Beyond simply serving as repositories for analog collections and manpower for creating digital assets, librarians and archivists have developed strategies to synthesize digitization workflows with digital preservation and DH initiatives (Dalbello, 2011; St. Jean et al., 2011; Senchyne, 2016). Although libraries, museums and archives have different approaches to organizing, curating and providing access to their collections, they do so by drawing on a shared set information science practices and methods for cataloguing and managing content—which is to say, for creating and maintaining metadata and databases (Given & McTavish, 2010; Corrado & Jaffe, 2017 Feinberg, 2017). While metadata and databases have become almost colloquial concepts in research, there are nuances and complexities to disciplinary understandings of what constitutes metadata, and the function of a database

Manage your data

(Liew, 2016: Terras, 2015). Foundational and contextual knowledge about information science strategies for discussing metadata and databases offers researchers opportunities to improve their methodological approaches to planning data collection, analysis, reporting and preservation procedures.

While there are certainly data and digital asset management practices and practitioners that fall outside the scope of information science, as a discipline, information scientists work in sectors and institutions that provide access to objects and infrastructures necessary for humanities and DH work. As an umbrella term then, information science encompasses a range of theoretical, practical and technical work. Our broad overview of four sub-disciplines offers a means for researchers to use precise language to communicate their disciplinary and project approaches to creating, using and sharing a preserving data.

8.3.1 Knowledge organization

Broadly speaking, knowledge organization brings together theories and practices for classifying and indexing information (Taylor, et al., 2017). More than simply tagging and describing content, knowledge organization explores the social and cultural processes that produce certain attitudes and approaches to categorizing and classifying information. The practice of knowledge organization, ties into knowledge management which is the function of learning orientation, knowledge sharing, organizational memory and knowledge reuse. Knowledge management can aid with creating value strengthened by developing relationships with stakeholders. Information organizations can manage social capital through knowledge management processes including:

1. Learning orientation,
2. Knowledge sharing,
3. Organizational memory
4. Knowledge reuse which ties into information management, digital curation and research data management.

There is a great deal of research that can help us understand knowledge organization as a social and technical practice. Much of Geoffrey Bowker's work critiques frameworks and practices used to produce and maintain standards for organizing and managing information. Much of Bowker's work (e.g. *Sorting Things* co-authored with Susan Leigh Star, and *Between Meaning and Machine* co-authored with David Ribes) requires readers to pause and analyse their approach(es) to organizing information—in both digital and analog formats. Bowker and his co-authors explore the implications these choices have on users' understandings of information. A key claim in his work is that information is a socially constructed and mediated artifact. He guides the reader towards justifying and accepting this adoption through analyses and discussions of how personal, social and cultural contexts can, and should, change to reflect needs and interests.

While Bowker's work does not specifically address the technical facets of knowledge representation, it does shed light on library and information sciences' interest in problematizing assumptions about institutional practices and traditions. Elaine Svenonious' work, however, does address the technical practices library and information scientists engage in while making decisions about how they classify and represent information. Her work (e.g. *The Intellectual Foundation of Information Organization* and *Design of Controlled Vocabularies*) contextualizes the role(s) technology play in conceptualizations of information organization practices. She draws careful connections between these decision-making processes effect practices across cultural heritage institutions—libraries in particular.

Both Bowker and Svenonious draw our attention to the potential for change in understandings of information, and the ways changes require critical engagement by information professionals. One could argue that these critical engagements and reflective practices allow us to organize and manage knowledge.

8.3.2 Information management

While knowledge organization explores the social and cultural implications of classification and categorization, information management contextualizes and evaluates methods and practices used to implement classification and categorization schemes. This can entail organizational, professional and disciplinary approaches, and often involves analyzing intersections between technical and professional practices (e.g. cataloguing and indexing). Christine Borgman provides us with a range of research that demonstrates how knowledge representation affect approaches to information management. As an active researcher (e.g. *From Gutenberg to the Global Information Infrastructure* and *Big Data, Little Data, No Data: Scholarship in the Networked World*), she demonstrates the roles data management can play in promoting new conceptualizations of knowledge. A key component of her findings and theories requires researchers and practitioners to recognize the potential benefits and challenges of interdisciplinarity. Her work requires that we consider the infrastructures and frameworks we (meaning researchers and practitioners) might use to conceptualize definitions of data *and* the technologies we use to preserve these data.

Information Management fits into the evolution of archival and preservation research because archiving practices share similar functions, which are ongoing maintenance and eventual archiving (storing) and deletion. However, as Gilliland-Swetland (2000) articulates, the GLAM sector needs continue investing in cross-institutional efforts to make their records publicly accessible and useable. Not in the least because it will provide wider access to heritage resources and objects regardless of format.

8.3.3 Digital curation

Practices and frameworks promoting preservation for the sake of reuse has emerged as an important area of practice in research across the humanities and social sciences. These initiatives have helped promote the concept and practice of digital curation, which has become a catch-all concept that covers a range of theories and practices relating to the creation, use, storage and retrieval and reuse of digital objects. Curation implies maintaining and enhancing value (Bashkar, 2017), which requires balancing two potentially competing interests. Maintenance implies a preservation of authenticity, while enhancement implies adding and/or expanding meaning, content and visibility. Frameworks and models can provide us with the means to balance these potentially competing demands. The DCC Curation Lifecycle Model, first described in Higgins, 2008 (see Figure 8.1), is a particularly influential model. While her framework is not without its limitations (see Constantopoulos et al., 2009), it is a foundational set of guidelines for identifying the processes involved in describing the creation, description, maintenance, storage, exchange and disposal of data. Oliver and Harvey (2016) analyze and contextualize the roles Higgins' model can play in promoting interdisciplinary endeavors to create, maintain and share data.

8.3.4 Research data management

As a discipline and as a practice, research data management (RDM) brings together institutional and disciplinary best practices with and legal requirements for handling research data. Closely related to digital curation, RDM introduces new strands research that focus specifically on identifying methods for defining data and evaluating infrastructures that facilitate the collection and distribution of research during *and* after a project's completion. There is a keen emphasis on institutional and researcher collaboration, which offers opportunities for RDM across academic and practitioner disciplines. While this flexibility presents opportunities for collaboration and cost sharing, it also leaves room for imprecisions and confusion. Identifying research practices and workflows can help us understand functions and transformations in data, or more succinctly, research data lifecycles. Humphrey (2006) presents a useful model for mapping stages of research onto the effects methodological approaches and technological processes will have on data (Figure 8.2).

Manage your data

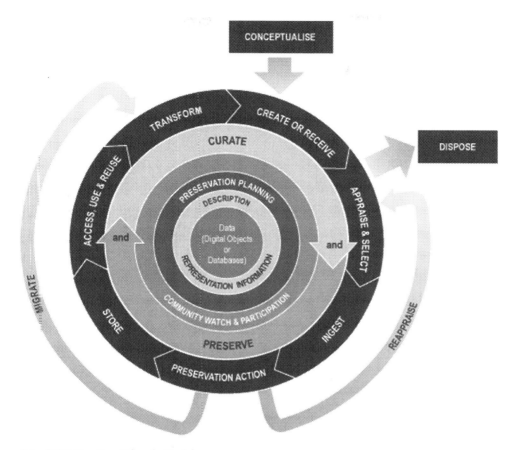

Figure 8.1 DCC Curation Lifecycle Model

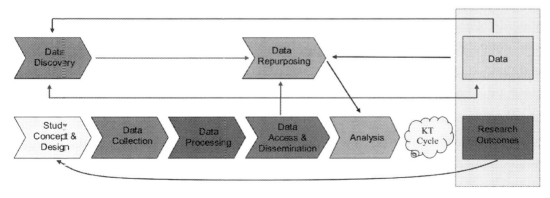

Figure 8.2 Humphrey's e-Science Data Management Model

Humphrey's model is agnostic in the sense it does not prescribe a specific methodology, infrastructure or discipline for working with data. This makes it suitable for interdisciplinary and collaborative projects and repositories. Of the many theories and frameworks that we could discuss, two are potentially of the greatest interest to DH: Crowdsourcing and Open Online Communities (OOCs). Crowdsourcing, at its core, is a combination of technical and institutional frameworks that facilitate user engagement with content (Dunn & Hedges, 2014; Owens, 2014). For digital humanists this opens up sources of practitioner, academic and general user engagement with multiple types of content in a variety of digital formats (Ridge, 2014). While crowdsourcing has drawn much attention in DH, OOCs remain understudied. OOCs play a greater role in data science and computer science communities, but like crowdsourcing, offer unique opportunities for re-presenting information to dedicated *and* new groups of users (Goggins et al., 2017).

8.4 Data management, research practices and research methods

Research methods, ideally, enhance the validity and reliability of research data. This is a rather technical way of saying that methods facilitate scholarly communication because they enable the management and exchange of knowledge. We maintain that in a multidisciplinary field like DH researchers will benefit from sharing a robust vocabulary for describing different approaches to managing, curating and preserving digital objects and data.

We've introduced terms, theories and practices that bridge humanities and social science approaches to creating, using and sharing digital and digitized objects. Contextualizing terms and introducing foundational theories presents opportunities to start using more precise descriptions of organizational and information needs, which, we feel, is fundamental to designing research methods and sustaining research projects. Beyond this though, it is possible to conceptualize having a foundational knowledge of multiple disciplinary practices enhances the potential for collaboration and co-production of digital content, which is a core and lasting goal in DH. Having a foundational knowledge of disciplinary approaches to describing information, data and curation facilitates interdisciplinary practices in several ways. We feel that researchers with the ability to discuss information, knowledge and data across disciplines are able to:

1. Adapt terminology to improve practices: Building budgets and setting goals through workflows that accommodate particular needs, interests and practices.
2. Frame terminology as a tool for building workflows: Using terminology to evaluate data management and IT infrastructures.
3. Share knowledge through information management: Drilling down and identifying areas for collaboration, delegation and outsourcing.

In the following sections we provide examples to support our claims. Our discussion of practitioner recommendations and experiences will explore the flexibility required to communicate research data management practices and highlight the roles a shared vocabulary can play in building partnerships between information professionals, DH practitioners and academics.

8.5 Facilitating communication and collaboration

In the previous sections, we presented our understanding of how information professionals engage with information management and digital curation and how they translate this work into DH methods. To contextualize and enhance our descriptions, we explored two questions by reaching out to colleagues and professional networks:

1. What methods do you use to discuss data management with your community of practice and/or clients?
2. What strategies do you use to interpret your colleague/clients' descriptions of data and data management practices?

Six people responded to our questions. Three respondents worked in academic library contexts and supported researchers across their faculties, two respondents worked as data management specialists for cultural heritage collections and one respondent coordinated research and development for a digital humanities lab. Respondents were from various parts of the world: The Netherlands, Australia, the United States, Spain and the United Kingdom. While this is a small sample and we can't draw any broad conclusions, we *can* use responses to highlight useful practices that facilitate clearer and more effective communication between information professionals and DH practitioners, and we have organized our summary of responses using three themes: Engaging with colleagues and clients; ongoing communication and collaboration; and sustaining research and improving practice.

8.5.1 Engaging with colleagues and clients

Our respondents all disclosed that their work requires negotiating a broad range of research methods and data management practices, which were discussed as frameworks for negotiating types of digital methods and formats researchers were aware of and comfortable using. Expanding on current practices and general knowledge was also a key theme in responses to our first question, and respondents generally shared the questions they asked their colleagues or clients during meetings. King's Digital Lab[1] provided two questions that reflect the general recommendations expressed in the other five responses:

1. What kind of data (type, format and size) are you expecting to create and/or process in your project or research?
2. Where are the datasets hosted if they already exist or where are you expecting to host them, and for how long?"

The first question creates opportunities to connect types of data to research methods, and the second question requires reflection and clarification on the particular preservation and curation practices involved in a research project. Instead of presenting plans and outlining best practices, it would seem more effective to ask questions and learning about research practices. Echoing this point, a colleague working in an Australian academic library stated that "researchers don't know enough about data management practices to describe [them] to me – I have to get the answers from them through questioning (no disrespect to my researcher!)" Understanding that information professionals and DH practitioners are prepared to engage in discussion about data management and digital curation highlights the need to invest in learning from one another and building a shared vocabulary to discuss information management practices.

8.5.2 Ongoing communication and collaboration

Since there is no one-size-fits-all DH project or DH practice, we reached out to a diverse range of scholars and practitioners. The types of projects and services described in responses extended from research library support for arts and humanities to classification and organization practices for a museum collection. Discussing types of practices and types of information revealed that identifying client/colleague/researcher needs required ongoing efforts by information professionals. By asking questions and engaging in conversations, we initiated conversations about data management and clarified approaches to curating, preserving and managing data. This being said, the process of clarifying approaches and building a shared vocabulary takes time and effort. One participant, a project manager at the Fundación Juan March, shared that

> Most of our methods are iterative and incremental. Thus, before we go and talk to our "clients" we generate quick prototypes that we can use to start discussing their requirements. Usually, this leads to a set of finer requirements that then get implemented and reviewed again. We have done this when creating digital collections/repositories using mockup tools that help us designing dummy interfaces" (Martinez Uribe, Fundación Juan March).

The iterative process used at the Fundación reflects the need to develop strategies that facilitate communication and, most importantly, minimize misunderstandings. Similarly, a colleague working in an American academic research library shared that building a shared vocabulary posed significant challenges. At the same time though, she reiterated that ongoing discussions presented opportunities for her to share her professional expertise and build up a shared vocabulary. She states that she

> "usually slip[s] a few words describing what I mean by preserving/archiving up front in the conversation to try to steer things that direction. If they're [the researcher] still getting conflated, asking questions can help clarify what each party thinks is being discussed before we wind up talking past one another."

8.5.3 Sustaining research, improving practice

Because data management and digital curation are iterative processes, it is important to develop sustainable practices—and not just for researchers. It is important to develop channels of communication between researchers/practitioners and information professionals. While discussing strategies and practices with colleagues, daily interactions were important to building mutual understandings of data management. Sarah Gillis, the associate registrar for collections documentation at the Worcester Art Museum (Worcester Massachusetts, United States) neatly expressed this: "Daily, I encounter different scenarios where I need to translate my lexicon for data management for collegial consumption, as well as talk through and guide my colleagues about what they think is data management versus what is more effective for their needs." Her regular conversations offer opportunities to connect with colleagues, learn their practices and to share her own expertise in more casual (but still professional) ways. This kind of slow, steady and shared communication is a process that reflects the need for sharing understandings data management facilitate collaboration and innovation, which encapsulates the spirit of DH.

8.6 Analysis

DH methods take shape in different ways throughout academic institutions. In our findings we noticed that practitioners are found in a broad range of departments, programs, technology groups, and libraries. According to the (2017; ECAR) DH comprises of faculty in programs formally designated as DH, faculty who identify as DH scholars and work in traditional departments and scholars who are doing work that could be considered DH but who may not self-identify as digital humanists. While some DH professionals cater to specialized groups of users, most data managers are working indirectly with the daily practices of data management and education. In an effort to find adoptable methods for data management practitioners, we reached out to colleagues through the email list serves of the International Federation of Library Associations and Institutions, to help us build a better understanding of what data managers are doing and what methods are being followed throughout the world. It is common to experience DH needs ranging from standard research computing services offered by campus IT; to those whom are made available by humanities scholars. Digital humanities practices vary fully within the institution and practice of where it takes place.

We learned that information professionals conduct similar activities when it comes to data management practices; some of which include actively being of assistance during their client's data management process. However, there are levels of involvement that data managers maintain, specifically when it comes to the decision-making process. There is an overall effort to serve as a point of reference but keep to the boundaries that are commonplace to prevent influencing data outcomes; intentionally these professionals are seemingly trying to be their client's point of reference throughout the evolutionary process of their data management process.

Manage your data

An excellent example of avoiding being influencers as data managers, but instead taking on the role of a trusty advisor comes from the Universiteit Twente, a public research university located in Enschede, the Netherlands. The University Library shared that it handles the data management process primarily with PhD candidates. The data management supervisors organize research seminars, during which they work with candidates throughout their data management process all the while ensuring not to tamper with or obstruct the candidate's research process. This particular organization does not interpret the client's descriptions of data management because their primary focus is on the overall metadata creation process so that the research can be reproduced.

In Contrast, the Fundación Juan March (www.march.es)—a non-profit organization founded in 1955 devoted to the promotion of arts, culture and science—reached out to our call about its practices. We found that the way data management is discussed among this community of practice is mostly iterative and incremental. Thus, before the institution convenes with their "clients" they generate quick prototypes that can be used to start discussing their client's requirements. This is a great approach, one that caters to the client's methods and content. The organization has found that this method leads to creating a set of finer requirements that then get implemented and reviewed—again, catering to the client's methods. The Fundación Juan March has done this when creating digital collections/repositories using mockup tools which in the end help among many areas, particularly in data management interface design.

When it comes to data management practices and strategies librarians at Juan March shared that they try to listen to their client's practices and needs first of all. This is crucial, as sometimes their needs are somehow disconnected from their data practices. For instance, the institution shares that from experience they may need to frequently analyse visitor's data but, because they collect and store data in different excel files it can be difficult to identify or extrapolate trends from it. Based on this, we learned that it is not a lack of data that prevents collaboration or information sharing; instead, emerging or tacit data management practices effect how much data can be shared.

Our respondent from the University in Southern Australia shared that they assist their clients with traditional literature searches, literature reviews, and most recently have become focused on research data management by addressing with their clients the requirements of data management practices. Rather than addressing the benefits of making research data open, accessible and findable in order to be reused, these professionals "plant the seed" about the benefits of making data open.

Open Data as defined by the Open Data Handbook, is data that can be freely used, re-used and redistributed by anyone—subject only, at most, to the requirement to attribute and share alike.[2] Moreover, Open Data is a entire topic related to the idea that some data should be freely available for all to use and re-publish as they wish, without restrictions from copyright patents. Although this idea is now being considered by clients wanting to publish their findings, there have been some linked issues with instructional intellectual property and legal issues associated with these adopted practices that is beyond the scope of this chapter.

One of the participants who reached out to us shared that when it comes to working with colleagues on the various facets of data management there will be challenges associated with the kinds of data that they have. In this case, one of the respondents works with physical object files in a museum's permanent collection (as well as temporary works, such as items on loan) located in the New England region of the United States. This respondent reported that they used to have an antiquated filing system based on the geography of the object's origin, then the classification. Here the culture/creator of the work may no longer be alive or involved with the content to make changes and decisions. This makes for a challenging process when this or any institution attempts to retrieve files, as files can go missing without the appropriate care or plan. This example lets us know that there are known challenges when it comes to working with clients and achieving the process of data management.

Information professionals strive to be educators, innovators and savers of data. The process becomes much more difficult as sometimes data managers have to deal with managing data without the creators being present. In the event that creators are not present, coming up with plans that work as a universal fit is a challenge because—unfortunately—that is not the way data management works. Data differs when it comes to how it is created and kept. The nature of data can be broken down into categories, yet even then they may not fit. Some basic reporting data categories include: transactional, master, reference, and metadata. Reporting data is that related to enterprise and intended for transactional purposes. Transactional data is best described as business type related to events that involve buying and selling. Master data refers to data related to things, items and people. Reference data is used to describe data that can be organized by a number system; for example, information institution resources are organized using classification systems that include letters, patterns, numbers and subject headings.

Finally, there is metadata, a descriptor of other data about that particular datum. This includes the data size, resolution, author information, creation information, and so on. This is great area to explore while learning what DH practitioners do when managing data. Most practitioners deal with educating their clients about the importance of metadata, and for many clients it is all quite new to them. Demonstrating to clients how the various types of data they manage (e.g. interview transcripts in word docs; recorded interviews in mp3 format; photographs etc.) affect storage requirements and options creates space and opportunities to discuss details about data sets and, in the long term, encourage researchers to proactively manage their own data before sharing it or depositing it in an institutional repository. As one of our participants mentions "it is up to me to describe it." Having these categories allows professionals to get a better scope of the types of data their clients are creating and managing and can be useful when creating a plan towards organizing their data.

8.7 Recommendations for professionals

How can practitioners describe the overall process of data management? This question is especially important because not every researcher knows the process. Here are a few recommendations that we gathered from our respondents and our own experiences with data management:

- Whether practitioners work directly or indirectly with the data management process it is important to note that when it comes to discussing data management, it becomes a one to one process where practitioners listen to their clients' needs and coordinate a plan that will fit their management style.
- Pay attention to your client's needs, ask them questions about what they wish to accomplish and why they think it is important that they manage their data.
- The client must first identify for themselves that their data has value, and thus proceed with a plan that suits the purpose of the data and how the data is intended to be used and by whom.
- As mentioned, there is no one-size-fits-all approach to data management. The process varies, depending on the type of data and the client's data use.
- In order to successfully carry out the data management process, it all starts out with coming up with a data management strategy: one that supports the data created, stored and managed by the client.
- Administer a data management process, which includes the process for which the client will ensure accessibility, reliability and adequate storage for uninterrupted future access.
- Focus on creating a hands-on strategy to improve the quality of the client's data. This is done by working closely with the client and being attentive to the client's needs.
- Establish an approach on normalizing data which is an important task. Doing so reduces data redundancy and without this consideration it is difficult to store digital objects.
- Carrying out the normalization process is the key to data consistency and allows for the practitioner to have a better handle of the client's data in the case that the client decides to store all related data items together, which is essential to the data management process.
- Discuss data storage—this is a very important step in bringing your client's data management plan to fruition.

Manage your data

- Establish intellectual property rights and go over ethics and privacy. These are important elements, especially since they involve securing the client's data and overall safety and security of their intellectual property as it pertains to the institutional policies.

In interdisciplinary and interdepartmental contexts like foresight and strategic planning committees, training events, and grant workshops it is important to build rapport and common ground. We have based our recommendations on findings from a range of conversations and we think that, when organized into recommendations, they can help researchers and practitioners co-create talking points and build appropriate and sustainable agendas and action items. Moulding these strategies to in-house practices and standards for data management is achieved by working closely with the client and being attentive to the client's needs. Practitioners can achieve this by ensuring that the data management strategy that is being created fully supports all data types stored in-house and by their clients. We hope that, in addressing these areas this chapter presents the point of view of several unique information institutions and that in learning their methods, practitioners can adopt new ways to manage research data.

Notes

1 King's Digital Lab is a consultancy service based at King's College London. Lab members provide a range of research and technical support for DH practitioners.
2 Link to the Open Data Handbook: https://opendatahandbook.org/guide/en/what-is-open-data/

References

Bashkar, M. (2017). Curation: *The Power of Selection in a World of Excess*. London: Piatkus

Borgman, C. (2003) *From Gutenberg to the global information structure: Access to information in the networked world*. Cambridge, MA: MIT Press.

Borgman, C. (2016). *Big data, little data, no data: Scholarship in the networked world*. Cambridge, MA: MIT Press.

Bowker, G. & Starr, S. (2000). *Sorting things out: Classification and its consequences (inside technology)*. Cambridge, MA: MIT Press.

Bush, V. (1945). As we may think. *The Atlantic, 176*(1) pp. 101–108

Constantopoulos, P., Dallas, C., Androutsopoulos, I., Angelis, S. Deligiannakis, A., Gavrilis, D. …Papatheodorou, C. (2009). DCC & U: An extended digital curation lifecycle model. *The International Journal of Digital Curation, 4*(1), 34–45. http://doi.org/10.2218/ijdc.v4i1.76

Conway, P. (2015). Digital transformations and the archival nature of surrogates. *Archival Science, 15*(1), 51–69. http://doi.org/10.1007/s10502-014-9219-z

Corrado, E. M., & Jaffe, R. (2017). Access's unsung hero: The [impending] rise of embedded Metadata. *International Information and Library Review, 49*(2), 124–130. http://doi.org/10.1080/10572317.2017.1314142

Dalbello, M. (2011). A genealogy of digital humanities. *Journal of Documentation, 67*(3), 480–506. http://doi.org/10.1108/00220411111124550

Dunn, S. & Hedges, M. (2014). How the Crowd Can Surprise Us: Humanities Crowdsourcing and the Creation of Knowledge. In M. Ridge (Ed.), *Crowdsourcing our Cultural Heritage* (231–246). New York, NY: Ashgate

ECAR Working Group (2017). Building capacity for digital humanities: A framework for institutional planning.

Etzel B., Thomas P. (1996) Personal information management. In: *Personal Information Management*. Palgrave, London

Feinberg, M. (2017). Reading databases: slow information interactions beyond the retrieval paradigm. *Journal of Documentation, 73*(2), 336–356. http://doi.org/10.1108/JD-03-2016-0030

Gilliland-Swetland, A. (2000), "Enduring Paradigm, New Opportunities: The Value of the Archival Perspective in the Digital Environment", *Library Hi Tech*, Vol. 18 No. 4, pp. 383–386. https://doi.org/10.1108/lht.2000.18.4.383.4

Given, Lisa M.; McTavish, L. (2010). What's old is new again: The reconvergence of libraries, archives and museums in the digital age. *Library Quarterly, 80*(1), 7–32.

Goggins, S., Million, A. J., Link, G., Germonprez, M., & Schuster, K. (2017). The Open Community Data Exchange: Advancing Data Sharing and Discovery in Open Online Community Science. In Matei, S., Jullien, N., & Goggins, S. (Eds.), *Big Data Factories: Collaborative Approaches* (pp. 23–36). Cham, Switzerland: Springer Nature.

Green, H. E., & Courtney, A. (2015). Beyond the scanned image: A needs assessment of scholarly users of digital collections. *College & Research Libraries, 76*(5), 690–707. http://doi.org/10.5860/crl.76.5.690

Higgins, S. (2008). The DCC curation lifecycle model. *International Journal of Digital Curation 3*(1), 134–140

Humphrey, C. (2006). e-Science and the Life Cycle of Research, 3. http://doi.org/https://doi.org/10.7939/R3NR4V

Huvila, I. (2015), "The unbearable lightness of participating? Revisiting the discourses of "participation" in archival literature", *Journal of Documentation*, Vol. 71 No. 2, pp. 358–386. https://doi.org/10.1108/JD-01-2014-0012

Lansdale, M. (1988). The psychology of personal information management. *Applied Ergonomics, 19*(1), 55–66. https://doi.org/10.1016/0003-6870(88)90199-8

Liew, Chern L.; Cheetham, F. (2016). Participatory culture in memory institutions: Of diversity, ethics and trust? *D-Lib, 22*(7/8), 12–17. http://doi.org/10.1045/july2016

Liu, A. (2016). N+1: A Plea for Cross-Domain Data in the Digital Humanities. In M.K. Gold & L.F. Klein, (Eds.), *Debates in the Digital Humanities 2016* (pp. 559–568). Minneapolis: University of Minnesota Press.

Moore, G. (1965). Cramming more components onto integrated circuits. *Electronics, 38(8). Retrieved from* https://newsroom.intel.com/wp-content/uploads/sites/11/2018/05/moores-law-electronics.pdf

Oliver, G & Harvey, R. (2016). *Digital Curation.* Facet Publishing: London

Owens, T. (2014). Making Crowdsourcing Compatible with the Missions and Values of Cultural Heritage Organizations. In M. Ridge (Ed.), *Crowdsourcing Our Cultural Heritage* (269–280). New York, NY: Ashgate

Poeter, D. (2015). How Moore's Law changed history (and your smart phone). *PC Magazine. Retrieved from* https://uk.pcmag.com/cpus-components/41195/how-moores-law-changed-history-and-your-smartphone

Ribes, D. & Bowker, G. (2009). Between meaning and machine: Learning to represent the knowledge or communities. *Information ad Organization, 19*(4) pp. 199–217.

Ridge. M. (2014). Crowdsourcing Our Cultural Heritage: Introduction. In M. Ridge (Ed.), *Crowdsourcing Our Cultural Heritage* (1–16). New York, NY: Ashgate

Sagner Buurma, R., & Tione, L.A. (2016). The Sympathetic Research Imagination: Digital Humanities and the Liberal Arts. In M.K. Gold & L.F. Klein, (Eds.), *Debates in the Digital Humanities 2016* (pp. 274–279). Minneapolis: University of Minnesota Press

Senchyne, J. (2016). Between Knowledge and Metaknowledge: Shifting Disciplinary Borders in Digital Humanities and Library and Information Studies. In In M.K. Gold & L.F. Klein, (Eds.), *Debates in the Digital Humanities 2016s* (pp. 368–376). Minneapolis: University of Minnesota Press.

St. Jean, B.; Rieh, S.; Yakel, E. & Market, K. (2011). Unheard voices; Institutional repository end-users. *College & Research Libraries* 77(1) pp. 21–42

Sula, C. A. (2013). Digital humanities and libraries: A conceptual model. *Journal of Library Administration, 53*(1), 10–26. http://doi.org/10.1080/01930826.2013.756680

Sundt, C. L. (2013). Research resources at our fingertips. *Visual Resources, 29*(4), 269–272. http://doi.org/10.1080/01973762.2013.846774

Taylor, A., Joudrey, D. & Wisser, K. (2017). *The Organization of Information.* Santa Barbara, CA: Libraries Unlimited

Terras, M. (2015). Opening access to collections: The making and using of open digitised cultural content. *Online Information Review, 39*(5), 733–752. http://doi.org/10.1108/OIR-06-2015-0193

9

THE LIBRARY IN DIGITAL HUMANITIES

Interdisciplinary approaches to digital materials

Paul Gooding

9.1 Introduction

Digital Humanities and Library & Information Studies (LIS) share a common interest in the collection, organisation, preservation, and use of digital materials. The academic library acts as a hub for digital humanities activities on many campuses, and this close relationship has led scholars to extensively interrogate how library services can support, and contribute to, DH (Green, 2014; Hartsell-Gundy, Braunstein, & Golomb, 2015). What little work exists that focuses on the nexus of information studies and digital humanities has attempted to establish common intellectual ground (Robinson, Priego, & Bawden, 2015), to compare each discipline's respective strengths and weaknesses (Koltay, 2016), or to express the ways in which DH can enrich the study of information work (Clement, 2016). In response, it has been noted that training for librarians must change in order to meet the changing demands of their scholarly communities (Moazeni, 2015). To date, however, we have been less successful in expressing the direct contribution of LIS to knowledge creation in DH, and several scholars have noted the erasure of library and archival scholarship from the humanities (Caswell, 2016; Whearty, 2018). This erasure is paralleled elsewhere, due to the distributed nature of LIS research; its researchers inhabit not only departments of information studies, but are dispersed across DH centres, and departments spanning the arts, humanities, social and computational sciences. They contribute to knowledge across the academy by this very act of dispersal, while drawing on their own intellectual history, disciplinary and professional knowledge within several disciplines.

In this chapter, I will concentrate on two key questions: why is LIS as a field of study so underrepresented in the DH literature? And how are methods derived from LIS advancing work in, and on, the digital humanities? In order to answer these questions, I will explore three interwoven topics that provide a framework for understanding the contribution of information studies: first, how communities of practice within each field are influenced by our epistemological perspectives; second, how the imbalance in recognising academic labour in DH has been addressed in the literature; and third, how user studies represent a divergence in practice that emphasises the unique, values-led contribution that scholars of information studies make to the intellectual development of digital humanities. The chapter will conclude by discussing how research inspired by both DH and information studies approaches questions of method that engage with both fields as truly interdisciplinary spaces.

9.2 Digital humanities in the library

The title of this chapter was inspired by a recent book, *Digital Humanities in the Library* (Hartsell-Gundy et al., 2015), which explores the role of subject specialist librarians in relation to DH. The volume makes a valuable contribution to our understanding of how specialist library roles are adapting to changing research and infrastructural needs for the humanities in the United States of America. The conceit behind placing DH within the library is quite accurate, at least in the United States and United Kingdom. In both countries, DH centres are often physically located in close proximity to university libraries, which provide space and expertise to support DH teaching and research (Burns, 2016; Kretzschmar Jr & Gray Potter, 2010; Svensson, 2012). The continued shrinking of permanent or tenure-track jobs, and the clear intellectual overlap offered by alt-ac jobs in the gallery, libraries, archives and museums (GLAM) sector, has led many postdoctoral humanities scholars to view the library sector as a logical home for their work. The intellectual link is clear for DH researchers, many of whom bring computational skills and work on problems that are also central to LIS:

> Motivated to theorize the digital, networked information systems that they construct, those DH scholars are expressing their desire to connect their training in the humanities with theories around topics such as information organization, information behaviour, information retrieval, sociotechnical systems, human-computer interaction, computer-supported co-operative work, and information systems (Clement & Carter, 2017, p. 1395).

The result is an influx of so-called 'non-credentialed' librarians from DH-related backgrounds[1]—highly skilled researchers with relevant knowledge, but without formal accredited qualifications in librarianship—into libraries and archives. Michelle Caswell expresses despair at this influx of humanists, noting that routes into library and archival careers are sometimes viewed as an alternative for those who are unsuccessful in obtaining permanent research posts:

> As if being an archivist was a fallback career that did not require its own postgraduate-level education and training. As if every act was not laden with theory. As if archival studies could not offer its own important intellectual contribution (Caswell, 2016).

Her despair is representative of a continuing pattern of decline in the number of jobs requiring Masters in librarianship over more than twenty years (Grimes & Grimes, 2008). DH is not the cause of deskilling in libraries and archives, but it is one facet of a longer-term shift in the skills required in the information sector. Indeed, DH competencies are increasingly finding their way into the curriculum of taught library courses (Moazeni, 2015; Sula, 2013) and vice versa (Warwick, 2012). Bethany Nowviskie notes the positive aspect of this infiltration:

> PhD-holding librarians and alt-ac digital scholarship staff come at their work from a certain useful vantage. They have performed scholarship and experienced our humanities collections, interfaces, and services as students, as researchers, and as teachers – in a word, as library users. They are our new colleagues, who have taken a look at librarians from the other side of the reference desk (Nowviskie, 2013, p. 58).

I will pick up on the significance of this outside perspective later, as it is characteristic of the way that LIS adopts ideas from other disciplines and intellectual traditions. Information studies can be understood as a "field of study" (Hirst, 1974), which allows new methods and theory to cross-pollinate its practice and

The library in digital humanities

scholarship. New epistemological practices can be transformative for research into information. As a result of these complementary forces, DH research often takes place in libraries and archives, or in collaboration with librarians, and addresses what can be understood to constitute traditional library activities (Sula, 2013, p. 17). The results of such collaborations are frequently published in major LIS journals, but it has been argued that the opposite is rarely true except in the case of studies that directly address this interaction between DH and libraries (Robinson et al., 2015, p. 46). The preponderance of such studies demonstrates that the significance of DH for libraries is firmly established.

What, though, if we flip the sentence around and ask not what DH is doing in the library, but what LIS *as a field of study* is doing in DH? The spaces, and practices, of our libraries are in the process of being reordered, but a glance at the DH literature suggests this process is unilateral. Theories and methods that define the "meta-discipline" of information studies (Bawden, 2015) are underrepresented in relevant areas of DH, but a similar erasure has not occurred for computer science, literature, or history. When Borgman, for instance, asked where the social sciences are in DH, she referred to the body of work "that has informed the design of scholarly infrastructures for the sciences, and is a central component of cyberinfrastructure and eScience initiatives" (2009) rather than cognate work from information studies. This is despite the presence of several leading DH scholars that have a background in libraries. This chapter will explore the methodological implications of that erasure.

9.3 Hierarchies: Where is LIS in the digital humanities?

My reversal addresses the uneven relationship between DH and LIS, whereby it is assumed that the former acts upon the latter, performing fundamental change upon a physical institution and its staff. Focusing on how DH changes the library fits the normal order of technological discourse whereby it is often assumed that the new, seemingly more complex innovation must inevitably enact transformation upon the traditional institutions that it operates within, and upon. By adopting this narrative, we produce echoes of an outdated academic hierarchy that positions library and archival staff as in servitude to the 'real' academic business of knowledge production (Rockenbach, 2013, pp. 4–5). The digital humanities have begun to redefine how the library operates as a space for scholarship, by entering its physical and virtual spaces; its jobs; its curriculum; and its publications. The library is thereby judged by the extent of this alteration. Sarah Buchanan, however, provides a note of difference to this link by presenting DH and libraries in a bilateral process of knowledge exchange. She describes the relationship thus:

> It recasts **the scholar as curator and the curator as scholar** [original author's emphasis], and, in doing so, sets out to reinvigorate scholarly practice by means of an expanded set of possibilities and demands, and to renew the scholarly mission of museums, libraries, and archives (Buchanan, 2010).

Despite this, there is an imbalance in the terminology applied to each field by many writers. They recognise the broad practice-based contribution of librarianship to DH—in teaching (Burns, 2016; Green, 2014); facilitating research (Sula, 2013); and resource creation and training (Hauck, 2017). But Hauck's description of the direct involvement of library staff, for instance, is typically self-effacing: "librarians are encouraged to contribute their skills to digital humanities projects as full partners doing what they already do quite well" (Hauck, 2017, p. 435). *Quite well*. Compare this modesty with the language used by Buchanan to describe DH: "revolution," "fundamental reshaping," "transformative" (2010).

Michelle Caswell's work has become a recent touchstone because it addresses the erasure of archival studies scholars from debates in the humanities. She argues that humanities scholars view "the archive" as a theoretical space in relation to the systems and structures of Foucault, or Derrida's death drive; whereas archival scholars focus on archives as a plural representation of "the archival":

> For archival studies scholars and practicing archivists, archives – emphasis on the "s" – are collections of records, material and immaterial, analog and digital (which, from an archival studies perspective, is just another form of the material), the institutions that steward them, the places where they are physically located, and the processes that designated them "archival" (Caswell, 2016).

As a result, there are two parallel tracks of discussion into archives, and the fields are not taking part in the same conversations, establishing a shared language, or benefiting from mutual exchange of ideas. Caswell diagnoses this as a failure of interdisciplinarity in relation to archives for humanities scholarship. This failure leads to gaps in vocabulary, citation practices that reinforce the status quo, and a resultant inability to engage with the specific interventions of information studies in a truly interdisciplinary conversation. The following section will address how the nature of interdisciplinarity is itself a product of how each community of practice has emerged and cohered around particular intellectual structures.

9.4 What does it mean to be an interdisciplinary field?

Vakkari notes that "to define universals is always an effort" (1994, p. 1). Indeed, the process of arriving at a universal definition of DH has been a key challenge for the field. The definitional drive of DH seems to continue unabated, with each new attempt filtered through the disciplinary or methodological frames of the definer. Here, though, I have shied away from the idea of universal definitions of LIS and DH, and focused more on the multiple spaces they inhabit—on *how* they operate as interdisciplinary fields. Klein's broad synthesis of work into interdisciplinarity can assist in defining its nature and scope:

> Interdisciplinarity has been variously defined in this century: as a methodology, a concept, a process, a way of thinking, a philosophy, and a reflexive ideology. It has been linked with attempts to explore the dangers of fragmentation, to re-establish old connections, to explore merging relationships, and to create new subjects adequate to handle our practical and conceptual needs. Cutting across all these theories is one recurring idea. Interdisciplinarity is a means of solving problems and answering questions that cannot be satisfactorily addressed using single methods or approaches (Klein, 1990, p. 196).

Two important points emerge from Klein's definition. First, interdisciplinarity involves solving problems with reference to a variety of methods and approaches from more than one discipline. Second, Klein emphasises that in order to cross disciplinary boundaries, it is necessary that the boundaries are defined in some form. These boundaries are derived from the values, assumptions, and methods of an academic field that give it a community identity and cohesion. DH and information studies both provide a central space for multiple disciplines to approach a shared problem, but the extent to which this is truly interdisciplinary depends on each scholar's approach.

I have focused here on definitional work that enhances our understanding of how each field operates as a convergence point for several disciplinary approaches. For LIS, the key works in this area have focused on the scope and nature of the field. Lyn Robinson, for instance, defines LIS as follows:

> A field of study, with human recorded information as its concern, focusing on the components of the information chain, studied through the perspective of domain analysis, and in specific or general context is based on a rather longstanding perspective of the field, combined with more modern insights (Robinson, 2009, p. 587).

The library in digital humanities

Her use of the term "field of study" is meant in the sense introduced by Paul Hirst (1974); it is indicative of a field that is focused on a particular subject or topic area, and that uses any methods or forms of knowledge that may be helpful in studying it. Most contemporary definitions of LIS are in rough alignment with Bate's claim that its focus is "the study of the gathering, organizing, storing, retrieving, and dissemination of information" (Bates, 1999).

However, Hirst's term is not unproblematic as an explanation of the field. His "field of study", as originally developed, refers to fields that are not additive to the scholarship on a topic; for instance, Hirst argued that educational theory was a field of study because it produced no unique forms of understanding about education that were additional to the fundamental disciplines (Hirst, 1966). Biesta argues that constructing educational studies as a field of study both denies autonomous disciplinary status to the field, and "locates all the 'rigorous work' within the fundamental disciplines" (Biesta, 2011). The challenge, then, is to interrogate how LIS has provided a unique contribution to their domains of knowledge. Here, Bates argues strongly for what makes LIS unique and significant:

> We are always looking for the red thread of information in the social texture of people's lives. When we study people, we do so with the purpose of understanding information creation, seeking, and use. We do not just study people in general (Bates, 1999, p. 1048).

Bawden expands upon this to propose that information studies gains its unique identity through a focus upon the human information chain, by describing it as a "multidisciplinary field of study, involving several forms of knowledge, given coherence by a focus on the central concept of human recorded information" (Bawden, 2007). As such, LIS has been a voracious adopter of methods from other disciplines. It engages with the computer sciences, through Human-Computer Interaction, informetrics, and informatics. It draws upon the social sciences through ethnography, case study research, surveys, and questionnaire research. It engages critically with the humanities by engaging with texts as theoretical spaces that are in conversation with the people that create, curate, and use them, and the interfaces through which they are presented. By noting this broad sphere of influence, we arrive with a conception of the field that hints at its unique contribution to digital humanities. We may cautiously say that the social sciences are interested in the people, and the structures, that overlap with the information life cycle; and that the arts and humanities are interested in studying information in relation to the outputs of human culture. LIS, though, is ultimately interested in overlapping questions that assist us to understand how information is created, transmitted, and used in a variety of contexts. It operates as a field of study that draws on a multidisciplinary tradition, in aid of a focused study on recorded information.

Despite this, the organisational structure of the field within universities is not always clear, and broad interdisciplinarity becomes a vehicle that normalises LIS practices within specific disciplines; in other words, to make them invisible within alternative epistemological frameworks. I saw this process in action first-hand in my first postdoctoral position. Despite being a trained librarian, whose PhD work spanned libraries and digital humanities, I was employed as a Research Fellow in DH, in a department of media studies. Here, my work was understood not by its difference, but by its similarity: a well-meaning colleague, explaining how my work could be made relevant to my colleagues, told me that it could be simply boiled down to 'reception studies for libraries.' By focusing on what they saw as clear synergies, their comment unintentionally erased the entire tradition of my field's approach to information behaviour and user studies. Koltay, though, argues that the distributed nature of LIS within academic structures is actually a strength:

> People doing work in this field are not always found in departments of that name. Even, when there are LIS departments they are to be found in different areas of the academic structure: technical schools, humanities faculties, social science faculties, business schools, etc. Neither this is a weakness. On the contrary, it is strength, because it ensures that the discipline should always find a home for itself (Koltay, 2016, p. 786).

It is a *form* of strength, certainly, that LIS, and its human practitioners, are flexible— peripatetic even— in managing to fit their careers into the structures of the modern academy. But because our research is often done under the auspices of other disciplines, it is thus adapted to local contexts and ways of knowing. As a result, it is perhaps unsurprising that pinning down the unique contribution of LIS is so difficult (Vakkari, 1994).

In this respect, information studies shares something with DH, which is famous for its lack of definitional agreement. As a field of study, LIS draws on critical and methodological approaches from across the humanities, social sciences, and computing, to inform its work. DH, too, can be understood as a field for which multidisciplinary approaches are essential. The extent to which this myriad of methods is truly interdisciplinary is contested, and some have argued that most definitions of DH have failed to fully engage with its necessarily interdisciplinary scope. Alan Liu, for instance, argues that:

> Digital humanists are unlikely to come to clarity about their naming or usage conventions, and about the concepts these express, until they engage in much fuller conversation with their affiliated or enveloping disciplinary fields (e.g. literary studies, history, writing programs, library studies, etc.), cousin fields (e.g. new media studies), and the wider public about where they fit in, which is to say, how they contribute to a larger, shared agenda expressed in the conjunction and collision of many fields (Liu, 2013).

In 2011, Matthew Jockers and Glenn Worthey introduced the concept of the "Big Tent" to capture the nature of the relationship between DH and other disciplines. It was intended as a joyful expression of the diversity of DH practice, for the DH2011 conference, expressing "wonder and appreciation for the many-splendored field of DH, for its practices of creative exuberance, for its opening of the scholarly senses to new and revolutionary ways of seeing and thinking about the humanities" (Jockers & Worthey, 2011).

The commendably inclusive big tent can also be seen as a pragmatic, flexible term that helps to give strength in numbers to a growing discipline (Terras, 2011)—but there has been a push back against the amorphous nature of the activities within that tent. The presence of interdisciplinarity relies on a visual demarcation between the disciplines in question (Klein, 1990), and DH is regularly framed as being committed to inter-disciplinary work. Differing models have been proposed to explain how interdisciplinarity occurs within DH. Svensson (2012, p. 46) refers to "trading zones", a term which describes 'places' where interdisciplinary work occurs, and intersectional work is carried out while different traditions are maintained. Robertson (2016) argues that DH should be viewed as a house with many rooms, with disciplines establishing their own spaces connected by various entry points and communal spaces. Both share a common desire to engage in interdisciplinary work, but with defined boundaries evident between the various disciplines. On the other hand, one implication of the big tent is that those boundaries are not always visible; and smaller fields can become embedded to the point of erasure.

In 2006, Harold Short and Willard McCarty attempted to map the extent of humanities computing, the forerunner term to digital humanities, to capture the diversity of work in the field. The resultant "methodological commons" was imagined as a series of convergence points between many disciplinary groups and modes of knowledge, focused on those methods and tools central to the practices of the DH community, including data and data structures, modelling core materials, and tools modelling formal methods (Siemens, 2016). The commons share a logic with the field of study, in that the disciplines contribute their modes of knowledge to a central area of inquiry. Indeed, Siemens draws upon the methodological commons to propose that we can understand DH as a community of practice:

> If what brings us together as a community is our practices, the notion of the methodological commons helps us understand key elements of the work we have done, our work now, and our work as we imagine it in the future (Siemens, 2016).

The library in digital humanities

This community of practice sits between the methods of the disciplines of the social sciences, arts, humanities, and the physical and computational sciences. Notably, though, it excludes other fields of study including information studies. To be flippant, librarians don't get their own bubble in the methodological commons of the digital humanities.

Given that both DH and LIS can be understood alternatively as meta-disciplines, or fields of study, with theory and methods derived from a wide variety of core disciplines, that question that arises is why is LIS so poorly represented in DH, when the opposite is not true? Caswell is one of several scholars (Cook, 2006; Whearty, 2018) who argue that there is a 'refusal' to engage with library and archival studies:

> Almost none of the humanistic enquiry at "the archival turn"… has acknowledged the intellectual contribution of archival studies as a field of theory and practice in its own right, nor is this humanistic scholarship in conversation with ideas, debates, and lineages in archival studies (Caswell, 2016).

This is framed as a gendered and structural failing, relating to the status of the profession as predominantly female, professional in the sense that it is not academic, and service orientated. Cook, for instance, points to the fact that in Canada, archivists were referred to as "handmaidens of historians" (2006) until the 1980s. He argues that this act of side-lining bears similarities to the silencing of women in social and historical memory, relegated to anonymous supporters of male accomplishment:

> Archivists have remained invisible in the construction of social memory, their role also poorly articulated and rarely appreciated. I might go further to say that just as patriarchy required women to be subservient, invisible handmaidens to male power, historians and other users of archives require archivists to be neutral, invisible, silent handmaidens of historical research (Cook, 2006).

DH scholars have been key contributors to work that unpicks the technical infrastructures of humanities research, providing key insights into the aspects of power, gender, and race that are associated with academic institutional hierarchies and ways of working. More importantly, many are taking steps to develop *new* infrastructures and methods in light of insights from intersectional feminist theory (Brown, Clement, Mandell, Verhoeven, & Wernimont, 2016), black studies (Gallon, 2016), and postcolonial theory (Olsen & Risam, 2016). In doing so, they foreground the absence of these voices from previous debates. The erasure of LIS scholarship is different: the voices have been present, but due to the dispersed nature of the field there has been a failure to engage directly with work that was hidden in plain sight. The flexible, fluid status of the field within the interdisciplinary commons of DH means that it is unclear to many what exactly the theory and methods grounded within LIS uniquely bring to DH, precisely because they now appear indistinguishable.

I have argued that DH and information studies can be understood as convergence points between various disciplines. Both additionally share a keen awareness of the role of service. DH has often been situated as a service centre with universities, but those in the field have worked hard to assert their own academic identity. LIS, however, is more closely aligned to the service-oriented value system (Bates, 1999, p. 1049) that is actively embedded within the professional values of librarianship. When it comes to professional practice, this is an admirable ethos, but inadequately expresses the unique contribution of the scholarship that derives from these values. So far, I have focused on my first question: why is LIS as a field of study so underrepresented in DH? I have broken down various aspects of this question: the idea of the field of study, the place of LIS in digital humanities discourses; and the debates over the erasure of information studies scholarship in the humanities. The rest of this chapter will attempt to answer my second question: how are methods derived from LIS advancing work in, and on, the digital humanities?

9.5 Information studies, and values-based methods

Bates (1999) proposes that information studies has tended to follow the "value neutral" science or engineering model, while professional librarianship has followed a more service-based model. However, the influence of DH has helped to foreground the theoretical component of information management. Such work builds on Haraway's idea of becoming answerable to address how feminist theory can intervene in our concepts of objectivity:

> Feminist objectivity is about limited location and situated knowledge, not about transcendence and splitting of subject and object. It allows us to become answerable for what we learn how to see (Haraway, 1988, p. 583).

In doing so, DH scholars can address the theoretical subtext of systems and working practices that either assume objectivity or adopt pragmatic approaches in response to technical limitations (Drucker & Nowviskie, 2004). This has been reflected in renewed calls to activism on the part of the digital humanities. Traditionally, developing library systems, and information resources, would have been seen as service work, whereas it has been argued that the future of DH lies in demonstrating that such service-based roles are in themselves intellectual contributions:

> To be an equal partner – rather than, again, just a *servant* – at the table, digital humanists will need to find ways to show that thinking critically about metadata, for instance, scales into thinking critically about the power, finance, and other governance protocols of the world (Liu, 2011).

Liu foregrounds the importance of power structures as they relate to information systems, and Tanya Clement further addresses this point when she argues that the digital humanities have renewed calls to activism for the role of the broader humanities as a different way of looking at technological questions. The projects she cites are powerful precisely because they seek to dismantle and rebuild information systems through humanistic perspectives that focus on situatedness and subjectivity:

> The authors – some of whom have published as digital humanities scholars and all of who are influenced by both information studies and the humanities – reorient seemingly objective representations of life and culture – space, time, and image – through changes in encodings, both computational and taxonomic (Clement, 2016).

The point of difference of these projects is their answerability, the act of being humanistic rather than scientific; and it is this difference that denotes the unique contribution of DH to questions in information studies. Likewise, I will argue here that a focus within LIS on the use and users of information systems is one of its key theoretical and methodological contributions to DH. The reframing of DH service as a unique intellectual contribution to academic knowledge is a point of difference to LIS, which emphasises service as a core value. This difference is evidenced by the secondary importance of users in many DH resources. Robertson, for instance, argues that "the most common use to which digital humanists, including some historians, have the put the web has been the distribution and presentation of material to other scholarly researchers" (Robertson, 2016). He notes that Kirschenbaum, for instance, responded to complaints against the usability of the *William Blake Archive* by noting that "while we are happy to have users from so many different constituencies, the site's primary mission has always been expressly conceived as scholarly research" (Kirschenbaum, 2004). There is an element of intention to this statement: the non-scholar is not addressed directly because they are not the intended

The library in digital humanities

audience. It is not unusual to focus largely upon the target audience of a particular resource, even within LIS; Simon Tanner, whose Balanced Value Impact Model addresses the need to demonstrate the value and impact of digital resources through systematic assessment and evaluation, similarly defines impact in terms of intention:

> The measurable outcomes arising from the existence of a digital resource that demonstrate a change in the life or life opportunities for which the resource is intended (Tanner, 2012).

Tanner provides a model for collecting data to report value to funders, government, and management. In common with work in the digital humanities, though, it is not explicitly concerned with addressing unintended audiences. It is not my intention to argue that either approach must do so, merely that instead they reflect extensively on the creation and value of digital resources while focusing on aspects of information work that engage only partially with the service-based tradition of information studies work. On the other hand, many writers from that tradition have posited service as a key value for librarianship (Finks, 1989; Lankes, 2011; Shera, 1972). They thus foreground a values-based approach that more broadly addresses the user communities of library. Ranganathan, for instance, considered the library to be a "growing organism" (1931) comprising books, staff and readers, with growth and change in any one of these groups affecting the others. In this tradition, the existence of users also demonstrates a change in how we perceive a digital resource, and by modelling and understanding information behaviour we are thereby able to illuminate aspects of change that are hidden when addressing intention in resource creation. LIS therefore differs from humanistic approaches in that the object of attention is the user as a concrete presence—much as Caswell proposes that archivists view the archive in concrete rather than purely theoretical terms.

9.6 The methodological importance of user studies in the digital humanities

The value of user studies, then, is to allow us to understand how user behaviour exists in conversation with other factors. By addressing users in this way, the values of library practice can both inform our research and allow us to more broadly engage with humanistic and social science questions. While I have noted the self-effacing nature of librarianship, I would argue that professional and scholarly values that encompass service-based librarianship can help to place critical constructions of the library as central in user studies of digital resources (Gooding, 2017, p. 142). In an era when digital resources are challenging our theories of who, or what, a user might actually be, information studies can identify who those users are in reality, what behaviours they are engaged in, the methods they use in their work, and their current and future information needs. Gorman and Clayton define the case study as:

> An in-depth investigation of a discrete entity… on the assumption that it is possible to derive knowledge of the wider phenomenon from investigation of a specific case or instance (Gorman & Clayton, 2005, p. 47).

User studies are built on the logic that although each user is an individual, there are common activities undertaken by researchers (Unsworth, 2000) that allow us to study information behaviour within a defined community (Bawden & Robinson, 2013). For this reason, it is common to adopt a case study approach for researching information behaviour.

I have previously argued that exploring the development of information behaviour in relation to digital resources is a complex task that relies on a multifaceted approach to collecting and analysing data (Gooding, 2017). Others have also warned of the weakness of narrow approaches to data collection, which risk providing an evidence base too narrow to derive meaningful analysis of wider socio-cultural aspects of information sources. This limitation extends to a reliance on solely qualitative, or quantitative research methods:

> Whereas qualitative techniques alone risk missing the big picture due to their necessary small-scale nature, quantitative techniques risk being superficial or misleading if they are not complemented by supporting qualitative analysis (Thelwall, 2009, pp. 1–2).

Thelwall's insight applies particularly to the narrow adoption of methods for analysing user behaviour online. Web log analysis has been adopted as a common method of data analysis and applied to several studies of digital resources in the humanities (Gooding, 2016; Warwick, Terras, Huntington, & Pappa, 2008). It is a relatively unobtrusive way to track real user behaviour without bias being introduced by a researcher through interviews or observation. As part of a larger group of webometric methods, web log analysis thus provides a direct method of what people have actually done, rather than what they remember doing or what they believe they do. However, adopting a data-driven approach can make it difficult to derive deeper insights into the relationship between a digital resource and the broader information practices of a user community:

> Studies which rely solely on webometrics inevitably understand user behaviour in terms of the website infrastructure rather than as a mediated relationship between user and content. Webometric analysis can only reveal how a website is used and not the motivating factors which encourage a user to return or leave without engaging (Gooding, 2017, pp. 82–83).

Thus, while web log analysis provides robust insights into user behaviour, mixed methods approaches are better suited to developing theoretical and practical models of information behaviour. The empirical tradition of library research, which arguably emerges from a historical view of information work as a profession in the positivist tradition, has given way over time to a pragmatic acceptance that mixed methods are vital to allow deeper insights to emerge by placing methods in conversation with each other. This methodological triangulation is accepted as a valid approach to case study research, where the research method regularly drives which methods are adopted for a particular study. Triangulation of methods in LIS therefore works something like the macroanalytic lens in the digital humanities, by allowing us to adopt both macro- and micro-level perspectives to a case, or cases.

This approach has informed several studies that relate to digital resources and the digital humanities. The ones I draw attention to here either provide models for evaluating digital resources (Tanner, 2012), or undertake evaluation of specific resources (Hughes, Ell, Knight, & Dobreva, 2015; Meyer & Eccles, 2016; Warwick et al., 2008), and all adopt mixed methods approaches that include various forms of web log analysis, stakeholder interviews, focus groups, qualitative and quantitative surveys, and citation analysis. These studies constitute a large subset of work within the digital humanities and demonstrate that deep methodological engagement with the question of the user is a key characteristic of LIS work in the digital humanities. One way, then, of approaching problems through an interdisciplinary DH/LIS lens that is specifically 'information studies' in nature, is to adopt a focus on the user that is absent from so much work in the digital humanities. In this work, the user is both an abstract concept for theorisation and an individual member of a concrete user community relating to a specific resource. But what insights into the user community can this approach bring? What happens when we view the user not as a recipient of the tools created by digital humanists, but as an individual within larger social, economic, and professional structures that sit outside the structures of the academy? By way of illustration, I will briefly elaborate on my own work in this area.

During my PhD, I undertook case studies of users of two digitised collections; The British Library's Nineteenth Century Newspapers (BNCN), and Welsh Newspapers Online (WNO). Inspired by user

The library in digital humanities

studies in digital humanities, I adopted a mixed methods approach which incorporated web log analysis, citation analysis, surveys, and interviews. Initially, I focused on the 'intended community' for digitised newspaper collections: the academic community, and particularly historians. However, during the user survey, I received several responses that forced me to realign how I approached my research question. A distinct user group, precariously employed academics, noted concerns about their ability to access the paywalled BNCN between contracts. Some expressed disappointment that they would have to pay for the resource at the precise moment they could least afford it, while another related the problem to larger issues with accessing scholarly materials while between academic posts: "once I'm no longer employed, how am I to keep up with research to get another job when I can't afford access to sources and journals?" (Gooding, 2014, p. 283).

Whereas my initial research questions adopted a narrow perspective of the user, these responses inspired me to investigate the personal and social factors that affect access to digitised resources. Access is a function of an individual's geodemographic status (Harris, Sleight, & Webber, 2005), so I set out to gather and map demographic data that related to access to digitised newspapers. The visualisation built upon a single point of logic derived from the work of geodemographics:

> While the location of individual users gives us a superficial idea of where people are using a digitised collection, it tells us nothing about their socio-economic status. Instead, grouping users together based on their demographic status allows us to discover general information about that population to compare them to other distinct populations (Gooding, 2017, p. 253).

There are huge individual benefits to being allied to information rich institutions, so we must bear in mind that an access map built upon individual location tells us nothing more than where those who definitely have access are located in the world when they take advantage of that access. We learn nothing of those who are deprived access, and little about the demographics of those we study. This led me to conclude that, for subscription resources, the single strongest indicator of an individual's ability to access digitised newspapers was their institutional affiliation. As a result, I could identify geographical trends in relation to accessing institutions. I could also group communities of users based on extant demographic data relating to each institution. I therefore collated a list of subscribing institutions for two key subscription digital newspaper resources: BNCN, and the Times Digital Archive. The main subscribers were global tertiary education institutions, major national and research libraries, and public library services in the United Kingdom. I geocoded these institutions: specific university and national libraries became node points, and public library services represented the entire geographical area they served to reflect the presence of multiple physical access points. I then compiled detailed demographic data from extant datasets: for HE and FE institutions, I gathered statistics for student populations, budgetary information, and university rankings; for public libraries, I included regional populations; total library spend per capita; and indices of relative deprivation from the British government (2011).

My results found that there were genuine inequalities in access: the ability to access a chosen resource correlated closely with those universities with the highest reputations, budgets, and student communities. Similarly, free access to digitised newspapers in British public libraries correlated strongly to the most populous, least deprived areas where individuals already benefited from more expansive life opportunities on average. I chose to describe digital resources as "unequally free": a term that recognises that digital resources are often free, but "only if you meet certain criteria such as membership of a specific organisation or residence in a particular location" (Gooding, 2017, p. 163).

My work to map the use of digitised newspapers, then, fits the model of the field of study in that it draws upon multidisciplinary perspectives. It draws on work in the digital humanities to inform visualisation, both through the underlying technical method, and by focusing on deconstructing the human implications of a particular dataset or tool. In doing so, it restructures the task of mapping usage of digital resources away from questions of individual mobility, and towards the geodemographic implications of the structures that users work within. By adopting a user-focused, rather than resource-focused approach, it also accounts for the possibility that questions may arise that require us to go beyond the intended community to explore broader implications for precariously employed researchers, non-academic users, and non-users. I chose this work, which sits within the established methodological tradition of user studies in digital humanities, not because it is the best, or the only, example of such work. Instead, it demonstrates how user-focused perspectives from information studies can broaden our analysis of the tools and infrastructures that constitute so much digital humanities work. It also emphasises that library values are derived from a long body of theoretical work in LIS, in the same way that other work in DH applies theoretical and critical perspectives from other domains that have been underrepresented in humanities scholarship. In doing so, we can see how a study informed by both DH and LIS can broaden the questions we ask of our information systems, our digital resources, our computational tools, by grounding work in a productive debate between humanistic theory and the social and human applications of these technologies.

9.7 Conclusion

I have argued here that information studies and digital humanities share several characteristics: they both encompass research questions relating to the life cycle of recorded information; they both operate as a field of study, or a community of practice, that derives methods from several disciplines; and they are both methodological in nature. This shared interest has led to productive interdisciplinary work by many scholars whose work spans the intellectual tradition of both fields. Despite this, work from LIS is underrepresented in much of the DH literature: its sources are not cited; its epistemological foundations, where addressed, are represented as practice-based rather than intellectually derived; and there continues to be a focus on the 'Digital Humanities in the Library'. It is clear that DH has had major implications for libraries that justify this focus: several prominent researchers are undertaking exciting work into information studies problems that incorporate the intellectual impetus provided by digital humanities. However, this chapter has laid out a methodological, and an intellectual, contribution for what LIS does extremely well: translating its service-based values into epistemological and methodological approaches that can broaden the focus of research into information systems in the digital humanities.

I have interpreted the values of information studies to be centred on the library as a service, with a resultant desire to identify user communities in order to tailor this service according to identified needs. We can see this reflected in work that spans DH and LIS: these interventions address the ways that varied methodological approaches to user studies that can inform how we develop digital resources, interpret their value and utility, and understand how they intersect with changing models of user behaviour. This is distinct from work derived from DH, which is often about the implications of humanistic thinking for the development of digital resources and infrastructure: for instance, the scholarly process of "building" hermeneutic tools that incorporate humanistic methods; and the application of theory to the development of tools and infrastructure. I would sound a note of caution here: in arguing for the importance of research driven by the longstanding values of the library profession, we must also be open to the idea that this epistemological framework is not universal. The user is *not* at the heart of some work, and neither must it be to make it robust and meaningful. The definitional impulse of DH struggles to reach consensus precisely because it is far from simple to determine a universal set of values that define the field. Instead, I will conclude by proposing that we need to be explicit in addressing the values, and the disciplinary traditions, that underpin work in the digital humanities: rather than agreeing on universal values, we must be clear what our own values are, and how they might speak to specific communities of practice more than others. Claire Warwick is not alone in arguing that the big tent model for DH has

The library in digital humanities

led to a culture of niceness that can stand in the way of developing effective communities of practice with distinct focuses and values:

> It may be that DH will have to let go of our ideas of niceness and methodological agreement, and accept the likelihood that different schools and methods of doing DH will emerge. This may entail public battles, schisms, and regroupings, but it does not necessarily threaten the integrity of the discipline; it may even be a sign of strength and confidence (Warwick, 2016).

If we choose to consciously address how and where DH scholars differ in their approaches, we can better understand the nature of interdisciplinarity when applied to DH work. Our methods, and objects of study, bring us together as a community, but this understanding necessitates truly interdisciplinary collaboration, in Klein's (1990) sense that interdisciplinarity still recognises disciplinary boundaries. A culture of co-citation, and co-reading (Whearty, 2018), is similarly necessary to address multilateral modes of enquiry. However, I do not see this driving us apart: instead, I hope that by providing a clearer sense of how different communities of practice make a distinct contribution to our shared literature, we will be better positioned to recognise not just the labour of librarians, but also the intellectual contribution that information studies makes to the digital humanities.

Note

1 The library job market has been covered extensively in the literature, from the "Shambrarian" through to the role of formal Masters programmes in Librarianship (MLS in the USA).

References

Bates, M. J. (1999). The Invisible Substrate of Information Science. *Journal of the American Society for Information Science, 50*(12), 1043–1050. https://doi.org/10.1002/(SICI)1097-4571(1999)50:12<1043::AID-ASI1>3.0.CO;2-X

Bawden, D. (2007). Organised Complexity, Meaning and Understanding: An Approach for a Unified View of Information for Information Science. *ASLIB Proceedings, 59*(4/5), 307–327. https://doi.org/10.1108/00012530710817546

Bawden, D. (2015). On Not Being A Weak Discipline. Retrieved September 18, 2019, from https://theoccasionalinformationist.com/2015/07/06/on-not-being-a-weak-discipline/

Bawden, D., & Robinson, L. (2013). No Such Thing as Society? On the Individuality of Information Behaviour. *Journal of the American Society for Information Science and Technology, 64*(123), 2587–2590.

Biesta, G. (2011). Disciplines and Theory in the Academic Study of Education: A Comparative Analysis of the Anglo-American and Continental Construction of the Field. *Pedagogy, Culture & Society, 19*(2), 175–192. https://doi.org/10.1080/14681366.2011.582255

Borgman, C. (2009). Scholarship in the Digital Age: Blurring the Boundaries Between the Sciences and the Humanities. Presented at the Digital Humanities 2009, Maryland, USA. Retrieved from https://works.bepress.com/borgman/216/

Brown, S., Clement, T., Mandell, L., Verhoeven, D., & Wernimont, J. (2016). Creating Feminist Infrastructures in the Digital Humanities. Presented at the Digital Humanities 2016, Krakow. Retrieved from http://dh2016.adho.org/abstracts/233

Buchanan, S. (2010). Accessioning the Digital Humanities: Report from the 1st Archival Education and Research Institute. *DH Quarterly, 4*(1). Retrieved from http://www.digitalhumanities.org/dhq/vol/4/1/000084/000084.htmlaccessed

Burns, J. A. (2016). Role of the Information Professional in the Development and Promotion of Digital Humanities Content for Research, Teaching, and Learning in the Modern Academic Library; An Irish Case Study. *New Review of Academic Librarianship, 22*(2–3), 238–248. https://doi.org/10.1080/13614533.2016.1191520

Caswell, M. (2016). "The Archive" Is Not an Archives: On Acknowledging the Intellectual Contributions of Archival Studies. *Reconstruction: Studies in Contemporary Culture, 16*(1). Retrieved from https://escholarship.org/uc/item/7bn4v1fk

Clement, T. (2016). Where is Methodology in Digital Humanities. In *Debates in the Digital Humanities* (2nd Edition). Minneapolis MN: University of Minnesota Press. Retrieved from http://dhdebates.gc.cuny.edu/debates/text/65

Clement, T., & Carter, D. (2017). Connecting Theory and Practice in Digital Humanities Information Work. *Journal of the Association for Information Science and Technology, 68*(6), 1385–1396. https://doi.org/10.1002/asi.23732

Cook, T. (2006). Remembering the Future: Appraisal of Records and the Role of Archives in Constructing Social Memory. In *Archives, Documentation, and Institutions of Social Memory: Essays from the Sawyer Seminar* (p. 170). Ann Arbor: University of Michigan Press.

Department for Communities and Local Government. (2011, March 24). Statistics: English Indices of Deprivation 2010. Retrieved January 16, 2013, from https://www.gov.uk/government/publications/english-indices-of-deprivation-2010

Drucker, J., & Nowviskie, B. (2004). Speculative Computing: Aesthetic Provocations in Humanities Computing. In S. Schreibman, R. Siemens, & J. Unsworth (Eds.), *Companion to Digital Humanities (Hardcover)*. Oxford: Blackwell Publishing Professional. Retrieved from http://www.digitalhumanities.org/companion/

Finks, L. W. (1989). What Do We Stand For? Values Without Shame. *American Libraries, 20*(4), 352–354.

Gallon, K. (2016). Making a Case for the Black Digital Humanities. In *Debates in the Digital Humanities*. Minneapolis MN: University of Minnesota Press. Retrieved from http://dhdebates.gc.cuny.edu/debates/text/25

Gooding, P. (2014). *Search All About It: A Mixed Methods Study into the Impact of Large-Scale Newspaper Digitisation*. University College London, London.

Gooding, P. (2016). Exploring the Information Behaviour of Users of Welsh Newspapers Online through Web Log Analysis. *Journal of Documentation, 72*(2), 232–246.

Gooding, P. (2017). *Historic Newspapers in the Digital Age: "Search All About It."* Abingdon: Routledge.

Gorman, G. E., & Clayton, P. (2005). *Qualitative Research for the Information Professional* (2nd edition). London: Library Association Publishing.

Green, H. E. (2014). Facilitating Communities of Practice in Digital Humanities: Librarian Collaborations for Research and Training in Text Encoding. *The Library Quarterly: Information, Communication, Policy, 84*(2), 219–234. https://doi.org/10.1086/675332

Grimes, M. F., & Grimes, P. W. (2008). The Academic Librarian Labor Market and the Role of the Master of Library Science Degree: 1975 through 2005. *The Journal of Academic Librarianship, 34*(4), 332–339. https://doi.org/10.1016/j.acalib.2008.05.023

Haraway, D. (1988). Situated Knowledges: The Science Question in Feminism and the Privilege of Partial Perspective. *Feminist Studies, 14*(3), 575–599.

Harris, R., Sleight, P., & Webber, R. (2005). *Geodemographics, GIS and Neighbourhood Targetting*. Chichester: John Wiley & Sons.

Hartsell-Gundy, A., Braunstein, L., & Golomb, L. (Eds.). (2015). *Digital Humanities in the Library: Challenges and Opportunities for Subject Specialists*. Association of College & Research Libraries.

Hauck, J. (2017). From Service to Synergy: Embedding Librarians in a Digital Humanities Project. *College & Undergraduate Libraries, 24*(2–4), 434–451.

Hirst, P. (1966). Educational Theory. In J. W. Tibble (Ed.), *Educational Theory*. London: Routledge and Kegan Paul.

Hirst, P. (1974). *Knowledge and the Curriculum*. London: Routledge and Kegan Paul.

Hughes, L. M., Ell, P.., Knight, G. A. G., & Dobreva, M. (2015). Assessing and Measuring Impact of a Digital Collection in the Humanities: An Analysis of the SPHERE (Stormont Parliamentary Hansards: Embedded in Research and Education) Project. *Digital Scholarship in the Humanities, 30*(2), 183–198.

Jockers, M., & Worthey, G. (2011). Introduction: Welcome to the Big Tent. Retrieved September 17, 2018, from http://dh2011abstracts.stanford.edu/xtf/view?docId=tei/ab-005.xml

Kirschenbaum, M. G. (2004). "So the Colors Cover the Wires": Interface, Aesthetics, and Usability. In S. Schreibman, R. Siemens, & J. Unsworth (Eds.), *Companion to Digital Humanities (Blackwell Companions to Literature and Culture)* (Hardcover). Oxford: Blackwell Publishing Professional. Retrieved from http://www.digitalhumanities.org/companion/

Klein, J. T. (1990). *Interdisciplinarity: History, Theory, and Practice*. Detroit: Wayne State University Press.

Koltay, T. (2016). Library and Information Science and the Digital Humanities: Perceived and Real Strengths and Weaknesses. *Journal of Documentation, 72*(4), 781–792.

Kretzschmar Jr, W., & Gray Potter, W. (2010). Library Collaboration with Large Digital Humanities Projects — Lit Linguist Computing. *Literary and Linguistic Computing, Advance Access*. Retrieved from http://llc.oxfordjournals.org/content/early/2010/10/19/llc.fqq022.short?rss=1

Lankes, R. D. (2011). *The Atlas of New Librarianship*. Cambridge Mass.: The MIT Press.

Liu, A. (2011, January 7). Where is Cultural Criticism in the Digital Humanities? Retrieved November 13, 2018, from http://liu.english.ucsb.edu/where-is-cultural-criticism-in-the-digital-humanities/

Liu, A. (2013). Is Digital Humanities a Field? - An Answer from the Point of View of Language. Retrieved from http://liu.english.ucsb.edu/is-digital-humanities-a-Field-an-answer-from-the-point-of-view-of-language/

Meyer, E. T., & Eccles, K. (2016). *The Impacts of Digital Collections: Early English Books Online & House of Commons Parliamentary Papers.* London: JISC. Retrieved from https://papers.ssrn.com/sol3/papers.cfm?abstract_id=2740299

Moazeni, S. L. (2015). Integrating Digital Humanities into the Library and Information Science Curriculum. *Public Services Quarterly*, *11*(3), 225–231.

Nowviskie, B. (2013). Skunks in the Library: A Path to Production for Scholarly R&D. *Journal of Library Administration*, *53*(1), 53–66. https://doi.org/10.1080/01930826.2013.756698

Olsen, P., & Risam, R. (2016). Postcolonial Digital Humanities. In *The Encyclopedia of Postcolonial Studies* (pp. 1–6). American Cancer Society. https://doi.org/10.1002/9781119076506.wbeps297

Ranganathan, S. R. (1931). *The Five Laws of Library Science.* Bombay: Asia Publishing House.

Robertson, S. (2016). The Differences Between Digital Humanities and Digital History. In *Debates in the Digital Humanities*. Retrieved from http://dhdebates.gc.cuny.edu/debates/text/76

Robinson, L. (2009). Information Science: Communication Chain and Domain Analysis. *Journal of Documentation*, *65*(4), 578–591. https://doi.org/10.1108/00220410910970267

Robinson, L., Priego, E., & Bawden, D. (2015). Library and Information Science and Digital Humanities: Two Disciplines, Joint Future? Presented at the 14th International Symposium on Information Science, Zadar, Croatia. Retrieved from https://openaccess.city.ac.uk/id/eprint/11889/

Rockenbach, B. A. (2013). Digital Humanities in Libraries: New Models for Scholarly Engagement. *Journal of Library Administration*, *53*(1), 1–9. https://doi.org/10.1080/01930826.2013.756676

Shera, J. H. (1972). *Toward a Theory of Librarianship and Information Science.* Centre or the Study of Democratic Institutions. Retrieved from http://revista.ibict.br/ciinf/index.php/ciinf/article/viewFile/1643/1251

Siemens, R. (2016). Communities of Practice, the Methodological Commons, and Digital Self-Determination in the Humanities. *Digital Studies/Le Champ Numérique.* https://doi.org/10.16995/dscn.31

Sula, C. A. (2013). Digital Humanities and Libraries: A Conceptual Model. *Journal of Library Administration*, *53*(1), 10–26. https://doi.org/10.1080/01930826.2013.756680

Svensson, P. (2012). Beyond the Big Tent. In M. K. Gold (Ed.), *Debates in the Digital Humanities*. Minneapolis MN: University of Minnesota Press.

Tanner, S. (2012). *Measuring the Impact of Digital Resources: The Balanced Value Impact Model.* London: King's College London. Retrieved from http://www.kdcs.kcl.ac.uk/fileadmin/documents/pubs/BalancedValueImpactModel_SimonTanner_October2012.pdf

Terras, M. (2011, July 26). Peering Inside the Big Tent: Digital Humanities and the Crisis of Inclusion. Retrieved November 8, 2018, from http://melissaterras.blogspot.com/2011/07/peering-inside-big-tent-digital.html

Thelwall, M. (2009). *Introduction to Webometrics: Quantitative Research for the Social Sciences.* Morgan and Claypool Publishers. Retrieved from http://www.morganclaypool.com/doi/pdf/10.2200/S00176ED1V01Y200903ICR004

Unsworth, J. (2000). Scholarly Primitives: What Methods do Humanities Researchers Have in Common, and How Might our Tools Reflect This? Presented at the Humanities Computing: Formal Methods, Experimental Practice, King's College London. Retrieved from http://people.brandeis.edu/~unsworth/Kings.5-10/primitives.html

Vakkari, P. (1994). Library and Information Science: Its Content and Scope. In *Advances in Librarianship* (Vol. 18, pp. 1–55). Emerald Group Publishing Limited. https://doi.org/10.1108/S0065-2830(1994)0000018003

Warwick, C. (2012). Institutional Models for Digital Humanities. In *Digital Humanities in Practice* (pp. 193–216). London: Facet Publishing.

Warwick, C., Terras, M., Huntington, P., & Pappa, N. (2008). If You Build It Will They Come? The LAIRAH Study: Quantifying the Use of Online Resources in the Arts and Humanities. *Literary and Linguistic Computing*, *23*(1), 85–102.

Whearty, B. (2018). Invisible in "The Archive": Librarians, Archivists, and The Caswell Test. *English, General Literature, and the Rhetoric Faculty Scholarship*, *4*. Retrieved from https://orb.binghamton.edu/english_fac/4

SECTION II

Convergence and collaboration

10

HUMANS IN THE LOOP

Epistemology and method in King's Digital Lab

James Smithies and Arianna Ciula

10.1 Introduction

The first occurrences of the English word 'laboratory' date back to the end of the fifteenth and beginning of the sixteenth century. Ben Jonson used the word in a masque performed at the court of James I in 1610, in which Mercury drives alchemists out of a laboratory in favour of Prometheus, Nature, and twelve "sons of nature" (Kohler, 2008, p. 756). In the Western tradition, laboratories were integral to the development of natural philosophy during the Enlightenment, and fundamentally entangled with the development of experimental science in the late sixteenth and early seventeenth centuries. Drawing on a flowering of activity in these 'mechanical arts' across Europe, Francis Bacon famously recommended to Queen Elizabeth I that she establish libraries and zoos and botanical gardens to better understand the natural world (Merchant, 2008, pp. 735–736). These prototypical laboratories took the alchemical tradition, where people attempted to turn base metals into gold, and reoriented them towards mathematically-grounded methods based on observation and repeatability. Bacon described the rationale for this in one of the foundational texts of modern scientific method, *Novum Organum* (1620):

> We must not only search for, and procure a greater number of experiments,
> but also introduce a completely different method, order, and progress of
> continuing and promoting experience. For vague and arbitrary experience
> is (as we have observed), mere groping in the dark, and rather astonishes
> than instructs. But when experience shall proceed regularly and
> uninterruptedly by a determined rule, we may entertain better hopes of the
> sciences. (Bacon, 1902, p. 80)

In the centuries that followed, laboratories became the "myth-laden headwaters of scientific knowledge" (Barben, Fisher, Selin, & Guston, 2008, p. 988) where methods like these were deployed in increasingly controlled 'clean' environments enabled by a mixture of tools and methods. Andrew Pickering's claim (1995, p.7) that the laboratory method is as much "performative" as procedural is telling: laboratories have come to symbolise not only science but a mode of techno-scientific instrumentalism that lies at the heart of modern industrial capitalism.

This is in tension with the values of many humanities researchers, but it is important not to lose sight of the rich historical connections between science and the humanities and their origins in the tradition of natural philosophy that led to the modern laboratory system (Bod, 2014).[1] According to the seminal paper by Eugenio Garin (1969), the birth of scientific method originated in a convergence, bridging the fourteenth and the sixteenth centuries, between the *critical* work by humanists (indistinguishable from the scientists or the philosophers of the time) and the 'mechanic' contributions of artisans (painters, architects, engineers): between the techniques of the machinists and historico-philological techniques. Even at a quick glance over its multifaceted and possibly not yet fully explored history, the laboratory seems to sit at the crossroad of recurring revisions of the relation between *homo faber* and *homo sapiens*. These revisions have informed and continue to inform the epistemologies, the economies, and the cartographies of knowledge in the modern age.

Discussing early modern experimentation, Ursula Klein (2008) argues that laboratories and the "hybrid experts" operating in them produced things as well as knowledge and "bridged the gap between the intuitive, local knowledge of apprenticed craftsmen and the rational, text-based knowledge of university-educated scholars":

> [...] experimental inquiry into nature was interconnected with technological innovation and the economic system of labor more broadly. The early modern laboratory was the outcome of a long tradition in which innovative forms of labor, technical expert knowledge, and text-based philosophies developed in tandem. [...] handiwork was tied to some forms of advanced expertise, including text-based knowledge. In other words, the ancient separation of hand and mind, highlighted by Shapin, was restructured and slowly abolished in this mixed expert tradition. [...] These hybrid experts, fostered by mercantilist states, argued emphatically in favor of an amalgamation of experimentation, hands-on knowledge, mathematics, and conceptually driven analysis that partly relied on knowledge transmitted by texts, diagrams, and other forms of representation. [...] The mediating tradition of hybrid experts, highlighted above, developed new forms of useful knowledge present neither in the tradition of scholars nor in that of ordinary craftsmen. These ranged from ineffable bodily skills to connoisseurship of materials, tacit and verbal, to articulated know-how, to methods of measuring, data gathering, and classification, all the way to conceptually driven analysis and work on paper using various kinds of paper tools to construct intelligible representations (Klein, 2008, pp. 779–781).

According to Graeme Gooday (2008), use of the term 'laboratory', over the *longue durée*, offers ample evidence for "a multifarious, heterogeneous, and mutable entity" (p. 788). Over history, the laboratory has diversified in its forms and evolved in status, arguably becoming emblematic of an experimental but also materialist and hence situated epistemology.

The development of conceptual and institutional apparatuses capable of supporting this evolution are revealing. David Livingstone notes that the physicist James Clerk Maxwell had to argue strongly for the development of laboratory science in the nineteenth century, against colleagues and administrators used to much less practical research methods. His experience reveals the "intimate connections between claims to scientific knowledge and the places of knowing", along with the more quotidian need to explain sometimes challenging new practices to sceptical research communities. Maxwell's appeal to "a strategic alliance [...] between philosophy and the factory" secured at the same time a space and a *raison d'etre* for what became the Cavendish Laboratory in Cambridge—aptly located on the New Museum Site—in the 1870s. "[T]he new physical laboratory was a spatial and symbolic intervention into the University's scholarly domain" (Livingstone, 2000, p. 288). This kind of institutional 'conceptual work' has direct parallels in the vision statements and business cases of our own era, appealing for a share of resources and infrastructures in humanities faculties, institutes, and centres as well as in the galleries, libraries, archives and museums sector (GLAM).

Cognizance of this historical connection provides an important opportunity for reflection, especially given contemporary trends towards datafication, quantification of the self, and the entanglement of society and culture with computing technologies. Laboratory methods are entering (or re-entering under new guises) the humanities and are an important component in the humanist search for knowledge. The history of laboratories demonstrates their plasticity. A great variety of different kinds of laboratories have emerged and disappeared over the years, from floating river barges used to collect and examine marine life to an unsustainable herbarium at a major United States research university that was demolished to build a stadium. Far from been immune from what goes on outside their space, "[l]aboratories, like individuals, have to a large extent thrived or languished according to how effectively they have dealt with the rest of the world" (Gooday, 2008, pp. 785–786).

Many early laboratories were heavily criticised by the scientific community, and many only lasted as long as their founding scientist. In some cases this had profound effects on the reception of laboratory science itself. As Andrew Pickering (1995) notes, for example, the failure of the tools and methods associated with microscopic morphology in the nineteenth century led to a more general suspicion about the value of laboratories that supported those approaches. When bold claims being made by morphologists were undermined by new approaches, critics took aim at the laboratory system more broadly, claiming that the large capital investment and ongoing costs for their maintenance and support could be better used elsewhere. They felt modern, highly controlled, laboratories industrialised scientific method at the expense of individual genius and argued for a return to less institutionalised settings. Nature, rather than sterile rooms in research-intensive universities, was the appropriate experimental setting, despite the difficulties that created in the development of robust scientific methods (Pickering, 1995, p. 457).

The heterogeneous nature of laboratory science continues to this day: wet labs studying plants or animals; genomic laboratories sampling and analysing gene sequences; metallomics labs exploring the composition of materials; field laboratories processing samples gathered from rivers and lakes; chemistry laboratories creating everything from industrial chemicals to shampoo; linguistics laboratories studying language acquisition and development; archaeology and art history laboratories applying material sciences methods to analyse artefacts of the past. Research facilities like CERN's Large Hadron Collider or the United Kingdom's Diamond Light Source synchrotron, are in many senses laboratories too. However large and complex they might be, they are still merely sites that enable research through the provision of infrastructure, tools, and methods. This is a view of laboratories that intersects with the broader notion of the generic 'research facility', an even more ill-defined label common in national and international research discourse. In simple terms, however, it is enough to remember that laboratories are profoundly defined by the space they inhabit and their situatedness.

10.2 The sociology of the laboratory

So-called 'laboratory studies' have been commonplace in Science and Technology Studies (STS) since Bruno Latour and Steve Woolgar embedded themselves in a neuroendocrinology laboratory as cultural anthropologists in the 1970s. The field has resulted in sophisticated (and sometimes contentious) understandings of what laboratories are and how they function,[2] complemented by systematic historical reflections on the poietic relation between subjects and objects of sciences.[3] STEM laboratories have "become a theoretical notion in our understanding of science" (Knorr-Cetina, 1992, p. 116), acting as a synecdoche for not only experimental method but (more problematically) also epistemological purity and the human drive towards truth. This is far less true for humanities laboratories, of course, even if they have not been immune to the rhetoric of the "progressivist" laboratory discourses and "the desire to be modern" (Tollebeek, 2014, p. 137). Humanists have a complex relationship to experimentation, quantification, and engineering, and digital humanities (DH) laboratories are rare enough that we have not yet had time to define their form and function, let alone their place in the symbology of epistemology and method. There is no reason, for example, that they even need to be situated within universities or the cultural heritage sector: the form can evolve over time according to the needs of the knowledge ecologies they support. This is primarily because digital humanities is a new field and few laboratories have been subjected to detailed study,[4] but it also reflects resistance to tools, methods, and organizational structures perceived to be influenced by STEM models—themselves associated with managerialism and capitalist economics (Clement, Emerson, Losh, & Padilla, 2018).[5] Early scientific laboratories were resisted for the same reason, interestingly enough, because they were believed to be "congruent with the new managerial hierarchies and procedures of large-scale industrial capitalism" (Kohler, 2008, p. 678).[6]

Comparison with scientific laboratories only goes so far—their epistemological and methodological goals are fundamentally different—but as Rens Bod (2014) and others have noted, cross-pollination between science and the humanities is more common and historically grounded than many people think. Both traditions have a common ancestry in natural philosophy, centuries of collaboration, and shared tools and methods. Moreover, the research traditions that evolved from natural philosophy instantiated social and moral infrastructure—such as the seminar model in philology and history, research groups and schools, large collective projects,[7] national and international networks, public funding, the professionalisation of disciplines—alongside technical and procedural methods (standardised methods of text collection, division of labour, the settings and handling of equipment). Laboratories are "implicated in th[e] very matrix of the modern" (Kohler, 2008, p.765) and benefit from what sociologist Zymunt Bauman (2000) refers to as "liquid modernity", the continuous reconfiguration of practices, institutions and methods. R. G. Collingwood noted the self-conscious attitude towards research method this produces in his 1924 commentary on the history of ideas, *Speculum Mentis*:

> the empirical scientist respects fact, but it is a peculiar kind of fact that he respects; it is not fact as it grows, tangled up in the growth of the everyday world, but fact passed through the sieve of his own abstract methods, fact refined and expurgated, the fact of the laboratory. (Collingwood, 1924, p. 203)

It is important to correct the view of laboratories, held by many humanists, as deterministic factories that inevitably imply the use of a narrow set of (empirical) methods. A laboratory represents "a social form that travels and is easy to adopt, because it seems rooted in no particular cultural soil but, rather, in a universal modernity" (Kohler, 2008, p. 766). Rather than implying an inevitable drive towards positivism and industrial capitalism, laboratories allow us to subvert and mutate experimental method and culture.

As Karin Knorr-Cetina (1992, p. 116) notes, "the study of laboratories has brought to the fore the full spectrum of activities involved in the production of knowledge", creating a rich store of critical insight. DH laboratories can be guided by a significant critical tradition that takes into account myriad factors, from epistemological and methodological to cultural, historical, economic, political. In doing so they might avoid mistakes made by colleagues in other fields and design their spaces and activities in ways that strengthen the core humanities disciplines. In addition, because they are highly invested in the study of human artefacts, the humanities (including DH) are well positioned to creatively draw from a more inclusive legacy of models and metaphors of knowledge production and praxis beyond mainstream laboratories, from the design studio and maker space to the press.[8] The "social worlds" approach articulated by scholars such as Knorr-Cetina (1981), Fujimura (1987), and Star (1988) in the 1980s is particularly useful. These writers claimed that (regardless of their research focus) laboratories are best viewed as complex *discursive* arenas, segmented into multiple different social worlds cooperating and sometimes competing for resources, viewpoints, funding sources, tools, and so on. The "n-dimensional" (Star, 2010, p. 602) social world of laboratories make them good examples of what Star refers to as "boundary objects": sites, concepts, or objects that facilitate work and communication across an extremely wide range of communities. Boundary objects "are a sort of arrangement that allow different groups to work together without consensus. However, the forms this may take are not arbitrary. They are essentially organic infrastructures" (Star & Griesemer, 1989).

King's Digital Lab can certainly be characterised as an n-dimensional boundary object. It was established in 2015, an outgrowth of the rapidly expanding Department of Digital Humanities (DDH) at King's College London. The current model of department + lab is the product of over 50 years[9] experimentation in digital humanities (formerly 'humanities computing') and ongoing efforts to stay at the forefront of a rapidly evolving field.[10] The department and laboratory evolved from the Centre for Computing and the Humanities (1995)[11] and the Centre for e-Research (2008), which were combined as DDH in 2012. Rapid growth of digital humanities as a field, and burgeoning student numbers, led to an increasing focus on teaching and a desire to bring new tools and methods to bear on software development projects and their supporting infrastructure. Software engineering capabilities (staff and infrastructure) were restructured out of the department into a stand-alone laboratory and asked to increase digital capability not only in DDH, but also in the wider faculties of Arts & Humanities, and Social Science & Public Policy.

The laboratory is conceived as both a research unit (producing research outputs) and research facility (providing access to tools and expertise to enable research), balancing the need for practical digital humanities scholarship with industry-standard approaches to software development, infrastructure maintenance, and financial management. The lab functions in the context of an evolving university-wide eResearch strategy that seeks to increase digital research capability across all disciplines and work towards the efficient integration of research capability with core data management, library, and archival systems. The lab's social world is therefore radically n-dimensional, encompassing not only the local and global digital humanities communities but also cognate fields in the arts and humanities and social sciences, funding agencies, and institutional teams involved in IT, HR, business support, and finance.

10.3 Infrastructure: Human and technical

KDL methods are designed to manage the complexity of working in an n-dimensional environment, building on concepts of postphenomonology, postfoundationalism, and entanglement described by Smithies (2017). The assumption is that laboratory methods need to cut through a "mangle" (Pickering, 1995) of epistemological, technical, human, and financial issues, which collide in the physical and intellectual space of the laboratory. This extends to the provision of career development processes for staff, involving defined 'Research Software' roles (Analyst, UI/UX Designer, Engineer, Systems Manager, Project Manager) aligned to the Agile DSDM® and Skills Framework for the Information Age® (SFIA) industry standards. To ensure staff are provided with robust career paths, and acknowledged as skilled professionals, core lab staff are employed on permanent full-time contracts, aligned to both academic and professional service (IT) tracks. Fixed term staff are employed sparingly, and only to 'scale up' when demand requires it. At the time of writing the lab comprised a Director, Deputy-Director, Research Software Engineers (1 principal and 3 senior), two UI/UX Designers (1 senior), Research Software Project Manager, Senior Research Software

Systems Manager, two contractors, two research associates and two student interns. Academic Affiliates and Research Fellows provide intellectual input, in addition to the many Primary Investigators (PIs) and project owners from King's College London and external universities, the cultural heritage sector, and industry. The lab hosts guest speakers and runs workshops and hackfests like most digitally-intensive research units (Smithies, 2018).

It is worth noting that the lab's approach to HR career development, as described in Smithies (2019), is conceived as a 'research method' in its own right. It assumes that diversity is a key method for fostering creativity and quality, based on an emerging consensus that not only is diversity ethically necessary, but an effective way to ensure quality (Ensmenger, 2012; Abbate, 2012). More pointedly, as Marie Hicks notes, there is strong evidence to suggest the British computing industry collapsed and was overtaken by Silicon Valley in the late twentieth century specifically because of state-sanctioned gender discrimination (Hicks, 2017). Our underlying assumption is that "labor—and gendered labor, specifically—made computing what it is today, far more so than the hardware or exceptional individuals who are often the focus of computing histories" (Miltner, 2019, p. 164): the methodical development of diverse human 'infrastructure' is a key factor in successful digital research laboratories. Optimal diversity is some way off (especially when contractual status, seniority, and ethnicity are taken into account) but at the time of writing this stance has led to a movement from six men and one woman, to seven men and six women. Seven languages, across nine nationalities, are spoken in the lab.

As with STEM laboratories, this lab is tightly integrated into the corporate life of the university. Much leaner policy documents are used now, but almost 100 pages of business, operations, and human resource plans were produced to guide the lab through its first years. The daily rate for development is set at cost-recovery level, in recognition of the scholarly value the lab offers colleagues within the university, its contribution to the wider university research environment, and its contribution to knowledge and society. Infrastructure is designed and managed by the lab and supported by a cost-recovery model under-pinned by Faculty. Laboratory staff are represented on major faculty committees and contribute to administrative life alongside other 'standard' departments. The philosophy of the lab thus problematises the provision of digital research capability (in a collaboration between academic and administrative teams within Faculty) across all aspects of its operations: epistemological, methodological, infrastructural, operational, and financial. Rather than being a space dominated by material equipment, the lab functions as a complex socio-technical system, with a variety of humans in the loop. In reductive terms this 'operational method' provides the bedrock upon which all other methods sit.

KDL's technical infrastructure is as important to its work as its sociology. As Anna Foka et al. note in their discussion of HumlabX at Umeå University, "[t]he turn to digital research infrastructures is a call for the humanities to review the categories that have so far helped us make sense of the sociotechnical reality we study. As technology progresses, we need to invent new concepts, relationships, and vocabularies to understand its impact" (Foka et al., 2018, p. 273). We could add to this the need for new methods and epistemologies, to help us understand how technology can be used to answer new and existing research questions. Research infrastructures like laboratories generate both opportunities and constraints. This is perhaps *the* fundamental insight gained from operating the lab in the four years it has existed. Unlike traditional humanities disciplines, where methods can (to a significant degree) be divorced from their immediate operational context, methods used in humanities laboratories are inextricably tied to their human and technical infrastructure, operational capabilities and funding model.

King's Digital Lab manages about 90 projects, including up to 30 that are active in some form, and ~5 million digital objects. Its infrastructure comprises over 200 virtual machines, running Debian and Ubuntu Linux and a software stack that includes a range of legacy software (Java, PHP) but primarily Django Python, Javascript, and associated management tools (Solr/Elastic Search, Vagrant, Docker, Travis).[12] Additional servers are used for centralised services such as image storage, mail and user authentication. A major new hardware upgrade was completed in mid-2018, replacing end of life hardware with

Humans in the loop

Figure 10.1 Migration of ca.170 virtualised servers to upgraded KDL infrastructure (summer 2018)

5 Dell R640 servers (Intel Xeon Gold 6154 3GHz, 18 cores 25MB Cache, 512MB RAM, upgradeable to 768RAM), a largely solid-state SAN (44 x 960GB SSD disks, 6 x 6TB 7.2k spinning disks) comprising 35TB RAID6 and an 18TB slow archive (Figure 10.1). Lab infrastructure is connected to the university network (and from there the UK's national high-speed research network) via a 10GB connection. The entire system is backed up to King's College London's enterprise backup system daily. Cloud services such as Amazon Web Services, Linode, and Microsoft Azure are considered where they seem appropriate (for example for experimental work, or short-term analysis), and High Performance Computing (HPC) facilities are available via the university's eResearch team.

Lab methods rely on control and management of this 'full stack' infrastructure, which was implemented at significant cost and will need to be renewed every five years.[13] As dry as the details may be to the uninitiated, this infrastructure is the digital equivalent of flasks, beakers, and centrifuges. It is not suited to tasks such as simple data storage (which can be handled more cost effectively on central university infrastructure), simple web hosting (where external parties install and manage the applications themselves), digital preservation (which often uses cheaper and slower hardware), or high performance computing (which requires greater compute capacity and access to powerful graphics processing units (GPUs)). It is designed to support the kinds of tools and methods that the lab excels and has expertise in, or aims to develop capacity in, such as image-intensive websites, domain-specific data models, digital scholarly editions, map-based interfaces, text and network analysis, data visualisation and analysis, and digital object repositories.

10.3.1 Key methods: Design, build, maintain and monitor

The lab's infrastructure therefore includes obvious technical and human elements, but there are significant procedural elements too. These procedural elements can be viewed as methods for "technological mediation" (Kiran, 2015, p.123): the self-reflexive and circular interaction of humans and the technological world. Although derived from industry, they have been heavily adapted for a research context, and are central to the daily life of the lab.[14] It is difficult to understate the importance of this suite of methods. In a classic essay in *Social Studies of Science* in 1987, Joan Fujimura (1987) noted that laboratory methods exist to allow the alignment of different 'worlds', through a process of 'articulation' undertaken by team members as they design, build, and maintain their experiments or research projects. Alignment between the 'social world' of the laboratory (the host organization and collaborators, their administration, funding requirements, and processes), the 'laboratory' (available expertise, time, resource, equipment) and the 'experiment' (access to materials, algorithms, databases) is necessary before a given experiment or project can be undertaken. 'Articulation' takes place largely through conversations and workshops, supported by a range of design methods (see below) that help assess feasibility and define the tools and methods that will be used in the experiment or project. In KDL's case, for example, a project with existing funding requiring a relatively simple historical database or scholarly edition would be very easy to 'articulate' because the social world, laboratory, and project, are already well aligned. The only issue would be staff availability, and perhaps issues related to digitization or copyright. At the other end of the scale, major Horizon 2020 projects, involving multiple UK and European partner institutions, large distributed datasets, and advanced algorithmic analysis requiring high performance computing are also possible, but require significant articulation.

Few projects fall completely outside KDL's capabilities, but in some cases a recommendation is made to engage a different laboratory or centre with more suitable expertise, or an attempt is made to partner with another team or vendor, to ensure the research can be conducted at a high standard. External collaboration often involves colleagues (and Principal Investigators) at external universities with expertise in a particular research domain, or involves people from the creative arts, or the GLAM sector. It is worth noting that KDL's philosophy (and formal strategy) embraces a range of projects, requiring the team to explore both straight-forward projects in need of little articulation and complex ones demanding a lot. The point is that, as Fujimura notes, "technology alone cannot make problems doable [feasible]. *Doability is better conceptualised as the alignment of several levels of work organisation*" (Fujimura, 1987, p. 258, emphasis in original). Lab methods allow articulation across social, laboratory, and experiment to occur as smoothly as possible and in doing so extend the capabilities of the lab, and open up new possibilities for research and collaboration. More detailed methods, such as digitization, TEI-XML text encoding, or natural language processing occur within individual projects, of course,[15] but they are almost wholly dependent upon these higher-level methods of laboratory management.

The lab's full software engineering process is enabled and monitored by the lab Project Manager.[16] This person chairs a weekly project planning (PP) meeting, involving the entire team, where new project ideas are assessed against the lab's workload, funding strategy, research interests and technical capability. Involving the whole lab taps into the 'hive brain', or collective intelligence, of the team and allows holistic decisions to be made: these meetings are integral to the communal philosophy of the lab, and represent the first step towards the articulation (in Fujimura's terms) of the problem. About three new projects ideas are assessed in this manner each week: over 100 each year.

10.3.1.1 Design

Projects that move beyond the PP meeting are assigned a Research Software Analyst (RSA) and move into the 'feasibility' phase of the design process, guided by software engineering methods tailored for a research environment from Agile DSDM®.[17] The RSA will meet with the relevant partner, usually the Principal Investigator (PI), to discuss their project's often very preliminary idea, recommend tools and methods, and define and prioritise technical requirements. Tools might range from a digital repository to a text processing algorithm, methods from algorithmic analysis to oral interviews or manual interpretation of sources: it is

Humans in the loop

the analyst's job to understand the research domain and work with the partner to determine the optimal way to answer the research questions. Requirements are prioritised using the Must have/Should have/ Could have/Will not have (MoSCoW) for short[18] method, and costed using a standard spreadsheet tool that includes rates for labour and technical infrastructure (including CPU, RAM, and disk space). Methods for estimating the time it will take to build each component of the project are largely tacit, relying on the experience of the analyst and their colleagues. This reliance on tacit knowledge is a well-known aspect of laboratory method across all disciplines, and an important factor in the success of laboratory research. If tacit knowledge is lost, through the departure of key staff members, a lab's research capability can be seriously undermined (Polanyi, 2009).[19]

After internal peer review, and approval from the lab director, the feasibility document is slightly updated and sent to the partner as a Product Quote (PQ). When funding is not already secured, this forms the technical basis of a grant application, including its technical costs and expectations for research data management and sustainability. At the time of writing the lab is placing greater attention on its design methodology in this preliminary phase, leading to a sometimes longer process that allows more complex and risky projects to be undertaken. The intention is to align technical development (based on Agile DSDM® methods) to the Double Diamond design process recommended by the UK Design Council (2015). This process is divided into four phases (Discover, Define, Develop and Deliver), and aims to balance free expression with the progressive articulation of high-quality products. In KDL's case, this means digital tools that enable high quality, reproducible, and sustainable research outputs.[20] Double Diamond is being explored in recognition of the difficulty of engaging in cutting-edge design practices in environments dominated by research and engineering cultures: dedicated effort is needed to convince colleagues of the need to invest in adequate design discovery to ensure elegant, accessible and user-centred research tools are produced.[21]

In some cases, the design phase will result in a decision not to move forward with the project. In other cases, decisions are made to undertake preliminary exploratory workshops to produce design models rather than actual products, due to technical complexity and cost. Sometimes the risk of failure will be so high that the project is taken out of the main Agile software engineering process and 'incubated' using '10% time' allocated to staff members to work on projects of personal interest to them.[22] Sometimes, a decision is made to produce a proof of concept (PoC) at low cost, to better understand the research problem, model data, and experiment with risky new methods.[23]

A more challenging example, which illustrates the problems associated with articulating new methods in labs like KDL, lies in a project led by Ligeia Lugli, Newton Fellow at King's College London. The project aims to track 'Conceptual change in Buddhist Sanskrit literature through corpus data', using neural networks developed by computer scientists and linguists. Senior Research Software Engineer Geoffroy Noël and Senior Analyst Paul Caton led the work for KDL with seed-funding supported by Faculty, undertaking extensive feasibility testing to prove the methods could support a major funding bid. Over several weeks Noël and Caton worked with Lugli to define her requirements, which aimed to produce a system capable of segmenting strings of Sanskrit text to a high enough quality that a human researcher could complete the task. As possible technical solutions were being considered, Lugli became aware of a new Sanskrit parser, and asked if KDL could test it using a sample corpus (Reddy et al., 2018). Noël began the work as part of the normal Agile feasibility phase, requesting additional time and resource as various issues, including not only technical complexity but the need for a more powerful computer, became apparent. In normal circumstances it would not have been feasible to continue without external funding, but KDL was engaged in a concerted effort to increase capability in machine learning (ML) at the time and the project was an excellent way to achieve this.

Through careful management, Noël and Caton were able to build and test several models based on a deep sequential segmenter described in the paper provided by Lugli, using that team's open source code and training set. They then measured the recall performance of those models on Lugli's samples, which were Buddhist variants of Sanskrit. Surprisingly the results highlighted the inability of a state-of-the art neural network to generalise to a small corpus containing some new words and longer sentences. This apparent setback actually allowed Dr. Lugli to instead craft her own segmentation heuristics in R with very promising results and that new development was rapidly integrated into our feasibility study. This was enough to deem a larger project feasible, and a Product Quote was produced as input to future grant proposals. The care and investment required to articulate Lugli's research problem should be readily apparent. The laboratory's software engineering methods include a degree of flexibility, but some research projects fall outside the normal pattern of activity. It was only possible to articulate 'Conceptual Change in Buddhist Sanskrit Literature' because the project aligned well to faculty and university strategic priorities (to increase capacity in machine learning), and the lab budget topped up by faculty seed-funding could accommodate limited additional expense to support that.

It is perhaps unfortunate that KDL cannot support all the research ideas it is presented with, but it is no different in this way to a genomics laboratory or high-energy physics facility: every laboratory is limited in intellectual, technical, and financial capital and needs to decide for itself (in consultation with its primary community) what methods it should specialise in. KDL staff are consistently involved in multiple project ideas requiring in-depth feasibility analysis, sometimes requiring recourse to workshops, proof of concept models, or preliminary data modelling. This usually occurs in emerging technologies, or areas DH at King's have not worked in before, and can be considered normal for a research laboratory in any field. Although the lab's design methods have evolved in the past four years and have reached a satisfactory level of refinement and rigour, the sustainability of a research facility operating in an n-dimensional environment inevitably relies on a certain degree of flexibility that allows for its design methods to be fine-tuned in response to exploratory research areas and emerging technologies.

10.3.1.2 Build

Because it is an essential activity that usually occurs before funding has been granted, and in many cases will not result in a successful funding bid regardless, funding projects that require extensive feasibility analysis can be difficult, making it important that a steady stream of projects fall within the boundaries of the lab's normal research model. This is the case with perhaps 70% of project ideas. In normal circumstances, the Product Quote drafted during the Design phase is produced in relatively straight-forward fashion, taken out of storage when funding is granted, and a project team established to work with the partner and their researchers to build the tool, website, archive, or visualization. The feasibility process will have defined high-level requirements (see Figure 10.2), ensured the project is technically feasible, and defined the amount of funding available to deliver it, but a lot of work remains to be done.

After development environments have been established on KDL's server infrastructure, using operating system templates tailored to the team's development stack, this work is managed through iterative design and software engineering methods allocated into standard Agile 'increments' usually delivered at the end of a two-week 'time-box', dedicated for development work. For a mid-size project like Gordon McMullan's *Shakespeare in the Royal Collections* (ShaRC; McMullan et al., 2019), funded by the AHRC, this requires allocation of a lead Research Software Analyst[25] to guide the project and a wider team of Research Software Designer(s), Research Software Engineer(s), and a Research Software Systems Administrator. The Principal Research Software Engineer will provide oversight and ensure it is aligned to work that needs to be delivered for other projects.[26] In this way, the high-level requirements contained in the PQ can be divided into more tightly defined detailed requirements, and the project integrated into broader lab workflows. Fortnightly time-boxing meetings determine what work will be undertaken in each increment,

Humans in the loop

Priority	Requirement
M	Taxonomic data model for Shakespeare-related items in the Royal Collections and Royal Archives
M	Metadata schema that facilitates multiple associations among records
M	Site that can store, search across, and display a set of digital objects representing those items (likely to be approx 2500 objects)
M	Site that can store, search across, and display a set of metadata records associated with the digital objects
S	Admin interface that allows direct metadata record creation on site
S	Map functionality showing location of items by royal residences
S	Timelines placing items in historical context
C	Integration of 3D visualizations of key rooms at Windsor Castle (creation of 3D images would be by 3rd party)
W	Public interaction with/contributions to site

Figure 10.2   Shakespeare in the Royal Collections (ShaRC) high level requirements.[24]

in close consultation with project partners and the wider project team to ensure the budget is spent in an optimal way. Projects will often compete with other work for priority within the lab, so the weekly project planning meeting mentioned above—attended by all lab staff to maximise the range of available viewpoints - is held to manage workflow issues. In addition, the Principal Research Software Engineer coordinates a three-month planning meeting ('quarterly time-boxing') to provide the team with a means to control its workload within a medium-term horizon, and provide the Project Manager and Research Analysts with an overview of available resources in the medium term. Brief daily 'stand up' meetings (previously in face to face mode and now moved to a dedicated virtual channel of communication to enable flexible working), attended by development team members, are used mainly for a brief mutual update on daily workflow, but also to identify choke points and emerging issues. All time spent on a project is logged using the ActiveCollab project management tool, which is also used for document and task management, and budgeting.

The build process is iterative and unfolds in close collaboration with the wider project team. It is characterised by deep intellectual engagement as detailed tools and methods such as user interface design, data modelling, and system design are deployed. This is where post-foundational research methods (Smithies, 2017) are most intensively used, in a reflexive process of discovery, experimentation, deployment, and improvement between the technical and research teams (Smithies, 2017, pp. 153–202). This is the point in the software engineering cycle where design artefacts such as John Bradley and Harold Short's 'factoid' data model are produced (Pasin & Bradley, 2015), where map-based search interfaces such as the one produced by Neil Jakeman for *Atlantic Europe in the Metal Ages* are realised (Koch et al., n.d.), and where the TEI markup schemas and data analysis methods developed by Paul

Caton (and expressed using designs produced by Ginestra Ferraro) for *The Values of French* emerged (Gaunt et al., 2015–2020).[27]

Technical work occurs on both local development environments installed on laptops and PCs, and a staging server used for testing and iteration. In many ways, the build phase best demonstrates the unique value of research software engineering teams. The design phase requires close collaboration between technical and research leads, but the build phase puts these relationships to the test, requiring close ongoing collaboration, deep engagement with the subject matter and research questions, ongoing creativity and problem solving, frequent review meetings and the negotiation of not only research methods (with their attendant affordances and constraints) but time, budget, and other external pressures.

A key moment in the build phase is realised when the budget diminishes to a point where the project needs to transition towards go-live, or 'production'. This is often a testing time, involving negotiation about which 'Could' MoSCoW requirements agreed to in the PQ can be delivered. All going well, assuming a high quality PQ has been produced and the build phase has not met with significant unexpected technical difficulties or found itself exploring unexpected avenues (as sometimes needs to occur as the research process evolves), the lab's project manager announces 'change freeze': the point at which new features will no longer be added, and all resources will be deployed towards quality assurance and deployment processes. This is also the stage in the process where a Service Level Agreement (SLA), defining the terms and length of maintenance, and expectations for long-term archiving and sustainability, is produced. That document is signed by the partner, usually the PI, and KDL Director, and viewed as the authoritative 'acceptance to service' authorizing go-live of the public site.[28]

10.3.1.3 Maintain

Laboratory methods do not halt after go-live. Projects, such as *The Values of French*, are often deployed in an iterative fashion, progressively adding content for months or sometimes years after core development has stopped. All online projects require ongoing maintenance, of both the operating systems/server, and application. These are usually scheduled yearly or bianually depending on perceived risk, but occasional additional maintenance is sometimes needed if (for example) a vendor releases a version of their internet browser that breaks functionality on a website, or (as occurred with the so-called 'Heartbleed' bug; US Department of Homeland Security, 2014) a previously unknown security vulnerability is uncovered that requires immediate resolution. Continuous changes in the wider university technical environment, undertaken by the central IT team to improve and secure core services, sometimes also entails work by the laboratory team, to ensure their core systems remain aligned to IT standards or projects are updated to account for architectural changes that were not present when the project was designed. All of these scenarios, and more, need to be accounted for in the lab's methods, balancing the research needs of the project partners and their associated research communities, with the security of the lab, wider university's networks and data, and sometimes national or international policies.[29]

This is managed through the broader framework of the lab Software Development Lifecycle (SDLC; see King's Digital Lab, 2018): a set of methods derived from the software industry but adapted to the lab's research environment. In alignment with Agile DSDM methodology, the SDLC drives all project phases (from pre to post-project) including the design and build processes described above (see Figure 10.3). It frames a wider process that includes maintenance and archiving or 'Application Lifecycle Management' (ALM) and 'Research Data Management' (RDM). These methods are sometimes merely procedural, related to process and project management, and sometimes highly technical, related to Continuous Integration (CI) used to manage the programming process, and DevOps used to manage server software. A full archiving and sustainability process (Smithies, Sichani, Westling, Mellen, &

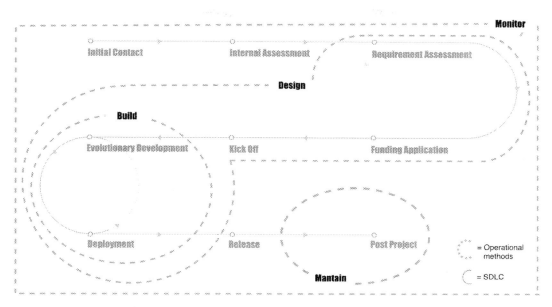

Figure 10.3 Integration of KDL SDLC with the lab operational methods

Ciula, 2019; King's Digital Lab, 2019) guides the final stages of projects, when funding has ended and decisions need to be made about its future. This involves a series of steps to assess the scholarly value of the site, its technical complexity, costs for ongoing maintenance, and possible routes to ongoing funding. Additional work is done if needed to explore migration to other hosts, or the best methods for archiving.

10.3.1.4 Monitor

The process of 'articulation' referred to by Fujimura and explored in depth by a range of Science and Technology Studies researchers, expands the notion of laboratory method outwards from the tools and methods used to answer research questions and disseminate knowledge to the wider context of the laboratory in its intellectual, socio-cultural, and business contexts. Although by no means the only mode of digital humanities research—or necessarily the best—laboratories benefit the community not only in the resources they offer and the research opportunities they present, but in the macroscopic scale or "wider social canvas" (Gooday, 2008, p.786) they beg to be interpreted through. In many ways they present an uncomfortable lens into the machinery of contemporary academic research—highlighting the dependence on scale, volume, and administrative necessity—and the tension between economic and epistemic visions.

This entanglement with socio-cultural and administrative necessities is nowhere more apparent than in the methods needed to monitor the daily work of the laboratory, the progress of projects, and the outcomes of research activity. This is not to mention the need to account for and manage the financial aspects of the laboratory, including in the case of King's Digital Lab (at the time of writing) a requirement to recover at least 70% of operational costs through external funding. This figure is designed to balance the need for sustainable income streams with a recognition that research activity cannot be measured by commercial norms: cost recovery rather than profit is the primary goal, with a view to increasing capability, and offering a reasonable amount of freedom to follow hunches and experiment with risky techniques. A detailed funding strategy with targets for both funding bids and other external income is used for that purpose, recalibrated each year and reviewed each quarter.[30] Progress is reported to faculty in quarterly and annual reports, along with financial accounting methods required by central university administration. Given the assumptions outlined earlier in this chapter, and the inherent complexity of laboratory operations, we assume administrative and financial realities will evolve over time.

Conclusion

In this chapter we sketched the n-dimension environment of a research lab and its methods by drawing from an historically and sociologically informed reference framework as well as from the empirical evidence provided by King's Digital Lab's operational model. The chapter leaves out the 'material truth' (Baird 2003, p.54) of the laboratory, however (the models that are produced in the design process or the working knowledge embedded in the instruments of a build phase are not described here), to foreground the operational methods which align the lab's research environment with its wider multi-faceted context of production—itself comprising cultural, epistemological, methodological, infrastructural, human, and business resources and constraints. What emerges is a view of an arts, humanities, and social science research facility that functions in a multidimensional context, where research is shaped in negotiation with human, financial, and technical factors. The focus on design and build methods, leading to maintain and monitor methods, exemplifies the processes of articulation evolved in a specific epistemological and operational context, designed to engage with a demanding workflow of heterogenous projects at scale, and managed by a highly collaborative team of hybrid experts.

While acknowledging that the formalisation of operational methods at King's Digital Lab is organic and *in fieri*—under constant (creative) pressure from time, and evolving financial, political, and epistemological issues—its key methods are designed consciously and in cognizance of the team's duty of care to research traditions and colleagues. It is an example of a research software engineering facility adapted to a Digital Humanities and Social Science context—one of many configurations possible.

Notes

1 For the connections between Italian humanism and laboratory science as well as more generally between historical and philological sciences and historical natural sciences, see also Pyle (2010).
2 For canonical examples of the field see Latour & Woolgar (1979); Knorr-Cetina (1981, 1999); Winner (1986); Longino (1990); Pickering (1992).
3 See for example: Daston (2000); Daston & Galison (2007).
4 A study of HumLabX at Umeå University is a notable recent exception. See Foka, Misharina, Arvidsson, & Gelfgren (2018). For a discussion on the heterogeneity of DH labs see also Lane (2016).
5 Thomas Gieryn (2008) concludes his paper on the design of the Clark Center at Stanford University as the new stereotypical placeless place for the Biomedical Engineering and Sciences lab architecture with a reflection on the endemic tension in science between economic and epistemic visions.
6 See also Schaffer (1998).
7 For a discussion of how Classics paved the way in the origins of collaborative research in the nineteenth century, anticipating also the resistance to positivistic methods and the criticism of its legacy, see Baertschi (2014).
8 Wai-te-ata Press at Victoria University of Wellington (New Zealand) is a remarkable example of a digital humanities lab revitalising, disrupting and appropriating the press model; see Sydney Shep's presentation (Institute of Historical Research, 2018).
9 For a snapshot on this recent institutional history see Short, Nyhan, Welsh, & Salmon (2012).

10 We refer to the labels 'digital humanities' and 'humanities computing' as commonly accepted chronological distinctions in the field (the first one used in particular from the end of the 1940s and replaced by the second one in the early 2000s). For more details, both on their connotations and the historical development they represent in the evolution of digital humanities in the Western and English-speaking tradition, see Nyhan & Flinn (2018, pp.1-8).

11 CCH itself evolved from an initiative known as the Research Unit in Humanities Computing, established in 1992 (Short et al., 2012).

12 See https://stackshare.io/kings-digital-lab for a complete list.

13 KDL technical infrastructure is managed by Tim Watts and Brian Maher who led the recent upgrade and coordinate its operational methods.

14 Software engineering methods were designed and implemented by Miguel Vieira and Paul Caton, and have evolved with the input of various team members. Design methods are led by Ginestra Ferraro and Tiffany Ong. Project management methods are led by Pam Mellen.

15 These methods are of obvious relevance to the research conducted by KDL, but not the focus of this paper.

16 At the time of writing, Pam Mellen.

17 In some cases someone other than an RSA will be assigned, perhaps for small projects that don't require a full software engineering process, or if someone else in the lab has particularly relevant understanding of the research problem or solution.

18 Must, Should, Could, Won't have this time (see Agile Business Consortium, 2014 and in particular https://www.agilebusiness.org/content/moscow-prioritisation).

19 For a digital humanities example, see Nowviskie (2014).

20 This process is led by Ginestra Ferraro, Senior Research Software UI/UX Designer.

21 Archetype.ink, a simple website marketing an open source tool used for manuscript analysis, is one of the first results of this focus (Stokes et al., 2017).

22 This is only possible if the project is of genuine interest to a KDL staff member, who is free to allocate their 10% time as they please. This is the case for Elliott Hall's *Digital Ghost Hunt* project, which went on to receive funding from the UK Arts & Humanities Research Council (AHRC) in 2018 and 2019 (Hall, Bowtell, Krell & Westling, 2019).

23 This approach was used for the *Georgian Papers Programme* (GPP), a partnership between the Royal Collection Trust (RCT) and King's College London, and the Omohundro Institute of Early American History and Culture and the College of William & Mary (Royal Collection Trust, & King's College London, 2015). KDL used internal funding from RCT and King's to produce a PoC data integration workbench, designed to integrate digital content across disparate sources, and allow users to update metadata. It involved the development of an extensive information architecture, and a basic web application. It has resulted in a much more detailed PQ that defines the technical requirements for a complete product that is being funded from various sources.

24 Paul Caton, for Gordon McMullan, 'Shakespeare in the Royal Collections product quote'. King's Digital Lab, 2017.

25 Often but not always the person who wrote the PQ.

26 Project management is another area in need of continuous improvement and fine-tuning for KDL. Indeed, due to the substantial number of projects sprinting in each timebox, the intersections between the build and monitor processes (see below) require team work and close partnerships especially between the Principal RSE role and project management roles, currently shared across lab manager and analysts.

27 Geoffroy Noël was lead software engineer on this project.

28 At the time of writing, methods and processes of release management and user acceptance are priority areas the lab is aiming to refine further.

29 KDL has formal and informal relationships with many international partners, from single individuals to research institutions and funders. While it is not in the remit of this chapter to describe how the national and international landscape impacts the n-dimensional environment of the lab, it is worth noting that (especially national and international) research policies concerning digital research infrastructures are evolving as we write and could provide both further constraints to KDL, as well as opportunities for expansion or collaboration. See in particular UK Research and Innovation (2018).

30 In the 2017–2018 financial year King's Digital Lab was involved in over 80 project ideas (ranging from concept development to grant submission), and grant applications totalling ~£26 million.

References

Abbate, J. (2012). *Recoding gender: Women's changing participation in computing*. Cambridge, Mass: MIT Press.

Active Collab. (2007, 2019). ActiveCollab. Retrieved 8 February 2019, from ActiveCollab website: https://activecollab.com/

Agile Business Consortium. (2014). *The DSDM Agile Project Framework Handbook*. Retrieved from https://www.agilebusiness.org/resources/dsdm-handbooks

Bacon, F. (1902). *Novum Organum [1620]* (J. Devey, Ed.). New York: P. F. Collier.

Baertschi, A. M. (2014). 'Big Science' in Classics in the 19th Century and the Academicization of Antiquity. In R. Bod, J. Maat, & T. Weststeijn (Eds.), *The Making of the humanities. volume III: The making of the modern humanities* (Vol. 3, pp. 133–249). Amsterdam: Amsterdam University Press.

Baird, D. (2003). Thing knowledge: Outline of a materialist theory of knowledge. In H. Radder (Ed.), *The philosophy of scientific experimentation* (pp. 39–67). Pittsburgh, Pa.: University of Pittsburgh Press.

Barben, D., Fisher, E., Selin, C., & Guston, D. H. (2008). Anticipatory Governance of Nanotechnology: Foresight, Engagement, and Integration. In E. J. Hackett, *The handbook of science and technology studies: Third edition* (pp. 979–1000). Cambridge, MA: MIT Press.

Bauman, Z. (2000). *Liquid modernity*. Hoboken: Wiley.

Bod, R. (2014). *A new history of the humanities: The search for principles and patterns from Antiquity to the present*. Oxford: Oxford University Press.

Clement, T., Emerson, L., Losh, E., & Padilla, T. (2018). Reimagining the Humanities Lab. In É. Ortega, G. Worthey, I. Galina, & E. Priani (Eds.), *Digital humanities 2018: Book of abstracts/Libro de resúmenes* (pp. 55–59). Mexico City: Red de Humanidades. Retrieved from https://dh2018.adho.org/reimagining-the-humanities-lab[s5]

Collingwood, R. G. (1924). *Speculum mentis, or, the map of knowledge*. Oxford: The Clarendon Press.

Daston, L. J. (Ed.). (2000). *Biographies of scientific objects*. Chicago: University of Chicago Press.

Daston, L. J., & Galison, P. L. (2007). *Objectivity*. New York: Zone Books.

Design Council. (2015, March 17). The Design Process: What is the Double Diamond? Retrieved 8 February 2019, from Design Council website: https://www.designcouncil.org.uk/news-opinion/design-process-what-double-diamond

Ensmenger, N. (2012). *The computer boys take over: Computers, programmers, and the politics of technical expertise*. Cambridge, Mass: MIT Press.

Foka, A., Misharina, A., Arvidsson, V., & Gelfgren, S. (2018). Beyond humanities qua digital: Spatial and material development for digital research infrastructures in HumlabX1. *Digital Sholarship in the Humanities*, *33*(2), 264–278.

Fujimura, J. H. (1987). Constructing `Do-able' Problems in Cancer Research: Articulating Alignment. *Social Studies of Science*, *17*(2), 257–293.

Garin, E. (1969). Gli umanisti e le scienze. In *L'Età nuova: Ricerche di storia della cultura dal XII al XVI secolo.* (pp. 451–475). Napoli: A. Morano.

Gaunt, S., Morcos, H., Rachetta, M. T., Ravenhall, H., Ventura, S., Caton, P., … Husar, M. (2015, 2020). Homepage | The Values of French. Retrieved 8 February 2019, from The Values of French website: https://tvof.ac.uk/

Gieryn, T. F. (2008). Laboratory Design for Post-Fordist Science. *Isis*, *99*(4), 796–802.

Gooday, G. (2008). Placing or Replacing the Laboratory in the History of Science? *Isis*, *99*(4), 783–795.

Hall, E., Bowtell, T., Krell, M., & Westling, C. (2019). The Digital Ghost Hunt. Retrieved 8 February 2019, from https://digitalghosthunt.com/

Hicks, M. (2017). *Programmed inequality: How Britain discarded women technologists and lost its edge in computing*. Cambridge, MA: MIT Press.

Institute of Historical Research. (2018, October 23). Sydney Shep (Victoria University of Wellington)—The Digital Handmade: Reimagining Nineteenth Century New Zealand Printing History. Retrieved 8 February 2019, from Digital History Seminar website: https://ihrdighist.blogs.sas.ac.uk/2018/08/sydney-shep-the-digital-handmade-reimagining-19thc-new-zealand-printing-history/

King's Digital Lab. (2018). A Software Development Life Cycle for Research Software Engineering. Retrieved 18 October 2019, from Sdlc-for-rse website: https://github.com/kingsdigitallab/sdlc-for-rse

King's Digital Lab. (2019). Archiving and Sustainability | King's Digital Lab. Retrieved 7 March 2019, from King's Digital Lab website: https://www.kdl.kcl.ac.uk/our-work/archiving-sustainability/

Kiran, A. H. (2015). Four Dimensions of Technological Mediation. In R. Rosenberger & P.-P. Verbeek (Eds.), *Postphenomenological investigations: Essays on human-technology relations* (pp. 123–140). Lanham: Lexington Books.

Klein, U. (2008). The laboratory challenge: Some revisions of the standard view of early modern experimentation. *Isis*, *99*(4), 769–782.

Knorr-Cetina, K. (1999). *Epistemic cultures: How the sciences make knowledge*. Cambridge, Mass: Harvard University Press.

Knorr-Cetina, K. D. (1981). *The manufacture of knowledge: An essay on the constructivist and contextual nature of science*. Oxford: Pergamon Press.

Humans in the loop

Knorr-Cetina, K. D. (1992). The Couch, the Cathedral, and the Laboratory On the Relationship between Experiment and Laboratory in Science. In A. Pickering (Ed.), *Science as practice and culture* (pp. 113–138). Chicago: University of Chicago Press.

Koch, J. T., Vetch, P. H., Karl, R., Cunliffe, B., Bray, P., Cleary, K., … Jakeman, N. (n.d.). Search | Atlantic Europe in the Metal Ages. Retrieved 8 February 2019, from Atlantic Europe in the Metal Ages website: http://www.aemap.ac.uk/search/

Kohler, R. E. (2008). Lab history: Reflections. *Isis*, *99*(4), 761–768.

Lane, R. J. (2016). *The big humanities: Digital humanities/digital laboratories*. Milton Park, Abingdon, Oxon; New York, NY: Routledge.

Latour, B., & Woolgar, S. (1979). *Laboratory life: The social construction of scientific facts*. Princeton University Press.

Livingstone, D. N. (2000). Making Space for Science. *Erdkunde*, *54*(4), 285–296. https://doi.org/10.3112/erdkunde.2000.04.01

Longino, H. E. (1990). *Science as social knowledge values and objectivity in scientific inquiry*. Princeton, N.J.: Princeton University Press.

McMullan, G., Retford, K., Barnden, S., Tamblin, K., Caton, P., Loboda, O., & Vieira, J. M. (2019). Shakespeare in the Royal Collections. Retrieved 18 October 2019, from Shakespeare in the Royal Collections website: http://sharc.kcl.ac.uk/

Merchant, C. (2008). 'The violence of impediments': Francis Bacon and the origins of experimentation. *Isis*, *99*(4), 731–760.

Miltner, K. M. (2019). Girls Who Coded: Gender in Twentieth Century U.K. and U.S. Computing. *Science, Technology, & Human Values*, *44*(1), 161–176.

Nowviskie, B. (2014). *Speaking in Code: An NEH Summit on the Social and Intellectual Implications of Tacit Knowledge Exchange in Digital Humanities Software Development* (National Endowment for the Humanities Final Report and White Paper No. 109227). Retrieved from University of Virginia Library Scholars' Lab website: https://securegrants.neh.gov/publicquery/main.aspx?f=1&gn=HD-51674-13

Nyhan, J., & Flinn, A. (2018). *Computation and the Humanities Towards an Oral History of Digital Humanities*. Retrieved from http://link.springer.com/978-3-319-20170-2

Pasin, M., & Bradley, J. (2015). Factoid-based prosopography and computer ontologies: Towards an integrated approach. *Literary and Linguistic Computing*, *30*(1), 86–97. https://doi.org/10.1093/llc/fqt037

Pickering, A. (Ed.). (1992). *Science as practice and culture*. Chicago: University of Chicago Press.

Pickering, A. (1995). *The mangle of practice time, agency, and science*. Chicago: University Of Chicago Press.

Polanyi, M. (2009). *The Tacit dimension*. Chicago: University of Chicago.

Pyle, C. M. (2010). Bridging the Gap. A Different View of Renaissance Humanism and Science. In R. Bod, J. Maat, & T. Weststeijn (Eds.), *The making of the humanities. volume 1—Early modern Europe* (Vol. 1, pp. 39–58). Amsterdam: Amsterdam University Press. Retrieved from doi: 10.5117/9789089642691

Reddy, V., Krishna, A., Sharma, V. D., Gupta, P., Vineeth, M. R. & Goyal, P. (2018). Building a Word Segmenter for Sanskrit Overnight. *ArXiv:1802.06185 [Cs]*. Retrieved from http://arxiv.org/abs/1802.06185

Royal Collection Trust, & King's College London. (2015). Georgian Papers Programme. Retrieved 8 February 2019, from Georgian Papers Programme website: https://georgianpapersprogramme.com/

Schaffer, S. (1998). Physics Laboratories and the Victorian Country House. In C. Smith & J. Agar (Eds.), *Making space for science: Science, technology and medicine in modern history*. (pp. 149–180). London: Palgrave Macmillan.

Short, H., Nyhan, J., Welsh, A., & Salmon, J. (2012). "Collaboration Must Be Fundamental or It's Not Going to Work": An Oral History Conversation between Harold Short and Julianne Nyhan. *Digital Humanities Quarterly*, *6*(3). Retrieved from http://www.digitalhumanities.org/dhq/vol/6/3/000133/000133.html

Smithies, J. (2017). *The Digital Humanities and the Digital Modern*. Basingstoke: Palgrave Macmillan.

Smithies, J. (2018). *From Lab to University: Towards an Institutional RSE Career Pathway*. Presented at the Research Software Engineering 2018, Birmingham University. Retrieved from https://jamessmithies.org/blog/2018/09/03/lab-university-towards-institutional-rse-career-pathway-rse-2018/

Smithies, J. (2019, February 7). The Continuum Approach to Career Development: Research Software Careers in King's Digital Lab. Retrieved 8 February 2019, from King's Digital Lab—Thoughts and reflections from the Lab website: https://www.kdl.kcl.ac.uk/blog/rse-career-development/

Smithies, J., Sichani, A. M., Westling, C., Mellen, P., & Ciula, A. (2019). Managing 100 Digital Humanities Projects: Digital Scholarship & Archiving in King's Digital Lab. *Digital Humanities Quarterly*, *13*(1). Retrieved from http://www.digitalhumanities.org/dhq/vol/13/1/000411/000411.html

Star, S. L. (2010). This is Not a Boundary Object: Reflections on the Origin of a Concept. *Science, Technology, & Human Values*, *35*(5), 601–617.

Star, Susan Leigh. 'Introduction: The Sociology of Science and Technology'. *Social Problems* 35, no. 3 (1988): 197–205.

Star, S. L., & Griesemer, J. R. (1989). Institutional Ecology, 'Translations' and Boundary Objects: Amateurs and Professionals in Berkeley's Museum of Vertebrate Zoology, 1907-39. *Socistudscie Social Studies of Science, 19*(3), 387–420.

Stokes, P. A., Brookes, S., Noël, G., Jakeman, N., Ferraro, G., & Ong, T. (2017). Archetype. Retrieved 8 February 2019, from Archetype website: https://archetype.ink/

Tollebeek, J. (2014). A Domestic Culture: The Mise-en-scène of Modern Historiography. In R. Bod, J. Maat, & T. Weststeijn (Eds.), *The making of the humanities. volume III: The making of the modern humanities* (Vol. 3, pp. 129–143). Amsterdam: Amsterdam University Press.

UK Research and Innovation. (2018). Infrastructure—UK Research and Innovation. Retrieved 8 February 2019, from UK Research and Innovation website: https://www.ukri.org/research/infrastructure/

US Department of Homeland Security. (2014). *OpenSSL 'Heartbleed' vulnerability (CVE-2014-0160).* Retrieved from United States Computer Emergency Readiness Team website: https://www.us-cert.gov/ncas/alerts/TA14-098A

Winner, L. (1986). *The whale and the reactor: A search for limits in an age of high technology.* Chicago: University of Chicago Press.

11

THE WARBURG
ICONOGRAPHIC DATABASE
From relational tables to interoperable metadata
Richard Gartner

11.1 Introduction

This chapter details work undertaken at the Warburg Institute in London to convert a database of iconography from a bespoke application to one grounded in interoperable metadata standards. The Institute has compiled over many years a unique database for art history arranged by iconographic subject. This invaluable resource was created using the database package mySql and as such is only accessible via the Institute's website. To enable it to be shared more widely amongst the community of scholars, the project described here attempted to translate its metadata from database tables to fully interoperable and established standards

To do this required two distinct stages. The first involved the creation of a 'data model', an overall map of the content of the database that defines both the metadata fields contained within it and their interrelationships. This 'data model' was then 'serialized', translated into pre-existing metadata standards from the library community: these then became the containers within which the database's contents could be held, processed and shared. None of this work was undertaken with a completely blank slate. The 'data model' was based on a well-established community standard known as CIDOC-CRM, an abstract 'conceptual model' which defines the core concepts and relationships that populate a metadata scheme of this kind. The serialized metadata was entirely based on well-established mechanisms already in place in digital libraries.

This chapter introduces the Warburg Institute, its place in the history of iconography and the database itself. It then describes the thought processes behind each stage of the project, the construction of the data model and its serialization. It ends by discussing the next steps necessary to realize the ambitions of the project to open up the Institute and its database to the wider community.

11.2 The Warburg Institute and iconography

The art historian and cultural theorist Aby Warburg (1866–1929) gives his name to one of world's leading centres for interdisciplinary studies in the humanities and sciences, the Warburg Institute in London. Warburg used his primary academic interest, the transmission and reception of the classical tradition in Western (particularly Renaissance) culture, to illuminate his wider interests in anthropology, history and the visual arts. His most important physical legacy was the Kulturwissenschaftliche

Bibliothek Warburg, the private library for cultural studies which he established in Hamburg in 1926 to house his extensive collection. His most important intellectual legacy in the eyes of many scholars, and possibly his most perplexing, is his Bilderatlas, literally an atlas of images, to which he gave the name Mnemosyne (memory).

In this project Warburg covered 40 wooden panels in black cloth and attached over 1000 images, not just photographs of acknowledged artworks but also images from newspapers, magazines and more ephemeral sources. Very little annotation adorns Warburg's creation apart from titles to each panel—anything from *Migrations of the ancient gods* to *From the Muses to Manet* to *The classical tradition today*. Warburg attempts to communicate his ideas through the juxtaposition of these images and leaves much of the interpretation to those who view the Atlas. Many have been the scholarly pages devoted to unravelling the often cryptic messages encoded in this network of images.

Warburg's interest in the image and its ramifications inspired much of the scholarly work undertaken at the Institute founded in London in 1933 that bears his name. One of the acknowledged founders of the discipline of iconology, Erwin Panofsky (1892–1968), carried out much of his pioneering research at the Institute. Fritz Saxl (1890–1948) and Ernst Gombrich (1909–2001), two illustrious names from art history in the United Kingdom, both served as its directors. But it is to the art historian Rudolf Wittkower (1901–1971) that is owed one of the unique resources of the Institute, its Photographic Collection.

This collection contains, in the words of its website, "physical photographs of sculptures, paintings, drawings, prints, tapestries and other forms of imagery… [including] tens of thousands of late nineteenth and early twentieth century photographs and slides, together with hundreds of thousands of images added since the Institute came to London in 1933" (Warburg Institute, 2018). More important than its size, historical provenance and scope is the unique way in which it is organized, by iconographic subject, not artist or period.

Wittkower, the first curator of the collection, devised a taxonomy based on iconographic types in the 1930s. This subject index, currently numbering some 18,000 categories, forms the basis on which the folders of the collection are organized. Reflecting its provenance and the academic interests of its progenitors, this index is highly detailed in its categorization of European iconography but rather less so in the case of others: it does, however, provide at least summary, and often more detailed, overviews of Islamic, Egyptian, Indian and Mesopotamian iconography (Warburg Institute, n.d.).

No other iconographic collection is arranged so comprehensively by subject as that of the Warburg which makes it a unique resource for art historians. It is particularly valuable for researchers who wish to trace the development of given subjects or stories, their diachronic journey through the history of art and the patterns of their appearances in this history. No other resource allows analyses of these types to be carried out with such ease; this has ensured the centrality of the collection in the study of iconology.

11.3 The Warburg Iconographic Database

Since 2010, the Photographic Collection has been undertaking an extensive digitization programme: to date approximately 80,000 of the Collection's 400,000 images have been scanned and added to its database. The bulk of these relate to the theme of classical antiquity and its influence on later periods, one of Aby Warburg's principal scholarly interests (Duits, 2018, p.162). The continued digitization programme is mainly funded by external grant income, particularly from the Kress Foundation who in recent years has funded the conversion of several tranches of the collection.

The Iconographic Database employs an extended version of Wittkower's classification scheme, translated into a facetted taxonomy (Duits, 2018, p.162). This extends considerably the granularity of the subject index to the paper collection, usually by adding extensive sub-facets to the categories of the original classification. Up to eight taxonomic levels are available to record an iconographic subject; this allows very detailed descriptions, for instance:

RELIGIOUS ICONOGRAPHY

- Typology and Prophecy
- Cycles
- Manuscripts and Prints
- Speculum humanae salvationis
- Chapter 34: Pentecost
- Chapter 34c: The Israelites receive the Ten Commandments
- Variant: An angel giving the tablets of the Law to Moses

The Warburg taxonomy forms a complement to IconClass, a widely-established standard for the classification of iconographic subjects (IconClass, 2018). This scheme, which has been in development since its inception in the 1970s, comprises approximately 28,000 concepts arranged hierarchically into ten broad categories, like the Dewey Decimal Classification on which it is partly modelled. The depth of its constituent subject areas varies, but it is particularly strong in the representation of biblical subjects and classical mythology.

Although there is considerable overlap between the two taxonomies, the Warburg's scheme is more detailed in many areas. One example of this is the mythological story of Apollo and Daphne, a single facet in IconClass. In the Warburg taxonomy, the story is sub-divided into eight facets, some of which are divided further. The facet detailing Daphne's transformation into a laurel tree, for example, is sub-divided a further eight times to reflect different stages of her transformation (Duits, 2018, p.162): these go into such details as transformations involving only her arms and hair, arms and toes, arms and feet, and her complete metamorphosis. Such details are not available in the broader taxonomy that is IconClass.

One further notable feature of the Warburg taxonomy is its malleability as a reflection of current iconographical research. The scheme is as a much a research output as a classification mechanism, reflecting new insights into iconography which emerge as a result of the scholarly investigations of the Photographic Collection's staff. As their research uncovers areas which require changes to the taxonomy these are readily and easily made, much more speedily than the mechanisms for amendments to the IconClass scheme allow. The Warburg taxonomy is thus a dynamic entity, changing frequently to represent the latest developments in iconographic research.

At present the Iconographic Database and its constituent metadata is stored in a series of mySql tables and interfaced by a set of PHP scripts. The taxonomy itself is encoded in a series of eight tables, each containing one level of the hierarchy. At the top of the taxonomic tree is a table containing the 15 top-level categories which form the starting point for exploring the semantic space beneath:-

ANTIQUITIES
ARCHITECTURE
ASIAN ICONOGRAPHY
ERANOS ARCHIVE
GESTURES & EXPRESSION
GODS & MYTHS
HISTORY
LITERATURE
MAGIC & SCIENCE
ORNAMENT
PORTRAITS

PRE-CLASSICAL ICONOGRAPHY
RELIGIOUS ICONOGRAPHY
RITUAL
SECULAR ICONOGRAPHY
SOCIAL LIFE

Lower-level tables are slightly more complicated as they require columns to indicate the parent of each term. A further complication arises from the occasional need to arrange the facets at a lower level in something other than alphabetical order; the books of the Old Testament, for instance, begin:

Genesis/Exodus/Leviticus/Numbers/Deuteronomy/Josue (A.V. Joshua)/Judges

These are more logically rendered in the order in which they appear than alphabetically. One column in all of the tables below the top level, therefore, provides a numerical indicator of a term's sequencing.

Encoding a complex taxonomy of this type within the relational tables of a database such as mySql presents multiple problems. The hierarchical structure of such a taxonomy fits clumsily into the relational structure, requiring a complex set of links or joins between tables to record its multiple levels. Links within these chains are easily broken, particularly if, as is the case here, the taxonomy is revised on a regular basis.

Even more problematic is the limited interoperability of a taxonomy encoded as a set of relational tables. It is difficult to share such a scheme with, or transfer it to, other systems except by a direct export and import of the tables. Translating it to systems not based on mySql requires significant data editing to retain the hierarchies of its internal structure. There is, therefore, the significant risk that the research encapsulated in the taxonomy, which is potentially of value to a wide scholarly community, remains hidden within the depths of the mySql labyrinth on the Warburg's servers.

Some other features of the metadata within the Database as a whole are also impediments to its interoperability. This screenshot of thumbnails depicting Daphne's transformation reveal an inconsistent set of captions: the first image, on the far left, indicates that this is a plate from the works of Ovid (but not which one) from the second half of the 15th century, the second that it is from a manuscript of [Konrad] Celtis, the fourth from works by Cambiaso. The others only indicate places of provenance and dates. (See Figure 11.1)

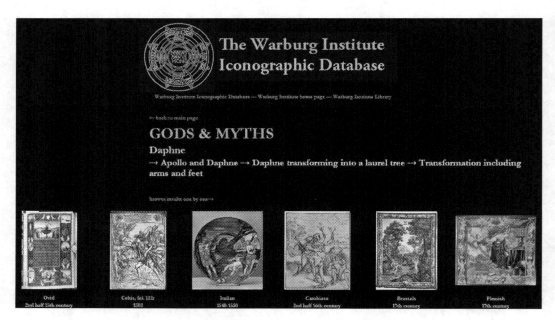

Figure 11.1 Warburg Institute Iconographic Database: browsing the taxonomic hierarchy

The Warburg iconographic database

Figure 11.2 Warburg Institute Iconographic Database: keyword search

This inconsistent set of captions is generated from each item's metadata: in the case of Ovid and Celtis from a field giving brief bibliographic information on the source of the photo, in the case of Cambiaso from an author/creator field. The others, those giving place names, are also, rather confusingly, from an author-creator field; in these cases the caption records the geographic provenance of a work when the artist is not named.

These generated captions are understandable when read in the context of the taxonomic hierarchy within which the image finds its place but make little sense outside it. Carrying out a search for 'Daphne', for instance (Figure 11.2), returns a set of thumbnails without the taxonomic description but with the cryptic captions alone.

This problem arises as a result of the image-level metadata within the Database containing no cataloguer-supplied title or caption field: because the metadata was initially devised for use in the context of the extensive taxonomy this appeared redundant. If, however, it is desired to share the Database outside the specific context of the interface within which it is currently presented this would present significant problems of comprehensibility.

Some means of producing meaningful titles or captions for each image therefore appears necessary. In some instances the images themselves may have titles: this will be so for many paintings, for instance. Where this is not the case consistent rules for generating these titles are necessary. The large number of images, and the relatively small amount of staff time available for any possible re-cataloguing of this material, means that these titles will generally have to be auto-generated by applying a set of consistent rules, resorting to manual generation only where this is not possible (hopefully in a small number of cases only).

11.4 The move to interoperability

The case for moving the Database and its metadata from the confines of mySql tables to more interoperable formats seemed compelling. Such a move would allow the Photographic Collection to widen its reach well beyond the Institute itself by sharing its taxonomy and the Database with others who could make use of it.

In particular, it was felt that its taxonomy offers a viable complement, or even alternative, to IconClass for those who require much more detailed and granular descriptions of iconographic subjects than the more established standard could offer.

Two stages were identified to enable this move to interoperability. The first was the definition of a clearer data model for the Database than the one that was currently locked away in its tables. This would involve, for instance, the rectification of omissions such as the image titles noted above as well as a consolidation of existing fields and structures to ensure a greater overall coherence for the metadata landscape.

The second stage would be the serialization of the data model into an interoperable metadata syntax. The term 'serialization' here means the translation of the abstract data model into concrete metadata records encoded in a machine-readable format. A serialization specifies how the abstractions of a model can be converted into something that can be stored and transmitted digitally, the metadata records that form the basis of a curated collection.

To begin, serialization requires two sets of choices to be made, the first of the encoding mechanism to be used and the second of the metadata schemes employing that mechanism, either pre-existing or newly designed. It was decided to use, if at all possible, pre-existing encodings and schemes which had found their place in the digital library and digital humanities communities instead of creating bespoke schemes specifically for the Database. This would avoid having to duplicate earlier work and ensure that the metadata so painstakingly compiled for the Database could more readily be transferred to, and used by, others.

11.5 Two approaches to interoperability

Two approaches to metadata interoperability predominate in the area of digital asset management. The first tends to aggregate all of the metadata for a complex digital object into a single hierarchy, usually encoded in the widely-used markup language XML (eXtensible Markup Language). This is the strategy adopted by one of the most commonly applied metadata schemas for digital libraries, METS (Metadata Encoding and Transmission Standard), a 'packaging standard' which allows all metadata for an object, usually encoded in several different schemas, to be conjoined into a single, logical hierarchical structure (Gartner, 2008).

An alternative approach that has been articulated by some practitioners of digital asset management (for instance (Lagoze et al., 2006)) argues that RDF-based networks of semantic linkages are the most appropriate method for serializing a data model of this kind. This is the approach taken by the widely-used Fedora Commons repository system (Fedora Commons, 2013) which employs an architecture of this kind, the Fedora Content Model Architecture (Fedora Commons, 2002). In this methodology, a complex set of RDF statements expressing semantic linkages (such as isPartOf, isConstituentOf or isDependentOf) is used to express the relationships within and external to a complex digital object. It is often advocated for use in rapidly-changing metadata environments, either on its own (Waddington et al., 2016) or in conjunction with XML schemas (Gartner & Hedges, 2013).

This latter approach allows an easy translation of a diagrammatically-expressed data model into a form that can be readily machine-processed, but there are many reasons for preferring the former which utilizes the more rigid hierarchies of an XML architecture. The complexity of data modelling involved in developing coherent ontologies, data cleansing problems and skills shortages have been cited as particular issues for RDF-based approaches to metadata, particularly in the library sector (Hawtin et al., 2011). They also present problems for digital preservation owing to their incompatibility with the package-based models on which current practices are based: in particular, the blurred boundaries of RDF-based metadata make it difficult to establish domains of responsibility for preservation (Gartner, 2016, p.92).

The Warburg iconographic database

For these reasons, the former, METS-based, approach was chosen for the conversion of the Database. Once this choice was made, the next stage was the definition of a data model. Before this could be drawn up, however, it was necessary to consider whether the model should itself draw on a wider and more abstract framework, commonly termed a 'conceptual model'.

11.6 Stage one: The data model

Designing a data model for the Iconographic Database was an opportunity to take an entirely fresh look at its overall design unencumbered by its current manifestation as a series of mySql tables. Such a model has two sets of components, the metadata facets to be included and their semantically-expressed relationships, both of which are essential in a viable data model. The facets comprise the semantic units of metadata necessary to describe the items in the Database, essentially the 'labels' with which these are tagged: they may include concepts such as artists' names, subject terms, places of origin and so on. Equally important are the linkages between these which give an overall shape to the data model: these form the joins that assign a given work of art to its place of origin or its artist, for example. A fully-developed data model must establish coherence in both of these essential components.

Rather than starting with a completely blank sheet, it proved better to build such a model on the foundations of a pre-existing conceptual model. There are many advantages to using such a model when undertaking an exercise such as this. It can act as a checklist of fundamentals, ensuring that, in carrying out the exercise of defining a data model from scratch, nothing vital is omitted. Because a conceptual model is usually built on the collective expertise of established practitioners, it can usually be relied upon to present a coherent, thought-out synthesis of best practice and so can help ensure that one's designs do not head off tangentially from what is required. It can, therefore, potentially save a significant amount of time and effort when approaching the task of designing a data model from scratch. Too rigid an application of a conceptual model such as this, however, has the potential to act as something of a straitjacket if it is allowed to constrain one's ideas or force them into a form in which one's requirements are not met. This is a particular danger if an inappropriate model is chosen. It is important to be selective and critical when choosing one and to be flexible in its application. It may act as a foundation or framework but should not form the entire edifice on which a data model is built.

The model chosen for this project was CIDOC-CRM (http://www.cidoc-crm.org/). This is widely established as a semantic framework within the heritage sector, particularly the GLAM (galleries, libraries, archives and museums) domain. It originated as a way of formalising the description of curated objects in these collections and forms the basis of several important data models such as Europeana (Charles & Isaac, 2015; Olensky, 2010) and FRBRoo (Riva & Žumer, 2017; Riva & Oliver, 2015; Bekiari et al., 2015).

CIDOC-CRM is designed to enable the exchange of cultural heritage information through the definition of high-level concepts for objects and their environment: specifically it provides

"definitions and a formal structure for describing the implicit and explicit concepts and relationships used in cultural heritage documentation…to promote a shared understanding of cultural heritage information by providing a common and extensible semantic framework that any cultural heritage information can be mapped to" (http://www.cidoc-crm.org/)

CIDOC-CRM is not without its problems or issues. It has been criticised for often requiring application-specific extensions, for allowing multiple representations of the same attributes, and for the complexity of the chains of concepts in which it records information (Hasihofer, 2009). It has also been deprecated for providing no guidance on mapping external metadata schemes to the model, which may often lead to problematic inconsistencies, and for giving no advice on encoding, storing, or processing this mapped metadata (Nussbaumer & Haslhofer, 2007, p.5).

Richard Gartner

Nonetheless, the provenance of CIDOC-CRM in the GLAM sector makes it an obvious choice for a relatively smooth fit with the requirements of the Iconographic Database. Most of the problems highlighted above can be obviated by the use of established interoperable standards such as those used in this project: these can resolve issues of ambiguous representations, inconsistent mappings and the paucity of guidance on encoding and also avoid the need to employ application-specific extensions. When used as the conceptual basis for a data model which is then serialized into established standards, it presents few problems as an underlying framework for metadata.

1. At its highest level, CIDOC-CRM divides its classes into four categories:-Space-Time, which covers a broad sets of concepts such as era or period, place and time span
2. Events, which includes when things come into existence or leave it and events that involve people
3. Material Things, tangible objects
4. Immaterial Things, intangible concepts or components of information

Below this level are narrower classes which form the components of a data model. These may include such concepts as Man-made Thing, Conceptual Object, Temporal Entity, Time Span, Symbolic Object and Actor.

Classes in CIDOC-CRM are accompanied by an extensive set of properties which may be used to join them semantically. Those referencing a time span, for instance, including Temporal Entity, Period, and Event, may be joined to other classes by such properties as has time-span, took place at, at some time within, and had at most duration. In all, 148 properties are available to link the 90 entities within the CIDOC-CRM class hierarchy, allowing a rich and complex web of data to be modelled.

The data model for the Iconographic Database was compiled by the Deputy Curator of the Photographic Collection, Dr. Rembrandt Duits, who created and designed the Database from its initial inception. His model, expressed in terms of the CIDOC-CRM ontology, takes the form shown in Figure 11.3.

At the centre of the diagram are the four core components of the Database: the image itself, the work of art in which it is instantiated, the photo that represents the work of art and the digital file in which the photo is encoded and stored. The image is conceived as a Symbolic Object, defined by CIDOC-CRM as a "sign of any nature, which may serve to designate something, or to communicate some propositional content." (http://www.cidoc-crm.org/Entity/e90-symbolic-object/version-6.2). The photo itself and the work of art are both Man-made Things, "discrete, identifiable man-made items that are documented as single units... [which are] either intellectual products or man-made physical things, and are characterized by relative stability" (http://www.cidoc-crm.org/Entity/e71-man-made-thing/version-6.2.1). The digital file is an Information Object, "identifiable immaterial items...[which] have an objectively recognizable structure and are documented as single units...[and do] not depend on a specific physical carrier" (http://www.cidoc-crm.org/Entity/e73-information-object/version-6.2).

The most abstract component, the image, has three linkages, one to the work of art that it represents, another to its classification in the taxonomy and a third to the photo in cases where this represents only part of the art work but is nonetheless a self-contained image (for instance, a photo of a single panel with a saint from a larger altarpiece). The other three components require a much more extensive set of linkages to describe them adequately.

The work of art represented in the image has ten linkages to other classes. The first of these provides information on its physical location (Place appellation in the CIDOC-CRM scheme): this may describe its current location or those which it occupied in the past, the latter employing a Time span class linked to the buildings cited in order to provide temporal information of its historical locales. The work itself may be assigned a time span to indicate particularly the diachronic dimensions of works that are no longer in existence. A further class allows inventory numbers or identifiers to be assigned to the work and the Actor class allows the essential component of the artist who created the work to be linked to it.

The Warburg iconographic database

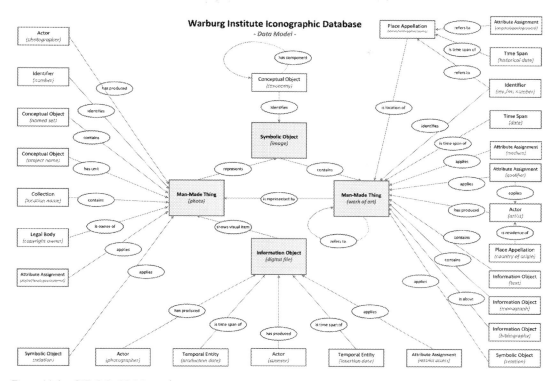

Figure 11.3 CIDOC-CRM ontology

Contextual information is very important for a work of art and so several linked classes provide this type of background metadata. These include details of monographs or other textual items in which the work of art is to be found and also a bibliography of secondary literature which discusses it. A final class allows the work to be related to others by any relevant criteria.

The photograph of the work of art has an equally rich set of linkages available. Here the CIDOC-CRM Actor class identifies the photographer who captured the image in the photograph. As is the case for the work of art itself, an identifier class is essential for the efficient management of the photograph: this is the identifier used for the physical copy held in the Photographic Collection where available. To place the photograph in context, it can be associated with the Conceptual objects 'Named set' (which refers to specific sub-collections within the Collection of which it is a part) or 'Project name' (if it was produced in the context of a particular project originating in the Institute). Its physical location is also recorded in a location name element.

As many parts of the Collection owe their origins to specific funded projects, there is space in the data model for a project name and also to record the often complicated copyright information associated with a photograph. A final class, the CIDOC-CRM Attribute assignment (an assertion about the properties of an object), indicates whether the photograph was captured in analogue or digital form.

It is important to distinguish the photograph from the digital object in which it is stored in the Database: the latter requires a distinct set of administrative and technical metadata. In addition to employing the Actor class for the person responsible for the digital file (for instance, the scanner operator), it is also used to identify the sponsor who made possible the digitization: this is important as large parts of the conversion of collections to digital form were only made possible through grants from external bodies (such as the Samuel H. Kress Foundation who have funded this for significant parts of the Database).

Two Temporal Entity classes identify the production date of the digital object (the date of its initial digitization) and its insertion into the Database: the latter can often be considerably later than the former owing to the need to find time and personnel to carry out the rigorous cataloguing necessary to ensure its scholarly value. A final class, in this case an Attribute Assignment, details access restrictions on the digital file: in some cases, viewing is limited to thumbnails only for copyright reasons.

Despite its apparent complexity, this data model fits readily into the CIDOC-CRM scheme: every component readily finds a place within the extensive set of classes and properties that it provides. Undertaking this exercise in the context of CIDOC-CRM, rather than beginning with an entirely blank sheet, proved a highly effective way of concentrating attention on the essentials of what such a data model is trying to do. The constraints and discipline of working within the context of the broader model ensured a coherent overall scheme was readily produced.

This was particularly important in the definition of the four core components at the centre of the diagram. It is important to separate out the abstract concept of an 'image' from its physical or digital manifestations and the work of art in which it is instantiated. It is to this abstraction that classification metadata about an iconographic subject is most effectively attached and so its definition as a symbolic object is an essential part of the model. Without CIDOC-CRM as a prompt, it would have been possible to conflate this abstract but essential concept with its manifestations and so lose important descriptive functionality from the model.

11.7 Stage two: Serializing the model

Once the data model is fully mapped out in this fashion, the next stage of the conversion of the Database is its serialization into interoperable metadata standards. Two sets of choices must be made at this stage: the first is the syntax, or encoding mechanism, within which the metadata will be held, the second the choice of standards employing that syntax which will form the containers for it.

The choice of syntax for the Database was relatively easy to make. XML, the eXtensible Markup Language, is one of the most widespread languages for encoding interoperable metadata for many important reasons. Because it is encoded as text, it is software independent and so ideal as a mechanism for data transfer. It is one of the most robust formats for archival purposes, in part for the same reason: despite the frequent obsolescence of data formats, text seems the least likely of all to be unreadable many years in the future.

Despite the simplicity of its encoding mechanism, XML is capable of encoding complex data structures, often with much greater clarity than the relational tables which have held sway over database design for so long. It is particularly effective at recording hierarchical relationships, such as those which predominate in the taxonomy of the Database. XML allows its metadata elements to be nested within each other so modelling these hierarchies elegantly and efficiently. It is for this reason that it is used particularly in environments where hierarchical models prevail, such as text encoding (the Text Encoding Initiative (TEI) (Text Encoding Initiative, 2013) and archival description (the Encoded Archival Description (EAD) (Library of Congress, 2017).

The choice of XML for an encoding medium is relatively simple to make: the choice of the XML schemas in which the metadata is to be held is rather more difficult. This is because of the sheer number of standards around, many of which overlap in their functions. Not for nothing did the computer scientist Andrew Tannenbaum quip "the nice thing about standards is that you have so many to choose from" (Tannenbaum, 2003, p.254). Luckily for the Warburg Iconographic Database a number of established standards stood out.

For the taxonomy an obvious contender was the Metadata Authority Description Schema (MADS) (Library of Congress, 2011), one of a family of bibliographic schemas produced by the Library of Congress. The Library of Congress website describes it as "an XML schema for an authority element set that may be used to provide metadata about agents (people, organizations), events, and terms (topics, geographics,

The Warburg iconographic database

genres, etc.) ". As such, it is ideal for encoding a taxonomy of subject terms. MADS allows each subject term to be encoded in a separate file or an entire collection of such terms to be listed together in a single 'MADS collection': the latter approach was chosen for the Database as it allows the taxonomy to be treated, and if necessary interchanged, as a single entity.

At the top of the hierarchy in the taxonomy are the 15 top-level categories described above. A sample entry for one of these takes this form:-

```
<mads>
    <authority ID="vpc-cat1-9">
        <topic valueURI="http://warburg.sas.ac.uk/vpc/id/cat1/9"
            authorityURI="http://warburg.sas.ac.uk/vpc">Magic and
Science</topic>
    </authority>
</mads>
```

The topic itself is recorded, unsurprisingly, in the <topic> element. It is assigned a unique URI (the valueURI attribute) by which it is referenced from outside the MADS file: the authorityURI attribute indicates that this URI is assigned by the Warburg Institute Photographic Collection. Each record in MADS is given a unique ID (the ID attribute of <authority>) by which it is referenced from within the MADS file itself.

Below this top level, the MADS record for a given topic is similar except for the inclusion of a reference to its immediate parent. One level down from Magic and Science, for instance, is the topic Astronomy and Astrology

```
<mads>
    <authority ID="vpc-cat2-71">
        <topic valueURI="http://warburg.sas.ac.uk/vpc/id/cat2/71"
        authorityURI="http://warburg.sas.ac.uk/vpc">Astronomy and
astrology</topic>
    </authority>
    <related type="broader"
            xlink:href="#vpc-cat1-9">
            <topic>Magic and Science</topic>
    </related>
</mads>
```

This only differs from its parent element by the inclusion of a <related> element with a type attribute set to 'broader'. The crucial link to its parent is made by the xlink:href attribute in which the internal ID of its parent (in this case vpc-cat1-9) is given. Each level down the hierarchy is treated in the same way: a <related> element uses an xlink:href attribute to reference its parent.

In this way, a thread is built up which allows each subject term to trace its line from the top of the hierarchy. The entire taxonomy can readily be contained in a single file: this represents its canonical or definitive version and in this form it can be transferred across systems and archived for long-term preservation.

The relative complexity of the hierarchical chains of the MADS format, and in particular the necessity of an integrated system of internal IDs without any broken linkages, may make it difficult to maintain the taxonomy manually if encoded in this form. For this reason, the MADS file is the output from the system in which the taxonomy is maintained and edited, not the primary mechanism by which these operations are performed. At present it is generated by a simple Python script which interrogates the mySql tables in which the Database is currently stored. The script iteratively runs through the levels of the taxonomy, generates the <mads> elements for each and, for any below the top, inserts references to its parent element.

The structure of a MADS file, based as it is on a chain of internal references, is logical and simple to process but relatively difficult for humans to decode: for this reason, alternative 'views' of the same data may be generated to make this chain of linkages easier to read. One of these is an XML file in which the thread for each topic is fully expanded: the subject noted earlier, for instance, an angel giving the tablets of the law to Moses, would have an entry as follows:

<category category-uri="http://warburg.sas.ac.uk/vpc/id/cat8/1474">RELIGIOUS ICONO-GRAPHY/Typology and Prophecy/Cycles/Manuscripts and Prints/Speculum humanae salvationis/Chapter 34: Pentecost/Chapter 34c: The Israelites receive the Ten Commandments/Variant: An angel giving the tablets of the Law to Moses

An 'expanded' version of the taxonomy of this kind may readily be used to generate the thread of topics in the user interface as shown in Figure 11.1.

For the item-level records for each image, another XML-based standard from the same 'family' of schemas produced by the Library of Congress was an obvious choice. METS, the Metadata Encoding and Description Standard (Library of Congress, 2014a) is, in the words of its website, 'a standard for encoding descriptive, administrative, and structural metadata regarding objects within a digital library'. It is designed to accommodate the complex array of these three types of metadata which are essential for describing and administering a digital object and is widely used amongst practitioners of digital asset management.

METS is a packaging standard for metadata, not a schema for descriptive or administrative metadata in its own right. It does not, for instance, contain any elements for bibliographic description or technical information about an object, nor any rights metadata necessary to enforce its intellectual property rights. Instead it acts as a container for other standards containing metadata of this kind, each of which has a logical place within the METS architecture. The one type of metadata encoded directly in METS is structural, the internal structure of a complex digital object, which is recorded in a hierarchical map within its architecture.

Three XML standards are embedded within the METS record for an image in order to record the extensive metadata mapped out in the data model described above. The first, and most extensive, of these is MODS (Metadata Object Description Schema) (Library of Congress, 2010), another standard from the same Library of Congress family as MADS and METS. This schema is a set of bibliographic elements intended primarily, but not exclusively, to provide descriptive metadata for objects in library collections. It is derived from MARC21, the primary bibliographic standard for library catalogues, but adds a number of elements which are specifically relevant to digital objects.

Two MODS files are embedded within the METS file for any given image: the first relates to its digital manifestation, the second to the work of art that it depicts. These two conceptually distinct items have separate locations within the METS architecture, the former within its container element for descriptive metadata, the latter within a subset of its administrative metadata section containing 'source metadata', that which relates to the analogue original from which a digital object is derived. This division neatly carves us the four core concepts of the data model, the first covering the Photo and Digital File, the second the Image and Work of Art.

The majority of the descriptive metadata for any given image relates to the work of art that it depicts and so goes into the MODS file within the source metadata section. This includes such standard information as artists' names, dates of creation, physical location, bibliographic citations referencing the work and details of the book or manuscript in which it is found (if any). It can also include more atypical bibliographic metadata, such as auction dates, where these are necessary to identify the previous location of a work of art.

The Warburg iconographic database

The most intellectually important metadata in the MODS file detailing the digital manifestation is its iconographic subjects: these are recorded by simple references to their URIs in the MADS file discussed earlier:

```
<mods:subject valueURI="http:/warburg.sas.ac.uk/vpc/id/cat6/2727"/>
<mods:subject valueURI="http:/warburg.sas.ac.uk/vpc/id/cat3/680"/>
<mods:subject valueURI="http:/warburg.sas.ac.uk/vpc/id/cat5/1274"/>
<mods:subject valueURI="http:/warburg.sas.ac.uk/vpc/id/cat3/2862"/>
```

For each subject, the valueURI attribute contains the URI of the <topic> element's valueURI attribute in the taxonomy MADS file.

In addition to this subject information, this section is limited to an identifier for the image, a note of the sub-collection of the Database to which it belongs, and information on the metadata record itself, including details of any funding which supported its creation.

In addition to an image's descriptive metadata and that of the work of art that it depicts, technical information on its provenance is important to record. In the case of the Iconographic Database this is limited to recording the date and time of its creation and the photographer who captured it. To do this, metadata is embedded in the section of the METS file containing digital provenance metadata using a further standard, PREMIS (PREservation Metadata: Implementation Strategies) (Library of Congress, 2008).

PREMIS, also maintained by the Library of Congress, is in the words of its website "an international standard for metadata to support the preservation of digital objects and ensure their long-term usability". It can be used to record, with some verbosity it must be said, an extensive set of metadata relating to the creation of an object and its digital life thereafter. In the Database it is used to record the image creation date and the name of its photographer.

Although the PREMIS schema is relatively verbose, it is logical and easy to accommodate when processing in a live system. The single event captured in the Iconographic Database can, of course, be supplemented by much more extensive listings, but, at present, this 'audit trail' of actions performed on the object is limited to its creation, the only event recorded in the database. It is hoped that new versions of the database will allow the recording of more extensive details of image's lifecycle in order to enhance its preservation in the long term.

The final component of the complex digital object that is an image in the Database is a listing of the files of which it is comprised. METS has a section for this as well, the file section.

Three files for a single image are recorded here, an archival, uncompressed TIFF image as originally captured, a full-size JPEG for delivery and a smaller JPEG which acts as a thumbnail for browsing.

Despite the apparent complexity and verbosity of the METS serialization of the data model, every component has a logical and unambiguous location within its architecture. At an initial glance, it may appear that the hierarchies of a METS file, and of the schemas used within it, make a potentially disjoint match with the distinctly non-hierarchical linkages of the data model in Figure 11.3. In practice, METS and these schemas allow a fluid set of linkages to operate within their architectures, cutting across these hierarchies as required, and so no significant mismatch occurs. Every component and linkage in the Data Model can be accommodated within the serialization as it is detailed here.

11.8 The next steps

This two stage process of metadata redesign has produced a robust data model that meets fully the intellectual and scholarly requirements of this unique database, the only one currently in existence that takes iconography as the primary focus for its survey of art history. A data model that did not meet these needs would have reduced severely the value of this resource, particularly in simplifying its iconographic backbone to a point where its raison-d'etre would be lost. The serialization into the well-established XML schemas of MADS, MODS, PREMIS and METS has captured this data model in all of its richness and reified its abstraction into a tangible set of metadata records in fully interoperable formats which can form the basis of delivery systems on any platform.

The next steps to be taken are the re-design of the Iconographic Database system to one that incorporates this newly-designed metadata as the basis of its operations. This will involve the creation of two user-interfaces, one for the delivery of the Database to its end users, the other (perhaps more complex) to allow the creation and editing of its constituent records. Despite its well-proven functionality within its user base, the current interface is relatively clunky and unattractive and so will need revising to enhance the profile of the Database amongst a wider cohort of potential users. This important work will be passed to professional designers, from whom tenders are being sought at the time of writing.

An important principle that must be established for the new interface is that the system which delivers it must be based on the canonical, XML-serialized form of the metadata. While the new system may not itself be one which is itself fully XML-compliant, it must be able to import directly from the MADS and METS files and export to them seamlessly and fluently. These files form the definitive 'statement' of the Database's metadata and so the core on which the system will operate, whether this is done directly or indirectly though real-time import and export functionalities.

Several possible platforms currently exist which could readily host the next version of the Database. Although investigations are still on-going, it appears that Islandora (Islandora, 2013), a modular digital asset platform built on the Fedora Commons repository, will be able to accommodate the requirements mapped out for this revision. Islandora is likely to be a suitable platform because it is open-source and so readily customizable, and also because it is based on a sound metadata core which can accommodate METS, MADS and MODS relatively easily.

Whatever platform is chosen in the relatively near future, the strategy outlined above is designed specifically to ensure the viability of the Database in the much longer term. The use of XML and these well-supported schemas will ensure that its metadata will be readily transferrable to any future system when the platforms that are currently available are long obsolete. The metadata discussed here is very much the infrastructure on which any superstructure resides and so the work that has gone into ensuring its robust format and content is essential, arguably more so than that which goes in to the comparatively ephemeral interfaces by which it is made available to users.

Conclusion

The approach discussed throughout this chapter demonstrates how a highly valuable and scholarly resource can move from a skilful but relatively ad hoc construct to a more solid and interoperable basis. This is not to underestimate the work that went into its initial creation, which produced a system finely attuned to the needs of its user constituencies and one which developed an important resource in its own right, the taxonomy which forms the backbone of the Database. The move from relational tables to interoperable metadata discussed here aims to open this resource to a much wider user base and to allow its unique approach to art history to find a foothold in the scholarly landscape outside the Warburg Institute.

The move to interoperability must be made in a methodical and logical way if the richness of a resource such as this is not to be lost in the process. The challenge in such a case is always to avoid simplifying not only the content of its constituent metadata but also the chain of linkages within which this content is embedded. Interoperability may be more easily achieved by simplification of this kind, reducing the complex structures of a metadata environment to something 'flatter' and so uncomplicated, but this should be resisted: the scholarly worth of this resource in particular lies as much in the intellectual structures embedded within it and the unitary metadata components that they contain.

The Warburg iconographic database

Three components to the process of moving to interoperability have been highlighted in this chapter, all of which are important to ensuring that it is achieved in a robust and usable fashion. The first is to ensure that there is, if at all possible, a solid standards-based backbone to the process as a whole. There are many good reasons for ensuring community-based standards underpin such an exercise, including the avoidance of redoing work already done by experts in the field and ensuring that the end product does not exist in a silo of its own construction.

Standards underpinned this project at both its inception and final manifestation. The construction of the data model was based on the conceptual model of CIDOC-CRM which focused thoughts at this abstract stage, providing a framework on which it could be built and separating out concepts, such as symbolic, man-made and information objects, which require separate treatments when drawing up their more concrete manifestations as metadata. It is, of course, not essential to employ a conceptual model of this type when drawing up a data model and it should certainly be avoided if it involves distorting one's requirements to ensure conformance with it in an over-rigid way. It is, however, an important and useful tool when applied appropriately and where it has clear relevance to the metadata environment being constructed.

The second component to the process is the compilation of an overall data model at an appropriate level of abstraction. This is where one should attempt to codify the landscape of the metadata requirements for the redesign and, just as importantly, to establish their interrelationships in a coherent overall structure. Overall coherence is important to ensure a robust structure which will be easy to maintain and develop further. It is, therefore, important to concentrate on the 'big picture' at this stage, not to become overwhelmed with details which can obscure this. This is the stage where serious questions about the purpose of the metadata redesign need to be asked and answered and when it is important to take a critical view of what is produced. This is much easier to do when one has an abstract view, unencumbered with excessive detail, of the scheme as a whole.

Putting together such a data model diagrammatically, as in Figure 11.3, is an excellent way of clarifying one's thoughts at this important stage. It can make more concrete the abstractions with which one is juggling at this point, enabling them to become something more tangible and malleable. Establishing the structural links between the components of a data model becomes easier and clearer when everything is laid out in this diagrammatic form as does the sense of an overview of the environment being created as a whole.

The third component is the serialization of the data model into concrete schemas which will form the containers in which the metadata will be held, preserved and disseminated. This process has three subcomponents to it. The first is the choice of the syntax for encoding the metadata: here we have chosen XML for the various reasons described above. The second is the choice of schemas that employ this syntax. Many factors may go in to this choice, including an assessment of their functionality, their provenance and the sectors in which they originated. Some reasons for the choices made in this case have been cited earlier: the overriding factor was, and has to be, their ability to absorb the data model without distorting it or excising its significant features. A detailed examination and assessment of potential schemas is a vital part of the process and plenty of time and attention should be expended on this.

The final sub-component is the translation of the data model into the schemas themselves. This is a skilled and often complex procedure, requiring a thorough understanding of the data model and the semantics of the chosen schemas. There is not always a one-to-one match from a component in the data model to an element in an XML schema: often a combination of elements and attributes is necessary to express the semantics of components accurately and without distortion. At each stage of the translation it is necessary to ask if this has been achieved and whether anything is missing in the serialized form of any given component: if so, one must go back to the beginning and start the process again. As is the case in the compilation of the data model, it is necessary to be critical of one's work and to be ready to take another approach if anything is lost of the richness of the model from which it is drawn.

This discussion should make it clear that the process as a whole is more than a simple translation of a set of metadata elements. In the case of a relational database of this type such an approach would be more of a hindrance than a help as the architectures of semantic data models and XML are much more elegant and flexible than the rigid structures of relational tables.

Even without these architectural considerations, the process has to be seen as a way of rethinking the Database and its rationale. Examining its metadata requirements in this way, mapping out its structures and clarifying the rationale behind its components and their interrelationships allows a critical assessment of its functions and their respective priorities. From here it is possible to improve it in more ways than ensuring the interoperability of its metadata alone. Inconsistencies and redundancies can be removed, priorities established and serious consideration given to its user constituencies and how their needs can be met.

Not for the first time, metadata can prove itself a way to question and clarify far more than the ways in which something is described and administered: it can seed considerations of the rationale behind a system at a far more basic level and so transform it as a whole. For the Warburg Institute, and art history in general, this process of assessment and clarification offers the possibility of opening up this important, and in many ways unique, resource to the wider scholarly community beyond its current limited domain.

Acknowledgments

The author acknowledges with thanks Dr. Rembrandt Duits, the Deputy Curator of the Photographic Collection at the Warburg Institute, for his assistance in the compilation of this chapter.

References

Bekiari, C. et al. (2015) *Definition of FRBRoo: A conceptual model for bibliographic information in object-oriented formalism.* Den Haag: IFLA.

Charles, V. & Isaac, A. (2015) Enhancing the Europeana Data Model (EDM). [online]. Available from: http://pro.europeana.eu/publication/enhancing-theeuropeana-data-model-edm (Accessed 12 April 2018). [online].

Duits, R. (2018) 'Classified iconography: a new data model for the Warburg Institute Iconographic Database', in *Proceedings of the IEEE 5th International Symposium on Emerging Trends and Technologies in Libraries and Information Services.* 2018 Bennett University, Noida: IEEE UP Section (India). pp. 161–164.

Fedora Commons (2013) Fedora Commons [online]. Available from: http://fedora-commons.org/ (Accessed 11 June 2013).

Fedora Commons (2002) The Fedora Content Model Architecture (CMA) [online]. Available from: http://fedora-commons.org/documentation/3.0b1/userdocs/digitalobjects/cmda.html (Accessed 9 December 2011).

Gartner, R. (2016) *Metadata: shaping knowledge from antiquity to the semantic web.* Basel: Springer-Verlag.

Gartner, R. (2008) Metadata for digital libraries: state of the art and future directions. [online]. Available from: https://www.jisc.ac.uk/media/documents/techwatch/tsw_0801pdf.pdf (Accessed 3 December 2018).

Gartner, R. & Hedges, M. (2013) 'CENDARI: establishing a digital ecosystem for historical research', in 7th IEEE International Conference on Digital Ecosystems and Technologies. 2013 pp. 61–65.

Hasihofer, B. (2009) CIDOC CRM in practice: experiences, problems and possible solutions. [online]. Available from: https://www.slideshare.net/bhaslhofer/cidoc-crm-in-practice (Accessed 12 May 2018). [online]

Hawtin, R. et al. (2011) Review of the evidence for the value of the 'linked data' approach: final report to JISC [online]. Available from: http://ie-repository.jisc.ac.uk/559/1/JISC_Linked_Data_Review_Oct2011.pdf (Accessed 27 July 2012).

IconClass (2018) Outline of the Iconclass system [online]. Available from: http://www.iconclass.org/help/outline (Accessed 21 August 2018).

Islandora (2013) Islandora Website [online]. Available from: http://www.islandora.ca/ (Accessed 12 June 2013).

Lagoze, C. et al. (2006) Fedora: an architecture for complex objects and their relationships. *International Journal on Digital Libraries.* 6 (2), 124–138.

Library of Congress (2017) EAD: Encoded Archival Description Official Site [online]. Available from: http://www.loc.gov/ead/ (Accessed 4 April 2017).

Library of Congress (2011) Metadata Authority Description Schema (MADS) - (Library of Congress) [online]. Available from: http://www.loc.gov/standards/mads/ (Accessed 24 November 2011).

The Warburg iconographic database

Library of Congress (2014a) Metadata Encoding and Transmission Standard (METS) Official Web Site [online]. Available from: http://www.loc.gov/standards/mets/ (Accessed 19 September 2014).

Library of Congress (2010) Metadata Object Description Schema: MODS [online]. Available from: http://www.loc.gov/standards/mods/ (Accessed 28 January 2010).

Library of Congress (2008) PREMIS data dictionary for preservation metada, version 2.0. [online]. Available from: http://www.loc.gov/standards/premis/v2/premis-2-0.pdf (Accessed 13 May 2013). [online].

Nussbaumer, P. & Haslhofer, B. (2007) Putting the CIDOC CRM into practice-experiences and challenges. [online]. Available from: http://eprints.cs.univie.ac.at/404/1/covered.pdf (Accessed 12 May 2018).

Olensky, M. (2010) Semantic interoperability in Europeana: An examination of CIDOC CRM in digital cultural heritage documentation. *Bulletin of IEEE Technical Committee on Digital Libraries*. 6 (2).

Riva, P. & Žumer, M. (2017) FRBRoo, the IFLA Library Reference Model, and now LRMoo: a circle of development. [online]. Available from: http://library.ifla.org/2130/ (Accessed 4 December 2018).

Riva, P. & Oliver, C. (2015) 'Beyond FRBR: FRBROO and the consolidated FRBR model', in Canadian Library Association Conference. 2015 [online]. Available from: http://library.ifla.org/id/eprint/2130 (Accessed 1 December 2018).

Tannenbaum, A. (2003) *Computer networks*. Upper Sadle River: Prentice Hall PTR.

Text Encoding Initiative (2013) TEI: Text Encoding Initiative [online]. Available from: http://www.tei-c.org/index.xml (Accessed 7 October 2013).

Waddington, S. et al. (2016) 'PERICLES–Digital Preservation through Management of Change in Evolving Ecosystems', in *European Project Space (EPS) event organized in Colmar, July 2015, associated with the set of conferences ICETE (12th International Joint Conference on e-Business and Telecommunications), ICSOFT (10th International Joint Conference on Software Technologies), SIMULTECH (5th International Conference on Simulation and Modeling Methodologies, Technologies and Applications) and DATA (4th International Conference on Data Management Technologies and Applications)*. 2016 pp. 51–74.

Warburg Institute (n.d.) Photographic Collection Index. [online]. Available from: https://warburg.sas.ac.uk/sites/default/files/files/test%20subfolder/pcindex.doc (Accessed 21 August 2018).

Warburg Institute (2018) Warburg Institute: Photographic Collection [online]. Available from: https://warburg.sas.ac.uk/library-collections/photographic-collection.

12

INFORMATION COMMUNICATION TECHNOLOGIES, INFRASTRUCTURE AND RESEARCH METHODS IN THE DIGITAL HUMANITIES

A.J. Million

12.1 Introduction

Technical barriers and resource limitations often prevent humanists from employing digital methods in the production of scholarship. For example, a scholar with a background in comparative literature may be familiar with literary traditions in multiple cultures and speak several languages. However, this scholar also may lack the requisite training to compare literary works using computationally-enhanced distant reading techniques. To address technical and resource barriers to the production of scholarship, this chapter discusses information communication technologies (ICT) and research infrastructures. The traditional view of systems infrastructure holds that it acts as a form of "substrate" that extends the work of individuals. While this view is accurate, work in the field of computer-supported cooperative work (CSCW) also demonstrates that infrastructure is relational. Because systems infrastructure is relational, it is difficult to develop tools that meet the needs of a diverse audience, and this creates implications for digital humanities (DH) work.

In this chapter, I argue there is an increasing need for humanists who use digital methods to think and act as managers. To make this point, I define my terms, discuss why humanists encounter barriers to the application of digital methods, and present three solutions rooted in the idea of *collaboration*.[1] While discussing collaboration, I focus on the potential afforded to humanists through the development of ICTs that automate digital methods. Equally important, I describe how these tools may "scale-up" to create transformative infrastructures that allow humanists to draw on a shared set of resources to produce unique, high-impact work. To learn if such large-scale infrastructures are used in DH work, I also present findings from a qualitative analysis of Association of Digital Humanities Organizations (ADHO) conference papers. I conclude that infrastructure is rarely used, so I proceed to argue that humanists should employ an "all of the above" collaborative strategy to produce scholarly works. Employing an all of the above strategy means that humanists must act as project managers while finding ways to navigate diverse, local research landscapes, and I conclude by discussing this point as it relates to infrastructural potential.

12.2 Digital research methods in the humanities

In the humanities, mediated scholarship has become increasingly common. For example, high-profile DH projects have found coverage in newspapers like *The New York Times* and *Guardian*, but the number of disciplines in the humanities, and complexities associated with ICT use, mean that it is not always possible for humanists to employ digital methods (Lea, 2016; Schuessler, 2017). Taking care not to over-generalize, a basic summary of DH methods illustrates this point; for example, humanists may use technology to conduct:

- Social network analyses;
- Model topics;
- Visualize textual data (e.g., Drucker 2011);
- Analyze bibliometrics; and
- Conduct cultural criticism (e.g., Liu, 2012).

This list is not representative of the digital humanities, but it reflects the diversity of research and scholarly approaches that humanists may employ using technology.

12.3 Collaboration and the co-production of scholarship

Acknowledging that humanists possess a wide range of training, and that they operate in diverse contexts, a practical question to ask is: how can they use digital methods when they lack the skills and resources to do so? That is, how can humanists use ICTs in novel and interdisciplinary ways? Sidestepping questions about the nature of the digital humanities (Berry, 2012; Gold, 2012) and how humanists are trained, I argue that a potential solution lies in collaboration and the co-production of scholarship. Through collaboration and collective action, humanists can work together (directly and indirectly) to finish projects, leverage organizational support environments, and develop ICTs to automate tasks. Below, I expand upon this argument for the humanities as a cohesive field of study.

Taken from organizational management literature, the idea of a *collaborative advantage* offers one way to think about collaboration among humanists (Kanter, 1994). Defined by Huxham and Vangen (2008), collaborative advantages are "things to be achieved that could not have been [… accomplished] by one person or organization acting alone," and the concept applies to all types of activity. Noteworthy examples include nonprofits fighting poverty as part of an ad-hoc network (Kania & Kamer, 2011), software companies working with competitors to develop tools (Levy & Germonprez, 2015), and even humanistic work like Google's (n.d.) Library Digitization project. Although it is not always acknowledged, the production of scholarship is fundamentally a social exercise, and this means humanists can employ a range of strategies to use digital methods in partnership with others. Sir Issac Newton once attributed his success to "standing on the shoulders of giants," and the many different ways that scholars collaborate are central to humane and scientific progress.

12.3.1 Digital labs

Take, for example, the concept of an organization. *Organizations* are structured groups of individuals "with a particular purpose" like conducting research (Oxford, n.d.). At the institutional level, one way that universities can help humanists produce scholarship is to create a research lab with the explicit purpose of supporting academics without technical training. For instance, the Price Lab for Digital Humanities at the University of Pennsylvania (https://pricelab.sas.upenn.edu) provides one example worth reviewing. The Center for Digital Humanities (https://cdh.ucla.edu/labs) at UCLA represents another example, and with this approach universities create "spaces" that offer technical expertise, hardware, software, and other resources. A strength of this institutionalized approach is that it provides regular, structured support for humanists to extend their work.

Although it makes sense for many universities to create labs for humanists, this particular strategy is not always practical. For instance, many small and under-resourced universities cannot afford to create labs. At the University of Pennsylvania, an exceptionally well-funded Ivy League institution, the Price Lab (n.d.) was only made possible by two large donations that exceeded $9 million dollars. Theories of innovation also show that large universities can provide more support to employees than their smaller counterparts (Rogers, 2003). Furthermore, leadership and administrative priorities may stymie the formation of labs, and not all humanists work in universities in the first place.

12.3.2 Project-based collaboration

Recognizing that an institutional approach is imperfect, a second way that humanists can sidestep barriers to the production of scholarship is for them to collaborate with other researchers directly. Scholars do not have to limit their work to single universities, and it is common for scientific researchers to sub-specialize and band together in distributed networks. As a consequence, the number of scientific, co-authored papers has grown since the late nineteenth century (Bastian, 2015). Humanists who work in environments without institutional support can partner with others, and attending conferences provides networking opportunities for humanists to seek research support. Furthermore, ADHO hosts a conference that brings together DH scholars to share their work, attend topical workshops, and identify new research opportunities. The Association for Computers and the Humanities is an organization based in the United States (http://ach.org/conferences) that hosted an inaugural conference in 2019, and there are many other avenues for humanists to find research partners. Yet, here too remain problems; not all humanists are comfortable networking with colleagues, and among small groups, competing priorities and time limitations may complicate research. Travel to conferences may also be cost-prohibitive, so additional research strategies are needed.

12.3.3 ICTs and infrastructure

Acknowledging the need for humanists to employ research strategies that mitigate barriers to the use of digital methods, I argue a third solution relates to ICTs and computational infrastructure. To bypass technical and resource-related problems, software developers can develop tools that humanists can use to carry out work like conducting social network analyses, analyzing bibliometrics, and producing new forms of cultural criticism.

High-profile examples of ICTs permitting new digital scholarship within the humanities are already widespread and discussed in the DH literature. Take, for example, Omeka (http://www.omeka.org). Omeka is a free, open source content management system (CMS) first designed for the production of digital collections at George Mason University in the United States. Initially developed in 2008 Omeka allows users to publish and exhibit cultural heritage objects by using a push-button interface. Concurrently, Omeka also extends its core functionality with site-based themes and plugins while employing an unqualified version of the Dublin Core metadata standard. An advantage of using Omeka is that it allows end-users to publish content to the Web without knowledge of HTML, CSS, and programing languages. Relatedly, Scalar (http://www.scalar.me/) is another platform designed with scholarly needs in mind, but it focuses less on collections of digital material than individual, mediated texts. Since this is the case, Scalar provides built-in support for textual visualization and Web-based analysis (Roman, 2018). For both tools, humanists can contract with third-parties to host content, and an associated consequence is they face fewer barriers to the publication of digital scholarship than ever before.

While humanists can use a CMS to publish digital scholarship, they are just one type of ICT that automates previously manual work. Ashley Maynor (n.d.), a Digital Humanities Librarian at New York University provides a list of 100+ ICTs that humanists can use to extend their scholarship (https://guides.nyu.edu/dighum/tools/). References to ICTs are also common in DH literature as well: *Table 12.1* lists select tools referenced by humanists in peer-reviewed articles. Some of these tools were created specifically for humanists, but many more of them are commercial products used by a broader audience.

ICT, infrastructure and research methods

Table 12.1 Select ICTs Used in Humanities Scholarship

ICT	Description of Tool	Reference
ArcGIS	Commercial, cloud-based geographic information systems and analysis tool.	(Varner, 2016)
Annotation Studio	Annotation tool for pedagogical use.	(Hwang & Ronchetti, 2014)
Gephi	Network analysis and data visualization software package.	(Liu, 2013)
GitHub	Web-based, version control program.	(Reed, 2014)
Jupyter Notebook	Data analysis tool meant for creating and sharing documents that contain code, equations, and text.	(Hiippala, 2016)
Omeka	Open source Web publishing platform, based on WordPress.	(Kucsma, Reiss, & Sidman, 2010)
Zotero	Popular citation management tool.	(Spiro, 2012)

Research-enhancing ICTs are not limited to single tools, and this point bears mentioning. Oftentimes, tools can be linked together, and standards provide a way for tools to offer a substantially greater reach (and impact) than they could otherwise have on their own. Collaborative in nature, *standards* in the digital humanities are particularly useful for knowledge organization and refer to "codified rules and guidelines for the creation, description and management of digital resources" (Gill & Miller, 2002, para. 14). Using standards, organizations like the Wikimedia Foundation can embark on large-scale, ambitious projects like "creating a more consistent, structured way of entering and retrieving" metadata for digital content in Wikimedia Commons (Morgan & Fauconnier, 2018). Furthermore, by employing this approach, the Wikimedia Foundation is partnering with galleries, libraries, museums, and archives worldwide so they can upload content to make it more accessible. Organizations like the German Federal Archive have already done so, and this represents another example of the benefits that ICT-use and collaboration may potentially afford.

Setting aside the example of the Wikimedia Foundation, anecdotal evidence suggests that a broader shift is taking place in relation to the ICTs that are used by digital humanists. Although its potential has yet to be realized, libraries, archives, museums, and organizations that store and preserve large collections of electronic information have begun using tools that support linked-data standards. Speaking about this point, in 2016, the Academia Sinica Center for Digital Cultures organized the "Knowledge Organization and Cultural Heritage: Perspectives of the Semantic Web" conference. Reporting on conference proceedings, organizers concluded that, "from the Semantic Web perspective, knowledge organization systems and knowledge organization methods are in the midst of a paradigm shift" (Zeng & Chen, 2018, p. 18). The promise of linked, open data and associated standards are that they facilitate improved instrumentation that enables researchers to better carry out their work. Other types of standards extend the work of humanists. For example, Omeka was successful in part because it used hardware and software that was user-friendly and available to variety of end-users. Unsurprisingly, standards are very important to the development of popular ICTs used within the humanities.

Concluding my discussion of ICTs as a mechanism for humanists to employ digital methods, a brief word needs to be said about systems infrastructures. Single ICTs can extend the abilities of humanists, but when they occupy a central place in humane work, they become infrastructure. Thus, *infrastructure* is the "basic systems and services" that support humanists in their use of digital methods (Cambridge, n.d.); it is pervasive, often used, and a type of substrate upon which activities are layered. Not all ICTs used by humanists are infrastructure, but when combined with standards, many of them scale-up. Extended more broadly, then, ICTs that are infrastructure represent something transformative—a way for humanists to automate away barriers to the use of digital methods at-scale. In particle physics, the European Organization for Nuclear Research's Large Hadron Collider is infrastructure, because it provides data to physicists who could not otherwise be able to collect it. In the humanities, more mundane tools like Zotero may be thought as infrastructure, because it dramatically simplifies writing and document citation processes, but the potential for other infrastructural systems also exist. I return to this point at the end of the chapter.

12.3.4 The limits of infrastructure

The field of CSCW provides a useful explanation of why computational infrastructure is an imperfect way to address many of the barriers that humanists face to the production of scholarship. Normally, when researchers talk about ICTs as research infrastructure, they portray it as substrate. For example, online applications require physical hardware (e.g., Web servers, Ethernet cables) and technical standards (e.g., HTTP, TCP/IP) to function. This means that underlying system components "count" as infrastructure, because new tools and work practices can be layered on top them; however, a more nuanced portrayal of infrastructure exists.

In 1996, Star and Ruhleder presented a technology adoption case-study centered p.on a tool named the Worm Community System (WCS). The WCS was built for the genomic research community to help sequence the genome of *c. elegans*, a nematode, and the system was meant to facilitate work by over 1,400 scientists worldwide (pp. 114–15). WCS development was supplemented with user testing and active feedback from genomic researchers who reported that the system met their research needs; however, it was not adopted (p. 116).

To explain why the WCS was not adopted by the genomic community, Star and Ruhleder (1996) turned to the topic of infrastructure. First, they noted that the WCS was developed around the time the modern Internet began to take root. This meant some researchers preferred to use simple tools like e-mail and early Web-browsers to work with their colleagues. Many other researchers did not log onto the system. Second, however, Star and Ruhleder presented a much more basic reason that the tool was unsuccessful: large-scale online infrastructure is characterized by an internal tension. On one hand, WCS users engaged in highly technical scientific work and had needs that varied because of local research contexts (p. 117). Many of these needs were not supported by the WCS, so these "rigidities" required users to find workarounds to accomplish their goals. However, because users relied on so many workarounds, the WCS needed to be recalibrated. This "back and forth" dynamic created tension that could not be solved using a "lowest common denominator" software development approach or by establishing standards (p. 112).

Learning from their experience working on the WCS, Star and Ruhleder (1996) came to an important conclusion. According to their work, infrastructure is not merely a form of substrate upon which other tools are layered, but something relational that emerges in practice. To determine when infrastructure emerges, then, they presented eight indicators. According to Star and Ruhleder, infrastructure:

1. Is embedded within other structures, social arrangements, and technologies;
2. Does not have to be reinvented for new tasks;
3. Has a scope or reach beyond single events and/or use-cases;
4. Is learned as part of a community of practice;
5. Is shaped by the conventions of users;
6. Embodies standards that plug into other tools and infrastructures;
7. Is built on a "installed base" that determines its strengths and weaknesses; and
8. Becomes visible when it breaks (p. 113).

In the sections that follow, I use several of these indicators to frame a discussion of digital methods in the humanities. Based on my work evaluating ADHO papers, I argue that large-scale ICT infrastructure tends to be rare, because most of the tools that authors used required reinvention or had single use-cases.

12.4 Research methods

To evaluate the extent that ICT infrastructures are used by humanists in their research to produce scholarly works, in the summer of 2018, I analyzed digital humanities research. Central to my study was Star and Ruhleder's (1996) definition of infrastructure and the concept of collaboration, but these ideas did not frame my research strictly, nor did I ask formal research questions. Instead, my goal was to evaluate the broader state of the field by examining DH literature and to learn the extent that large-scale infrastructure was used by humanists to employ digital methods in their work.

As a preliminary research step, I decided to examine papers that were presented at the 2017 ADHO annual conference in Montreal, Canada. While I could have examined other DH papers, ADHO papers were ideal; the conference was attended by a large international audience, is well-regarded, and represents a major venue in which humanists discuss their use of digital methods. Compared to many DH journals, ADHO paper abstracts are freely available, and papers were published at a single point in time rather than being staggered throughout a calendar year (Lewis et al., 2017). Once I determined that ADHO conference papers represented a suitable data point to learn if ICT infrastructures are used by humanists, I chose to limit my analysis to full-length papers written in English. There were 32 "panel" presentations, 99 "full-length" papers, 132 "short" papers, 5 "virtual short" papers, and 117 "posters." Examining full-length papers streamlined the research process and represented a methodologically sound sampling procedure, given that papers were reviewed by in-field experts and reported about complete projects. Examining posters and/or short papers would have skewed my sample by drawing attention to small projects that require a minimal investment of time or incomplete work that may remain unfinished.

After downloading full-length paper abstracts, I set out to create a snapshot of the ICT infrastructures that humanists used to create scholarly works. In this sense, I used a strategy akin to *infrastructure inversion*. Presented by Bowker and Star (2000), this method calls for researchers to defamiliarize themselves with infrastructure that is used in the production of knowledge (Kaltenbrunner, 2015). This approach is geared for the study of scientific and humanistic inquiry, and it holds that work is "embedded" within interrelated social and technical systems. For instance, as a research strategy, infrastructural inversion has been used by researchers to investigate how things like classification systems are embedded in research flows that advance a range of social, cultural, and scientific goals (Edwards, 2010; Jensen, 2008; Shankar, 2004). In my study, I did not focus on specific hardware, software, standards, and other infrastructural elements, but I did examine the extent to which scholarship was enhanced and extended by ICTs.

After framing my research, and selecting which data to examine, my next step was to read ADHO papers and analyze them. To accomplish this, I employed what Saldaña (2016) refers to as an open, inductive approach to qualitative coding. I coded text at the paper-level, and in particular, I used this approach for three mezzo-level categories that intersect with ICT infrastructure, which are indicative of project-based research practices in DH work: 1) *research methodologies*, 2) *study topics*, and 3) *data types*.

While coding, I created open codes for each of the three categories above to "reveal what is unseen" in terms of the ICT infrastructure that humanists used. During a preliminary study phase, I coded ADHO papers, took notes, tabulated author counts, and began thinking about how to organize findings. For mezzo-level categories, I coded each paper using one code; for instance, a paper that conducted *citation analysis* using *computational methods* was coded using the term for research methodologies I felt was best. To make my qualitative codes more meaningful (and accurate), in a second phase, I combined redundant categories and re-coded conference papers using my new categories. I listed all of the collected papers in Excel with code classifications, my notes, author counts, and information that shed light on the type of work reported in papers, as well as the extent to which humanists rely on large-scale ICT infrastructure. In doing so, I also assumed that using ICTs automated all, or part, of the research process described therein.

12.5 Findings

Altogether, I analyzed 91 (or roughly 92%) of the full-length conference papers that were presented at ADHO, and this suggests my findings were indicative of larger trends in the humanities. I excluded eight papers from my analysis, because they were written in French (n=4) and Italian (n=4), and one limitation is my findings (likely) privileged scholarship and research practices used by the English-speaking world. The papers I analyzed were written by an average of 2 authors, and this suggests most paper authors collaborated with colleagues during the research process. Despite this, however, I did not find evidence that large-scale collaborations are common, or that humanists leveraged ICT infrastructures to sidestep problems associated with the use of digital methods.

Supplementing what I found by coding ADHO papers, I also identified several high-level trends while reading published paper abstracts. For instance, most papers tended to discuss single projects and case studies. References to research lab support were rare, and there was also substantial attention paid to textual analysis; most studies examining textual artifacts framed work as a "microanalysis" or "macroanalysis" project (Jockers, 2014), meaning that ICT use was limited to single, discrete projects. Some papers did talk about standards, or depend on infrastructural collections of digital content, but once again, the dominant focus was generally on single-use ICTs and time-bound research methods—neither trend aligned with Star and Ruhleders' portrayal of infrastructure.

12.5.1 Research methods used in papers

Regarding the research methods that humanists used in ADHO papers, I identified a total of 17 strategies (see *Table 12.2*). Four methods, in particular, accounted for two-thirds of all accepted papers: *computational methods* (n=28), *lessons learned* (n=24), *tool or methodological presentations* (n=9), and *best practices* (n=7). These categories suggest that humanists employed bespoke research methods supported by data scientists (in most cases) and large-scale ICT infrastructure did not regularly help scholars carry out work.

Table 12.2 Methodology, Topic, and Data Source of ADHO Full-Length Papers

Method	#	Topic	#	Data Source	#
Computational methods	28	Research methods	27	Project or tool development	29
Lessons learned	24	Domain-specific	15	Academic literature	12
Tool or methodological presentation	9	Mapping, visual media, and visualization	14	Digital monograph collection	12
Best practices	7	Ethics, minorities, and at-risk populations	9	Lab notes	11
Critical theory	4	Pedagogy	9	Miscellaneous digital archival content	6
Theory development	3	Standards	7	Popular culture	4
Bibliometrics or citation analysis	2	Gamification	2	Interviews	3
Digital forensics	2	--	--	Other	3
Opinion	2	--	--	Digital manuscript collection	2
Standards development	2	--	--	Public repository metadata	2
Survey	2	--	--	Social media	2
Usability testing	2	--	--	Art exhibition	1
Narrative	1	--	--	Survey	1
Oral history	1	--	--	--	--
Phenomenology	1	--	--	--	--
Proceedings	1	--	--	--	--
Traditional statistical analysis	1	--	--	--	--

Take, for example, the papers I classified as using computational methods. This category was my largest, and it referred to humanists employing computationally-enhanced research approaches like topic modeling or sentiment analysis. One typical paper described an attempt by the authors to find the minimum textual sample size needed to attribute authorship in monographs (Eder, 2017). At first glance, it appears that the use of computational methods might have helped humanists to produce scholarly work, but the nature of work described suggests ICT-use was extremely localized. The ICTs used to conduct data analysis also included programs like RStudio or iPython; and, based on the relational CSCW definition of infrastructure I presented earlier these tools were not infrastructure, because most data transformations had to be reinvented for use in new projects.

Rather than employing research methods and/or ICTs that could be employed in a variety of contexts, most papers discussed the intricacies of single projects within sub-areas of the humanities. Lessons learned was my second most common methodology code, and this shows how authors tended to describe their research experiences to conference attendees. Bahde and Crawford (2017) wrote about combining Web-based archival finding aids with data visualizations at Oregon State University. Other methodologies explicitly presented new research methods and tools for research. Noteworthy examples related to measuring the overall completeness of metadata records in Europeana and "best practices" for teaching and research in the digital humanities (e.g, Cummings, 2017; Király, 2017), but again, these tools and methodologies were not cross-cutting across papers in the way that ICT infrastructures would be expected.

12.5.2 Research topics

Evaluating the foci of ADHO papers provided additional evidence that humanists did not use ICT infrastructure to address, or sidestep, methodological research limitations. As illustrated in *Table 12.2*, three codes described 57% of the topics of ADHO papers. These codes were: *research methods* (n=27), *domain specific* scholarly projects (n=15), and *mapping, visual media, and visualization* (n=14). This topical emphasis on research methods, and domain-specific material, reinforces the argument that humanists did not use infrastructure often.

Take, for example, the large number of papers that related specifically to novel digital research methods. In one case, a team of researchers presented the development of a new tool for supporting distant reading in Polish literature (Piasecki et al., 2017). Another presented a methodology for examining editorial changes in manuscript drafts using the book *The Martian* as an example (Ketzan & Schöch, 2017). In general, there appeared to be substantial interest in sharing new digital methods, which sometimes led to domain-specific projects. Kim et al. (2017) used computational methods to examine emotion developments in story genres, and consequently they helped to answer questions debated by scholars in the field of literary analysis. Yet, the research methods presented in domain-specific papers were meant for narrow sub-disciplines and not the humanities as a whole. In short, this suggests diversity among communities of practice within the humanities meant no single ICT could support every method humanists might hope to use, regardless of if they embodied standards or not.

12.5.3 Data types and an unexpected finding

Finally, my coding of data sources also shed light on the ICTs used in DH research, as well as their instructional nature. As shown in *Table 12.2*, my codes revealed that paper data generally came from author recollections about *project or tool development* (n=29) and *lab notes* (n=11). This data also (generally) described how authors developed software and completed projects, but not was all as it seemed.

Narrative reports about project and tool development were the most common type of data presented in ADHO papers, but surprisingly, three other qualitative codes suggested ICT infrastructure is used by humanists, thus contradicting my previous findings: academic literature, digital monographs, and digital archives. Take, for example, my code *academic literature* (n=12). Although it was not infrastructure in the sense that humanists used it to analyze datasets, many drew from digital repositories to read others' work and publish their own. Applegate (2017) provides an example in that she drew from other critical theorists to inform her discussion of university politics. Many of these publications came from library databases, and more still came from open access journals. Keeping with the CSCW definition of infrastructure, then, academic literature was embedded in the practices of humanities work. Additionally, scholars did not have to reinvent this literature for new tasks, it could be used for other projects, and the content it described was learned in the disciplinary sub-areas (i.e., communities of practice) were authors conducted their research and shared their scholarship.

My interpretation of academic literature in online repositories as infrastructure extends to the use of *digital monograph collections* (n=12) and *digital archival content* (n=6). For example, One study used a collection of historical, digital copes of the *Oxford English Dictionary* to document the evolution of words (Williams, 2017). Other studies drew on collections of content, data, and metadata to carry out work. All of these resources were provided via the Internet, enhanced scholarship, and were scholarly products themselves. Whether through computationally-enhanced humane projects, or traditional ones that depend on digital versions of electronic content, a linkage in papers classified as using these data sources was that authors depended on sources as infrastructure—research data infrastructure.

12.6 Discussion and implications

I began this chapter by noting that, sometimes, humanists cannot employ digital methods as desired. To resolve problems, humanists can partner or collaborate with others. Software development also represents a collaborative strategy that humanists can employ; and, when ICTs "scale-up" they become infrastructure that may automate work in the humanities. However, despite this, ADHO authors did not use infrastructure often.

Star and Ruhleder (1996) argue that ICT infrastructure is relational, and using their work as a guide, one explanation for the apparent rarity of infrastructure relates to diversity in the humanities. Paper authors reported using ICTs to carry out work, but diversity among them (as it relates to their skills, backgrounds, and interests) means they came from very different communities of practice. Some AHDO papers were written by librarians. Others were written by authors in radically different fields, such as music theory.

Describing ICT development, Edwards (2010) provides insight into why software fails to scale-up and become infrastructure. He says that the underlying dynamic of infrastructure is a constant "oscillation between a desire for smooth system-like behavior and the need to combine [tool] capabilities no single system can yet provide" (p. 12). Applied to research methods within the digital humanities, a conclusion to draw is that ADHO authors did not use infrastructure, because no system could support the needs of all humanists concurrently. Furthermore, this dynamic also explains why humanists presented lessons learned, talked about building new tools, and offered novel research methods to conference attendees. Below, I discuss project management and present it as an "all of the above" stratagem for humanists to produce scholarly works.

12.6.1 Project management

According to the Project Management Institute (n.d.), a *project* is temporary. All projects have beginnings, ends, and a set of resources to draw from. Additionally, projects are unique and center on meeting an objective or goal. *Project management*, on the other hand, is defined as the "application of knowledge, skills, tools, and techniques to project activities to meet […] project requirements" (para. 5).

Given that in my findings: humanists used bespoke computational methods, ICT infrastructure was rarely used, and many papers were domain specific, there is evidence that humanists should employ project management strategies to carry out work, assuming they do not already. In her survey of digital humanities labs, Zorich (2008) observes how these labs sometimes offer project-management services. Posner

(2013) calls attention to overlooked administrative needs in DH library support, and in doing so speaks about a near constant need for "project management expertise" (p. 47). Quan-Hasse and colleagues' (2014) observe that Hispanic Baroque humanists employ different collaborative approaches than traditional scientific researchers, and one implication is they need to use different networking strategies to successfully employ digital methods in complex environments. Referencing the WCS in Star and Ruhleder's work (1996), digital humanists using project management strategies appears to resemble genomic researchers use of tool "workarounds" (or other tools) when infrastructure did not meet their needs.

Guidance for humanists at the individual-level appears to be lacking, but fortunately the Project Management Institute (n.d.) offers help. On their website, the Institute says that successful project management falls into five steps. These are:

1. Initiating;
2. Planning;
3. Executing;
4. Monitoring and controlling; and
5. Closing.

These processes are somewhat oversimplified, but nevertheless, they connect to Star and Ruhleder's (1996) idea of infrastructure during phases two, three, and four. Planning, executing, and monitoring/controlling DH projects, for example, all require that humanists leverage available resources. This includes ICT infrastructure, but also DH labs, the skills of collaborators, and more.

Siemens (2009) provides arguably the most concrete available guidance for humanists in DH environments, and her work expands on strategies that humanists can employ in the "planning," "executing," and "monitoring" phases of project management. Reporting on research examining DH research teams in Canada, England, and the U.S., she makes five recommendations for humanists who use digital methods in their work. Her recommendations include: guaranteeing team member commitment, providing leadership, training researchers, and balancing digital and in-person communications.

Lacking humanities-wide infrastructure, there is no one "correct" way for humanists to manage projects and employ digital methods, but project collaboration tools may assist humanists in doing so. Asana, Slack, and Trello are all tools used in the software development community and may be thought of as support infrastructure. For instance, Asana (http://www.asana.com) and Trello (http://www.trello.com/) are Web-based management applications that support the "planning," "monitoring," and "closing" phases of DH projects. Each tool allows researchers to create to-do lists, set deadlines, and assign team member responsibilities. Slack (http://www.slack.com) is a Web-based collaboration tool for coordinating discussion among online teams, and relatedly, it can enhance the "initiating," "planning" and "monitoring" phases of scholarly collaboration. Project management does not have to take place online, but by connecting scholarly objectives to the resources available, humanists can work more efficiently whenever barriers to the use of digital methods arise.

12.6.2 Infrastructural potential

Based on my findings, and the literature that I reviewed, it is challenging for humanists to build infrastructural systems. In 2008, Juola argued "killer apps" cannot be built in the humanities, whereas Van Zundert (2012) later argued that large-scale research infrastructures are a "dead end." The diversity of small ICTs I found in my study reinforces arguments made by both scholars; however, because infrastructure emerges in practice (as per the CSCW definition), and because ADHO papers described new tools and digital methodologies, Juola and Van Zundert's assessment of infrastructural potential appears to be limited.

In my study, scholarly material, digital monographs, Web-based archival collections, and other resources "counted" as infrastructure. These systems met the conditions of Star and Ruhleder's (1996) definition:

they were embedded within a larger research environment, did not have to be reinvented, had a scope or reach beyond single projects, and were learned as part of a community of practice. Additionally, these digital content collections were shaped by the conventions of users (e.g., interface design), built on (metadata) standards, possessed an installed base that determined strengths and weaknesses, and were likely to become visible when only they break.

Given this counterpoint, a conclusion to draw is that large-scale ICT infrastructures retain their potential. In the humanities, digital collections enhance scholars' ability to use digital research methods (Zhang et al., 2015). Infrastructure providing access to Web content is different than the tools used to analyze it, but ADHO papers also described humanists seeking collaborative advantages by sharing ICTs and research methods. This suggests that new forms of infrastructure may emerge moving forward, and this potential should be recognized.

Concusion

To conclude this chapter, I cannot say where new humanities infrastructure might emerge in the future, if at all. That said, the research methods I utilized provided a template for humanists to remain abreast of ongoing developments. In my findings, humanists used ICTs that were highly localized and required training (e.g., SQL, Python, R), but future studies might determine this is not the case.

I examined AHDO research at the paper-level, but future research could examine individual tools referenced in papers while tracing their utilization over time. As humanists learn to use different tools, and are trained in different ways, this may shape the research infrastructures that humanists use, as well as the shape of the discipline. Alternatively, new user-friendly, less costly ICTs may also emerge. As a case-in-point, JuypterHub (https://jupyter.org/hub/) is a Web-based platform for computation and analysis that allows users to analyze, transform, and visualize datasets without configuring local hardware. JuypterHub has a steep learning curve, but developments in tools like it means the availability of ICTs to humanists is not static. New forms of infrastructure may emerge, and in the meantime, humanists need only employ project-management skills to carry out their work.

Ending with a quick reference to project management, a last point needs to be made about digital collections in the humanities. Star and Ruhleder (1996) point out infrastructure that is invisible until it breaks, but my data shows building and preserving digital collections is increasingly central to humanities scholarship (Upadhyay & Upadhyay, 2017). Preserving digital content is a management issue (Corrado & Sandy, 2017), and often this work is entrusted to librarians and archivists. Whoever maintains this infrastructure, however, can employ the skills I referenced earlier from the domain of project management, but an unresolved question relates to how long collections ought to be retained.

Acknowledgements

This material is based upon work supported by the U.S. National Science Foundation under Grant No. 1822228.

Note

1 By collaboration, I refer to collective acts that help bring about a given end.

References

Applegate, M. (2017). Digital Humanities as Critical University Studies. In *Digital Humanities 2017 Conference Abstracts*. Montreal: McGill University. Retrieved from https://dh2017.adho.org/abstracts/190/190.pdf

Bahde, A., & Crawford, C. D. (2017). Data Visualization in Archival Finding Aids: A New Paradigm for Access. In *Digital Humanities 2017 Conference Abstracts*. Montreal: McGill University. Retrieved from https://dh2017.adho.org/abstracts/556/556.pdf

Bastian, H. (2015). Science and the Rise of the Co-Authors. *Absolutely Maybe*. Retrieved from https://blogs.plos.org/absolutely-maybe/2015/11/25/science-and-the-rise-of-the-co-authors/

Berry, D. M. (2012). Introduction: Understanding the Digital Humanities. In D. M. Berry (Ed.), *Understanding Digital Humanities* (pp. 1–20). London: Palgrave Macmillan.

Bowker, G. C., & Star, S. L. (2000). *Sorting Things Out: Classification and Its Consequences*. Cambrige, MA: MIT Press.

Cambridge (n.d.). Infrastructure. Retrieved from https://dictionary.cambridge.org/us/dictionary/english/infrastructure/

Corrado, E. M., & Sandy, H. M. (2017). *Digital preservation for libraries, archives, and museums*. London: Rowman & Littlefield.

Cummings, J. C. (2017). A World of Difference: Myths and Misconceptions about the TEI. In *Digital Humanities 2017 Conference Abstracts*. Montreal: McGill University. Retrieved from https://dh2017.adho.org/abstracts/529/529.pdf

Drucker, J. (2011). Humanities approaches to graphical display. *Digital Humanities Quarterly*, *5*(1), 1–21.

Eder, M. (2017). Short Samples in Authorship Attribution: A New Approach. In *Digital Humanities 2017 Conference Abstracts*. Montreal: McGill University. Retrieved from https://dh2017.adho.org/abstracts/341/341.pdf

Edwards, P. N. (2010). *A Vast Machine: Computer Models, Climate Data, and the Politics of Global Warming*. Cambridge, MA: MIT Press.

Gill, T., & Miller, P. (2002). Re-inventing the wheel? Standards, interoperability and digital cultural content. *D-Lib Magazine*, *8*(1). https://doi.org/10.1045/january2002-gill

Gold, M. K. (2012). *Debates in the Digital Humanities*. Minneapolis, MN: University of Minnesota Press.

Google. (n.d.). Library Partners. Retrieved from https://books.google.com/googlebooks/library/partners.html

Hiippala, T. (2016). Semi-Automated Annotation of Page-Based Documents within the Genre and Multimodality Framework. In *Proceedings of the 10th Sighum Workshop on Language Technology for Cultural Heritage, Social Sciences, and Humanities* (pp. 84–89). Association for Computational Linguistics.

Hwang, H. K., & Ronchetti, M. (2014, June). Q-Book: Multimedia Annotation Tool for e-Books. In *EdMedia: World Conference on Educational Media and Technology* (pp. 2543–2551). Association for the Advancement of Computing in Education.

Huxham, C., & Vangen, S. (2008). Realizing the Advantage or Succumbing to Inertia? In *Collaborative Governance: A New Era of Public Policy in Australia* (pp. 29–44). Canberra: ANU Press.

Jensen, C. B. (2008). Power, technology and social studies of health care: An infrastructural inversion. *Health Care Analysis*, *16*(4), 355–374.

Jockers, M. L. (2014). *Text Analysis with R for Students of Literature*. New York: Springer.

Juola, P. (2008). Killer applications in digital humanities. *Literary and Linguistic Computing*, *23*(1), 73–83.

Kaltenbrunner, W. (2015). Infrastructural inversion as a generative resource in digital scholarship. *Science as Culture*, *24*(1), 1–23.

Kania, J., & Kamer, M. (2011). Collective Impact. *Stanford Social Innovation Review*. Retrieved from https://ssir.org/articles/entry/collective_impact

Kanter, R. M. (1994, July 1). Collaborative Advantage: The Art of Alliances. *Harvard Business Review*. Retrieved from https://hbr.org/1994/07/collaborative-advantage-the-art-of-alliances

Ketzan, E., & Schöch, C. (2017). What Changed When Andy Weir's The Martian Got Edited? In *Digital Humanities 2017 Conference Abstracts*. Montreal: McGill University. Retrieved from https://dh2017.adho.org/abstracts/317/317.pdf

Kim, E., Padó, S., & Klinger, R. (2017). Prototypical Emotion Developments in Adventures, Romances, and Mystery Stories. In *Digital Humanities 2017 Conference Abstracts*. Montreal: McGill University. Retrieved from https://dh2017.adho.org/abstracts/203/203.pdf

Király, P. (2017). Measuring completeness as metadata quality metric in Europeana. In *Digital Humanities 2017 Conference Abstracts*. Montreal: McGill University. Retrieved from https://dh2017.adho.org/abstracts/458/458.pdf

Lea, R. (2016, September 15). "It's like hitting a painting with a fish:" Can computer analysis tell us anything new about literature? *The Guardian*. Retrieved from http://www.theguardian.com/books/2016/sep/15/what-is-the-point-of-cultural-analytics-computers-big-data-literature

Lei Zeng, M., & Shu-Jiun Chen, S. (2018). Knowledge organization and cultural heritage in the semantic web—A review of a conference and a special journal issue of JLIS. *DHQ: Digital Humanities Quarterly*, *12*(1).

Levy, M., & Germonprez, R. M. (2015). Is it egalitarianism or enterprise strategy? Exploring a new method of innovation in open source. In *21st Americas Conference on Information Systems, AMCIS 2015*. Americas Conference on Information Systems.

Lewis, R., Raynor, C., Forest, D., & Sinclair, S. (2017). Digital Humanities 2017: Conference Abstracts. Montreal: McGill University. Retrieved from https://dh2017.adho.org/abstracts/DH2017-abstracts.pdf

Liu, A. (2012). Where Is Cultural Criticism in the Digital Humanities? In M. Gold (Ed.), *Debates in the Digital Humanities*. City University of New York.

Maynor, A. (n.d.). Digital Humanities: Tools & Software. Retrieved from https://guides.nyu.edu/dighum/tools

Morgan, J. & Fauconnier, S. (2018). What galleries, libraries, archives, and museums can teach us about multimedia metadata on Wikimedia Commons. Retrieved January 31, 2019 from https://wikimediafoundation.org/2018/01/29/glam-multimedia-metadata-commons/

Oxford. (n.d.). Definition of Organization. Retrieved September 30, 2018, from https://en.oxforddictionaries.com/definition/organization

Piasecki, M., Walkowiak, T., & Maryl, M. (2017). Literary Exploration Machine: New Tool for Distant Readers of Polish Literature. In *Digital Humanities 2017 Conference Abstracts*. Montreal: McGill University. Retrieved from https://dh2017.adho.org/abstracts/526/526.pdf

Posner, M. (2013). No half measures: Overcoming common challenges to doing digital humanities in the library. *Journal of Library Administration*, *53*(1), 43–52.

Project Management Institute. (n.d.). What is Project Management? Retrieved from https://www.pmi.org/about/learn-about-pmi/what-is-project-management

Price Lab for Digital Humanities. (n.d.). What We Do. Retrieved August 25, 2018, from https://pricelab.sas.upenn.edu/about/what-we-do

Quan-Haase, A., Suarez, J. L., & Brown, D. M. (2015). Collaborating, connecting, and clustering in the humanities: A case study of networked scholarship in an interdisciplinary, dispersed team. *American Behavioral Scientist*, *59*(5), 565–581.

Reed, A. (2014). Managing an established digital humanities project: Principles and practices from the twentieth year of the William Blake Archive. *DHQ: Digital Humanities Quarterly*, *8*(1).

Rogers, E. M. (2003). *Diffusion of Innovations*. New York: Free Press.

Roman, G. T. (2018). Review: Scalar and Omeka. *Journal of the Society of Architectural Historians*, *77*(1), 122–123.

Saldaña, J. (2016). *The Coding Manual for Qualitative Researchers*. London: Sage.

Siemens, L. (2009). 'It's a team if you use "reply all"': An exploration of research teams in digital humanities environments. *Literary and linguistic computing*, *24*(2), 225–233.

Spiro, L. (2012). *This is Why We Fight: Defining the Values of the Digital Humanities* (pp. 16–34). Minneapolis: University of Minnesota.

Shankar, K. (2004). Recordkeeping in the production of scientific knowledge: An ethnographic study. *Archival Science*, *4*(3–4), 367–382.

Schuessler, J. (2017, October 30). Reading by the Numbers: When Big Data Meets Literature. *The New York Times*. Retrieved from https://www.nytimes.com/2017/10/30/arts/franco-moretti-stanford-literary-lab-big-data.html

Star, S. L., & Ruhleder, K. (1996). Steps toward an ecology of infrastructure: design and access for large information spaces. *Information Systems Research*, *7*(1), 111–134.

Upadhyay, S., & Upadhyay, N. (2017). Future directions and a roadmap in digital computational humanities for a data driven organization. *Procedia Computer Science*, *122*, 1055–1060.

Varner, S. (2016). Library Instruction for Digital Humanities Pedagogy in Undergraduate Classes. In *Laying the Foundation: Digital Humanities in Academic Libraries* (pp. 205–222). West Layfette: Purdue University Press.

Van Zundert, J. (2012). If you build it, will we come? Large scale digital infrastructures as a dead end for digital humanities. *Historische Sozialforschung*, *37*(3), 165–186.

Williams, D. A. (2017). Opening up the Oxford English Dictionary: What an enhanced legacy dataset can tell us about language, lexicography, literature, and history. In *Digital Humanities 2017 Conference Abstracts*. Montreal: McGill University. Retrieved from https://dh2017.adho.org/abstracts/234/234.pdf

Zeng, M. L., & Chen, S. J. (2018). Knowledge Organization and Cultural Heritage in the Semantic Web-A Review of a Conference and a Special Journal Issue of JLIS. *DHQ: Digital Humanities Quarterly*, *12*(1).

Zhang, Y., Liu, S., & Mathews, E. (2015). Convergence of digital humanities and digital libraries. *Library Management*, *36*(4/5), 362–377.

Zorich, D. (2008). *A Survey of Digital Humanities Centers in the United States*. Council on Library and Information Resources: Washington, D.C.

13

MAPPING SOCIO-ECOLOGICAL LANDSCAPES

Geovisualization as method

Foka Anna, Cocq Coppélie, Buckland Phillip I. and Gelfgren Stefan

13.1 Introduction: From manual cartographies to digital geographies

Mapping means to sketch and plan, to delineate and to represent things and ideas, most often in geo-spatial terms. Cartography, the practice of drawing and studying maps, has been used extensively in the past beyond the discipline of geography and is now increasingly digital: deep digital geovisualizations can represent several layers of data.[1] A deep, or multilayered map, a geovisualization of data can encapsulate a number of different approaches with layers of geographical, historical, archaeological, literary, philosophical, scientific, anthropological, sociological, and even theological data. Current and ongoing projects seem to further facilitate the addition of spatial metadata by proxy: locatives, or events, for example. Global vocabularies help compose gazetteers that can work across platforms and ontologies for even free-tagging metadata have the potential to add extra, organized spatial information on map environments in relation to both texts, monuments, and artefacts (see for example the use of the platform Recogito in Foka, Barker, Konstantinidou & Åhlfeldt 2019).

A synthesis of disciplinary approaches for the capturing of spatial data and the production of relevant spatial metadata helps weaving together multiple observations, impressions and memories to a specific location. Deep maps therefore can function, often simultaneously, as databases, repositories, and data visualization interfaces. In doing so, they can operate as a platforms while at the same time they are both a process and a product. For example, landscape analysis with Geographical Information Systems (hereon GIS) offers an up-to-date method that includes contextual aspects in layers in order to e.g. render other processes behind narratives (Tangherlini 2013). The application of digital cartographic methodologies for studying data in space has been singled out as having the potential to further expand historical understandings of place, culture, and society as geographical networks, and has been treated with enthusiasm (Schriebman et al. 2004; Frischer et al. 2006: 163–82; Dunn et al. 2019).

Digital cartographic methods can map out and relate detailed geographic data to primary sources in order to perceive larger societal patterns in a designated geographical space, a birds-eye' view a derivative of machine or hyper reading of data in space. High-granularity maps can reveal the complexities of more localised sets of data, for a close reading of space. For at least three decades now (Schriebman et al. 2004; Mahony & Bodard 2010: 1–14; Barker et al. 2010 and 2012: 185–200, Landeschi 2015 103–13), digital maps have provided insight into aspects of historical urban development and have facilitated critical discussions of the application of digital tools for mapping, methodologies for handling geodata and their limitations; for example, while the use of web-based geovisualizations is often a stand-alone methodology of studying historical notions of place, the World Wide Web tends to amplify some concepts of place while reducing others (Dunn 2019).

Against this backdrop, this chapter begins by discussing methodological limitations; more precisely, the methodological complexities of capturing and rendering spatial data:

1. Space as a chronotope[2]: i.e. where geographical space is understood as an event that takes place in a designated time and a designated space, thus encapsulating both geographical and temporal data. The depiction of the combination of both space and time, is fraught with difficulties which geovisualization can help problematise or resolve. Digital cartography is aligned with manual maps: where place may remain a static instant on a map, or a time period with start and end, and therefore rarely represented accurately, GIS methodologies present us with the potential to allow for geovisualizations as portals into different spatial and temporal components of a dataset.
2. The issue of fragmentation, transparency and visualizing spatial accuracy. Fragmentation may refer to data (poor space and time coverage) or understanding (lack of knowledge, insufficient data for drawing robust conclusions). Digital methodologies provide enhanced scope for addressing these issues, as the analysis and examples below aim to show.
3. Geovisualization is understood as a set of conceptual methodologies that holds many possibilities, yet many visualizations tend to be tailored to specific research questions and are not always able to provide adequate solutions for representing other aspects of the data. At the other extreme, more generally applicable or abstract geovisualizations may not reveal detail that researchers need to be able to gain insights into specific research questions. In this respect, whilst any solution may help a particular area of science or even a conceptual and particular research question, they undoubtedly risk limiting the capacity for research outside the scope of the original design.

To illustrate different angles of this discussion, this chapter provides a transparent assessment of three otherwise unrelated mapping interfaces, conceptually designed for three different projects. The projects are: 1) the Strategic Environmental Archaeology Database (SEAD, www.sead.se), 2) Mapping Linguistic Landscapes and 3) Mekhane (www.mekhane.com). The first project, SEAD (www.sead.se, Buckland 2014a), is a research data infrastructure for storing, managing and analysing multidisciplinary paleo-environmental data.[3] The project includes powerful in-house querying and limited visualization tools as well as providing a source of spatiotemporal data for other systems. The second project, Mapping Linguistic Landscapes, aims to create an understanding of the materialization of languages in urban and rural landscape. The project shows where, when and what languages are addressed and represented, and thereby gives an indication of the inclusion and exclusion of various linguistic groups in public spaces. The third project, Mekhane is a repository of information about research-driven 3D renderings of ancient cities. It further provides the user with a visualization of the geographical reach of antiquity. For example, a user can see how many times digital models of Rome were made in other places. Mekhane aims at providing the user with an understanding of ancient place and its contemporary reconstruction in one single interface. In the geovisualization analysis that follows, we suggest that places, structures, and materials with GIS may be used to uproot well-established notions of space and place in relation to landscapes, cultures, media, and societies (White 2010; Frank 2012). We then discuss the limitations of geovisualizations.

Limitations related to cartography, a textual and visual exercise of space in essence, were identified long before the advent of digital technology. For example, *Periegesis Hellados* (*Description of Greece*) is a traveling narrative of space: a cultural geography of Greece comprised by 'the things that *deserve* to be recorded.' (Pausanias, *Description of Greece* 1.39.3); maps and narratives about space can be very conceptual, subjective, comprised by a specific selection of data. In the study of folk traditions and

Mapping socio-ecological landscapes

narratives, the early historic-geographic method developed by Julius and Kaarle Krohn (1926), strove for the reconstruction of the original form of a story or a tradition and for the mapping of its diffusion. It aimed 'to explain the similarities of stereotyped, complex forms of folklore as the result of shared origin and migration' (Kvideland, Sehmsdorf and Simpson, 1989:5). The historic-geographical method has been criticized for the loss of subjective and local variation (Christiansen, 1945; Cocq 2008) and the mapping of intangible cultural heritage with cartography may contribute to a misinformed geographical representation. Similar concerns have been raised by some archaeologists on the use of GIS in archaeology, including the suggestion that the technology removes the human, subjective aspects of interpreting data (Connolly & Lake, 2006; see Landeschi 2018 for a review of discussions with respect to the use of 3D GIS).

Landscape studies enable new approaches, which are, in turn, facilitated by new technological opportunities, and have even targeted global initiatives, such as the safeguarding of tangible, natural, and intangible cultural heritage (see Kirshenblatt-Gimblett 2014). Nature and culture in their tangible (landscapes, species, and villages) and intangible forms (rituals, entertainment and other habitual and temporary practices) often have spatial extensions In an Icelandic context, for example, where perceptions on individuality and variation differ from the context of the historic-geographical method, the interoperability and connection of maps and databases is seen as "an important tool for re-opening the field of local folklore and regional identity" (Gunnell 2010:157). Pálsson (2018) demonstrates the effective use of GIS for examining networks of social and resource connectivity in eighteenth century Iceland, but also comments on the tendency of archaeology to construct networks by connecting nodes with little consideration of the meaning or contents of the lines themselves. The robustness of social and environmental interpretations based on these networks may be difficult to evaluate. This is not unique to archaeology, and there is further a need for a transparent assessment of the processes of visualizing and linking data (Vitale 2016). The application of geovisualizations, does not remove the complexities associated with traditional cartography, and even introduces new challenges to the visualization of spatial data and interpretations.

While traditional print cartography can only visualize place as static geometries on a map, digital platforms provide a capacity for easily distributed updates, interoperability, and interactivity. This is not automatic, however, and digital maps are often created to display a static visualization of the spatial nature of a phenomenon. Interactivity is enabled by allowing the user to affect the visible content of the map, such as the selective visualization of points representing a particular type of archaeological site, or a particular time period. GIS methods can be used to connect to continuously updated databases, in real time, allowing for real-time querying, updates and corrections to be reflected on maps which may be static snapshots of the data. In this respect, digital maps do not necessarily have to be frozen in the same way that a paper map, which is more difficult to update, and absolutely impossible to animate.

Visualizing research data in space is bound up with issues of historical representation and identity formation, fragmented by and refracted through various moments of intersection between space and time. Our visual depiction of past landscapes, on the other hand, is based on snapshots of environments in space and time as provided by different lines of empirical data; for example, the variation in the diversity of plant or animal species found in geological samples or finds from archaeological sites. Visualization of these landscapes requires the interpolation or extrapolation of these data, and their spatial implications, following established, but not always transparent workflows and algorithms, using calibration data derived from contemporary ecology.[4]

The aforementioned case studies help identifying the validity of geovisualization as a research, educational, and dissemination tool. In foregrounding the role of digital technology among disparate projects, this research takes as its starting point the inherent statistical bias, in that any sample never truly represents

Foka Anna, Cocq Coppélie, Buckland Phillip I. and Gelfgren Stefan

the entirety of what it is designed to study; all datasets are broken in the sense that they represent only part of any sampled aspect of reality. Ultimately, we argue that visualizing place and space within a historical context is of dual significance that corresponds both to historical and current interest; for example it extends annotated scans of archaeological excavations to urban planning of local municipalities who could use the former when planning interventions on the territory. Rather than concentrating on the properties of geovisualization as such we focus on the new possibilities that can be found for creative research and expression which integrate affective history with more traditional modes of understanding (Turkel 2011). In the following sections, we address and highlight methodologies for mapping for each of the case studies, gathering evidence from multiple disciplines, including environmental archaeology, ethnography and linguistics, classics and media studies.

13.2 The Strategic Environmental Archaeology Database—SEAD

The SEAD system is primarily a resource for the storage and dissemination of data for archaeology and Quaternary[5] science. It contains numerous virtual constituent databases[6], the largest of which is the BugsCEP fossil insect database (Buckland 2014b). This represents the identification of over 700 000 individual fossil insect remains, deposited in the ground over thousands of years, and primarily from sites throughout Europe (Figure 13.1). Every site has a unique identifier which can also be used to find or share the site SEAD's data browser (see www.sead.se).

Environmental archaeologists and Quaternary scientists use these data to derive information on past climates, environments and human activities, using the assumption that any species found in the past will have required conditions similar to those in which it is found at the present day (this is the basis of palaeoecology, the study of past environments and climates, and environmental archaeology, see Reitz & Shackley 2012 for an overview). Each of the points on the map represents a *site* - shorthand for a collection of soil samples from either an archaeological excavation or a suitable organic deposit, such as a peat bog or lake sediment. Each sample represents a snapshot of some aspects of the environment around it during the time in which the sediment was deposited. The analogy of a pitfall trap is often used in that a depression in the ground will accumulate material until it becomes full. If we later extract the material from this depression we are in effect sampling the environment of the time of deposition.

Interpreting the implications of the fossil insects found in a soil sample is subject to a multitude of limits and assumptions (see Buckland *et al.* 2018a), but the goal is most often some form of representation of the environment which is relevant to a particular research question. This question may be as linguistically simple as 'how has the landscape changed around this site in the past' (according to the insects), but most often includes an interest in details such as changes in the proportion of woodland or water over time. Differences in the numbers and species of insects found between samples are assumed to represent changes in the environment over time at the site. Our capacity to identify these changes is controlled by several factors, including: 1) The ability of the samples and the enclosed fossils to reflect the changes, 2) The temporal resolution of the samples, and 3) The nature of the depositional environment we are trying to reconstruct. The geographical area represented by the fossils in any sample, or how much of the landscape around the point of deposition they reflect, is a complex issue which will not be covered here (but see Buckland *et al.* 2018a and Mitchell 2011 for general introductions).

The environmental and climatic requirements of 1000's of insects have been classified in the BugsCEP database (Buckland 2014b). By compiling these data for the species found in any sample, and treating them to some simple statistics, we can quantify the environmental and climatic implications of the sample. The results can be visualized in many ways, but a simple set of bar charts, where each chart represents the relative importance of a particular type of environment, is the preferred format in palaeoentomology

Mapping socio-ecological landscapes

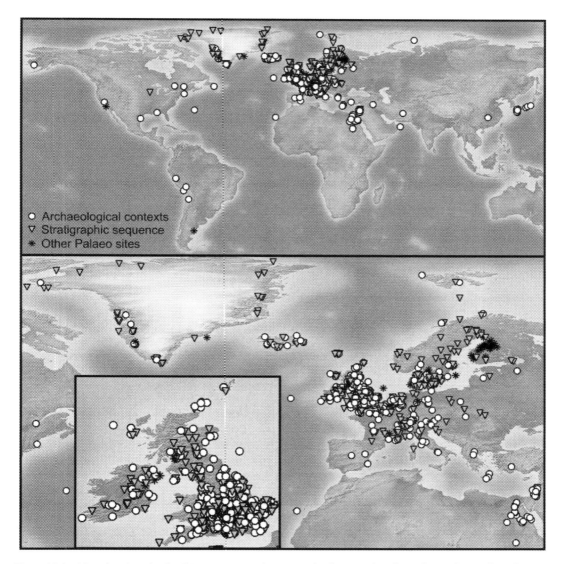

Figure. 13.1 Map showing the fossil insect sites in the SEAD database. Archaeological sites derive their data from archaeological excavations; Stratigraphic sequences may be associated with these, but are more often peat or lake cores from Quaternary science/geological studies; Other Palaeo sites are where fossils have been found in context which do not fit these descriptions. In all cases, a point on the map indicates the geographical location of insect fossils dated to either a period or date in the past

(the study of fossil insects) (Figure 13.2). The diagram can be read, from bottom to top, as changes in the environment at the site over time; the temporal resolution of each sample indicated by the vertical thickness of each bar, although in this example only information on the depth of the samples is available. Changing temperatures are shown as a span of potential ranges (or variation over the temporal extent of the sample) for winter and summer (on the left), with the mean temperature indicated as a line within the summer bars. Figure 13.2 shows the changes in temperature and environment which occurred between ca 20 000 and 11 000 years ago at Glanllynnau, north west Wales (Coope & Brophy,

Foka Anna, Cocq Coppélie, Buckland Phillip I. and Gelfgren Stefan

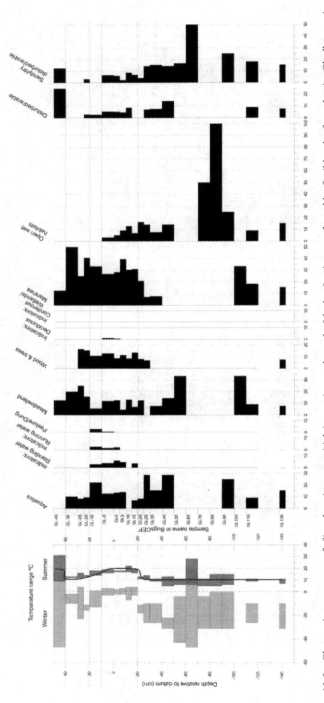

Figure 13.2 Changes in temperature (left) and environment (right) over time at the end of the last Ice Age as reflected by fossil beetles from the site Glanllynnau, in what is now north west Wales, UK. Modified from Buckland 2014b, using data from Coope & Brophy (1972). The transition from the Ice Age into a warmer climate is seen at about −20cm, during which wetlands and woodlands replace the earlier, more open environments. (The data behind this figure are available by searching for Glanllynnau in the SEAD portal at www.sead.se)

1972), including the transition from Ice Age temperatures to a warmer period (the Bölling/Alleröd Interglacial), a return to Arctic temperatures in the Younger Dryas, and the start of the warmer Holocene period (the uppermost sample). Cold periods are reflected by less complex, unstable, open and wet landscapes, whereas warm periods by stable, mixed landscapes with more trees.

The methodology behind Figure 13.2 allows us to visualize, in a controlled, reproducible, scientific[7] manner, changes over time. It is a powerful tool for understanding changes over time, and can be repeated for any site in the SEAD database, and the data source or statistics behind the visualization changed as deemed appropriate for the particular research questions. In theory, we could visualize the spatial extent of these changes by placing similar figures at multiple points on a map (e.g. selected sites from Figure 13.1). This is, however, a cumbersome solution for a static map, and while it could be a useful data exploration tool, it is doubtful that the addition of interactive features (such as site or time selection) of such an information intensive map would provide for an intuitive overview of past changes over space and time. The commonly accepted solution is to create a series of maps of coloured points, or interpolated temperature or environment surfaces between the points for selected time slices (see Coope et al. 1998 for an example using Glanllynnau and other data). These maps could be relatively easily connected to a time slider to allow a user to see changes over space and time, but it is very difficult to visualise more than one variable on such a surface map. The key problem here, is how to display more than 20 aspects of environmental change (e.g. temperature, extent of woodland etc.) in an intuitive way. The SEAD project is exploring alternatives, including 3D landscape visualizations with symbolic indications of key environmental indicators, and semantic linking between different types of data.

The approach of SEAD is far from objective or neutral in terms of the role of the technology in the research process. The web and mapping interface relies on a highly normalized relational database which is designed to closely model the structure of its source research projects and data. Although the visualization system allows for new patterns to be observed, and interesting theories to be tested, on environmental change throughout time and space, it also relies on the classification of organisms according to well established literature (see Buckland 2014b). Much of the data in SEAD are derived from standardised analysis methods, essentially the counting and classification of organisms and the measuring of sediment properties. There is much metadata connected to this, but a structured data and interface model easily replicates traditional analysis pathways to provide an efficient set of tools for analysing unconventionally large amounts of data outside of the scope of original creation. However, for more innovative exploratory data analysis, a model based on unstructured data, and visualization tools developed to look for unexpected patterns and relationships may be more interesting. Methodological approaches from big data analysis and critical humanities would undoubtedly be beneficial when designing these.

13.3 Mapping linguistic landscapes

The relationship between migration, linguistic diversity, and the hierarchy of languages in urban environments is addressed within the project Mapping Multilingualism. The project, initiated in 2016, includes scholars in minority studies and language education. It investigates how languages, as they materialize in the landscape, contribute to the making of public spaces. It focuses on visible languages (on public, private and commercial signs, on billboards, etc.) in a traditionally linguistically rich area of Sweden, the region of Norrland. Through a mixed-methods approach and the combination and layering of quantitative and qualitative data, the project can analyse which languages are visible and which are not, and relate these findings to demographic, socio-economic, educational and linguistic characteristics of different spaces. This enables us to understand how urban and rural places are constructed by the use of Indigenous, minority and majority languages, and to investigate and describe the role of language in place-making and in relation to various groups in the population.

Spatial analysis is central to the project's methodological approach and in this purpose, and is supported by a deep map, a multi-layered geovisualization. A digital visualization of photos of linguistic expressions is created by producing a map displaying where and when different languages are materialized in the city.

The photos are coded and assigned characteristics such as language, position, type of sign, sender, addressee etc. and placed geographically on a map with filterable categories. Geographical places are here a point of entry and of focus for compiling data from the different sources, and in analyzing these data in relation to geographical and social contexts. The digital map constitutes a methodological hub for the spatial analysis: the topographical exploration through layering of different kind of data enables a geovisualization of the selected places and explore place-making processes.

The map is interactive and the user can access detailed information on an image or a group of image intuitively, by clicking on an icon for the item (see Figure 13.3). This form of deep mapping enables us to conduct a spatial analysis for the exploration of the different layers of information. The textual data as indicated by the signs have a clear spatial dimension; the signs themselves are placed at specific locations in the geovisualization of the linguistic landscape and are presented as points on a digital map and linked to information about content and context.

As mentioned earlier and in reference to previous uses of cartography, one of the main challenges of mapping is to avoid recreating static representations of place as 'one point maps'. Moreover, the field of linguistic landscape studies has been criticized for being limited to qualitative data, and thereby leading to "the counting of languages" (Moriarty, 2014, p. 458). Also, place has often been interpreted as fixed and static instead of dynamic, fluid and changing (Ben-Rafael; Shohamy & Barni, 2010). Mapping multilingualism strives for rendering the dynamism of languages and their uses. The geovisualization method in layers, corresponds not only to different data, but also to different periods of time, and comprises one of the basic methods to meet this challenge: data collected through ethnographic fieldwork (photo documentation) are about a specific time and event; socio-demographic register data based on individual data describes the characteristics of the population (such as country of birth, residential address, and occupation); social media data can provide samples for a specific time laps, for instance during a particular cultural event. By navigating through different time periods on the same space (a specific town or neighbourhood), the user of the geovisualization can get insight into the flow and dynamism of linguistic landscapes.

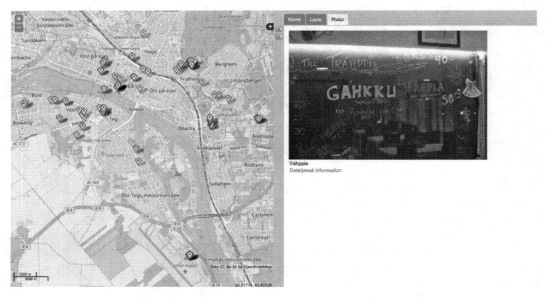

Figure 13.3 A mapping layer of the city of Umeå, Sweden, with photographic detail sign at the Sámi cultural house Tráhppie

Contextualizing the data is yet another challenge that the research team strives to address in order to limit the risk of fragmentation. Geovisualization might be misleading and give the web-user a false impression that it is comprehensive and includes all data that exist. The project seeks therefore to provide contextual information about the data collection process and the process of designing a geovisualization that aims at linking datasets. This will be achieved by adding annotations and field notes to the map. Preferably, this should be complemented without risking slowing down the navigation on the map. A possible solution that the research team considers would be a separate window that does not appear as a layer, but still can be browsed and searchable through keywords.

The project team found that the selection of data is key in countering the risk of representing language use at a frozen time at a defined place. A central aspect is not only to strive for a variety of data for the geovisualization (ethnographic, demographic, quantitative and qualitative), but also the transparency of the selection in itself. The design challenge here is to let the white spots on the map (in time and place) be visible and motivated for the user when navigating the map. Thus, the necessary contextualization mentioned above should not be restricted to the data, but should include the choices made by the researchers.

Thereby, the map is intended to constitute not only a mode of geovisualization, but also and foremost a method for the exploration of place-making with respect to spatial and temporal variations and including the rendering the context of the research process. These considerations open for other possible applications in forthcoming research, such as examining the relation between the visibility of languages and their vitality, or addressing societal challenges such as social inclusion.

13.4 Mekhane

Mekhane (http://www.mekhane.com) is an online database for born-digital reconstructions of ancient buildings and cities in the Mediterranean region. The project team combined methods from architecture, media, and classical reception studies for the purpose of gathering, organising and visualizing data on a mapping interface. Users can create an account free of charge, and after signing generic terms of service, they can contribute sets of data about both the digital reconstruction and the actual ancient site that served as inspiration (see Figure 13.4). The Mekhane team's geovisualization challenge was to connect ancient

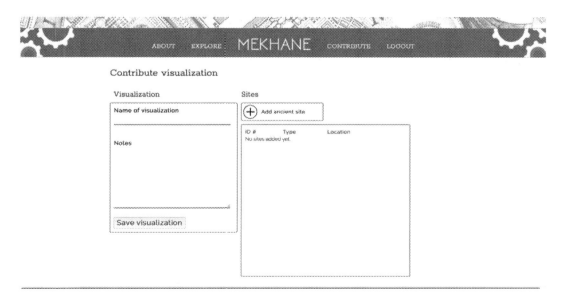

Figure 13.4 Mekhane's data aggregation interface

places and the geographical origin of contemporary reproductions in one single mapping interface. The Mekhane team envisioned this as a tool for those interested in studying the role of digital technology in the discipline of classical reception studies, and seek a way to represent the impact of the born-digital representations of the ancient world.

The system was developed around a principle of avoiding the devotion of time and resources to building new, self-contained applications. Emphasis was placed on the reuse and extension of data and tools that have already been produced and are open source and sustainable. The use of standardized software was based methodologically on the fact that they are open source, simple, versatile and sustainable. OpenLayers (https://openlayers.org) was used as it allows a dynamic map in any web page; it can display map tiles, vector data and markers loaded from any source.

A second important methodological choice was to utilize tools that already have a community around them. The project needed to connect and link data that is open and available. In order to make this a useful tool and to connect it to other ancient geospatial analysis platforms, Mekhane is further linked to existing gazetteers including Pleiades (https://pleiades.stoa.org) and DARE, the Digital Atlas of the Roman Empire (https://dh.gu.se/dare/).

In doing so the project connected to a global network of gazetteers through Pleiades (which covers the ancient world) and DARE. Mekhane then enables the user to identify a string of letters (e.g. R-O-M-E) but also then to align that reference to an appropriate authority file, a URIs (Uniform Resource Identifiers) numbers for places, which allow them to be disambiguated from each other.

Third, the project attempted to use a Linked Open Data model for connecting online resources. A gazetteer is, in simple terms, a geographical index or a dictionary (see White, 1968). Gazetteers are pivotal to geovisualization as they contain information about geographical coordinates, names, periods and time-spans, which, to begin with 1) differ across the centuries examined, 2) may be contested across different current national histories and geographies. Handling places which do not already exist in a gazetteer presents problem for projects which rely on connecting to them, as new places could not be easily entered by laymen. The complexity of handling such places for Mekhane was partly because of the gazetteers requiring a closed system for curation purposes, and partly because entering a new place requires entering of a number of parameters which may exceed what could be expected of the more casual users.

When building Mekhane, the methodology followed was based on a single, overarching aim: to be as inclusive as possible regarding data entries.

This type of methodology presupposes the need to carefully select data so that information is deposited within the Mekhane environment, and it requires that the user moves beyond the gazetteer framework and allows the user to manually mark a place on a map. The problem with this methodology is that it breaks integration with the rest of the mapping ecosystem (see Figure 13.5). Only the parts of the data in Mekhane specified using a gazetteer would be exportable to the rest of the ecosystem. It may risk enabling undesirable behaviour from the user, where the selection of place by map becomes preferred over finding the place in a gazetteer, since the former may often be the easier and faster approach. The independent/ internal solution for locating places on a map is a temporary solution that may not be compatible with other gazetteers. It is possible that Mekhane could find other more complete gazetteers in the future, or become a gazetteer in its own right, or just that existing gazetteers will grow to cover a larger number of places thus rendering any places selected by map obsolete.

Another methodological issue was visualizing time periods: again, the issues were primarily ontological: libraries for the parsing of ancient dates at the time of development were scarce, so the Mekhane team had to write their own. Later digital resources for the geospatial analysis of events, such as the project Periegesis (http://www.periegesis.org) draw upon time period and data gazeteers such as PeriodO (http://www. perio.do) and Trismegistos (https://www.trismegistos.org).

Mapping socio-ecological landscapes

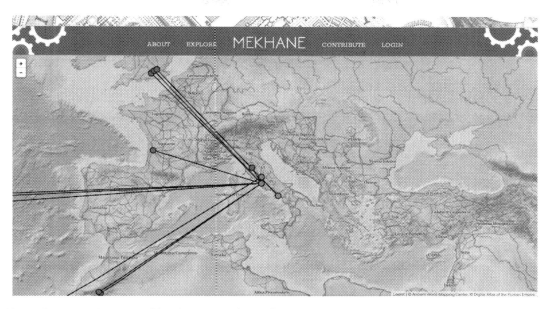

Figure 13.5 Zooming out: Mekhane's mapping tile interface in relation to mapping certain reconstructed sites from Italy. The orange dots represent location of original site and the blue the site of reconstruction

While the mekhane operates as a repository for temporal information, the only way to solve this would be to include any time period. There is also the consideration that if one wants to store these dates as Unix timestamps, one needs to run a 64bit operating system to handle the resulting very long integers. Striking a balance between the amount and precision of data requested to be input by the user, user friendliness and accessibility. This is especially important in a crowdsourced applications as the contributors are in fact voluntary laymen, some of whom may have older computers.

Handling the list of production technologies, from which a user could choose when registering a place, also presented a problem. A normalized list[8] was most desirable, but entailed limiting the number of possible technologies the user could choose. Whilst this allowed multiple levels of technology to be included, a discussion was required on the appropriate level to present the technologies—e.g. just "3D scanning" or give the option of selecting the specific type of 3D scanning used. An option for technologies used which did not exist in the predefined list was also problematic, in that it would break the normalization of the database unless a more complex solution for entering lists was coded. The solution the team applied was to use a tree-list where the broad categories such as "3D scanning" were included, but also subcategories to each of them. Both the overlying categories and the subcategories are selectable. This way the user may select their specific version of 3D scanning used, or if it does not exist in the Mekhane interface list, they can simply select the top category of "3D scanning". An annotated "other" field was provided to capture technologies not found in any list. This means the user could select 'other' then enter a note on what the other was. The list of entries was periodically evaluated and new categories inserted into the normalized list manually. The visual representation of different technologies was achieved by using different colours.

To conclude, while gazetteers of the ancient world and contemporary places provide us with the possibility of visualizing past and present, it is a complex task to create common vocabularies for spatial or temporal data, and to connect disparate places in disparate times in the same mapping interface. Data fragmentation is also an issue. The Mekhane team is thus currently adding entries which are then in turn visualized as single points on a map and connected by lines to indicate the connection between two points, ancient site and contemporary digital rendering of the past.

13.5 General considerations regarding the visualizations for geospatial analysis

From these explorations it derives that precisely because space and time are dynamically bound up with each other, it is difficult to map geographies of culture by conventional GIS. There are, for example design challenges: to integrate ground-up, localised points of view with broader bird's-eye horizons, and to incorporate disparate kinds of data, linked together by common references through annotation and categorization, essentially by identifying an ontology of sources. Digital maps are primarily directed toward critical visualizations, such as bringing new knowledge to an already solidified scholarly notion within a discipline. SEAD's online interface (Figure 13.6; www.sead.se; http://supersead.humlab.umu.se) provides a faceted browser to allow users to filter which sites are displayed on the map, and provides a number of other data visualizations to help the user explore the data and identify relationships or patterns across space and time.

In the case of Mekhane, the humanistic aim is to visualize the impact of classical material cultures within contemporary digital media and to examine this relationship in depth in order to identify how

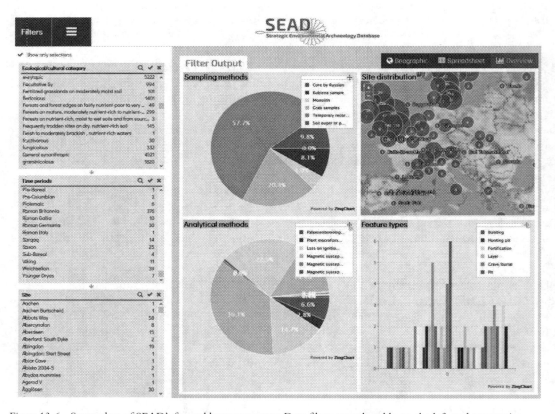

Figure 13.6 Screenshot of SEAD's faceted browser system. Data filters are selectable on the left, and summaries of the filtered results are shown in the panels on the right. Alternative views are included with either point or aggregated point maps and spreadsheet views. Individual site datasets are accessed by clicking on a site the map

Mapping socio-ecological landscapes

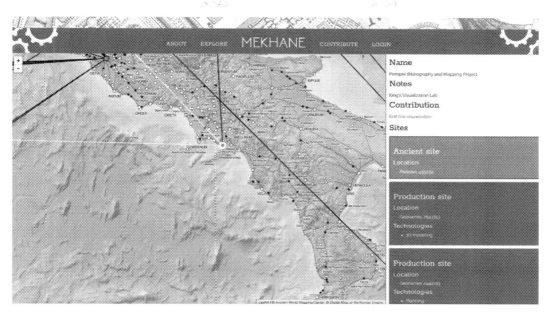

Figure 13.7 Pompeii Bibliography and Mapping Project as shown in Mekhane's repository. An example is Kings Digital Visualization Lab (Kings College London) Pompeii Bibliography and Mapping Project

often cultural heritage visualizations are not restricted to a national initiative (see Figure 13.7). In the case of Mapping Linguistic Landscapes, the purpose of the visualization model is not only to display multilingualism or point to the lack of representation of multilingualism —it also illustrates how linguistic landscape studies can go beyond "the counting of languages" (Moriarty 2014) and problematize linguistic landscaping by visualizing its relation to demographic data.

Switching between *close* and *distant* reading, facilitates individual movements through complex data, and builds in critical awareness of these technologies and the data they present. It is thus worthy to examine further how one may expose and analyse textual space beyond two-dimensional Cartesian mapping. With advances in web-mapping and digital texts, there is a demand for new research methodologies, based on using maps to visualize dynamic patterns as events, and to analyse them as flows and transformations. The close versus distant concept may also be applied to other forms of data, and the large scale overviews presented in SEAD's browser (Figure 13.6 provide distant views aggregated or summarised from the details available in the close viewing of datasets or site based environmental visualizations (Figure 13.2).

Conclusion

In this article, we have highlighted how geovisualization methodologies for socio-ecological landscapes provide opportunities for a deeper and more nuanced contextual reading of historical material. Digital cartography can and should be seen as a tool that incorporates various sets of research methods. In this sense, technology can hardly be seen as a neutral component of the process that leads to new knowledge. Making use of GIS visualizations as a method and tool means that we are facing a number of different choices - which materials must be selected, how the material must be adapted to fit into a digital platform, the very design properties of that platform, the extent to which they control software visualization, and so on.

While digital tools admittedly enable the rapid dissemination and analysis of both old and new issues, we must still say that the visualization tool and process should be viewed through a critical humanistic approach.

Foka Anna, Cocq Coppélie, Buckland Phillip I. and Gelfgren Stefan

Converting empirical data to any kind of visualization thus requires a traditional humanities research and critical analysis. But when used correctly, it visualization is a tool that can bring new research questions and thereby contribute with new knowledge and understanding. Questions and ideas are influenced by the digital context in a complex relationship. The effects of digital material and processing on historiographical development need to be thoroughly studied in future research in order to better understand contemporary and future knowledge production, its merits and shortcomings. Digitization can contribute to the development of knowledge, but it should not be an end in itself, and neither should data visualization.

Notes

1 For a general discussion on cartography, chorography and their tradition as knowledge production methods see Dunn 2019. See also Hepworth 2016: 280–302 on visualization as tool and a methology more generally.
2 From Piccini 2015: Media archaeology is not simply an addition to the familiar archaeological hermeneutics by comparing, for example, the description of the "pre-cinematic" image sequences on the ancient Trajan's Column in Rome to technologies like chronophotography. The media-archaeological task is rather to reveal the *discontinuity* of the media-artifactual message when compared with traditional cultural artefacts by describing their implicit techno-mathematical operations.
3 Palaeoenvironmental data generally refers to data on past environments, including the fossil organisms and chemical or physical properties recorded from archaeological and geological samples.
4 See Newell, R., and Canessa R. (2015) and Buckland *et al.* 2018b.
5 The Quaternary period is the last 2.588 million years, roughly equivalent to the period in which human-like species have existed.
6 Essentially databases contained within a larger database, but maintaining their own identity.
7 Rather than artistic—it is perhaps not a visually stimulating figure.
8 i.e. a hierarchical list with groups containing several items per group.

References

Barker. E., Bouzarovski, S., Pelling, C., and Isaksen, L. 2010. 'Mapping an ancient historian in a digital age: the Herodotus Encoded Space-Text-Image Archive (HESTIA)'. *Leeds International Classical Studies*, 9(2010) article no. 1. http://www.leeds.ac.uk/classics/lics/

Buckland, P. I., (2014a). SEAD—The Strategic Environmental Archaeology Database. Inter-linking multiproxy environmental data with archaeological investigations and ecology. In: Graeme E., Sly, T., Chryssanthi, A., Murrieta-Flores, P., Papadopoulos, C., Romanowska, I., & Wheatley, D., (Eds.), CAA2012, *Proceedings of the 40th Annual Conference of Computer Applications and Quantitative Methods in Archaeology* (CAA), Southampton, England..

Buckland, P.I. (2014b). The Bugs Coleopteran Ecology Package (BugsCEP) database: 1000 sites and half a million fossils later. *Quaternary International*, *341*, pp.272–282.

Buckland, P.I., Buckland, P.C., & Olsson, F. (2018a). Paleoentomology: insects and other arthropods in environmental archaeology. In *Encyclopedia of global archaeology* (2nd ed.). Cham. https://doi.org/10.1007/978-3-319-51726-1_2333-2

Buckland, P. I., Dell'Unto, N., & Pálsson, G. (2018b). 'To tree, or not to tree? On the Empirical Basis for Having Past Landscapes to Experience. *DHQ: Digital Humanities Quarterly*, *12*(3). http://digitalhumanities.org/dhq/vol/12/3/000383/000383.html

Christiansen, R. T. 1945. 'Et eventyrs krokveier'. *Festskrift til Konrad Nielsen*. Oslo.

Cocq, C. (2018). *Revoicing Sámi Narratives. North Sámi storytelling at the turn of the 20th century*. Sámi Dutkan 5, Umeå Universitet.

Conolly, J., & Lake, M. (2006). *Geographical information systems in archaeology*. Cambridge University Press.

Coope, G. R., & Brophy, J. A. (1972). Late Glacial environmental changes indicated by a coleopteran succession from North Wales. *Boreas*, *1*(2), 97–142.

Coope, G. R., Lemdahl, G., Lowe, J. J., & Walkling, A. (1998). Temperature gradients in northern Europe during the last glacial–Holocene transition (14-9 14C kyr BP) interpreted from coleopteran assemblages. *Journal of Quaternary Science: Published for the Quaternary Research Association*, *13*(5), 419–433.

Dunn, S, Earl, G. Foka, A. Wooton, W. (2019) The Birth of the Digital Object Itinerary. In Tula Giannini and Jonathan Bowden (ed.) *Museums and Digital Culture: New Perspectives and Research*, London and New York: Springer: 253–271.

Mapping socio-ecological landscapes

Dunn, S. (2019) *A History of Place in the Digital Age*, Routledge:London.

Barker, E., Foka, A. and Konstantinidou, K. (2020) 'Coding for the Many, Transforming Knowledge for All: Annotating Digital Documents', *PMLA the Journal of the Modern Language Association of America* 135(1): 195–202

Frank, Z., & Berry, W., (2010). The Slave Market in Rio de Janeiro circa 1869: Context, Movement and Social Experience. *Journal of Latin American Geography*, 9(3), 85–110. doi:10.1353/lag.2010.0033

Frischer, B., Abernathy, D., Giuliani, F. C., Scott, R. T., and Ziemssen, H. 2006. 'A New Digital Model of the Roman Forum'. In *Imaging Ancient Rome* edited by Haselberger, L. and Humphrey, J., Portsmouth, *RI: Journal of Roman Archaeology*, 163–8

Gunnell, T. 2010. 'Sagnagrunnur: A New Database of Icelandic Folk Legends in Print'. *Folklore: Electronic Journal of Folklore*, 151–162.

Hayles, N. K. (2012). "How We Read: Close, Hyper, Machine". *ADE Bulletin*. 152 (1). doi:10.1632/ade.152.0

Hepworth, K. (2016). History, power and visual communication artefacts, *Rethinking History*, Routledge: London 20:2, 280–302.

Isaksen, L.; Barker, E.; Kansa, E. C. and Byrne, K. (2012). GAP: a neogeo approach to classical resources. *Leonardo*, 45(1) pp. 82–83.

Kirshenblatt-Gimblett, B. (2014). Intangible heritage as metacultural production. *Museum International*, 66(1–4), 163–174. http://www.michaelfehr.net/Museum/Texte/heritage_MI.pdf

Kvideland, R., Sehmsdorf, H. K. and Simpson, E. 1989. *Nordic folklore: recent studies*. Bloomington: Indiana University Press.

Landeschi, G. (2018). Rethinking GIS, three-dimensionality and space perception in archaeology. *World Archaeology*, 1–16.

Mahony, S., and Bodard, G. (2010). Introduction. *In Digital Research in the Study of Classical Antiquity*, edited by Mahony, S. and Bodard, G., Surrey Ashgate: 1–14.

Mitchell, F. J. (2011). Exploring vegetation in the fourth dimension. *Trends in Ecology & Evolution*, 26(1), 45–52.

Moriarty, M. (2014). Languages in motion: Multilingualism and mobility in the linguistic landscape. *International Journal of Bilingualism*. Vol 18, Issue 5.

Newell, R., and Canessa R. (2015). Seeing, Believing, and Feeling: The Relationship between Sense of Place and Geovisualization Research., *Spaces & Flows: An International Journal of Urban & Extra Urban Studies* 6.4 (2015).

Nygren, T., Foka, A., and Buckland, P. (2014). Digital History in Sweden. *H-Soz- Kult*, Humbolt: Humbolt University Press.

Pálsson, G. (2018). Storied Lines: Network Perspectives on Land Use in Early Modern Iceland. *Norwegian Archaeological Review*, 51(1–2), 112–141.

Pausanias. *Pausanias Description of Greece* with an English Translation by W.H.S. Jones, Litt.D., and H.A. Ormerod, Volumes I-II. Cambridge, MA, Harvard University Press; London, William Heinemann Ltd. 1918. (first edition)

Piccini, A. (2015). Media Archaeology: an Invitation, *Journal of Contemporary Archaeology*, 2 (1). DOI:10.1558/jca. v2i1.27134

Reitz, E., and Shackley, M. (2012). *Environmental archaeology*. Springer Science & Business Media.

Schreibman, S., Siemens, R., Unsworth, J. (2004). *A Companion to Digital Humanities*. Oxford: Blackwell.

Tangherlini, T.R. (2013). "The Folklore Macroscope: Challenges for a Computational Folkloristics." The 34th Archer Taylor Memorial Lecture. *Western Folklore* vol 72(1): 7–27.

Turkel, W. J. (2011). Intervention: Hacking history, from analogue to digital and back again, *Rethinking History*, 15:2, 287–296,

Vitale, V. 2016. 'Transparent, Multivocal, Cross-disciplinary: The Use of Linked Open Data and a Community-developed RDF Ontology to Document and Enrich 3D Visualisation for Cultural Heritage'. in Boddard, G. and Romanello M. *Digital Classics outside the Echo-Chamber* London: Ubiquity Press.

White, R. (2010). What is spatial history? Retrieved from http://www.stanford.edu/group/spatialhistory/cgi-bin/site/pub.php?id=29&project_id=

White, Robert C. (1968). "Early Geographical Dictionaries," *Geographical Review* (Volume 58, Number 4, 1968): 652–659.

14

GIS FOR LANGUAGE STUDY

William A. Kretzschmar, Jr. and Alexandra Petrulevich

14.1 Introduction

Space is one of two basic ways in which we perceive the world around us, along with time. We see in spatial terms, and we hear sounds that appear closer or further away. As Lakoff and Johnson (1980/2003) and Steen (2011) have pointed out, we use spatial metaphors frequently to interpret the world around us. Assessment of people's ability with spatial relations is part of common intelligence testing. Still, most people live their lives with quite different perceptions of the space around us. Gould and White (1986) describe the mental maps that each of us maintains, and demonstrate that our perceptions of space are colored by relative distance and mixed with many other kinds of information. We are required, then, to develop special methods for the analysis of space that make up for our failures in perception, ones that permit exact and replicable measurement and validation, and these methods are best carried out with digital assistance.

Geographic information systems (GIS) is a framework used for spatial analysis across a large number of disciplines covering a set of digital tools to collect, manage, analyse, and visualise spatial data. GIS for language study is a relatively new phenomenon within digitally oriented linguistics that took shape at the end of the so-called "spatial turn" within the humanities in the beginning of 00s. Early applications of GIS in linguistics, sometimes termed geolinguistics, pre-date this development by at least twenty years (e.g. Thomas, 1980, Mackey, 1988, Mark & Csillag 1989, see Hoch & Hayes, 2010 and Dell'Aquila, 2010 for an overview). Pederson (1986, 1988,) inaugurated the plotting of dialect data by microcomputer, followed closely by Kirk and Kretzschmar (1992), who built a GIS using geographical base maps. The first interactive GIS for linguistic data on the Web appeared in 1996 (Kretzschmar, 1996). Today, GIS for language study is an established approach to spatial analysis of language data comprising a substantial and growing amount of literature and reaching out to yet new branches of language science such as philology. However, GIS is still seldom included into conventional linguistics curricula at universities, which often feature formal or text-based corpus methods without reference to geography, or typological studies that assume but do not discuss particular geography. Furthermore, bespoke methodologies and common standards for data collection, management, and visualisation in linguistic research utilising GIS are still being discussed and developed.

The areas of application of GIS for language study range from the fields where mapping and spatial perspectives have played a crucial role since their establishment such as general linguistics, dialectology and onomastics (e.g. Kretzschmar, 1992a, Ormeling, 1992, Lee & Kretzschmar, 1993, Goebl, 2006,

Kretzschmar, 2006, Luebbering, Kolivras & Prisley, 2013, Corbett, 2013, Gammeltoft, 2016, Gawne & Ring, 2016, Syrjänen et al., 2016, Eppler & Benedikt, 2017) to those branches of linguistics where the interest in spatiality and spatial aspects of data is growing such as philology and language planning and policy (e.g. Williams & Van der Merwe, 1996, Wrisley, 2014, Petrulevich, Backman & Adams, 2019). Moreover, GIS-based approaches to data visualisation and spatial analysis have been utilised in studies of language contact (Williams, 1996), language change (Bye, 2011, Teerarojanarat & Tingsabadh, 2011), linguistic landscapes (Holder, 2007), and sociolinguistics (Veselinova & Booza, 2009, Dell'Aquila, 2010). The variety of areas of application implies a variety of field-specific research questions, methodologies, and theoretical frameworks. At the same time, it is important to bear in mind that GIS is not a neutral set of tools ready to be adapted for the next linguistic project, but rather a complex framework based on spatial theory and associated with a certain area of scientific inquiry, Geographic Information Science (GIScience) (Mark, 2003, McMaster & Usery, 2004, Longley et al., 2015). Any linguistic study employing GIS is by definition an interdisciplinary enterprise. It is thus of crucial importance for linguists working with GIS to acknowledge and engage with the fundamental concepts of geography and cartography (e.g. Lameli, Kehrein & Rabanus, 2010, pp. 1–145). Adopting a more pronounced theoretical awareness of the implications of GIS usage is a necessary prerequisite for fruitful collaboration with other GIS subjects in both hard sciences and the humanities.

GIS-based language research begins with a spatial research question. What is the spatial distribution of a language feature or a set of language features? Are there any spatial patterns? Does the spatial distribution of the language feature correlate with the spatial distribution of other non-language variables? The spatial component of the research question has implications for the datasets needed to answer the question. The language data have to be spatially referenced, i.e. provided with coordinates. In addition, other types of data might be needed, for instance topographic data or early modern road network data for investigation of dialectal diversity in relation to topography in a geographical area. In general, the goal is to analyse data visually or statistically to reveal patterns in spatial distribution of variables under study, compare the distribution of several variables, predict the distribution of a variable through data modelling, observe changes in spatial distribution over time, and unveil the reasons behind the observed patterns of distribution.

GIS makes it possible to bring together, integrate, and aggregate different types of data such as topographical data, elevation data, administrative data, census data, and different types of language data, relevant for answering a specific research question. GIS enables work at any level of scale, from neighborhoods to nations to transnational regions, so that investigators can consider language data below, at, or above the level of an individual language. The data are organised in separate data layers, ideally one data layer per data type. The data layers can be processed or adapted to suit the project, for example allowing to exclude geographical areas or variables not of interest. The fundamental advantage of GIS is the capability to process and manipulate large quantities of otherwise disparate spatial and attribute data. This in its turn makes it possible to test multiple hypotheses and create new predictive models for the same dataset. The results of the work can be exported as maps or graphs since GIS provides a range of output options.

The current chapter will present a concise guide into the methodology of using GIS for language study exploring data management, spatial referencing, and computational analyses, as well as data visualisation. The chapter contains some introductory remarks on the basic concepts of GIS, but it is not meant to be a general introduction to GIS or GIScience (see e.g. Heywood, Cornelius & Carver, 2011, Longley et al., 2015, Chang, 2016 for such an introduction). Section 14.2 provides an introduction to geographical modelling of linguistic data including an overview of related literature. In section 3 we address the data and data management procedures needed to carry out GIS-based linguistic research. In addition, the section includes a discussion on data quality, a major issue in GIS. Section 14.4 deals with two major types of methods in GIS-driven spatial analysis of linguistic data, computational analyses and data visualisation. In this section we address a number of challenges associated with GIS for spatial analysis in linguistics, for instance using multi-dimensional scaling to assess similarity of individual variables and operationalisation of abstract concepts to allow visualisation by mapping.

GIS is not the only way of conducting spatial analysis in linguistics. For instance, phylogeography and phylolinguistics offer other approaches to statistical spatial analysis of language data not dealt with in this chapter.

14.2 Geographical modelling of linguistic data

When we represent spatial information, as on a map, we are making a model (see Kretzschmar, 1992b). Models are separate from reality but describe or predict particular aspects of reality. They are thus more manageable than reality because they make big things smaller (whole cities or countries in a small image) or small things bigger (bar and ball representations of molecules). Models need not have physical form: the general form of a model in equation form is $a + b + c + \ldots + E$, where a number of variables are chosen to describe or predict aspects of reality with all other aspects not chosen for specific representation included in the final error term (E). People who make models always have to choose which aspects to include in their modes, and also have to decide how to represent them. Weather maps may show satellite images or radar, known as raster maps because the maps are composed of an array of locations (like pixels on a computer screen or television, or squares on a chess board), each of which is colored to represent data (like the green color often used for rain on computer or television weather maps) or is otherwise associated with data. Alternatively, in what is known as vector format, weather maps can show graphical elements like isobars or lines for fronts, perhaps with L or H labels, or labels for wind speed or temperature. People who make models should be systematic in the creation of the representation (show all the points or elements/labels for the scale and area represented), but they can create them at any level of scale (say, local or national). These decisions about how to make models always reflect the maker's theoretical foundations and assumptions. The more explicitly the ideas involved in the model are discussed, the more usable the model will be. The London Charter (http://www.londoncharter.org/) is an attempt to address the general issue of making models in the digital humanities.

In recent years, the Google API (programmers' interface) has become the expected public norm for computer maps, though of course there are many other options for experts. Google maps are highly scalable, from viewing a whole country or region at once right down to finding one's own neighborhood and house. There is a place to click to show a satellite image (a raster map) or a road map (a vector map). In some ways raster images appear to be simpler for developers because they are just rows and columns of pixels. On the other hand, the relationship between the pixels and the information that we want see in the map may not be very clear. Vector maps can make it easier to manage information by packaging it into perceptual objects (like lines for roads).

Linguistic maps can be made with either the raster or vector method. Figure 14.1 shows a raster map of where people were likely to say *quarter of* when telling the time (as opposed to *quarter to*, *quarter till*, or many other responses) in the Linguistic Atlas Eastern States data. The survey area has been divided into a grid of about 3000 squares, each .2 degree of latitude by .2 degree of longitude. Each square is colored according to the likelihood of finding *quarter of* there, darkest for high probability down to no coloring for lowest probability.

This style of map shows patches of different levels of probability. *Quarter of* is more likely to appear in northern parts of the survey area, though it also occurs in other places and its use is not predicted to be uniform in the North.

GIS for language study

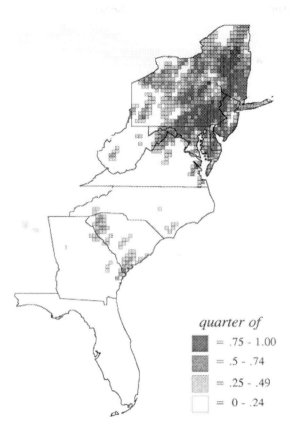

Figure 14.1 Quarter of in the Eastern States

Figure 14.2 shows a map of national regions prepared by William Labov using the vector style.

Here we see lines drawn on the map intended to represent different dialect regions. We also see symbols of different colors that indicate phonetic realizations of different speakers. In this style of map the lines represent generalizations of the map maker (not all of the data points within them are the same). Both the vector and the raster methods model the language behavior of speakers in the chosen areas, just with different theoretical assumptions and decisions about representation.

A characteristic feature of GIS models is that they contain layers of information. Computer mapping uses the layer principle to establish a base map and to add user-selectable layers, each of which contains a different kind of information. Thus, the $a + b + c + \ldots$ of the standard model formula has the a on one layer, the b on another layer, the c on yet another layer, with as many more layers as there are aspects represented in the model. In Figure 14.1, for instance, one layer shows the outlines of American states; it could be left out, but it helps the user to understand the area of the survey. Another layer is the grid units. The third layer is information about the likelihood of *quarter of*, represented in the coloring. In Figure 14.2, one layer is the base map showing state boundaries. Another layer is the lines indicating dialect regions. A third layer is the locations for speakers. A fourth layer is the shapes of the symbols. Finally, a fifth layer is the color of the

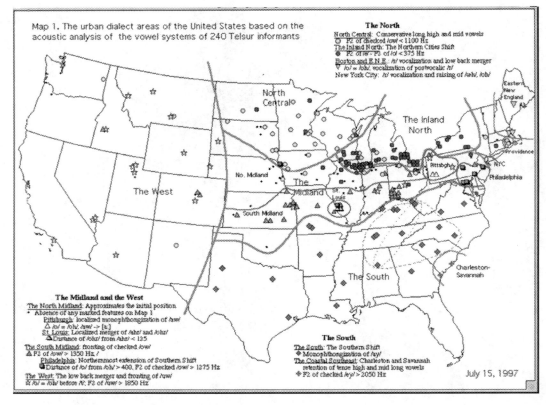

Figure 14.2 Map of national regions prepared by William Labov using the vector style

symbols. The map also has labels, and these can be considered a layer in themselves even though they do not represent data. Each of the figures thus shows that the map presented is actually a composite set of layers.

14.3 Data and data management

As it has been pointed out in Section 14.1, a spatial research question is a necessary point of departure for all the data work, regardless of whether a new GIS-compatible dataset is created from scratch or if relevant datasets are fetched from a third party. The data have to be collected, put in a database, edited or "cleaned" and spatially referenced in order to be used in a GIS-based analysis. It is important to note that the results of any GIS analysis will greatly depend on how well the research question has been defined and what sort of data have been used to answer that question. The computer science saying "garbage in, garbage out" is highly applicable in this case. In other words, the data quality issues need thorough consideration for all types of data you have accumulated for your project.

14.3.1 Data types, data acquisition and spatial referencing

The GIS data can be divided into two major subgroups, spatial or geospatial data and attribute data. Spatial data need not represent geographical space. For example, a common application of GIS spatial analysis is the enhancement of photographs. An example from linguistics is analysis of data in F1/F2 space (Kretzschmar, Kretzschmar, and Brockman 2013). Spatial data commonly describe physical objects of the

GIS for language study

real world. The main component of such spatial data is information on geographic locations represented by geographical references such as coordinates. Spatial data often include additional attribute data or non-spatial characteristics of the dataset, e.g. type of locality. However GIS can process many different types of attribute data and aggregate many different attributes for one geographical feature. Language data can thus be seen as a type of attribute data in a GIS project.

GIS utilises three types of two-dimensional geometric objects, points, lines, and areas or polygons, to represent more complex three-dimensional geographical entities of the real world. Depending on the scale of the map a point can be a major city or a village or a tree. Lines represent objects with some length, e.g. roads or rivers. Polygons have length, width and area and are suited to represent such features as countries, administrative units or lakes or forests. The choice of the spatial data type depends on the resolution appropriate for the project and the scale of the map involved. For instance, for an investigation of linguistic diversity in a major city one might want to work with polygon data rather than points representing different neighbourhoods.

Spatial data can be acquired in a number of ways, e.g. by browsing for and downloading the data from national governmental agencies and public sector organisations, European data initiatives (e.g. European Data Portal or INSPIRE) and other commercial or free online spatial resources. The same goes for spatially referenced language data available for free or licensed use, e.g. linguistic atlases (Glottolog, LAP, Ethnologue, WALS Online, WLMS) or place-name gazetteers and databases (DigDAG, Geonames, iDAI.gazetteer, Pleiades). Since common standards for both spatial data and language data are still being developed, the different datasets may need to be converted to a single standard to be able to use them in GIS. For instance, the data can be in different coordinate systems or map projections which will cause problems when overlaying the dataset layers.

If the data needed for your GIS project is not available you might need to digitise a spatial dataset, e.g. an older paper map, or geocode a language dataset manually. Georeferencing is the process of making analogue maps GIS-compatible by matching a set of fixed reference points with known coordinates on the scanned image of the map to the corresponding points in the chosen GIS coordinate system (for an example, see Macniven, 2015, pp. 41–44). Language data need to be spatially referenced, i.e. assigned coordinates such as latitude and longitude, in order to be combined with other types of data in GIS. For the Linguistic Atlas Project, interview locations were geocoded by looking up the names of localities in standard databases, an application of a vector object (a named community) to a geographic location (longitude/latitude coordinate) that could be used in either raster or vector analysis. In communities with multiple interviews, longitude/latitude coordinates for each interview were assigned to intersections near the address of the speaker (not to their actual street addresses!) using online maps. People interviewed for the LAP have a right to privacy, and it has been standard LAP practice to suppress information–like street addresses and names of people or community institutions to which the people belonged–in order to protect their identities. Current research involving human subjects is monitored at universities and often other facilities (such as hospitals) by an Institutional Review Board, to which investigators should report their plans for the protection of subjects' privacy and for ethical maintenance of data. Spreadsheets are still the prevalent way of organising, storing, and managing language datasets. However multi-tabular SQL relational databases are a better option for dealing with GIS-compatible datasets, because the database approach implies that the data have been processed in a uniform fashion using the same formats and most importantly the same principles for defining and organising attributes. Data input or encoding is the most important and time-consuming tasks in a GIS project since the output will have a direct impact on the results of any further analysis.

14.3.2 *Data quality issues*

There are a number of requirements posed on both spatial and language datasets to assure the data are appropriate to use in scientific research. Accidental and systematic errors can be introduced into the data at many levels, such as during data collection, processing, or digitisation. The quality standard for spatial data includes such parameters as accuracy, precision, completeness, compatibility, consistency, and applicability (e.g. Heywood, Cornelius & Carver, 2011, pp. 310–314). In linguistics, there are as well articulated standards for language data requiring the data to be objective, reliable, valid, and representative (e.g. König, 2010, pp. 494–511; there remain serious questions about how such data can be "representative," see Kretzschmar, 2015: Chapter 7.). However using language data in GIS implies compliance with spatial data standards such as data completeness, which is not always recognised in linguistic research (Briscoe, 2009, pp. 19–28, 43–49). Moreover, re-using data or combining a number of different datasets, which is commonplace in the GIS-based approach, requires reliance on someone else when it comes to data quality and it may be necessary to access data collection documentation or other metadata for quality control.

Re-using data from linguistic atlases in GIS may cause problems since the data may have a different resolution or may have been collected for a purpose different than that of the current project. For example, Figure 14.1 relies on 1162 speakers to make a map of the Eastern States, while Figure 14.2 uses 240 speakers to make a map of the entire nation. Data collection through digitisation of older linguistic maps for locations can result in a highly imprecise spatial dataset. The same goes for spatially referencing the linguistic results of field work that are not primarily accumulated for a GIS-compatible dataset and thus may have insufficient or imprecise spatial information and lack documentation of data collection (e.g. Briscoe, 2009, pp. 43–49; see Gawne & Ring 2016 for a helpful and up-to-date introduction into mapmaking for language documentation). Veselinova & Booza (2009) provide another example of challenges associated with re-using data for linguistic research. They have investigated linguistic diversity by using the US Census 2000 data. Mapping languages spoken at home documented in the dataset has proven difficult for a number of reasons, one of them being the discrepancies between the language classification used in the census and in linguistics respectively. In name studies, combining spatial data fetched from an external gazetteer and a place-name dataset can constitute a problem if there is a mismatch between the temporal prerequisites and the resolution of the datasets (Petrulevich et al. 2019, see Section 14.1). The first step in amending the data quality problems is to recognize them as well as to discuss the fit for use issue explicitly, i.e. the applicability of the imperfect data for a GIS project. In many cases there are simply no other data available to use.

14.4 Methods and applications

In this section, we go through GIS-based mapping techniques such as area-class maps based on Voronoi polygons and kernel density estimation as well as essential geostatistical methods for analysis of geographical variation in language such as point-pattern analysis and Levenshtein distance methods. Appropriate software package are needed in order to use the visualisation techniques and analytical methods presented. Since the market of both licensed and open-source GIS software and their different versions is changing rapidly we are not including any survey or guide of the available options (for a recent overview see Kretzschmar, 2013b, pp. 58–59, Gammeltoft, 2016). The most widely known licensed software include ArcGIS from ESRI and MapInfo® Pro from Pitney Bowes, while QGIS (www.qgis.org/en/site/) is one of the most commonly used free open-source packages. The GIS software provides a set of pre-programmed options for statistical analysis. However it might be a good idea to learn a scripting language such as Python for performing customised statistical operations or integrate your GIS software with the statistical programming language R, for further functionality in statistical computing. Use of programming tools like Python and R have allowed the Linguistic Atlas Project, for instance, to make its own GIS applications without having to pay for ArcGIS or to ask assistants to engage in the long training program required for its use. Collaboration with geographers can be a fruitful option.

14.4.1 Statistical approaches

Analysis of spatial patterns relies on the property of "complete spatial randomness" (CSR). If a perceived pattern is spatially random, then the pattern just belongs to the perception of the analyst (as Gould and White 1980 argue is quite possible). Alternatively, patterns may be more uniform than CSR (such as the location of the black and white squares of a chessboard) or more clustered than CSR (such as the high proportion of the population in urban areas as opposed to having people in a random or even spread across the land).

A good example of analysis of CSR comes from point pattern analysis. In this technique, a grid layer is applied to the area of interest, and the analyst counts the number of data points that occur in each region. Acoustic phonetic analysis is commonly performed in F1/F2 space, which consists of frequency measurements in Hertz of the spoken signal; F1 refers to the first formant (harmonic) above the fundamental frequency, and F2 refers to the second formant above the fundamental frequency. Plotting the F1 frequency on the y axis and the F2 frequency on the x axis, as if these occurred in the lower-left quadrant of an x/y plot, yields a visualization that matches traditional vowel charts (i.e., the high-front/i/vowel as in FLEECE is at the upper left of F1/F2 space, the high-back/u/vowel as in GOOSE is at the upper right, and the low-front/æ/vowel as in TRAP is at the lower left. Traditional analysis of F1/F2 space grew from the use of just a few tokens, owing to the difficulty of making measurements, but now it is possible to acquire a large number of tokens from forced alignment of transcripts with sound files and associated automatic formant extraction (as in Olsen et al. 2017).

In Figure 14.3 (http://lap3.libs.uga.edu/u/jstanley/vowelcharts/), F1/F2 space have been overlaid with a 12 x 12 grid, and points plotted for realizations of the GOOSE vowel by three non-African American speakers from the state of Georgia (522 tokens). Point pattern analysis shows that the points are clustered, as shown by the shading. There is one darkest grid unit with the most tokens (H9), another one with the next most tokens (G9), and then a number of grid units with a smaller density of tokens. Grid units with no tokens are not labeled. It is possible to carry out a statistic to show whether the data over all are statistically significantly clustered or trend towards clustering (see Kretzschmar 2009), but that procedure has not been carried out here.

It is also possible to consider the arrangement of locations only with respect to each other, whether they are "neighbors" or more remote from each other. One can calculate distances between different locations. In real geographic space, a familiar example is the calculation of the most direct route between two places on a map, as on the familiar Google sites that will provide driving directions between two addresses. "Distance" can also be interpreted in ways other than miles or kilometers. For instance, Jean Séguy (1971) pioneered "dialectometry" on data from the *Atlas linguistique de Gascogne* by calculating the "linguistic distance" between pairs of places, for him the number of different responses from a list of questions. The best current work in dialectometry has come from John Nerbonne and his associates (e.g. Nerbonne & Heeringa, 2001). Nerbonne has applied the Levenshtein distance metric to assign distances between pairs. Levenshtein uses string edit calculations to determine distance: the difference between any two forms, say "dog" and "dogs," is the number of changes one has to make to get from one to the other (the distance is 1 between "dog" and "dogs" to add the −s). Nerbonne has aggregated Levenshtein distances across a number of variants to calculate the overall distance between two places, and then produces maps by methods such as MDS (see below) as in Figure 14.4 (from www.let.rug.nl/~kleiweg/lamsas/).

More recently, various statistics have been used to derive abstract, non-geographic distances for GIS applications, notably multi-dimensional scaling (MDS), which computes the Euclidean distance between points in N dimensions corresponding to variables of interest to the analyst. In such analysis, the notion of "similarity" depends upon complex mathematical calculations which position data points in abstract, non-representational space. In such cases the analyst must use care not to interpret results just in terms of a visualization in the two or three dimensions that we can immediately perceive, but to take account of the mathematics that generate the visualization. A good example of the use of cluster analysis is Grieve, Speelman, and Geeraerts (2013).

The most recent quantitative movement has arisen from the discovery that human language is a complex system (Kretzschmar 2009, 2015; Burkette and Kretzschmar 2018). Complex systems, whether in human populations (language, economic markets), biological systems (ecology, the human immune system), or physical systems (quantum mechanics, fluid/air dynamics), are characterized by the interaction of many elements and the emergence of stable patterns. In language, the pattern that always emerges from

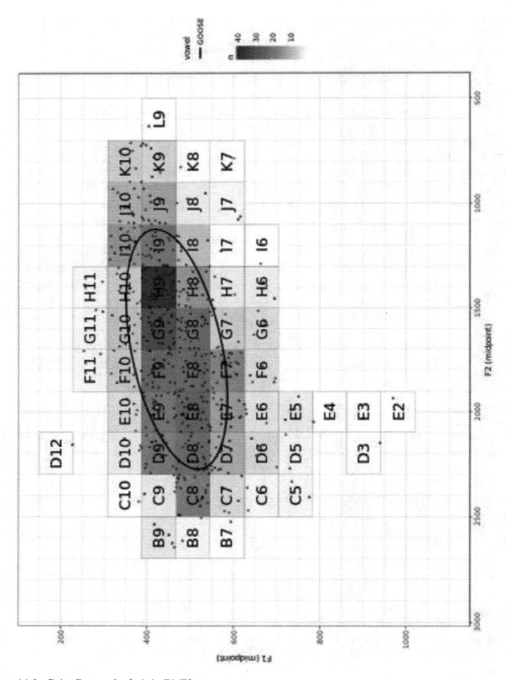

Figure 14.3 Point Pattern Analysis in F1/F2 space

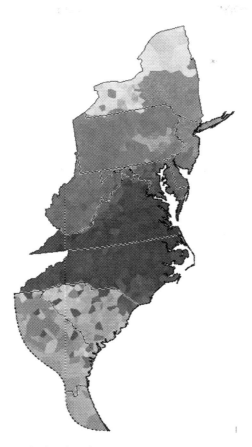

Figure 14.4 Levenshtein Distance displayed with MDS

Souce: http://www.let.rug.nl/~kleiweg/lamsas-old/results/plain-1162-Mds.gif

interaction of speakers is a nonlinear frequency pattern, in which a few variants of some linguistic features are extremely common, a few variants are moderately common, and most variants seldom occur. This pattern occurs at every level of scale (say, at the national, regional, local, and individual levels). Figure 14.5 shows the frequency pattern of the grid units from Figure 14.3.

In geographical terms, the result is the clustered appearance of data on maps, as in Figure 14.1. All linguistic features demonstrate this pattern. While all locations tend to share all of the variants that occur more than a few times, particular variants may be more much more common in particular areas—thus the clusters. Statistical procedures that capitalize on this fact about language include density estimation (a form of discriminant analysis; see Kretzschmar, 2017 for discussion of a multivariate form of density estimation) and spatial autocorrelation (see Lee and Kretzschmar, 1993). The nonlinear distributional pattern is also the basis for validation of a GIS-based computer simulation for language diffusion, built as a cellular automaton so that it applies procedural mathematics rather than numerical statistics (see Kretzschmar, Juuso, & Bailey, 2014).

14.4.2 Data visualisation

Data visualisation via mapping is a way of storing, organising, presenting and analysing the data. Maps have been heavily used in different branches of linguistics since the establishment of the field. Ideally, the visualisation in itself is sufficient for drawing some preliminary conclusions about the spatial distribution of a

William A. Kretzschmar, Jr. and Alexandra Petrulevich

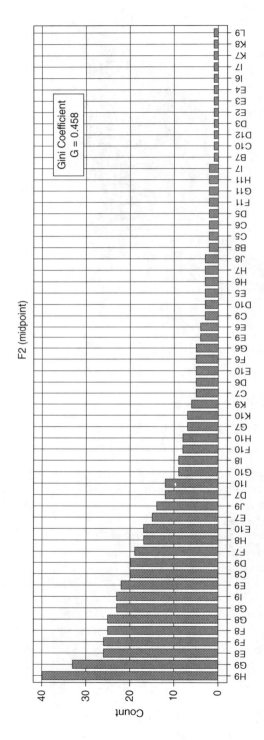

Figure 14.5 Frequency pattern from Georgia GOOSE tokens

Source: http://lap3.libs.uga.edu/u/jstanley/vowelcharts/

certain variable. However, a map is essentially a simplified or generalised two-dimensional model of the real world and as such can give misleading ideas about both spatial data and spatially referenced language data. The mapping process of linguistic data is always grounded in an implicit or explicit theoretical standpoint. For dialectology, Kretzschmar (2006) discusses two, a deductive or Neo-Grammarian approach that focuses on isoglosses and establishing dialectal areas with more or less discrete borders (Figure 14.6), and an inductive or French approach that sees geographical variation in language as a continuum. Isoglosses are lines drawn on a map that are supposed to represent the limit of occurrence of some linguistic feature, and bundles of isoglosses that run in approximately the same place are taken to represent boundaries between the separate language systems that many linguists prefer to discuss. The continuum approach prefers to see gradual, quantitative differences across areas, not sharp breaks represented by isoglosses. In other words, there is a need of both theoretical and methodological awareness when discussing or re-using the results of the mapping work of other linguists as well as when designing maps of your own.

The methodology behind traditional linguistic mapping and analogue thematic maps, e.g. isoline and choropleth maps in dialectology, have been heavily criticised for a number of flaws (e.g. Dahl & Veselinova, 2005; Pi, 2006; Hoch & Hayes, 2010; Lameli, 2010, pp. 574–582; Kretzschmar, 1992, 2013a & b; Luebbering, Kolivras & Prisley, 2013). Most of the maps are based upon a number of extensive generalisations about

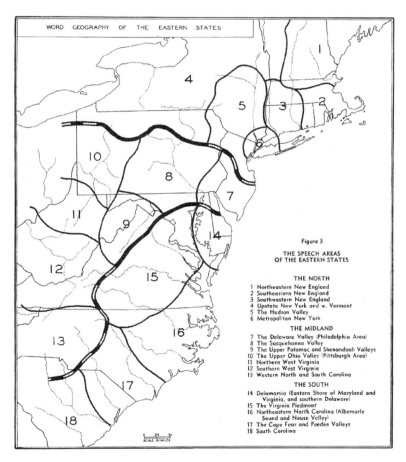

Figure 14.6 A linguistic thematic map showing the speech areas of the US Eastern States

Source: reprinted with permission from Kurath, 1949, Figure 3

the language phenomena mapped. For instance, arbitrary and highly subjective choices may lie behind suggested boundaries between languages or dialectal areas. These boundaries are often represented as discrete lines thus concealing or ignoring the multi-variate or multilingual characteristics of the studied dialect or linguistic space (Figure 14.6). Furthermore, although conceived as purely descriptive models linguistic maps can easily be perceived as implicit predictive tools. The datasets used to produce the maps are usually samples and as such they by definition do not cover the entire population of the mapped territory and fail to meet the requirements of data completeness posed by spatial theory (see Section 14.3.2). As Luebbering, Kolivras & Prisley (2013, p. 583) put it, the appropriate mapping unit for a linguistic map is an individual speaker provided the data is informant-based. Instead, linguists tend to operate with areal, administrative units when collecting and aggregating their data. Another issue related to data sampling and mapping in linguistics concerns representativity and perception of power. These critical and ethical aspects of linguistic mapmaking have to a large extent been ignored, but the questions of whose linguistic data are represented or marginalised in a map and why need to be addressed (see discussion in Lameli, 2010, pp. 583–585, Luebbering, Kolivras & Prisley, 2013, pp. 582–583, Gawne & Ring, 2016, pp. 196–197). For these reasons, re-using or re-producing data from older analogue linguistic atlases in GIS may be problematic and requires thorough understanding of the choices behind the original material, see Section 14.3.2.

In many cases, GIS is capable of solving the problems outlined above. However, this does not mean that GIS is free from generalisation. As has been stated earlier, in GIS complex three-dimensional spatial reality is distilled down to a definite number of operationalised concepts and two-dimensional representations. In linguistics, different GIS mapping techniques have been proposed or utilised to produce maps and mapping resources meeting a wide range of requirements in the fields of dialectology, dialectometry, linguistic diversity, language documentation and description, place name studies, philology etc. In this subsection, a limited number of applications of these techniques are considered including dynamic interactive mapping of place-name data in philology as well as quantitative approaches to visualising language data through mapping. A comprehensive overview of linguistic mapping and cartography is given in Lameli, Kehrein & Rabanus, 2010.

The choice of an appropriate mapping technique depends on the methodological, technical, user-related, and aesthetic requirements you pose on the end product. The basic questions concerning map design always include those about the purpose of the map, its scale and projection, the features mapped, and the method of representation (Girnth, 2010, Heywood, Cornelius & Carver, 2011, p. 36, Gawne & Ring, 2016, pp. 198–200). Sibler et al. (2012) posit a comprehensive list of methodological and aesthetic requirements for mapping single morphosyntactic features. The list covers capabilities to account for co-occurrence of multiple variants of the same feature and fill in missing values as well as visual attractiveness and easiness of perception. As stated in Section 14.3.2, it is necessary to provide accurate documentation of a dataset to allow data re-usage. In the same way, it is important to include necessary annotation, e.g. a legend, when presenting mapping results

Visualisation of spatially referenced data via GIS mapping is a relatively new approach in the field of philology (Wrisley, 2014, Petrulevich, Backman & Adams, 2019). One of the very recent examples is the interactive spatial-temporal resource Norse World. The main objective of the project is to provide an innovative infrastructure with mapping capabilities for research on spatiality and worldviews in medieval literature from Sweden and Denmark. The primary data include attestations of foreign place names and other spatial references in the corpus of East Norse literary texts. The end-user interface employs dynamic GIS-based mapping via the Leaflet Library and the Leaflet.markercluster plugin to highlight the quantitative aspects of the data, i.e. how frequently localities are mentioned in the corpus (Figure 14.7). This visualisation technique data opens new possibilities to explore the material quantitatively that did not exist before.

In this case, the shortcomings of the interactive mapping and clustering come from operationalisation of the abstract concepts of place and time as perceived by medieval people in Scandinavia (Petrulevich, Backman & Adams, 2019). The Norse World project geocodes heterogeneous spatial references from a

GIS for language study

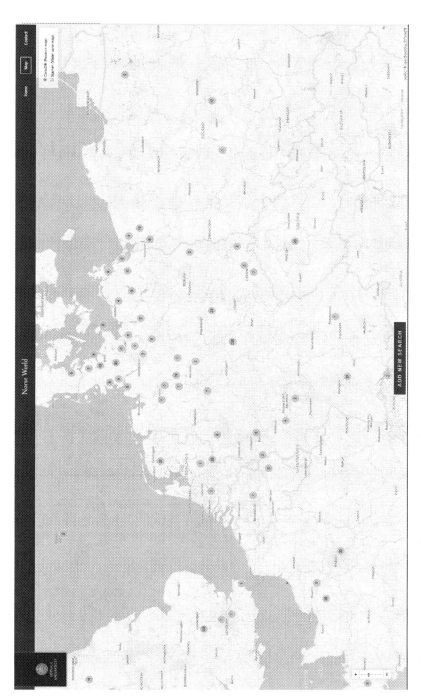

Figure 14.7 Interactive clustering technique employed in the Norse World

Source: © 2018 Norse World, © Leaflet, © OpenStreetMap, © CartoDB

variety of medieval sources by re-using spatial data from a number of standard gazetteers such as Geonames. As a result there is a major spatial and temporal discrepancy between the multi-layered raw data, their attribute counterparts and the spatial data. However geocoding for visualisation purposes still allows meaningful spatial grouping of data and thus making sense of thousands of attestations of foreign place names in the corpus.

One of the developments in mapping techniques in dialectology include area-class maps based on Voronoi (Thiessen) polygons (Lee & Kretzschmar, 1993, Goebl, 2006, 2010, Nerbonne, 2009, 2010, Sibler et al. 2012). The main advantage of introducing Voronoi diagrams instead of mapping linguistic features by areal or administrative units is that the entire area of survey is divided into regions or cells based on calculated distances to pre-defined sets of points (for example, the survey sites). Each Voronoi cell thus contains all points closer to a particular pre-defined point than to any other (Figure 14.8). Linguistic data is usually collected from a limited number of informants thus not covering the entire parish or municipality or other mapping unit (see above). The procedure of dividing the entire area under study into cells based on survey sites allows to eliminate the holes in the data or, in other words, the problem of incomplete data. The Voronoi diagram is a suitable method for generating area-class maps of distribution patterns of single

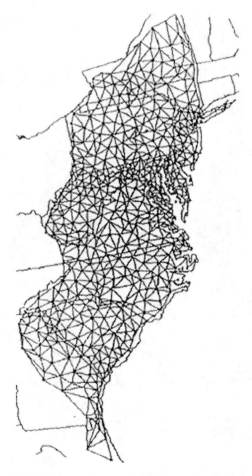

Figure 14.8 Visualisation of the LAMSAS survey data employing Voronoi polygons and Delauney triangles
Source: reprinted with permission from Kretzschmar, 2013, Figure 3.7

attributes or linguistic features. However, the maps of the kind are assumed to be vulnerable to short-range spatial variation and uncertainties that may affect the mapping results (Sibler et al. 2012).

This disadvantage can be redressed by introducing spatial interpolation methods such as kernel density estimation (KDE; Rumpf et al. 2009, 2010, Sibler et al. 2012). The KED method is a way smoothing the data and thus eliminating any eventual "noise" such as short-range spatial variation. As explained in Kretzschmar 2017, the kernel method produces a generalization based on the data, rather than a more direct visualization. Figure 14.1 illustrates density estimation using the nearest-neighbor method, which shows clusters; the kernel method would produce a visualization something like a target which suggests that the data has a central tendency but would conceal the clusters. "Noise" might be something analysts need to see, depending upon their theoretical stance and assumptions, and a smoothed visualization may give an impression based more on the smoothing than the data. As we have suggested, models using GIS can show quite different visualizations from the same data, and so the makers of GIS models should always declare what ideas drive their models.

Conclusion

The current chapter has introduced some basic concepts and principles behind geographical modelling of linguistic data and the GIS-based approach to spatial analysis in linguistics. The best sort of linguistic map, especially one prepared by computer, is the map that the analyst can actually make and use. It is important for analysts to make their own maps, because maps are sensitive to the different theoretical assumptions of their makers: the same data can generate many different maps. This is especially true in a quantitative GIS, whose goodness of fit to the data may not be entirely clear. The two main divisions in quantitative methods, calculation of relationships of the data to CSR, and dialectometric calculations of "linguistic distance," are both useful so long as they fit the larger models of their practitioners. GIS makes linguistic maps better than traditional linguistic maps. However, we need to maintain appropriate respect for all the aspects of the map as a model in order to make good maps. And we should never forget what Gould and White have taught us, that our mental maps are always based on perceptions and mixed with other information, so that a GIS must be the beginning of our analytical story and not the end.

References

ArcGIS. (2018). Retrieved from https://www.arcgis.com/index.html

Briscoe, Ulla. (2009). *Geolinguistic GIS Applications: Aspect of Data Quality in Mapping Lesser-Used Languages*, Master thesis, Centre for Geoinformatics (Z_GIS), Salzburg University.

Burkette, Allison, & William A. Kretzschmar, Jr. (2018). *Exploring Linguistic Science: Language Use, Complexity and Interaction*. Cambridge: Cambridge University Press.

Bye, Patrik. (2011). "Mapping Innovations in North Germanic with GIS", in Language Variation Infrastructure, ed. by J. B. Johannessen. *Oslo Studies in Language* 3:2, 5–29.

Chang, Kang-tsung. (2016). *Introduction to Geographic Information Systems*. Eighth edition. New York, NY: McGraw-Hill Education.

Corbett, Greville G. (2013). "Number of Genders", in *The World Atlas of Language Structures Online*, Matthew S. Dryer and Martin Haspelmath (eds.).(Leipzig: Max Planck Institute for Evolutionary Anthropology). Retrieved from http://wals.info/chapter/30

Dahl, Östen & Veselinova, Ljuba. (2006). Language Map Server. *ArcUser Online*. Retrieved from https://www.esri.com/news/arcuser/0206/language_ms1of2.html

Dell'Aquila, Vittorio. (2010). "23. GIS and sociolinguistics", in *Language and Space: An International Handbook of Linguistic Variation* 2. Language Mapping. Part I. Part II: Maps, ed. by Alfred Lameli, Roland Kehrein, and Stefan Rabanus (Berlin, Boston: De Gruyter Mouton), 458–482. Handbücher zur Sprach- und Kommunikationswissenschaft 30:2.

DigDAG. (2018). Retrieved from http://digdag.dk/

Eppler, Eva & Benedikt, Josef. (2017). "A perceptual dialectological approach to linguistic variation and spatial analysis of Kurdish varieties". *Journal of Linguistic Geography* 5, 109–130.

The Ethnologue: Languages of the World. (2018). Retrieved from https://www.ethnologue.com/

European Data Portal. (2018). Retrieved from https://www.europeandataportal.eu/

Gammeltoft, Peder. (2016). "Names and Geography", in *The Oxford Handbook of Names and Naming*, ed. by Carole C. Hough (Oxford: Oxford University press), 502–512.

Gawne, Lauren & Ring, Hiram. (2016). "Mapmaking for Language Documentation and Description". *Language Documentation & Conservation* 10, 188–242.

Geonames. (2018). Retrieved from https://www.geonames.org/

Glottolog. (2018). Retrieved from https://glottolog.org/

Goebl, Hans. (2006). "Recent Advances in Salzburg Dialectometry". *Literary and Linguistic Computing* 21:4, 411–435.

Goebl, Hans. (2010). "22. Dialectometry and quantitative mapping" in *Language and Space: An International Handbook of Linguistic Variation* 2. Language Mapping. Part I. Part II: Maps, ed. by Alfred Lameli, Roland Kehrein, and Stefan Rabanus (Berlin, Boston: De Gruyter Mouton), 433–464. Handbücher zur Sprach- und Kommunikationswissenschaft 30:2.

Gould, Peter, & White, Rodney. (1986). *Mental Maps*. 2nd ed. London: Routledge.

Girnth, Heiko. (2010). "5. Mapping language data", in *Language and Space: An International Handbook of Linguistic Variation* 2. Language Mapping. Part I. Part II: Maps, ed. by Alfred Lameli, Roland Kehrein, and Stefan Rabanus (Berlin, Boston: De Gruyter Mouton), 98–121. Handbücher zur Sprach- und Kommunikationswissenschaft 30:2.

Grieve, Jack, Dirk Speelman, & Dirk Geeraerts. "Multivariate Spatial Analysis of Vowel Formants in American English." *Journal of Linguistic Geography* 1 (2013), 31–51.

Heywood, Ian, Cornelius, Sarah & Carver, Steve. (2011). *An Introduction to Geographical Information Systems*. Fourth edition. Harlow: Prentice Hall.

Hoch, Shawn & Hayes, James J. (2010). "Geolinguistics: The Incorporation of Geographic Information Systems and Science". *The Geographical Bulletin* 51, 23–36.

Holder, Nick. (2007). "Mapping the Roman Inscriptions of London". *Britannia* XXXVIII, 13–34.

iDAI.gazetteer. (2018). Retrieved from https://gazetteer.dainst.org/app/#!/home

INSPIRE Knowledge Base. Infrastructure for spatial information in Europe. (2018). Retrieved from https://inspire.ec.europa.eu/

Kirk, John, & Kretzschmar, Jr., William A. (1992). Interactive Linguistic Mapping of Dialect Features. *Literary and Linguistic Computing* 7, 168–175.

Kretzschmar, Jr., William A. (1992a) "Interactive Computer Mapping for the Linguistic Atlas of the Middle and South Atlantic States (LAMSAS)." In *Old English and New: Essays in Language and Linguistics in Honor of Frederic G. Cassidy*, edited by N. Doane, J. Hall, and R. Ringler, 400–414. New York: Garland.

Kretzschmar, William A., Jr. (1992b). Isoglosses and Predictive Modeling. *American Speech* 67, 227–249.

Kretzschmar, Jr., William A. (1996). "The LAMSAS Internet Site", paper presented at NWAVE, Las Vegas.

Kretzschmar, Jr., William A. (2006). "Art and Science in Computational Dialectology". *Literary and Linguistic Computing* 21:4, 399–410.

Kretzschmar, Jr., William A. (2009). *The Linguistics of Speech*. Cambridge: Cambridge University Press.

Kretzschmar, Jr., William A. (2013a). "GIS for Language and Literary Study", in *Literary Studies in the Digital Age: An Evolving Anthology*, ed. by Kenneth M. Price, Ray Siemens. Retrieved from https://dlsanthology.mla.hcommons.org/

Kretzschmar, Jr., William A. (2013b). "Computer mapping of language data", in *Research Methods in Language Variation and Change*, ed. by Manfred Krug, Julia Schlüter (Cambridge University Press: Cambridge), 53–68.

Kretzschmar, Jr., William A. (2015). *Language and Complex Systems*. Cambridge: Cambridge University Press.

Kretzschmar, Jr., William A. (2017). "Good Maps." In *From Semantics to Dialectometry, Tributes 32*, ed by. M. Wieling, M. Kroon, G. van Noord, and G. Bouma (London: College Publications), 211–220.

Kretzschmar, Jr., William A., Ilkka Juuso, and Thomas Bailey. (2014). "Computer Simulation of Dialect Feature Diffusion." *Journal of Linguistic Geography* 2, 41–57.

Kretzschmar, Jr., William A., Brendan Kretzschmar, and Irene Brockman (2013). "Scaled Measurement of Geographic and Social Speech Data." *Literary and Linguistic Computing* 28, 173–187.

Kurath, Hans. (1949). *A Word Geography of the Eastern United States*. Ann Arbor: University of Michigan press. Studies in American English 1.

König, Werner. (2010). "28. Investigating language in space: Methods and empirical standards", in *Language and Space: An International Handbook of Linguistic Variation* 1. Theories and Methods, ed. by Peter Auer and Jürgen Erich Schmidt (Berlin, Boston: De Gruyter Mouton), 494–511. Handbücher zur Sprach- und Kommunikationswissenschaft 30:2.

Lakoff, George, & Johnson, Mark. (2003). *Metaphors We Live By*. Chicago: University of Chicago Press, 1980. Republished with new afterword, 2003.

Lameli, Alfred. (2010). "32. Linguistic atlases – traditional and modern", in *Language and Space: An International Handbook of Linguistic Variation* 1. Theories and Methods, ed. by Peter Auer and Jürgen Erich Schmidt (Berlin, Boston: De Gruyter Mouton), 567–592. Handbücher zur Sprach- und Kommunikationswissenschaft 30:2.

GIS for language study

Lameli, Alfred, Kehrein, Roland & Rabanus, Stefan (eds.). (2010). *Language and Space: An International Handbook of Linguistic Variation* 2. Language Mapping. Part I. Part II: Maps. Berlin, Boston: De Gruyter Mouton. Handbücher zur Sprach- und Kommunikationswissenschaft 30:2.

Leaflet: An open-source JavaScript library for mobile-friendly interactive maps. (2018). Retrieved from https://leafletjs.com/

Leaflet.markercluster plugin. (2018). Retrieved from https://github.com/Leaflet/Leaflet.markercluster

Lee, Jay & Kretzschmar, William A. Jr. (1993). "Spatial analysis of linguistic data with GIS functions". *International Journal of Geographical Information Science* 7:6, 541–560.

LAP (Linguistic Atlas Project). (2018). Retrieved from http://www.lap.uga.edu/

Longley, Paul A., Goodchild, Michael F., Maguire, David J. & Rhind, David W. (2015). *Geographic information science & systems*. Fourth edition. Hoboken, New Jersey: John Wiley & Sons.

Luebbering, Candice R., Kolivras, Korine N. & Prisley, Stephen P. (2013). "Visualizing Linguistic Diversity Through Cartography and GIS". *The Professional Geographer* 65:4, 580–593.

Mackey, William Francis. (1988). "Geolinguistics: Its Scope and Principles", in *Language in Geographic Context*, ed. by Colin H. Williams (Clevedon: Multilingual Matters), 20–46. Multilingual matters 38.

Macniven, Alan. (2015). *The Vikings in Islay: The Place of Names in Hebridean Settlement History*. Edinburgh: John Donald.

MapInfo® Pro. (2018). Retrieved from https://www.pitneybowes.com/us/location-intelligence/geographic-information-systems/mapinfo-pro.html

Mark, David M. & Csillag, Ferenc. (1989). "The Nature of Boundaries on 'Area-Class' Maps". *Cartographica: The International Journal for Geographic Information and Geovisualization* 26:1, 65–78.

Mark, David M. (2003). "Geographic Information Science: Defining the Field", in *Foundations of Geographic Information Science*, ed. by Matt Duckham, Michael F. Goodchild and Michael F. Worboys (New York: Taylor & Francis), 1–17.

McMaster, Robert B. & Usery, E. Lynn. (2004). *A Research Agenda for Geographic Information Science*. Boca Raton: CRC Press.

Nerbonne, John. (2009). "Data-Driven Dialectology". *Language and Linguistics Compass* 3:1, 175–198.

Nerbonne, John. (2010). "24. Mapping aggregate variation", in *Language and Space: An International Handbook of Linguistic Variation* 2. Language Mapping. Part I. Part II: Maps, ed. by Alfred Lameli, Roland Kehrein, and Stefan Rabanus (Berlin, Boston: De Gruyter Mouton), 476–501. Handbücher zur Sprach- und Kommunikationswissenschaft 30:2.

Norse World. (2018). Retrieved from https://norseworld.nordiska.uu.se/

Nerbonne, J. & Heeringa, W. (2001). "Computational comparison and classification of dialects". *Dialectologia et Geolinguistica* 9: 69–83.

Olsen, Rachel M., Michael Olsen, Joseph A. Stanley, Margaret E. L. Renwick, & William A. Kretzschmar, Jr. (2017). "Methods for transcription and forced alignment of a legacy speech corpus." *Proceedings of Meetings on Acoustics* 30, 060001; doi: http://dx.doi.org/10.1121/2.0000559.

Ormeling, Ferjan. (1992). "Methods and possibilities for mapping by onomasticians". *The Cartographic Representation of Linguistic Data. Discussion Papers in Geolinguistics* 19–21, ed. by Peeters, Yvo J. D. and Williams, Colin H., 50–67. Selected Papers from a Geolinguistic Seminar (Le Pailly, France, September 10–13, 1992).

Pederson, Lee. (1986). "A Graphic Plotter Grid". *Journal of English Linguistics* 19:1, 25–41.

Pederson, Lee. (1988). "Electronic Matrix Maps". *Journal of English Linguistics* 21, 149–74.

Petrulevich, Alexandra, Backman, Agnieszka & Adams, Jonathan. (2019). Medieval Macrospace Through GIS: The Norse World Project Approach. In: Cartographic Journal. https://www.tandfonline.com/doi/full/10.1080/00087041.2019.1596341.

Pi, Chia-Yi Tony. (2006). "Beyond the Isogloss: Isographs in Dialect Topography". *Canadian Journal of Linguistics* 51:2–3, 177–184.

Pleiades. (2018). Retrieved from https://pleiades.stoa.org/

QGIS. (2018). Retrieved from https://www.qgis.org/en/site/

Rumpf, Jonas, Pickl, Simon, Elspaß, Stephan, König, Werner & Schmidt, Volker. (2009). "Structural Analysis of Dialect Maps Using Methods from Spatial Statistics." *Zeitschrift für Dialektologie und Linguistik* 76:3, 280–308.

Rumpf, Jonas, Pickl, Simon, Elspaß, Stephan, König, Werner & Schmidt, Volker. (2010). "Quantification and Statistical Analysis of Structural Similarities in Dialectological Area-Class Maps". *Dialectologia et Geolinguistica* 18:1, 73–100.

Séguy, Jean. "La relation entre la distance spatiale et la distance lexicale." *Rev. Linguist. Rom.* 35 (1971), 335–57.

Sibler, Pius, Weibel, Robert, Glaser, Elvira & Bart, Gabriela. (2012). "Cartographic Visualization in Support of Dialectology", in *The 2012 AutoCarto International Symposium on Automated Cartography, Columbus, Ohio, USA, 16 September 2012–18 September 2012.*

Steen, Gerard. (2011). "The Contemporary Theory of Metaphor — Now New and Improved!" *Review of Cognitive Linguistics* 9, 26–64.

Syrjänen, Kaj, Honkola, Terhi, Lehtinen, Jyri, Leino, Antti & Vesakoski, Outi. (2016). "Applying population genetic approaches within languages: Finnish dialects as linguistic populations". *Language Dynamics and Change* 6:2, 235, 283.

Teerarojanarat, Sirivilai & Tingsabadh, Kalaya. (2011). "Using GIS for Linguistic Study: a Case of Dialect Change in the Northeastern Region of Thailand", in *International Conference: Spatial Thinking and Geographic Information Sciences 2011*, ed. by Asami, Y. (Elsevier Procedia), 362–371. Procedia Social and Behavioral Sciences 21.

Thomas, Alan R. (1980). *Areal Analysis of Dialect Data by Computer: A Welsh Example.* Cardiff: University of Wales Press.

Veselinova, Ljuba Nikolova & Booza, J.C. (2009). "Studying the multilingual city: a GIS-based approach". *Journal of Multilingual and Multicultural Development* 30:2, 145–165.

WALS (The World Atlas of Language Structures Online). (2018). Retrieved from https://wals.info/

WLMS (World Language Mapping System) (2018). Retrieved from http://www.worldgeodatasets.com/language/

Williams, Colin H. (1996). "Geography and Contact Linguistics", in *Kontaktlinguistik. Ein internationales Handbuch zeitgenössischer Forschung* 1, ed. by Hans Goebl, Peter H. Nelde, Zdeněk Starý and Wolfgang Wölck (Berlin: Walter de Gruyter), 63–74. Handbücher zur Sprach- und Kommunikationswissenschaft 12:1.

Williams, Colin H. & Van Der Merwe, Izak. (1996). "Mapping the Multilingual City: A Research Agenda for Urban Geolinguistics". *Journal of Multilingual and Multicultural Development* 17:1, 49–66.

Wrisley, David J. (2014). "Spatial Humanities: An Agenda for Pre-Modern Research". *Porphyra* 22, 96–107.

SECTION III

Remediation and transmission

15

(DIGITAL) RESEARCH PRACTICES AND RESEARCH DATA

Case studies in communities of sociolinguistics and environmental humanities scholars

Vicky Garnett and Eliza Papaki

15.1 Introduction

From November 2017 to October 2018, the DARIAH Community Engagement Working Group[1] investigated matters of self-identity and whether this is reflected in the manner in which data is managed. In particular, we were interested in how researchers may identify themselves within the context of Digital Humanities, and whether or not their scholarly practices reflected their own academic identities. We studied the tools and methodologies employed by researchers at different career levels, and in different academic fields. This chapter showcases some of the results of this study.

15.2 Background

Attempting to give a definition to the term "Digital Humanities" can prove challenging. Historically, the term "Digital Humanities" derived from the term "Humanities Computing" in 2004 when the first 'Companion to Digital Humanities' was published[2]. However, while the field has been active for more than a decade, its definition keeps changing, because it is a constantly developing environment (Gavin & Smith, 2012).

With so many different definitions comes inspiration for more creative solutions. Discussions on what defines Digital Humanities have been captured in interview series, workshops or DH Days gathering different definitions from researchers in the field. Examples include training websites such as DariahTeach[3], or randomly presented definitions on 'What Is Digital Humanities?' (Heppler, 2015). It seems therefore that while there is not one unifying definition, there is a large and growing literature invested in defining it.

15.2.1 Academic identities

This complexity in terms of definition relates to the equal complexities it creates for researchers attempting to identify themselves as digital humanists. Linda Evans, reflecting on Clegg's (2008) terms of self-identification, suggests that the interpretation of identity is formed through the application of labels to oneself, as she puts it "*self*-labelling and *self*-designation" (Evans, 2015, p. 259, original emphasis). She goes on to say that "Self-reports are [...] the only reliable identity-indicators" (ibid, our editing).

Bauman (1996) points to the fluid nature of self-identification, noting that an individual would not want a fixed identity, preferring to 'keep the options open' (ibid: 18), and moreover may find themselves holding multiple and even contradictory identities. In an academic context, this is perhaps most relevant to those working within an interdisciplinary field of research.

Yet while the self-designation aspect to self-identification (including in the context of academia) is a strong and important element, Taylor (1989) notes the influence of 'a defining community' on a person's process of self-identification. This community can help the individual to contextualise their own place in the (academic) world through use of a shared 'language' and understanding. Jenkins (1996) adds that self-identification can be continuous and reflexive, combining internal notions of self with external definitions of oneself applied by others, once again adding in this product of community-driven identity.

This fluid and continuous nature of self-identity within academia can be influenced by changes at a policy level, as Henkel (2005) discusses. While framing her argument within the biosciences, the motivations of funding and reward are equally applicable to the Humanities and Social Sciences. Henkel acknowledges this draw (or indeed push) towards interdisciplinary and multi-modality within research, but concludes that while the dominance of discipline as a means of defining oneself has been challenged in recent years, it is still a 'strong source of academic identity, in terms of what is important and what gives meaning and self-esteem' (Henkel, 2005, p. 173).

While there has been a push towards interdisciplinarity since Henkel's study, challenges persist for those who wish to adopt a more interdisciplinary academic identity (Burgess, Garnett, O'Connor, & Ohlmeyer, 2018). This is reflected in the results of the SPARKLE project (Edmond et al., 2015), where participants did not self-identify primarily as digital humanists, despite having a sense of technology influencing their work. Lyall, speaking at a workshop in Dublin on Interdisciplinary Research in 2016 noted that dismissive attitudes towards interdisciplinary research endure where researchers have difficulties publishing interdisciplinary papers in well-regarded journals (Lyall, quoted in Burgess et al., as above). This difficulty is extended to challenges in obtaining funding for interdisciplinary research: better to stick to a single field where it is easier to both get published and win funding than to start swimming in uncharted waters.

15.2.2 Research communities

According to Wenger (1998), there are four components identifying learning, namely: meaning, practice, community and identity.

These components of learning are defined as follows:

1. **Meaning**: talking about our ability to experience the world as meaningful;
2. **Practice**: talking about shared historical and social resources, frameworks and perspectives that sustain mutual engagement in action;
3. **Community**: talking about the social configurations in which our enterprise is defined and our participation is recognisable as competence;
4. **Identity**: talking about how learning changes who we are.

Here we focus on 'Practice' and 'Community', approaching and analysing the term "communities of practice" as an overlay concept of research communities. According to Kuhn's "The Structure of Scientific Evolutions", there are different research paradigms rooted in research communities and practice (Kuhn, 1970). These paradigms can be characterised by different elements, namely:

- they can be centred around a specific problem, or set of problems, regarded as particularly significant in relation to the advancement of knowledge;
- they can be about shared practice and shared understanding about which research techniques are appropriate for investigating that issue;

- they can involve a sense of shared identity, which can be reinforced both through the processes of information exchange of the particular community (specialist publications and conferences) and through the interpersonal networks that practitioners establish in relation to their area of research.
- And fourth, these paradigms operate through groups of practitioners operating in research communities.

Therefore, research communities can exist at a number of levels. At the highest level, such a community is formed by all those engaged in scientific research. At a lower level there are communities operating at the level of subject disciplines, and within these there are sub-communities linked to particular areas and sub-disciplines. Communities, in other words, can exist at different levels and will vary in size. They can be quite small, particularly in the case of 'cutting edge' research, and membership of one community does not automatically exclude membership of another. It is a common practice that researchers can be in multiple communities according to their interests, affiliation, or status.

Rethinking for a moment the term 'research communities' to the concept of 'communities of practice' (Lave & Wenger, 1991; Wenger, 1998; Wenger & Snyder, 2000), this last term derived from social learning theory and developed largely in connection with the management of knowledge in formal organisations, capturing also practices of researchers within academic institutions and research organisations. Compared with formal groups created within organisations, who follow a specific structure, tasks and identity, communities of practice can, and do, transcend boundaries of departments, organisations, locations and seniority. The idea behind these communities of practice is that they come into existence through the need to collaborate and learn. Following this, it is possible to have virtual communities based entirely on communication technologies that eliminate the need for face-to-face contact.

What brings them together as a community, though, is that they share a common purpose (Johnson-Lenz & Johnson-Lenz, 1999, cited in Denscombe, 2008) and that common purpose reflects a need to know what each other knows (Brown, cited in Denscombe, 2008). "Communities of practice are groups of people who share a concern or a passion for something they do and learn how to do it better as they interact regularly", according to Wenger-Trayner & Wenger-Trayner (2015). Members of such communities can interact in different ways and have different goals, however they are bound together due to the common (research) interests and knowledge that they want to exchange. Some examples of activities that such communities develop (as listed by wenger-trayner.com, as above) are:

- Problem solving
- Requests for information
- Seeking experience
- Reusing assets
- Coordination and strategy
- Building an argument
- Growing confidence
- Discussing developments
- Documenting projects
- Visits
- Mapping knowledge and identifying gaps

Depending on where the concept of communities of practice is applied (research, education, web, etc), the scientific domain, the goals of a community and its members, different kinds of activities are developed that best represent the common needs, interests and gaps.

The term 'communities of practice' has acquired some negative connotations as it raises concerns that it might elevate practice-based knowledge above more theoretical and abstract forms of knowledge. However, according to the Mixed Methods approach (Denscombe, 2008; Johnson, Onwuegbuzie, & Turner, 2007;

Maxwell & Loomis, 2003), communities of practice have been treated primarily as a description of how research communities operate, rather than prescribing a path that ought to be followed. In this respect, there is no clear distinction between practitioners and researchers. Therefore, in this chapter, when referring to 'communities of practice' we refer to communities of researchers who work within academic and research institutions.

15.2.2.1 Research infrastructures for research communities

Research infrastructures (RIs) offer a means in which research communities can come together. According to the European Commission, RIs are facilities, resources and services used by the science community to conduct research and foster innovation[4]. They may include major scientific equipment (or sets of instruments); skilled personnel engaged in services, competence development and outreach; knowledge-based resources such as collections, archives or scientific data; and e-infrastructures, such as data and computing systems and communication networks[5]. Research infrastructures can be single-sited (a single resource at a single location), distributed (a network of distributed resources), or virtual (the service is provided electronically). Based on this nature and scope, the ways research communities interact with research infrastructures is potentially rich.

Mapping this interaction to the activities communities of practice develop, based on Wenger (Wenger, 1998), research infrastructures function as the space for problem-solving and requesting information, either by accessing knowledge and resources, or by communicating with the community. The nature of RIs as networks of people, knowledge and expertise enables seeking experience, discussing developments and growing confidence scientifically as members of a recognised and established infrastructure. Finally, a significant part of activities undertaken in RIs has to do with strategic thinking, understanding and representing a research community. Members of such networks are therefore exposed to coordination and strategy activities, mapping knowledge and identifying gaps of a research field.

Within the Humanities and Social Sciences, and in a European context, examples of RIs include DARIAH (Digital Research Infrastructure for Arts and Humanities), CLARIN (Common Language Resources and Technology Infrastructure), and CESSDA (Consortium of European Social Science Data Archives) to name a few. We briefly discuss the role of RIs for research communities as part of this chapter.

15.2.3 Scholarly practices

15.2.3.1 Data management within scholarly practices

Moving on to research practices and day-to-day research workflows, the discussion here renders from the scholarly research primitives and practices, outlined by Palmer et al (Palmer, Teffeau, & Pirmann, 2009) and Unsworth (Unsworth, 2000). As suggested in the EHRI[6] deliverable report 16.4 'Researcher Practices and User Requirements', working practices within the broad Humanities field share common fundamental processes across disciplines (Angelis et al., 2013); these fundamental processes have been defined and approached several times, leading to various interpretations of scholarly activities. By reviewing literature and other various taxonomies to approach and define research practices for the context of this study, a long list of different practices was retrieved which captures the research process in detail. Here, we mostly adopt the following "principles" or "primitives":

Palmer's Scholarly Principles (2009)
- Searching
- Collecting

- Reading
- Writing
- Collaborating
- Cross-cutting:
  - ♦ Monitoring
  - ♦ Note-taking
  - ♦ Translating
  - ♦ Data Practices

Unsworth's Scholarly Primitives (2000)
- Discovering
- Annotating
- Comparing
- Referring
- Sampling
- Illustrating
- Representing

Though these practices can be applied to all Humanities researchers, further literature captures more specialised research workflows according to different sub-disciplines. For example, Kemman et al. identify four stages of scholarly research for oral historians as 'exploration and selection', 'exploration and investigation', 'result presentation' and 'data curation' (Kemman, Scagliola, de Jong, & Ordelman, 2014). On the other hand, Rutner and Schonfeld in their 2011–2012 ITHAKA report on "Supporting the changing research practices of historians" define a whole different set of research practices mainly based on the nature of collaboration of historians with librarians for research content (Rutner & Schonfeld, 2012).

Depending on the specialised needs of each discipline, the scholarly content and discipline-specific tools, research practices can vary. For the purposes of this chapter, we have taken practices and primitives from both Palmer et al. and Unsworth that correspond closely to the two case studies presented in this chapter; Sociolinguistics and Environmental Humanities.

15.3 Methodology

The research followed a mixed methodology approach consisting of desk research, online surveys, case studies and interviews. Employing this methodology, we aimed to shape an overview of the research practices in the Social Sciences and Humanities, to understand and document research workflows and perceptions or interactions with research infrastructures and to analyse these practices in terms of disciplinary similarities and differences. Moving from an overview of the field to more in-depth analysis of two particular research communities through case studies, this mixed methodology approach would suggest patterns for the wider Humanities and Social Sciences disciplines.

15.3.1 Survey methodology

The survey comprised three main sections, focusing on communication methods within research communities, their research practices and use of digital tools, and whether or not they participated in research infrastructures during their research. It was conducted in early Spring 2018 and promoted via group mailing lists within the humanities and social sciences, on social media and through our own academic networks.

15.3.2 Interviews to form case studies

Following the survey, we decided to focus on two case studies, Sociolinguistics and Environmental Humanities. This would allow us to investigate in more depth how researchers within two specific communities identify themselves, how they communicate among themselves, and how they identify and handle research data: be it data they are finding and using, or data they are generating themselves.

Interviews were conducted within each community, with at least one participant in each at the early career and senior career level. Various researchers were contacted that matched these criteria and were geographically dispersed to explore possibilities of collaboration to this research. For the most part, potential participants were recruited through our own social networks (such as colleagues, previous project partners, etc) while we also reached out to interested respondents to our online survey. Four participants, two from each discipline, expressed interest and availability for this research. These interviews were held either face-to-face, or virtually through Zoom. In all cases, the interviews were anonymised for the purposes of this chapter.

Questions already addressed through the online survey were taken into consideration when developing the interview structure, such as:

- Research communities' with which participants engage most closely
- Academic role
- Use of digital tools
- Familiarity with research infrastructures

The interview structure was then designed based on the discussion on research primitives by John Unsworth, cross-referenced with the work on research practices by Carole Palmer[7].

15.3.3 Analysis of data

The transcribed interview data were collaboratively analysed and thematically coded according to the following areas:

- Research communities and self-identify
- Research practices and data
- Communication among communities
- Interaction with research infrastructures.

This analysis aimed to understand and document research practices within Sociolinguistics and Environmental Humanities, mainly with a view to identifying similarities and differences among these two communities that may suggest patterns for the wider social sciences and humanities.

The final aspect of the analysis concerned the mapping of the data to research practices and research primitives from the literature. This opened up interesting discussions of how RIs are or can be part of the research workflow.

15.4 Results of survey

The survey had 40 responses in total, from respondents at academic institutions all over Europe. The range of disciplines was also wide, covering literature studies, linguistics, gender studies, art and art history, classics and geohumanities, to name a few.

Research practices and research data

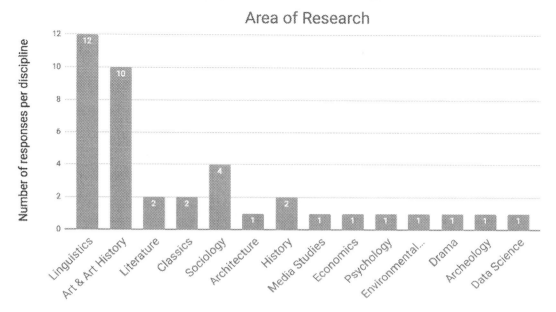

Figure 15.1 Area of research

We present the results thematically, beginning with how the respondents identify and interact with their research communities, on to how they conduct research (and manage data), and finally if and how they interact with RIs.

15.4.1 *About the respondents*

15.4.1.1 *Responses by broad discipline*

The respondents were asked about their research area, and naturally the responses we received varied. To try to arrive at some meaningful consensus, we grouped them together by their broad area of research. The three largest groups were Linguistics, Art & Art History, and Sociology (see Figure 15.1).

15.4.1.2 *Responses by career level*

The responses we received were largely given by those in more senior positions, however we did still get a reasonable amount of responses from mid and early-career researchers.

15.4.2 *Identifying and interacting with research communities*

The majority of respondents (87.5%) identified their research community primarily through discipline or area of research. Other research communities appear to be by methodology, or a combination of discipline and methodology. None of our respondents to this survey mentioned their affiliation to a research community by career level or by geographical context (see Figure 15.2).

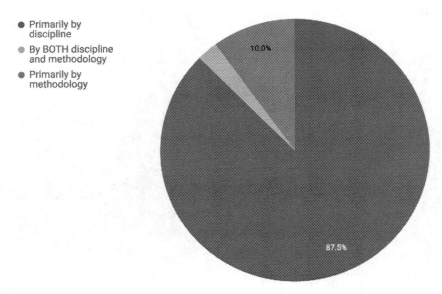

Figure 15.2 How do you identify your research communit(ies)?

15.4.3 *Communications within communities*

Perhaps unsurprisingly, virtual communication dominates among our respondents, either through mailing lists, or more interactive means such as social networking media like Facebook, Twitter and (to a lesser extent) LinkedIn. Yet, despite this, the face-to-face interaction of conferences is still well represented. Attendance at conferences is of course costly, and requires a time-commitment, but with nearly 39% of the overall responses noting conferences as a means of communication with peers in their community, they are still seen as a highly effective mode of interaction (see Figure 15.3).

When we break this down by career level, we see similar patterns, but with some interesting nuances. Conferences are as we've seen, most popular overall, which was also evident when asked how they keep up to date with any new developments or publications in their field. This pattern is also reflected when we break the results down by career level (see Figure 15.4).

Mailing lists were the second most popular communication method when we look at the respondents as a whole, but while they are indeed popular, this seems to be mostly among the early-career researchers, with fewer responses among mid-career researchers and senior researchers.

Social media, such as Facebook, Twitter and LinkedIn, were less popular overall, but still showed some interesting patterns. Facebook Groups are most popular among the senior researchers, falling among mid-career researchers, and lower still among the early-career researchers. Yet Twitter use is a lot higher among mid-career researchers, and very low among early-career researchers. LinkedIn use is non-existent among our early-career respondents, and still fairly low among mid and senior-career researchers.

Research practices and research data

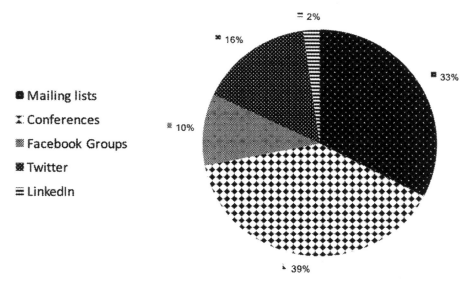

Figure 15.3 How do researchers communicate within their communities?

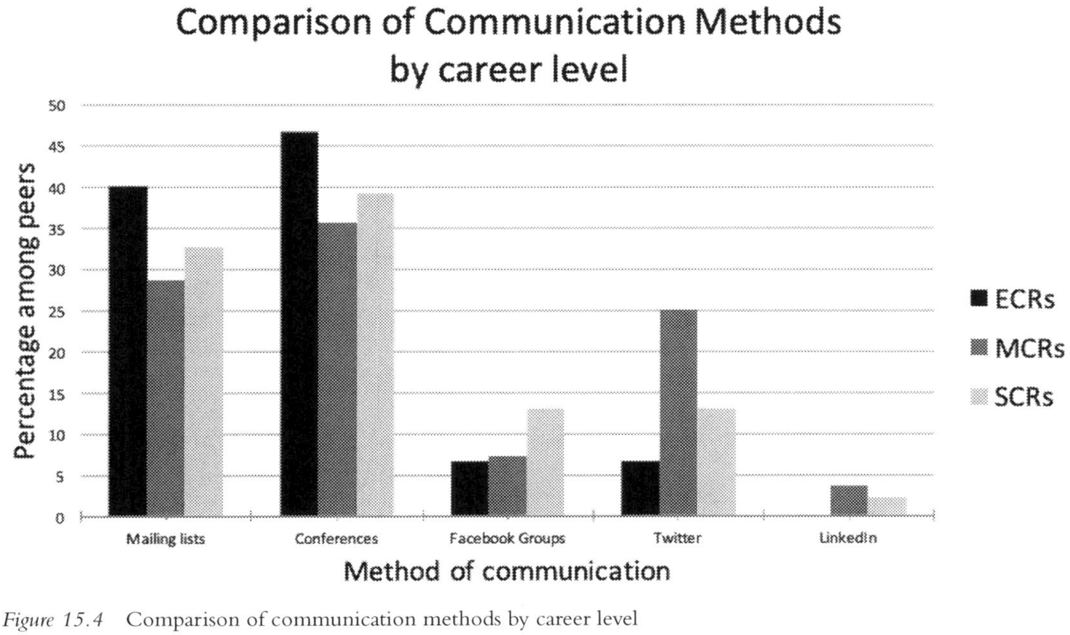

Figure 15.4 Comparison of communication methods by career level

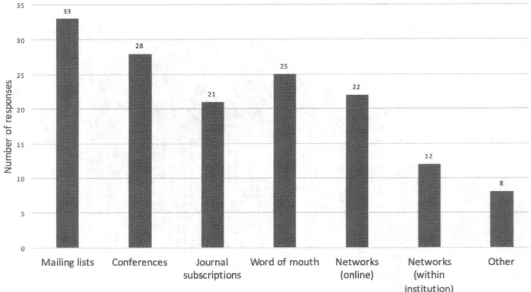

Figure 15.5 How do you keep up to date on new publications/developments in your field?

Noting that these modes by which researchers communicate could be considered the more 'active' approach, we also asked our survey respondents how they 'received' information about new developments in their field (see Figure 15.5).

The idea of what it means to 'communicate' with other researchers was somewhat altered when we asked people to discuss what role they took in these modes of communication (see Figure 15.6). Overall, almost everyone reported communicating via mailing lists or face-to-face at conferences (see Figure 15.5.), but the largest number of respondents said that they were more of a 'lurker' in mailing lists (31.6%) (see Figure 15.6), frequently being more passive and less likely to post anything themselves. The second largest grouping (19%) was as a member of a social media group (such as a Facebook group, or possibly a LinkedIn group).

15.4.4 Conducting research and data management

When asked about use of digital tools as part of their research, 75% of all respondents said that they used them, with 15% saying they didn't, and 10% not entirely sure. This leads to an interesting question about what constitutes a 'digital tool': how do researchers categorise the tools they use, and by extension, how digital do they believe their own research is?

To investigate this further, we asked respondents to name digital tools they used as part of their research. We deliberately gave no prompt in this regard, so as to leave it open for the respondents to decide what they categorise as 'digital'. The results were, as might be expected, both varied and illuminating.

Overall, we had 103 individual responses in terms of digital tools, as many of our 40 respondents listed multiple tools. In order to try to break this down into something more meaningful, we have grouped them according to shared features and functions. We have tried to make these categories as broad as possible, so

Research practices and research data

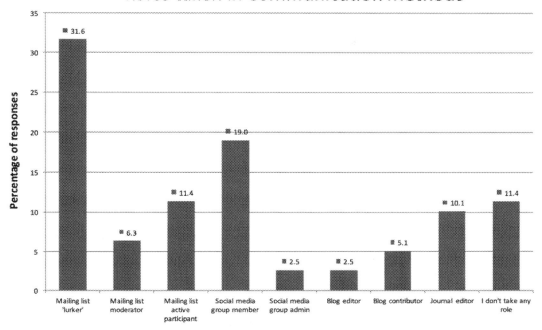

Figure 15.6 Roles taken in communication methods

as to try to avoid too much of our own unconscious bias into this categorisation, but we acknowledge that it is possible some may have crept in along the way.

The categories used are:

- Audio Editing Software (such as 'Sony Soundforge')
- Bibliography tools (such as 'Mendeley' and 'Zotero')
- Coding Languages (such as 'XML' and 'SQL')
- Corpora, Databases and Repositories (such as COPAC, JSTOR and Google Books)
- Data Management, Processing and Visualisation (such as MaxQDA, Elan and MS Excel)
- Imaging Software (such as AutoCAD and SketchUp Adobe)
- Social Networking tools (including Social Media, such as Twitter, and networking platforms, such as Sketchfab)
- Writing Tools (such as LaTeX and Scrivener)

The idea of what constitutes a 'digital tool' varies considerably, with many listing more generic and commonplace tools such as Microsoft Office products (e.g. Word or Excel), or Adobe products. As the tools become more specialised, we also see use of tools such as R and SPSS for statistical analysis; Praat, Atlas. ti, ELAN and NVivo for annotation (particularly of speech and videos); GIS tools for spatial analysis; and Citation Software such as EndNote; writing tools such as Scrivener and LaTeX; and social media, such as Academia.edu, Facebook and Twitter being noted in particular. In addition to these software items, we also see respondents noting publication repositories such as JSTOR, Google Books and even in one case the 'institutional library' as a digital tool.

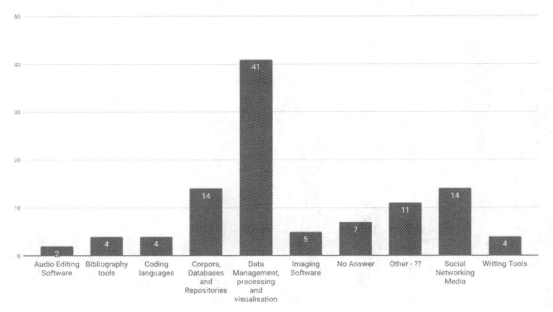

Figure 15.7 Responses to 'what digital tools do you use?'

As the largest category, we will take a look at the types of tools mentioned regarding 'Data Management, Processing and Visualisation' (see Figure 15.7).

The most commonly used tool among our respondents is that which assists with statistical and quantitative analysis (see Figure 15.8). This included tools such as R, RStudio and SPSS. As the figure shows, 'Spreadsheets' have been categorised separately to this. While spreadsheets (Excel, Google Sheets) are also commonly used to format and analyse data in a quantitative way, they can also be used for data management.

Phonetic Software is the next largest category, which was mainly software such as PRAAT. As our largest group of respondents were linguists, this is perhaps not surprising, and shows a more discipline-specific level of categorisation.

We received few responses that could not be categorised and were analysed as 'Other responses', which varied from digital data types, to search engines and the Internet.

15.5 Case studies

The online survey gave us some background into how different sub-communities might communicate, and what they considered to be digital practices. However, it didn't provide us with context for these results, and what factors might be informing these practices. To investigate further, case studies were conducted with Sociolinguists and Environmental Humanists to discuss in more depth how researchers within these two specific communities identify themselves, how they communicate among themselves, and how they identify and handle research data. As discussed above, the structure of interviews we conducted with these researchers was framed in the context of the scholarly primitives identified by both Palmer et al., (2009) and Unsworth (2000).

Research practices and research data

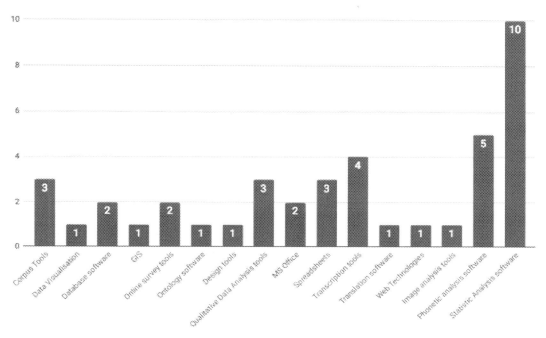

Figure 15.8 Types of data management, processing and visualisation tools

As previously outlined, in addition to categorisation by discipline, within each community we tried to approach and interview researchers from different career levels: early-career researchers, mid-career or senior-career researchers. The categorisations are outlined in Table 15.1, retaining career status by coding their practices as 'EC' for early-career researchers, and 'SC' for senior-career researchers.

Table 15.1 Categorisation of case study interviewees

Code applied	Interviewee	Country
SL(SC)	Senior Career Sociolinguist	Ireland
SL(EC)	Early Career Sociolinguist	Belgium
EH(SC)	Senior Career Environmental Humanist	France
EH(EC)	Early Career Environmental Humanist	Ireland

15.5.1 Case study—sociolinguists

15.5.1.1 Research communities and self-identify

SL(SC) identifies her research communities as primarily within the field of sociolinguistics, with sub-communities falling under that category. She also identifies herself with communities at a geographic level: a national or European context. SL(EC) identifies herself on a disciplinary level as both a Sociolinguist and Geolinguist, due to the nature of her research. Similar to SL(SC), SL(EC) identifies herself as part of multiple groups either within her institution, her geographical region or at a broader European level. These multiple research groups seem to be formed on specific topics, methodologies, resources or career-level status.

Within the interview, both SL(SC) and SL(EC) did not identify themselves as 'digital humanists', either considering themselves as more 'traditional scholars' or stating that they do not make great use of digital practices.

15.5.1.2 Research practices and data

15.5.1.2.1 Obtaining data

The data handled by both interviewees are mainly recorded interviews (in most cases researcher-generated), their transcriptions and survey data. SL(SC) notes that most of her data are generated specifically for her use, and are rarely taken from another researcher or collection in a cultural heritage institute. For this reason, most of the issues in obtaining her data are focused around ethical approval, rather than any issues negotiating licensing and copyright of data. Similarly, SL(EC), who obtains data that she has either generated or gathered from existing datasets in repositories, seems to be mostly concerned with issues of managing, storing and preservation of her data rather than copyright issues.

15.5.1.2.2 Data types

Both interviewees manage similar data types: mainly recorded interviews, which follow a process of being converted into a digital format (mp3 and WAV) in order to be transcribed. SL(SC) also makes use of observational data, which is based around surveys and other non-linguistic data on her participants. Similarly, SL(EC) mentions making use of surveys online or via "paper service", conducted in an educational context. Finally, the interview datasets taken from SL(EC)'s institutional repository were originally in analogue format, but have since been digitised and published online via institutional websites.

15.5.1.2.3 Data analysis and management

SL(EC) analyses her data for both qualitative and quantitative information. For the qualitative type of research, she uses Word documents, while for larger datasets she would consider software such as NVivo. For quantitative analysis of the data, SL(EC) uses coding in R for the statistical analysis and Excel spreadsheets to mark basic information. SL(SC) also refers to the use of Excel spreadsheets for processing and analysing her data, but also as a way to store any qualitative data she observes as she works through the survey and interview data. Both interviewees make use of transcription and annotation tools such as Elan.

Both interviewees store their data locally on their computers and also within their institutions' networks. SL(SC) notes, however, that this can be problematic for open and FAIR[8] data sharing (Wilkinson et al., 2016). SL(EC) also raised an issue of the need on one hand, to secure this data in a trusted repository in the future—possibly even making them available online—and on the other hand, the potential risks for the researcher of losing control over data if entrusted to bigger repositories. This concern lies mainly in relation to ethical and licensing issues that may arise and require clarification. At the time of interview, SL(EC) used a Dropbox filing system, structuring her data independently.

15.5.1.2.4 Data citation practices

Both interviewees employ similar practices for citation, yet both seem to be less familiar with *data citation* practices and subsequently do not have a methodology for citing datasets. They mostly rely on publication citation practices (using bibliographic tools) and on published data in order to refer back to publications for comparison or simple reference.

15.5.1.2.5 Open data, open access, open science

Both SLs are aware of the Open Science initiatives and recognise the shift towards Open Access. However, they do express some concerns. SL(SC) is very much in favour of sharing knowledge but she has concerns regarding the loss of 'ownership' over data. It seems that she is more in favour of sharing the resulting knowledge obtained from the data than her actual data. SL(EC)'s skepticism lies more on the fact that she does not see a similar shift in terms of training and education. Handling data, particularly interview datasets, can be a quite sensitive issue and SL(EC) underlines the need for research training in terms of ethics and proper open access practices.

15.5.1.3 *Communications among research communities*

The use of social media in communications among a research community seems to be a personal preference. In this case, both interviewees say that they are not really "sharers" when it comes to communicating successes or asking for advice through social media, at least not in a systematic way. SL(EC) in particular prefers to share problems or successes on her research with colleagues that are in her immediate vicinity rather than reaching out to the wider scientific community via established networks or platforms.

Both SLs highly value face-to-face communications within the community via conferences or meetings as a way of fostering a network and developing new ideas. SL(SC) notes in particular that one of the most successful conferences she attended was specifically designed entirely around discussion and networking. Both are also part of discipline-specific mailing lists, which are mostly valued by the SL(EC) in terms of keeping up to date with discipline news.

Interestingly, SL(EC) brings in the discussion the importance of sharing scientific knowledge with non-specialists crowds. In addition to scientific publications, SL(EC) has published in more "traditional" journals while also being active in events and presentations with non-scientific audiences.

15.5.1.4 *Interaction with research infrastructures*

Although both SLs are familiar with research infrastructures (RIs), and in particular CLARIN, they characterise them as 'difficult to use' without any additional support. Both indicated a lack of clarity of how RIs work or what the benefits of engaging with RIs are for researchers. SL(EC) also stresses the need for training in introducing such concepts and practices from an early stage in a researcher's career. While the importance of using, engaging with and networking within an RI is acknowledged, in the busy researcher' life, one has to be clear of the benefits before s/he goes on to invest time and effort in them.

15.5.2 Case study—Environmental humanists

15.5.2.1 Research communities and self-identify

EH(SC) discusses research communities within the context of academic discipline as a starting point, naming at least three research fields with which she identifies: geohumanities, computational linguistics and Digital Humanities.

In addition to research area, EH(SC) mentions geographical location, specifically within France, in the context of her research community, mentioning tools and infrastructures available to colleagues 'here in France'. EC(SC) also indicates a 'community' in discussion around data practices and various aspects of research. While she doesn't explicitly indicate if she means 'community' at a disciplinary or a geographic level, the context suggests a disciplinary research community.

EH(EC) almost exclusively looks to discipline as a means of identifying his research community, first noting the discipline of his previous academic studies, before noting his role within Environmental Humanities and the team he currently works with. He notes the multidisciplinary aspect of his work, and of the team. EH(EC) also identifies his community at an institutional level and occasionally at a national level, and in regard to his position within the team.

15.5.2.2 Research practices and data

15.5.2.2.1 Obtaining data

EH(SC) mentions that she and her colleagues work a lot with heritage data, making use of structured information from archives. Often this requires permissions from the archive or library.

EH(SC) also generates her own data by creating a corpus where a similar corpus is unavailable, although she questions where the line is drawn between obtaining data and generating data. Her rationale is that she regularly annotates existing corpora, or connects datasets to create a new corpus. Her research makes use of semantic web technologies such as Linked Open Data content, SPARQL Endpoints, DBPedia, or downloadable datasets.

Much of the data EH(EC) deals with is obtained through archives, memory institutions and other academic institutions, both within Ireland, and further afield. Often datasets can be behind paywalls, although here EH(EC) notes the benefits of being part of a large funded project that has the means to obtain licenses for data use. Where data is provided by an institution, it is done so through a Creative Commons license, or Fair Use. With these datasets, EH(EC) participates in generating new data through deep mapping and visualisations.

15.5.2.2.2 Data type

EH(SC) works mostly with textual data sets, and corpora. She also makes use of structured data that comes from archives or libraries and legacy data types that require digitisation. As this makes use of books readily available in hard copy, EH(SC) freely admits that they do not take 'particular care to preserve the copies' because they are so abundant. EH(EC) and members of his project also work with textual or map-based data. He notes the variety of resources that match the multidisciplinary nature of the team, with plankton indexes sitting alongside seventeenth century trade books, for example.

15.5.2.2.3 Data analysis and management

For EH(SC), data is stored locally, with support from Huma-Num (TGIR—Très Grande Infrastructure de Recherche)[9], a large infrastructure for the humanities in France, which provides for storage of larger datasets. EH(SC) makes use of a 'git' or other versioning tools to manage data in order to record changes that have been made by individuals within the project.

EH(EC) and his colleagues make use of metadata standards as part of their data management practices, typically Dublin CORE and Darwin CORE. EH(EC) notes also that the project has a dedicated data manager, who works alongside the team to ensure good practice. Further data management is conducted using tools such as Omeka, Dropbox Business, EndNote. To analyse their data, the team makes use of digital tools such as GIS (ArcGIS and QGIS), R, Optical Character Recognition, Spider, and MAXQDA.

15.5.2.2.4 Data citation practice

EH(SC) is keen to ensure that she cites data as much as possible, not only for the good of the wider community, but because it is how she would like her own data to be treated. She notes that it is often easier to cite data if it is already held in a recognised data repository, ideally with a DOI or unique reference provided to make the dataset more identifiable. She also notes that sometimes the authors of datasets might provide their own suggestions for how to cite the data. However, where suggestions and existing references are not available, she makes use of templates for data citation, which might come from the wider (disciplinary) community through conferences. She also notes that if none of these previous options are available, she will try to cite a publication where the data is introduced for the first time by the data's creator. EH(SC) also notes, however, that within her community, data papers are quite common, making it easier to cite data and tools created by colleagues in a clear and more standardised way.

On the other hand, EH(EC) was perhaps less familiar with the concept of data citation, but did note that the team uses Omeka to generate citations for maps and similar resources using Dublin CORE.

15.5.2.2.5 Open data, open access, open science

EH(EC) works closely with the project data manager to make their project database searchable through the project website. They also link any secondary resources they have to the original website to ensure provenance is maintained. However, it is not clear how this will be maintained after the project ends.

EH(SC) is very conscious of trying to make the datasets she and her team generate as open as possible, noting that they have a plan to deposit the code or data in an online repository. Again, this is supported through Huma-Num.

In her opinion, the research community as a whole should be 'careful not to inhibit people in sharing data by putting the bar too high'. Instead, she feels that researchers should feel empowered to share their data, even if they do not feel it can be "100% reproduced or […] 100% reused". She also notes that within her community there is increasing acceptance of the FAIR Principles.

While EH(SC) doesn't want to be pessimistic, she has concerns around the 'General Data Protection Regulation' (GDPR)[10] and how that is going to affect the work within her research community.

15.5.2.3 Communications among research communities

EH(EC) plays a very active role in communicating and disseminating outputs from the project he works on. Most of this communication is done through social media and the project website, although he acknowledges the participation of other team members in larger national and multinational networks working at a disciplinary level. The project also makes use of a mailing list that is maintained 'in-house' to disseminate any news about the project.

When communicating with her community, EH(SC) does make use of social media, particularly Twitter, but she is also cautious around the idea of using it to ask for any help in her research. But she notes that she is not against it and doesn't discount the possibility of using it for feedback or help. Instead, she prefers to interact with her community in what she calls 'traditional ways'; for example via emails or personal contact at conferences. This is echoed by EH(EC), who says that if he needs to discuss a research problem, he will speak to people he already knows quite well who will be able to assist him.

EH(SC) likes to present ongoing work at conferences as she finds this more useful for feedback, keen to ensure that even work in its early stages is communicated online through project websites in order to gain insight from the community.

15.5.2.4 Interaction with research infrastructures

EH(SC) is quite well versed with digital research infrastructures, as she plays a very active role in both CLARIN and DARIAH at a European level, as well as Hum-Num at a national level. She is aware of the supports in place within RIs and online repositories and tries to make the best of what is offered. She notes in particular how helpful RIs have been with data citation and data standards to ensure her data is published in the correct way. She notes that having such facilities in place "takes a lot of the pressure of practical issues away".

While EH(EC) and his project members participate in large networking initiatives, he is less familiar with digital research infrastructures. He has heard of DARIAH, but is not very familiar with what it can do for researchers, or the benefits such research infrastructures hold beyond the networking initiatives.

15.6 Discussion

15.6.1 Self-Identity, communities and communication

Henkel (2005) pointed to the discipline as a strong source of academic identity, linked to self-esteem. For early-career researchers in particular, this is their primary mode of self-identification, and therefore the principle means by which they identify their research community. The disciplinary field is the 'defining community' suggested by Taylor. Furthermore, of the four interviewees, only one was comfortable applying the label 'Digital Humanities' to her research, with the other three interviewees shying away from the term, and indeed using labels at a disciplinary rather than interdisciplinary level. Even those who have a good knowledge of technology within their field were more inclined to consider themselves 'traditional' rather than 'digital' humanists.

As noted among our survey respondents and our interviewees, (particularly in the case of SL(EC)), the pressure to publish could be the driving factor that leads academics to identify by discipline, allowing them to 'stick to what they know' in terms of prestige in journals, and with whom to discuss their work. This disinclination to apply interdisciplinary labels reflects the findings of Burgess et al. (2018), which looked to publication as one of the influences behind such motivations (or lack thereof). Taking the interdisciplinary route means risking publication in an unknown field, and uncertainty that it will be seen by peers, leading to a drop in bibliometric scores, and thus potentially harming future career prospects. To identify as an interdisciplinary scholar is still perceived as a risk to publication and funding, despite the responses of EH(SC) where she reflects that access to interdisciplinary pan-European initiatives such as DARIAH and CLARIN have 'taken the pressure away' when citing her own data and that of others.

Additionally, while none of the survey respondents identified geographic area as a research community, interviewees added geographic-region groups or project-specific groups to the discussion as one the research communities with whom they identify or collaborate. Equally, no one in our survey mentioned career level as a research community, but within the interviews, the early-career researchers did mention groupings and networking based on the early-career experience, indicating that they perhaps innately, if not overtly, feel some level of collegiality with that cohort.

The sense of common purpose within a research community (Denscombe, 2008) is present among these interviewees, though. While the common purpose may not be at an interdisciplinary level, the community in which they each operate does engage in collaboration and regular interaction, as discussed by Wenger-Trayner and Wenger-Trayner (2015), with a view to learning more about the discipline. This is often done through mailing lists or face-to-face interaction at conferences, rather than through more structured platforms such as Research Infrastructures. Despite increasing numbers of research groups and networks that are shaped digitally, participants mentioned that usually their points of contact for such communications are the people or colleagues in their vicinity or institution. Proximity seems therefore to have a role in such communication and dissemination practices. Such practices are reinforced by the idea that face-to-face interactions are still very important for research. All case study participants seemed to agree that conferences are still a more preferable way of networking and presenting work to the community. Social media and dissemination platforms were mentioned in all interview discussions as an accepted and valid way of communicating research. However, if such dissemination practices are not enabled by project funding, as in the case of EH(EC), then their use for communicating individual research comes down to personal preference. Mailing lists on the other hand are used by everyone as they don't require active participation. Most participants were members of different mailing lists primarily to gather information about their research community.

Indeed, the discussion on how researchers tend to communicate their work, their research successes or failures, led to an interesting observation that such practices are at the end "a personality thing". This was a suggestion made from participants SL(SC), SL(EC) and EH(SC), saying that they are all aware of these practices within their research communities or institutions but they are not really following this trend. How researchers communicate and disseminate their research through social media or other dissemination platforms, such as ResearchGate, is ultimately a personal decision and practice. Interestingly, all participants described in a similar way the recent practices they had noticed being used for wider dissemination of research successes. However, as they don't personally embrace these habits, they stand a bit critical or just neutral in such practices. The low-use of social media among early-career researchers could perhaps point to an anxiety around whether or not what they write or say could potentially be misinterpreted or seen as 'foolish' and therefore harmful to their future careers. The mid-senior level researchers may feel a little more comfortable in their field to be able to communicate in this manner. Social media has a reputation for being somewhat antagonistic, and perhaps the early-career researchers would rather not engage in any potential conflict or discourse in which they are not entirely comfortable with their level of expertise.

15.6.2 Community-based research practices in data management and citation

Of our two case studies, the Environmental Humanities scholars demonstrated a wider use of digital tools and methodologies to manage and analyse their data than the Sociolinguists. The Environmental Humanities scholars listed many more digital tools and methods they use for obtaining, organising and analysing their data, such as Linked Open Data and SPARQL Endpoints for obtaining data, and a 'git' or data end-code for versioning. EH(SC) in particular makes use of digital research infrastructures to publish and publicise her data. EH(EC) notes how he and his colleagues make use of digital data standards to organise their data, as well as digital tools such as GIS for analysis and Omeka for publishing, visualisation and referencing.

The issue of digital tools and methodologies directly links to identities, despite being somewhat contradictory. The survey data showed us the plethora of digital tools that many of the respondents use (or consider both 'digital' or as a 'tool'), yet almost none of them offered 'Digital Humanities' as their scholarly identity. Similarly, both sociolinguists describe themselves as 'old fashioned' or 'traditional' in their methods of data management and analysis, both making extensive use of spreadsheets to organise their qualitative and quantitative data. Both do note, though, that their data practices could be more digital. For example,

SL(SC) mentions her participation in a working group within her institution to enhance the digital data storage facilities and practices. SL(EC) notes how she would like to be able to use more digital techniques to organise and open up her data, but feels under pressure to concentrate on publishing and disseminating her research. When annotating and analysing her data, however, SL(EC) does make use of tools such as ELAN and NVivo. Which again begs the question of just how digital does a researcher have to be before they feel comfortable calling themselves a 'digital humanist'? It is also interesting that the perception of the non-digital humanist being 'old fashioned' persists, despite non-digital and digital research methodologies sitting side-by-side in many discipline-specific journals, both having been peer reviewed and considered significant contributions to the field.

As we did not discuss Data Citation in our survey, we have no insight from that body of results. However, among our interviewees, only EH(SC) noted specific processes she goes through, such as using existing templates, citing a DOI, or creating bespoke templates for use in data citation. EH(EC) mentioned citing maps through Omeka, and specifically referencing back to source websites. EH(EC)'s practices, however, were closer in style to SL(SC) and SL(EC), both of whom noted that they were more likely to fall back on a journal article, book or chapter from the original user of that data, rather than citing the data separately. Speculation around whether or not this makes one field more 'clued in' to data citation practices is nonsensical. However, if seen as a whole, it does show that among the pan-disciplinary scholarly community, data citation is still a little-known practice, with even less agreement as to what 'best practice' should be.

Conclusion

The reluctance to adopt an interdisciplinary identity persists among many scholars within the broader Humanities. While there are those who are happy to self-identify with such fields as 'Digital Humanities' in addition to their original field of study, the hesitation to identify as such can come from a lack of familiarity outside their more traditionally-established discipline, even if they are already making use of digital means of analysis and scholarship. Many of our respondents to both the interviews and the survey indicated digital tools and services in their workflow, yet only one of our interviewees specifically declared affiliation with the 'Digital Humanities' research community. This suggests that, while many may acknowledge the field of Digital Humanities, attend the conferences and use computational methodologies or digital tools, very few are prepared to step beyond their 'primary' discipline when identifying their community of scholarly practice.

We suggest this is perhaps due to a desire to remain where they are comfortable, where they can reinforce their self-esteem, and a concern that publications in a more interdisciplinary field may not be seen within their more monodisciplinary community. This is felt most keenly among the early-career researchers in our case studies, for whom the pressure to publish in order to widen future career prospects, especially within academia, is of high priority and thus potentially affects perceptions of belonging to more interdisciplinary fields, such as Digital Humanities, or even collaborating within interdisciplinary spaces, such as research infrastructures. In this case, it seems that Digital Humanities is considered mainly as a broader field entailing digital methodologies, projects and tools which are applied to discipline-specific strands of research.

In terms of belonging to a community, the results from the survey and case studies suggest that (geographical) space creates a sense of belonging. In particular, while the geographical area was not overtly expressed when interviewees were asked to identify themselves within a research community, it seems that it does play an important role in terms of being part of different research groups (geographic region groups, project specific groups). This was also the case with career level. Drawing more on results from the survey, the early-career researchers did not identify as part of a community based on their status or career level despite mentioning groups and networking based on the early-career

Research practices and research data

experience. Perhaps not surprisingly, this suggests that the way researchers tend to identify themselves falls strictly within the context of their scientific area rather than any other factor (methodology, geography, career-level).

The use of digital tools and methodologies did not seem to significantly affect the researchers' self-perception. While researchers use increasingly more digital tools and methodologies in their research, they appear to be reluctant in presenting themselves as digitally literate as they do not consider their level of digital expertise high enough to mark their transition from 'old-fashioned' to 'digital humanist'.

Finally, communication practices seem to have smoothly transitioned into new, more digital formats. The use of social media to communicate, share knowledge and, in particular, research successes is part of every researchers' life either as active users or as observers. Far from suggesting this use as best practice in terms of communications, our interviewees agreed on the common practices and different perceptions when using and reaching out to the community through social media, retaining their individual taste in their communications. Apart from personal preferences, career level seems to have a role in how communication practices are formed. Early-career researchers tend to be less confident in using social media and expressing opinions openly and widely. Despite a trend for more research groups and networks to be shaped digitally, and communication practices becoming increasingly virtual, researchers in all career levels state the importance of communicating, meeting and exchanging knowledge and ideas face-to-face with the community through conferences and scientific gatherings.

Notes

1 The DARIAH Community Engagement Working Group, https://dariahre.hypotheses.org/ (retrieved 28th March 2019)
2 What's "digital humanities" and how did it get here? (21st October 2012), https://blogs.brandeis.edu/library/2012/10/09/whats-digital-humanities-and-how-did-it-get-here/ (retrieved 10th November 2018)
3 Introduction to Digital Humanities. (n.d.). Retrieved from https://teach.dariah.eu/
4 European Research Infrastructures. (2019, March 13). https://ec.europa.eu/research/infrastructures/index.cfm?pg=about (retrieved 26th March 2019)
5 Science Europe Shaping the future of research. (n.d.). https://www.scienceeurope.org/policy/policy-areas/research-infrastructures/ (retrieved 26th March 2019)
6 European Holocaust Research Infrastructure (EHRI), https://www.ehri-project.eu/, retrieved 9th April 2019
7 The full list of questions can be found in Garnett, V., Papaki, E. (2018) *Barriers and Pathways to Community Engagement* (pp.26–27), available at https://dariahre.hypotheses.org/939#more-939 (Retrieved 28th March 2019) .
8 FAIR Principles, where data is 'Findable', 'Accessible', 'Interoperable', and 'Reusable'.
9 Huma-Num : L'infrastructure des humanités numériques. (n.d.). Retrieved October 22, 2018, from https://www.huma-num.fr/
10 GDPR, introduced in May 2018, https://ec.europa.eu/commission/priorities/justice-and-fundamental-rights/data-protection/2018-reform-eu-data-protection-rules_en (retrieved 28th March 2019)

References

Angelis, S., Benardou, A., Constantopoulos, P., Dallas, C., Fotopoulou, A., Gavrilis, D., … Links, P. (2013). *Researcher Practices and User Requirements* (Project Deliverable No. Deliverable 16.4). European Holocaust Research Infrastructure.

Bauman, Z. (1996). From pilgrim to tourist–or a short history of identity. *Questions of Cultural Identity*, *1*, 18–36.

Burgess, M., Garnett, V., O'Connor, A., & Ohlmeyer, J. (2018). *Interdisciplinarity for Impact: Workshop Report*. Retrieved from Irish Research Council website: https://www.tcd.ie/trinitylongroomhub/assets/documents/2018-FinalReport.pdf

Denscombe, M. (2008). Communities of practice: A research paradigm for the mixed methods approach. *Journal of Mixed Methods Research*, *2*(3), 270–283.

Edmond, J., Bagalkot, N., & O'Connor, A. (2015). *Toward a Deeper Understanding of the Scientific Method of the Humanist*: https://hal.archives-ouvertes.fr/hal-01566290/ accessed 14 April 2020

Evans, L. (2015). Reflections: Academic identity and the changing European landscape. *Academic Identities in Higher Education: The Changing European Landscape*, 241.

Gavin, M., & Smith, K. M. (2012). An interview with Brett Bobley. *Debates in the Digital Humanities*, 61–67.

Henkel, M. (2005). Academic identity and autonomy in a changing policy environment. *Higher Education*, *49*(1–2), 155–176.

Heppler, J. A. (2015). What is Digital Humanities? [Website]. Retrieved 9 April 2019, from What Is Digital Humanities? website: https://whatisdigitalhumanities.com/

Jenkins, R. (1996). *Social Identity*. (1st ed.). London: Routledge.

Johnson, R. B., Onwuegbuzie, A. J., & Turner, L. A. (2007). Toward a definition of mixed methods research. *Journal of Mixed Methods Research*, *1*(2), 112–133.

Johnson-Lenz, P., & Johnson-Lenz, T. (1999). Awaking technology. *Retrieved November*, 30, 2007.

Kemman, M., Scagliola, S., de Jong, F. M., & Ordelman, R. J. (2014). Talking with scholars: Developing a research environment for oral history collections. *Communications in Computer and Information Science*, *416*.

Kuhn, T. S. (1970). *The Structure of Scientific Revolutions*. (2nd enl. ed.). University of Chicago Press.

Lave, J., & Wenger, E. (1991). *Situated Learning: Legitimate Peripheral Participation*. Cambridge University Press.

Maxwell, J. A., & Loomis, D. M. (2003). Mixed methods design: An alternative approach. *Handbook of Mixed Methods in Social and Behavioral Research*, *1*, 241–272.

Palmer, C. L., Teffeau, L. C., & Pirmann, C. M. (2009). *Scholarly Information Practices in the Online Environment: Themes from the Literature and Implications for Library Service Development*. Retrieved from Online Computer Library Center website: http://www.oclc.org/content/dam/research/publications/library/2009/2009-02.pdf?urlm=162919

Rutner, J., & Schonfeld, R. C. (2012). *Supporting the Changing Research Practices of Historians*. Ithaka S+ R New York, NY.

Taylor, C. (1989). *Sources of the Sself: The Making of the Modern Identity*. Harvard University Press.

Unsworth, J. (2000). *Scholarly primitives: What methods do humanities researchers have in common, and how might our tools reflect this. 13*, 5–10.

Wenger, E. (1998). Communities of practice: Learning as a social system. *Systems Thinker*, *9*(5), 2–3.

Wenger, E. C., & Snyder, W. M. (2000). Communities of practice: The organizational frontier. *Harvard Business Review*, *78*(1), 139–146.

Wenger-Trayner, B., & Wenger-Trayner, E. (2015). Introduction to communities of practice [Website]. Retrieved 29 November 2018, from Wenger-trayner.com website: http://wenger-trayner.com/introduction-to-communities-of-practice/

Wilkinson, M. D., Dumontier, M., Aalbersberg, Ij. J., Appleton, G., Axton, M., Baak, A., … Bourne, P. E. (2016). The FAIR Guiding Principles for scientific data management and stewardship. *Scientific Data*, *3*.

16
COMPUTATIONAL METHODS FOR SEMANTIC ANALYSIS OF HISTORICAL TEXTS

Barbara McGillivray

16.1 An interdisciplinary contribution to semantic change

A large part of humanities research relies on interpreting the meaning of written text. This is a complex task, because meaning is affected by a variety of factors, including linguistic context, stylistic choices, register conventions, cultural constraints, and metaphorical usages. Among the different types of linguistic meaning, words play a prominent, though not exclusive, role.

Over the past years large digital text collections have become available to the scholarly community, and can be searched by sequences of characters or words. For example, we can search for the string *happ* in a collection and be presented with all texts containing the words *happy*, *happiness*, and *happily*. However, semantic search (i.e. search at the level of meaning) is still in its infancy. If we wanted to search for synonyms of *happy* like *glad* or *delighted*, we would need to specify them manually in a dedicated search. This is because associating meaning to words in context requires a significant effort to interpret the texts.

It is clear that the traditional approach of interpreting word meaning with the help of dictionaries and close-reading of texts is not scalable beyond a limited set of texts and the analysis of individual words. At a large scale, the statistical analysis of word patterns has proven to support semantic analysis, and language dynamics can be dealt with in probabilistic terms, as advocated by Jenset and McGillivray (2017:44). Based on this principle, recent advances in computational linguistics have shown the potential of these methods for historical semantic analyses (cf. the survey in Kutuzov et al. 2018), thanks to which researchers can detect linguistic, cultural, and social trends at a large scale which might be overlooked when relying on manual inspection alone.

However, this research has been confined within the limits of the natural language processing community, leading to serious methodological limitations for its applicability to humanistic research questions. Ancient languages, older time periods, and non-standard texts can be of great interest to humanities research. At the same time, they present unique challenges that usually concern the relatively limited size of the corpus of texts, as well as its specific composition and lack of balance between genres, authors, styles, and registers, and the evolving linguistic norms over the time periods covered. These challenges are mostly avoided by computational systems, which mainly focus on texts written in recent time periods (usually the last three centuries) and very large balanced datasets for modern languages (mostly English) that are stylistically more homogenous and formally more standardized. Work on addressing these challenges has only just started (cf. McGillivray et al. 2019), and it promises to bring impactful results for the humanities community by supporting the work of historians, literary scholars, classicists, and historical lexicographers.

It can also improve search on historical texts, allowing readers of historical library collections to search for concepts and meanings over time. In analogy with the use of "historical" and "diachronic" in linguistics, here by "historical text" I mean any text that is object of humanistic enquiry and whose temporal dimension is considered critical to the analysis from the point of view of its language.

In this chapter I present an overview of the current state of the art in the analysis of semantics phenomena in historical texts at scale, highlighting its critical aspects and proposing a new approach which joins together the expertise of computational specialists with that of humanities scholars. This innovative perspective promises to open up a new research paradigm for computationally-enhanced humanities scholarship and is in line with recent trends in Artificial Intelligence research (cf. e.g. Battaglia et al. 2018), which recognize the need for more sophisticated and interpretable models that are closer to the complexities of human intelligence.

16.2 Three reasons why semantics in historical texts is difficult

16.2.1 Why is semantics so hard?

Change and variation are inherent and persistent in all human languages (Kay 2015). Over time, new words enter the lexicon, others become obsolete, and existing words acquire new meanings, expanding or restricting their scope. The mapping between linguistic forms (such as words) to their meaning is not explicit in language, and the study of word meaning (known in linguistics as *lexical semantics*) has attracted the attention of linguists for a long time (cf. e.g. the review in Koptjevskaja-Tamm 2016).

One important and frequent semantic phenomenon is *lexical polysemy*, whereby words display several meanings. For example, the word *head* in English can refer to a body part or to a group leader. Another critical aspect concerns the nature of language as a dynamic system (Traugott 2012). Word meaning may change over time, giving rise to *semantic change*; consequently, words associated to certain concepts can be different in different eras. A classic example is the English adjective *gay*, which originally meant 'happy' and 'joyful', but over time it has increasingly often been used to refer to homosexual men. Polysemy and semantic change are closely related: the original meaning of a word may coexist with a newer one, and sometimes it ends up being limited to particular contexts. For example, the noun *tweet* means the chirp of small birds, and in recent years it has acquired the new meaning of a post on the social media platform Twitter. Nowadays we are more likely to find the bird-related meaning of *tweet* in texts about birds, while the social media meaning is probably considered the most common one.

Linguists have identified various processes responsible for lexical polysemy (Bréal 1883; Ullmann 1962; Blank 1999; Koch 2016). For example, the same word may have a more concrete and a more abstract meaning, and the two may be related via metaphoric links; cf. *grasp,* which means 'seize' in the physical domain, and 'understand' in the mental domain. In other cases, words may have opposite polarity values depending on context, and this coexistence may occur over time; for example, the adjective *sick* acquired the positive connotation of 'excellent', first observed in 1983, alongside the original negative connotation of 'ill' (cf. entry 'sick, adj. and n.' in Oxford English Dictionary). Sometimes a new meaning replaces the old one via metonymic change (e.g. *happy* changed its meaning from 'favourable' to 'feeling pleasure'), extension (e.g. the English word *camp* originally had a restricted military meaning and was then extended to mean encampment in general), or narrowing (e.g. the English word *meat* originally meant food in general, and then restricted its meaning to the current one).

Semantic phenomena are grounded in linguistic, cognitive, social, cultural, and contextual factors, occur due to specific (and often changing) linguistic contexts or language-external events (Stehling 2014), and their dynamic mechanisms are often led by innovative language users and communities (Traugott 2012; Andersen 2001). Most of us will have witnessed the change in meaning of the English word *friend* after the rise in popularity of the social media platform Facebook. To take a historical example,

Computational methods for semantic analysis

the semantic ranges of the Latin word *uirtus* were deeply affected as the values and conceptual systems of Latin speakers changed over the course of the rise of Rome and the conversion of the Roman world to Christianity. *Virtus*, originally meaning something close to 'manliness', extended to comprise violence, Christian virtue, and miracles. This word also acquired parts of the semantic range of Greek *andreía* (Clackson and Horrocks 2007:197), showing how interactions between speakers of different languages are one of the causes for these changes.

The semantic analysis of texts is challenging because of the complex interplay of phenomena I have outlined. When focussing on historical texts, this task becomes even more challenging, as we will see in the next section.

16.2.2 *The complications of historical texts*

If we have access to large amounts of texts, we may be able to identify a word's semantic change by observing the way in which the word is used over time. For example, the usages of the word *friend* in social media are likely to differ from the ones in more traditional sources. In our analysis we may detect clues such as references to Facebook or to the online setting of the discourse, or we may resort to native speakers' intuition. This is made easier by the large availability of contemporary textual material.

The situation changes when considering texts from earlier periods in history, and particularly ancient texts. Let us take the example of the Ancient Greek word *mus,* for which dictionaries list the following meanings: 'mussel', 'muscle', 'whale', and 'mouse'. Imagine that we are reading a late medical text, and that this is the first text we have access to that displays the use of *mus* as 'muscle'. Can we conclude that at the time when the text was written the medical meaning had just emerged in the language? Or could it be that the 'muscle' meaning was always uniquely associated to medical contexts? How can we find out which meaning is the most likely one in a series of Ancient Greek texts, so that we can search for only those texts that display the medical meaning of *mus* without reading them all? In order to answer these questions, deep analyses are necessary on the texts available to us. In the next section I will discuss the challenges of performing such analyses given the available search tools, and highlight how this hinders Digital Humanities research.

16.2.3 *The inaccessibility of semantics*

Historical collections of texts in digital form are essential resources for academic and non-academic purposes. Over the past few decades, massive digitization efforts have provided the community with large corpora that offer new and exciting research opportunities. To focus on just a few examples, we can name the Europeana collections, the Perseus Digital Library, Early English Books Online, and the Darwin Correspondence Project. In spite of the efforts to add metadata and link these collections, we are still far from taking full advantage of the rich content they offer, particularly for what concerns accessing their semantic level.

At the present, digital text collections of interest to the Digital Humanities community can normally be searched by sequences of characters (with or without wildcards), words, manually-curated keywords, or metadata fields (such as year of publication, author, text type, etc.). However, there is a demand to offer a more advanced functionality that better addresses the needs of the community, independently from the accidents of digitization and choice of content of the relevant digitization projects. As we have seen, such functionality involves the semantic level of analysis of the texts, which would allow users, for example, to identify content relevant to abstract concepts, or to find texts displaying specific meanings of words. Adding a diachronic dimension would also make it possible to run these searches according to specific historical periods. This would enable researchers to redefine the sorts of questions they can ask of texts and would open up whole new research directions. Consider, for example, the Latin word *passio*, which originally

263

meant 'suffering' or 'experience' and in the Christian era extended its range to mean 'emotion', with particular reference to the suffering and death of Christ and the martyrs (Auerbach 1937). In spite of what looks like a linear change, instances of the meaning 'passion' in the modern sense of 'strong emotion' are found in Christian authors as well, and discovering such nuances using existing textual search tools requires a series of time-consuming searches of the word *passio* in conjunction with words related to human feelings, for instance. A semantic search facility based on automatic methods would make this task significantly easier, and much more accessible to those without expert knowledge of the historical language in question, thus offering new insights into the language and the culture of the time.

Over the past few decades the corpus linguistics community has developed search tools for exploring corpora, including historical ones, such as the interface for Google Books developed by Davies (2014) and the Latin corpus LatinISE available on Sketch Engine (McGillivray & Kilgarriff 2013). Mostly independently from the development of Digital Humanities projects building large textual collections such as Europeana, corpus linguists have also engaged in the task of incorporating semantic information in the texts by performing what is known in linguistics as semantic annotation (Jenset and McGillivray 2017: 117–125). This involves interpreting a variety of different linguistic phenomena, including assigning the relevant meaning of a word in its context or detecting classes of named-entities such as people, organizations, locations, and time expressions. An example of a historical corpus with manually added semantic annotation is the Ancient Greek portion of the PROIEL corpus (Haug et al. 2009; 40–3), which consists of animacy tagging following the framework by Zaenen et al. (2004), and associates every Greek noun lemma (or dictionary-entry form) in the corpus to labels such as 'HUMAN', 'ORG' (organizations), 'ANIMAL', 'VEH' (vehicles), 'CONC' (concrete entities), 'PLACE', 'NONCONC' (non-concrete, inanimate entities), and 'TIME'. The presence of this type of annotation allows the users of the corpus to identify references to place names, for example, without the need to search a list of all Ancient Greek place names. A different type of semantic annotation of historical texts is reported in Declerck et al. (2011) for the Viennese Danse Macabre Corpus, which contains German texts from 1650 to 1750. The annotation identifies different conceptualizations of the theme of death, thus allowing to retrieve the corpus passages in which death is personified as a figure, for instance.

Manual semantic annotation is very time-consuming and cannot usually be extended from one set of texts to another. Therefore, some attempts at performing semantic annotation in automatic ways using computational tools have also been made. Archer et al. (2003) adapted the UCREL Semantic Analysis System to a historical corpus, thus allowing meaning-based text searches based on the Historical Thesaurus of English, which contains almost 800,000 words from Old English to the present day, arranged into fine-grained hierarchies.

Computational experiments towards historical semantic search that do not rely directly on manual semantic annotation or on existing thesauri, and are therefore generalizable to more languages and texts, have just started (Hellrich & Hahn 2017), and so far have been limited to a few corpora; Hellrich and Hahn (2017) focus on the English and German fiction portions of Google Books Ngram Corpus, the Corpus of Historical American English, the Deutsches Textarchiv, and the Royal Society Corpus. As in the case of corpus linguistics, such computational research has mostly developed independently from Digital Humanities environments. This can explain why Digital Humanities scholars as a group are still far from adopting such advanced functionality, and more interdisciplinary efforts are required to turn this work into impactful contributions to the community, as I outline in the next section.

16.2.4 Impact of historical semantics research

Identifying and understanding semantic phenomena at scale was unthinkable a couple of decades ago, and is now gradually getting within the reach of a growing group of scholars, both within the linguistics community and beyond, thanks to the development of advanced computational systems in this area. Semantic distant reading of large textual collections, if conducted in a methodologically accurate way, would open up a range of new possibilities in Digital Humanities research, especially in the area of cultural conceptual analysis (cf. Grondelaers et al. 2012 and Recchia et al. 2017). For example, we may expect the word *sleep* not to have changed its semantics between 1960s and 1990s, but the computational model by Gulordava and Baroni (2011) discovered indicators of potential changes, leading to the acquisition of more negative connotations of this word in relation to sleep disorders over time.

When analysing historical periods remote from our time, distant-reading approaches enable us to detect semantic associations and clusters that may challenge our assumptions, and raise interesting epistemological questions about concepts (Gavin 2016). Instead of using static lists of words to refer to concepts, and then analysing the distribution of those words, thus imposing a fixed conceptualization over a diachronic dataset, we can use data-driven methods to adjust concept-to-word mappings and thus reflect semantic changes in the data over time (Wevers et al. 2015).

In spite of the high potential impact of historical semantic research, however, the scholarly community has not yet found an optimal methodological configuration to tackle its challenges. In the next section I will review previous work in this area, underlining the different disciplinary approaches followed. As highlighted by Jenset and McGillivray (2017:137–142), "the scholarly communities of Natural Language Processing, Digital Humanities, and corpus linguistics would benefit from a deeper level of interaction and awareness of each other's fields" (Jenset and McGillivray 2017:125,137), and this applies to historical semantics at least as much as to other research areas.

16.3 Interdisciplinary pitfalls

16.3.1 Qualitative studies and computational studies

Within the humanities scholarly community researchers have investigated the history of words' meaning as a way to better understand social and cultural systems (Williams 1976), adopting research tools of various disciplinary approaches.

Building on previous tradition represented by scholars such as Benveniste (e.g. Benveniste 1969), in the second half of the last century philological methods have been employed in cultural history for the study of individual terms (cf. Lau 1975, Kenny 1995, Wierzbicka 1997). In the field of linguistics, recent years have witnessed a growing level of activity in the development of theories of lexical semantics (Taylor 2004, Geeraerts 2010; Goddard and Wierzbicka 2014).

Within historical research, the study of the history of concepts (Koselleck's 2006 *Begriffsgeschichte*) is closely connected with historical semantics, since concepts can be mapped to linguistic terms, and the study of the semantic evolution of key terms has been interpreted as the study of the evolution of the corresponding paradigmatic ideas and their effect on society.

The main limitation of all these qualitative studies is their narrow scope, which can be explained by the fact that individual scholars can only manually process a restricted amount of texts and focus on a small number of words, and often have to resort to secondary sources to support their analyses. What is lacking is a general overview of the evidence basis covering a large range of words and meanings (Williams 1976), as a way to investigate major cultural and social changes.

In a separate area of the academic community, the fields of computational linguistics and natural language processing have devoted much attention to semantics topics for some decades. The aim in this context is to arrive at computer algorithms that can automatically detect specific semantic phenomena in texts (such as semantic similarity between words, phrases, or sentences), with a view to solving practical applications such as automatic question answering or machine translation, as well as to deepen our understanding of language and its dynamic and complex mechanisms. Current computational approaches to semantics share a usage-based perspective on meaning, following the simple yet powerful intuition of the so-called distributional hypothesis, formulated by Firth (1957:11) as "you shall know a word by the company it keeps". In distributional approaches, semantic properties of words can be at least partially determined by analysing their distributional properties (Lenci 2008). Based on this view, for example, from the fact that two words like *boundary* and *limit* are found in texts in similar contexts displaying words like *outside*, *within*, *beyond*, *demarcate*, and *place*, we would conclude that *boundary* and *limit* are (at least in some contexts) synonyms of each other. Based on the distributional hypothesis, corpus linguistics and computational linguistics have applied various statistical techniques and measures to analyse word behaviour in context. The simplest distributional scheme has been successfully employed by corpus linguistics and lexicography for a few decades now and involves a more or less manual analysis of concordances (lists of words presented in their corpus context) and analyses of co-occurrence patterns such as collocations. More recently, based on the analogy between words on the one hand and geometrical objects (specifically vectors) on the other, computational distributional semantics has employed techniques from geometry to calculate various measures of "closeness" between vectors and interpret these in terms of semantic similarity between words. In recent years more advanced approaches, some of which involve neural network models, have been developed to represent semantic and syntactic profiles of words via so-called embeddings, with some very successful results (Bengio et al. 2003; Mikolov et al. 2013a,b).

The concerns of the computational linguistics community have traditionally been on modern languages and synchronic approaches, which have more direct and obvious links with commercial applications in today's world. However, over the past decade, computational and quantitative approaches to historical linguistics in general, and historical semantics in particular, have received increasing attention among computational linguists. This has been enabled by a combination of favourable factors, such as the growing amount of available digital material and the development of new algorithms. Such recent developments open up a range of possibilities to investigate historical linguistic phenomena at an unprecedented scale and in new ways (cf. Jenset and McGillivray 2017). In the context of semantics, distributional methods have proved to be very powerful, and their application to historical corpora spanning over longer or shorter time periods has the potential to shed new light into how configurations of words and meanings are embedded in their historical era and change over time.

The basic idea behind computational methods in historical semantics consists in building semantic spaces from text data to reflect the historical period of the corpus in question, with its conceptual and cultural frame of reference. In diachronic studies, semantic spaces are built corresponding to different time periods and the same words are mapped across these spaces. A change in the geometrical location of the vector of a given word in relation to other words over time can be measured and then interpreted as a signal for semantic change.

One of the most commonly used corpora in this line of research is the multilingual Google Books n-gram Corpus (Lin et al. 2012), which contains sequences of five words (5-grams) from texts of over 6% of the books ever published. Studies such as Hamilton et al. (2016) have highlighted well-known macroscopic examples such as the change in meaning of the word *gay* from 'happy' to 'homosexual'. In the context of classical languages, Boschetti (2010) used the Thesaurus Linguae Graecae corpus to measure semantic relations between words with vector spaces, and Rodda et al. (2017) used the same corpus and a distributional approach to explore the change affecting the Ancient Greek vocabulary from the pre-Christian to the Christian era. Some research has focussed on shorter time periods (Yao et al. 2017; Basile & McGillivray 2018) and other studies have analysed the semantic features of communities (Del Tredici et al. 2018) and semantic change (e.g. Kulkarni et al. 2015; Shoemark et al. 2019) using data from social media platforms. While focussing on large diachronic spans allows us to detect lasting linguistic changes affecting semantics, using data from short time spans can lead us to identify ephemeral phenomena which reflect shorter-term cultural and social changes, for example the recently emerged meaning of *snowflake* as 'shy person'.

16.3.2 Interdisciplinary gaps

The impact of computational semantics research has only reached a small group of "early adopters" (cf. e.g., Heuser et al. 2016) and not yet the mainstream Digital Humanities community. The current situation can be partially explained by limited interdisciplinary communication. On the one hand, computational researchers have not sought enough input from humanists while formulating research questions, devising evaluation strategies, and choosing the datasets to analyse. This limits the margins of improvement of computational research, as it restricts the scope of investigation to a limited group of datasets and languages consisting of large, general corpora of modern languages, or a few widely used diachronic (but problematic) corpora such as Google Books. On the other hand, computational methods have not yet been adopted to their full potential to answer humanities research questions, which restricts the advancement of humanistic fields of enquiry as well.

Quantitative and computational methods have a long history of criticism in the humanities. One common view is that these methods should only be employed in certain research areas, excluding semantics because of its complexity; for an overview of these criticisms, see Jenset and McGillivray (2017:81–96). In the field of general linguistics, both Sampson (2001) and Talmy (2007) put forward the idea that qualitative methods and introspection are superior to quantitative ones when trying to investigate semantics. In historical linguistics, Campbell (2013, 491) writes that quantitative methods "hold out promise" of understanding the effect of usage frequency on lexical change, but does not talk positively about their use in other areas.

In spite of such criticism, statistical methods are particularly well suited to the particular case of historical texts and languages, because the lack of native speaker competence in those languages naturally points to the use of written texts as primary source of evidence for the investigation (Jenset and McGillivray 2017).

Lack of communication between different scholarly communities leads to problems in the design and implementation of the research studies. A common limitation of computational semantic research is the lack of a satisfactory level of granularity in the analysis and the fact that linguistic complexities are often not adequately considered in the study design, for example the effect of the size of the textual context on the type of semantic change detected (e.g. pragmatic vs. propositional change).

Another problem has to do with the distributional approaches themselves, which assume that a word's semantics can be represented geometrically based on co-occurrence statistics, i.e. how many times other words are found in its contexts, defined typically as a window of a few words to the left and to the right of the word of interest. However, co-occurring words in a fixed context window do not fully describe a word's semantics. For example, there can be elements of background knowledge which are assumed in the text and which point to a particular meaning of a word as the more likely one; there can also be particular stylistic conventions that allow certain meanings and not others. From a study we have conducted on Ancient Greek (McGillivray et al., 2019), we have found that in only about half of the cases the meaning of a word in the texts can be inferred based on its context words, and that in all other cases access to other sources of knowledge is needed.

Furthermore, the use of computational methods based on word embeddings in historical semantics have been criticized when taken at face value without proper calibration. The methods themselves are poorly validated, and recent studies have highlighted that they can lead to artificially skewed and distorted results (Hellrich & Hahn 2016; Koplenig 2017; Dubossarsky et al. 2017). Finally, computational approaches tend not to account for contextual features, such as the historical environment, the author's stylistic choices, or geographical and social factors.

16.4 Bridging the gap between disciplines

The current situation calls for a whole new approach to the area of historical semantics, and the research community is now ready for a major methodological leap forward to address existing challenges. Importantly, the current disciplinary and scientific environment provides a positive driving force to this. Many see the combination of qualitative and quantitative approaches (so-called 'close reading' and 'distant reading') as the way to proceed in Digital Humanities (Digital Humanities Manifesto 2.0; Berry 2011), and the ambition to reach across the Science/humanities divide is a highly ambitious effort, also reflected in the activities of early adopters groups such as the Stanford Literary Lab. This is echoed in the data science community, with an increasing emphasis on human-centred data science, focussed on interpretability of machine learning models and a more active role of human input in algorithms (Chen et al. 2016), and on an increased interest towards hybrid approaches combining structure-based methods with deep learning in artificial intelligence (Battaglia et al. 2018). I argue that, by relying on the complementary combination of skills (either realized in a team or within the same individual researcher), it is possible to drive this methodological shift by combining computational modelling of semantic analysis with humanistic insights, thus pushing the boundaries of what academic disciplines separately have achieved so far.

How can such a disciplinary combination be fruitfully implemented in the semantic analysis of historical texts? Based on the arguments put forward so far, I propose the following list of priorities to address this question and offer an interdisciplinary contribution in the area of semantic analysis of historical texts, aiming to bridge the gap between humanistic expertise and computational approaches:

1. Define appropriate research questions which deal with the concerns of humanists;
2. Set the right expectations when assessing the accuracy of automatic systems that aim to scale up manual analyses;
3. Develop new paradigms for the evaluation and criticism of computational models for lexical semantic change;
4. Define a systematic approach to analysis and data annotation;
5. Avoid over-simplification of the original research questions thus allowing for the research to be relevant to Digital Humanities, and involve humanistic expertise at all stages of the process, from study design to data collection, implementation decisions, evaluation, and deployment;
6. Aim to develop new computational methods, if state-of-the-art ones are not adequate.

16.4.1 Relevant research questions

Regarding question 1, in the case of historical semantic analyses the concerns of historians, philologists, lexicographers, linguists, and other humanities researchers should be considered in order to ensure that the work addresses their needs; otherwise, the risk is for computational research to miss out on valuable input from humanities researchers.

So far, the focus of semantic change research in the NLP community can be summarized as being on different variations of the following question: can we build an automatic system that predicts when a word changed meaning in a given time span and beats the state of the art? On the other hand, from the point of view of Digital Humanities research, more relevant questions include: what is the relation between specific cultural events and semantic change? Which different types of semantic change can be recognized in relation with language-internal and language-external events? Can we automatically detect the most likely meaning of a word in a particular set of texts of interest, given their historical and literary context? Can we identify subtle changes in word meaning? Can we detect semantic change from small corpora (i.e. the particular ones of interest)? Approaching the research from a nuanced perspective and defining the questions in such a way that they address the concerns of humanities researchers makes it more likely to meet expectations and realize full impact.

16.4.2 Setting the right expectations in evaluation

Related to the point made above regarding research questions, setting the right criteria about what the computational system is expected to achieve and what is not expected to achieve is of critical importance for the success of a research project. Scaling up qualitative analyses requires a new mindset on the part of the researchers involved. Automatic systems can be built to imitate human performance to some extent, but they will highlight any inconsistencies or under-specification in the annotation and would suffer from lack of data. It is important to set the right expectations so that the automatic systems can be used productively, without competing with the human analysis, but complementing it.

Perrone et al. (2019) further developed the statistical model for semantic change detection of Frermann and Lapata (2016) by extending this model to Ancient Greek, whose corpus of texts is qualitatively different in terms of size, time span covered, lack of balance in the genres, and chronological gaps. Furthermore, the main audience of this work includes classicists and historical linguists, for whom an evaluation based on matching automatic analysis with manual analysis is the most intuitive one. Their expectations concern exploring questions about the semantics of Ancient Greek words and how it relates with historical, stylistic, cultural, and geographical factors. Their threshold for "trusting" an automatic system is very high: if the system's analysis is not seen to be at least as good as human analysis, it is not likely to be adopted by the community. This problem can be addressed by resorting to the original research questions as a basis to decide on the evaluation approach.

16.4.3 Develop new paradigms for the evaluation and criticism of computational models for lexical semantic change

The previous question raises the critical topic of how to evaluate computational models. Evaluation procedures in NLP aim to beat the state of the art. This means that computational semantics systems are typically evaluated directly in terms of how they perform compared to previous systems, and/or indirectly based on the accuracy of applied tasks that they relate to. In the former case, evaluation metrics on standard datasets are usually employed to assess the systems. Such standard datasets include semantically annotated corpora like SemCor (Landes et al. 1998) and tend to be drawn from a small group of such resources, given the amount of time and effort needed to create them and given the need for a standard approach to evaluation.

On the other hand, when evaluating systems indirectly against specific tasks, the choice is usually driven by application areas of interest to the NLP community. To take an example, word sense disambiguation systems aim to assign the correct meaning of a word in a given context and can be evaluated based on how much they help towards improving the accuracy of machine translation systems. For instance, how can knowing when the English noun *plane* refers to an aircraft or to a geometrical object help in automatic translation of *plane* as *aeroplano* vs. *piano* in Italian?

When dealing with historical texts, this approach to evaluation is likely to fail for two fundamental reasons. First of all, annotated datasets are hard or sometimes impossible to find, and building semantically annotated historical corpora is very time-consuming. Moreover, because different historical periods and languages have different features which affect word semantics, creating a corpus for one period and one language is only going to help scholars interested in that particular period and that particular language.

Secondly, even if annotated datasets or tasks were to be made available, historical datasets do not typically lend themselves easily to being evaluated against application-oriented tasks, as it is customary in natural language processing, and therefore this line of action is not likely to meet the needs of the Digital Humanities community. Exceptions to this claim exist, but are very few. Frermann and Lapata (2016) aimed to model the change in meaning of English words in a general corpus covering the time period 1700–2010 and used a time-assignment task to evaluate their model, based on the intuition that knowing how the semantic profile of a word changed over time can help assign a given historical word usage to its correct meaning. They measured the degree to which their model helped the accuracy of a system aimed to identify the time in which a text was written. Their research, however, stayed within the confines of the natural language processing field.

16.4.4 A systematic approach to analysis and data annotation

While aiming to automate the semantic analysis of historical texts, and therefore develop computer algorithms that perform this analysis, a range of interesting problems emerge. For example, which semantic framework to use? As outlined earlier in this chapter, important considerations have been put forward by scholars to define the theoretical foundations of semantic analysis. When the ultimate goal of the research is to provide insights into cultural and social trends in history, researchers have traditionally provided evidence of their analysis in a non-reproducible fashion, focussed on the scholarly and intellectual results rather than on the research process that led to them. This is what Jenset and McGillivray (2017:8–10) call the "example-based approach". In contrast, when switching from purely qualitative analysis to quantitative methods, a systematic approach and a more stringent attitude towards data collection and annotation are necessary to enable the computational implementation step.

Annotating samples of the data is often required for the purpose of training and/or testing machine learning algorithms, and corpus annotation (Jenset and McGillivray 2017:10–12) necessitates clear guidelines spelling out thought processes which tend to be implicitly stated in qualitative studies. In the case of semantic annotation of historical texts, we may consider the opportunity to refer to external resources like dictionaries or previous studies for an inventory of word meanings. In McGillivray et al. (2019), we chose an Ancient Greek-English dictionary (Liddell et al. 1996) and a philological study (Pollitt 1974) to annotate the meaning of three words in Ancient Greek texts. A significant body of research in corpus and computational linguistics has been devoted to the task of annotating corpora, and historical corpora in particular (cf. e.g. Passarotti et al. 2009; Jenset and McGillivray 2017: 98–129), and it is going to be beneficial for the Digital Humanities community to engage with this research. This is likely to result in a more robust and reproducible approach to the analysis.

16.4.5 Involving humanistic expertise

McGillivray et al. (2019) is the first study aimed at semantic change modelling in Ancient Greek. Previous work such as Rodda et al. (2017) used distributional semantics models to compare the semantic spaces of Ancient Greek words in two corpora, one for the pre-Christian era and one for the Christian era, highlighting interesting changes between the two time periods in terms of groups of semantically similar words. McGillivray et al. (2019) approach the topic from a different perspective, aiming at providing a model that maps the gradual change in distribution of the words' different senses over time in the history of Ancient Greek from the seventh century BC to the fifth century AD. The goal is very ambitious, as no similar analysis has been done before for this language, the closest precedents being dictionaries and qualitative studies. Historical dictionaries report words' meanings and, for each of them, a few dated quotations from authors employing those meanings, but they do not give any indication of the relative distribution of these meanings over time, apart from some sporadic qualitative indications like "rare" or "common", which are impossible to quantify reliably. Qualitative studies have also adopted an example-based approach whereby quotes from different authors are listed in correspondence with different meanings, and derived from a more or less extensive and systematic analysis of the sources, but do not aim at a full overview of lexical semantics in Ancient Greek history. This is understandable, as implementing such an analysis manually would require going through each text written in this language and recording the meaning of each word, an impossible task for anyone.

When attempting to tackle this problem computationally, McGillivray et al. (2019) relied on the model developed by Perrone et al. (2019), which in turn was inspired by Frermann and Lapata (2016). However, the presence of classicists in the team of this project meant that some important intuitions were suggested early on in the study and accounted for computationally. Specifically, it was observed that polysemy and semantic change are particularly hard to tease apart in the case of ancient languages, and genre plays a particularly critical role in the semantics of Ancient Greek words. Moreover, given the features of the corpus at our disposal —the Diorisis Ancient Greek corpus (Vatri & McGillivray 2018), the largest that could be built based on the digital resources available — it was not possible to aim at a balanced representation of genres, as was done for English by Frermann and Lapata (2016). For example, in the case of the word *mus*, the meaning 'muscle' is associated with a technical genre such as medicine, indicating that genre might play a stronger role than diachrony in determining the distribution of senses over time. These observations led to the development of a new computational model, responding to the last of the points advocated above.

16.4.6 New computational methods

Truly cutting-edge computational research in historical semantics should involve the development of innovative and impactful methods, which are built to answer questions relevant to humanists.

We have observed that computational historical semantics methods tend to focus on distributional data, but do not account for contextual features, which however are very important in determining word meaning. In the case of Ancient Greek semantics, Perrone et al. (2019) implemented the intuition that distributional context needs to be accompanied by genre in a statistical model for word semantics, alongside time. Because the corpus of Ancient Greek contains a limited and highly skewed set of texts, drawing random samples from a very large number of observations that approximate the language as a whole is bound to fail dramatically. This situation is common to many historical datasets and poses a general challenge to computational historical linguistics. Therefore, it is crucial to build statistical models that explicitly incorporate confounding variables like genre. The further back in time the texts are dated, the more acute this problem becomes because of gaps in the data. Another important insight that was gained from the interdisciplinary composition of the project's team was that there is a genuine fuzzy boundary between polysemy and semantic change from our viewpoint as contemporary and non-native speakers of Ancient Greek. The only evidence source we have is the high degree of semantic variation observed in the corpus at our disposal, so it is even more important to map and relate this variation to different confounding variables such as genre.

Current semantic change approaches in natural language processing simply focus on time as the only variable determining polysemy, and this leads to some macroscopic results for modern languages (such as *gay* shifting from 'happy' to 'homosexual'). However, this approach risks missing more subtle nuances, and because of the lack of a systematic evaluation framework for such methods, we cannot exclude this risk. In the case of ancient languages, semantic nuances are dominant, and macroscopic semantic changes are very rare. All these reasons point to the need for new computational models that work better for historical languages. Perrone et al. (2019) and McGillivray et al. (2019) describe this model, which provides for each genre the estimated probability distribution of each sense over time.

Conclusion

I have detailed the state of the art of computational approaches to historical semantics, which suffers from a disconnection with the Digital Humanities and humanities communities. On the one hand, computational disciplines try to automate analysis tasks and often fail to fully appreciate the concerns and research goals of the humanities. On the other hand, humanities scholars often struggle to imagine the potential of computational methods or to appropriately judge the results of automatic analyses over manual ones. I have motivated the need for more work that hinges on the active involvement of humanists' expertise in the design and implementation of computational models, so that they can fully account for the complexities of the data and the research questions. The solution I have suggested in this chapter takes the first steps in the direction of allowing us to use computers to scale up manual analyses of word semantics over time and provides a case study on Ancient Greek. The proposed approach addresses some of the challenges of the Ancient Greek corpus, including lack of balance between the genres represented therein and data sparsity (for a discussion of these challenges in historical corpora, cf. McGillivray 2014). This is achieved by incorporating a linguistic intuition (i.e. the need to use genre information in the computational models) which had not been accounted for in previous computational models. Future work could address the role of different types of historical texts in shaping this research proposition. Importantly, I have also advocated for a new attitude towards the evaluation of computational models of semantics, which sets realistic expectations on the results of automatic analysis, while recognizing the merits of a more systematic approach to the analysis of the data. More challenges lie ahead, including the need to address complexities such as subtle semantic changes and to account for language-external factors such as historical events and social structures. New computational research has proposed ways to incorporate knowledge bases in semantic models (cf. e.g. Ziegler et al. 2017; Boghrati et al. 2015), and humanistic scholarship is certainly going to provide plenty of evidence on which to build such advanced models, while making sure they answer the questions humanists care about.

Acknowledgements

This work was supported by The Alan Turing Institute under the EPSRC grant EP/N510129/1.

References

Andersen, H. (2001). Markedness and the theory of linguistic change. In Andersen, H. (Ed.), *Actualization: Linguistic change in progress*. Amsterdam & Philadelphia, John Benjamins, 21–57.

Archer, D., McEnery, T., Rayson, P., and Hardie, A. (2003). Developing an automated semantic analysis system for early modern English. In *Corpus Linguistics 2003 Conference*, Lancaster University, 22–31.

Auerbach, E. (1937). Remarques sur le mot "passion". *Neuphilologische Mitteilungen*, 38 (3), 218–224.

Basile, P. and McGillivray, B. (2018). Exploiting the Web for Semantic Change Detection. In: Soldatova, L., Vanschoren, J., Papadopoulos, G. and Ceci, M. (Eds.), *Discovery Science: 21st International Conference, DS 2018, Limassol, Cyprus, October 29–31, 2018, Proceedings*. Cham: Springer.

Battaglia, P. W., Hamrick, J. B., Bapst, V., Sanchez-Gonzalez, A., Zambaldi, V., Malinowski, M., Tacchetti, Raposo, D., Santoro, A., Faulkner, R., Gulcehre, C., Song, F., Ballard, A., Gilmer, J., Dahl, G., Vaswani, A., Allen, K., Nash, C., Langston, V., Dyer, C., Heess, N., Wierstra, D., Kohli, P., Botvinick, M., Vinyals, O., Li, Y. and Pascanu, R. (2018). Relational inductive biases, deep learning, and graph networks. *ArXiv*:1806.01261. https://doi.org/10.1002/gps.2367.

Bengio, Y., Ducharme, R., Vincent, P., Jauvin, C. (2003). A Neural Probabilistic Language Model. *Journal of Machine Learning Research* 3, 1137–1155.

Benveniste, E. (1969). *Le vocabulaire des institutions indo-européennes*. Paris: Minuit.

Berry, D. M. (2011). The Computational Turn: Thinking About the Digital Humanities. *Culture Machine*, 12(0), 1–22.

Berry, D. M. (2011). The computational turn: Thinking about the Digital Humanities. *Culture Machine*, 12(0), 1–22. http://www.culturemachine.net/index.php/cm/article/view/440

Blank, A. (1999). Why do new meanings occur? A cognitive typology of the motivations for lexical semantic change. *Historical Semantics and Cognition*, (13), 6.

Boghrati, R., Garten, J., Litvinova, A. and Dehghani, M. (2015). Incorporating Background Knowledge into Text Classification. *Proceedings of 37th Annual Conference of the Cognitive Science Society*, 244–249.

Boschetti, F. (2010). *A Corpus-Based Approach to Philological Issues*. Ph.D. thesis, University of Trento.

Bréal, M. (1883). Les lois intellectuelles du langage: fragment de sémantique. In *Annuaire de l'Association pour l'Encouragement des Études Grecques en France*, 17, 132–142.

Chen, N–C, Kocielnik, R. et al. (2016). Challenges of Applying Machine Learning to Qualitative Coding. In *CHI 2016 workshop on Human Centred Machine Learning (HCML 2016)*.

Clackson, J. and Horrocks, G. (2007). *The Blackwell History of the Latin Language*. Oxford and Malden, Mass: Blackwell.

Davies, M. (2014). Making Google Books n-grams useful for a wide range of research on language change. *International Journal of Corpus Linguistics*, 19(3), 401–416.

Declerck, T., Czeitschner, U., Moerth, K., Resch, C., and Budin, G. (2011). A text technology infrastructure for annotating corpora in the eHumanities. In Gradmann S., Borri F., Meghini C., Schuldt H. (Eds.), *Proceedings of the International Conference on Theory and Practice of Digital Libraries (TPDL–2011)*, 457–60.

Del Tredici, M., Fernández, R., and Boleda, G. (2019). Short-term meaning shift: an exploratory distributional analysis. In *Proceedings of the 2019 Conference of the North American Chapter of the Association for Computational Linguistics: Human Language Technologies, Volume 1 (Long and Short Papers)*. Minneapolis, Minnesota.

Digital Humanities Manifesto 2.0. Several authors. Available at www.humanitiesblast.com/manifesto/Manifesto_V2.pdf

Dubossarsky, H., Grossman, E. and Weinshall, D. (2017). Outta control: Laws of semantic Change and inherent biases in word representation models. In *Empirical Methods in Natural Language Processing (EMNLP), Copenhagen, Denmark*, 1147–1156.

Firth, J.R. (1957). A synopsis of linguistic theory 1930–1955. In *Studies in Linguistic Analysis*, 1–32. Oxford: Philological Society. Reprinted in F.R. Palmer (Ed.), *Selected Papers of J.R. Firth 1952–1959*, London: Longman (1968).

Frermann, L. and Lapata, M. (2016). Bayesian model of diachronic meaning change. In *Transactions of the Association for Computational Linguistics*, (4), 31–45.

Gavin, M. (2016). The Arithmetic of concepts: a response to Peter de Bolla. http://modelingliteraryhistory. org/2015/09/18/the-arithmetic-of-concepts-a-response-to-peter-de-bolla/

Geeraerts, D. (2010). *Theories of Lexical Semantics*. Oxford: Oxford University Press.

Goddard, C. and Wierzbicka, A. (2014). Words & Meanings: *Lexical Semantics across Domaines, Languages & Cultures*. Oxford: Oxford University Press.

Grondelaers, S., Speelman, D. and Geeraerts, D. (2012). Lexical variation and change. In D. Geeraerts, and H. Cuyckens (Eds), *The Oxford Handbook of Cognitive Linguistics*. Oxford: Oxford University Press.

Gulordava, K., Baroni, M. (2011). A distributional similarity approach to the detection of semantic change in the Google Books Ngram corpus. In: *Proceedings of the EMNLP 2011 Geometrical Models for Natural Language Semantics (GEMS 2011) Workshop*, 67–71.

Hamilton, W. L., Lescovec, J. and Jurafsky, D. (2016). Diachronic Word Embeddings Reveal Statistical Laws of Semantic Change. *Annual Conference of the Association of Computational Linguistics 2016. Association for Computational Linguistics (ACL)*.

Haug, D., Jøhndal, M., Eckhoff, H., Welo, E., Hertzenberg, M., and Müth, A. (2009). Computational and linguistic issues in designing a syntactically annotated parallel corpus of Indo-European languages. *Traitement automatique des langues* 50, 17–45.

Hellrich, J., & Hahn, U. (2016). Bad Company — Neighborhoods in Neural Embedding Spaces Considered Harmful. *Proceedings of the 26th International Conference on Computational Linguistics (COLING-16)*, 2785–2796.

Hellrich, J., and Hahn, U. (2017). Exploring Diachronic Lexical Semantics with JESEME. In *Proceedings of ACL 2017, System Demonstrations*, 31–36.

Heuser, R., Moretti, F. and Steiner, E. (2016). Mapping London's emotions. *New Left Review*, 101 (2016): 63–91.

Jenset, G. B. and McGillivray, B. (2017). *Quantitative Historical Linguistics. A corpus framework*. Oxford: Oxford University Press.

Kay, C. (2015). *English Historical Semantics*. Edinburgh: Edinburgh University Press.

Kenny, N. (1995). Interpreting concepts after the linguistic turn: The example of curiosité in Le Bonheur des sages/ Le Malheur des curieux by Du Souhait (1600)'. In *Interpréter le Seizième Siècle*, Michigan Romance Studies, XV, 1996, 241–70.

Koch, P. (2016). Meaning change and semantic shifts. In Juvonen, P. and Koptjevskaja-Tamm, M. (Eds) *The Lexical Typology of Semantic Shifts*. De Gruyter, Berlin.

Koplenig, A. (2017). Why the quantitative analysis of diachronic corpora that does not consider the temporal aspect of time-series can lead to wrong conclusions. *Digital Scholarship in the Humanities*, 32(1), 159–168. https://doi. org/10.1093/llc/fqv011

Koptjevskaja-Tamm, M. (2016). "The lexical typology of semantic shifts. An introduction". In Juvonen, P. and Koptjevskaja-Tamm, M. (Eds). *The Lexical Typology of Semantic Shifts*. Berlin: De Gruyter.

Koselleck, R. (2006). *Begriffsgeschichten*, Frankfurt am Main: Suhrkamp.

Kulkarni, V., Al-Rfou, R., Perozzi, B., Skiena, S. (2015). Statistically significant detection of linguistic change. In: *Proceedings of the 24th International Conference on World Wide Web*, 625–635.

Kutuzov, A., Øvrelid, L., Szymanski, T. and Velldal, E. (2018). Diachronic word embeddings and semantic shifts: a survey. In *Proceedings of the 27th International Conference on Computational Linguistics*, 1384–1397.

Landes, C. L. S. and Fellbaum, C. (1998). Building semantic concordances. In Fellbaum, C. (Ed.), *WordNet: An Electronic Lexical Database*, 199–216, Bradford Books.

Lau, D. (1975). *Der lateinische Begriff Labor*. Munich: Wilhelm Fink.

Lenci, A. (2008). Distributional approaches in linguistic and cognitive research. *Italian Journal of Linguistics*. 20:1–31

Lau, D. (1975). *Der lateinische Begriff Labor*. Munich: Wilhelm Fink.

Lin, Y., Michel, J.B., Aiden, E.L., Orwant, J., Brockman, W. and Petrov, S. (2012). Syntactic annotations for the Google books ngram corpus. In: *Proceedings of the 50th Annual Meeting of the Association for Computational Linguistics, Jeju, Republic of Korea, 8–14 July 2012*, 169–174.

McGillivray, B. (2014). *Methods in Latin Computational Linguistics*, Leiden: Brill.

McGillivray, B., Hengchen, S., Lähteenoja, V., Palma, M. and Vatri, A. (2019). A computational approach to lexical polysemy in ancient Greek. *Digital Scholarship in the Humanities*, https://doi.org/10.1093/llc/fqz036

McGillivray, B. and A. Kilgarriff (2013). Tools for historical corpus research, and a corpus of Latin. In Bennett, P., Durrell, M., Scheible, S., and Whitt, R. J. (Eds.), *New Methods in Historical Corpus Linguistics, Volume 3 of Corpus Linguistics and Interdisciplinary Perspectives on Language*, Tübingen: Narr.

Mikolov, T., Chen, K., Corrado, G., and Dean, J. (2013a). Efficient Estimation of Word Representations in Vector Space. In *ICLR: Proceeding of the International Conference on Learning Representations Workshop Track, Arizona, USA*, 1301–3781.

Perrone, V., Palma, M., Hengchen, S., Vatri, A. Smith, Jim and McGillivray, B. (2019). GASC: Genre-Aware Semantic Change for Ancient Greek. In: *Proceedings of the 1st International Workshop on Computational Approaches to Historical Language Change 2019, ACL 2019, Florence, Italy, 2 August 2019*.

Pollitt, J. J. (1974). *Ancient View of Greek Art*. New Haven: Yale University Press.

Recchia, G., Jones E., Nulty, P., Regan, J., and de Bolla, P. (2017). Tracing shifting conceptual vocabularies through time. In: Ciancarini P. et al. (Eds.), Knowledge Engineering and Knowledge Management. EKAW 2016. *Lecture Notes in Computer Science, vol. 10180*. Cham: Springer.

Rodda, M.A., Senaldi, M.S. and Lenci, A. (2017). Panta Rei: Tracking Semantic Change with Distributional Semantics in Ancient Greek. *Italian Journal of Computational Linguistics*, 56, 103–127.

Sampson, G. (2001). *Empirical linguistics*. London & New York: Continuum.

Shoemark, P., Ferdousi Liza, F., Hale, S., Nguyen, D. and McGillivray, B. (2019). Room to Glo: A Systematic Comparison of Semantic Change Detection Approaches with Word Embeddings. In: *Proceedings of 2019 Conference on Empirical Methods in Natural Language Processing and 9th International Joint Conference on Natural Language Processing, Hong Kong, China, November 2019*

Talmy, L. (2007). Lexical typologies. In T. Shopen (Ed.), *Language Typology and Syntactic Description*, 66–168. Cambridge: Cambridge University Press.

Taylor, J.R. (2004). *Linguistic Categorization*. Third edition. Oxford: Oxford University Press.

Traugott, E. C. (2012). On the persistence of ambiguous linguistic contexts over time: Implications for corpus research on micro-changes. *Corpus Linguistics and Variation in English*, 231.

Ullmann, S. (1962). *Semantics: An Introduction to the Study of Meaning*. Basil: Blackwell.

Vatri, A. and McGillivray, B. (2018). The Diorisis Ancient Greek Corpus. *Research Data Journal for the Humanities and Social Sciences*, 3:1.

Wevers, Melvin, Kenter, Tom, and Huijnen, Pim (2015). Concepts Through Time: Tracing Concepts in Dutch Newspaper Discourse using Sequential Word Vector Spaces. In *Book of abstracts of DH2015*.

Wierzbicka, A. (1997). *Understanding Cultures Through Their Key Words: English, Russian, Polish, German, and Japanese*. Oxford: Oxford University Press.

Williams, R. (1976). *Keywords. A Vocabulary of Culture and Society*. London: Fourth Estate.

Yao, Z., Sun, Y., Ding, W., Rao, N., Xiong, H.: Dynamic Word Embeddings for Evolving Semantic Discovery. Technical report (2017). https://doi.org/10.1145/3159652.3159703, arXiv:1703.00607

Zaenen, A., Carletta, J., Garretson, G., Bresnan, J., Koontz-Garboden, A., Nikitina, T., O'Connor, M. C., and Wasow, T. (2004). Animacy encoding in English: Why and how. In Webber, B. and Byron, D. K. (eds.), *Proceedings of the ACL2004 Workshop on Discourse Annotation*, Volume 17, Barcelona, 118–25

Ziegler, K., Caelen, O., Garchery, M., Granitzer, M., He-Guelton, L., Jurgovsky, J., Portier, P., and Zwicklbauer, S. (2017). Injecting Semantic Background Knowledge into Neural Networks using Graph Embeddings. *2017 IEEE 26th International Conference on Enabling Technologies: Infrastructure for Collaborative Enterprises (WETICE)*, 200–205.

17

ENCODING AND ANALYSIS, AND ENCODING AS ANALYSIS, IN TEXTUAL EDITING

Christopher Ohge and Charlotte Tupman

17.1 Introduction: Textual scholarship, encoding, and new modes of reading

Regardless of whether one views editorial work as merely mechanical or as heroic scholarly work, it is undeniable that it is a useful means of preserving and organising information (and of course it *is* heroic).[1] The word 'editor' comes from *editio*, which in its original sense could also denote a representation or exhibition, not merely the publishing of a work. Engaging in editing means entering into a long-standing tradition of textual exhibition in which an edition is a product of analysis, arguments and decisions as to the significance of the material. Yet even in book-making we are still producing something with dynamic processes, and now with the help of digital methods, the edition can take on new dimensions of exhibition.

Textual editing for digital publication encompasses not only the consensus of practitioners in philology, bibliography and textual scholarship, but also the creation of a computational pipeline that both curates the text and provides a structure for text analysis. The aspect of consensus bespeaks a praxis of digital scholarly editing that should, alongside the necessary theoretical debates about the nature of texts or the proper ways to choose and emend texts, be grounded in a spirit of pragmatism and thus a consideration of what actually works well in practice for the material under study. Elena Pierazzo rightly pointed out that in the strong and spirited debates between editorial theorists, 'the question has very rarely been which editorial framework was best for the type of document under consideration'.[2] The tendency is to posit what the author may have wanted, or what readers want now. We explore another relevant question: what do the documents require, and for what purpose? Textual editing is about making something—namely, assembling and building a text out of raw materials—and pragmatism provides a framework for making and knowing that allows editors to embrace the messy differences of the ideas within the web of cultural heritage.[3]

Editing also encompasses information management—namely, the guiding of information in a way that is useful to others. The philosopher C. S. Peirce often focused his attention on the dynamic processes whereby research moves toward reducing doubt and fixing belief in the abstract. His contemporary colleague William James invoked the physicist James Clerk Maxwell by asking for the 'particular go' of such research—'true ideas are those that we can assimilate, validate, corroborate and verify'.[4] This concept of the 'particular go' of ideas can be extended to the random detritus of textual production and cultural memory, but also to the curiosity, questions, disagreements and doubts about those things. Under which conditions are we warranted to assert something about a text? What *makes* a digital edition reliable, and what makes it useful to users? Instead of being bogged down in a facts-first mentality about texts qua texts or texts qua works, we examine the surviving documentary evidence, raise our research questions and examine the best applicable methods, and then describe the facts in terms of a workable interface. This is to emphasise an enquiry-first approach, rather than a theoretical one; inductive, rather than prescriptive. A digital edition is not simply for presentational purposes (reading) or for thought experiments; it is also a tool for some use that needs a plan based on the terrain (the textual-documentary landscape) as well as maintenance and rethinking. So in a crucial sense the very activity of textual editing involves a lot of analysis—critical judgments, arguments and principles about how best to build editions that exhibit texts. But how does digital editing take encoding and analysis further, into the realms of computational pattern-recognition and reading that the human brain cannot achieve?

Encoding and analysis, and encoding as analysis: many researchers in digital humanities have practiced encoding and text analysis as separate tasks.[5] This split is unfortunate. Some textual scholars have dismissed text analysis as merely counting, and some text analysis experts disregard the importance of authoritative texts and versions structured in XML. What exactly is text analysis and why include it in an editing project? Text analysis is a computer-assisted calculation of word counts and other statistics (e.g. word and sentence lengths, lexical uniqueness, unique word frequencies, average word use, sentiments, and topics) in a textual corpus. As one preeminent text analyst John F. Burrows suggests, 'the real value of studying the common words rests on the fact that they constitute the underlying fabric of a text, a barely visible web that gives shape to whatever is being said'.[6] The divide between encoding and analysis is evident in the current MLA guidelines for scholarly editions, in which the words 'data mining' or 'text analysis' do not appear as essential criteria.[7] Tara Andrews has made up for that lack by including 'analysis' in her four-part list of desiderata for digital editions.[8] Even so, automation and systemisation to facilitate analysis can reduce the customisation and flexibility that is essential to TEI encoders. We would advocate a notion of analysis that aims to be more expansive, flexible and geared to new ways of reading editions. We encourage text encoding and analysis as complementary activities because of the ways that the analysis can reveal the 'barely visible' aspects of the edition. We see analysis as not just the *how* of encoding, but the *why*, as well as the *what for*—ultimately, the use of the edition's data. This involves both the decisions for robust semantic markup that will facilitate text analysis and data mining, and the text analysis tools themselves that will provide further insight into the edition. This might have particular resonance for certain genres (particularly fiction and poetry) that would be enhanced by analytical and interpretive encoding.[9] An edition that adopts these principles would, in an ideal scenario, allow a user essentially to 'check out' a digital edition and immediately receive statistics on its content that would facilitate reading and exploration.

How an editor does or does not succeed will depend not just on the strategies of encoding for an interface, but also on the extent to which the underlying data can be analysed with computers rather than merely read on the screen. This is not necessarily about the 'front end' of the edition (the digital edition, or web site), but rather the data files that make up the edition: XML files, tables (in .csv or .tsv), dataframes, images, and scripts in XSLT, JSON, JavaScript, Python, R and other languages. Textual editing now includes the building of a computational infrastructure for digital publication as well as facilitating new ways of reading editions that are not possible in analog formats.

The traditions of philology and textual scholarship shape computational methodology, but digital research has also re-oriented traditional editorial workflows. It is not our purpose here to survey the history of philology, bibliography and scholarly editing; foundational guides already exist.[10] Rather, we encourage text encoders to read the history of scholarly editing—the debates about texts, accuracy, the decisions that editors make, the ways in which they present their texts and their scholarship. Is an editor an arbiter or an archivist of the texts? Should editors keep versions of texts intact as they were presented to the public or saved in repositories, or should they create a new text that is more readable, accurate or faithful to the author's wishes? Does a reader enter the edition through a single base text, with a record of variants, or multiple versions of texts, or multiple interfaces? The answers will dictate how one encodes and analyses the edition, and those decisions are best situated within the continuing conversations of editorial practice.

Encoding and analysis in textual editing

G. Thomas Tanselle says in his 'Varieties of Scholarly Editing' that editing takes part in a tradition of historical research, and therefore editorial decisions stem from the scholar's attention to accuracy and facts.[11] However, Tanselle never adequately defines what he means by history—judging by his writings one could assume that he takes it for granted that history is merely the study of the past. But history is, to echo Yuval Noah Harari, the study of change—and the stories that make change. The textual scholar John Bryant has also argued that all texts are 'fluid', and culture is in a constant state of adapting its cultural heritage, echoing Ralph Waldo Emerson's aphorism in 'History' that 'there is properly no history; only biography' (as well as, 'The poets made all the words, and therefore language is the archives of history', in 'The Poet').[12] How best to represent that change is one of the chief tasks of the editor. And, when most people talk about textual scholarship, they usually mean the series of reforms of its predecessor—the field of philology represented at opposite ends by Karl Lachmann and Joseph Bédier—in the late-nineteenth and early-twentieth centuries, in which analytical bibliography and so-called 'copy-text' editing made scholarly editing seem more objective. These reforms, often grouped under the term New Bibliography, which were undertaken in a positivist intellectual era by luminaries in the field of early modern literature such as R. B. McKerrow, A. W. Pollard, W. W. Greg and Fredson Bowers, culminated in eclectic text editions, hybrid products of multiple versions put together by experts in the subject.[13]

As David Greetham has suggested, the critical editors of New Bibliography illustrated another iteration of a debate about the meanings of terms such as 'authoritative' as well as its constituents 'form', 'intention', 'material' and so on. 'The history of textual scholarship can therefore be seen as a series of arguments—often resulting in intellectual and scholarly and personal conflicts, even feuds—over the meaning and significance of its most important terms, from the classical period to the electronic environment of the twenty-first century', Greetham concludes.[14] Moreover, he shows that transcription and publication technologies have been useful to editors since classical times. Recent textual criticism has responded to the Greg-Bowers-Tanselle school of thought with ideas of textual authority that were indebted to mid- to late-twentieth-century literary criticism—particularly the French *critique génétique*—that gainsaid the seemingly obstinate fixity of the New Bibliographer's ideas of 'intention' and 'work'. Various ripostes might be classified as document-oriented (in the case of genetic text editing, fluid text editing) as well as reader-oriented (social text editing). A particularly useful feature of recent textual scholarship came from D. F. McKenzie and Jerome McGann's work examining the various social processes and 'bibliographic codes' before and after the publication of works, processes which undermine the assumptions of textual authority and intention that are central to New Bibliography.[15] Many of these editorial practices have developed very neatly in a digital context. For example, the social text theory elucidated by Ray Siemens suggests that editing involves 'communities of practice', which can be better realised in a digital environment.[16] It has not been sufficiently shown, however, how workable some of these new practices might actually be, particularly in an era when so many communities of practice are still siloed in academia and often working in precarious roles.

At the other end of the spectrum is a worry about how the field of digital textual scholarship has been dominated by a commitment to ideologies of post-modern reader-response and deconstructionist theories that deny the truthfulness of claims to accuracy, textual stability and authorial intention. In 'The Death of the Editor', J. Stephen Murphy suggests that recent editorial theorising has adopted the logic of Roland Barthes's 'Death of the Author' (i.e., that the unity of textual meaning lies not in the text itself but in its destination with the reader). Also, despite the reinvigoration of textual studies by many digital humanists, Murphy points out that their 'rhetoric may have been self-defeating' because it 'represents editors as antiquated, logocentric bullies opposed to readerly freedom and textual play'.[17] On one side is a theoretical attachment to 'the work' as an abstract reaching after the perfectly constructed eclectic text, and on the other is a relativism with regard to textual matters. Another way lies in between, particularly in the pragmatic ethos of digital humanities, to echo Christopher Ricks, to use 'hard thinking [that] is resolutely unelaborated beyond the exposition and application of principles'.[18] The important point is to take the debates seriously, and to make a principled judgment as to the most appropriate way to create a workable edition from the materials at hand.

The burgeoning digital methods evident in this Companion open up more avenues for debate in textual scholarship, but to evoke Ricks again, a fair amount of hard thought should be applied to editorial *and* computational methods; this means thinking about why the edition is being built, for what research purposes and how to make that research data accessible. Editing, according to A. E. Housman's concise definition, is the 'science of discovering errors in texts, and the art of removing them'.[19] Besides the apt reminder always to exercise doubt, Housman's lasting contribution was to emphasise the role of individual judgment in editing. Couple this, too, with Samuel Johnson's elegant maxim that in editing, a scholar is 'to correct what is corrupt, and to explain what is obscure'—but also to keep in mind, 'The editor, though he may less delight his own vanity, will probably please his reader more, by supposing him equally able with himself to judge of beauties and faults, which require no previous acquisition of remote knowledge'.[20] It is a constant negotiation for scholarly editors to decide the extent to which they should make themselves known by intervening in the construction and explanation of the contents of the edition, and it is now possible for that negotiation to be openly documented.

How has digital research re-oriented traditional editorial workflows? Text editing in print and digital involves an act of data modeling, which is based on the epistemological grounding of the editors. Pierazzo has posed an important question about whether the methodologies of editing can 'be pursued digitally or does the digital medium necessarily provide a new theoretical framework?'[21] This sets up a distinction between implementing old methods (and outputs) of editions versus creating a brand new methodology. While she leaves the question open, we argue here that old methods are informing digital editions at the same time as computational methods are enhancing what might be called the 'old' methods. Daniels and Thistlethwaite have asserted that 'Digital technologies have radically altered the traditional structure of habits in the scholarly workflow.'[22] All editors are output-driven, but some spend more time on analytical features. Others are more interested in presentation (reading texts). Also, even though 'user-driven' digital editions are a laudable goal, the purpose of the edition is still to employ the expertise of a textual scholar for the benefit of users. Even if we acknowledge that the 'user' is an abstraction that can never be reconciled with the myriad desires of scholars, students and general readers who use editions, it is still a pragmatic concept that grounds traditional approaches to the design of any digital object or software. Pierazzo is right to suggest that the workflow should be a primary concern in digital editing, along with producing the right type of edition as dictated by the material. The principles of the editors are also crucial (and are not always stated as often or as clearly as they might be). What is required in this rapidly advancing ecosystem of digital scholarship is a methodology grounded in pragmatist epistemology, one that seeks to use computers to make texts work better for research questions, and one that uses success in action to balance textual scholarship and the creation of a computational pipeline.[23]

The building of a computational pipeline should include decisions about the accessibility of data: a digital editor should consider whether their XML data is amenable to the analysis of researchers from outside the project. Tim Berners-Lee proposed five levels of open data specifications:[24]

★ Available on the web (whatever format) *but with an open licence, to be Open Data*
★★ Available as machine-readable structured data (e.g. Excel instead of image scan of a table)
★★★ As (2), plus non-proprietary format (e.g. CSV instead of Excel)
★★★★ All the above, plus: Use open standards from W3C (RDF and Sparql) to identify things, so that people can point at your stuff
★★★★★ All the above, plus: Link your data to other people's to provide context.

But data is not quite 'open' if a digital researcher needs a complicated specialist's manual to figure out how to analyse the layers that make up the edition. In other words, 'structured' data does not necessarily entail easily analysable data. What is missing in Berners-Lee's list of accessibility is analysability.

Encoding and analysis in textual editing

Berners-Lee's ideals can be enhanced with the desiderata set forth by Julia Flanders and Neil Fraistat,[25] that digital editions should be:

1. **interoperable** with each other and with other texts using professional standards such as the TEI;
2. **layered and modular,** so that the edition is separate from an interface which allows for redesigning interfaces;
3. **multimodal**, providing analysis of the text but also of other paratextual materials;
4. **dynamic**, encouraging user interaction;
5. **scalable**, allowing for microscopic and macroscopic inquiry;
6. **everted and interconnected**, so that edition data can be used by others;
7. **sustainable**, so the community can access the material.

As much as most scholarly editors would like to see these desires fulfilled, what Flanders and Fraistat suggest is not always practicable for scholars faced with time and resource constraints. It is hard to think of any current digital editions that successfully hit all seven targets, unless they are one of the rare, large-scale digital humanities projects that have attracted seven figures of funding. It is also arguable whether all editions should be dynamic, or whether interface needs to be a concern at all for those who simply want to preserve a small-scale text in an XML repository, which in itself should be considered a genuine service to scholarship. A minimalist—or minimal computing—approach to achieving all seven might be a laudable goal, but we would argue that the third point, that of multimodality (possibly combined with scalability and usability and interconnectedness), should be a primary concern to all editors, for it is an aspect of digital editing that is truly innovative in a way that printed books cannot be.

Constraint is an important factor that must be addressed in encoding, analysis, and workflow.[26] If you are a beginner to digital editions, it would be a mistake to think of the encoding as an encyclopedic markup enterprise. It can be intimidating to see the 23 Modules of the TEI Guidelines, and to wonder how one could understand all the possibilities that various elements, attributes and values can offer. Yet it is not the purpose of the edition to populate it with as many tags as possible. Rather, one should start by asking questions such as:

- How do the materials cohere with the methods of textual scholarship?
- What is the purpose of this edition?
- What are the arguments about the best way to organize and present the texts?
- What are the arguments for the significance of the text, and the priorities of its audience, and how do these affect our encoding choices?
- What analytical tools could enhance our understanding and demonstrate the significance of the research?

From there one can then construct an analytical model of encoding decisions to guide best practice. Sometimes, in order to accomplish the research aims based on the above analytical questions, a researcher will need to customise TEI or create new elements and attributes. That is entirely legitimate: there is a reason that the TEI Guidelines are not called the TEI Laws. They can be customised depending on the needs of researchers. The analytical dimension will also include some general principles about the goals of text analysis: what new forms of reading can brought to light as a result of the encoding?

A recent debate in textual scholarship between historical (or documentary) and critical ('copy-text') editors illustrates the importance of thinking in terms of encoding as analysis. By historical-documentary editions, we mean the transcription of a source text as exactly as possible; and by critical editions, we mean those that choose the most authoritative base text (often called the copy text) for the edition, the reading text of which will be emended if other authoritative readings exist in other versions (otherwise called 'witnesses'). One of the complaints about digital documentary editions—and their materialist cousins, genetic and versioning editions—is that they only work for a small audience of specialist scholars. Genetic editions aim to show the creative process in surviving documents, whereas versioning texts usually show documentary texts of multiple existing versions, usually in parallel. All of these editions are potentially unreadable or tedious, at worst; most people want to read one clean, accurate text.[27] The problem with that argument is that it is only forceful in the context of normal codex-based human reading processes. A complicated digital versioning text, or a transcription of a heavily revised and uncompleted manuscript, can be 'read' in a novel way with the tools of text analysis and querying. The text analysis can be an adjunct to the normal reading process (the edition should be machine-readable, after all). Moreover, as Bryant and other editors at the Melville Electronic Library have shown, the digital interface can make the reading process of difficult manuscripts smoother than that of their print predecessors by directly engaging the reader with the material context rather than relying on complex genetic symbols (especially when multiple reading interface options are involved).[28] The criticism leveled by Robinson against the limited page-by-page transcription of the digital documentary edition *Jane Austen's Fiction Manuscripts* does not take into account the intellectual value that text analysis could bring to that edition's XML data. His problem that we might 'distance ourselves and our editions from the readers' is actually more of an interface issue than a worry about the usefulness of the edition's data.[29] And let's not forget: humans are not the only readers now; the machines are too, and they can help humans find new information in complicated texts.

How, then, to begin? One simple place to start is to do what Syd Bauman, James Cummings, and Julia Flanders have suggested: create a spreadsheet of the kinds of elements that would be most useful to the project.[30] Researchers should also include a list of research hypotheses and intended analysis outcomes in this spreadsheet. In addition to the research questions that will guide the editing and encoding, one should also consider whether the edition data will be subject to analysis with Voyant Tools, AntConc, Python NLP, or R (or all of these in combination).[31] What kinds of information resulting from text analysis would benefit the research? The spreadsheet should identify at least two things: the set of elements, attributes and values, and the set of analytical aims of the encoding. A more advanced approach would be to implement the information from the spreadsheet into a project ODD file. ODD—which stands for 'one document does it all'—sets the constraints of encoding, along with the set of rules of the proper vocabularies and hierarchies. The Roma JS application, which is under development but available in beta, makes this process even easier to accomplish than it is with the TEI's existing Roma tool for generating customisation files.[32] Most TEI XML projects will only use around 25 or so elements, so there is actually no need to implement a TEI-all document template (which allows for around 500 elements), or to get overwhelmed with identifying a large group of elements for more sophistication.[33] The inclusion of an analytically-driven ODD file constrains the encoding in addition to bolstering the functionality of the finished edition.

17.2 Using EpiDoc to edit classical texts

For those less familiar with TEI and its scope, it is worth noting that there are subsets of the TEI designed specifically to constrain the available elements, attributes and values in order to encode particular types of texts: to take an example, the EpiDoc initiative produces a schema and guidelines for encoding scholarly editions of texts such as inscriptions and papyri (not limited to ancient materials).[34] EpiDoc caters not only for transcription and editorial interventions, but also for describing the object on which a text is written or inscribed, as well as its history. Rather than using the full set of options available within the TEI, the authors of EpiDoc have considered which elements an epigrapher or papyrologist will need to use to produce an edition. They have selected specific attributes and values for these elements in order to make the TEI as useful and relevant as possible to specialists in these areas, and the features that are expressed through EpiDoc are documented in a set of explanatory guidelines designed to help the user through the process of encoding.[35] In addition, there is a supportive community that runs training workshops and a mailing list for further discussion.[36] This approach has proved successful, in that EpiDoc is now considered

Encoding and analysis in textual editing

the standard method for encoding inscriptions and papyri for digital publication and interchange, without being prescriptive about the precise workflow that a project should follow.

It would be worth exploring how best to guide and inform those who plan to undertake such a project. The Women Writers project,[37] led by Julia Flanders at Northeastern University, has produced an extremely useful guide to strategy and workflow for encoding projects.[38] Although it is based on the encoding of early printed books, it serves a much wider set of users in offering a step-by-step guide to concepts, strategies, project management and design, including document analysis, markup, error-checking, post-processing and documentation. It is a valuable guide for anyone thinking of undertaking an encoding project, and the recommendations we make here build upon its foundation. How might appropriate workflows best be designed, from examining source materials to publishing and analysing data that serve a project's scholarly aims? In attempting to define a workflow, we should first establish what aims are being served. Those of the researchers on the project? Those of known groups likely to use the resource? Those of future or potential users with different/wider research questions? Financial practicalities, skill sets and varying availability of personnel throughout the project will also have their own influences on workflow. We make all the suggestions below with these caveats in mind.

To illustrate how an editorial workflow might be designed that caters to text encoding and analysis as complementary activities, we take the example of the work that an epigrapher typically undertakes when editing an inscription, or corpus of inscriptions, for digital publication, and how this might be enhanced to include plans for text analysis.[39] It seems timely to consider this, not least because a number of tools that could enhance such work are now available but are not as widely used as they could be, as noted recently by Bodard and Stoyanova when they remarked that 'We have yet to fully integrate any of this activity into the workflow of the epigrapher or papyrologist [...] and further training in this area would doubtless result in better integration with EpiDoc guidance'.[40]

The traditional editor of an epigraphic text will begin with the reading and transcription of the inscription from a combination of autopsy, photography and perhaps also the making of a 'squeeze' (an impression of the inscription made using squeeze paper, water and a specially made brush with tightly packed bristles designed to ensure an accurate rendering of the inscribed letters). In addition to traditional methods, digital techniques including RTI (Reflectance Transformation Imaging) can be included in the epigrapher's toolkit to enhance the reading of difficult or damaged letters.[41] If the text has been published, previous readings of the inscription will be considered, particularly where these were made when the stone was in better condition and more of the inscription was visible (for instance, before an inscription was damaged or exposed to weathering). Typically the epigrapher might work with a notebook and pencil before transferring their reading of the inscription to digital form.

Those who have been trained in EpiDoc encoding might create a 'born digital' text, entered immediately into a <div type="edition"> with minimal structural markup as a first step. Most epigraphers using traditional methods, however, will initially write up their reading of the text in their preferred text editor. They will record the diplomatic version of the text, i.e. what can be seen on the stone, and then as a separate task will produce an edited version that includes expansions of abbreviations, supplied letters or words, indications of unclear letters and so forth. At this stage the editor will include the 'Leiden conventions', sigla that indicate editorial interventions in the text, and will write an apparatus criticus discussing previous readings or unclear or otherwise notable sections of the text.[42] They will also consider details of the object on which the inscription appears, such as material, measurements and decorative features; previously known locations; dating criteria; letter heights; and bibliography. Finally, to explain the historical context of the inscription and its significance, the editor will write a commentary.

So far, this workflow would be familiar to any epigrapher working today, even if they might approach it in a slightly different order. Anyone considering a digital publication would familiarise themselves with the EpiDoc Guidelines[43] and take advice from the community mailing list[44] or one of the training workshops[45] as to the appropriate markup to structure the text and metadata, and to represent the editorial interventions in the text, but this aspect of the digital workflow is not markedly different from that of the print editorial workflow: indeed, the traditional workflow directly informs and influences the digital. The types of information recorded here are drawn from centuries of consensus about what epigraphic scholarship entails, epitomised by the gargantuan works of the *Corpus Inscriptionum Latinarum* and *Inscriptiones Graecae*.[46]

Where an encoded version of an epigraphic text begins to depart from the work of the traditional epigrapher is in the level of detail that can be achieved in the semantic markup of the edition. This goes beyond solely diplomatic transcription, encompassing more explicit details of editorial interventions as well as the encoding of information about specific entities within the text, and this stage is reflected in the digital workflow: a substantial amount of time is likely to be devoted to the encoding of entities that are identified as being of research interest to the project and/or its users. For instance, this might include encoding information about people or places that appear in the text, and providing links to internal or external authority lists containing further details about those entities, such as biographical details for people and coordinates for places, and possibly also some information about related entities. Whether or not the important entities have been established at the beginning of the project will depend on whether the content of the inscriptions was known before the project began, and often markup requirements will have to be adapted as new data come to light during the course of the work. However, in an ideal situation these entities will have been identified and decided upon before the project begins, so that effort is expended in the appropriate areas of the encoding process. It is always necessary to select the markup carefully: in a world where we could encode almost any aspect of a text and its physical support, the time, funds and available expertise will always be limiting factors (just as they are in non-digital projects). The digital workflow, then, might at this stage include the encoding of features such as places, events, dates, individuals, names, commemorative relationships, age, sex, social status, and occupation, depending on the focus of the project or that of its expected end users.

In a digital project, decision-making about the desired indices, tables of content, and other facets is ideally done at the earlier stages, to allow not only for planning the encoding that needs to be done in order to produce these features of the edition, but also to establish what *else* could be done beyond the markup itself. As Bodard and Stoyanova observe, 'the rigorous intellectual effort of indexing in a tradition[al] project is changed in the digital process, but not replaced by an automated process.' Referring to the order in which these skills are taught in EpiDoc workshops, they note that 'this structure follows the workflow of an epigraphic project, where the indices, tables of contents, lists of lemmata etc. are produced at the end of the project from the encoded XML files.'[47] While the generation of indices might still be done at the end of a project, the *thinking* about what indices are needed is best done as early as possible. The same is true for the creation and structuring of internal authority lists (and/or identification of the relevant external authority lists), although inevitably these will be populated as the project progresses.

The presentation of the texts (i.e. the design of the user interface) is likely to involve an iterative process of testing an initial design, receiving feedback and developing the interface further in several stages, whether the project uses the Kiln-based EFES (EpiDoc Front End Services),[48] an eXist-based approach with the EpiDoc stylesheets,[49] or a custom framework. Is the project intending to present users solely with the editors' readings and commentaries of the texts, or seek user annotations or submissions of new readings? If the latter, how much encoding knowledge is assumed on the part of the user? Should the interface allow for a relatively simple means of annotating a text, to encourage a greater level of participation amongst those who have not learnt to encode?

We are in agreement with Bodard and Stoyanova that were EpiDoc encoding skills to be taught alongside Linked Open Data (LOD) and Named Entity Recognition (NER) skills in Python or other languages, we would see the immediate benefits of encoding and text analysis as complementary and connected tasks.[50] In addition we would recommend the inclusion of text analysis tools such as Voyant[51] and AntConc,[52] at least in respect of making participants aware of their potential (even if teaching specific skills in using them is beyond the bounds of that particular workshop). The drive of projects such as Pelagios[53] to produce

Encoding and analysis in textual editing

user-friendly interfaces for the creation of LOD[54] (and, of course, Papyri.info[55] for the creation of EpiDoc encoding 'underneath the hood') means that confidence in at least some of these areas can be developed within the bounds of a relatively short learning time, although this is not a substitute for bringing in the appropriate expertise for a specific project, or for learning the fundamentals oneself, which will always bring a deeper understanding not only of what one is doing but of what might be possible. It is not within the scope of this chapter to debate the relative merits of user-friendly interfaces versus more in-depth training in the fundamentals of encoding and analysis, but what the former provides is the means for analytical tools to be explored by the epigrapher at the planning stages, and decisions made about how the encoding could be designed to facilitate further analysis. In doing so, we should plan for an iterative process, not least because experimentation is an important aspect of text analysis: while as researchers we have our own particular questions and priorities, we will inevitably need to modify or generate new questions as a result of undertaking this work.

17.3 Encoding and analysis in modern English texts

These considerations in epigraphy remain relevant to other time periods. Consider Philip Henslowe's diaries, written between 1592–1609, which detail his financial transactions, as well as fine-grained information about the daily operations of his playhouse. The manuscript is the best surviving source of information of English Renaissance theatre. This vital record has been published in print editions, but it is difficult to read and clearly aimed at specialists who already understand the linguistic and numerical data.[56] The recent addition of digital facsimiles of the original manuscripts has made it possible to create a digital edition, which is currently underway under the direction of Dr. Yuanbo (Edgar) Mao.[57] Any digital edition of a document like Henslowe's diary should be guided by analysis; the diary is a dataset, consisting as it does of rows of data relating to play titles, performance dates, loans and ticket sales. Examining the Foakes and Rickert edition of the following receipts from February 1592 (Figure 17.1) shows the difficulty of following a print edition for this kind of text:

Here is a draft TEI XML snippet of the same receipts from February 1592:

```
<div xml:id="f7r">
    <div xml:id="Receipt_159202">
        <!--Receipts from Feb_1592-->
        <!--receipts converted to pence-->
        <ab>In the name of god A men 1591<lb/>beginge the 19 febreary my<lb/>lord stranges
            mene A ffoloweth<lb/>1591</ab>
        <l>Rd at <bibl type="play" corresp="#FBAFB"><hi rend="italic">fryer
            bacvne</hi></bibl><date when="1592-02-19">the 19 of
            febreary</date>...satterdaye <num n="207">xvij s iij d</num></l>
        <l>Rd at<bibl type="play" corresp="#TBOA"><hi rend="italic"
            >mvlomvrco</hi></bibl><date when="1592-02-20">the 20 febreary</date>
            <num n="348">xxix s</num></l>
        <l>Rd at <bibl type="play" corresp="#ORL"><hi rend="italic">orlando</hi></bibl><date
            when="1592-02-21">the 21 of febreary</date>
            <num n="198">xvj s vj d</num></l>
        <l>Rd at <bibl type="play" corresp="#TSC"><hi rend="italic">spanes comodye donne
            oracioe</hi></bibl><date when="1592-02-23">the 23 of febreary</date>
            <num n="162">xiij s vj d</num></l>
        <l>......</l>
    </div>
</div>
```

[7]

In the name of god A men 1591
beginge the 19 of febreary my
lord stranges[2] mene A ffoloweth
1591

Rd at fryer bacvne the 19 of febreary . . satterdaye[3] . . xvij s iij d
Rd at mvlomvrco the 20 of febreary . . . . xxix s
Rd at orlando the 21 of febreary . . . . xvj s vj d
Rd at spanes comodye donne oracioe[4] the 23 of febreary . xiij s vj d
Rd at syᵣ John mandevell the 24 of febreary . . . . . . xij⁵ vj d
Rd at harey of cornwell the 25 of febreary 1591 . . . . . xxxij⁵
✗ Rd at the Jewe of malltuse the 26 of febrearye 1591 . . . . ls
—— Rd at clorys & orgasto the 28 of febreary 1591 . . . . . . xviij s
Rd at mvlamvlluco the 29 of febrearye 1591 . . . . xxxiiij s
Rd at poope Jone the 1 of marche 1591 . . . . xv⁵
Rd at matchavell the 2 of marche 1591 . . . . xiiij s
ne—— Rd at harey the vj the 3 of marche 1591 . . . . iiij¹ⁱ xvj⁵ 8 d
Rd at bendo & Richardo the 4 of marche 1591 . . . . . . xvj s
—— Rd at iiij playes in one the 6 of marche 1591 . . . . xxxj s vj d
Rd at harey the vj[5] the 7 of marche 1591 . . . . iij li
Rd at the lockinglasse the 8 of marche 1591 . . . . vij⁵
Rd at senobia the 9 of marche 1591 . . . . xxij s vj d
✗ Rd at the Jewe of malta the 10 of marche 1591 . . . . . . lvj s
Rd at harey the vj the 11 of marche 1591 . . . . xxxxvij⁵ vj ᵈ
—— Rd at the comodey of doneoracio the 13 march 1591–✗– . xxviiij⁵

(1) *xij.⁴ J. ha*] *xi* is written over *J*, *d* over *h*, and *a* stands free. The letters *J. ha* appear to be in the ink of the opposite page, which is dated 1591; they occur again on f. 7.
(2) *stranges*] *strangers* Greg.   (3) *satterdaye*] interlined.
(4) *oracioe*] so Malone; *oracoe* Greg; *i* and *o* are run together.
(5) *harey the vj*] *hary vj* Greg.

16

Figure 17.1   A scan of the February 1592 receipts from the Foakes and Rickert print edition of *Henslowe's Diary*

Encoding this project with TEI best practice in mind, one can not only structure the entries in the diary with descriptive markup, but also regularise the data for statistical analysis. The @when attributes in <date> elements regularise the data for the purposes of analysis, such that one could now identify all elements from February 1592 even if they are written in a different way. Moreover, the <num> elements and @n attributes exemplify good practice, but they also encapsulate encoding as analysis: while regularising the numerical values, a researcher should also aim to think about how to produce statistical calculations on Henslowe's recordings. That is, how could a digital edition improve the reading experience of the text? What text analysis tools would best suit this project? One could aim to include Python or R scripts for processing mathematical and subject calculations. Analysis of editions in this fashion can perform whole-text as well as node-level data mining.[58]

In bibliography and genetic criticism, marginalia studies stand out as another revealing example of encoding as analysis, particularly at the node level. *Melville's Marginalia Online* (MMO) is a highly functional

Encoding and analysis in textual editing

virtual archive, digital bibliography, and searchable edition of Herman Melville's library that is still very much in progress. The encoding decisions in the initial phase of the project could have followed the TEI, but the aim of the project was to create a searchable database of Melville's markings and annotations that matched the word-level results with their corresponding digital facsimiles. The resulting coordinate-capture XML encoding does just that:

```
<div id="2" x="277" y="2415" group="1" width="1299" height="129" type="checkmark"
    sealts="460_1_c011" attribution="HM" mode="comedy" play="1a">
    <w x="416">That</w>
    <w x="526">this</w>
    <w x="653">lives</w>
    <w x="726">in</w>
    <w x="815">thy</w>
    <w x="1023">mind?</w>
    <w x="1197">What</w>
    <w x="1344">seest</w>
    <w x="1469">thou</w>
    <w x="1574">else</w>
    <div id="3" x="277" y="2479" group="1" width="1075" height="74" type="underline"
        sealts="460_1_c011" attribution="HM" mode="comedy" play="1a">
        <w x="353">In</w>
        <w x="446">the</w>
        <w x="580">dark</w>
        <w x="836">backward</w>
        <w x="943">and</w>
        <w x="1124">abysm</w>
        <w x="1192">of</w>
        <w x="1345">time?</w>
    </div>
</div>
```

This is Melville's first marking (with an embedded additional marking) in *The Tempest*, from his seven-volume set of Shakespeare's plays. Each instance of marginalia is contained within a <div>, which includes several attributes identifying various bibliographic and holographic information. Clearly this is not TEI-compliant, but it is functional as to its purpose, which is to enable word searches of marginalia with corresponding highlighting of search results in the digital facsimile of the page from Melville's book. Of course TEI encoding would make it easier to refine analysis (of, say, marginalia differences between poetry and prose structures), and the project has plans to incorporate stand-off TEI to complement the existing coordinate-capture markup. Yet the fact that each instance of marginalia is encoded with a <div>, and that each <div> has additional attributes (such as the marking @type, the play's @mode, the play's @title, and the @sealts attribute, which identifies bibliographic information as well as the page number in a single value) means that the data is already amenable to text analysis. Also, each word encoded within a <w> allows for fine-grained markings-level and word-level analysis.

Complemented with the plan to encode Melville's marked texts were a series of XSLT and R scripts for performing text analysis on Melville's reading data.[59] With the services of Performant Software, MMO has also started to implement a complementary analysis interface, based on Voyant tools, which shows general statistics of reading data. The fragmentary nature of marginalia makes text analysis even more important as a tool for understanding. XSLT scripts created HTML tables of all the markings that could be sorted by word count as well as bar graphs of total words marked per play and play mode (comedy, history, tragedy). R code adapted from Jockers produce linguistic calculations on the lexical uniqueness of the markings. Other R code adapted from Silge and Robinson create sentiment analyses of Melville's marked content. And Voyant generates word clouds and graphs of most frequent word data. The illustrations and figures resulting from the text analyses illustrate Melville's varying forms of engagement in his readings, bringing into particular relief hitherto unanalyzed and under-appreciated aspects of his marginalia. Word frequencies point the way toward ideas and themes that interested him; lexical uniqueness and word-sentiment values of marked passages shed light on the rhetoric and perspectives to which he gravitated. The visualizations of reading evidence bolster conceptions of the writers that influenced him, including Melville's attending to Shakespeare's profundity in concise, philosophically bleak themes and perspectives. The node-level text analyses showed the value of using text analysis techniques to complement close reading, as we were able to show how his marginalia in Shakespeare inspired passages in *Moby-Dick*. Text analysis, therefore, does not always have to be concerned with large swaths of data; it can also enhance the reading of smaller data sets.

Another digital marginalia project, the Keats Library,[60] has encoded Keats's heavily marked copy of Milton's *Paradise Lost* in TEI, but the encoding encounters overlapping hierarchy problems, therefore requiring a 'Trojan Horse' markup scheme of using empty elements with @spanTo pointers to their corresponding @xml:id.[61] Here is how Dr Dan Johnson (Notre Dame) encoded Keats's marking at the beginning of *Paradise Lost*:

```
<pb n='3' xml:id='kpl1.3' facs = '9p290863t9m'/>
<lg>

    <l>OF Man's first disobedience, and the fruit</l>
    <l>Of that forbidden tree, whose mortal taste</l>
    <l>Brought death into the world, and all our woe,</l>
    <l>With loss of Eden, till one greater Man</l>
    <l>Restore us, and regain the blissful seat,</l>
    <l>Sing, heavenly Muse, that <mod rend='su' spanTo='#kpl1.003.0007'/>on the secret top</l>
    <l>Of Oreb, or of Sinai,<anchor xml:id='kpl1.003.0007'/> didst inspire</l>
    <l>That Shepherd, who first taught the chosen seed,</l>
    <l>In the beginning how the heavens and earth</l>
    <l>Rose out of chaos: Or if Sion hill</l>
    <l>Delight thee more, and <mod rend='su' spanTo='#kpl1.003.0012'/>Siloa's brook that flow'd</l>
    <l>Fast by the oracle of God<anchor xml:id='kpl1.003.0012'/>; I thence</l>
    <l>Invoke thy aid to my adventurous song,</l>
    <l><mod rend='lvs' spanTo='#kpl1.003.0015eol'/>That with no middle flight intends to soar</l>
    <l>Above the Aonian mount, while it pursues<anchor xml:id='kpl1.003.0015eol'/></l>
    <l>Things unattempted yet in prose or rhyme.</l>
</lg>
```

This is a workable solution for encoding marginalia in TEI, but unlike the Melville example, the transcription does not match up with the digital facsimile in the interface.[62] How does the descriptive markup facilitate analysis, and what kinds of text analysis could be accomplished? The marginalia encoding above is an impressive way to deal with the shortcomings of overlapping hierarchical markup. It is also not primarily intended for analysis; like many digital projects, it is designed for front-end viewing (users interacting with the finished interface) than it is for the ability to generate analyses within the project, or to produce alternative analyses of the data. Sometimes, as with the Melville example, editors must accept the gains and losses of TEI functionality as against the analysis.

Encoding and analysis in textual editing

As Berry and Fagerjord have observed, "The encoding system [...] need[s] to be carefully planned not only to enable effective data retrieval, but also in order to get data in…"[63] Here they touch on one of the key questions for encoding projects: in designing the markup, are we considering encoding primarily as a means of (a) recording and storing information about our texts; (b) disseminating our research findings to others via a project website; (c) enabling others to produce new analyses based on our data; or (d) some combination of all the above? The way we see the purpose of the encoding will inevitably shape our decisions about what to include and prioritise, and this should ideally be discussed at the initial design stages of a project, as it will influence the underlying framework as much as the web interface.

A similar back-end versus front-end crux shows in the Shelley-Godwin Archive digital edition of the *Frankenstein* Notebooks. An impressive work of documentary editing, the edition was also designed not for text analysis but for viewing on the Web. Again, this makes sense because we would expect most people to browse through a document-based edition on the Web, but there is currently no functionality for gaining access to a single concatenated XML file of all the Notebook transcriptions. If one were available, various text analyses would be made possible, from the more rudimentary sort of element searches (say, identifying all of Percy Shelley's edits to the manuscript and applying linguistic analyses) to stylometric analyses that could tease out the differences between Percy's language and Mary's. The current site, however, does not provide this: one can download all of the project's files (for which they should be commended), but due to the particular aims of that project their file system is almost inaccessible to the average outside researcher. The notebook XML is an index to the individual diplomatic transcriptions with <xi:include> elements that point to other XML files based on each transcription of the manuscript page.[64] Even with a combined XML file, one would still need to validate the XML against their schema in order to transform (or run analyses of) the XML, which puts up another barrier for the digital researcher outside of the project. This suggests that a workflow designed at once for valid TEI encoding and for text analysis should (regardless of the filing system and site architecture) at least make available a downloadable single XML file (or directory of XML files) amenable to analysis by others. A workflow designed with both encoding and analysis in mind could also make text analysis tools available on the front-end, but that would be more expensive than simply making available pared-down XML files. These questions ultimately come down to workflow design, and the efficiency of a researcher's workflow within a team.

At the risk of stating the obvious, the ethos of collaboration and teamwork in digital humanities should be applicable to digital editing projects. No one researcher will be able to do all the transcriptions, create a computational pipeline, and design a database and website—a selected team of professionals with complementary skills will bring all those pieces together. Yet it is crucial that digital editors create a workflow that includes encoding—ideally following TEI standards—while also keeping in mind how other digital researchers might want to access the project data for data mining and analysis.

One of the present difficulties is that projects rarely elucidate the decisions they made about workflow, and whether they saw text or data analysis as a crucial part of their documentation. Dunn has observed that workflows in arts and humanities 'are highly individual, often informal, and cannot be easily shared or reproduced.'[65] We would recommend that however individual a project's workflow might be, it is worth sharing the decision-making process as part of that project's outputs. The scarcity of such documentation is undoubtedly a barrier to creating improved processes through an understanding of the issues projects have encountered, how they have resolved them, what their priorities have been, and, if possible, what effects their decisions have had within and even beyond the project. Commitment to describing workflow might best be made at the point of applying for funding, as otherwise there can be a tendency to view workflow documentation as an output that fits firmly under the 'ideal world' umbrella, rather than being considered an important part of the project's outcomes.

Christopher Ohge and Charlotte Tupman

Conclusion: Encoding as analysis

With the above in mind, we set out here a suggested workflow for an encoding project that will promote analysis and knowledge production from the text. As noted, Flanders and her team at the Women Writers project published a guide that we consider highly effective and to which we are suggesting some additions and reordering rather than replacements.[66] Flanders and her collaborators set out seven main steps:

- **Planning your project**: representation of text, details of transcription and encoding, editorial method, and additional information such as glosses;
- **Project analysis**: duration of project, reasoning for encoding, editorial philosophy, considerations of audience, team, and how users will access text;
- **Document analysis**: similarities and differences amongst documents, genre, chronology, language, physical support, and legibility;
- **Transcription and markup**: digitising the text, encoding methods including automated markup, creation of template, stylesheet development;
- **Error checking**: proofreading for typographical errors and encoding errors, using tools and/or by hand;
- **Post-processing**: automated encoding, discovery and correction of errors, transformations to other formats for publication and archiving;
- **Documentation:** schema, encoding practices, editorial practices, tools and procedures.

While this is not quite a step-by-step guide, as several areas overlap and it is not always possible to divide the tasks quite so neatly, the main areas of the work of an encoding project are represented here. To this we would add an evaluation of text analysis between 'Document analysis' and 'Transcription and markup': in other words, after you have analysed your documents but before actually beginning your markup, it would be worthwhile to consider the types of text analysis that would be relevant, and how you could enable such analysis in the way you encode your texts. This could even include testing some of the available open source tools for text analysis.

We would also recommend that documentation be considered not as a separate step, but as an integral part of each stage. Many of us have encountered projects on which the documentation is left until the end and time runs out. To avoid this, it would be worth documenting the stages of the project, and the decisions made, as they happen. Our suggested workflow would, then, look more like this:

- **Planning your project + documentation**
- **Project analysis + documentation**
- **Document analysis + documentation**
- **Text analysis evaluation + documentation**
- **Transcription and markup + documentation**
- **Error checking + documentation**
- **Post-processing + documentation**

This that the project wants to optimise its encoded materials for text analysis by others, rather than undertaking the text analysis; if the latter, discussion should be included in the 'Planning your project phase' and the task itself following the markup phase.

The same principles that call for a standardised language of documentary editing in Classics should easily transfer to documents in modern literature. Yet, as Tanselle showed in his seminal article 'The Editing of

Encoding and analysis in textual editing

Historical Documents,' it is far from true that that has consistently happened:[67] for various reasons faithfulness and diplomacy can give way to modifications of original documents in the name of readability. Yet another problem with documentary editions is how to optimise the information in documents that are difficult to read in print.

A palpable challenge in the age of computers is the temptation to 'make it new'. This modernist doctrine did not advocate throwing out the old and coming up with something entirely new. The 'new' should be informed by, and in response to, tradition, as T. S. Eliot memorably put it in 'Tradition and the Individual Talent'. Textual editing is simply doing more with the aid of computers to guide research and reading practices. One way in which digital methodology and text analysis is in a sense 'new' is that it goes beyond texts into other data of culture. With the advent of digital curation, editions of material culture can be encoded and analysed for the benefit of literary culture and vice versa.

Any project will have its share of false starts and ill-judged decisions that lead to re-doing some of the work, and these 'failures' are of course helpful to document in themselves. But as the examples above suggest, old notions of print-based workflow stand in the way of an appropriate computational pipeline that would make analytically-informed, machine-readable documents complement text analysis tools that provide new modes of reading evidence. Part of the continuation of the print-based model is due to a belief that somehow print books are more lasting, that they do not exist in some immaterial form or ethereal cloud. But even digital projects rely on physical things, and all things decay. A print-out of an XML file will be more useful to future historians than printed books. Why? XML files include more information about a text—or group of texts—that make up an edition. As Greg Crane has pointed out, we are still in the incunabula phase of digital editions.[68] If that is true, it would be smarter to focus less on layered web applications and more on curating the underlying XML data—data which can be shared and used for digital text analysis to create new modes of reading and critical interpretation.

Notes

1 So said Greg Crane in his 2010 article 'Give us Editors! Re-Inventing the Edition and Re-thinking the Humanities', in J. McGann (ed.), *Online Humanities Scholarship: The Shape of Things to Come. Proceedings of the Mellon Foundation Online Humanities Conference at the University of Virginia, March 26-28, 2010* (pp. 81–97). Retrieved from http://cnx.org/content/col11199/1.1/ Editing is also 'messy, destabilizing, and above all, dynamic', Crane adds (p. 83).

2 Pierazzo, E. (2015). *Digital Scholarly Editing: Theories, Models, Methods.* Farnham, Surrey: Ashgate: 77.

3 Pierazzo 2015, pp. 88–90. Pierazzo surveys the 'epistemic virtues' that are part of textual scholarship ('truth-to-nature', 'objectivity' and 'trained judgment', as supplied by Daston and Galison), and what we are suggesting here is an alternative epistemology of pragmatism, or a success-in-action model that privileges coherence warranted assertibility in textual claims.

4 Quoted in Blackburn 2017, p. 63.

5 This was the subject of a panel at the 2012 Digital Humanities conference by Syd Bauman, David Hoover, Karina van Dalen-Oskam and Wendell Piez, Text Analysis Meets Text Encoding: 'Recent DH conferences have comprised, in addition to other activities, two distinct sub-conferences – one focusing on text encoding in general and TEI in particular, and the other on text analysis, authorship attribution, and stylistics. The separation between the two is so extreme that their participants often meet only at breaks and social events.' Given the fact that many practitioners of text analysis tend to be interested in txt files and very large data sets, it makes some sense that they would be less interested in the 'small data' of editions. Retrieved from http://www.dh2012.uni-hamburg.de/conference/programme/abstracts/text-analysis-meets-text-encoding.1.html

6 Burrows, J.F. (2004). Textual Analysis. In S. Schreibman, R. Siemens, J. Unsworth (Eds.), *A Companion to Digital Humanities.* Oxford: Blackwell. Retrieved from http://www.digitalhumanities.org/companion/. Burrows's 1987 study of Jane Austen, *Computation into Criticism.* Oxford: Oxford University Press, is still one of the finest examples of text analysis. Another recent one is Matthew Jockers's *Macroanalysis* (Urbana-Champaign and Chicago: University of Illinois Press 2013).

7 The Guidelines can be found at https://www.mla.org/Resources/Research/Surveys-Reports-and-Other-Documents/Publishing-and-Scholarship/Reports-from-the-MLA-Committee-on-Scholarly-Editions/Guidelines-for-Editors-of-Scholarly-Editions#editor. Of interest too is the MLA's recent white paper on electronic editions, 'MLA Statement on the Scholarly Edition in the Digital Age', https://www.mla.org/content/download/52050/1810116/rptCSE16.pdf. The words 'text analysis and data mining' do appear at the very end of the white paper, but only in the context of making print editions available online for such tasks, rather than being an essential aspect of the encoding process.

8 Andrews, T. (2013). The Third Way: Philology and Critical Edition in the Digital Age. *Variants,* 10, 61–76.

9 For more on analytic and interpretive encoding, see Chapter 17 of the *TEI Guidelines.* Retrieved from https://www.tei-c.org/release/doc/tei-p5-doc/en/html/AI.html.

10 The best are Philip Gaskell's *A New Introduction to Bibliography* (Oak Knoll, 1978), David Greetham's *Textual Scholarship: An Introduction* (Garland, 1994), and William Proctor Williams and Craig S. Abbott's *An Introduction to Bibliographical and Textual Studies* (1999).

11 Tanselle, G. Thomas. (1995). Varieties of Scholarly Editing. In D. Greetham (Ed.), *Scholarly Editing: A Guide to Research.* New York: Modern Language Association. 9–32: p. 9.

12 Bryant, J. (2002). *The Fluid Text.* Ann Arbor: University of Michigan Press.

13 See Tanselle's 'Varieties', pp. 18–22; also Suarez and Woudhuysen.

14 Greetham, D. (2013). A History of Textual Scholarship. In N. Fraistat & J. Flanders (Eds.), *Cambridge Companion to Textual Scholarship.* Cambridge: Cambridge University Press (pp. 16–41): p. 19.

15 McKenzie, D.F. (1999). *Bibliography and the Sociology of Texts.* Cambridge: Cambridge University Press; McGann, J. (1992). *A Critique of Textual Criticism* (Charlottesville: University of Virginia Press).

16 Siemens, R. (2016). Communities of practice, the methodological commons, and digital self-determination in the Humanities. *Digital Studies/le Champ Numérique.* doi: http://doi.org/10.16995/dscn.31

17 Murphy, J.Stephen (2008). Death of the Editor. *Essays in Criticism* 58.4, 289–310. p. 294

18 Ricks, C. (1981). In Theory. *London Review of Books* 3.7, 16 April 1981: 3–6.

29 Housman, A.E. (1921). The Application of Thought to Textual Criticism, originally published in *Proceedings of the Classical Association* 18, 68–69, and reprinted in Keleman, E. (2008). *Textual Editing and Criticism: An Introduction.* New York: Norton.

20 Johnson, S. Proposals for printing by subscription the dramatic works of William Shakespeare, corrected and illustrated by Samuel Johnson. In W. K. Wimsatt, Jr. (Ed.), (1960). *Samuel Johnson on Shakespeare.* New York: Hill and Wang, 19–20.

21 Pierazzo, E. (2015). *Digital Scholarly Editing: Theories, Models, Methods.* Farnham, Surrey: Ashgate: p. 15.

22 Daniels, J. & Thistlethwaite, P. (2016). *Being a Scholar in the Digital Era. Transforming Scholarly Practice for the Public Good.* Bristol: Policy Press. p. 9.

23 Pragmatism is not just a word that encompasses an attitude toward practice and practical success in action; it is also a logic that facilitates 'a method for the analysis of concepts' (Peirce, 'A Definition of Pragmatism,' p. 56). It bears reminding that later in the same piece (p. 57) he emphasises, 'Thinking is a kind of action, and reasoning is a kind of deliberate action.'

24 Tim Berners-Lee (2007). Linked Data. Retrieved from https://www.w3.org/DesignIssues/LinkedData.html

25 Fraistat, N. & Flanders, J. (2013). Introduction. In N. Fraistat & J. Flanders (Eds.), *Cambridge Companion to Textual Scholarship.* Cambridge: Cambridge University Press, pp. 13–14.

26 For more on this, see Bauman, S. (2008). Freedom to constrain: where does attribute constraint come from, mommy? Presented at Balisage: The Markup Conference 2008, Montréal, Canada, August 12–15, 2008. In *Proceedings of Balisage: The Markup Conference 2008. Balisage Series on Markup Technologies*, vol. 1. doi:10.4242/BalisageVol1.Bauman01

27 This debate is nicely summarised in Pierazzo 2015, pp. 78–9.

28 The obvious utility of this can be seen in the Melville Electronic Library's 'fluid-text' edition of *Billy Budd, Sailor,* which is based on Melville's final and uncompleted manuscript of his novella. The edition replaces the genetic symbols used by its print predecessor with TEI encoding that not only gives all of the evidence of the manuscript's genesis but also matches directly to the facsimile image of the surviving manuscript. It also has three reading views: a diplomatic transcription, a 'base' text that renders the revised manuscript, and a lightly edited reading text. Using text analysis, one could identify patterns, topics and other important aspects of the genetic data from this document-based text of *Billy Budd,* and an additional interface called 'revision narratives' guides the reader through the variants. The developers on the project are aiming to make a single, concatenated XML file available for researchers who might want to perform these kinds of analyses. See also Ohge, 'Melville Incomplete,' which surveys the gains of the MEL *Billy Budd* over its print predecessors.

29 Robinson, P. (2013). Toward a Theory of Digital Editions. *The Journal of the European Society for Textual Scholarship* 10, 126–127. doi: https://doi.org/10.1163/9789401209021_009

Encoding and analysis in textual editing

30 For the module's coursepack, see http://www.wwp.northeastern.edu/outreach/seminars/uvic_advanced_2015/venue/renear_mcgann.pdf (particularly pages 6 and 11–12).

31 For more on how to implement text analysis strategies with Voyant Tools, see Geoffrey Rockwell and Stéfan Sinclair's *Hermeneutica* (MIT Press, 2016; companion at http://hermeneuti.ca/). Jockers's *Text Analysis in R for Students of Literature* (Springer, 2014) is currently the best introduction to R programming for literary projects. Another very useful book is Julia Silge and David Robinson's *Text Mining with R: A Tidy Approach* (available online at https://www.tidytextmining.com/). The *Programming Historian* (https://programminghistorian.org/) also features excellent tutorials on AntConc, Python and R, among many other computing topics.). The *Programming Historian* (https://programminghistorian.org/) also features excellent tutorials on AntConc, Python and R, among many other computing topics.

32 The current Roma tool is available at https://roma.tei-c.org/. Roma JS code can be accessed at https://github.com/TEIC/romajs.

33 See Cummings, J. (2014). The Compromises and Flexibility of TEI Customisation. In C. Mills, M. Pidd & E. Ward. *Proceedings of the Digital Humanities Congress 2012*. Studies in the Digital Humanities. Sheffield: The Digital Humanities Institute. Available online at: https://www.dhi.ac.uk/openbook/chapter/dhc2012-cummings.

34 https://sourceforge.net/p/epidoc/wiki/Home/ For a survey of EpiDoc and its aims, see H. Cayless et al., "Epigraphy in 2017", *Digital Humanities Quarterly* 3.1 (2009). Available online at: http://digitalhumanities.org/dhq/vol/3/1/000030/000030.html

35 Elliott, T., Bodard, G., Mylonas, E., Stoyanova, S., Tupman, C., Vanderbilt, S. et al. (2007-2017). EpiDoc Guidelines: Ancient documents in TEI XML (Version 9). Available: http://www.stoa.org/epidoc/gl/latest/.

36 MARKUP list: https://lsv.uky.edu/scripts/wa.exe?A0=MARKUP

37 Women Writers Project (1996–2016). Northeastern University. Retrieved from http://www.wwp.northeastern.edu/

38 Women Writers Project Guide to Scholarly Text Encoding. (2007). Brown University Women Writers Project. Retrieved from http://wwp.neu.edu/research/publications/guide/index.html

39 For an introduction to epigraphy and the work of an epigrapher, see John Bodel's chapter 'Epigraphy and the Ancient Historian' in J. Bodel (Ed.), (2001). *Epigraphic Evidence. Ancient History from Inscriptions*. London and New York: Routledge (pp. 1–56).

40 Bodard, G. & Stoyanova, S. (2016). Epigraphers and Encoders: Strategies for Teaching and Learning Digital Epigraphy. In G. Bodard and M. Romanello (Eds.), *Digital Classics Outside the Echo-Chamber.* London: Ubiquity Press (pp. 51–68): 59. doi: https://doi.org/10.5334/bat

41 Mytum, H. & Peterson, J.R. (2018). The Application of Reflectance Transformation Imaging (RTI) in Historical Archaeology. *Historical Archaeology* 52: 489–503.

42 Krummrey, H. & Panciera, S. (1980). Criteri di edizione e segni diacritici. *Tituli* 2, 205–215; Panciera, S. (2006). I segni diacritici: riflessioni e proposte. In S. Panciera, *Epigrafi, Epigrafia, Epigrafisti. Scritti vari editi e inediti (1956–2005) con note complementari e indici Vol. II.* Roma: Edizioni Quasar. (pp. 1711–1717). The EpiDoc Guidelines have Leiden equivalence as a minimum, and in fact can be used to encode much greater detail than is permitted by the Leiden conventions.

43 Elliott, T., Bodard, G., Mylonas, E., Stoyanova, S., Tupman, C., Vanderbilt, S. et al. (2007–2017). EpiDoc Guidelines: Ancient documents in TEI XML (Version 9). Available: http://www.stoa.org/epidoc/gl/latest/.

44 MARKUP list: https://lsv.uky.edu/scripts/wa.exe?A0=MARKUP

45 EpiDoc training workshops: https://wiki.digitalclassicist.org/EpiDoc_Summer_School

46 The first volume to be produced by the *Corpus Inscriptionum Latinarum* (*CIL*) project under Theodor Mommsen was published in 1863. To date *CIL* encompasses some 17 volumes in 70 parts. *Inscriptiones Graecae* (*IG*) is a continuation of the original *Corpus Inscriptionum Graecum* directed by August Böckh. To date it has published 49 fascicules.

47 Bodard, G. & Stoyanova, S. (2016): 55.

48 EpiDoc Front End Services. Retrieved from https://github.com/EpiDoc/EFES

49 Pietro Liuzzo's eXist-db test app: https://github.com/EpiDoc/OEDUc

50 Bodard, G. & Stoyanova, S. (2016): 55.

51 Voyant Tools. Retrieved from https://voyant-tools.org/

52 AntConc. Retrieved from https://www.laurenceanthony.net/software/antconc/

53 Pelagios Commons. Retrieved from http://commons.pelagios.org/

54 Pelagios' Recogito tool for semantic annotation, for instance: https://recogito.pelagios.org/

55 Papyri.info. Retrieved from http://papyri.info/

56 The most recent print edition, edited by R.A. Foakes and R.T. Rickert, is largely an updating of W.W. Greg's 1904 London edition (*Henslowe's Diary*, by Philip Henslowe, 2nd ed. Cambridge: Cambridge University Press, 2002). Our thanks go to Dr Mao for sharing his XML on his project-in-progress.

57 The facsimiles of the Henslowe diary are available at http://www.henslowe-alleyn.org.uk/essays/henslowediary.html.

58 By 'node-level' we mean either XML elements (tags) or specific attribute values within those tags. In R, for example, one can do this with the XML library, which has the necessary functions for parsing XML documents (https://cran.r-project.org/web/packages/XML/index.html). MMO made significant use of the XML library package in R.

59 See Ohge, C. & Olsen-Smith, S. Digital Text Analysis at *Melville's Marginalia Online*, and Ohge, C., Olsen-Smith, S. & Barney Smith, E. (2018). "At the Axis of Reality": Melville's Marginalia in *Dramatic Works of William Shakespeare*. *Leviathan: A Journal of Melville Studies* 20.2: 1–16, 37–67.

60 Keats Library. Retrieved from http://keatslibrary.org/paradise-lost/

61 Trojan Horse markup uses empty elements to indicate the start and end of regions that cannot be contained within XML content elements. See Sperberg-McQueen's recent demonstration of 'Trojan Horse' markup at the 2018 Balisage markup conference: Sperberg-McQueen, M. (2018). Representing concurrent document structures using Trojan Horse markup. In *Proceedings of Balisage: The Markup conference 2018*. Balisage Series on Markup Technologies, vol. 21. doi: https://doi.org/10.4242/BalisageVol21.Sperberg-McQueen01

62 For a good overview of the problems of encoding marginalia in TEI, see Estill, L. (2016). Encoding the Edge: Manuscript Marginalia and the TEI. *Digital Literary Studies*, 1.1. doi:

63 Berry, D.M. & Fagerjord, A. (2017). *Digital Humanities. Knowledge and Critique in a Digital Age*. Cambridge: Wiley: 52.

64 For more on using <xi:include> for stand-off markup, see Chapter 16 of the *TEI Guidelines*. Retrieved from http://www.tei-c.org/release/doc/tei-p5-doc/en/html/SA.html#SASO

65 Dunn, S. (2016). Dealing with the Complexity Deluge. VREs in the Arts and Humanities. *Library Hi Tech* 27, 205–216.

66 Women Writers Project Guide to Scholarly Text Encoding. (2007). Brown University Women Writers Project. Retrieved from http://wwp.neu.edu/research/publications/guide/index.html

67 Tanselle, G.T. (1978). The Editing of Historical Documents *Studies in Bibliography*, 31, 1–56.

68 Crane. G. (2010): 81. For a more sustained treatment of some of these issues, see Cummings, J. (2018). 'A world of difference: Myths and misconceptions about the TEI', *Digital Scholarship in the Humanities*. doi: https://doi.org/10.1093/llc/fqy071

References

Andrews, T. (2013). The Third Way: Philology and Critical Edition in the Digital Age. *Variants*, *10*, 61–76.

Bauman, S. (2008). Freedom to Constrain: where does attribute constraint come from, mommy? Presented at Balisage: The Markup Conference 2008, Montréal, Canada, August 12–15, 2008. In *Proceedings of Balisage: The Markup Conference 2008. Balisage Series on Markup Technologies*, vol. 1. doi:10.4242/BalisageVol1.Bauman01

Bauman, S., Hoover, D., van Dalen-Oskam, K. & Piez, W. (2012). Text Analysis Meets Text Encoding. *DH2012 Book of Abstracts*. Retrieved from http://www.dh2012.uni-hamburg.de/conference/programme/abstracts/text-analysis-meets-text-encoding.1.html

Berners-Lee, T. (2007). Linked Data. Retrieved from https://www.w3.org/DesignIssues/LinkedData.html

Berry, D. M. & Fagerjord, A. (2017). *Digital Humanities. Knowledge and Critique in a Digital Age*. Cambridge: Wiley.

Blackburn, S. (2017). *Truth*. London: Profile Books.

Bodard, G. & Stoyanova, S. (2016). Epigraphers and Encoders: Strategies for Teaching and Learning Digital Epigraphy. In G. Bodard and M. Romanello (Eds.), *Digital Classics Outside the Echo-Chamber*. London: Ubiquity Press (pp. 51–68): 59. doi: https://doi.org/10.5334/bat

Bodel, J. (Ed.). (2001). *Epigraphic Evidence. Ancient History from Inscriptions*. London and New York: Routledge.

Bryant, J. (2002). *The Fluid Text*. Ann Arbor: University of Michigan Press.

Bryant, J., Kelley, W., & Ohge, C. (Eds.). (2019). Fluid-text edition of *Billy Budd, Sailor*. Melville Electronic Library. Retrieved from https://melville.electroniclibrary.org/versions-of-billy-budd.html

Burrows, J. F. (1987). *Computation into Criticism*. Oxford: Oxford University Press.

Burrows, J. F. (2004). Textual Analysis. In S. Schreibman, R. Siemens, J. Unsworth (Eds.), *A Companion to Digital Humanities*. Oxford: Blackwell. Retrieved from http://www.digitalhumanities.org/companion/

Cayless, H., Roueché, C., Elliott, T. & Bodard, G. (2009). Epigraphy in 2017. *Digital Humanities Quarterly* 3(1). Retrieved from http://digitalhumanities.org/dhq/vol/3/1/000030/000030.html

Crane, G. (2010). Give us Editors! Re-Inventing the Edition and Re-thinking the Humanities. In J. McGann (Ed.), *Online Humanities Scholarship: The Shape of Things to Come. Proceedings of the Mellon Foundation Online Humanities Conference at the University of Virginia*, March 26–28, 2010 (pp. 81–97). Retrieved from http://cnx.org/content/col11199/1.1/

Encoding and analysis in textual editing

Cummings, J. (2014). The Compromises and Flexibility of TEI Customisation. In C. Mills, M. Pidd & E. Ward. *Proceedings of the Digital Humanities Congress 2012*. Studies in the Digital Humanities. Sheffield: The Digital Humanities Institute. Retrieved from https://www.dhi.ac.uk/openbook/chapter/dhc2012-cummings

Daniels, J. & Thistlethwaite, P. (2016). *Being a Scholar in the Digital Era. Transforming Scholarly Practice for the Public Good*. Bristol: Policy Press

Dunn, S. (2016). Dealing with the Complexity Deluge. VREs in the Arts and Humanities. *Library Hi Tech*, 27, 205–216.

Elliott, T., Bodard, G., Mylonas, E., Stoyanova, S., Tupman, C., Vanderbilt, S. et al. (2007–2017). *EpiDoc Guidelines: Ancient documents in TEI XML* (Version 9). Retrieved from http://www.stoa.org/epidoc/gl/latest/

EpiDoc Front End Services. Retrieved from https://github.com/EpiDoc/EFES

Estill, L. (2016). Encoding the Edge: Manuscript Marginalia and the TEI. *Digital Literary Studies*, *1*(1). doi: https://doi.org/10.18113/P8dls115971

Foakes, R. A. & Rickert, R. T. (Eds.). (2002). *Henslowe's Diary*. 2nd ed. Cambridge: Cambridge University Press.

Fraistat, N. & Flanders, J. (Eds.). (2013). *Cambridge Companion to Textual Scholarship*. Cambridge: Cambridge University Press.

Gaskell, P. (1978). *A New Introduction to Bibliography*. New Castle, Delaware and Winchester : Oak Knoll.

Greetham, D. (1994). *Textual Scholarship: An Introduction*. New York: Garland.

Greetham, D. (2013). A History of Textual Scholarship. In N. Fraistat & J. Flanders (Eds.), *Cambridge Companion to Textual Scholarship*. Cambridge: Cambridge University Press (pp. 16–41): p. 19.

Housman, A. E. (1921). The Application of Thought to Textual Criticism. *Proceedings of the Classical Association*, *18*, 68–69, reprinted in Keleman, E. (2008). *Textual Editing and Criticism: An Introduction*. New York : Norton.

James, W. (1907). *Pragmatism*. New York: Longmans, Green & Co.

Jockers, M. (2013). *Macroanalysis*. Urbana-Champaign and Chicago: University of Illinois Press.

Jockers, M. (2014). *Text Analysis in R for Students of Literature*. New York: Springer.

Keats Library. Retrieved from http://keatslibrary.org/paradise-lost/

Krummrey, H. & Panciera, S. (1980). Criteri di edizione e segni diacritici. *Tituli 2*, 205–215.

McGann, J. (1992). *A Critique of Textual Criticism*. Charlottesville: University of Virginia Press.

McKenzie, D. F. (1999). *Bibliography and the Sociology of Texts*. Cambridge: Cambridge University Press.

Modern Language Association Committee on Scholarly Editions. (2016). *MLA Statement on the Scholarly Edition in the Digital Age*. Retrieved from https://www.mla.org/content/download/52050/1810116/rptCSE16.pdf

Murphy, J. S. (2008). Death of the Editor. *Essays in Criticism 58*(4), 289–310.

Mytum, H. & Peterson, J.R. (2018). The Application of Reflectance Transformation Imaging (RTI) in Historical Archaeology. *Historical Archaeology*, *52*, 489–503.

Ohge, C. (2019). Melville Incomplete. *American Literary History*, *31*(1), 139–150.

Ohge, C. & Olsen-Smith, S. (2018). Computation and Digital Text Analysis at Melville's Marginalia Online. *Leviathan: A Journal of Melville Studies*, *20*(2), 1–16.

Ohge, C., Olsen-Smith, S. & Barney Smith, E. (2018). "At the Axis of Reality": Melville's Marginalia in *Dramatic Works of William Shakespeare*. *Leviathan: A Journal of Melville Studies*, *20*(2), 37–67.

Panciera, S. (2006). I segni diacritici: riflessioni e proposte. In S. Panceira, *Epigrafi, Epigrafia, Epigrafisti. Scritti vari editi e inediti (1956-2005) con note complementari e indici Vol. II*. Roma: Edizioni Quasar. (pp. 1711–1717).

Peirce, C. S. (1998). How to Make our Ideas Clear. In *Chance, Love, and Logic*. Lincoln: Bison Books.

Peirce, C. S. (1997). A Definition of Pragmatism. In *Pragmatism: A Reader*. Ed. Louis Menand. New York: Vintage.

Pierazzo, E. (2015). *Digital Scholarly Editing: Theories, Models, Methods*. Farnham, Surrey: Ashgate.

Proctor Williams, W. & Abbott, C. S. (1999). *An Introduction to Bibliographical and Textual Studies*. New York: Modern Language Association of America.

Programming Historian. Retrieved from https://programminghistorian.org/

Ricks, C. (1981, April). In Theory. *London Review of Books*, *3*(7), 3–6.

Robinson, P. (2013). Toward a Theory of Digital Editions. *The Journal of the European Society for Textual Scholarship*, *10*, 126–27. doi: https://doi.org/10.1163/9789401209021_009

Rockwell, G. & Sinclair, S. (2016). *Hermeneutica*. Cambridge: MIT Press.

Siemens, R. (2016). Communities of Practice, the Methodological Commons, and Digital Self-Determination in the Humanities. *Digital Studies/le Champ Numérique*. doi: http://doi.org/10.16995/dscn.31

Silge, J. & Robinson, D. (2020) *Text Mining with R: A Tidy Approach*. Sebastopol: O'Reilly Media. Also available online, retrieved from https://www.tidytextmining.com/

Sperberg-McQueen, M. (2018). Representing concurrent document structures using Trojan Horse markup. In *Proceedings of Balisage: The Markup conference 2018. Balisage Series on Markup Technologies*, *21*. doi: https://doi.org/10.4242/BalisageVol21.Sperberg-McQueen01

Suarez, S. J. & H. R. Woudhuysen. (2010). *The Oxford Companion to the Book*. Oxford: Oxford University Press. Retrieved from https://www.oxfordreference.com/view/10.1093/acref/9780198606536.001.0001/acref-9780198606536-e-3354

Tanselle, G. T. (1978). The Editing of Historical Documents. *Studies in Bibliography, 31,* 1–56.

Tanselle, G. T. (1995). Varieties of Scholarly Editing. In D. Greetham (Ed.), *Scholarly Editing: A Guide to Research.* New York: Modern Language Association. 9–32.

The TEI Guidelines for Electronic Text Encoding and Interchange. Retrieved from https://www.tei-c.org/release/doc/tei-p5-doc/en/html/AI.html

Wimsatt, W. K. Jr. (Ed.), (1960). *Samuel Johnson on Shakespeare.* New York: Hill and Wang.

Women Writers Project (1996–2016). Northeastern University. Retrieved from http://www.wwp.northeastern.edu/

Women Writers Project Guide to Scholarly Text Encoding. (2007). Women Writers Project, Northeastern University. Retrieved from http://wwp.neu.edu/research/publications/guide/index.html

18

OPENING THE 'BLACK BOX' OF DIGITAL CULTURAL HERITAGE PROCESSES

Feminist digital humanities and critical heritage studies

Hannah Smyth, Julianne Nyhan and Andrew Flinn

18.1 Introduction

"Why are the Digital Humanities so white?" asked McPherson in 2012 to draw attention to how little theorised questions of race and other 'modes of difference' are in the field of digital humanities (McPherson 2012 p.139). Humanities computing, whence digital humanities (DH) emanated, was predominately text-oriented in method and content (see e.g. Oakman). The DH that emerged c.2004 would come to be described as a 'big tent' (Pannapacker 2011) that enfolded a diverse range of methods and content, including humanistic fabrication, gaming and augmented reality (Jones 2014). Despite the field's ostensible widening of scope (cf. Prescott 2012, interventions like McPherson's foregrounded DH's impoverished understandings of how frameworks like race, gender and power intersect to operate on and through the computational tools, resources and infrastructures that DH builds and uses. Key to this also are the DH methodologies and methods that (re)produce these frameworks. McPherson's perspectives were amplified in other writings, like those of Bianco and Liu. The latter asked 'where is the cultural criticism in digital humanities?' (Liu 2012). Bianco argued that DH represents a regression to a retrograde humanities that has not yet integrated:

> '…cultural and critical critique; political, institutional, and governmental analyses; feminism, critical race, postcolonial, queer and affect studies; biopolitics; critical science and technology studies' experimental methodologies; social theory; and, certainly, philosophical inquiry into the ontic and ontological.' (Bianco 2012 p.101).

And yet, green shoots can be noticed. A growing body of work is critiquing and challenging the implicit and explicit power dynamics that operationalise difference as a justification for the ascendency of one social group over another in the making and use of digital tools and resources (e.g. Risam 2018). Powerful arguments for why such perspectives matter, and should not simply be relegated to those who choose to 'yack' instead of 'hack'—as the albeit contested divisions between making and thinking in DH have been categorised—are also being made:

> "…the difficulties we encounter in knitting together our discussions of race (or other modes of difference) with our technological productions within the digital humanities (or in our studies of code) are actually an effect of the very designs of our technological systems, designs that emerged in post-World War II computational cultural" (McPherson 2012 p.140).

Hannah Smyth, Julianne Nyhan and Andrew Flinn

In line with the potential of critical theory, this body of work is not only critiquing such power dynamics, it is also seeking to redress. FemTechNet, for example, is "an international movement of feminist thinkers, researchers, writers, teachers, artists, professors, librarians, mentors, organizers and activists sharing resources and engaging in activities that demonstrate connected feminist thinking about technology and innovation" (FemTechNet 2019). Their interventions include the "Distributive Open Collaborative Course", a feminist re-thinking and re-implementation of the "Massive Online Online Course" (MOOC) format (Juhasz & Balsamo 2012). Moreover, building on the scholarship of women's studies, it is increasingly recognised that intersectionality should be a key tenet of methodology, analysis and interpretation in doing critical feminist DH because it is 'ethically and intellectually rich' (Ross 2018, p.220).

In this chapter we seek to draw attention to the resonances that exist between the field of Critical Heritage Studies (CHS) and Feminist Digital Humanities. In doing so we wish to also provoke new ways of thinking about methodological approaches, and about the nature of the 'research method' itself as a practice bound up in the same codifying structures we attempt to dismantle. Critical Heritage Studies is concerned with the power and knowledge systems at work in the relationships between people and heritage (Smith 2006, p.14). It is a rebuke to conventional heritage and heritage discourse, which is instead 'pluralising,' 'consciously post-Western,' and which aspires to be 'post-disciplinary' (Ashworth et al 2007; Winter 2013, p.451). Despite the centrality of heritage to the fields of Digital Humanities and Critical Heritage Studies they have largely proceeded in isolation of each other. Accordingly, Lutz has asked "In what ways can concepts of critical heritage studies ›animate‹ debates in digital humanities and vice versa to highlight the specific changes produced by the digital in the context of cultural heritage and memory work?" (Lutz 2017, p.17). We propose that an interlacing of the approaches of these fields to studies of the gendering of digital cultural heritage[1] resources would offer an important step forward.

Many scholars in Digital Humanities and Critical Heritage Studies are building on these critical debates in their fields to approach research in new ways. Nonetheless, we indicate in this chapter how normative methodologies and their processes are themselves a Western construct that further entrench exclusory, masculine paradigms that may limit creative potential and the exploration of epistemic alternatives. Yet we argue that methodologies may operate to construct but also *deconstruct* paradigmatic value systems. We should therefore appreciate their value as a critical intervention, as well as the value systems that created them.

Below we aim to give an overview of the scholarship on gender and digital humanities, and gender and heritage. We then discuss prominent trends in feminist digital humanities scholarship before discussing gender in relation to the foundational tenets of critical heritage studies. Observing that Digital Humanities and Critical Heritage Studies have recently turned to questions of how gender is performed by and through digital heritage, we propose that this suggests a fruitful way to bridge these currently largely unconnected fields. Finally, we discuss the role of oral history in undertaking research that could lead to deeper insights into gendering of digital cultural heritage as both product and process, as well as the ways in which it can and has been used in feminist research praxis. In this chapter, we focus primarily on feminist perspectives while recognising that the study of masculinity and masculine culture, along with gender fluidity and non-conformity, should also form part of enquiries into gender, digital humanities and digital cultural heritage.

18.2 Gender and digital humanities

In this section we discuss gender in the context of technology and digital humanities before giving an overview of recent Feminist Digital Humanities scholarship.

Gender is a cultural matrix that defines masculinity and femininity as separate and incommensurate (Abbate 2012, p. 3). Performances of masculinity and femininity are socially and culturally constructed and intersect with other power structures but are not contingent on biological sex. They are produced and re-produced by normative social roles and other dynamics between people and within society

Opening the 'black box'

(Butler 1999). Along with factors like race and class, purported gender differences and characteristics can be called on to justify discrepancies of power and privilege, the distribution of labour and access to economies of opportunity and influence among social groups.

The scholarship of Feminist Technology Studies has shown technology to be a central stage for the performance and even ratification of gender (e.g. Faulkner and Arnold 1985). With regard to the history of computing, for example, gendered labour segregation confined many women to the lowest-ranking posts and resulted in the devaluing and overlooking of their work (e.g. Light 1999; Abbate 2012). Likewise, gender stereotypes can influence what counts as technology (e.g. Cockburn and Ormrod 1993). In early computing projects, the work assigned to women typically covered computer operation and programming (Hicks 2017), which was seen as lower in status and less difficult than the hardware-oriented work done by men (Light 1999). In other words, technology is not neutral but has been created "in the interests of particular social groups, and against the interests of others" (Hamnett et al 1989, p.181). Computing in particular is "an explicitly hegemonic project built on labour categories designed to perpetuate particular forms of class status" (Hicks 2017 p.6).

Looking beyond computing, gender dynamics converge on DH via diverse processes, from the field's historical genealogies to the sociocultural dynamics that frame the contexts in which it is undertaken. For example, the library and archive sector with which DH is so connected is synonymous with feminised labour (Dean 2015; Caswell 2016). This suggests that much can be gained from studying digital resources, workflows and infrastructures as sites of power, that both inflect and are inflected by gender. Feminist Digital Humanities critiques need not be limited to the digital resource as it is made available through an interface, or via its underlying code or generative algorithms, but can extend to the histories, actors, organizations, and circumstances that participated in or shaped the elaboration of a resource (see Wernimont 2013).

Feminist DH scholarship may then be summarised as proceeding along the following axes: content, method, infrastructure, history and theory. Wernimont has explored the difficulties of locating feminist digital interventions in terms of content and problematised 'the idea that simply saving women's work in digital form is enough' (2013). A number of digital archive projects that spoke to questions of difference, some in the context of second-wave feminist recovery, were created within and without the digital humanities community in 1990s. High profile projects like Women Writers online and Orlando exist still but many others have disappeared or are effectively dead (Earhart 2012; Mandell 2015).

A good deal of research has sought to interweave DH methods and techniques with gender or feminist-led analyses of retro-digitised cultural heritage materials. For example, studies have examined the automatic gender classification of French and literary and historical texts (Argamon et al 2009a). Machine learning and text mining have been used to identify and analyse what are argued to be linguistic markers of gender, race and nationality in 20th Century Black Drama (Argamon et al 2009). In the 'Black Women Big Data' project, Brown *et al* tackle the 'intersectional nature of oppression' in the 'silencing digitized terrain' of digital libraries. Training algorithms to discover 'hidden' documents, they demonstrate how topic-modelling informed by a Black feminist (intersectional) interpretation of method can be used to recover Black women's narratives and create future models for disrupting traditional, biased analyses of textual corpora (Brown et al 2016). Weingart and Jorgensen hand coded mentions of body parts in canonical fairy tales and computationally analysed those references, noting that their findings reinforced that of previous feminist scholarship while being based on a more empirical approach (2013).

The interplay of gender, expertise and recognition in the field of DH itself is another area of ongoing enquiry. For example, Berens examined the intersectional human and machine processes that excluded Molloy's early hypertext *afternoon* from the electronic literature canon and Molloy herself, along with other female hypertext trailblazers, from tenured university posts (Berens 2014). The esteem that is given to coding, and how this can exclude women from prominent areas of DH research has been addressed (Jackson et al 2008; Posner, 2012). Despite some intimations (see Brown 2016), sustained analysis of how these debates essentialise gender has not been undertaken. A number of quantitative studies of the organisation and representation of the field of DH, as seen through conference, publication and other professional activities have also been undertaken, sometimes with gender as a point of focus (see Weingart and Jorgensen 2013).

Recent papers have discussed the transferrable lessons that Feminist Game Studies have for the project of articulating Feminist DH values (Losh 2015) and how an intersectional analysis could support the writing of alternate histories of DH and a more intellectually diverse research agenda that can accommodate studies of difference and cultural critique (Risam 2015). Addressed too has been the potential of philosophy of feminism scholarship to inform the articulation of epistemology in DH and Information Science, especially in the context of infrastructures (Clement 2015). Druckers' work on 'non-representational approaches to interfaces' also draws on feminist and related theories to critique universal and totalising portrayals of 'the user' and explore the affective, embodied and situated forms of knowledge (2013). Risam similarly critiques how normative 'human' subjects, predicated on and privileging masculine Global North identities, are encoded within AI and machine learning technologies and how these may be reinforced and legitimised in uncritical DH scholarship (Risam, 2019). Part of a recent volume dealing with intersectionality in DH, this critique comes alongside a series of essays bringing into conversation gender, queer, lesbian, postcolonial and posthuman perspectives with the diverse materialities and philosophical concerns of the contemporary digital humanities (Losh and Wernimont, 2019).

18.3 Gender and heritage

Although sustained theorizations of heritage specifically as it relates to gender are less common, there is a growing body of work dedicated to concepts around the gendered nature of heritage, heritage institutions, cultural heritage management, and to a lesser degree digital cultural heritage.[2] Gender is often understood solely as a women's issue and many case studies in heritage are, in this respect, concerned with issues of (mis)representation, marginalisation and (in)visibility (Smith 2008; Casserly and O'Neill 2017; Cramer and Witcomb 2018). What these tropes, value-systems, and absences of women in all walks of heritage tell us about masculinity and gender relations, as well as constructed, female social identities, receives comparatively less attention.

Cramer and Witcomb have shown how personalising historical women in exhibitions, as opposed to generalising in grand narratives, can allow for more critical perspectives where gendered experiences become more apparent (Cramer and Witcomb, 2018). Yet, what might be considered a language of exceptionalism has evolved around the reclamation of historically 'unsung women' (Lowenthal 2015, p.14). This may be strategic but tends to favour figures who were already privileged relative to their contemporaries, and more visible in the historical record and other material traces of the past because of their education, wealth, or status. Butler was somewhat prescient in warning that 'feminism ought to be careful not to idealize certain expressions of gender that, in turn, produce new forms of hierarchy and exclusion' (Butler 1999, p.viii). A gender approach to heritage is still a feminist one and requires 'not a monolithic emphasis on women, but an engendering of the past; it requires a consideration of gender as a process and a relation, and how masculinity has played out' (Engelstad 2007, p.218). The challenge is perhaps doing holistic gender work without re-obfuscating women in heritage, as has been the argument around, for example, women's history and the emergence of gender history (Casserly and O'Neill, 2017).

The issue of gender and heritage goes beyond absence, visibility or representation, concerning also methodologies, practices and interpretive assumptions based on normative ideas about gender and sexuality in academia and cultural heritage spaces (Reading 2015). It is about the division of labour in heritage research, preservation and management, both historically and contemporaneously (Mayo 1983, p.65; Levin 2010; Moravec 2017). Reading thus frames gender more broadly in relation to heritage in terms of '...how changing constructions of masculinity and femininity interact with what is valued and included as heritage' (2015, p.401).

Opening the 'black box'

The emerging 'gender archaeology' of the 1980s criticised archaeology for its role in substantiating a certain gender ideology, and mythology, about the social roles of men and women (Conkey and Spector 1984). Indeed, the recent furor over the gender of Bj 581—the skeleton of a (female) Viking warrior discovered in the nineteenth century– is an archetypal example of how deeply held assumptions around masculinity have and continue to bias archaeological interpretation even in the face of scientific evidence to the contrary (Hedenstierna-Jonson et al 2017; Norton 2017). And as demonstrated by Narayanan, the masculinity of urban heritage, combined with a lack of gender-conscious sustainable development, can have real and negative consequences for women's access to civic spaces in certain cultural contexts (Narayanan, 2014).

Indeed, masculinity, to a much greater extent than has been problematized, is a key subtext of the modern Heritage regime. The 'masculinity of heritage' as Smith says, is latent in the way heritage has been defined, valued and preserved in modern times: the monumental, the elite, the relics of androcentric histories of war, nationalism, colonialism, patrilineal monarchy, and patriarchal systems of governance (Smith 2008, p.161–2). A focus, in other words, on 'men and masculine pursuits' (Cramer and Witcomb 2018, p.3) has long been the gold standard for Heritage. Conkey and Spector impressed that gender biases were and are not exclusive to archaeology, rather they are a 'feature of our entire intellectual tradition' (Conkey and Spector 1984, p.3). Moreover:

> '…the expression of gender identities in heritage can never be understood to be politically or culturally neutral, as what is constructed has a range of implications for how women and men and their social roles are perceived, valued and socially and historically justified.' (Smith 2008, p.161)

In other words, the concept and consequences of gender do not exist in an intellectual vacuum, whether in analogue or digital contexts. So too it opens new areas of enquiry for a DH that has engaged little with heritage as a socially constructed phenomenon. The questions that this raises for digital heritage resources widen existing DH purviews to include an enquiry into issues like: what are the gendered and/or sex-differentiated power relations at play in the heritage process, the meanings, silences and contestations they produce? How is the discourse around heritage gendered? How have normative conceptions of gender been reproduced or challenged in conventional and counter heritages? And perhaps most importantly, what are the material consequences for individuals and society?

To adequately synthesize a constellation of studies over the past thirty years of the heritage field is not possible here and would be to repeat what has been done elsewhere (Reading 2015; Wilson, 2018). It will be more useful here to consider gender in relation to some of the foundational Critical Heritage Studies issues. Lowenthal says that heritage was once 'limited to the annals of kingship and conquest and the deeds of great men' and 'now dwells on the everyday lives and aspirations of "people without history"' (Lowenthal 2015, p.14). Critical Heritage Studies question the conventional and naturalised power structures that dictate what heritage is or isn't, what should or should not be preserved, who is or is not visible or included in heritage and the heritage process. It is especially concerned with challenging the dominance of Western or Eurocentric heritage discourse and elitist heritage structures, decolonizing heritage and advocating a 'pluralising,' 'multi-vocal,' 'participatory' even 'eclectic' heritage (Hall 2001, p.92; Smith 2006, p.12; Ashworth et al 2007, p.45, 50; Association of Critical Heritage Studies, 2012; Flinn and Sexton 2013). It increasingly looks to the relationship between heritage, social justice, human and cultural rights (Duff et al 2013; Coombe and Weiss 2015; Lynch 2017), and as Winter says, critical heritage should also 'be about addressing the critical issues that face the world today' such as multiculturalism, climate change, sustainability, and conflict resolution (Crooke 2001; Harrison 2013; Winter 2013, p.533; Harvey and Perry 2015). CHS is also, as mentioned above, heavily preoccupied with identity and the politics of recognition. Arguably then, a gender perspective might logically find more currency within the same rights-based, dissonant and transformative worldview within the core discourse of critical heritage. After all, gender-based discrimination and oppression, violence and sexual crime against cis-gender women and trans- men and women have legal and political heritages that continue to be unravelled at differing pace in different cultural contexts worldwide. Women's rights and LGBTQ+ rights are human rights. Men and women are inheritors of, and have played different parts in, anthropogenic climate change through shifting gender roles in production (Merchant 1990; Chakrabarty 2009). The consequences and legacies of war and civil conflict are gendered and, as Ward reminds us, often do little to advance gender relations (Ward, 2006, p.282). We are also seeing a period of significant flux regarding gender identities and gender relations in the public space. These are all global and personal, political and emotional issues affecting humanity and what it means to be human that are entangled with heritage yet remain subsidiary to the dominant trends within CHS. Indeed, the growing feminist and gender critique within heritage studies was born in response to a conspicuous 'gender blindness' in the field described by Reading as an ignorance resulting from the 'earlier dispersal of studies across the multidisciplinarity of heritage studies' (2015, p. 339).

The intervention of digitality in the heritage sphere adds further layers to this gender-heritage complex not least as it ties in with the notions about power and knowledge structures that are central to CHS. It poses myriad questions about the nature of engagement, interpretation, cultural encoding, and accessibility that may be gendered or have gendered consequences. Wilson has gone so far as to describe gender as 'the fundamental mode of critique for the modern era' (2018, p.9). Already we can begin to see common cause with feminist DH. We will now propose that questions of how gender is performed by and through digital heritage, to which DH and CHS have recently turned, suggests a fruitful way to bridge these currently largely unconnected fields. We emphasise scholarship relevant to the issue of 'content', given the attention that Wernimont has given to the difficulties of accounting for this in digital heritage.

18.4 Digital heritage as bridge

The digital context in which heritage now finds itself, and where it is produced and reproduced, has implications for how gender plays out within it. Digitality has undoubtedly opened doors for 'gender mainstreaming' and a more participatory culture in heritage, being an environment in which—at great velocity—many voices can speak louder from the margins, new information can be reached, shared and mobilized. Or as UNESCO puts it 'access to this heritage will offer broadened opportunities for creation, communication and sharing of knowledge among all peoples' (UNESCO, 2003). However, nothing should be assumed about the power plays of cultural heritage on the internet. Horst and Miller are concerned with what opportunities 'the digital' offers our understanding of what it is to be human and they remind us of 'humanity's remarkable capacity to re-impose normativity just as quickly as digital technologies create conditions for change' (Horst and Miller 2013, p.13). Wilson reminds us that normativity is itself a 'site of control and domination' whether you exist within it or without (Wilson, 2018, p. 7). This has implications for thinking about gender (and race and class) and the reproduction of pre-digital patterns such as systems of social inequality, exclusions, hegemonic narratives, and soft power (Taylor and Gibson 2017). Further, this universalizing discourse of world heritage coupled with digitisation and 'open access' is not always appropriate to the value systems of Indigenous peoples to whom they may pertain. While digital heritage initiatives can be well-meaning and facilitate forms of repatriation in some contexts, in others they can operate to undermine efforts at 'decolonizing' heritage when they do not respect the knowledge systems, intellectual property and human rights of their subjects (Delva and Adams, 2016; Taylor and Gibson, 2017).

The so-called 'democratisation' of heritage through digitization and digital technologies is also fraught with caveats and requires a critical eye towards the processes at work in the mediation of digital objects that is true for all digital cultural heritage (Bishop 2017; Taylor and Gibson 2017). While the digital allows for a displacement of traditional powers structures in heritage, there are still people behind the creation and curation of digital heritage meaning that its processes remain situated and culturally coded (Cameron and Kenderine 2007). What has, is and will be collected, preserved, privileged and disseminated by digital

Opening the 'black box'

means is not a neutral endeavour (Gauld 2017): cultural knowledge systems (Mason 2007), metadata, digital cataloguing, descriptions and arrangements in online collections and exhibitions can all operate to sustain or challenge the gender *status quo ante* in terms of findability, interpretation and agency in the digital space. Bishop has argued that digital databases and their search pathways have altered the information seeking behaviours of the public and academics but particularly historians, requiring feminist historians to 'read against the grain' and to 'question absence as well as presence' (Bishop 2017, p.771). Furthermore, what heritage becomes digital at all may be contingent on funding, policy, or national commemorative agendas that favour safe, canonical narratives tending towards white, male, heteronormative biases. This also throws into sharp relief the convergence of neoliberal economic policies and heritage practices (Cifor and Lee 2017; Moravec 2017). Furthermore, we must remember that the digital does not equate with accessibility (Reed 2014). As Bishop says, it is largely 'a first-world democratisation,' which gives little account of the 'digital divide,' the limitations on poorer women's access to, participation or inclusion in, digital cultural heritage particularly in the global south (Bishop 2017, p.771). These are just some of examples that demonstrate the messy ties between analogue, digital and human as they relate to gender in the field of heritage and which necessitate a practice of what might be called Critical Digital Heritage.

It is thus within this new digitality that feminist DH and critical heritage studies converge and pose novel theoretical and methodological questions. Concerns with 'rethinking canons and periodization, globalizing humanities research, addressing new media, and foregrounding politics and issues of power' are shared across each school of thought. More specifically, both feminist DH and what Wilson (2018, p. 6) describes as 'Critical Gender Heritage Studies' recognise and seek to theorize and challenge the default masculinity, euro-centricity and whiteness of their fields that is wrapped up in a presumed objectivity, neutrality and openness, as well as patriarchal, colonial 'origin narratives' (Wernimont and Losh, 2016, p.40; Ross, 2018). Such narratives speak to and legitimise certain identities while obfuscating or actively delegitimising others. Both fields also thus recognise, as Ross says, 'the impossibility of impartiality' and the need for a powerful, 'liminal,' and transformative critique of the disciplinary 'core' (Wernimont and Losh, 2016; Wilson, 2018, p.9; Ross, 2018, p.217). Winter has gone so far as to say that some critical approaches to heritage can be so strident as to be anti-heritage (Winter, 2013). Undeniably, similar currents are emerging in critical and feminist DH, and wider society, with concerns over the techno-social implications of our digitally embedded lives (Losh and Wernimont, 2019), producing as they do new inequities and unforeseen consequences for which more technology may be inadequate in remedying. 'Algorithmic universals' are indeed anything but, and have repeatedly proved biased in their outputs, with consequences ranging from corporate embarrassment to influencing real-world racial, homophobic or sexualised violence (Noble, 2018; Risam, 2019, p. 46).

Feminism is about more than women and gender; it is about power and concurrent dynamics of privilege that pervade our social realities (D'Ignazio and Klein, 2019). These dynamics have material consequences for peoples and societies, and transformation requires not just theoretical critique but also active methodological de-centring. Furthermore, intersectional feminist and gender analyses have been challenging narratives and praxis across a variety of disciplines that bear upon DH and CHS for some time. As such we must also actively avoid appropriation, and give recognition to the labour and intellectual contributions that predate and coexist with the current critical turn, within and beyond the canon of these disciplines and practices (Wernimont and Losh, 2016).

18.5 Methodologies

How, then, might we take up the challenge of examining the systemic gendered structuring of white privilege and patriarchy within heritage, particularly what has been dubbed the Authorised (Digital) Heritage Discourse (Caswell et al 2016; Smith, 2006)? How can we examine heritage both as product and process? How can we discover (perhaps not just to understand but also to counteract and reverse) the ways in which intersectional identities are hidden and marginalised in digital heritage materials? Which methodologies can assist researchers to explore the 'black box' of heritage processes, for example, the erasure of the feminised labour that underpins digital heritage?

A critical digital heritage study of gendered heritage processes will require a suite of methodologies and approaches. We might argue that an ethnographic approach to heritage processes and production and the organisations and systems that produce them is necessary given the tacit assumptions, informal practices and prevailing dominant orthodoxies and cultures at work in the production and presentation of AHD. The need to engage with the social process of heritage and public history production, in a sustained and deep fashion, to understand the public manifestations of dominant and exclusive narratives embedded in exhibitions and digital displays has been widely acknowledged since MacDonald's influential appraisal of exhibitions at the London Science Museum (Macdonald 2002). Such an embedded and critically engaged approach would enable researchers to explore these practices in the context of the dominant ethos of society rather than simply focusing on the final heritage production itself as neutral space, or by taking rhetorical explanations and justifications of purpose by heritage institutions for granted (MacDonald et al 2018). We acknowledge the need to pay attention to the development, qualities and affordances of digital heritage and digital archive resources and the need to develop/adopt/adapt research tools and methods that are appropriate for these digital environments. However, we must also recognise that the digital heritage environment is one that results from human agency, social structures and human-led decision-making processes. The humanities, ethnographic and social science research methods that seek to explore critical questions around the gendering of digital heritage will therefore share much in common with the methods and approaches that we would employ to study the processes underpinning non-digital [heritage] productions and environment.

Within this field of the (organisational) ethnography of heritage institutions, professions and academic disciplines, one established critical humanistic research approach (Plummer 2001; Stanley 2013) we advocate is qualitative interviewing and life stories, in particular oral history. The practice of oral history has a long and close relationship with feminist and gender studies. At times, oral history has been identified as a specifically feminist research practice (concerned with hidden histories, power relations in research and society, and intersubjectivities). Feminist oral history practices ('research by, on, and for women' Iacovetta et al 2018) have specifically been employed across a range of research subjects including the recovery of hidden or otherwise forgotten histories; the unpicking of how the structuring of gendered relations over time has impacted lives, careers, work places, families, organisations, etc; and as a tool associated with advocacy and struggles for raising the profile of women and women's contributions. Several research initiatives into the historical incarceration of women and institutional abuse in Ireland have utilized oral history as a core methodology to give voice to the voiceless of the past. The 'Waterford Memories Project' for example applies oral history within a digital humanities framework to investigate institutions for research, preservation, pedagogical and restorative social justice ends (The Waterford Memories Project, 2015).[3] Similarly, 'Industrial Memories' was a digital humanities response to the 2009 Ryan Report into historical child abuse in Church institutions in Ireland. A public, multimedia database and data analysis resource of the report and its witness testimony was created to interrogate and understand its full weight and complexity, the experiences of victims, and in turn the interconnectedness of power and patriarchal oppression in this particular cultural context (Industrial Memories, 2018). The subjectivities and intersubjectivities of oral history making thus further align with feminist theory and praxis. Ross insists on the impossibility of impartiality and objectivity in research. They are, in themselves scientific, masculinist constructs that have operated to maintain gendered (as well racial, classist, colonial etc.) power structures within humanities fields such as archives, history, literature, and digital humanities itself (Ross, 2018, p. 217). As Cook put it, in the eyes of post-modern archival—and indeed, wider humanities—thought '[N]othing is neutral. Nothing is impartial. Nothing

Opening the 'black box'

is objective'. (Cook, 2001, p. 7) The answer then, propose Ross and others, is a highly reflexive partiality in doing feminist, digital archival work (Cifor and Wood, 2017, p. 3; Ross, 2018, p. 217). And it is here also that oral history finds currency as a feminist DH methodology.

The history of the interconnectedness of feminist research and oral history, and the evolution of the application of oral history approaches (ones that focus on the past and those actions/motivations/challenges that might otherwise be hidden or invisible) has been discussed and critically analysed at length, not least in the edited volumes *Women's Words—the feminist practice of oral history* (Gluck and Patai, 1991) and its recent pluralised successor *Beyond Women's Words— feminisms and the practices of oral history in the twenty-first century* (Srigley et al, 2018). The latter volume, in addition to documenting a number of theoretical, decolonising and intersectional debates and applied developments in oral history as a methodology, also examines the impact of digital environments on feminist oral history. This is examined in terms of the creation of digital oral history archives that document the experience of women, in particular lesbians (Chenier 2018), 'feminist engagements with heritage culture' and questions of representation (Shea, 2018). A recent project of the Black Cultural Archives (BCA), an oral history of the Black Women's Movement, applied such feminist engagements. A community archive in south London, BCA is 'a national institution dedicated to collecting, preserving and celebrating the histories of diverse people of African and Caribbean descent in Britain'. (Black Cultural Archives, 2018a) This feminist oral history project in its methodology explicitly sought 'to present Black history by members of the Black community. To this end, the oral history interviews were undertaken by female, Black volunteers.'(Black Cultural Archives, 2018b) Similarly, the women's testimonies were the central reference point in creating interpretive text and shaping appropriate themes and audio excerpts for a future digital platform, in order that their voices and perspective be respected and salient at every level of the project.[4]

Relevant to the critical debates we are interested in here are suggestions of fundamental incompatibility between feminist sensibilities 'such as respect for the narrators, and the digital's pace, openness and impersonal, profit-driven nature' and the continued relevance of critical questions relating to the impact of race, gender, class that privilege what gets digitised and what gets posted and accessed (Iacovetta et al, 2018, pp. 11–12). Indeed, what is occluded or undervalued when the knowledge that tends to be privileged in digitisation and digital humanities research continues to be largely textual rather than oral? Ross (Ross, 2018, p.220) further reminds us that digital platform design itself dictates the nature of its feminist engagements or otherwise, be it 'welcoming or exclusionary, open-ended or teleological, user-centred or dictatorial, plural or definitive.' Feminist DH might animate alternative digital heritage content, platforms and interfaces underpinned by feminist methodologies and epistemologies, in for example, constructing digital oral histories. Hall demonstrates a fine-grained approach in creating the digital exhibit 'Women Sing the Blues,' into which non-linearity, complexity and interactivity is in-built to engage women's interpretations of songs, and interpret the feminist genealogies of blues music heritage as a process through time (Hall, 2018). Perhaps similar modalities might be fruitful in creating digital oral history platforms by engaging the aesthetic, theoretical and historical and facilitating alternative ways of knowing (Hall, 2018). Feminist DH applied in curating oral histories can thus be more analytically and interpretively powerful, as well as more ethical, in the process of critical digital heritage.

In our own practice we have used oral history as a primary methodology to critically explore the (hidden and gendered) histories of digital humanities. We have explored the careers and contributions of the key figures and pioneers (Nyhan and Flinn, 2016) and the hidden and feminised labour that lay behind the work of some of these key canonical figures. The canonical history of Digital Humanities emphasises technological progress and narratives of 'great men', especially Fr Roberto Busa SJ (1913–2011). Nyhan has used oral history to uncover the nature of the contributions that were made to Busa's renowned *Index Thomisticus* project by the mostly female key punch operatives who worked on the project from c.1954–67. They worked for Busa in the keypunch school that he set up in Milan in 1956 and also in the Literary Data Processing Centre (CAAL) that he set up around the same time. Though their work has been overlooked and devalued by Busa, and by much of the scholarship written about the project by other scholars, they made an immense contribution to Busa's research by transcribing onto punched cards ""natural texts containing 12,000,000 words in 9 different languages in the Latin, Hebrew, Greek, and Cyrillic alphabets" (072_1968)". They worked with Busa until c.1967 when, as he later described it, "I completed the punching of all my texts" (Busa 1980 p.85). Oral history has thus played a key role in uncovering details of everyday significance of their work. Also, by uncovering the nature of the womens' contributions, and the processes that served to devalue and ultimately silence them and their work, we can get an insight into how knowledge was defined at the beginning of DH and into the categories of people who were considered able to make that knowledge. This raises crucial questions about the 'deep history' of digital cultural heritage tools and resources and the gendered practices that underpinned them and that remain little understood.

Conclusion

This chapter has given an overview that is by no means exhaustive of the current critical debates in Digital Humanities as they relate to intersectional feminist theory and practice. In conversation with the founding principles of Critical Heritage Studies and its own set of gender and feminist debates, we have demonstrated how Feminist DH and (Gender) CHS have strong practical and analytical links and are in many ways ideologically aligned. Lastly, we have proposed and rationalised oral history as conceptually allied, and a potential tool, in feminist DH work.

> 'If we do not want to be complicit in the oppressive conditions created by our tools, our theories, and our institutional structures, then we have an obligation to do something about them.'(Wernimont and Losh, 2016, p.38)

Digital oral history making is just one potential tool for broader feminist digital humanities practice. Ethnographic methods are colonial in origin but institutional ethnographies of, for example, technology corporations—many of which have a large stake in digital cultural heritage—can shift the research gaze to expose the workings and/or exploitations of white, normative, neoliberal power structures that are both human and computational (Noble, 2018; Thylstrup, 2018). There is no silver bullet approach and we would argue, as with any robust research and analysis, that a suite of methodologies are possible and necessary; what matters in the end is how they are understood, critiqued and operationalised for intersectional, feminist ends (Wernimont, 2013).

Notes

1 The UNESCO Charter on the Preservation of the Digital Heritage says that: 'The digital heritage consists of unique resources of human knowledge and expression. It embraces cultural, educational, scientific and administrative resources, as well as technical, legal, medical and other kinds of information created digitally, or converted into digital form from existing analogue resources.' (UNESCO 2003)
2 Only as recently as 2014, a UNESCO report on Gender, Heritage and Creativity for the first time acknowledged that gender does play an apparent role in the "identification, protection, conservation, presentation and transmission to future generations of the cultural and natural heritage" as defined in Article 4 of the World Heritage Convention.' (UNESCO 2014, p. 61)
3 See also 'Justice for Magdalenes Research,' www.jfmreasearch.com, and 'Archiving Personal Histories: The Tuam Mother and Baby Home,' https://www.nuigalway.ie/about-us/news-and-events/news-archive/2019/january/nui-galway-launch-project-to-archive-personal-histories-of-the-tuam-mother-and-baby-home.html
4 This is based on recent work carried out by one of authors during an EU-funded secondment in partnership between UCL with BCA.

Opening the 'black box'

References

Abbate, J. (2012) *Recoding Gender: Women's Changing Participation in Computing*, Cambridge, Mass: MIT Press.

Argamon, Shlomo, et al. (2009a) "Gender, Race, and Nationality in Black Drama, 1950–2006: Mining Differences in Language Use in Authors and Their Characters." *Digital Humanities Quarterly*, 3, no. 2 (June).

Argamon, Shlomo, et al. (2009) "Vive La Différence! Text Mining Gender Difference in French Literature." *Digital Humanities Quarterly*, 3, no. 2 (June).

Ashworth, G. J., Graham, B. J. and Tunbridge, J. E. (eds) (2007) *Pluralising Pasts: Heritage, Identity and Place in Multicultural Societies*. London: Pluto Press.

Association of Critical Heritage Studies. (2012) *History—2012 Manifesto*. Available at: http://www.criticalheritagestudies.org/history/ (Accessed: 1 August 2018).

Berens, K. I. (2014) "Judy Malloy's Seat at the (Database) Table: A Feminist Reception History of Early Hypertext Literature", *Literary and Linguistic Computing* 29(3), pp. 340–348. https://doi.org/10.1093/llc/fqu037.

Bianco, J. (2012). "Skye: The Digital Humanities Which Is Not One", in Gold M. K. (ed) *Debates in the Digital Humanities*, Minneapolis: University of Minnesota Press, pp. 96–112.

Bishop, C. (2017) "The Serendipity of Connectivity: Piecing Together Women's Lives in the Digital Archive", *Women's History Review*, 26(5), pp. 766–780. doi: 10.1080/09612025.2016.1166883.

Black Cultural Archives (2018a) *Our Mission*. Available at: https://blackculturalarchives.org/about/ (Accessed: 12 September 2018).

Black Cultural Archives (2018b) *Subject Guide: The Black Women's Movement*. Available at: https://static1.squarespace.com/static/5a01baa7d7bdcee985c80c15/t/5a08920ae2c483d6cb7d8229/1510511116192/2016_Womens-Movement-updated.pdf (Accessed: 12 October 2018).

Brown, N. M. et al. (2016) "Mechanized Margin to Digitized Center: Black Feminism's Contributions to Combatting Erasure within the Digital Humanities", *International Journal of Humanities and Arts Computing*, 10(1), pp. 110–125. doi: 10.3366/ijhac.2016.0163.

Busa, R. (1980) "The Annals of Humanities Computing: The Index Thomisticus." *Computers and the Humanities* 14 (2): 83–90. https://doi.org/10.1007/BF02403798.

Butler, J. (1999) *Gender Trouble : Feminism and the Subversion of Identity*. New York: Routledge.

Cameron, F. and Kenderdine, S. (eds) (2007) *Theorizing Digital Cultural Heritage: A Critical Discourse*. Cambridge Mass., MIT Press. Available at: https://www.dawsonera.com:443/abstract/9780262269742.

Casserly, M. and O'Neill, C. (2017) "Public History, Invisibility, and Women in the Republic of Ireland", *The Public Historian*, 39(2), pp. 10–30. doi: https://doi.org/10.1525/tph.2017.39.2.10.

Caswell, M. L. (2016) "The Archive' Is Not an Archives: On Acknowledging the Intellectual Contributions of Archival Studies", *UCLA*. https://escholarship.org/uc/item/7bn4v1fk.

Chakrabarty, D. (2009) "The Climate of History: Four Theses", *Critical Inquiry*, 35(2), pp. 197–222. doi: 10.1086/596640.

Chenier, E. (2018) "Oral History's Afterlife", in Srigley, K., Zembrzycki, S., and Iacovetta, F. (eds) *Beyond Women's Words: Feminisms and the Practices of Oral History in the Twenty-First Century*. London: Routledge, pp. 304–312.

Cifor, M. and Lee, J. A. (2017) "Towards an Archival Critique: Opening Possibilities for Addressing Neoliberalism in the Archival Field", *Journal of Critical Library and Information Studies*, 1(1), pp. 1–22. doi: 10.24242/jclis.v1i1.10.ISSN.

Cifor, M. and Wood, S. (2017) "Critical Feminism in the Archives", *Journal of Critical Library and Information Studies*, 1(2), pp. 1–27. doi: 10.24242/jclis.v1i2.27.

Clement, T. (2015) "An Information Science Question in DH Feminism', *Digital Humanities Quarterly* 9(2).

Conkey, M. W. and Spector, J. D. (1984) "Archaeology and the Study of Gender", *Advances in Archaeological Method and Theory*, 7, pp. 1–38. Available at: http://www.jstor.org/stable/20170176.

Cook, T. (2001) "Archival Science and Postmodernism: New Formulations for Old Concepts", *Archival Science*, 1(1), pp. 3–24. doi: 10.1007/BF02435636.

Coombe, R. J. and Weiss, L. M. (2015) "Neoliberalism, Heritage Regimes, and Cultural Rights", in Meskell, L. (ed) *Global Heritage: A Reader*. Somerset, Wiley Blackwell. doi: 10.2139/ssrn.2644495.

Cramer, L. and Witcomb, A. (2018) "'Hidden from View"?: An Analysis of the Integration of Women's History and Women's Voices into Australia's Social History Exhibitions', *International Journal of Heritage Studies*, 25(2), pp. 1–15. doi: 10.1080/13527258.2018.1475409.

Crooke, E. (2001) "Confronting a Troubled History: Which Past in Northern Ireland's Museums?", *International Journal of Heritage Studies*, 7(2), pp. 119–136. doi: 10.1080/713772347.

Dean, G. (2015) "The Shock of the Familiar: Three Timelines about Gender and Technology in the Library", *Digital Humanities Quarterly* 9(2).

D'Ignazio, C. and Klein, L. (2019) "Introduction", in *Data Feminism*. MIT Press. Available at: https://bookbook.pubpub.org/pub/dgv16l22 (Accessed: 28 March 2019).

Delva, M. and Adams, M. (2016) "Archival Ethics and Indigenous Justice: Conflict or Coexistence?", in Foscarini, F. et al. (eds) *Engaging with Records and Archives: Histories and Theories*. London: Facet Publishing, pp. 147–172. doi: 10.29085/9781783301607.009.

Duff, W. M. et al. (2013) "Social Justice Impact of Archives: A Preliminary Investigation", *Archival Science*, 13(4), pp. 317–348. doi: 10.1007/s10502-012-9198-x.

Drucker, J. (2013) "Performative Materiality and Theoretical Approaches to Interface", *Digital Humanities Quarterly*, 7(1).

Earhart, A. (2012) "Can Information Be Unfettered? Race and the New Digital Humanities Canon", in M. K. Gold (ed), *Debates in the Digital Humanities*, Minneapolis: University of Minnesota Press.

Engelstad, E. (2007) "Much More than Gender", *Journal of Archaeological Method and Theory*, 14(3), pp. 217–234. Available at: http://www.jstor.org/stable/25702342.

Faulkner, W. and Arnold E. (eds) (1985) *Smothered by Invention: Technology in Women's Lives*. London: Pluto Press.

FemTechNet (2019) http://femtechnet.org/publications/manifesto/

Flinn, A. and Sexton, A. (2013) 'Research on Community Heritage: Moving from Collaborative Research to Participatory and Co-Designed Research Practice', *CIRN Prato Community Informatics Conference 2013*, pp. 1–14.

Gauld, C. (2017) "Democratising or Privileging: The Democratisation of Knowledge and the Role of the Archivist", *Archival Science*, 17(3), pp. 227–245. doi: 10.1007/s10502-015-9262-4.

Gluck, S. B., and Patai, D. (eds) (1991) *Women's Words: The Feminist Practice of Oral History*. London and New York: Routledge.

Grahn, W. and Wilson, R. J. (eds) (2018) *Gender and Heritage: Performance, Place and Politics*. London and New York: Routledge.

Hall, J. (2018) "Using a Feminist Digital Humanities Approach", *Frontiers*, 39(1), pp. 1–23.

Hall, S. (2001) "Constituting an Archive", *Third Text*, 15(54), pp. 89–92. doi: 10.1080/09528820108576903.

Hamnett, C., McDowell L., and Sarre P. (1989) *Restructuring Britain: The Changing Social Structure*. London: Sage Publications.

Harrison, R. (2013) *Heritage: Critical Approaches*. London; New York: Routledge.

Harvey, D. and Perry, J. A. (eds) (2015) *The Future of Heritage as Climates Change: Loss, Adaptation and Creativity*. London: Routledge.

Hedenstierna-Jonson, C. et al. (2017) "A Female Viking Warrior Confirmed by Genomics", *American Journal of Physical Anthropology*, 164(4), pp. 853–860. doi: 10.1002/ajpa.23308.

Hicks, M. (2017) *Programmed Inequality: How Britain Discarded Women Technologists and Lost Its Edge in Computing*, 1st edn. Cambridge: MIT Press.

Horst, H. and Miller, D. (2013) "The Digital and the Human: A Prospectus for Digital Anthropology", in Horst, H. A. and Miller, D. (eds) *Digital Anthropology*. Bloomsbury Publishing, pp. 12–43. doi: 10.1093/obo/9780199766567-0087.

Iacovetta F., Srigley, K., and Zembrzycki, S. (2018) "Introduction", in Srigley, K., Zembrzycki, S., and Iacovetta, F. (eds) *Beyond Women's Words: Feminisms and the Practices of Oral History in the Twenty-First Century*. London: Routledge, pp. 1–24.

Industrial Memories (2018) *Industrial Memories, University College Dublin*. Available at: https://industrialmemories.ucd.ie/ (Accessed: 5 April 2019).

Jackson, L. A., Zhao, J., Kolenic, A. III, Fitzgerald, H. E., Harold, R., and Von Eye, A. (2008). "Race, Gender, and Information Technology Use: The New Digital Divide. *CyberPsychology & Behavior*, 11(4), pp. 437–442. http://online.liebertpub.com/doi/pdf/10.1089/cpb.2007.0157

Jones, S. E. (2013) *The Emergence of the Digital Humanities*. New York: Routledge.

Juhasz, A. and Balsamo A. (2012) "An Idea Whose Time Is Here: FemTechNet – A Distributed Online Collaborative Course (DOCC)'. *Ada: a Journal of Gender, New Media, and Technology, No. 1*. (November). https://adanewmedia.org/2012/11/issue1-juhasz/.

Levin, A. K. (ed.) (2010) *Gender, Sexuality and Museums: A Routledge Reader*. Routledge. Available at: https://www.dawsonera.com:443/abstract/9780203847770.

Light, J. S. (1999) "When Computers Were Women", *Technology and Culture*, 40(3), pp. 445–483.

Liu, A. (2012) "Where is Cultural Criticism in the Digtial Humanities", in M. K. Gold (ed) *Debates in the Digital Humanities*, Minneapolis: University of Minnesota Press, pp. 490–509.

Losh, E. and Wernimont, J. (eds) (2019) *Bodies of Information: Intersectional Feminism and Digital Humanities*. Minneapolis: University of Minnesota Press.

Lowenthal, D. (2015) *The Past is a Foreign Country—Revisited*. Cambridge: Cambridge University Press.

Lutz, S. (2018) "{D1G1TAL HER1TAGE}. From cultural to digital heritage", *Hamburger Journal für Kulturanthropologie (HJK)*, (7), pp. 3–23.

Lynch, B. (2017) "The Gate in the Wall: Beyond Happiness-Making in Museums", in Onciul, B., Stefano, M. L., and Hawke S. (eds.) *Engaging Heritage, Engaging Communities*, Woodbridge and New York: Boydell Press, pp. 11–29.

Macdonald, S. (2002) *Behind the Scenes at the Science Museum*. Berg.

Macdonald, S., Christine G., and von Oswald, M. (2018) "No Museum is an Island: Ethnography Beyond Methodological Containerism", *Museum and Society*, 16(2), pp. 138–156. doi: https://doi.org/10.29311/mas.v16i2.2788

Mandell, L. C. (2015) "Gendering Digital Literary History'. In *A New Companion to Digital Humanities*, John Wiley & Sons, Ltd. pp. 511–523. https://doi.org/10.1002/9781118680605.ch35.

Mason, I. (2007) "Cultural Information Standards—Political Territory and Rich Rewards." in Cameron F. and Kenderdine S. (eds.) *Theorizing Digital Cultural Heritage: A Critical Discourse*, Cambridge: MIT Press, pp. 223–43. https://doi.org/10.7551/mitpress/9780262033534.003.0012.

Mayo, E. P. (1983) "Women's History and Public History: The Museum Connection", *The Public Historian*. [National Council on Public History, University of California Press], 5(2), pp. 63–73. doi: 10.2307/3377251

McPherson, T. (2012) "Why Are the Digital Humanities so White? or Thinking the Histories of Race and Computation", in M. K. Gold (ed) *Debates in the Digital Humanities*, Minneapolis: University of Minnesota Press, pp. 139–160.

Merchant, C. (1990) "Gender and Environmental" *The Journal of American History*, 76(4), pp. 1117–1121. doi: 10.2307/2936589.

Moravec, M. (2017) "Feminist Research Practices and Digital Archives", *Australian Feminist Studies*, 32(91–92), pp. 186–201. doi: 10.1080/08164649.2017.1357006.

Narayanan, Y. (2014) "Quo Vadis, Delhi? Urban Heritage and Gender: Towards a Sustainable Urban Future", *International Journal of Heritage Studies*, 20(5), pp. 488–499. doi: 10.1080/13527258.2013.771790.

Noble, S. U. (2018) *Algorithms of Oppression : How Search Engines Reinforce Racism*. New York : New York University Press.

Norton, H. (2017) *How the Female Viking Warrior Was Written Out of History, The Guardian*. Available at: https://www.theguardian.com/science/2017/sep/15/how-the-female-viking-warrior-was-written-out-of-history (Accessed: 14 August 2018).

Nyhan, J. and Flinn A. (2016) *Computation and the Humanities: Towards an Oral History of Digital Humanities. Springer Series on Cultural Computing*. Springer International Publishing.

Onciul, B., Stefano, M. L. and Hawke, S. (eds) (2017) *Engaging Heritage, Engaging Communities*. Woodbridge and New York: Boydell Press. Available at: http://www.jstor.org/stable/10.7722/j.ctt1kgqvrc%0A.

Pannapacker, W. (2011) "'Big Tent Digital Humanities,' a View From the Edge, Part 1'". *The Chronicle of Higher Education*, 31 July 2011, Sec. Advice. http://chronicle.com/article/Big-Tent-Digital-Humanities/128434/.

Plummer, K. (2001) *Documents of Life 2: An Invitation to a Critical Humanism*. London: SAGE Publications Ltd.

Posner, M. K. (2012) "Some Things to Think About Before You Exhort Everyone to Code", *Miriam Posner's Blog*. http://miriamposner.com/blog/some-things-to-think-about-before-you-exhort-everyone-to-code/

Prescott, A. (2012) "Consumers, Creators or Commentators? Problems of Audience and Mission in the Digital Humanities", *Arts and Humanities in Higher Education*, 11(1–2), pp. 61–75. doi: https://doi.org/10.1177/1474022211428215.

Reading, A. (2015) "Making Feminist Heritage Work: Gender and Heritage", in Waterton, E. and Watson, S. (eds) *Handbook of Contemporary Heritage Research*. Basingstoke : Palgrave Macmillan, pp. 397–413.

Reed, B. (2014) "Reinventing Access", *Archives and Manuscripts*, 42(2), pp. 123–132. doi: 10.1080/01576895.2014.926823.

Risam, R. (2019) "What Passes for Human? Undermining the Universal Subject in Digital Humanities", in Losh, E. and Wernimont, J. (eds) *Bodies of Information: Intersectional Feminism and Digital Humanities*. Minneapolis: University of Minnesota Press, pp. 39–56.

Ross, S. (2018) "Toward a Feminist Modernist Digital Humanities", *Feminist Modernist Studies*, 1(3), pp. 211–229. doi: 10.1080/24692921.2018.1505821.

Shea, M. (2018). "Feminist Oral History Practice in an Era of Digital Self-Representation", in Srigley, K., Zembrzycki S., and Iacovetta F., (eds) *Beyond Women's Words: Feminisms and the Practices of Oral History in the Twenty-First Century*. London: Routledge, pp. 283–297.

Smith, L. (2006) *Uses of Heritage*. London; New York: Routledge. doi: 10.1007/978-1-4419-0465-2_1937.

Smith, L. (2008) "Heritage, Gender and Identity", in Graham, B. and Howard, P. (eds) *The Ashgate Research Companion to Heritage and Identity*. Abington: Routledge. doi: 10.4324/9781315613031.ch9.

Srigley, K., Zembrzycki, S. and Iacovetta, F. (eds) (2018). *Beyond Women's Words: Feminisms and the Practices of Oral History in the Twenty-First Century*. London: Routledge.

Stanley, L. (2013). *Documents of Life Revisited: Narrative and Biographical Methodology for a 21st Century Critical Humanism*. London: Routledge. https://doi.org/10.4324/9781315577869

Taylor, J. and Gibson, L. K. (2017) "Digitisation, Digital Interaction and Social Media: Embedded Barriers to Democratic Heritage", *International Journal of Heritage Studies*. Routledge, 23(5), pp. 408–420. doi: 10.1080/13527258.2016.1171245.

The Waterford Memories Project (2015) *The Waterford Memories Project*. Available at: https://www.waterfordmemories.com/home (Accessed: 5 April 2019).

Thylstrup, N. B. (2018) *The Politics of Mass Digitsation*. Cambridge and London: MIT Press.

UNESCO (2003) *Charter on the Preservation of the Digital Heritage*. Available at: http://www.unesco.org/new/fileadmin/MULTIMEDIA/HQ/CI/CI/pdf/mow/charter_preservation_digital_heritage_en.pdf (Accessed: 28 February 2018).

UNESCO (2014) *Gender Equality, Heritage and Creativity*. Paris: UNESCO. Available at: http://www.unesco.org/new/en/culture/gender-and-culture/gender-equality-and-culture/the-report/ (Accessed: 5 March 2018).

Ward, M. (2006) "Gender, Citizenship, and the Future of the Northern Ireland Peace Process", *Eire-Ireland*, 41(1), pp. 262–284. doi: 10.1353/eir.2006.0012.

Weingart, S. and Jorgensen, J. (2013) "Computational Analysis of the Body in European Fairy Tales", *Literary and Linguistic Computing* 28(3), pp. 404–416. https://doi.org/10.1093/llc/fqs015.

Wernimont, J. (2013) "Whence Feminism? Assessing Feminist Interventions in Digital Literary Archives", *Digital Humanities Quarterly*, 7(1). Available at: http://www.digitalhumanities.org/dhq/vol/7/1/000156/000156.html.

Wernimont, J. and Losh, E. (2016) "Problems with White Feminism: Intersectionality and Digital Humanities", in Crompton, C., Lane, R. J., and Siemens, R. (eds) *Doing Digital Humanities: Practice, Training, Research*. 1st edn. Routledge, pp. 35–46.

Wilson, R. (2018) "The Tyranny of the Normal and the Importance of Being Liminal", in Grahn W. and Wilson R. (eds.), *Gender and Heritage: Performance, Power and Place*, London and New York: Routledge, pp. 3–14.

Winter, T. (2013) "Clarifying the Critical in Critical Heritage Studies", *International Journal of Heritage Studies*, 19(6), pp. 532–545. doi: 10.1080/13527258.2013.818572.

19
HOW TO USE SCALAR IN THE CLASSROOM

Christopher Gilman, Jacob Alden Sargent and Craig Dietrich

19.1 Introduction

19.1.1 An instruction sheet for recommended practices

Scalar is an online platform for authoring media-rich, long-form academic content, designed to provide scholars with a web-based option for publishing monographs and long-form articles. In recent years, as digital archives have become accessible to undergraduate students, Scalar has seen increasing use in college classrooms for student and collaborative student-faculty projects. In addition to Scalar's standard affordances for authoring in a web-based environment (e.g., on an edit page with form fields and a WYSIWYG editor), Scalar's unique features, such as technical bridges to digital archives and path-based, non-hierarchical navigation, enable novel learning activities to teach students discursive and information literacies while engaging in public authorship.

As a scholarly authoring tool designed from the ground up for academic use, Scalar departs from mainstream media applications in its design and usage. The idiosyncrasies of Scalar, paradoxically, make it an excellent vehicle for student learning, if educators can navigate its complexity. Common challenges facing educators include: how to teach students the fundamental principles and functionality of the platform; how to manage collaborative design and authorship processes with many participants; how to scope, structure, and sequence in-class activities; and, how to edit and publish final products created during the ebb and flow of an academic term. The challenges compound already vexing questions involving digital-era vernacular: how should scholars do *media import*, are *annotations* part of an argument, what does it mean to create multiple *pathways* through a scholarly text? Working with Scalar requires a high level of intentionality to explain its nuances in comparison with other scholarly and commercial environments, and thereby introduces a transferable critical frame for understanding other forms of authorship for the web.

The Occidental College Center for Digital Liberal Arts (CDLA) is a small staff of disciplinary specialists, technologists, and librarians that provides student and faculty research consultations, digital project support, and curricular integration of scholarly technology. Scalar co-creator Craig Dietrich joined Occidental in 2017, when the CDLA had already introduced Scalar in pilot course collaborations with faculty and was looking to regularize and expand the scope of their implementation. Dietrich informed in-class activities with insights from work being conducted at other institutions, and provided previews of new but untested features that might be useful for teaching, such as Scalar's Editorial Workflow (added in early 2019). Dietrich's presence at Occidental has helped make Scalar a centerpiece technology for interdisciplinary curricular work at Occidental. With this chapter we hope to assist other efforts to use the sophisticated but challenging scholarly tool in the classroom.

19.2 Considering Scalar's use

19.2.1 A common design language for the duration of a term

Given the ubiquity of digital devices, apps, and websites that offer "born-digital" content, authoring inside Scalar can help students understand the relationship between their own information usage and their teachers' scholarly practices. Educational institutions seeking to publicly showcase student research, writing, and information literacy skills, are contending with a gap in the respective habits of mind in the use of digital information sources, especially rich media content, between faculty and students. For teachers, new opportunities to develop courses using Scalar have arisen through external grant funding for curriculum innovation or internal initiatives to "flip" classrooms. An integration of Scalar in the classroom may also come about through incremental changes to teaching practices or desire to expand the scope of a class from writing print papers to writing online. When viewed as a learning tool, Scalar's discrete functions, like media import, annotation, and tagging, can help students be more transparent in their research and writing process. As these skills are integrated with digital and information literacy concepts, students can also reflect on how their information habits and expectations align with "traditional" and "digital" scholarship.

However the consideration of Scalar for curricular implementation is first approached, the decision should rest upon a firm imperative that integration be conceived holistically within the entirety of a course's academic term. In our experience, best results come from understanding Scalar as a series of potential learning activities, rather than as a media production tool with a particular feature set to be mastered. Tasks such as creating an account and joining a shared Scalar book, to media import and annotation, to pages, paths, and tags, move students through increasingly complex components of a design language deployed incrementally throughout the course schedule, tied to learning goals and methodological outcomes.

For those hesitant to commit to a full implementation it may help to consider an alternative. It is not uncommon for curious faculty to deploy Scalar as an experimental add-on in an existing lecture course, perhaps reserved for the last few weeks of a term. This approach, we assert, risks counterproductive student and faculty experiences, reinforces arbitrary lines demarcating "traditional" scholarship from digitally inflected disciplines, and leaves little space for thoughtful metacognitive reflection while authoring content. In such circumstances, when Scalar is incorporated as an afterthought, students are often left wondering why they needed to go through what feel like burdensome steps to post text and media for a teacher. The holistically integrated approach requires substantial up-front commitment and intentional design, but it is more likely to result in positive student and faculty engagement with course themes and materials, and the creation of web-based publications positively received by readers inside and outside of the campus community.

To provide context for general project ideas and learning activities, we present a single "case study" of a substantial Scalar integration in an upper-division Spanish course. The course availed us of a number of enabling circumstances: course development funds, collaboration with Dietrich and other Scalar developers, openness to fundamental experimentation with curriculum design, and a media-rich research project that engaged with various cultural forms (e.g., portraiture, book arts, novels, television, and film). While this particular course may have had an unusual confluence of resources and expertise, it should be understood as a highly scaffolded experiment for the exploration of a wide range of pedagogical possibilities. Below, we distill the course design principles and assignments into lessons that can be repurposed at a more modest scale.

19.3 Planning a term

19.3.1 Everything that is done in Scalar is a learning activity

For a course integrating Scalar, three structural concepts for the class should be considered: first, Collections-based Research, a collaborative, faculty-guided inquiry into a key question using a finite, curated set of works or objects (e.g., short stories, oral histories, music event posters, paintings, or zines); second, regular,

How to use scalar in the classroom

in-class "lab" time devoted to hands-on group and individual work in Scalar; and third, time in the class schedule to pause and reflect upon the form and organization of the Scalar book as it develops. These structures require advance planning and should preferably enlist the collaborative contribution of a Digital Humanities specialist, instructional designer, or librarian.

19.3.1.1 Collections-based research (CBR)

The animating idea behind CBR is to involve undergraduate students directly in the process of an authentic, open-ended inquiry task relevant to a teacher's own research agenda, and to develop curated collections of primary materials, such as paintings, photographs, sound files, specimens or artifacts as the starting point of curriculum design. In the example of this case study, the professor identified a corpus of video materials that students investigated with her guidance. This material may already be online in an existing archive or library such as YouTube, the Internet Archive, or Scalar-partner Critical Commons. If not, the project workflow should include preliminary work assembling and hosting primary content. As recommended in Scalar documentation, video clips should be housed externally from Scalar in an online archive so that they can be "imported" into a Scalar book rather than be hosted as large media files on the server on which Scalar is operating.

Using a CBR approach allows students to look and listen more closely and get beyond the tasks of seeking and choosing information (media) in support of a pre-existing thesis or to use as illustration. In research assignments that leave students to their own devices at the end of the term to choose a topic and find resources, students often have little guidance on what kinds of information, in what modes and formats, will be relevant. When faculty guide the collaborative curation of a set of primary objects, students can move beyond the threshold concept of research as inputting terms into a search bar and sifting through returns to more complex, inductive analytical tasks. The constraint in content selection also reduces intellectual labour on the part of the faculty member to consider the near-infinite possible range of material collected by students.

Early in course planning, consider: .

1. **Who can help you?** Locate your support network of library or technology expertise or a digital humanities specialist. Include them in the development of your syllabus from the beginning rather than coming to them with a request for a workshop (or two) to teach the tool.
2. **What is the collection of materials the students will examine?** Consider its scope, format, and possible places to locate the materials. Scalar's media import feature links directly to several prominent affiliated archives and widely used repositories. This is also a step that librarians can help support.
3. **Will you involve students in the selection of materials for the class collection or pre-determine the materials?** If involving students, consider how central evaluation and selection of works are to your learning goals. If you prefer to pre-determine the materials, will you have students upload them and provide metadata as a way to understand citation and context?
4. **What is the relationship between students' individual work and group work?** Will students do preliminary work as a team and produce individual analyses, or vice versa?

19.3.1.2 In-class labs

Regularized hands-on work in labs gives students time to absorb important skills while also drawing explicit connections between what they are putting into Scalar and the themes, materials, and skills of the course. An early assignment to select images from an archive, for example, can be a moment to reflect upon questions of authorship, representation, and accessibility. Soon after selecting images, lab time can focus on creating spatial annotations. In Scalar, annotation of still imagery entails drawing boxes over selected areas to highlight details, then inputting a title and descriptive or interpretive commentary. This "backward," or inductive approach to image analysis provides a first live opportunity for students to write text in the platform. To the extent that every form of content in Scalar becomes a discrete page, including annotations, students are thereby introduced to Scalar's fundamental "idiosyncrasy" of flattened content hierarchies. As students move through project work during the term, they will be less likely to develop notions of "normal" versus "abnormal" workflows based upon staged text composition in a word processing platform prior to pasting into Scalar.

As you develop your course schedule consider:

1. **When can you hold a lab?** Are there opportunities to add a low-unit lab to your existing course? Is it possible to devote a particular day of the week to hands-on work and "flip" some of your content delivery? If not, is it possible to flip some of the Scalar delivery through structured homework assignments?
2. **Where can you hold a lab?** Rooms with collaborative tables and projection may be hard to come by for the entire term but may be possible to book for specific sessions. Consider doing a technology survey with students so that they can communicate their technology and device needs directly to you if your room does not have devices available.

19.3.1.3 The Scalar book as documentation of collective process

The prioritization of course learning goals over project production entails prior acceptance of a somewhat unexpected genre of digital scholarship. With CBR and labs helping to drive the course schedule and assignments, the resulting Scalar book may look less like a ready-to-publish monograph and more like a combination of syllabus, learning management tool, process documentation, and student work. To frame this new hybrid product, faculty has taken to writing introductory essays that can become part of a teaching dossier or a publication. Because the book does not submit to a clear-cut distinction between "content" and course delivery mechanism, the syllabus should include "pauses" along the way that allow for a reflection on:

- Page length: making sure each page, which was written by individual students, are of similar length to avoid some pages being short and others noticeably longer, and consider whether each page will display the individual page author or if this will be left out in favor of a shared identity;
- Including media: having consistency in the placement of media in text pages including their size, relative position, and inclusion of annotations;
- Layout: if using Scalar "layouts" considering what messages are conveyed by, for example, Scalar's Splash Page and Image Header layouts;
- Interactive elements: when and why interactive elements, such as Scalar's Map and Timeline layouts and widgets, are included.

With a hybrid work product that involves student work, supporting curricular materials, and process documentation, we recommend a subsequent editorial process that refines and curates the collective document and frames the book for the reader with the professor's voice and teaching practice. While it is important for the course integration with Scalar to be collaborative, it can also be useful to identify in early conversations who will be doing what kind of labour. For example, a Digital Humanities specialist with design experience could take on the role of "technical editor," making sure pages in the Scalar book are consistent in form. The teacher could take on the "content editor" role ensuring that content (page texts, annotations, media metadata, etc.) are complete and error-free. This role might require the teacher to suspend prior assumptions about originality and authenticity of student-produced content as coursework; the teacher can clarify in the syllabus that, as the content editor, they will be making small and possibly substantial changes to student writing should the project be made public.

How to use scalar in the classroom

19.4 Course scaffolding

19.4.1 Use live examples from the course material.

In developing curriculum according to the Collections-Based Research (CBR) model, a central tenet is to integrate critical analytical skills from the outset of the syllabus. The first units of instruction might include, for example, production activities that explore and reflect upon online archives. By the mid-point of the course, students will be sufficiently prepared to thoughtfully select, annotate, and analyze media and related text, and place them into complex combinations. Annotations and other writing applied to the media can be created according to themes identified collaboratively in teams and in consultation with the teacher.

SPAN 320, "Golden Age of Spanish Literature and Film," was taught at Occidental College in Los Angeles in the Fall semester of 2017 by Professor Felisa Guillen, a Faculty Fellow of the Center for Digital Liberal Arts (CDLA), whose curriculum development efforts were supported by a grant from the Andrew R. Mellon Foundation. The course goals were to teach students spoken and written Spanish language skills as well as to develop critical digital information literacies and primary research practices using digital tools. The resulting Scalar book is entitled <u>Variantes de Cervantes: Representaciones del autor en el cine y la television</u> (Variants of Cervantes: Representations of the Author in Cinema and Television) <http://scalar. cdla.oxycreates.org/variantes-de-cervantes>. As is standard for the college's academic semester, the course was fifteen weeks long. At other institutions, the duration of a term may vary significantly. In our estimation the absolute length of a semester is not as important as the relative time and sequencing of activities inside Scalar relative to time devoted to other course activities.

The course involved undergraduate students directly in the process of an authentic inquiry task relevant to the teaching faculty member's own research agenda, and constrained to a curated collection of primary source materials. For SPAN 320, Professor Guillen had identified a corpus of cinematic and televised video materials that students investigated under her guidance. She describes the intellectual contribution of this research project in the introduction to the completed Scalar book, here translated into English by Guillen:

> In European book publishing since the second half of the 16th century it has been common practice to include a portrait of the author in the preliminary pages of his work. However, the contemporary reader of Cervantes will not find in the editions of his novels a pictorial semblance of the author. The reason for this absence has been the cause of much speculation, also encouraged by the ambiguity of the words of Cervantes himself. As is well known, in the "Prologue to the reader," at the beginning of his Exemplary Novels (1613), the author alludes to a possible portrait by Juan de Jauregui. Since such a visual portrait does not accompany the text of his novels, Cervantes creates a verbal self-portrait to compensate for that absence, imagining the description that could complement the image.
>
> Released from the spatial limitations of a visual portrait, Cervantes incorporates into his self-portrait biographical and literary aspects that would not fit in a single and fixed image as those of the illustrations of his time, nor in the painting that for a long time was considered as the true portrait by Jauregui, today considered by critics to be a "real fake." The expressive freedom exercised by Cervantes himself in his verbal self-portrait has given rise to writers', artists' and filmmakers' representations of the author from very different perspectives according to the vision of the creators, the historical circumstances, and the characteristics of each artistic medium. In this sense, the five biographical films about Cervantes that are analyzed in this project serve to examine how cinema and television propose a multifaceted and dynamic representation of the author that transcends the goal of memorializing or providing a "true portrait" of Cervantes.

The course also included a one-credit hour Digital Liberal Arts Lab, conducted in English, which met weekly for the duration of the term. The lab sessions were taught collaboratively by staff of the CDLA and included guest lectures, workshops and visits by colleagues from Occidental College, University of

Figure 19.1 Students collaborating on data entry in the digital liberal arts lab

Southern California, and University of California, Los Angeles. The lab scaffolded students' critical analytical skills and iteratively developed their proficiencies in using Scalar through a series of preliminary activities and exercises (Figure 19.1).

For the defining task of the term, students and professor researched, critically analyzed, and contextualized changing representations of the sixteenth-century Spanish novelist Miguel de Cervantes in cinema and television. They relied upon the scholarly video hosting site Critical Commons as a repository for media clips and commentary, and Scalar for comparative analysis in long-form text (having imported the Critical Commons videos into Scalar). Students worked in six teams of three, each addressing a different film or television episode. Individual student analyses, by group and written as Scalar pages, were bundled into Scalar paths, and synthetic conclusions were derived inductively through comparison of tagged annotations and other presentation affordances of Scalar (e.g. timeline and force-directed visualization). By the end of the course, the class had utilized almost all features of the platform. The completed Scalar book self-reflectively includes process documentation, preliminary activities for scaffolding student learning, instructions and lesson plans, all placed into path and consolidated using the book's Table of Contents feature (Figure 19.2).

Students were prepared for individual and group analysis of video clips during a preliminary series of activities related to the construction of facial representations in the sixteenth-century context, and more general human patterns of image and text perception. Their work began early in the course to learn the principles and practices of curating a shared collection of materials that the students subsequently investigated as objects of inquiry. The intent of introducing historical and theoretical frameworks was to

How to use scalar in the classroom

Disciplinary	Information Literacy	Spanish Language Development
• Comparative inter-media analysis of text, imagery, and moving imagery • Historical / longitudinal study of subjective self-representation • Coordinated and collaborative research techniques • Focused extraction of information as evidence from cultural phenomena via close observation	• Finding, collecting, curating, annotating, critically analyzing rich media archival content • Ethically participating in digital humanities knowledge communities • Collaborating effectively in structured team-based scholarly production activities with embedded faculty participation	• Writing analytically in a sophisticated and persuasive way. • Acquiring and consolidating control of complex lexical, grammatical, syntactic and stylistic features of the language. • Organizing and crafting discourse that is appropriate to the text modality and the target culture

Figure 19.2   Integrated course learning goals

help narrow the scope of inquiry and selection criteria; the course historically contextualized looking—tracing the (masculine) "gaze"—during the simultaneous rise in the latter sixteenth-century Europe of anatomical theaters, Elizabethan drama, group portraiture, and the printed novel.

19.5 Detailed assignment examples

19.5.1 Incorporate Scalar into the day-to-day activities of a class

The following assignments were developed and deployed in SPAN320, "Golden Age of Spanish Literature and Film," in 2017. The course assignments were divided roughly into two sections. The first, entitled "Reading Faces," included an *Ekphrasis* activity, and presented examples of portraiture in the late sixteenth and early seventeenth century to orient students to visual conventions of the period of study. For skill development students created spatial annotations. The second unit of the course, "Moving Images" centered upon a group-based critical analysis of living portraiture in film focused on representations of Cervantes in cinema and television. This section began with students making clips of video from a DVD and uploading them to Critical Commons. Clips were then imported into Scalar where video annotations were added. Thus, two sets of annotations—image and video—were created that were then managed via Scalar tags (each annotation was tagged to form meta-groups of annotations).

19.5.1.1 Reading faces

Ekphrasis is a term borrowed from the ancient Greek word ἔκφρασις or "description," to apply to a series of cultural practices at the intersection of text and visual imagery: poetic "translations" of a painting, for example, or detailed enumeration of elements of a work of art for interpretation and critical analysis. The corollary phenomenon, a painting derived from a work of literary text, represents an inversion of the practice.

Following an ekphrastic line of inquiry, students created collective comparative visual analyses of portraits of the novelist Miguel de Cervantes Saavedra (1547–1616), and playwright William Shakespeare (1564–1616), using Scalar's spatial (image) annotation feature. The sequence of activities began with several lab sessions devoted to basic technology skills, such as image acquisition, metadata, adding to a Scalar book, and the annotation feature, as well as a preparatory lesson about visual literacy (Figure 19.3).

On the first day of the ekphrasis unit, students were each instructed to create and name a Scalar page, and then write, directly into the page's WYSIWYG editor, spontaneous descriptions of two relevant historic

Cervantes

There is a painting. Begin by imagining a black rectangle, longer in height than width. Near the center of this rectangle is a human face (1), whose chin (2) rests on a collar (3) of creamy white ruffles (4). The body of this human is not visible below the ruffles (5), there is only blackness. The ruffles (6) waver around the neck (7) of the human approximately 26 times going back and forth from looking like raindrops and upside down raindrops in a pattern. The head (8) sits on the ruffles (9) softly, almost disembodied. A pointy, grey beard (10) rests above the near center of the ruffles (11) and continues up the jawlines (12) of the face (13) in soft lines. One ear (14) is visible where the grey beard (15) meets a darker grey hairline (16). Pouty pink lips (17) seem to barely hold up a grey mustache (18) in the shape of a boomerang. The face (19) is turned slightly almost in profile, allowing only one nostril (20) to be visible. The nose (21) is small but has a soft point and a large bridge at the top, perfect for resting glasses. Dark brown eyes (22) in full, almond shaped sockets droop slightly below thin and long brown eyebrows (23). The hairline (24) recedes to create a point on a large forehead (25). There is writing (26) on the top and the bottom of the painting, slightly too faint to read, possibly saying a name and date of the painting.

Parts

1. Face
2. Chin
3. Collar
4. Ruffles
5. Neck
6. Head
7. Beard
8. Jawlines
9. Ear
10. Hairline
11. Lips
12. Mustache
13. Nostril
14. Nose
15. Eyes
16. Eyebrows
17. Forehead
18. Writing

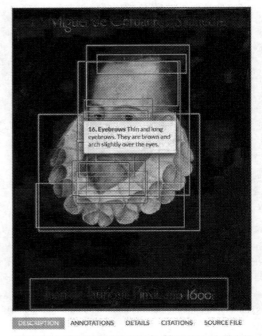

Figure 19.3 Screen capture of ekphrasis activity on a Scalar page with student description of an annotated image of Cervantes.

How to use scalar in the classroom

SPAN 320 "Ekphrasis of Two Faces" Data

Parts	Cnt	Ave	SD	Ratio	AA	BSF	CHG	CW	DB	ER	ET	JB	JD	LH	LBO	MS	NA	NH	OK	SP	SC	WA
Face	10	3.10	2.64	3.23	2	1	1	7		3	2			8	1				1			5
Beard	13	4.38	2.50	2.96		2		2	5	4	4	3	4	2	7	6		4			3	11
Collar	12	4.67	4.03	2.57		4	12	1	1			1	2	3	3	11		5			10	3
Head	8	3.25	4.30	2.46		13			1	1		1			6				2		1	1
Hair	11	4.73	2.80	2.33	4	3	3		4		10	4	6	1		2					9	6
Eyes	11	6.27	3.26	1.75	6		5		7		6	3	4	15	3			7			6	7
Eyebrow	12	6.92	3.50	1.73	5		4		8	7	8	5		16	9			2	6		5	8
Mustach	10	6.40	3.92	1.56	11		6		6		5	2			12	5		3			2	12
Lips	9	7.33	2.60	1.23				7	10		3			7	11	7		9	4	8		
Forehea	8	7.50	5.50	1.07	1		2		2					10	17	10		10	8			
Nose	9	8.67	2.83	1.04	12				9		7			6	14	8		8	5			9
Figure	1	1.00		1.00																	1	
Hairline	4	5.50	3.32	0.73	3				3	6					10							
Ears	6	9.00	2.90	0.67			9		8	9				5							9	14
Ear	5	7.60	5.08	0.66	15										9	1			6	7		
Chin	4	6.75	4.43	0.59											2				11		4	10
Shirt	1	2.00		0.50																		2
Facial H	4	8.50	4.20	0.47	10		8												3			13
Neck	3	7.00	3.46	0.43		5	11								5							
Jawline	3	8.33	4.51	0.36	13										8							4

Cervantes | Shakespeare

Figure 19.4   Screen capture of Google Sheet where students entered tallies of observed details

portraits of Cervantes and Shakespeare in a timed writing activity of 20 minutes—with explicit instruction to avoid interpretation and analysis. Then, over a series of lab sessions, students itemized and numbered each detail they observed, and collectively collated all their observations into a spreadsheet to determine what were the most salient features in the portrait.

Students then agreed upon a controlled list of terms for describing the respective portraits. Next, students each entered their respective lists of details in a shared spreadsheet (Figure 19.4). To establish a ranking of saliency, a synthetic score for each described detail was determined by the number of students who mentioned it divided by the number of its position in a sequence (e.g. 1 = first, 2 = second, etc.). Rankings of items were presumed to indicate the perceived importance to a viewer.

As a lab activity this broader exercise in quantification served two purposes: it developed students' patience and attention to detail as a visual literacy skill; and, it cultivated an essential cooperative group dynamic in following detailed directions toward a collaborative finding (Figure 19.5).

19.5.1.2 Moving pictures

After ekphrasis, students shifted to individual and group interpretation of cinematic clips in activities related to facial representations in a sixteenth-century context, and more general human patterns of image and text perception. Students learned the principles and practices of curating a shared collection of materials as exhibits and essayistic Scalar paths using a variety of digital processes. In the lecture and discussion component of the course run concurrently with the in-class lab, Professor Guillen addressed the ten target works of cinema and television, and on the basis of discussion and collaborative analysis

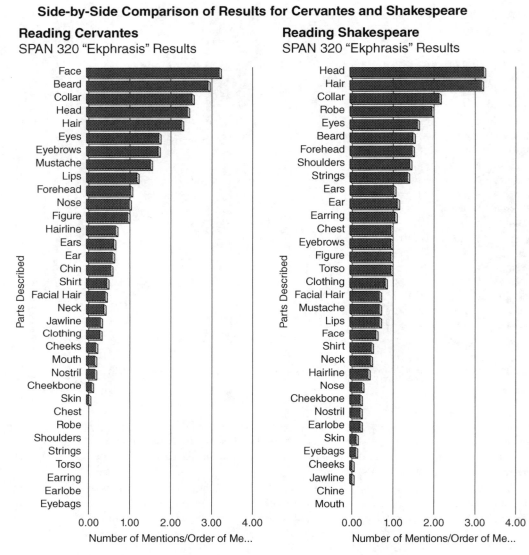

Figure 19.5 Data visualization of class observations of Cervantes and Shakespeare portraits

discerned the set of group topics relevant to each selected work, as well as a set of themes that intersected multiple works. This collective study of representations of Cervantes constituted the core contribution to the Scalar book.

To prepare students for the immediate technical and conceptual tasks of scholarly analysis of media, the CDLA invited Steve Anderson, UCLA Professor of Theater, Film and Television and Principle Investigator of Critical Commons, to conduct a hands-on workshop about copyright, fair use, and scholarly commentary using Critical Commons. Students worked in groups to review their assigned media, select longer clips for study, and upload their selections to Critical Commons as the media

How to use scalar in the classroom

repository (and online community on its own). Clips were then imported into Scalar for closer analysis using the time-based (video) annotation feature.

The second sequence of in-class labs required students to work in teams of two or three, collectively assigned to a different film or television series. Each individual participant submitted a Scalar page with embedded media (video and images) as well as annotations and tags that could be shared across the Scalar book and used by all participants collaboratively:

1. Text: approx. 1500–2000 words;
2. Media: curated selection of (approx. 7–10) items with complete and accurate metadata;
3. Annotations: highlighting details of media, with commentary and discussion;
4. Tags (optional): adding media and annotations to a controlled vocabulary of distinctive features (each vocabulary term as a Scalar page that becomes a tag of media and annotation pages).

The sequence of in-class lab activities for "Moving Pictures" paralleled and advanced students' skills for working in Scalar. The ekphrasis activity, "Reading Faces" (described above), dealt with: 1) close looking and page creation; 2) image import and metadata; 3) text markup; 4) annotation, then doing it again with another example, and then doing it again in Spanish. For "Moving Pictures," students engaged in: 1) close viewing; 2) clip extraction; 3) uploading using Critical Commons and adding commentary; 4) annotation. (For detailed descriptions of the instructions given to students, see Appendixes 1 and 2.) Students, now fluent in the language of Scalar and grounded in the analytical approaches of the course, worked more fluidly in groups to design their Scalar paths for the completion of the shared Scalar book.

19.6 Lessons from the case study

19.6.1 *Transferable principles for Scalar-based assignment design*

- Students benefit from guided hands-on instruction to become comfortable and proficient with Scalar and its features.
- Step-by-step detailed instructions are useful for in-class labs and for scaling assignments across terms or courses. In a pinch, instructions can be repurposed into homework modules emailed to students or posted to the learning management system.
- Reading is fundamental: before students practice clicking and choosing, instruction can begin with a close analysis of media *that is relevant to the course.* We try to avoid using throwaway or generic examples as practice.
- Once students are grounded in analysis, build the Scalar book inductively through assignment stages. Start with file organization, then media annotation, then text pages with embedded media, then paths.
- Every Scalar book benefits from both a good *technical* editor and *content* editor.
- Metacognition is essential to student learning: as busy as a term may be, it helps to build in moments during hands-on instruction to pause so that students can reflect on their process and demonstrate understanding of underlying principles.
- Once a course is over it is often difficult to return to the project and edit to standards of faculty scholarship. Unless you plan to use it for a research publication, allow the project to be seen as student work—including its blemishes and learning moments. As genuine curricular material it is likely to be more valuable to teaching colleagues.

Christopher Gilman, Jacob Alden Sargent and Craig Dietrich

Appendix 1: Week-by-week in-class lab session outline for SPAN 320

Week	Lab Plan
1 8/31	***Ekphrasis: "Ut pictura poesis" (reading images and vice versa)*** • Log in to Critical Commons / Scalar • **Activity** (in Scalar): *Ekphrasis* exercise (students write a descriptive paragraph of Cervantes portrait, then Shakespeare. *Notes: individual student writings will demonstrate: 1) selectivity of details; 2) sequence of priority*
2 9/7	**Digital Humanities and the "Idea of the Commons"** • Guest presentation and workshop w/ Steve Anderson, UCLA *Notes: Anderson will describe the history and thought behind Critical Commons and Scalar, esp. using copyrighted resources for academic fair use, contributing to the intellectual community w/ curated collections and commentary. He will also provide some guidance on film scholarship, esp. how to select and isolate clips as fundamental units of analysis.*

3 9/14	**Parts v. Wholes**
	
	• Presentation/Discussion
	  ♦ Lessing. *Laocoon*
	  ♦ Sawday. *The Body Emblazoned*
	  ♦ Eisenstein. *Laocoon.*
	• Activity
	Creative Commons login and procedures

4 9/21	**Reproduced Portraiture and Book Arts in the Age of Cervantes** • Visit Occidental Special Collections with guest presentation by Helena Vilar de Lemos, Book Arts Specialist
5 9/28	**The Writer's [Male] Gaze, Physiognomy and the History of Human Anatomy** • Guest presentation and workshop with Alexandra Sherman, Occidental Professor of Cognitive Science • Conduct eye tracking exercise w/students looking at portraits. • Review statistical analysis of Ekphrasis sequence of characteristic details *Markup and coding: what did you note first, then second, etc. What is the relationship between two sequential descriptions; and what is the statistical occurrence across the class? (comparing where eyes go in reading a face w/ word sequence in describing a face.*
6 10/5	**Learning Spanish through Research and Multimedia** • Yovanna Cifuentes, Language Education Specialist, CDLA (conducted in Spanish)
7 10/12	LAB CLOSED
8 10/19	**End of Ekphrasis / Group Assignments** • Ekphrasis upload (in Spanish) • Review of assignment • Formation of teams • Assignment of films to teams (mixed groups based on language proficiency) • How to watch the film (tagged notes and rough time-stamp) Each group watches their film. Guidelines (see questions I created over summer) Every group member takes notes in Google Docs Download **MPEG Streamclip**

How to use scalar in the classroom

Week		Lab Plan
9	10/26	**From Critical Viewing to Annotation**
		• Come with a carefully chosen clip / notes • Trim video • Upload video clip to Critical Commons / enter commentary • Use Annotation tool to annotate video using notes • Create individual Scalar pages
10	11/2	**Multimedia Analysis (Still and Video Annotation)**
		• Making and annotating stills • Related imagery • Cross-annotation • Page design
		Have a draft of their paper by then.
11	11/9	**Book-Making 1 (Collaborative Content-Driven Scalar Production)**
		• Categorization of ideas • Creating paths
	11/14	**Annotation of 1 clip**
12	11/16	**Book-Making 2:**
		• Categorization of ideas • Creating paths • The "big picture" (presentation of Exploding Tongues) • Lorem Ipsum 1500 words • Build all media
	11/21	**Rough Draft of Text w/ media** *Due*
13	11/23 11/28	**Thanksgiving Break**
14	11/30	**Critical Commons Redux**
		• Revising commentaries • Inputting overview
15	12/5 Last day	Project Showcase

Appendix 2: Ekphrasis sample assignment details in stages

Part 1. Ekphrasis

1. Create a page in Scalar.
2. Title the page with your last name, first name.
3. Enter description "Ekphrasis by Firstname"
4. View projected image of a portrait of Cervantes, and write a simple, detailed description paragraph in the Scalar WYSIWYG editor (10 mins.)
5. View projected image of a portrait of Shakespeare, and write a simple, detailed description paragraph (10 mins.)
6. Add the names Cervantes and Shakespeare above each paragraph, highlight each, select menu H1 and change formatting to Heading 3.

Part 2. Image upload

1. Open the Scalar book.
2. Open a new browser window, look up Miguel de Cervantes in Wikipedia, click on his image, and click the blue More details button to go to Wikimedia Commons. Find the globe icon and click "Use this file/on the web." In the popup window, select and copy the **second item (FILE URL:).**
3. In Scalar, roll over the Import Menu icon (an arrow pointing down into bin), and select the last menu option, **Internet media files**
4. Paste your copied URL into the **Media file URL** field. Just above in the **Description** field enter "Cervantes media import by Yourfirstname." For the title, return to the Wikimedia Commons page, and copy the title in Spanish in the blue Description field, including his vital dates. Then add a comma, and 1600 for the date. Then click **Save and view.**
5. Edit your media file by clicking the pencil edit icon. Click **Metadata**, and then **Add additional metadata.** Select all boxes in the **Featured** category, and click the blue **Add fields** button in the bottom right.
6. In the new metadata fields, copy and paste metadata from the Wikimedia page:

    a. dcterms:date [1600]
    b. dcterms:source [Real Academia de la Historia]
    c. iptc:By-line [Attributed to Juan Martínez de Jáuregui y Aguilar (1583–1641)]
    d. dcterms:coverage [Spain]
    e. dcterms:spatial [Madrid, Spain]
    f. dcterms:temporal [1547–1615]
7. Then click **Save and view**

Part 3. Text markup

1. Go to Scalar table of contents, and find your own ekphrasis page by clicking the carrot to the right of "Ekphrasis of Two Faces…" and select it.
2. Click the pencil icon to edit the page
3. In your paragraph text, identify each instance of a facial part (e.g. nose, eyes, etc.) or clothing and accessories (e.g. collar), and insert a number in parentheses in sequence (1), (2)… before each one. If a part is repeated, mark with (1a)…Do not number text or background. IMPORTANT: DO NOT CHANGE, EDIT, OR CORRECT YOUR TEXT!
4. Below your paragraph, write Parts in italics
5. Under Parts, use the number icon in the toolbar to create a list. Write down just the name of the part in order of occurrence in the paragraph
6. Highlight the name Cervantes, and click the leftmost blue "play" button in the toolbar to "Insert Scalar Media Link"
7. In the Select content menu, look for your own bar in the Description column "Cervantes media import by Yourname," and click the play thumbnail on the far left to load.
8. In the popup window, select Size: Medium, Align: Right, and Caption: Title and Description, then click **Continue.**

Part 4. Annotation

1. Open a new window for the course Scalar project so you have two side by side, and find your own page
2. In the new screen, roll over the caption under Cervantes image, and click on **Details**
3. Click **Scalar URL** to go to the Media page
4. In the menu bar at the top right of your screen select the paper clip icon to **Annotate**

How to use scalar in the classroom

5. The annotation editor will appear and ask you to Click and Drag to draw a box. Using your list of Parts, draw a box around each of the parts in order. If you want to change size or location of the box, use the +/- tools
6. In the blank "Add a comment," write the number, insert a period and name of the part only, then hit **Save**.
7. In the Description field below, type "Interpretive analysis by Yourname."
8. In the Content field, type in a brief (2 sentence) prose description and interpretation. This statement is subjective and interpretive, but should be reasonable to anyone looking at this same image. Then click **Done.**
9. Repeat for all Parts on your list.
10. When you have finished all your annotations, return to your page from the Contents menu. Click the **edit** pencil icon, roll over the blue highlighted Cervantes name, and click the gear icon. Select all annotations to be displayed, and choose "None" as Featured Annotation. Then click **Continue.** In your editing interface, click **Save and display.**
11. You are done! Now do the same thing for Shakespeare!

Part 4a (Homework). Cervantes cleanup and Shakespeare thereafter

1. Open up two windows with the class Scalar project, so you can see these instructions **and** the page you are editing. Go to Scalar table of contents, and find your own **ekphrasis** page by clicking the carrot to the right of "Ekphrasis of Two Faces…" and select it. If you have more items to complete or correct, click the pencil icon to edit the page. Here's what you might need to correct: a) **only** facial parts and clothing are to be described; b) **only** nouns are to be included in the list of parts.
2. Repeat all the steps in Parts 2–4, but replace Shakespeare for Cervantes. Note, also, that the date 1600 should be adjusted to 1610.
3. As a check, the metadata from the Wikimedia page should look like this:

    g. dcterms:date [1610]
    h. dcterms:source [National Portrait Gallery]
    i. iptc: By-line [Attributed to John Taylor]
    j. dcterms:coverage [England]
    k. dcterms:spatial [London, England]
    l. dcterms:temporal [1564–1616]

Part 5. Reassembling parts

4. Data cleanup: Open your own ekphrasis page, and check for missing or insignificant elements
5. Controlled vocabulary: collective agreement on terminology for list of parts. Facilitator enters into Sheet
6. Open Google Sheet spreadsheet
7. Find your initials in the header, and enter in the ordinal number of each part you listed.
8. Discuss individual v. collective ordering of facial parts

Part 6. Ekphrasis en Español

1. Create a new page in Scalar.
2. Title the page with Ekphrasis in Spanish by your first name (all in Spanish).
3. Enter description "Ekphrasis of Cervantes portrait by yourname"
4. Input your Spanish-language ekphrasis text, using the "paste as plain text" button (clipboard with T on the left side of the toolbar)

5. Insert inline Scalar media link, using the second blue "play" button from the left in the toolbar. Search for your own imported media of Cervantes by typing your own name in the search field and selecting the media you, yourself, imported. Select medium size and align right. Suppress all previous annotations (in English)
6. Click the blue Save and view button at the bottom of the input screen.
7. Find your Cervantes image using the Dashboard (wrench icon), selecting the media tab and searching for your name, or by finding the Scalar link in "Details" under the image as it appears in your page.
8. Enter in all your annotations in Spanish just as you did with English. There will be a lot of annotations to deal with, so be patient! When you are done with annotations, make sure to edit your page (pencil icon), roll over the image thumbnail, and click on the gear icon to pull up the formatting options. Suppress all English annotations and activate all Spanish, then select "none."
9. Tagging: select the relationships tab below the WYSIWYG editing window, and choose "Tag" at the bottom of the menu. You will use both tagging options. Click each link to "choose…" and select your English-language ekphrasis page titled with your name.
10. Click Save and view.

Appendix 3: Moving Images Sample Assignment Details in Stages

Participants in SPAN 320 Digital Liberal Arts Lab work in teams to analyze cinematic and television representations of Cervantes. Each student produces a multi-page (2–3) path with approximately 5–7 pages of conventional text (@ 1500–2000 words), and approximately 7–10 video annotations of the group-assigned video content, with comparative use of video stills, other imagery and annotations. Pages and media in individual paths will be selectively incorporated into other non-linear project elements, using tagging, paths, timeline, or other features of Scalar, in response to commentary and input by Professor Guillen and others.

Part 1. Analytical viewing

1. Open your group Google Doc for viewing notes
2. Read specific instructions to access your film/TV episode (each film is different). Then:

   ♦ view your video fully as a group
   ♦ identify prospective sections of video you might use for your Scalar paths, and take notes collaboratively in your Google Doc.
   ♦ choose one clip that you know you want to use in lab 10/26 for uploading to Critical Commons, and importing to Scalar.

Part 2. From analytical viewing to MPEG Streamclip

How to use scalar in the classroom

Screenshot showing menu option to upload a file to the MPEG Streamclip software.

Screenshot showing where the playhead slider is located in the MPEG Streamclip interface. Also highlights indication of In and Out selections.

1. At least one member of your group should download the video file of your film/TV episode onto a laptop.
2. If you haven't already, download MPEG Streamclip onto your computer and install it.
3. From your notes, select one clip that you would like to upload to include in the Scalar project (you will select more in the future, but today's exercise is to get you comfortable with the process).
4. Open MPEG Streamclip.
5. Go to Files > Open Files and select your group video.
6. Use the slider below the video to fast forward to the starting point of your clip. Once you have positioned the play head at the starting point, press I on your keyboard (or Edit > Select In). This sets the In point.
7. Locate the end of the clip, and press O on your keyboard (or Edit > Select Out). This sets the Out Point.
8. Once your In and Out Points are set, select Edit > Trim (or Cmd+T) to trim the clip. When you play back the clip after trimming, it will only play the short portion between the In and Out points you just set.
9. Select File > Save As and title your clip. Be sure to give it a different title than the full video to ensure you don't overwrite the full video.

Christopher Gilman, Jacob Alden Sargent and Craig Dietrich

Part 3. From MPEG Streamclip to Critical Commons

Screenshot of the page in Critical Commons to upload a video clip.

Screenshot of the page in Critical Commons where user adds commentary about a video clip.

How to use scalar in the classroom

Commentary page in Critical Commons indicated published status after saving commentary.

1. Visit the Critical Commons website and log into your account.
2. Click on Upload in the top navigation.
3. Fill in all the required fields and any optional fields for which you have information. Tag your clip SPAN320 and any other descriptive keywords useful for categorizing the clip. Add your video clip file and click Save changes at the bottom of the page. The description field is not your commentary, just a brief one sentence description of why you are sharing this clip.
4. After the file is uploaded, transcoding will begin and you are prompted to add commentary on the clip. This is where you should enter the short notes you took about this clip – the information that made this clip important to your analysis. You also need to title your commentary. Once finished, click Save and you will see that the clip goes from a status of Private to Published.

Part 4. From Critical Commons to Scalar media

Screenshot showing how to access Critical Commons importer via the import menu in Scalar toolbar.

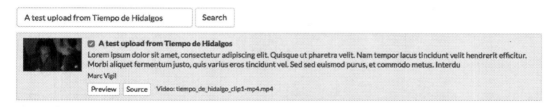

Screenshot showing an item ready to be imported into Scalar.

1. Visit the Scalar book.
2. Select the **Import Media menu icon > Affiliated archives > Critical Commons**
3. Search for your clip by title on the Critical Commons Importer page. Once you have found your clip, tick the box next to the clip and click the Import Selected button at the bottom of the page.
4. On the next page, edit metadata fields as needed. For example, the dcterms:publisher field is carried over from the Distributor field in Critical Commons, but the Publisher (i.e. the studio that produced the film or TV series) may be different from the company that distributes it. Click Continue.
5. You can now check the media page and this video clip can now be embedded in any page within the Scalar book.

Part 5. From Scalar media to Scalar annotation

Video annotation in Scalar is time-based, and allows critical analysis of "clips within clips." Each annotation can be displayed as its own interactive illustration in a page of text, or a full clip can be displayed with multiple annotations. Each student should create an annotation to the shared video clip.

1. To annotate video, click the paper clip Annotate icon. Click the + button and use the video viewer and play button to find in and out points for the "clip within a clip" you wish to annotate, and click the green Set buttons to mark those points.
2. Title each annotation with a succinct name to describe what it is you are saying. In the Content field, enter the full text of your analysis of this section of a clip. LEAVE THE DESCRIPTION FIELD BLANK. (Note: this is a correction of previous instructions! If the description is filled in, only it will appear on the text page; if it is not filled in, the full annotation, with media, will load and display on the page if it is set to do so.)
3. Click Save, then Done.
4. Once entered, annotations can be edited as their own Scalar page, to include media and create relationships, such as Paths and Tags. To further edit the annotation click the annotation title link or search for the annotation in the Book or Dashboard.

Part 6. From Scalar annotation to Scalar page

Annotations can serve as "clips within clips" in a Scalar page with proper settings.

1. Each group member should create a New page by clicking the plus button. These pages will begin your group project work, so title them appropriately, including the name of the film or television serial you are analyzing (in Spanish). In Description, include your own name, e.g. "Film analysis by Chris"
2. Input some temporary dummy text. Highlight text and click the blue "Insert Scalar Media link" button or move the cursor to a desired spot in the text and click the "Insert inline Scalar Media link" button. In the "Select content" dialog box scroll, find and select your group's clip. Click anywhere on the bar except the blue link text (if you click the link, it will open the video clip in a new tab, so just click open the last tab).
3. In the "Media formatting options" dialog box, select desired size and position, and change "Create new line…" to "Wrap text…"
4. For caption, select Title and Description (for now…your judgment may change on this later)
5. Select only your own annotation and leave it selected as the Featured Annotation.
6. Click Done, then Save and view at the bottom of the page editor screen.
7. Check to see that your annotation loads automatically in your page.

Part 7. From amateur to intermediate

Until this point, all instruction in Scalar has been directed and uniform. Now, you will gradually transition to small group and independent research and production work outside of lab, and productive, hybrid learning and research consultations with each other, Professor Guillen, CDLA staff, peer-learning support and Scalar help guides.

1. For a little "clean-up" from last week's Annotation work, each group should open the Dashboard (wrench icon) find their own media clip and look to see whether a duplicate was made. If so, look at how many annotations were made on each and decide among group members which one should be retained and which deleted. For those whose annotations will be deleted, copy any meaningful annotation text and recreate your own on the single shared clip.

2. Note that instructions last week (Part 5. above) incorrectly advised you to add a summary of the annotation in Description. Upon further investigation it was discovered that leaving Description blank allows for robust annotation. Every student should go back and edit their annotation to remove description.
3. Constructing a Path. Each group should find their own group Scalar path in the Moving Pictures path. You will notice that the Visual Path layout presents your clip as background to the link to your path. Open and edit your group Path. At the bottom of the editing page, tab to Styling, and from the menu select Key Image. Scroll through the list of media items and select or confirm the film clip you uploaded. As you import the remainder of your film clips, you will review this selection and decide which you would like to represent your project. Then tab to layout menu where it says Basic, and switch it to Splash (not Book Splash). Then Save and view.
4. Developing your skillsets and expressive choices. Click to the next page in this path to view and learn about various features of Scalar for integrating media with text. The page should be self-explanatory. Review the text and annotations, and discuss which of these you would like to start with your group.

Part 8. Film clips

This is the first full-day lab session, with hands-on project work time for importing all video clips and learning how to annotate video.

1. Video annotation, you should recall, is a means to create "clips within a clip." Each individual project page should have a minimum of three video annotations (that is, your own analysis of a portion of a clip that might be shared with other members of your group.
2. Groups that elect to provide transcriptions of difficult audio Spanish dialog can subtitle clips using Camtasia, which is a licensed software available in all computers in the Critical Making Studio. Original clips without titles must also be imported, and transcriptions should be included as one annotation of the video.

Part 9. What is an annotation?

Review of one sample video annotation per group. Annotations should have the following elements and qualities:

- Succinct title (noun phrase or short sentence) that clearly identifies what the annotation is about, so it can be used or read by others outside its immediate context.
- Body text of approx. 3 sentences, including: contextual "ekphrasis" style description, so viewer knows what you're talking about; analysis, interpretation, and/or commentary on the clip.

Part 10. Multimedia

This lab is devoted to importing, annotating and adding multimedia content to your paths, including imagery and stills (screen grabs) of video clips. Professor Guillen has provided scans of texts that include images and metadata for your use. For any images you intend to use as Scalar media, a high-resolution scanner will be brought to lab. Do not use a screen grab of her PDF(!) as image quality will be too low.

1. The scanner will be set up with the Varelas Innovation Lab built-in Mac Mini computers. "Keeper" scans should be uploaded to the **SPAN 320 Materials > Still Images Google Drive before being uploaded to Scalar via Import menu > Local media files**.

2. Each uploaded image should have relevant metadata included upon upload. Remember, you can add appropriate fields by clicking the tab Metadata > Add additional metadata, and selecting from the options. Hint: try to keep with "Featured" fields to reduce unnecessary complexity.
3. Every image that has been scanned from <u>Miguel de Cervantes: de la vida al mito</u> should have an additional metadata field. Click the Metadata tab > Add additional metadata and select dcterms, and select the box for bibliographicCitation. Cut and paste these full citations in the metadata field then add the page number: Lucía Megías, José Manuel. Miguel De Cervantes: de la vida al mito. Madrid, Biblioteca Nacional de España, 2016.

The other book is:

- Cervantes Saavedra, Miguel de. Novelas exemplares. Madrid, 1614. Facsim. Ed. Alicante: Biblioteca Virtual Miguel de Cervantes, 2001.

Part 11. Editing and stylistic consistency: Formatting, style, font, page titles, and so on

You have all submitted rough draft texts and imported media, then taken a long, well-deserved Thanksgiving break. This lab and set of guidelines and instructions are devoted to the important work of ensuring basic editorial standards of coherence, consistency and uniformity among your individual and small group submissions, as well as catching up on those Scalar proficiencies that may have slipped past you the first time or two. Please refer to instructions on the following page for advanced suggestions on how to annotate using rich media.

- **TEXT.** All body text should be input directly or pasted in using the Paste as plain text or Paste as Word tools (clipboards with T or W, respectively) in the upper left of the editing screen. Otherwise you will have non-standard fonts or formatting from excess code. If you already pasted text directly in the screen, you will have to do it again and rebuild your page.
- **TITLE.** The title of your page should individually reflect the subject matter of your critical analysis, and not be the name of the media you are analyzing. Your page should begin directly with body text, and not include a header or other information typical of a course paper.
- **CITATIONS.** All citations will appear in a single Works Cited page. Add any new citations to this list, and include in your text an MLA citation, (Author, Date), highlight this citation, and click the Insert Scalar Note (third blue icon from the left), then search "Works Cited" to call up the link.
- **FORMATTING.** You should use the media formatting options in the popup to arrange and size media in an intentional and thoughtful way to enable viewer/readers to understand importance and relationships of media in combination. Wrap text around media, and choose left or right side to best position items in relation to text. Master the difference between Scalar Media Link and Inline Scalar Media Link to make your choices between the two purposeful.
- **ANNOTATION.** Remember that you have to activate any annotations you want to appear on your page! Click the pencil edit icon and hover over the media icon to enable re-formatting of the media, then select annotations by clicking the eyeball icon, and toggle to "None."

20
DISCOVERING DIGITAL HUMANITIES METHODS THROUGH PEDAGOGY

Kristen Mapes

20.1 Introduction

An understanding Digital Humanities as a field is enriched through exploration of the way that it is introduced to students. This study examines the methods and approaches to teaching Digital Humanities in the context of ten "Introduction to Digital Humanities" courses during the timeframe of 2014–2018. It builds on curricular studies conducted by Terras and Spiro, aiming to update them and to define the corpus of study more narrowly to discover how DH as a field is framed (Terras, 2006 and Spiro, 2011). I also build on Sula, Hackney, and Cunningham's study, which looked at Digital Humanities programs through their requirements and descriptions but not at the level of the individual course (2017). Sula, Hackney, and Cunningham specifically pointed out that studying curriculum—both at the programmatic and course level—illuminates and reflects some of the larger tensions in the field around what it means to do DH. I also explore the relationship between pedagogy in the introductory DH classroom and the research, publication, and presentation practices of the instructors to discover whether the DH work in the classroom carries over into the instructors' DH work outside of it.

I entered into the study particularly interested in the relationship between the introductory DH classroom and university infrastructures for Digital Humanities, such as the DH Center or DH Lab, especially infrastructures present in libraries. I discovered that my expectation that there would be a strong relationship between libraries/librarians and the introductory DH classroom is not supported by this syllabus corpus. Indeed, these syllabi show that while there is a priority in bringing in guest speakers and exposing students to the professional community and its practices a practice of bringing libraries into direct contact with the course is absent.

Lisa Spiro's framing of Digital Humanities as centered around a set of values (openness, collaboration, collegiality and connectedness, diversity, and experimentation) in 2012 established a lens through which to examine DH activity and a proxy for a definition that is freed from disciplinary boundaries methodological list-making[1]. I apply this values-driven approach to ask how the field of DH defines itself as demonstrated by how practitioners choose to teach the introductory DH course:

- Are the values of the field taught to students?
- What methods are emphasized and what classroom approaches are taken to train digital humanists?
- How does teaching DH relate to an instructor's DH work writ large, especially in light of a framework in which DH emphasizes collaboration and experimentation?

By asking these questions of a corpus of syllabi, we learn about the state of the field beyond the individual classroom.

20.2 Background

DH carries a range of meanings depending on the context, but it has coalesced into an institutionally recognized field in many universities, with the attendant course offerings. In conjunction with this growth in curricular programs, there have also been publications and discussions around what DH pedagogy is and should be.

Melissa Terras' article in Literary and Linguistic Computing in 2006, "Disciplined: Using Educational Studies to Analyse 'Humanities Computing'", explored the framing of Humanities Computing as a field through its educational expression and participation of scholars at conferences to discover which disciplines were participating in and influencing the emerging field (Terras, 2006). Following on Terras' study of Humanities Computing curriculua, Lisa Spiro's presentation at the 2011 Association of Digital Humanities Organizations (ADHO) DH conference, "Knowing and Doing: Understanding the Digital Humanities Curriculum" reported on a study not only of curricular programs writ large but examined DH syllabi in depth (Spiro, 2011). A more detailed analysis of the findings of these two studies will be discussed later in relation to the findings made here.

Digital Humanities Pedagogy: Practices, Principles and Politics (Hirsch, 2012) included chapters discussing program and course structures, class assignments, and theories of pedagogy. The volume showed the role of DH pedagogy in a range of classroom types (e.g. first-year writing and public history) while highlighting discussions about the intersection of DH values and the classroom (e.g. collaboration, openness, and experimentation). Hirsch's introduction to the volume laid out the stakes of DH pedagogy: "there is no better way to stabilize a field than through pedagogy [… and] canons play an integral role in reshaping our fields" (Hirsch, 2012, p. 13). Teaching forces us to give the field shape and to establish reference texts, a process which establishes the field and creates new scholars in it. The volume did not provide a blueprint for DH pedagogy, but instead addressed issues in the field. At the same time, the *Debates in Digital Humanities*' 2012 edition included a section devoted to "Teaching the Digital Humanities" with eight chapters, ranging from discussions of assignment types (Kelly, Sample, Owens, Gold and Groom) to DH pedagogy in different institutional contexts (Alexander and Frost Davis) to critique of the absence of pedagogy in DH writing (Brier). With the publication of these two volumes, DH pedagogy entered the conversation. Already in 2012 questions that continue to be explored in this study were being raised, especially around issues of teaching in relationship to research and in questioning what teaching DH on the ground means in the classroom and as expressed through the values and methods introduced to students.

Since 2012, there have been many articles and discussions about pedagogy, including a special issue of the College English Association's journal *CEA Critic* on Digital Humanities Pedagogy in 2014, edited by Ann R. Hawkins. Leigh Bonds' essay "Listening in on the conversations: An overview of digital humanities pedagogy" provides a survey of the contemporary discussion, pointing out that "the ideas shared in these conversations on DH pedagogy reflect the active learning strategies promoted by education researchers" (Bonds, 2014, p.152). Bonds notes the prevalence of collaboration, project analysis, and experimentation as hallmarks of the DH classroom, but the context about whether these approaches are unique to DH or whether they are simply best practices for teaching in general is an intriguing question.

Digital Humanities Quarterly's "Imagining the DH Undergraduate: Special Issue in Undergraduate Education in DH", edited by Murphy and Smith, in 2017 showed examples of DH approaches to specific classroom and experiential learning contexts (Hswe, LaLonde, Miffitt, O'Sullivan, Pickle, Piekielek, Ross, and Rozo), as well as sections on DH teaching in the disciplines and the relationship between tool development and the DH student. These articles show the range of activities that can be undertaken in the DH classroom. The focus on the disciplinary context for DH teaching that comes through in the issue builds on Ryan Cordell's essay, "How not to teach digital humanities", from the 2016 edition of *Debates in Digital Humanities*, in which he argued that Digital Humanities teaching should be integrated into disciplinary courses rather than taught as "DH qua DH". In this vein, Battershill and Ross' 2017 volume *Using Digital*

Humanities in the Classroom is specifically written for instructors teaching in the disciplines who would like to add digital humanities to their courses, rather than for instructors looking to teach an introductory course in digital humanities.

While the debate about whether digital humanities should continue as its own field or be subsumed into the differing humanities (and beyond) fields in which it operates is interesting, this study examines the state of the field as it stands, and how that is reflected through the DH courses which are taught. Of particular interest to this study was Scott Selisker's reflective essay, "Digital humanities knowledge: Reflections on the introductory graduate syllabus", also from the 2016 *Debates* volume. The chapter discussed the tensions at play in the creation of an introductory DH syllabus, including how to balance methods and tools, especially addressing the question of "how much programming?". Stephen Ramsay's chapter in *Digital Humanities Pedagogy*, "Programming with Humanists: Reflections on raising an army of hacker-scholars in the digital humanities" (2012), also discussed this question, as did Nick Montfort's chapter in the *New Companion to Digital Humanities* in 2015, "Exploratory programming in digital humanities pedagogy and research." There is no consensus on whether DH pedagogy must include programming, as much as Montfort makes a compelling argument and a passionate plea for it. Consequently, this study asks if programming is taught at the introductory level of DH.

While the literature around pedagogy and DH has grown in recent years, especially since Spiro's study of DH syllabi in 2011 and the publication of *Digital Humanities Pedagogy* in 2012, there remains a divide between the continued discussions of the future of DH as a field and the role of pedagogy in the field. For example, Svensson's chapter on "Sorting out the Digital Humanities" in the *New Companion to Digital Humanities* in 2016, which looked for approaches to "resolving the key tensions" in the field in order to move DH and the humanities forward, emphasized "us[ing] infrastructure as a way of channeling resources" to be an inclusive space, and "requires the digital humanities to have integrity and the ability to empower the development of research and education".[2] And yet, such an essay addressing the field and its role within the university, and indeed within the humanities, does not address pedagogy at all. The only time "pedagogy", "teaching", or "education" are raised throughout the essay is the one instance of "education" in the abstract. This critique of Svensson's essay is not particular to him but raises the point that DH pedagogy and DH writ large are inextricably related and yet pedagogy is often only briefly mentioned when scholars discuss DH outside of pedagogy specific contexts. When we talk about DH values such as collaboration and project work, we are often relying on the work of students, whether undergraduate or graduate. The students may be a part of our courses, participating in a larger project during a single term; they may be hired as an employee or intern to gain experience in the field outside of a course; or, they may be a graduate assistant tasked with shepherding along a faculty project.[3] The role of the classroom and of students in DH writ large cannot simply be an afterthought.

Even beyond formal project collaborations with students, the DH classroom is a project unto itself. Instructors and students learn together what new technologies and questions may be used and asked. As new tools and techniques are developed, the course instructor may not have any formal training in them, and as such may be learning alongside their students. Because DH courses often strive to bring in students from multiple disciplines and DH as a whole seeks to embrace many disciplinary approaches and perspectives, we listen to the approaches our students bring to the conversation. The DH classroom as collaboration stems from the experimentation that we undertake with methods and tools as well as from the dialogue built into an interdisciplinary (or at least multidisciplinary) context itself. In this study, we see examples of the classroom as DH project: Shawn Graham's course is framed around the collective writing of an undergraduate DH textbook by the students; and, in my course, students undertake a large DH project of their own, with class time devoted to shared learning and troubleshooting through the project creation process.

Curricular programs in digital humanities (and similarly titled fields, such as digital cultural studies, digital liberal arts, and digital history) have become common at both the undergraduate and graduate level, particularly in North America and Europe, growing in number substantially since 2008 (Sula, Hackney, and Cunningham, 2017). Directories of programs (DARIAH[4], Advanced Degrees in DH[5], Programs Data[6]) now serve to introduce potential students and academics across the field to this activity on the ground. Sula, Hackney, and Cunningham scanned thirty-seven programs in 2015 to discover what trends existed on the programmatic level, collecting data such as: titling of programs, programming requirements, experiential or internship requirements, and the institutional locations of program administration. While looking for similarities across programs, the study emphasized the importance of the local context for shaping what DH curriculum means on any one campus.[7]

Since most Digital Humanities programs are not degree granting (across both undergraduate and graduate levels—the highest percentage of degree granting programs is for masters degrees, at 22% [Sula, Hackney, and Cunningham]), the impact of individual courses within a program rather than on the program as a whole may carry more weight because students do not encounter as many courses in DH as they would if it were their major or degree. Sula, Hackney, and Cunningham's study points out its inability to explore the role of critical theory and critical thinking in these programs solely through the program descriptions alone, as "local interpretation" influences how reflection is presented and integrated into the classroom. Individual syllabi provide a more direct approach into these sorts of questions, revealing the DH methods and values implemented in the classroom. Examining syllabi of DH instruction shows at a more granular level the methods and approaches to DH as they are actually taught.

Sula, Hackney, and Cunningham also noted a lack of attention in program descriptions to terms associated with the work of librarianship and archiving, fields which have a strong affiliation with DH[8]. Libraries and librarians are involved in many ways: providing lab space, technology and support, material for digitization and collections for analysis; in class visits, as embedded librarians, and as instructors for credit-bearing courses; and, as project leaders and research collaborators. Using the TaDiRAH taxonomy[9] to categorize digital humanities activity, Sula et al observed a scholarly disconnect, in which the work done by faculty, which includes collaborations with librarians and involves activities of "storage", "preservation", "organizing", and "editing", are not seen as fully scholarly work in the same way as "analysis", "critical thinking", and "project management". The lack of inclusion of activities relating to librarianship in DH program descriptions, according to Sula et al, "seems constituent with claims made by librarians that their expertise in technology, information organization, and scholarly communication is undervalued in the field, whether instrumentalized as part a service model that excludes them from the academic rewards of and critical decision-making in DH work [...] or devalued as a form of feminized labor." With this observation about the absence of library work in DH program descriptions in mind, this study looked for evidence for the work of librarianship in individual syllabi.

Among the key concepts discussed in Spiro's findings are "data and databases" and "openness and copyright", which point to areas in common with libraries and archives [Spiro 2011]. This close reading of a sample of syllabi pays particular attention to the methods taught in DH courses, but it also notes whether there is a course collaboration with a librarian or archivist (e.g. class visit, embedded librarian, co-teaching).

20.3 Creating the corpus

This examination explores the field of digital humanities as expressed through the syllabi of ten introductory courses, and to see what methods and values are taught in the field as well as how the teaching of the field does or does not intersect with the research program of the instructors. While a small corpus has limitations, it allows for individual assessment of the content that takes into account the nuance of context and allows for a look at the research practices of the instructor.

The corpus (Table 20.2) was formed around several requirements. All courses needed to be titled either "Introduction to Digital Humanities" or something very similar for two reasons. First, courses specifically titled "Digital Humanities" were included to examine how digital humanities is taught as a discipline. Second,

Discovering digital humanities methods

Table 20.1 Requirements for selection

Requirements for selection
Titled "Introduction to Digital Humanities" or very similar
Taught 2014–2018
English language
Must be available freely online (either through an institutional/ subject repository or as a public website)

the aim was to compare similar courses and not attempt to compare courses across disparate disciplinary fields. In rder to build on and compare with earlier work, the courses must have been taught since Terras', Spiro's, and Sula, Hackney, and Cunningham's studies and be as recent as possible at the time of writing, so the timeframe was restricted to 2014–2018. The courses had to be taught in English, based on my own linguistic limitations. The syllabi had to be available freely online, either through an institutional or subject repository or a public website. Open access is a value of the digital humanities, and while more nuance is being introduced into the field about when openness is and is not appropriate, it is still a priority on the whole, and so evaluating courses shared in this way suits the norms of the field (Table 20.1).

In addition to the above criteria for corpus creation, I also aimed to be inclusive in my selections. I attempted to include a balance between undergraduate and graduate level courses. I sought gender diversity among course instructors and geographic diversity of institutions where the courses were taught. I looked for a variety of institutional types to reflect the range of contexts for introductory DH courses—whether at large, public, research universities or smaller private institutions or another type entirely. Finally, I tried to capture a variety of disciplinary backgrounds among the instructors (LIS, history, literature, area studies).

There were challenges to compiling this corpus despite recent efforts from around the field to create repositories for Digital Humanities syllabi. The search for syllabi explored Humanities Commons, Lisa Spiro's Zotero group on Digital Humanities Education[10], and the "Advanced Degrees in Digital Humanities" Github page[11]. I also consulted the Digital Humanities in the Classroom online Scalar book[12], focusing particularly on the chapters "Designing Syllabi" and "Teaching Graduate Students", which led me CUNY's DH syllabi list[13] and Scott Weingart's curated list of syllabi[14]. Finding a balance of syllabi between undergraduate and graduate courses was initially a goal for the corpus, but considering the other requirements, it had to be abandoned. Most of the syllabi with the title requirements I was looking for were for graduate courses, a challenge which reflects Terras' finding in 2006 that most curricula around DH were at the graduate level (Terras 2006, p. 234). Another challenge in creating the corpus was finding courses titled "Introduction to Digital Humanities" or very similar. I set this parameter to ensure continuity across the courses and to avoid comparing courses from different disciplines which might incorporate DH[15]. Initially, I planned for the corpus to build on Sula, Hackney, and Cunningham's programmatic study by compiling syllabi only from institutions listed in the study or DARIAH's programs list. However, finding syllabi published online became a challenge, so I opened the corpus creation up to any introductory DH course at any university. The largest challenge was not finding syllabi, but rather finding syllabi within the timeframe which fit the parameters I set forth.[16]

The corpus includes ten syllabi—four at the undergraduate level, and six at the graduate level —the vast majority of which are from the United States, with one each from Canada, Ireland, and the Netherlands. This heavy United States focus and entirely Western corpus is a result of the parameters set along with the way DH is framed globally. Because the study examines syllabi which were posted publicly online, different cultural norms around open access and sharing of syllabi have likely excluded different English-language syllabi from this corpus. These parameters, while leaving many courses out, nevertheless allow the study to focus on how DH as DH is advertised to students and framed by instructors and institutions. While DH— called "digital humanities" or something else— operates in many contexts successfully, the aim of this study is to discover how it is framed in courses explicitly devoted to it.

Kristen Mapes

Table 20.2 The corpus

Course Level	Institution	Instructor	Term & Year	Title of Course/Module	Link
Undergraduate	University of California, Los Angeles (US)	Miriam Posner	2017 – Fall	Introduction to Digital Humanities (DH101)	http://miriamposner.com/classes/dh101f17/
Undergraduate	Brigham Young University (US)	Brian Croxall	2017 – Fall	Introduction to Digital Humanities (DIGHT215)	http://briancroxall.net/f17dh/
Undergraduate	Universiteit Leiden (Netherlands)	Paul Vierthaler	2018 – Fall	Hacking the Humanities: An Introduction to Digital Humanities and Text Mining [title on registrar's page] Hacking the Humanities: Programming and Analysis [title on syllabus] (5170V01)	https://static1.squarespace.com/static/58b89382db29d626268df4f4/t/5b962cb270a6adfadf488aa7/1536568498723/HackingFall2018.pdf
Undergraduate	Michigan State University (US)	Kristen Mapes	2018 – Fall	Introduction to Digital Humanities (DH285)	http://www.kristenmapes.com/dh285fall2018/
Graduate	Pratt Institute (US)	Chris Alen Sula	2015 – Spring	Digital Humanities I (LIS657)	http://chrisalensula.org/wp-content/uploads/syllabus657-s15.pdf
Graduate	University of Texas, Austin (US)	Tanya Clement	2015 – Fall	Introduction to Digital Humanities (INF383H)	https://www.ischool.utexas.edu/sites/default/files/images/webform/DHFall2015Syllabus.pdf
Graduate	Lehigh University (US)	Amardeep Singh & Edward Whitley	2015 – Fall	Introduction to Digital Humanities	http://www.electrostani.com/2015/08/fall-teaching-digital-humanities.html
Graduate	Bowling Green State University (US)	Andrew M. Shocket	2016 – Spring	Introduction to Digital Humanities (ACS6820/HIST6820)	http://intro-dh-2016.andyschocket.net/syllabus/
Graduate	Maynooth University (Ireland)	Susan Schreibman	2017 – Fall	Digital Humanities: Theory and Practice (AFF601) [required intro module for MA in DH]	http://madh.maynoothuniversity.ie/aff601/?page_id=265
Graduate	Carleton University (Canada)	Shawn Graham	2017 – Fall	Introduction to Digital Humanities (DIGH5000)	https://hcommons.org/deposits/item/hc:15465/

Discovering digital humanities methods

20.4 The corpus

20.4.1 Approaching the introductory course

As Hirsch discussed the role of pedagogy in solidifying the field of DH, Selisker noted that "syllabi themselves not only map out a (necessarily limited) picture of the field, but they also make an argument for what kind of knowledge is being produced in the course" (Selisker 2016). How we approach this question in introductory courses tells us something about the field according to those who teach it. There are several ways to discover how these instructors present DH through their course design. Nine of the ten courses dedicated at least one class session to explaining what DH is, often incorporating a bit of DH history into the discussion and reading (either in that session or at some point during the term). Croxall's was the one course that did not incorporate a formal introduction to DH. For courses titled "Introduction to DH", this attention is not surprising.

The introductory DH course, whether at the undergraduate or graduate level, requires a balanced approach to acclimating students to new modes of creation (e.g. visualization, websites, video) alongside new methods of inquiry (e.g. text analysis, mapping, network analysis) all while incorporating discussions of metadata, structures of power, and the archive into the mix.

How, then, do instructors balance all of the competing needs of the introductory DH classroom? Each instructor studied has taken a different approach. Posner focused on the structures that underlie DH work, spending more time than other courses on power and the archive, metadata, and inequality and big data. In some ways, Posner's course centered DH around the question, "what is data, how has it been used, and how might it be used?" Singh and Whitley similarly brought social justice approaches and values directly into the DH classroom. By contrast to a focus on data, Croxall's course asked what new methods of analysis can be applied to literary text. It was the only course that assigns several works of literature to the students and did a deep dive of those works through digital methods. My course used the Harlem Renaissance and its historical context as a framing topic for a wide ranging look at DH, with more of a focus on the digital project as text than the other courses. Vierthaler's course was the only one of the four centered on programming, with a heavy emphasis on text analysis methods as well as some data analysis, although Shocket's course also required the students to gain a basic set of programming skills.

Many of the courses set aside time to work on projects together and taught students how to troubleshoot and teach themselves through tutorials. For example, Graham's integration of Programming Historian tutorials into the syllabus demonstrates how digital humanists gain expertise outside of the classroom setting. These activities, in the classroom and outside of it, collectively serve to model DH approaches to work that students can continue beyond the term, a useful strategy for seeding DH values and behavior considering the competing topics and methods vying for time in the course of a single term.

I will explore the syllabi in further depth below, discovering trends for undergraduate level courses and for graduate level courses.

20.5 The undergraduate syllabi

20.5.1 Co-instruction and guest speakers

Of the four undergraduate courses, two had teaching assistant(s), and a third had a formally embedded librarian [Table 20.3]. While the size of the courses is unknown, the prevalence of multiple instructors in some form is not surprising. Teaching an introductory course of this nature to undergraduates requires a mix of skill sets—theories, methods, technologies—that usually transcends the expertise of a single instructor. In addition, troubleshooting with students on technical assignments requires one-on-one time that quickly extends beyond the resources of one instructor. I contend that the role of instructor support in a DH course is different than that required by an introductory humanities methods course. The university has often established institutional frameworks for supporting students as they learn the skills to succeed in

Kristen Mapes

Table 20.3 Undergraduate course teaching assistance

Instructor	Instruction Assistance	Guest Speakers - From outside the home university	Guest Speakers - From inside the home university
Posner	TA (2)	2	2
Croxall	None	0	0
Vierthaler	TA	0	1
Mapes	Embedded Librarian	2	2

the non-DH classroom. Writing centers are one of the key support services for curricula (in the U.S.), and as digital assignments become more prevalent, these centers are looking for ways to contribute to student learning in these new modes, but they are still in the process of thinking through what that means and how to do it. Writing Centers may still be of assistance in the DH course (indeed, they are mentioned explicitly in two of the syllabi [Vierthaler & Mapes]), but they are not equipped to troubleshoot the range of technologies encountered during these courses. DH Centers and labs, especially in libraries, play a key role in consultation and support for DH faculty and seem poised to play a role in the classroom as well, but they are not explicitly discussed in any of these syllabi.[17]

Along with teaching assistants and embedded librarians, three out of the four courses brought speakers into the class at some point in the semester. These guest speakers included colleagues and students from within the course's institution [Table 20.3], with visits ranging from guest lectures on a particular topic to leading a workshop on a method. Just as frequently, however, speakers were brought in from outside the institution. Posner brought in two speakers, one from industry and one from government, to speak on areas of expertise, and these visits show a focus on how DH methods are employed beyond the academy. I brought in two speakers virtually to discuss DH projects with the class. Only one course (Croxall's) did not incorporate guest speakers into the course. The prevalence of guest speakers also points to the need for expertise in the introductory DH classroom beyond what one instructor can provide, supporting the value of knowledge as collaborative and the need to gather expertise from a wide range of experts. All knowledge does not rest with the instructor; instead, they are part of a larger community of learning and practice that admits what it doesn't know and seeks to learn together in community.

20.5.2 Course design and the project

The role of the digital humanities project as an object in the field is discussed often in the context of evaluation for tenure and promotion and in relation to the results of grant funded research. The concept of the DH project is also at the root of some of the skills associated with the work of DH. It is not surprising to discover, then, that most of the courses incorporated discussion and critique of DH projects into the assignments and/or class activities. My course is structured around critiquing DH projects throughout the semester, through assignments, class discussion, guest visits, and in the final project grading rubric. Posner brought project critique into the beginning of the term and continued to introduce concepts through a combination of readings and example projects. Croxall's course discussed a few projects, although class time appeared more focused on discussing readings than evaluating projects. Vierthaler's course focused on programming and so had a different orientation to DH that involved no detectable project evaluation.

After learning about digital humanities through project examples, the courses often culminated in the creation of a final project. From the undergraduate corpus, three courses have a large, final project (Posner, Vierthaler, Mapes) (See Table 20.4). The other course had four projects throughout the semester (Croxall). Project work in the DH classroom can resurface the old hack versus yack debate, but all of the courses work to balance critique and making. This mix is natural for a classroom setting, as students in the humanities are generally called upon to practice making scholarly arguments through written papers, oral presentations,

Discovering digital humanities methods

Table 20.4 Project work days

Instructor	Project work days
Posner	2
Croxall	6
Vierthaler	0
Mapes	6

and other forms. The DH classroom in many ways simply expands these modes of creation. Through such expansion, however, the DH classroom also must introduce issues of working in those modes. For example, if the students are to create a public, digital edition of a text, as in my course where the class as a group worked on the Curatescape edition of Karen F. Taborn's 2018 guide, *Walking Harlem*, then they must learn about copyright, writing for a public audience, and the specifics of working on a digital platform (how information is structured, metadata, etc). Because new modes of production require new concepts for introductory students, the instructor must balance introducing a range of methods and modes over the course of the term with introducing the foundational concepts behind those structures, as well as the content being critiqued and discussed in those modes and projects.

Part of this balancing act between content and methods in a course, especially in relation to project work, is how much class time instructors devote to it. Most of the courses set aside class sessions for project work: Posner with a research-a-thon day and a project work day; Croxall by cancelling four class sessions in favor of project work (although that work was fully outside the classroom environment) in addition to two project days in class; and, my course setting aside six days for project work. Only Vierthaler's course had no such time allotted, and his was also the only course where students had a large individual final project.[18]

While not project work time, a hands-on approach to class sessions was visible in Posner's and Vierthaler's courses, which had built-in workshops throughout the term. Posner's course structure had two lecture meetings each week plus a lab meeting, which dedicated time to handling technical learning and troubleshooting as well as scaffolding final project work.[19] Vierthaler's daily class structure involved lecture and then workshop time to handle technical learning and troubleshooting. The number of dedicated project work days in my class were structured to allow for technical troubleshooting and mini-workshops on topics and tools as needed for student projects.

Prompted by Sula, Hackney, and Cunningham's observation about the absence of library related skills in DH program language as well as Terras' observation of the prevalence of librarians and LIS professionals in the field of DH, this study looked for any relationships with librarians or libraries in the syllabi. Of the four undergraduate courses, only mine incorporated a visit to a library or any explicit involvement with librarians. My course includes three visits to the University Libraries as well as the regular involvement of the embedded librarian in visiting class sessions and meeting with students individually on their final projects.

20.5.3 *Topics of instruction*

Looking at the table of topics explicitly covered in the syllabi, we can see a rather comprehensive list of the methods and tools of interest to the DH community writ large [see Table 20.5 above for a select list and Appendix A for the full list]. There are a wide variety of topics covered by each course, but relatively few that were taught in common among three of the undergraduate courses, with none that were taught in all four. The topics most frequently taught were: "What is DH?", visualization, text analysis, and mapping. Considering the discussion in the literature of programming and its relationship to DH pedagogy, it is notable that only one of the undergraduate courses featured programming, and only one other course (Posner's) introduced the concept of coding and basic HTML and CSS.

Kristen Mapes

Table 20.5 Most commonly taught course topics

Instructor	Course Level	What is DH (& history of DH)?	Visualization	Topic modeling	Text analysis (e.g. Voyant & NLTK)	Mapping	Networks
Posner	Undergraduate	1	1			1	1
Croxall	Undergraduate				1	1	
Vierthaler	Undergraduate	1	1	1	1		
Mapes	Undergraduate	1	1	1	1	1	1
UG Totals		*3*	*3*	*2*	*3*	*3*	*2*
Sula	Graduate	1			1	1	1
Clement	Graduate	1	1	1	1	1	1
Singh & Whitley	Graduate	1	1	1	1	1	1
Schocket	Graduate	1		1	1	1	1
Schreibman	Graduate	1	1		1	1	
Graham	Graduate	1	1		1	1	
Grad Totals		*6*	*4*	*3*	*6*	*6*	*4*
Total		**9**	**7**	**5**	**9**	**9**	**6**

By comparison with Weingart's analysis of the most popular keywords of the ADHO 2017 conference submissions, these top themes begin to align: text analysis was the most popular topic, with "archives, repositories, sustainability, etc" as the third most popular (Weingart 2016). Visualization was the sixth top topic, and "geospatial analysis, interfaces, & mapping" was seventeenth. If the popularity of topics at the DH conference is any indication, then these syllabi touch on topics at the heart of DH research and scholarly practice, showing a topical alignment between DH research and pedagogy.

While not reflected in the spreadsheet, there was a theme across several of the syllabi (especially in Posner's and my courses) relating to the digital archive and digital curation. Posner and I explicitly have class sessions on metadata, and both courses examined digital archives projects to varying degrees. If we are seeking to learn what DH is by how it is taught, then this simple quantified look does not tell us much. A few methods and topics are revealed, but there are more diverging approaches than anything resembling a cohesive approach. This discovery should not be surprising, since DH carries different meanings and priorities depending on the institutional context and the individual instructor.

20.6 The graduate syllabi

After going into depth about the undergraduate courses, I am most interested in asking what is different in the graduate courses. The most distinctive feature of graduate course syllabi was the importance of professionalization. Four of the six courses incorporated some mode of professionalization into class discussion and assignments, and each course did this in different ways, often in the form of the final project.[20]

20.6.1 Professionalization and the role of the project

The final assignment in Graham's course was a group project to create an undergraduate DH textbook, and the structure for grading that textbook was "⅓ research, ⅓ service, ⅓ teaching", just as Canadian and U.S. tenure stream faculty are usually evaluated. This assignment gave students practice thinking like faculty and framing their DH work in ways that are communicable to institutional assessors and academic peers. In creating a textbook for undergraduates, students learn to distill the information and methods they learn in their class into appropriate language and manageable pieces for the undergraduates that they may teach.

340

Discovering digital humanities methods

This approach seems to assume that graduate students go on to become tenure-stream faculty, which is interesting given that we know this is not always the case. DH has at times been framed as a career pathway to alt-ac careers beyond the tenure-track, either within or outside of the academy.[21]

Shocket's final project took a different angle regarding professionalization by structuring the project as a National Endowment for the Humanities Start Up Grant proposal. While the undergraduate courses often assigned a DH project as the final project, this assignment has students envision a DH project, challenging them to articulate scope, timeframe, costs, and so on without having them undertake the project itself in the course of a term. This adjustment familiarizes students with the process and genre of grant writing, which is needed in any DH job, whether on the tenure-track or otherwise. Even positions outside of the academy in non-profit or government environments need to write grant proposals. A grant writing assignment also teaches the students about DH project creation and management without having them begin projects that may be difficult to complete within the timeframe of one semester. While an undergraduate context may prioritize the experience of making a project, even if the product at the end of the term is a bit less polished, in graduate level context, the better use of time might be in planning for projects that can be undertaken later when the time allows.

The final project for Clement's course, part of a Library and Information Science program, involved group work (like Graham's course), but it involved working in pairs (as opposed to the class working as one large group) and took a direct approach to work in the Library and Information Science profession. The assignment was to assess the state of research infrastructure in a unit of the University Library. The students conducted interviews with administrators and faculty, wrote a report, and presented on it. In addition to the final project, Clement's course required students to create a workshop curriculum proposal with the aim of teaching the workshop at a professional conference. The combination of on the ground assessment and instruction in the form of workshops is directly in line with the regular work of library and archives professionals.

Sula's course, which was also part of a Library and Information Science program, devoted the most class time to the topic of professionalization and, especially, socialization into the profession. One week was on "DH and libraries", one on DH pedagogy, another focused on the state of higher education and scholarly communication, and one on "planning, funding, and digital preservation". These topics tie directly into the concerns and daily work of a librarian working in digital humanities or digital scholarship (DS) (the term increasingly adopted in libraries[22]). Sula's course did not have a final project per se, with grading instead broken into five equally weighted activities, one of which focused specifically on professionalization. That assignment was to create an instructional tutorial to be posted on a group DH Skillshare blog, which was meant to be used by newcomers to DH from beyond the class and beyond the university (DH Skillshare[23]). The creation of tutorial and documentation materials for methods and tools is work common to DH/DS librarianship. Another assignment was a "research experiment and report", which is similar to the DH project assignments of the undergraduate courses, but, like Shocket's recognition of the time constraints of a single term and the expectations of a professional DH project, scales the project down. The framing of it was an experiment meant to test a DH method on a humanities question. This focus on experimentation fits well into the values and ethos of DH as a space for play and failure.[24] Additionally, practice with experimentation and reporting on it aligns with the work of librarianship, as digital humanities and digital scholarship librarians are often called to be generalists in DH, consulting on a range of methods and across disciplines. Experience with testing methods and applying them to humanities questions equips the DH/DS librarian to undertake their own research as a professional and allows them the flexibility to work with faculty and students from a variety of methodological approaches and disciplines.

Singh and Whitley's course was structured similarly to Sula's in that there was not one final project, but a series of four projects that together formed a portfolio. One of the projects involved the class collaborating together on a Scalar website to create a digital edition and essays reflecting on Claude McKay's *Harlem Shadows*. The course as a whole took an explicitly social justice approach to teaching digital humanities, and the readings and project work sought to acculturate students to those concerns, in some ways reflecting Posner's focus in her undergraduate course in questioning the relationship between power and the archive. The *Harlem Shadows* project pushed the students to think about how to work in public and how to create a digital project, while the other assignments involved essay writing and working with data that did not require public publication.[25]

Schreibman's course reflects a unique structure and approach to professionalization because it had students enrolled in the Master of Arts in Digital Humanities as well as students in the MA in Historical Archives. While the readings and discussion appear to have been integrated throughout the term, DH students were required to take an additional "Research Skills Seminar", which met each week to cover a range of skills pertinent to graduate students, including a visit to the library, finding a research topic, and blog design. The two student populations also had different assignments: Digital Humanities students blogged throughout the term, while Historical Archives students wrote a "report on a scenario" relating to digitization and archiving. All students also had a video group project and a final essay to complete, although the DH students' final essays were longer. This bifurcated class structure reflects the institutional needs of different Masters programs, and the differing approaches to professionalization are notable. That DH students are required to blog reflects the values of working in public and of web design that are a part of the field, and the digitization and archives report aligns with work done in historical archives. That both types of students are brought together in this course reflects the role of digital humanities in the modern archives as well as the important role that archives play in digital humanities, even though the students were working within degree programs of differing lengths and requirements.

In addition to the professionalization work laid out in Sula's syllabus, the course prepared students to navigate the social world of DH and familiarized them with its norms for learning and communication. One week was devoted to "The culture of DH", and two of the assignments focused on professional acculturation: students were required to attend a DH event outside of class and write a report as an extended blog post, although the assignment was not required to be publicly shared. Students were also assigned one week during the term when they are responsible for monitoring Twitter to discover conversations in the field and report on the major themes in a Storify that was publicly shared and promoted. These two assignments pushed students to observe and participate in the DH community beyond the classroom and beyond their university.

Graham's course encouraged students to explore the DH community by pointing them to the DH Slack[26] and worked to professionalize them by framing class participation through the lens of "generous thinking" (Fitzpatrick 2016) and with a focus on collegiality (Spiro 2012).[27] While not in the mode of socialization, Schocket's focus on teaching students the methods and tools of DH through *Programming Historian* lessons acculturated them to the mode of learning that DH-ers adopt, as a willingness to learn new skills and experiment (and fail) are essential qualities for any digital humanist.

20.6.2 Libraries and librarians

Turning to the question of these courses and their relationships to librarians and libraries, I discovered more of a topical connection among the six graduate courses, but I saw a lack of formal relationships as in the undergraduate courses. Singh and Whitley's course included a visit by a librarian who led a workshop, and Schreibman's Research Skills Seminar visited the library. Surprisingly, neither of the LIS courses (Sula and Clement) included either a visit to the library or a guest speaker from a library. Instead, these two courses set aside a class period to discuss the topic of DH and Libraries (in Sula's course, that class was titled "Libraries", and in Clement's, it was titled "Digital Humanities Infrastructure I: Libraries and Centers"). Sula, Hackney, and Cunningham's study noted that the TaDirah terms "archiving, organizing, and preservation" were underrepresented in descriptions of DH programs and speculated that these activities may be found at the individual course level [Sula, Hackney, and Cunningham, 2017]. This study found that to be true (archiving and preservation in particular were discussed in a number of the courses), and yet the direct link of these topics with work in the field by librarians and archivists is not always made. Considering the aim of professionalization in the graduate level digital humanities classroom, the absence of librarians and libraries in the classroom is disappointing.

20.7 Comparing the corpus with historical studies

20.7.1 Modes of study

Terras' study observed that there was a lot of group work and assessment through project work in humanities computing courses (2006, p. 235). Spiro's study five years later saw frequent project assignments and group work as well (2011, p. 16 and 18). Project work has been discussed above, and it continued to be prominent in the introductory DH classroom in various forms. This study discovered that five of the ten courses required group work in graded assignments, and two additional courses involved group work in at least one class session[28]. Considering the prevalence of group work in this study and its consistency with Spiro's and Terras' findings, it is surprising that there is then a significant divergence from Spiro's finding that fifteen of the syllabi she examined explicitly listed collaboration as a learning outcome (2011, p. 18); by contrast, only one of the syllabi I studied (Croxall's) listed collaboration in the course goals or objectives.[29] These syllabi show that group work is integrated into the introductory DH class and is valued as a DH practice, and yet it is largely ignored as a formal course goal. In this light, I wonder to what extent the prevalence of group work truly reflects the values of DH as a field, or if group work has simply become a part of the university classroom writ large and is not notable as a specific goal for DH courses.

Another area of comparison over time is the role of working in public in the introductory DH classroom. Spiro noted that many courses involve blogging (37%) (2011, p. 19). My corpus includes four courses (40%) that required blogging, which aligns with Spiro's rate of blogging, an interesting continuity across time, considering popular rhetoric over the years about the rise and fall of the blog. Of the four courses that included blogging, there was an even split between undergraduate and graduate courses, as well as an even split (including between graduate and undergraduate) between writing on a course blog and having students create individual blogs as part of a larger aim to develop their digital presence [see Table 20.6].

Beyond blogging, I also looked for other forms of working in public. Four courses that did not have a blogging component did incorporate some form of public work, with a mix of one undergraduate and three graduate courses doing so. The undergraduate course, mine, involved the entire class working together on a digital project (in Omeka). This approach also held in Singh and Whitley's course, with the class creating a digital edition in Scalar together. The other two graduate courses, Graham's and Sula's, had

Table 20.6 Blogging

Instructor	Course Level	Blogging Type
Posner	Undergraduate	Course blog
Croxall	Undergraduate	Individual blog
Schreibman	Graduate	Individual blog
Shocket	Graduate	Course blog

Table 20.7 Public work

Instructor	Course Level	Working in Public in another form	Group or individual work
Mapes	Undergraduate	Class Omeka/Curatescape project (*Walking Harlem*)	Full class
Sula	Graduate	DH Skillshare + Storify	Individual
Graham	Graduate	Open textbook + Github	Full class and individual
Singh and Whitley	Graduate	Class Scalar project (*Harlem Shadows*)	Full class

the students create instructional materials (open textbook and skillshare) and practice community annotation (Github and Storify) publicly [see Table 20.7]. This mix between student levels shows an aspect in which the introductory DH classroom may focus on working together to create something in community for the sake of creating or building upon a digital project, for the experience of working on a project. By contrast, graduate courses are likely to have more of a focus on the professionalization of the individual students as they prepare for the particular activities of their careers and acculturate to the community, becoming digital humanists in the process.[30]

20.7.2 Topics of study

Methods observed in past studies bear relation to those taught in the syllabi studied here, especially regarding the prominence of text analysis. Terras noted a strong focus on text, including analysis and encoding (2006, p. 235), while Spiro also saw many classes focus on text (2011, p. 27). Nine of the ten courses included text analysis, indicating a continued prominence of this method in the field. Weingart's analysis of submissions to the ADHO 2017 conference supports the continued prominence of text, with "text analysis" assigned as the most common topic (2016). Only Posner's course did not include text analysis, likely due to the "focus on applications for structured data" rather than unstructured text (2017). While text remains prominent in the field and in introductory digital humanities courses, the role of text encoding in my corpus is much smaller than that seen in Terras' study. Only two of the ten courses in my study introduce TEI at all (Singh and Whitley's and mine); and, my course only briefly introduces it in the context of a class session on annotation. The relative absence of TEI could come from the North American focus of the corpus, by comparison to Terras' more European corpus.

Spiro pointed to a range of additional media types that appeared prominent in her study— video, audio, images, and games—which are not as prominent in this corpus (2011, p. 28–31). This discrepancy may be attributed in part to the wider range of courses included in Spiro's corpus, which included more digital media studies and digital culture courses than the very specific set of "Introduction to DH" courses included in this study. Only Graham's syllabus explored such a range of material explicitly. The one form of media beyond text that Spiro pointed to which appears prominently in this corpus is mapping. Mapping is on par with video as a popular material in Spiro's study, but here mapping was as commonly taught as text analysis and so was tied as the most popular method in DH, with only one course not teaching it (Vierthaler's) (Spiro, 2011, p. 32).

Aside from type of material of study, Spiro pointed out key concepts in her corpus: openness, network, data and database, and interaction (2011, p. 35–38). All of these methods, aside from interaction per se, appear in my corpus, with six courses teaching networks, four teaching some form of content management system, as well as a variety of introductions to data, including metadata, linked data, and data collection and cleaning (see Table 20.5 and Appendix A). Programming, as noted above, was taught in Vierthaler's course in depth and introduced in Posner's course, and at the graduate level was incorporated into Shocket's course and introduced, especially in the form of Github, in Graham and Singh and Whitley's courses (Appendix A). Similar to Spiro's expectation that programming would be more common in her corpus of

Discovering digital humanities methods

syllabi, I found that, across course levels, programming has not become the primary lens through which students are taught Digital Humanities (Spiro, 2011, p. 40).

20.8 Alignment of syllabi with DH values

Grounding DH in its values of openness, collaboration, collegiality and connectedness, diversity, and experimentation, as proposed by Spiro, this study asks if these values translate into the framing of DH presented to students in the introductory DH course. Indeed, we have seen these DH values expressed in the syllabi, indicating a link between DH research and DH work writ large. The classroom is a place of experimentation by nature, and the role of group work that we have seen in the syllabi studied above supports the role of collaboration in DH.

Openness comes into play in several ways, not least of which is that this corpus is comprised of syllabi that are publicly available, either through a subject repository or through the instructor's website. Many of the courses involve some form of working in public, bringing discussions about openness directly into the classroom. Spiro observed in 2011 that many of the course readings in syllabi were recent (since 2000) and publicly available online (p. 25). This study of recent syllabi makes this observation as well, as most of the readings and materials assigned were openly available. Openness in DH is a complex issue, with digital humanists serving as producers and consumers of content (text, tools, etc), and with a more nuanced understanding of what is appropriate to share openly versus when to keep something closed in the interest of safety, cultural sensitivity, or for other reasons.

Collegiality and connectedness come through especially in the graduate syllabi alongside the professionalization of the students into the field. As discussed above, several of the graduate courses explicitly expose students to spaces of communication and practices of collegiality in the field, whether through assignments (e.g. Sula's Twitter/Storify assignment) or grading frameworks (e.g. Graham's "collegiality/generous thinking" framing for class participation).

One challenge that DH has begun to work on is that of diversity. As part of the Western cultures in which all of these courses take place, and as part of the institutional histories and structures of the University, there are ways in which these courses and DH writ large are not as diverse in their student population, content, and approaches as they could be. By working with our students and acknowledging these structural legacies and our own limitations, we can begin to take apart some of the barriers to a more diverse and inclusive digital humanities. There is much work to be done, but through these values we have a path forward.

20.9 Relationship between teaching and research

After examining the syllabi in depth, I would like to return to the question posed above, asking how teaching DH relates to an instructor's DH work writ large. First, I looked at the instructors' backgrounds and location within their employing institutions, and then I explored their research to discover any relationships between their publicly available DH work and their DH teaching. Is the introductory DH classroom serving as a lab for developing robust DH research? Do these instructors incorporate DH pedagogy into public facing scholarship, presentations, and publications? If we see the Digital Humanities classroom as an environment in which the instructor learns from the students, then I would expect to find evidence of the DH classroom in the public work of its instructors.

20.9.1 Instructor background

A quick survey of the instructors looks at who they are and their location within their respective institutions. Of the eleven instructors, ten hold PhDs and all were in a position that involves some variation of continuing appointment or tenure, with seven tenured at the time of writing and four

Kristen Mapes

Table 20.8 Instructors

Name	Title	Institution	Background/Education
Miriam Posner	Assistant Professor of Information Studies and Digital Humanities	UCLA	PhD in Media Studies (+ CLIR Post-Doc)
Brian Croxall	Assistant Research Professor of Digital Humanities	BYU	PhD in English (+ CLIR Post-Doc)
Paul Vierthaler	University Lecturer (Assistant Professor) of Digital Humanities	Universiteit Leiden	PhD in East Asian Languages and Literatures
Kristen Mapes	Assistant Director of Digital Humanities	MSU	MLIS + MA Medieval Studies
Chris Alen Sula	Associate Professor, School of Information and Coordinator of Digital Humanities	Pratt Institute	PhD Philosophy
Andrew Shocket	Professor of History and American Culture Studies	Bowling Green State University	PhD History
Susan Schreibman	Professor of Digital Humanities and Director of An Foras Feasa	Maynooth University	PhD Literature
Shawn Graham	Associate Professor of Digital Humanities	Carleton University	PhD Archaeology
Amardeep Singh	Associate Professor of English	Lehigh University	PhD in English
Edward Whitley	Associate Professor of English	Lehigh University	PhD in English

pre-tenure [see Table 20.8].[31] Seven of the instructors had "digital humanities" in their job title. The prevalence of permanent job positions in this corpus, and in particular those explicitly tasked with doing DH, likely comes from the way syllabi were collected, in that people who are teaching a course more than once or who see the introductory DH course as part of their larger position or continued role at an institution are more likely to have developed the syllabus themselves and be in a position to share it publicly. By contrast, graduate students and post-docs may have been handed a syllabus or in some way not be in the position to share this form of work publicly. The position of this group of instructors lends itself to a discussion of the relationship between their teaching and other DH work.

Most of the instructors (six) have had a formal relationship with libraries and LIS in their professional careers. Posner and Croxall held CLIR post-doctoral fellowships in libraries, Sula and Clement trained librarians in LIS programs, Schreibman and Croxall worked in libraries for many years before holding their positions at the time of teaching these courses, and I hold an MLIS. Libraries and library science play a substantial role in the community and work of DH writ large, which is evidenced through participation in the largest conference in the field. Terras noted that the most represented discipline at the Association of Computing in the Humanities and the Association of Literary and Linguistic Computing Joint International Conference (ACH/ALLC) in 2005 was Library and Information Studies, with "staff from university libraries [...] also well represented" (2006, p. 239), and she discovered that "Library" was the academic department with the third largest showing among presenters (tied with Humanities Computing Centers, and only after LIS and English) (2006, p. 241). More recently, Scott Weingart's study of abstracts submitted to present at the ADHO 2017 conference were associated with the discipline of "Library and Information Science" third most frequently (after Computer Science and Literary Studies)—note that there were not separate categories for LIS and Libraries (Weingart, 2016). With this information in mind, the prevalence of instructors with a relationship to libraries is not surprising in introductory DH instruction.

Discovering digital humanities methods

I sought to learn the degree to which teaching in general, and teaching introductory DH in particular, plays in the presentation and publication work of these instructors, by looking at what was discoverable through institutional repositories, faculty pages, personal websites, and Google Scholar. A number of the instructors present at conferences about their teaching and/or write about DH pedagogy. Posner, Croxall, and I have work reflecting on our teaching in published and blog form and have participated in and/or organized conference events relating to DH pedagogy. Clement has also written about and edited a volume about DH pedagogy. Graham has written about teaching and foregrounds his students and his pedagogy on his extensive faculty page[32], and Singh's blog incorporates many posts reflecting on his teaching practice. Singh, Whitely, and Sula have undertaken DH work with their students. Singh and Whitely work directly with their classes to develop Scalar projects that they lead and shepherd from year to year. Sula has published and presented with students on studies of the field of DH and DH curriculum.[33] Shocket, Vierthaler, and Schreibman do not appear to have a direct relationship between their DH work outside and inside the classroom aside from the topic of study. This observation is based solely on what is publicly visible and does not reflect mentorship and advising and administrative work, which may involve more close collaboration with students and incorporate or build on DH pedagogy.

Conclusion

By examining a corpus of ten syllabi of introductory digital humanities courses, I investigated how digital humanities is framed and what methods are taught in order to learn what DH is. I have also explored the relationship between DH pedagogy and DH research. I have found the following three points to be the key take-aways:

First, we can indeed know something about what Digital Humanities is through these syllabi, and they show us that digital humanities is characterized by group, project work, which is often public facing and oriented toward experimentation (especially at the undergraduate level) and professionalization (especially at the graduate level). Ways of knowing in DH are multiple, as knowledge is shared among students, the instructor(s), and guest speakers. Digital Humanities can include many topics and methods, but text is at the heart of it, with digital archives, mapping, and networks as frequent methods as well.

Second, the world of Digital Humanities includes many centers and labs, and many libraries and librarians are deeply involved in the work of the field. Yet, the relationship between the introductory DH classroom and the library, and even Centers and Labs, is more tenuous than anticipated, considering this wider research and infrastructure context for DH.

Third, the relationship between the teaching and research agendas of the instructors is not as direct as it could be. However, a number of the instructors do present and publish (in peer-reviewed journals and books, and/or through their blogs) about their digital humanities courses and pedagogical approaches. The discussion in the field on this relationship continues actively, as seen in a conversation on the Humanist listserv, which continued on Twitter in November 2018[34]. In a thread about overwork and the framing of job advertisements, Roopika Risam made a passionate call for a more robust integration of Digital Humanists' teaching and research: "I cultivated a digital humanities practice where my research, teaching, and service are deeply integrated with each other. My classroom is a laboratory. It becomes a source of my research, it informs my DH building at the level of the institution, which is my service, also a source of research. Higher ed money is drying up —but hey, you should see the things people can do without it. The things they do with students. The research they produce. The deep integration of the holy trinity of teaching, research, and service they practice." (Risam, 2018). Risam's harmony between teaching and research shows that the values of DH as articulated by Spiro and supported by these syllabi can translate into robust DH work beyond the classroom.

Appendix A: Topics covered in syllabi

Topic	Grand Total	Undergraduate Courses (UG)					Graduate Courses (G)						
		Posner	Croxall	Vierthaler	Mapes	UG Total	Sula	Clement	Schocket	Schreibman	Graham	Singh & Whitley	G Total
What is DH (& history of DH)?	9	1		1	1	3	1	1	1	1	1	1	6
Text analysis (e.g. Voyant & NLTK)	9		1	1	1	3	1	1	1	1	1	1	6
Mapping	9	1	1		1	3	1	1	1	1	1	1	6
Visualization	7	1		1	1	3		1	1		1	1	4
Networks	6	1			1	2	1	1	1			1	4
Topic modeling	5		1		1	2		1	1			1	3
UX/Design/Usability	4				1	1	1			1	1		3
Content Management Systems (CMS)	4	1	1			2			1			1	2
Scholarly publishing & scholarly communication	3					0	1				1	1	3
Libraries & archives	3					0	1	1			1		3
Public humanities	3					0	1			1	1		3
DH culture	3						1	1	1				3
CMS – Wordpress	3		1			1			1			1	2
Github	3			1		1					1	1	2
Project management	3	1				1	1			1			2
Programming & Code	3	1		1		2					1		1
E-literature	2					0				1		1	2
Linked data	2					0				1		1	2
Pedagogy	2					0	1				1		2
Preservation	2					0	1			1			2
Social media	2					0				1	1		2
TEI	2				1	1						1	1
Stylometry	2		1			1						1	1
Accessibility	2				1	1					1		1
CMS – Omeka	2				1	1						1	1
Programming – HTML & CSS	2	1				1			1				1
Programming – Python	2			1		1			1				1
Crowdsourcing	2				1	1					1		1
VR	2	1			1	2							0
Image analysis	2		1		1	2							0
Metadata	2	1			1	2							0

(Continued)

Discovering digital humanities methods

Topic	Grand Total	Undergraduate Courses (UG)					Graduate Courses (G)						
		Posner	Croxall	Vierthaler	Mapes	UG Total	Sula	Clement	Schocket	Schreibman	Graham	Singh & Whitley	G Total
Digitization & OCR	**2**		1		1	2							0
CMS – Drupal	**1**					0						1	1
CMS – Scalar	**1**					0						1	1
CMS – ContentDM	**1**					0						1	1
Digital editions	**1**					0						1	1
Digital cultural heritage	**1**					0	1						1
Assessment and evaluation	**1**					0	1						1
Making	**1**					0		1					1
Data collection	**1**					0		1					1
Data cleaning	**1**					0		1					1
Web archiving	**1**					0				1			1
Games/ simulations	**1**					0					1		1
Sound	**1**					0					1		1
Minimal computing	**1**					0					1		1
APIs	**1**			1		1							0
Web scraping	**1**			1		1							0
Programming – Regex	**1**			1		1							0
Digital archives	**1**	1				1							0
Big data	**1**	1				1							0
Copyright	**1**		1			1							0
Media studies	**1**		1			1							0

Notes

1 As of the time of writing, Spiro's article has been cited 112 times, according to Google Scholar (https://scholar.google.com/scholar?cites=16959270652341829007), an indication of the impact of the article and her framework more generally.

2 "It is argued in this chapter that the only way to achieve this is to think of the digital humanities as an intersectional meeting place and trading zone, allow for engagement with the digital across different modes of engagement, and use infrastructure as a way of channeling resources and articulating an ideational underpinning. Such a model is not territorial, but requires the digital humanities to have integrity and the ability to empower the development of research and education." Sevensson 2016.

3 Liu discusses the teaching of humanities with technology as a shift from a teaching to a "co-developing" model (Liu 2009, p. 20).

4 https://registries.clarin-dariah.eu/courses/

5 https://github.com/dh-notes/dhnotes/blob/master/pages/dh-programs.md

6 https://github.com/dhprograms/data

7 "Many program specializations seem to follow from the flavor of DH at particular institutions". Sula, Hackney, and Cunningham, 2017.

8 Note, as evidence, the publication of several books on the topic: *Digital Humanities in the Library: Challenges and Opportunities for Subject Specialists*, edited by Arianne Hartsell-Gundy, Laura Braunstein, Liorah Golomb, ACRL Press, 2015; *Laying the Foundation: Digital Humanities in Academic Libraries*, edited by John W. White, Heather Gilbert, Purdue University Press, 2016; and, *Digital Humanities, Libraries, and Partnerships: A Critical Examination of Labor,*

Networks, and Community, edited by Robin Kear and Kate Joranson, Chandos Publishing, 2018, to name a few. The role of *dh+lib* (https://acrl.ala.org/dh/) as a post-publication peer review journal as well as a journal posting original content since 2012 and the creation of the Digital Scholarship Section in 2017 as part of ACRL (Association of College of Research Libraries) (http://www.ala.org/acrl/aboutacrl/directoryofleadership/sections/dss/acr-dssec) show the maturation of digital humanities and digital scholarship in libraries.

9 http://tadirah.dariah.eu/vocab/index.php

10 https://www.zotero.org/groups/25016/digital_humanities_education/items/collectionKey/MXXEMX7P

11 https://github.com/dh-notes/dhnotes/blob/master/pages/dh-programs.md

12 https://scalar.usc.edu/works/digital-humanities-in-the-classroom-a-practical-introduction/index

13 https://wiki.commons.gc.cuny.edu/dh_syllabi/

14 http://www.scottbot.net/HIAL/index.html@p=21794.html

15 For example, an introduction to digital history course will be different and not as directly comparable to an interactive digital narratives course, or an East Asian digital humanities course.

16 In particular, I expected to include at least one syllabus from the UK, but was unable to find an example of a syllabus that was actually used in the classroom. A sample syllabus from King's College London was available, but it is not included in the corpus because it is a draft that does not seem tied to a specific term in which it was taught. https://www.kcl.ac.uk/artshums/depts/ddh/modules/level7/7aavindh.aspx. I have found syllabi with similar challenges from University of Novia Gorica (Slovenia) [http://www.ung.si/en/study/school-of-humanities/study/2DH/course/271553/introduction-to-digital-humanities/], and from KU Leuven (Belgium) [https://onderwijsaanbod.kuleuven.be/syllabi/e/G0R03AE.htm#activetab=inhoud_idm15924416].

17 I incorporate several class visits to the Digital Scholarship Lab into the course, and the embedded librarian works in the Lab. Posner links to the Center for Digital Humanities' calendar for events info, but her syllabus does not talk about the Center explicitly. Singh and Whitley link to the Lehigh DH resources libguide in the readings, but any further involvement with resources on campus is not made visible in the syllabus analyzed.

18 My class also had a final project, and most students did it individually, although it had the option of being a group project.

19 See "Francesca's lab" page on course website: http://miriamposner.com/classes/dh101f17/francescas-lab/

20 Singh and Whitley's and Schreibman's courses may do this in practice, but it is not as visible in the syllabi as the other courses.

21 The degree to which digital humanities actually serves as this is contested. In particular, note Roopika Risam's 2013 post about MLA job ads, which notes the rhetoric of DH as being job-rich area and compares that rhetoric with actual job postings. http://roopikarisam.com/uncategorized/where-have-all-the-dh-jobs-gone/.

22 Note, for example, the Digital Scholarship Section of ACRL as an indicator.

23 https://studentwork.prattsi.org/dh/category/resources/skillshares/

24 Digital humanities as experimental is a theme in the field. See: Bethany Nowviskie, Skunks in the library: A path to production for scholarly R&D" *Journal of Library Administration* 53.1 (2013); Stephen Ramsay, The hermeneutics of screwing around; or what you do with a million books, in *Pastplay: Teaching and Learning History with Technology*, University of Michigan Press, 2014, p.111–120; Jesse Stommel, Digital Humanities is about Breaking Stuff, *Hybrid Pedagogy*, 2013, http://hybridpedagogy.org/the-digital-humanities-is-about-breaking-stuff/.

25 More about Singh's reflections on the course are available here: http://www.electrostani.com/2015/12/digital-teaching-notes-harlem-shadows.html

26 Read more about the DH Slack at http://blogs.lse.ac.uk/impactofsocialsciences/2016/07/13/using-slack-to-support-a-geographically-dispersed-community/

27 Graham does not explicitly cite Spiro on the topic of collegiality, but I contend that is the value he is channeling in the syllabus.

28 I provide the option for group work in the final project, although individual projects are also an option. Singh and Whitley had an assignment that involved the entire class and was graded, but the students work was more individually done. These cases bring collaboration into the classroom, but in a less integrated and robust way than the other five courses (Posner, Croxall, Clement, Schreibman, and Graham).

29 "To collaborate on research in a field that has traditionally privileged individual scholarship" (Croxall, 2017).

30 For publicly visible work, it is common for the syllabi to emphasize that students may choose pseudonyms and generally have control over the degree to which they share themselves publicly. While this issue of privacy versus openness is not uniformly addressed in the syllabi here, it does seem to be generally recognized. Note, for example, Posner's section on "Working in public" - http://miriamposner.com/classes/dh101f17/policies/working-in-public/.

31 I am in a continuing appointment role, Sula, Clement, Shocket, Graham, Vierthaler, Singh, Whitley, Croxall, Posner, and Schreibman all appear to be in tenure system positions.

Discovering digital humanities methods

32 https://carleton.ca/history/people/shawn-graham/
33 Sula, Hackney, and Cunningham, 2017, as well as http://chrisalensula.org/the-early-history-of-digital-humanities/
34 https://dhhumanist.org/volume/32/196/ and https://twitter.com/roopikarisam/status/1063471091069399042

References

Advanced Degrees in Digital Humanities. (2018, August 21). Retrieved from https://github.com/dh-notes/dhnotes/blob/master/pages/dh-programs.md

AFF601 Digital humanities: Theory and practice. (2017). Retrieved from http://madh.maynoothuniversity.ie/aff601/ and https://web.archive.org/web/20171117013634/http://madh.maynoothuniversity.ie/aff601/

Battershill, C., & Ross, S. (2017). *Using Digital Humanities in the Classroom: A Practical Introduction for Teachers, Lecturers, and Students*. Bloomsbury Publishing.

Bonds, E. L. (2014). Listening in on the conversations: An overview of digital humanities pedagogy. *CEA Critic 76*(2), 147–157. Johns Hopkins University Press. http://dx.doi.org/10.1353/cea.2014.0017

Clement, T. (2015). Introduction to digital humanities: INF 383H. Retrieved from https://www.ischool.utexas.edu/sites/default/files/images/webform/DHFall2015Syllabus.pdf

Cordell, R. (2016). How not to teach digital humanities. In M. K. Gold and L. F. Klein (Eds.), *Debates in the Digital Humanities*. University of Minnesota Press. Retrieved from http://dhdebates.gc.cuny.edu/debates/text/87.

Croxall, B. (2017). Introduction to digital humanities: DigHT 215, BYU, Fall 2017. Retrieved from http://briancroxall.net/f17dh/

Digital Humanities Course Registry. (2018). Retrieved from https://registries.clarin-dariah.eu/courses/

Fitzpatrick, K. (2016, October 2). Generous thinking: The university and the public good. Retrieved from http://www.plannedobsolescence.net/generous-thinking-the-university-and-the-public-good/

Gold, M. K. and Klein, L. F. (Eds.) (2012). *Debates in the Digital Humanities*. University of Minnesota Press. Retrieved from http://dhdebates.gc.cuny.edu/

Graham, S. (2017). DIGH5000 Introduction to digital humanities syllabus fall 2017 Carleton University. *Humanities Commons* http://dx.doi.org/10.17613/M6D50K

Hawkins, A. R. (2014). Digital Humanities Pedagogy [Special issue]. *The CEA Critic 76*(2).

Hirsch, B. D. (Ed.). (2012). *Digital Humanities Pedagogy: Practices, Principles and Politics* (Vol. 3). Open Book Publishers. http://dx.doi.org/10.11647/OBP.0024

Hirsch, B. D. (2012). </Parentheses>: Digital humanities and the place of pedagogy. In B. D. Hirsch (Ed.), *Digital Humanities Pedagogy: Practices, Principles and Politics* (Vol. 3). Open Book Publishers. http://dx.doi.org/10.11647/OBP.0024

Liu, A. (2009). Digital humanities and academic change. *English Language Notes*, 47(1), 17–35. Retrieved from https://liu.english.ucsb.edu/wp-includes/docs/writings/dh-and-academic-change-page-proofs.pdf

Mapes, K. (2018, November 11). Introduction to digital humanities (DH285) - Fall 2018. Retrieved from http://www.kristenmapes.com/dh285fall2018/

Montfort, N. (2015). Exploratory Programming in Digital Humanities Pedagogy and Research. In S. Schreibman, R. Siemens, and J. Unsworth (Eds.), *A New Companion to Digital Humanities* (pp. 98–109). John Wiley & Sons, Ltd. https://doi.org/10.1002/9781118680605.ch7

Murphy, E. C. and Smith, S. R. (2017). Imagining the DH undergraduate: Special issue in undergraduate education in DH [Special issue]. *Digital Humanities Quarterly* 11(3).

Posner, M. (2017). Introduction to digital humanities. Retrieved from http://miriamposner.com/classes/dh101f17/

Ramsay, S. (2012). Programming with Humanists: Reflections on Raising an Army of Hacker-scholars in the Digital Humanities. In B. D. Hirsch (Ed.). *Digital Humanities Pedagogy: Practices, Principles and Politics* (Vol. 3) (p. 227–239). Open Book Publishers. http://dx.doi.org/10.11647/OBP.0024

Risam, R. [roopikarisam] (2018, November 16). I already had some words for some snark on Humanist about this one, but let me tell you a few things about working at a regional comprehensive university. [Twitter thread]. Retrieved from https://twitter.com/roopikarisam/status/1063471091069399042

Selisker, S. (2016). Digital humanities knowledge: Reflections on the introductory graduate syllabus. In M. K. Gold and L. F. Klein (Eds.), *Debates in the Digital Humanities*. University of Minnesota Press. Retrieved from http://dhdebates.gc.cuny.edu/debates/text/68

Singh, A. (2015, August 25). Fall teaching: Digital humanities. Retrieved from http://www.electrostani.com/2015/08/fall-teaching-digital-humanities.html

Shocket, A. (2016). Intro to digital humanities 2016: ACS6820/HIST6820 Spring 2016 at BGSU. Retrieved from http://intro-dh-2016.andyschocket.net/syllabus/

Spiro, L. (2011). *Knowing and Doing: Understanding the Digital Humanities Curriculum* [DH 2011 conference presentation slides]. Retrieved from https://digitalscholarship.files.wordpress.com/2011/06/spirodheducationpresentation2011-4.pdf

Spiro, L. (2012). "This is why we fight": Defining the values of the digital humanities. In M. K. Gold and L. F. Klein (Eds.), *Debates in the Digital Humanities*. University of Minnesota Press. Retrieved from http://dhdebates.gc.cuny.edu/debates/text/13

Sula, C. A. (2015). Digital humanities I. Retrieved from http://chrisalensula.org/wp-content/uploads/syllabus657-s15.pdf

Sula, C. A. (2017, August 11) DH programs - Data. Retrieved from https://github.com/dhprograms/data

Sula, C. A., Hackney, S. E., and Cunningham, P. (2017). A survey of digital humanities programs. *The Journal of Interactive Technology and Pedagogy* (11). Retrieved from https://jitp.commons.gc.cuny.edu/a-survey-of-digital-humanities-programs/

Svensson, P. (2015). Sorting Out the Digital Humanities. In S. Schreibman, R. Siemens, and J. Unsworth (Eds.), *A New Companion to Digital Humanities* (pp. 476–492). John Wiley & Sons, Ltd. https://doi.org/10.1002/9781118680605.ch33

Terras, M. (2006). Disciplined: Using Educational Studies to Analyse "Humanities Computing." *Literary and Linguistic Computing*, 21(2), 229–246. https://doi.org/10.1093/llc/fql022

Vierthaler, P. (2018). Hacking the humanities: Programming and analysis. Retrieved from https://static1.squarespace.com/static/58b89382db29d626268df4f4/t/5b962cb270a6adfadf488aa7/1536568498723/HackingFall2018.pdf

Weingart, S. (2016, November 10). Submissions to DH2017 (pt. 1). Retrieved from http://scottbot.net/submissions-to-dh2017-pt-1/

21
COURSE DESIGN IN THE DIGITAL HUMANITIES

Benjamin Wiggins

21.1 More and Moore

In 1965, engineer Gordon Moore, the Director of Research and Development at Fairchild Semiconductors, wrote a polemic for *Electronics* on the future of his industry. With the amusingly utilitarian title, "Cramming More Components onto Integrated Circuits," the piece analyzed the relationship between unit cost and components per circuit to predict that integrated circuit complexity would rise roughly at a factor of two per year over the course of the next ten years (Moore, 1965). While Moore later revised his doubling period from every year to every other year, his predictions proved prescient and the argument came to be known as Moore's Law (Moore, 1975). Recently, the exponential behavior of the trend has stretched to around 30 months, but despite this lengthening, Moore's Law continues to function as a synecdoche for the exponential growth of computing power in the digital age (Clark, 2015 p. 114).

But while Moore is best remembered for the trend he identified, his original article dedicated less space to the trend itself than to its effects. The speed and economy of integrated circuits would, predicted Moore, "lead to such wonders as home computers—or at least terminals connected to a central computer—automatic controls for automobiles, and personal portable communications equipment" (Moore, 114) "Such wonders" now exist and, so long as Moore's Law remains at least reasonably law-like, many more technological wonders are sure to come. Irrespective of the promises and perils of each digital technology, the pace of change poses many challenges for those seeking to utilize them. For this reason, Moore's Law is at the heart of the challenges facing digital humanists today.

This chapter seeks to answer at least one of the challenges that the rapid pace of technological change presents to the digital humanities: how can instructors effectively teach the digital humanities in an era in which the power and potential of the digital grows and evolves so rapidly?

There is no simple answer to this question. And the problem is further compounded by the bureaucratic structures that underpin academia's typical calendars and often force faculty at colleges and universities to design a course months or years in advance of its offering. But it is not an intractable issue, and this chapter offers digital humanists practical solutions backed by evidence from the science of teaching and learning literature for keeping course content relevant in the face of the ever-shifting sands of digital technologies.

The "backward design" of courses has been foundational to the science of teaching and learning for over twenty years now and yet many instructors at the collegiate level fail to structure courses with the method's most basic question—*what are my objectives in this course?*—in mind (Tyler, 1949; Wiggins & McTighe, 1998). This start-at-the-end approach is critical to producing high quality courses generally and is perhaps even more critical to producing high quality digital humanities courses specifically, so I begin with an overview of backward design and its relationship to quick-changing fields of study.

Next, I place digital humanities courses within the context of the broader humanities curriculum. Regardless of the department or program in which a digital humanities course is housed, its function in a given curriculum is most closely akin to that of a methodology course. In this section of the essay, I illustrate how digital humanists can creatively draw upon the literature on teaching methodology courses.

Too often methodology courses focus on the theoretical arguments of how to study a given subject at the expense of the supplementary skills necessary for enacting a given research method. To avoid this mistake and to offer students practical preparation for research in the ever-changing field of digital humanities, I then move to a discussion of how to integrate the most important supplementary skill for any digital humanist: effective collaboration.

Given that this chapter wrestles with a field with such a wide array of standpoints, approaches, methods, technologies, and applications that it's been likened to the spectacular diversity of the "big tent" of a circus, it will likely fall short of the expectations of some readers (Svensson, 2012). Moreover, as it limits itself to the advanced undergraduate and graduate seminars introducing digital humanities, it will also likely fall short of the needs of scholars teaching in secondary or community education settings, libraries and cultural institutions, or the slew of other settings outside of colleges and universities where so much of education happens. Nevertheless, even readers whose expectations and needs this essay fails to specifically address will hopefully find some general insights that they can creatively apply to their specific teaching contexts. And while this essay is not specifically on diversity and inclusion in the digital humanities, it does recognize the field's important foregrounding of those values and works to infuse any advice it offers with ways to maintain and further that commitment (Spiro, 2012).

21.2 Designing backward

In *Understanding by Design*, the text that first applied "backward design" to education, Grant Wiggins and Jay McTighe introduce their work by humbly noting that it simply "may confirm much of what you believe and do as an educator" (Wiggins & McTighe, 2005). The basis of the backward design of curricula, courses, activities, assessments are, as Wiggins and McTighe admit, three questions that likely feel familiar to most teachers:

1. "What relevant goals (e.g., content standards, course or program objectives, learning outcomes) will this design address?"
2. "Through what … tasks will students demonstrate the desired understanding?"
3. "What learning experiences and instruction will enable students to achieve the desired results?" (Wiggins & McTighe, 2005)

And yet, without consistently considering this question throughout each stage of the design of educational practice, it is easy for any instructor to disregard the need for logical links between the goals, assessments, and experiences of any educational unit.

Tradition is a powerful force in course design and selecting content or activities because they have been taught by predecessors or peers is a rut that many instructors groove into. To illustrate this trap, Wiggins and McTighe offer a typical example of using "content-focused design" orientation instead of the "result-focused" approach of backward design:

"The teacher might base a lesson on a particular topic (e.g. racial prejudice), select a resource (e.g., *To Kill a Mocking Bird*), choose specific instructional methods based on the resource and topic (e.g. Socratic seminar to discuss the book and cooperative groups to analyze stereotypical images

Course design in the digital humanities

in books and on television), and hope thereby to cause learning (and meet a few English/language arts standards). Finally, the teacher might think up a few essay questions for assessing student understanding of the book" (Wiggins & McTighe, 2005 p. 15).

In this traditional approach, instructors often fail to connect activities to the overarching goals of the course and privilege "coverage" of factual information over the purposeful selection of material that relates to at least one overarching goal in the development of students' understanding. Backward design, on the other hand, offers instructors a formal structure that keeps the parts of any educational unit related to the whole of its aims.

The backward design of educational units—from an entire degree curriculum to a single activity—has proven to be good practice across disciplines. And three facets of that research point to its outsized potential for courses in the digital humanities.

The first facet of backward design that points to its potential for digital humanities education lies in its foundational relationship between "big ideas" and lasting skills. Though Wiggins and McTighe (and the many other educational scholars who have refined backward design in their wake) recognize that the goals of any educational experience are largely dependent on the subject and context in which they are taught, they advocate for instructors to set goals at the level of the "big ideas" of a given subject and context. "A big idea," they write, "is a concept, theme, or issue that gives meaning and connection to discrete facts and skills" (Wiggins & McTighe, 2005, p. 5). Developing an understanding of the concept of adaption in biology, the challenge of defining justice in law, and the distributive property in mathematics are all examples of the kind of goals Wiggins and McTighe suggest educators should design their courses around (Wiggins & McTighe, 2005, p. 5). In the case of the digital humanities, big ideas might include the understanding of the concept of distant reading, the challenges of representing uncertainty in data visualizations, and the architecture of artificial neural networks. Building courses from big ideas backward, maintains students' focus on the essential questions of the field that transcend any particular tool or application and offers digital humanists an important strategy for counteracting the fast pace of the field.

The second facet of backward design that illustrates its promise for digital humanities education is in the value it gains by forcing instructors to simultaneously be purposeful and transparent. "What is difficult for many teachers to see (but easier for students to feel)," write Wiggins and McTighe, "is that, without such explicit and transparent priorities, many students find day-to-day work confusing and frustrating." Confusion and frustration are particular perils of the digital humanities given the field's breadth and digital technology's constant fluctuation. Students may not understand why instructors chose to focus on online crowdsourcing instead of natural language processing or why instructors built an activity around the WordPress content management system instead of the Omeka content management system. But by designing curricula, courses, units, and activities around big ideas, digital humanities instructors are able to relate each part of their learning exercises to a critical, overarching whole. Such pervasive intentionality empowers instructors to share the reasoning behind the selection of their educational materials and the structure of their educational activities, which in turn helps to alleviate student confusion and frustration. Indeed, as the decade-long research studies of the University of Illinois at Urbana-Champaign and the University of Nevada Las Vegas's Transparency in Learning and Teaching (TILT) program has shown, assignments in which instructors transparently articulate their design choices and the assignment's relevancy to larger goals "contribute to increasing all students' success, especially that of underserved students" (Winkelmes, 2016).

The final facet of the backward design process with relevance to the digital humanities is in its transferability to the field itself. Incorporating an intentional design process into the work of building a curriculum or course and incorporating iterative design into each new offering of the units and exercises helps instructors think of themselves as designers and the concomitant transparency of backward design helps instructors to model design processes in their teaching. As digital preservation scholar Trevor Owens has written, meta-research scholarship has begun to show that the research process improves when "researchers adopt the role of designer and think through how formalizing the iterative practice of design could serve as a basis for research methods" (Owens, 2011). Tom Schofield, Mitchell Whitelaw, and David Kirk have further illustrated the importance of design to the digital humanities and have argued that the framework of "research through design" in particular is already resonant with the practices of digital humanists (Schofield et al., 2017). By transparently foregrounding the role of design in the construction of lessons, digital humanities instructors offer students an instance of "practicing-what-they-preach" as they center units and activities on the importance of the design process in digital humanities research.

21.3 Methodology

Lessons about or derived from the digital humanities have worked their way into a plethora of educational experiences across higher education. Lessons that may reasonably be housed under the tent of the field are now frequently included in the introductory courses of the humanities disciplines, advanced undergraduate and graduate seminars in the humanities, and extracurricular workshops. And the principles of the field are taught through the dozens of digital humanities centers, programs, majors, and minors that dot the higher-education landscape. Some of the field's literature has even made its way into the educational experiences of the arts, sciences, and social sciences. But what does a digital humanities course look like? To address the fast pace of the field, digital humanities courses can look toward a staple of curricula across the academia: the methodology course.

Methodology training is critical because it represents no less than the point at which students develop the ability to think like a researcher in their field. And despite continued debates about what constitutes the field of digital humanities, at perhaps its most elemental level, we might agree that the digital humanities utilizes digital technology to better answer humanistic research questions. Teaching digital humanities is then necessarily instruction about not only how to use digital technologies, but also how to imagine the ways such technologies can advance and augment the humanities' foundational methods of inquiry.

In fact, when we think of the digital humanities in relationship to humanities methodology generally we find that aspects of the digital humanities have long been present in the most analog of the humanities practices and that the same foundational techniques of the field persist in how we utilize digital technology. Jentery Sayers demonstrates precisely this point through his "ruination" of the field in his essay, "Dropping the Digital" (Sayers, 2016). In erasing the digital from a series of statements about the digital humanities, Sayers illustrates the continuity the digital humanities maintains with the humanities generally. Most notably, he places the digital under erasure in Matthew Gold's remark, "And the field of … humanities does move quickly." In his analysis of this remark, he notes that while networked technologies are indeed vaulting the speed of scholarship to a heretofore unseen pace, pre-digital methodological questions of ethics, structure, measurement, text, and context remain in every decision scholars make in relation to the digital. Moreover, Sayers draws upon Stephen Ramsay's work to show that what may typically be thought of as distinctly algorithmic and computational are actually part of the history of the core humanistic methodology of critical reading. "Critical reading practices already contain elements of the algorithmic…," writes Ramsay, "…the critic who endeavors to put forth a 'reading' puts forth not the text, but a new text in which the data has been paraphrased, elaborated, selected, truncated, and transduced" (Ramsay, 2011). In recognizing such continuity in methodology between the humanities and digital humanities, Sayers (via Ramsay and Gold) points toward a pedagogical strategy to counteract the speed of digital technology. While individual digital technologies might move rapidly, humanistic methodologies—how we approach our objects of study—remain rooted in the tradition of our fields.

Methodology training in the humanities generally and the digital humanities specifically, however, poses unique challenges. In their review of research methods courses in humanities disciplines—that is, art history,

Course design in the digital humanities

classics, history, linguistics, literature, media and performance studies, philosophy, and religious studies—Agnes Andeweg and Daphne Slob note that there is very little reflection on how to teach such coursework (Andeweg & Slob, 2017). But while explicit reflection on best practices for teaching methodology courses in the humanities is underdeveloped, Simon Mahoney and Elena Pierazzo have made a compelling case that when we teach digital humanities we must teach it in direct relation to methodology. With evidence from case studies about the educational experiences offered throughout the Department of Digital Humanities at King's College London, Mahoney and Pierazzo argue that digital humanities teaching should help students learn "how to do better or new research" (Mahony & Pierazzo, 2012). Given the centrality of technology to the digital humanities, though, instructors often focus on tools over methods. But as Manhoney and Pierazzo illustrate, teaching tools such as eXtensible Markup Language (XML) divorced from its specific application to humanistic questions leaves such lessons without a pedagogical underpinning and leaves students disinterested in both the discipline and the technology at hand. Alternatively, when digital humanities courses are constructed around the concept of the "research life cycle" and when each technology is shown in direct relationship to its domain-specific application, then students recognize "how such techniques could form the basis of a methodological approach to learn something new and exciting about the objects of their research" (Mahony & Pierazzo, 2012).

Though Andeweg and Slob find a lack of literature on teaching methodology in the humanities, they also note that a robust subfield in the science of teaching and learning literature has developed about teaching research methods in the basic, applied, and social sciences (Andweg & Slog, 2017). While looking to the scientific domains for suggestions on how to improve methodology instruction is not ideal for humanists, for better or worse, changing expectations from grant funders are demanding that projects in the humanities be presented similarly to those in the sciences. As English scholar Gabriele Griffin, has noted, increasingly grant funders are requiring that even humanists write formal methodology sections that explicitly outline plans for the management and sharing of data (even if humanists might not conceive of their research materials as data) (Griffin, 2013). Given such a convergence in expectations around developing an explicit meta-discourse for a project's research design, digital humanities scholars can find relevant lessons for teaching methodology in the generic literature on research design such as Ben Kei Daniel and Tony Harland's *Higher Education Research Methodology* and Mark Garner, Claire Wagner, and Barbara Kawulich's *Teaching Research Methods in the Social Sciences* (Daniel & Harland, 2018; Garner, et al. 2009). Similarly, such convergent grant expectations have also led to humanities and digital humanities-specific grant resources that guide scholars through how to write about research design such as Raphael Folsom's *How to Get Grant Money in the Humanities and Social Sciences* and the consortium-authored website Digital Humanities Data Curation (Folsom, 2019). Finally, while the literature on teaching methodology in the humanities remains minute, Mahoney and Pierazzo have developed a strategy for teaching the digital humanities as methodology. It follows three principles derived from a combination of the generic literature on teaching methodology and their own experience at one of the largest teaching organizations for the digital humanities:

- "The use of relevant examples, with the selection coming from the domain of the course participants;
- The use of exercises that are relevant for the participants, again by selecting material from the students' domains; and,
- Presentations of specific resources and supports that will be available to the participants after completion of the courses in order to allow students to accomplish research on their own." (Mahony & Pierazzo, 2012 p. 221)

In consistently making lessons about digital technologies relevant to the foundational methodologies of the humanities, instructors develop understanding about the big ideas both of how to design a research project and how to utilize digital tools to advance that research.

21.4 Collaboration

In teaching a digital humanities course as a methodology course, faculty teach students how to structure their thought as a researcher in their discipline would. The "big ideas" of a digital humanities course taught within a department of foreign language study and a media studies department will vary considerably, but one common thread that weaves together most digital humanities courses is an acknowledgment of the fact that digital humanities research necessitates collaboration in a way that traditional humanities research rarely did.

Of course, analog research methodology has long demanded collaboration with librarians, archivists, community members, students, and colleagues. Unfortunately, most of this collaboration has remained largely invisible and recognized informally, if at all. Now, though, working with librarians and archivists is more critical than ever as scholars navigate records in a time of uneven transition between physical and digital materials, partnering with communities no longer necessarily depends upon physical proximity thanks to the instant connections of digital communication technologies, and researching in partnership with students and colleagues at one's own institution and across institutions is more feasible than ever before thanks to digital project management systems that facilitate complex divisions of labor. Additionally, technologists—a broad classification that includes roles ranging from the contingent workers of information technology staffs to full-time researchers working in technology-rich fields such as computer science—have come to join the above pool of potential collaborators for humanists. And, recently, meta-discourse about research practices has encouraged humanists to reckon with the ethical necessity of making the invisible labor of research collaborations more visible and distributing credit more equitably.

With this increasing awareness of the need for collaboration has come an acknowledgement that collaboration requires specialized training for it to be done well. For over a half century now, the business and management subfields of team dynamics and project management have developed a scientific literature on effective collaboration in workplaces. Recently, this literature has even focused on research teams in higher education. And in just the last decade, digital humanists have begun to study collaboration in depth—an acknowledgement that the field depends upon collaboration and that its working environment contains unique needs and holds alternative values than private sector and scientific settings. Given such extensive demonstration of the importance of collaboration for research in general and digital humanities research in particular and given that it is an interpersonal skill with application to any methodology or technology, collaboration possesses a stability that overcomes the exponential pace of technological change. It is a formidable candidate for one of the handful of "big ideas" to center any digital humanities course around.

With such a wide array of approaches to collaboration, though, instructors dedicating time to the practice in their digital humanities courses will have to make decisions about which aspects to focus on in their course. Here, as elsewhere, instructors should ask themselves what activities will help students meet the objectives most important to the course. But while there are many aspects that instructors can focus on, the literature on collaboration in the digital humanities has coalesced around three themes: the importance of ethical collaboration, project management in group projects, and rapid collaboration. More themes will emerge as the literature develops further and instructors may find relevant lessons beyond the literature on collaboration in the digital humanities specifically, but looking into this literature can help instructors develop a plan for how to teach effective and transferable collaboration skills to their students.

In his essay, *Collaborative Research in the Digital Humanities*, Willard McCarty outlines the ethical tension that has existed in digital humanities research since its origins. He writes:

> "Socially the history of computing in the humanities has involved a long struggle to establish computing practitioners and non-technical scholars as equals in research … But again, collaboration (if the term is to be other than a euphemism of social control from above) must occur

Course design in the digital humanities

on the ground level. It must be work (*labor*) done together (*co*, from *cum*, 'with') in every sense. The technically focused researcher must work *with* not *for* the non-technically focused scholar, must serve the research co-authorially. Of course equality in research, where this is possible, brings with it equal demands on both sides, and so a host of questions about how both are to scale the steep learning curve that faces each. This in turn raises questions about how scholars are trained, and so about the institutional relationship between the sciences and humanities" (McCarty, 2012).

In this summary of the challenges that digital humanities collaboration poses, McCarty imagines the typical research relationship in the field as a partnership between the tech-savvy and the subject-expert. We must acknowledge that many other configurations of collaborations exist (and elsewhere McCarty does so), but the difficulty that McCarty points out—developing equality and shared ownership of the labor in research—is the pressing ethical question for any digital humanities collaboration. And it is a question that must be addressed not only in theory, but, more importantly, in training.

Like all other course content, what to teach about the ethics of collaboration is a negotiation between instructors and their institutional constraints, their disciplinary norms, and their students' needs and expectations. But instructors would do well to build lessons around the foundational questions of the collaboration such as how is work shared equitably and how is credit distributed proportionally. To wrestle with such ideas, digital humanities instructors can look to the intersection of mathematics and philosophy, particularly, the game-theoretical literature that has arisen around the problem of fair division. Rooted in Blaise Pascal and Pierre de Fermat's foundational work on probability, contemporary game theory has developed a host of tools to address the ethical questions of dividing a vast array of tangible and intangible entities fairly. And while game theory is literally theoretical, the subfield of fair division work brings theories of fairness to bear on real-world simulations that are often easy to simulate in a classroom setting and lend themselves to an active learning environment (Schubik, 2002).

Concurrent with lessons on the fair division of labor, instructors teaching the principles of effective collaboration should work through material on the division of the larger project into its component tasks. The division of labor gains a practical grounding when the team has a clear sense of the tasks at hand. Just as instructors work backward to develop the plan for meeting the objectives of their course, students in the digital humanities will need to work backward to develop a plan for meeting the objectives of their project. But rather than consult science of teaching and learning literature on backward design, students should be exposed to concepts from the field of project management. That field is a rather robust one with a massive professional training infrastructure that has been built largely outside of traditional higher education institutions, chiefly by the Project Management Institute and Association for Project Management. Given that the field of project management is, indeed, so sprawling and the semester so brief, instructors need to strip project management down to essential and relevant but still critical set of lessons.

Project management *qua* project management has its roots in Taylorism and was refined through neoliberalism and militarism—-isms that the humanities, in general, actively resists for ethical concerns. And yet, project management as concept is, as humanist Judy Hemming has suggested, nothing more than a "form of action…undertaken to make things better or stop them from getting worse" (Hemming, 2012 p. 375). If, as Hemming has convincingly illustrated, we teach university students the technical dimensions of project management in tandem with its political, social, economic, and ethical dimensions, then we can imbue students with practical skills to tackle not simply the problems motivated by profit, but also the skills to achieve objectives "in a way that relates to the operational world in which the project is embedded" be that the field of historical research or an anti-racist collective (Hemming, 2012).

To help wrest project management skills from their Tayloristic, neoliberal foundations, digital humanities instructors can draw their lessons from the burgeoning literature on project management processes in the digital humanities. For instance, librarians Brett Currier, Rafia Mirza, and Jeff Downing have written about the unique dimensions of project management in digital humanities and how they differ from its traditional, profit-motivated form (Currier et al., 2017). These scholars reduce traditional project management to four essential phases—conceptualization, planning, implementation, and termination—but then offer strategies for adapting them to the general ethos of the academy and of the field of digital humanities. Key considerations for project management include conceptualizing projects around mutually beneficial partnerships rather than around profit, planning projects around their contributions to a broader research field rather than around consumer needs, and concluding projects not when the market changes but rather wrapping up projects at their natural conclusion in a way that allows for archiving so that future generations of scholars may benefit (Currier et al., 2017). This study, along with dozens of others on project management in the digital humanities that have emerged in the last decade can help students to imagine alternative foundations for building and implementing projects in an efficient yet ethical way. As Christina Boyles et al., have shown, when the precarity of labor in digital humanities is recognized and grappled with, then students (and all other digital humanities practitioners) will be more likely to "sustain generative relationships that address the ethical dimensions of collaborative labor" (Boyles et al., 2018 pp. 693–699).

Just as the length of the bureaucratically focused academic calendar poses challenges to instructors designing courses, the brevity of the semester poses challenges to students tackling digital humanities projects. However, some recent literature on rapidly designing and building digital humanities projects offers instructors techniques for fostering projects across days or weeks rather than years. From 2010–2013, one of the leading centers for digital humanities in the United States, the Roy Rosenzweig Center for History and New Media at George Mason University, launched One Week | One Tool.[1] The program placed a multidisciplinary team of collaborators within a shared space to build a working humanities-focused software application within a single week. By all available accounts One Week | One Tool was productive and welcoming experience and resulted in multiple functioning digital humanities tools such as the Serendip-o-matic and Anthologize.[2] But more important than One Week | One Tool's outputs were the processes it introduced to digital humanities research. Drawing from both the old tradition of a communal barn raising and the recent working style of the "blitz weekend," the program built a structure for digital humanities research to be directly collaborative, consistently iterative, and fast.[3] More recently the University of Kansas Libraries and the University of Minnesota Libraries have repurposed the efforts of One Week | One Tool to craft a generic model for rapid production of research. Termed Research Sprints, these similarly time-bounded, collaborative events pair faculty and students with librarians and other research support professionals to complete small projects or components of larger projects in one week or less (Lach & Rosenblum, 2018; Inklebarger, 2019; Wiggins et al. 2019 pp. 420–422). Across the first few dozen of these sprints, multiple projects were centered on the digital humanities resulted in functioning tools such as a smartphone application for a public memory project on Emmett Till and significant research components such as a set of custom shapefiles to underpin the GIS mapping of historical waterways that have been subsumed by urbanization.[4]

While each of these working methods offer students in digital humanities courses examples of the field's practitioners crafting substantive projects quickly, both were focused on fostering the work of professionals rather than students and both events required levels of labor and financial resources that students rarely have access to. Nevertheless, because of the reflective literature from these projects and others, instructors in digital humanities can build exercises for students around the principles and methods that inspired and powered these projects. From One Week | One Tool, instructors can draw from the unconference principles that shaped its decision making and reimplement the instantaneous, networked feedback that drove its progress (Cohen, 2019). From Research Sprints, instructors can reach back to the Scrum techniques that structured its team dynamics and pace and reproduce the strategies to garner institutional support for such unique collaboration, if only on a smaller scale

Course design in the digital humanities

Lach & Rosenblum, 2018; Wiggins et al. 2019 pp. 420–422). Regardless of the particulars, if instructors commit time to the importance of effective collaboration, their students should find their work inside and out of the digital humanities better for it.

21.5 Bricolage

The digital humanities rest on shifting sands, but instructors can build effective courses by working backward from foundational big ideas through a thoughtfully scaffolded structure that supports the whole. For this sound structure, instructors can find models in methodological training. And to address the field's consistent and critical need for collaboration, instructors can dedicate significant energy to the unique skills necessary for working together ethically, efficiently, and quickly.

As anyone close to the field knows well, it is as difficult to define the digital humanities as it is to keep up with the field. But in spite of those difficulties, readers of this chapter may now begin to glimpse something axiomatic about our nebulous field: it is *bricolage* that is best taught with *bricolage*. The digital humanities is at its best when it creatively mortars together methods, tools, and perspectives that advance humanistic inquiry. And teaching such improvisational constructions requires instructors to look well beyond the digital humanities—to education, to design, to the sciences, to team dynamics, to industry, to ethics, and more—for inspiration. Whatever the focus of digital humanities lessons, a spirit of relentless bricolage should inhabit its content and drive its instruction.

Notes

1 Roy Rosenzweig Center for History and New Media, "One Week | One Tool: A Digital Humanities Barn Raising," One Week | One Tool, accessed June 8, 2019, oneweekonetool.org.
2 Roy Rosenzweig Center for History and New Media, "What It Is," Serendip-o-matic, accessed June 8, 2019, serendip-o-matic.com; Roy Rosenzweig Center for History and New Media, "Anthologize: Bits to Bookshelf," Anthologize, accessed June 8, 2019, anthologize.org.
3 Rosenzweig Center, "One Week | One Tool."
4 University of Kansas Libraries and University of Minnesota Libraries, "Portfolio," Research Sprints, accessed June 8, 2019, researchsprints.org/portfolio.

References

Andeweg, A. & Slob, D. (2017). "Humanities Research Methods in a Liberal Arts & Sciences Program" in *Transforming Patterns through the Scholarship of Teaching and Learning* edited by Katarina Mårtensson. Lund: Lunds Universitet, 34–39.
Boyles, C., et al. (2018). "Precarious Labor and the Digital Humanities." *American Quarterly* 70(3): 693–699.
Clark, D (2015). "Moore's Law Is Showing Its Age." *The Wall Street Journal* (July 16).
Currier, B.; Mirza, R. & Downing, J. (2017). "They Think All of This Is New: Leveraging Librarians' Project Management Skills for the Digital Humanities." *College and Undergraduate Libraries* 24 (2) 270–289.
Daniel, B.K. & Harland, T. (2018). *Higher Education Research Methodology*. New York: Routledge.
Folsom, R. (2019). *How to Get Grant Money in the Humanities and Social Sciences*. New Haven: Yale University Press.
Garner, M.; Wagner, C. & Kawulich, B. (2009). *Teaching Research Methods in the Social Sciences*. Burlington, VT: Ashgate Publishing.
Griffin, G. (2013). *Research Methods for English Studies*. Edinburgh: Edinburgh University Press.
Hemming, J. (2012). "Teaching Project Management: A New Perspective." *International Journal of Learning* 18 (3).
Inklebarger, T (2019). "Academic Speed Trials." *American Libraries* 50(1/2): 18.
Lach, P. & Rosenblum, B. (2018). "Sprinting Toward Faculty Engagement" in *Project Management in the Library Workplace* edited by Alice Daugherty and Samantha Schmehl Hines. Bingley: Emerald Group Publishing.
Mahony, S. & Pierazzo, E. (2012). "Teaching Skills or Teaching Methodology?" in *Digital Humanities Pedagogy: Practices, Principles, and Politics* edited by Brett Hirsch. Cambridge: Open Book Publishers.
McCarty, W. (2012). "Collaborative Research in the Digital Humanities" in *Collaborative Research in the Digital Humanities* edited by Willard McCarty and Marilyn Deegan. New York: Routledge.

Moore, G. (1965). Gordon. "Cramming More Components onto Integrated Circuits." *Electronics* 38(8)114–117.

Moore, G. (1975). "Progress in Digital Integrated Electronics." *Technical Digest of the International Electron Devices Meeting*: 11–13.

Owens, T (2011). "Please Write It Down: Design and Research in Digital Humanities." *Journal of Digital Humanities* 1(1).

Ramsay, S. (2011). *Reading Machines: Toward an Algorithmic Criticism*. Champaign: University of Illinois Press.

Sayers J. (2016). "Dropping the Digital" in *Debates in the Digital Humanities* edited by Matthew K. Gold. Minneapolis: University of Minnesota Press: 475–492.

Schofield, T.; Whitelaw, M. & Kirk, D. (2017). "Research through Design and Digital Humanities in Practice: What, How, and Who in an Archive Research Project." *Digital Scholarship in the Humanities* 32 (1): i103–i120.

Shubik, M (2002). "The Uses of Teaching Games in Game Theory Classes and Some Experimental Games." *Simulation & Gaming* 33 (2): 139–156.

Spiro, L. (2012). "'This Is Why We Fight': Defining the Values of the Digital Humanities" in *Debates in the Digital Humanities* edited by Matthew K. Gold. Minneapolis: University of Minnesota Press: 16–35.

Svensson, P (2012). "Beyond the Big Tent" in *Debates in the Digital Humanities* edited by Matthew K. Gold. Minneapolis: University of Minnesota Press: 36–49.

Tyler, R. (1949). *Basic Principles of Curriculum and Instruction*. Chicago: University of Chicago Press.

Wiggins, B., et al. (2019) "Research Sprints a New Model of Support." *Journal of Academic Librarianship* 45 (4): 420–422.

Wiggins, G. & McTighe, J. (1998). *Understanding by Design*. Alexandria, VA: Association for Supervision and Curriculum Development.

Wiggins, G. & McTighe, J. (2005). *Understanding by Design: Expanded 2nd Edition*. Alexandria, VA: Association for Supervision and Curriculum Development, 2005.

Winkelmes, M. et. al. (2016). "A Teaching Intervention that Increases Underserved College Students' Success." *Peer Review* 18, no. ½ (2016): 31–36.

22

CROWDSOURCING IN CULTURAL HERITAGE

A practical guide to designing and running successful projects

Mia Ridge

22.1 Introduction

Have you ever wanted to recruit hundreds of members of the public to assist with tasks like making cultural heritage collections findable online? Or to connect with passionate volunteers who'll share their discoveries with you?

Crowdsourcing in cultural heritage is a broad term for projects that ask the public to help with tasks that contribute to a shared goal or research interest related to cultural heritage collections or knowledge (Ridge, 2013). As participants receive no financial reward, the activities and/or goals should be inherently rewarding for those volunteering their time. This definition is partly descriptive and partly proscriptive, and this chapter is largely concerned with describing how to meet the standards it implies.

One of the key challenges that projects face is creating interfaces that turn a series of tasks that create and validate usable outputs, whether transcribing, describing, researching or contributing to source collections, into an enjoyable experience. As crowdsourcing is inherently productive in intent, each activity should contribute to a meaningful, collective goal. This chapter will help cultural heritage and digital humanities practitioners plan, design and document crowdsourcing projects with rewarding tasks and processes that contribute to a meaningful wider outcome. Understanding the motivations of cultural heritage organisations and the behind-the-scenes work that goes into building a crowdsourcing project should also help academics and others seeking to collaborate with or study crowdsourcing projects and cultural heritage institutions.

This chapter introduces key principles and stages in developing crowdsourcing projects and designing interfaces and communications that link to participant motivations. Based on the author's extensive practical experience and theoretical engagement with the field, it discusses topics including: choosing appropriate measures of success for evaluating projects; finding the right balance between productivity and engagement; validating and integrating the results of crowdsourced tasks into core collections systems; motivating organisations and volunteers to participate; and understanding the organisational and personal impact of crowdsourcing.

22.2 Crowdsourcing in cultural heritage

Crowdsourcing as we know it has been transformed by technology, but cultural heritage, scientific and other knowledge-based projects have a long history of asking people to voluntarily collect information and objects.[1] From the 1850s, Joseph Henry's meteorological observation project at the Smithsonian asked volunteers to submit weather observations via the still-new telegraph network (Smithsonian Institution Archives, 2012). Later, participants' own research and contact with the wider scientific community was facilitated through correspondence with the Smithsonian's second Secretary, Spencer F. Baird, so that each group benefitted in ways that were meaningful to them (Goldstein, 1994).

Some aspects of crowdsourcing—particularly 'citizen science' and 'citizen history'—also draw on a more recent history of public participation in scientific research (Bonney et al., 2009). Citizen science projects involve members of the public assisting professional scientists with research (Raddick et al., 2010), most commonly through data processing tasks like image classification but potentially also through fieldwork or observation tasks, data analysis or research design (Bonney et al., 2009). Humanities scholars interested in public participation in scholarly research may find the significant body of prior work on this topic by citizen science researchers particularly valuable.

An example from the humanities also neatly encapsulates many aspects of crowdsourcing. The editors of the Oxford English Dictionary (OED) appealed for examples and definitions of words from the public in the 1850s and in 1879 (Gilliver, 2012). Indexing, storing and managing the slips of paper subsequently received was a considerable task, as was coordinating and targeting requests for information about specific words. The OED continues to appeal to the public for help defining or providing examples of words in the present day.[2]

These early projects sought to gather data at a geographic and quantitative scale not possible for lone individuals by extending existing leisure activities like observing wildlife or reading historical books with additional documentation and communication tasks. However, the manual work of compiling the information received was time-consuming, and projects could easily fall behind in processing and analysing the incoming data.

The availability of the web as a platform has transformed crowdsourcing. Data can be easily entered via websites or applications, automatically validated against set criteria and aggregated with other data. Sites can acknowledge and thank contributors immediately, and if tasks are carefully designed, they can even provide instant feedback on the quality of contributions. For institutions that previously relied on volunteers having physical access to collections or records, remote contributions based on digital images relieves physical conservation requirements and pressures on venue space and hours.

Reaching potential participants is also easier online. Social media and specialist email lists or discussion boards can reach broad or niche audiences to advertise a project, according to the skills or numbers needed to complete tasks. In addition to traditional scholarly publications, email newsletters and blog posts can provide more timely and accessible updates on progress and developments. Unlike volunteer projects that require attendance at specific locations and times, crowdsourcing volunteers can contribute from anywhere in the world at any time of day or night, choosing tasks that match their interests and the time they have available.

22.3 Key conceptual and research frameworks

As evident in the paragraphs above, research on volunteer work in cultural heritage organisations and open source software has been particularly useful for thinking about fundamental aspects of participation in crowdsourcing. To understand participant motivations, I referenced research from related fields including citizen science, cultural heritage volunteering (Holmes, 2003), 'serious' leisure (Stebbins, 1997), commercial crowdsourcing, contributions to open source software and *Wikipedia*, and the emerging literature on cultural heritage crowdsourcing. While some aspects of volunteering enabled and mediated by online tools are novel (see for example Shirky, 2011), volunteers are still looking for a meaningful leisure activity that fits into their life: some just want casual activities they can pick up

Crowdsourcing in cultural heritage

whenever suits them, others want an opportunity to develop deeper skills and interests, or to socialise with other people with similar interests. Many of the skills needed to work with in-person volunteer or community programmes are similar to the community engagement and management skills needed for online projects.

As with traditional volunteering in cultural heritage venues, crowdsourcing is not merely an opportunity to get work done—it is also an opportunity to engage the public with collections, encouraging curiosity and learning as participants pay close attention to collection items. However, the need to justify the resources required to run projects designed to enhance collections can put pressure on projects to focus on productivity at the expense of participant enjoyment. This chapter will discuss some of the tensions between designing for productivity—the number of items processed and rate of data production—and for public engagement over the life of a project.

When thinking about the impact of interface, task and workflow design I drew on research from the fields of human-computer interaction, user experience design and usability. My views on the role of design in enabling curiosity and learning, and the potential of crowdsourcing for deeper engagement were informed by research on communities of practice (Wenger, 2010), learning through legitimate peripheral participation (Mugar, Østerlund, Hassman, Crowston, & Jackson, 2014), instructional design (Sharma & Hannafin, 2007; Wood, Bruner, & Ross, 1976) and museum studies.

While the availability of crowdsourcing platforms such as Flickr Commons, the Zooniverse Project Builder, FromThePage and Pybossa has reduced the technical overhead of setting up a project and managing the resulting data, it has also increased the competition for participants. Much of this chapter discusses design principles that will help projects attract and retain participants. While the underlying principles may hold, new and refined design techniques are still emerging. The best way to keep up is to try participating in newly launched or refreshed projects. This also provides valuable, grounded insights into volunteers' motivations, different types of barriers to participation, and the impact of communications and institutional processes. It also develops your ability to critically assess projects and define a shared language to discuss your own ideas.[3]

A brief note on language—throughout this chapter the shorthand 'crowdsourcing' will stand for 'crowdsourcing in cultural heritage and the humanities'. Discomfort with the term 'crowdsourcing' has led some to use terms such as 'community-sourcing' (Sample Ward, 2011), 'nichesourcing' (de Boer et al., 2012), 'micro-volunteering' (Lascarides & Vershbow, 2014) or 'targeted crowdsourcing' (Dafis, Hughes, & James, 2014). These terms acknowledge that the 'crowd' is often neither large nor truly anonymous. At times I use the acronym 'GLAMs' (galleries, libraries, archives and museums) as shorthand for 'cultural heritage institutions'. Crowdsourcing projects that seek to engage members of the public may also be described as a form of public history or public digital humanities. By enhancing digitised collection records, crowdsourcing in GLAMs can enable digital humanities projects, but the potential for more integrated projects between these groups is relatively little explored.

A single chapter cannot provide a definitive account of such a large, constantly changing topic. Instead, my aim is to provide a common language for discussing crowdsourcing, outline issues for consideration in planning and running projects, and provide pointers to further information. Many crowdsourcing projects are committed to transparency about their processes and results, contributing to a field rich in formal and informal publications,[4] including blog posts, conference presentations and newsletters from project stakeholders and contributors. Conference papers and publications on human computation, collective intelligence and computer-supported cooperative work (CSCW) contain deep technical expertise from specialist researchers in related fields, and are worth seeking out where relevant to specific design questions. Subjects not covered in this chapter include crowdfunding, user-generated content, the 'wisdom of the crowd', co-production or co-curation, or commercial crowdsourcing on platforms such as Amazon's Mechanical Turk.

Mia Ridge

22.4 Fundamental concepts in cultural heritage crowdsourcing

I will introduce some of the fundamental concepts in crowdsourcing by describing tasks commonly found in cultural heritage projects, with examples for each.

When teaching crowdsourcing, a simple, informal categorisation of participant actions can be used in conjunction with categories of task size and role.[5] Tasks are grouped into three types, according to their size and role: microtasks, macrotasks, and metatasks, which I will briefly define before describing participant actions.[6]

Microtasks are small, rapid, self-contained tasks. For example, the New York Public Library's *Building Inspector*[7] has broken down the task of checking building shapes and text transcribed from historical fire insurance maps into five extremely focused, tiny microtasks embedded in a specialised interface. Microtasks can be addictively satisfying because several can be completed in a short amount of time. Tasks such as tagging images are popular microtasks. In some cases, the simplicity of the task combined with the unpredictability of the items that appear in the queue can 'hook' participants.

Macrotasks are longer, and/or more complex tasks that often involve higher order decisions about what to record and how. The text transcription task in *Transcribe Bentham*[8] is a macrotask because the handwriting is difficult to decipher, whole pages are transcribed at a time (rather than line-by-line), and because participants can also 'mark-up' transcribed text to highlight insertions, deletions, etc., adding complexity to the task.[9]

Metatasks are activities that relate to the overall project, rather than individual tasks. This includes taking part in project design or analysis, and contributing questions, comments and answers to participant discussion fora. The *Old Weather* forum[10] is a justly famous example of the benefits of participant discussion, with a wealth of information shared and topics discussed.

Participant actions can be described according to how much creative freedom they have when completing the task and where it fits into the overall workflow. An informal categorisation I have found effective in teaching is: 'type what you see', 'describe what you see', 'share what you know', 'share what you have', 'validate other inputs'.

'Type what you see' tasks ask participants to type out or correct transcriptions from the item presented to them, and offer very little creative freedom. These tasks may be micro- or macrotasks. Transcription has been called a 'mechanical' task (Dunn & Hedges, 2012) but the difficulty varies according to the source material. Printed text is easier to decipher than unfamiliar older forms of handwritten text with unorthodox orthography that may require the transcriber to make difficult decisions. The National Library of Australia's *Trove* (Holley, 2009, 2010) platform for newspaper collections[11] includes functions to correct errors in automatically-generated text, and has been both hugely influential and productive (Holley, 2009, 2010). Other examples include the New York Public Library's *What's on the Menu* project.[12] Like *Trove*, the *Menu* interface shows the benefits of expert attention during the design process—the front page anticipates and addresses common barriers to participation, provides a range of tasks to suit different preferences, and the task itself is tightly focused on the transcription task, with items pre-processed to minimise distractions.

Transcription tasks may require a single contributor to transcribe an entire passage or page of text or audio, or they may break the task into smaller components (e.g. a line of text or a snippet of a recording). The British Library's *In the Spotlight*[13] project first asks participants to mark out the titles of plays on historical playbills; marked titles are then transcribed in a separate task. These tasks may not offer much creative freedom, but they can be immensely engaging, and lead to exploration of the collections and related topics outside the task.

'Describe what you see' tasks are designed to annotate items with additional information from formal taxonomies or informal folksonomies (Vander Wal, 2007), and includes identification and classification tasks such as tagging items with descriptive keywords. Image tagging on *Flickr Commons*[14] is perhaps not quite 'crowdsourcing', as the tagging activity can be spontaneous rather a response to direct requests from

Crowdsourcing in cultural heritage

the relevant GLAMs, but it provides a good example of the benefit of user-contributed keywords in aiding discoverability (Springer et al., 2008). Other early, influential projects include the art tagging projects steve.museum,[15] Brooklyn Museum's game, *Tag! You're It* (Bernstein, 2014), and *Waisda?* for video tagging (Oomen, Gligorov, & Hildebrand, 2014). The BBC's World Service Archive prototype used a combination of crowdsourcing and automated tagging on audio files (Raimond, Smethurst, & Ferne, 2014). Non-text forms of descriptive annotation include the Klokan *Georeferencer* implemented by the British Library[16] and the *Micropasts* 'photomasking' task that helps generate 3D models from photographs (Veldhuizen & Keinan-Schoonbaert, 2015).

'Share what you know' tasks may collect factual information or personal stories about collections by drawing on existing knowledge, or asking volunteers to conduct research. The *Lives of the First World War*[17] project asked participants to commemorate people who served in the war by 'sharing their stories, find their records and adding known facts', targeting the enthusiasm and research abilities of family and local historians. The Museum of Design in Plastics *10 Most Wanted* project crowdsourced research into their specialist collection (Lambert, Winter, & Blume, 2014), and comments on *Flickr Commons* sometimes note personal research or family stories about people, places, artefacts and events.

'Share what you have' projects collect items physically or digitally. RunCoCo's Community Collection Model (Berglund Prytz, 2013) has been adapted by Europeana for their First World War and Migration collecting projects.[18] The British Library's *UK Soundmap* project collected audio recordings over 2010–11.[19] The *Letters 1916–1923* project[20] digitises and transcribes items held in private and public collections.

Tasks to 'validate other inputs' can be designed to crowdsource quality control processes for content created in other tasks. They tend to occur within 'ecosystems' of tasks,[21] a design pattern in which task interfaces or applications are combined to process different aspects of the same source materials. *Building Inspector* is an example of this, as each of the five tasks offered contribute to the larger goal of digitising the maps. Validation tasks may be micro-, macro- or meta-tasks, and include checking tags or annotations added by others, or moderating forum discussions. Increasingly, participants are verifying the results of tasks by software, not people, as 'human computation' systems develop (Collings, 2015; Crowley & Zisserman, 2016).

22.5 Why do cultural heritage institutions support crowdsourcing projects?

Understanding why cultural heritage institutions undertake crowdsourcing projects provides important context, not only for measuring their success but also for understanding some of the barriers to success they face. The most obvious reason is that the size of the backlog of collection items needing transcription or description is beyond the scope of 'business as usual' projects. Resources are rarely available to adequately catalogue or describe in detail digitised collection items held by museums, libraries, archives and other institutions. Software designed to transcribe printed or handwritten text usually has some percentage of character- or word-level errors, hindering full-text search. Images, audio and moving image files often similarly lack detailed information about subjects depicted; audio transcription software may not be 100% accurate and cannot recognise subtle references to important individuals, events or subjects that a human can. If digital images or media files can be shared on crowdsourcing interfaces, tasks such as those discussed above can be applied to them.

Keywords and phrases suggested by the public can bridge the 'semantic gap' between the language used in catalogues designed for internal or specialist users, and the everyday language used by the public, to make collection items more discoverable (Trant, 2009).

As deeply specialist roles have been phased out and curatorial or reference teams are asked to cover longer periods or wider regions of specialist collections, it is increasingly likely that the most expert person on a specific item or collection may not work for the institution. Crowdsourcing can create opportunities for them to share their expert knowledge with an institution.

A number of projects have shown that crowdsourcing can create meaningful experiences with collections, and provide opportunities for learning and delight (Ridge, 2013, 2015). Well-designed projects can help people discover new interests, communities, or just encourage them to have a brief moment of deeper engagement with cultural heritage. This makes crowdsourcing a good fit for institutions whose missions encourage access, creativity, engagement or learning through their collections and knowledge.

22.6 Why do people contribute to crowdsourcing projects?

Understanding participant motivations is vital for designing successful projects that can attract and retain participants. Research on traditional volunteering, citizen science and GLAM crowdsourcing projects has provided insights into why people donate their time. Research into volunteering by psychologists Clary et al found six groups of motivations for volunteers: values ('altruistic and humanitarian concerns for others'), understanding (new learning experiences and the chance to practice knowledge, skills and abilities), social 'relationships with others', career-related benefits, ego-protective ('eliminating negative aspects surrounding the ego'), and enhancement (positive strivings for growth and development) (Clary et al., 1998). Research with museum volunteers found that 'doing something enjoyable', an interest in the subject, meeting people and 'making friends' were the main reasons for volunteering (Edwards & Graham, 2006).

Zooniverse projects have made a substantial contribution to research on motivations in citizen science. In one study, nearly 40% of *Galaxy Zoo* participants selected 'I am excited to contribute to original scientific research' as their main motivation, with the next most common primary motivation being: 'I am interested in astronomy' (Raddick et al., 2010). Alam and Campbell (2017) and Ferriter et al. (2016) have investigated how motivations change over time. A common thread across other projects is an interest in the subject (Eccles & Greg, 2014; Leon, 2014), with participants self-fashioning roles within a project to suit their interest (Das Gupta, Rooney, & Schreibman, n.d.).

When thinking about motivations in practical terms, I find grouping motivations relevant to heritage crowdsourcing into extrinsic, intrinsic and altruistic motivations is useful. Very few cultural heritage crowdsourcing projects support extrinsic motivations, such as tangible rewards.[22] Intrinsic motivations including fun, an interest in the subject and socialising are inherently rewarding and come into effect when an activity is worth doing for its own sake, regardless of external rewards (Csikszentmihalyi & Hermanson, 1995). Altruistic motivations include those related to the 'collective' or greater good, 'the importance attributed to the project's goals' (Nov, Arazy, & Anderson, 2011), and ideological values or principles. Jane McGonigal summarises much of the literature in her memorable overview of 'what humans crave' and 'what museums give us': '1. satisfying work to do 2. the experience of being good at something 3. time spent with people we like 4. the chance to be a part of something bigger' (McGonigal, n.d.).

22.7 Turning crowdsourcing ideas into reality

My analysis of non-commercial crowdsourcing projects (2015) found that successful projects have several features in common, including good publicity (whether through luck or design), well-designed task interfaces and processes, and messaging that presents the impact of the project on a shared, significant goal that links to participant motivations. Key challenges include recruiting and maintaining volunteer participation over time and integrating the results of crowdsourced tasks back into core catalogues, repositories or IT systems within the institution.

This section discusses important milestones in the process of planning, implementing and running crowdsourcing projects. Defining 'success' for your project will influence design decisions, as will the choice of source material and your desired outcomes. The exact order of decisions will vary according to the specific project, but you should expect that some decisions will be revisited as more information is gathered and allow for this when allocating resources. Designing iteratively also allows you to fine-tune

Crowdsourcing in cultural heritage

the prioritisation of efficiency and engagement, adjust workflow and quality controls measures as necessary, improve usability, and update text and tasks for specialist or generalist audiences as you learn from showing your project to potential participants.

Just as interfaces need to be carefully designed to maximise productivity and engagement, projects need to be carefully designed to ensure long-term success. Project design considerations include how the organisation sets up and resources a project, its coordination with other staff and work, and how it evaluates and responds to results. Decisions made in the planning phase will affect the implementation and running phases, so some points to consider for these later stages are discussed under the heading of planning.

22.8 Planning crowdsourcing projects

Key stages in the planning process include defining success for your project, managing any impact on the organisation, choosing source material and determining desired outputs, workflows and data re-use, communications and participant recruitment, and applying practical and ethical 'reality checks'.

Understanding the impact of logistical issues such as workflow, quality control and target systems for information collected through crowdsourcing by cultural heritage organisations should also help digital humanities researchers and practitioners interested in collaborating with GLAMs.

22.9 Defining 'success' for your project

Potential quantitative metrics for measuring the success of heritage crowdsourcing projects include: the number of hours participants have spent on a project; initial and sustained participation rates; participant retention; the extent and types of use of community discussion platforms; the number of tasks completed; and the percentage of tasks validated against required quality standards. Efficiency can be measured as the number of tasks accurately completed per volunteer minute. Valuable but less easily measured outcomes include the extent to which participants gain related skills and knowledge, or the number of new research questions or discoveries that emerge during a project. Qualitative measures include the extent to which participants expressed support or appreciation for the project, the number of participants who pursue activities related to their new interest, or some wider impact on participants' behaviour or attitudes.

Three definitions of success seem to have the most utility for project stakeholders: productivity, reach and engagement. However, two of these metrics are inherently opposed: time spent posting on discussion platforms or learning about collection items means less time is available to spend on the core task.[23] However, there is also an argument that both engagement and contributions are needed for citizen science projects to count as a success (Simmons, 2015). Accordingly, measurements of success should be judged and weighted according to the overall goals of an individual project.

Productivity is the simplest to define and to measure, and the easiest metric to design for. How many tasks have been completed to the standards required? Figures for prominent projects can be impressive, with *Trove* and Zooniverse contributions numbering in the hundreds of millions.[24]

Reach measures the number or type of people contributing to projects. This might be the 1.7 million (at the time of writing) volunteers contributing to Zooniverse or a small group of volunteers drawn to a highly specialist project. Reach can extend beyond individual participants to include those who access research that results from projects, or who are more easily able to find cultural heritage collections online.

Finally, you can consider how many participants become more engaged with the subject of the collections or disciplines (such as history or science) related to them. Engagement might appear as learning, attitude change, or other changes in behaviour linked to feelings or knowledge gained (Bitgood, 2010; Museums, Libraries and Archives Council, 2008; The Culture and Sport Evidence (CASE) programme, 2011). Once you have determined the most appropriate mix of success metrics, you can decide how you will measure and evaluate progress against them.[25]

22.10 Managing organisational impact

The Zooniverse guide to 'building a great project' begins '[k]now that you are making a commitment!' ('Part I: Building a Great Project', n.d.). Crowdsourcing projects require ongoing attention from staff and assessing whether you can provide resources for the life of the project is an important step in assessing the feasibility of a project. Staff can be supported by volunteers for some tasks, such as answering questions from other participants, but they must also have time to report on progress to internal and external stakeholders, and prepare newsletters and social media updates for outreach and marketing purposes.[26] Staff might also need support in gaining new skills such as community management or workflow integration.

Crowdsourcing projects can have an impact on the workload and outputs of departments across the organisation. For example, they can lead to increased attention to collections, and requests for new or reprioritised digitisation to keep items flowing into the platform. If your project is to generate metadata, annotations or other information about collection items, talking to the teams that manage the systems that store information about collections is vital. They can specify import formats and help you determine what information will be most useful to collect to improve catalogue or discovery systems. If information collected does not fit into existing interfaces (for example, your collections management system has no capacity to store user-generated content), where will it be kept? Ensure technical documentation is shared with relevant staff even if the platform is developed externally. The work of preparing material for ingest into the platform, and of reviewing and packaging task results for ingest into internal systems should also be included in overall resource plans.

Finally, an internal communications strategy, however informal, will help the rest of the organisation feel involved in the success of the project. You can share updates via internal presentations and emails, and invite staff to test interfaces, brainstorm ideas for outreach methods to reach potential participants, and plan publicity in physical venues.

22.11 Choosing source collections

Crowdsourcing relies on the availability of digitised collections. Digitisation can be expensive and time-consuming, so get estimates for delivery dates before building milestones around new digitisation. Source collections may also be determined by the goals of the project—research projects on a particular topic may choose items in a range of formats, while a project aimed at increasing discoverability might work through one format at a time.

Some content has a wider immediate appeal, and consequently makes the work of recruiting participants easier. Lascarides and Vershbow said 'it is much easier to get patrons excited about participation in a project if they are already excited about the source material' when describing the choice of material for what become *What's on the Menu* (2014). *DIY History* selects handwritten, historically significant, 'interesting' and extensive materials (DiMeo, 2014). They also note a preference for material is that is 'old enough' to avoid copyright and privacy issues. While collections that appeal to both casual viewers and scholars make attracting interest and justifying participation much easier, it is possible to create compelling stories about more obscure collections or to invite specialist communities to become involved.

22.12 Planning workflows and data re-use

The source material—text, digitised images, audio-video, etc.—and goals of the project determine the types of tasks that will be crowdsourced. Planning the workflows necessary to make data usable is part of the process of assessing the feasibility of a project: there is no point asking people to help create data or knowledge that you cannot use as intended. Creating a workflow plan is part of managing the organisational impact and integration of a project, and should ensure that you can move digitised source material into your crowdsourcing platform, then move validated data to the system (which might be a collections management system, web publishing system etc.) in which it can be used. Collections management staff can advise on the most useful data for discoverability or help work out how to publish research datasets. Any changes required are likely to take time to implement so begin conversations with relevant departments as early as possible.

Source items might need pre-processing before they are presented in tasks. For example, some projects categorise manuscript items by how easy or hard they are to transcribe. Some pre-processing tasks can be built into the task ecosystem, such as Fossil Finder,[27] which asked participants whether a photo was 'good enough to study', instructing them, 'If it is too blurry, dark, noisy, or bushy then bin it!'. Workflow also includes task validation and quality control processes, although these are usually built into the crowdsourcing platform. Data might also need post-processing to convert it into formats suitable for ingest and sharing with project contributors.[28]

Workflows should be tested as early as possible to allow time to manage any logistical, technical, legal or institutional issues that arise. This behind-the-scenes work ensures that new items can be easily added to the platform, and that data created is put to work as soon as possible, helping demonstrate the value of volunteer contributions to all.

Workflow systems should be designed for modularity to allow for changes in other platforms over time. Collections management systems can be refreshed, new tasks with different export formats devised – or you may start to integrate machine learning processes to create human computation systems. Finally, in order to re-use content created by volunteers, you should ensure that you have put in place terms and conditions that give you the right to use the data.

22.13 Planning communications and participant recruitment

There is someone, somewhere, interested in every single thing collected by a cultural heritage institution. The hard part is finding them and reaching them with a compelling invitation to join your shared endeavour.

Without participants, there is no project, so invest time in planning your communication strategy. Publicity material, including posts on social media, text on project sites, must clearly explain the project's goals and tasks without jargon or assumptions about what recipients already know. For example, testing for *In the Spotlight* found that not everyone was familiar with terms like 'transcription' or understood why it cannot be done automatically. As you develop prototype interfaces, test and revise messages until they effectively motivate target participants to complete their first task.

Marketing and outreach may not come naturally. It can help to find out (or remind yourself) what people already love about the relevant collections—what stories do they share with front-of-house or social media staff about them, or why do they already value them? Similarly, you can involve existing communities of interest in the process of designing the project (bearing in mind that they will not be able to represent the needs of novices with those collections). You might find them on listservs or discussion forums, social media hashtags or via academic or community contacts.

Clary et al found that messages that resonate with recipient motivations have enhanced 'persuasive impact' and help volunteers find more enjoyable and satisfying roles that match their motivations (1998).[29] Furthermore, volunteers whose experiences matched their motivations were more satisfied and more likely to intend to continue volunteering (1998), suggesting that the text used to market and describe projects could be as important as interface and task design. Favourite examples of 'straplines' that encapsulate the goals and attitudes of projects include: 'With a few keystrokes, you could bring a family together';[30] 'We know the names of these children; can you help us tell their stories?';[31] 'Kill Time. Make History.';[32] 'Historians need your help!'.[33]

371

22.14 Final considerations: practical and ethical 'reality checks'

Having defined success for your project, talked to teams across your organisation, chosen your goals and source material, and considered workflow, a final 'feasibility check' can be useful. Will anyone have the necessary skills and knowledge to undertake the task you propose, and can you motivate them to take part?

You can talk to potential contributors and undertake usability testing on early paper or digital prototypes of your interface to check whether the tasks proposed make sense and whether they would be motivated to do them. These 'reality check' conversations will also help determine whether you have a compelling 'marketing' story about the difference the project makes that would convince people to donate time to your project, allowing you to refine or abandon an idea.

The final 'reality check' for a planned project is reviewing your plans to ensure that it meets the ethical standards required. For example, organisational policies about volunteering may apply, or there may be local norms about responsibility and fairness. Once you have determined the ethical principles that apply, ensure they are enacted in practices such as task and interface design, communication strategies and data access plans. For example, you may value transparency about process and outcomes, but as this can be challenging for cultural heritage and academic projects, you could initiate internal conversations about publishing more information than usual to meet those goals.

Project teams generally believe that they must honour participants' time and contributions, and honour any commitments they make to them.[34] (Having seen stakeholders on some early projects disappear after launch, I tend to use a 'party' metaphor :if you have invited people into your space, as a host you are bound to stay and provide for their basic needs.) The European Citizen Science Association's Ten Principles of Citizen Science lists some practical ways in which ethical considerations may be operationalised (2015). Discussion of 'what ethical practice looks like on a daily basis' at an expert workshop on crowdsourcing organised at the Digital Humanities 2016 conference (DH2016 Expert Workshop, 2016) included: timely and responsive communication, defining benefits to each party, communicating expectations and keeping promises to volunteers, ensuring participants' right to access and re-use data, data protection (for records related to recent generations), acknowledging and crediting participants; considering participant experience alongside goals and efficiency; and updating ethical practices as necessary. Models for crediting participants could be drawn from traditional volunteer programmes, and might include letters of reference or certificates of participation in addition to credit on academic outputs.

22.15 Developing and testing crowdsourcing projects

In this section I will discuss key points and general principles for implementing crowdsourcing projects, including task design, documentation and tutorials, quality control and ensuring that designs work as well as possible through usability testing. It is important to note that basic usability (minimising dissatisfaction) is rarely enough; websites should both offer pleasing features that encourage users to return and minimise annoyances for users. The details of effective task design will depend on your goals and source materials. 'User experience' design, also known as UX, includes the visible aspects of backend workflow, instructional and marketing text, and so on in addition to interface and interaction design.

Critical points when a quality user experience matters include successfully 'onboarding' a participant so that they can complete their first task, and maintaining participation despite changes over time. As crowdsourcing is a voluntary activity, it is vital to minimise barriers to participation, points of friction and demotivators.

Barriers to participation include compulsory registration (Budiu, 2014), so some projects do not require registration, and some Zooniverse projects have successfully deployed a design pattern called 'lazy registration' ('Lazy Registration design pattern', n.d.). Being clear about how data will be used helps. Rose Holley's 2010 summary of research on participation in *Distributed Proofreaders*, *FamilySearch Indexing*, *Wikimedia* and

Trove reported that volunteers 'do not want to feel that their work can be commercially exploited' (2010). A study of *Old Weather* found that stopping participating is strongly associated with an anxiety about the quality of contribution (Eveleigh, Jennett, Blandford, Brohan, & Cox, 2014). Competitive models like gamification-style leaderboards are an easy way to recognise individuals who have completed more tasks, but they favour those with more free time, and there is some evidence that some participants are deterred by competition (Eveleigh, Jennett, Lynn, & Cox, 2013) (Preist, Massung, & Coyle, 2014).

Usability tests can be conducted throughout the development process, as you can test existing projects, paper prototypes and work-in-progress. Tests can be informal ('guerrilla' usability tests are free apart from the time required to talk to participants) or formal, but the benefits are invaluable. Usability tests allow you to understand and devise creative solutions to problems uncovered. They will help you identify and remove barriers to participation, define rewards appropriate to your goals and community and ensure that the project maximises the return on investment.

22.16 Designing the 'onboarding' experience

In user experience design, 'onboarding' refers to orienting people to the features of a site and helping them start to use it (Hess, 2010). Ideally, the first page that potential participants see shows (not tells) them what the project aims to do, how their help can make a difference, and where to start the task. For example, *What's on the Menu* has manicules (pointing hands) pointing to a button labelled 'Help transcribe'. As discussed earlier, a good communication strategy should include a strong strapline that give a sense of the larger challenge that tasks will contribute to, and ideally connect to probable motivations for action.

The landing page should also include 'social proof' that others have already chosen to participate (Mitra & Gilbert, 2014).[35] For example, the front page of *What's on the Menu* prominently lists the number of dishes transcribed so far and *Trove* lists the number of corrections already made on a given day, the number of items tagged that week, and the number of comments added that month, showing how updates can be tailored to the frequency of different tasks (a method that supports less active projects).

Some projects feed participants tasks from a queue of material, while others leave the choice of material up to the participant. Providing initial tasks from a queue minimises the number of decisions a participant has to make, which helps reduce cognitive load (the amount of mental effort required to operate a system or learn new information; Whitenton (2013)). This, in turn, leaves more mental resources for learning the task.[36] Feeding the first tasks to participants also allows a project to begin with 'golden tasks', tasks to which the answer is known, so they can assess the participant's performance (De Benetti, 2011).

The *Smithsonian Transcription Center* provides many ways for a participant to find content that they might be interested in, including themes (such as 'Civil War Era' or 'Field Book Project'), source organisations (specific museums or archives), featured projects and those with recent activity. The *Notes from Nature* collection pages list the average time per record (ranging from 3 minutes to 15 minutes) as well as the average 'difficulty' (ranging from 'easy' to 'very hard').

22.17 Task design

Nielsen's usability heuristics contain many principles relevant to crowdsourcing projects, including: keeping users informed of the system status through appropriate feedback; speaking the users' language; preventing errors; supporting recovery from error when errors do occur; following platform conventions; minimising memory load by making actions and options visible; and (where necessary) providing concrete instructions that focus on the users' task (1995).[37]

In design principles specific to crowdsourcing, task 'size' can be measured in terms of the amount of source material to process, the time per task, modularity (whether tasks are independent and asynchronous) and cognitive load (roughly, the amount of mental effort required).[38] Research has found that microtasks lead to fewer mistakes and an 'easier' experience.[39] They provide opportunities to learn the skills required for more complex tasks but are easier for novices to complete. If you have to design macro- or more specialist tasks, ensure that motivational text and recruitment are strong enough to match the size or complexity. Finding the sweet spot between tasks likely to attract participants, that provide useful data and are possible within the resources available can require some creativity.

Most crowdsourcing projects report that up to 80–90% of the work is done by 10% of participants and many other participants contribute a small amount each.[40] Given the role 'super-contributors' play in a projects' productivity, it could be tempting to optimise designs for their need but projects must cater for both casual and super contributors.

22.18 Documentation and tutorials

Ideally, interactive tutorials would show new participants how to complete the task successfully while letting them try it, rather than read about it, but the user experience design and technical resources required to do so are rarely available,[41] many tutorials appear as modal windows overlaid over the task window.[42] However, many users automatically close tutorials without reading or watching them, so it is important to have a visible link for a Help page that includes the tutorial and/or more detailed documentation.

Help text, whether on the task interface or a separate page, should help reassure potential participants by anticipating and answering their questions. It should be clear and unambiguous, and available at the point at which it is needed (Nielsen, 1995), address 'boundary cases', and ideally provide examples of what is expected (Kittur et al., 2013). Balancing the need for simplicity with the need for flexibility is a challenge for projects working with materials that may contain unexpected or inconsistent information. Producing good tutorials and documentation can take several iterations. Including tutorials and help text in usability testing will highlight issues, and test participants may provide more user-friendly alternatives for language used.

22.19 Quality control: validation and verification systems

Even the most highly skilled and well-intentioned volunteer makes occasional mistakes, and crowdsourcing projects usually carefully check the information they receive. Most methods involve comparing two or more task results for the same source against each other, with a simple 'majority rules' decision to accept the most common answer. The most appropriate method for reaching consensus will depend on the material, even for 'type what you see tasks', where small differences in punctuation may make transcriptions fail 'exact match' tests. Ben Brumfield has provided a useful overview of quality control methods for transcription (Brumfield, 2012a). Verifying tags is difficult to do automatically without excluding potentially valuable unique tags from contributors with specialist knowledge,[43] but verification tasks can help.[44]

22.19.1 Rewards and recognition

Public recognition of volunteer contributions is important, and can be built into many points of the project interface and communications. Some projects name contributors in project updates[45] or list them as co-authors on journal articles.[46] Describing, or even better, showing the impact of contributions towards a project's goals can powerfully link to participant motivations (Rotman et al., 2012).

Metrics for recognition should be chosen carefully. Ben Brumfield has a story that illustrates the dangers of external motivators like leaderboards, where contributors may focus on aspects that are quantified on a leaderboard at the expense of more important but unquantified tasks (Brumfield, 2012b).

Crowdsourcing in cultural heritage

22.20 Running crowdsourcing projects

The key challenge in running a project is motivating continued participation. In this section I discuss expectations around launching projects, the effect of media stories, consider the role of participant discussion, ongoing communications and maintaining participation, and planning for a 'graceful exit'.

Participatory projects can be challenging for organisations used to 'launch and forget it' exhibitions and publications. Ideally, iterative design processes can continue after launch. Participants tend to have creative ideas for new tasks,[47] suggest sensible tweaks to existing tasks and text, and report bugs. Over the longer term, an interface that looks good in 2019 may look dated in 2022, or you may want to take advantage of emerging technologies. It is important to allow resources for post-launch.

22.21 Launching a project

You've planned, designed and tested your project. You've prepared a press release and social media posts. Launch day will (hopefully) be busy. Allow time for answering participant queries and media enquiries, and be prepared to load new material if the first batches are completed.

When your project launches, some of the first visitors will be participants from other projects, and colleagues from academia and cultural heritage institutions. The first group often has a highly sophisticated understanding of crowdsourcing, and will be looking for markers of quality including the importance of the task, the availability of data and how participants are credited or rewarded. The second group will be curious about your project design. Their positive reports may help build your word of mouth marketing.

Pieces in 'traditional' media can be very effective in attracting visitors, some of whom may become participants. It is difficult to disentangle the role of luck in getting media and popular attention but a quirky story or topic, relationships with an existing community, being the first of its type, or an opportunity to access highly-valued content or expertise seem to help. More targeted publicity may reach a smaller number of people, but those reached may be proportionally more likely to participate. *History Harvest* and *Letter in the Attic*[48] found that 'face-to-face contact' at local events and groups was more effective than media attention at gaining contributions (Latimer, 2009).[49]

22.22 The role of participant discussion

Some crowdsourcing projects provide ways for participants to communicate with each other via a discussion forum,[50] on social media, or through comments on specific items.[51] Some participants may prefer to comment directly to project staff rather than post in public. Posts might discuss difficulties, help answer queries, collect lessons learnt over time, share stories about interesting finds or potential discoveries, and provide feedback or suggestions for improvement to project stakeholders. Conversations on forums can have important learning outcomes (Mugar, Østerlund, Jackson, & Crowston, 2015) and provide social opportunities that motivate ongoing participation (Holmes, 2003). Participants' expectations about the presence of project staff on discussion forums vary, and projects should be careful about how these forums are described so that their expectations are not disappointed.

22.23 Ongoing community engagement

Once a project is up and running, marketing efforts generally need to shift from participant recruitment to participant retention. This is also an opportunity to shift from talking about the project to talking about the impact of the project. You can thank participants individually or collectively, share progress reports and participants' findings and questions, and provide information about how contributions have been used (an important factor in ongoing motivation; Rotman et al. (2012). The *Smithsonian Transcription Center* has been carefully designed to provide multiple opportunities for celebrating success, with small-scale, niche projects within the larger project.[52]

One of the benefits of *In the Spotlight* is the opportunity to amplify the expertise and curiosity of participants (for example, we published a blog post from one participant, Edward Mills, on the British Library's Digital Scholarship blog (2017)). My hope is that posting updates from participants encourages more activity, which I can then share, in a 'virtuous circle'. Even the most ardent fans of a project may forget to revisit it unless it has become a daily habit (even then, it is liable to be interrupted by changes in routine). Regular updates remind participants to come back to a project.

Ongoing communications, whether simple quantitative progress updates, answering questions or liaising with experts to pass on information on the impact of the project, can require significant amounts of time. However, anecdotally, it seems that paying attention to activity on a project reaps rewards in ongoing participation.

22.24 Planning a graceful exit

Whether a project finishes because volunteers have completed all the available tasks, key team members move on or funding ends, planning a graceful finish is the best way to honour the work of the project team and volunteers alike. It is important to let volunteers know when the end of a project is in sight, giving them time to complete personal tasks, download data and finish conversations. You should document the final outcomes, deposit any resulting datasets in a repository, and (ideally) submit project URLs to regional or international web archives.

22.25 The future of crowdsourcing in cultural heritage

As the increasing success of machine learning-based projects such as *Transkribus*,[53] which aims to teach computers to read handwriting, shows, many tasks currently crowdsourced can increasingly be performed by software. Computer vision technologies can increasingly identify even obscure or historical subjects in a picture (Collings, 2014) (Willett, n.d.).

As computers get better at microtasks such as text transcription and image classification – tasks that many crowdsourcing participants find satisfying, and that may be important first steps in developing new interests—what impact will this have on crowdsourcing projects and participants? 'Human computation' systems that deploy the particular skills of people and machines in order to efficiently complete tasks can help meet the challenges of large-scale collections. However, if they are used in GLAMs, they should be carefully designed to allow for engagement and enjoyment of collections while not unnecessarily duplicating effort that could be better done by software.

To finish on a positive note, these new technologies can also be harnessed to make crowdsourced microtasks even easier.[54] The success of OCR correction projects like *Trove* shows that providing some pre-processed data might actually make tasks easier, and therefore more enjoyable.[55] Pre-processing items might allow tasks that can be performed on mobile and tablets devices to be created, and machine learning technologies could be used to provide personalised feedback on participant tasks, helping them feel more confident and learn skills more quickly.

Acknowledgements

I would like to thank participants and supporters of crowdsourcing projects I've created, including *Museum Metadata Games*, *In their own words: collecting experiences of the First World War*, and *In the Spotlight*. I would also like to thank my co-organisers and attendees at the Digital Humanities 2016 Expert Workshop on the future of crowdsourcing. Especial thanks to the participants in courses and workshops on 'crowdsourcing

Crowdsourcing in cultural heritage

in cultural heritage', including the British Library's Digital Scholarship training programme, the HILT Digital Humanities summer school (including a session with Ben Brumfield) and scholars at other events where the course was held, whose insights, cynicism and questions have informed my thinking over the years. Finally, thanks to Meghan Ferriter and Victoria Van Hyning for their comments on this manuscript.

Notes

1 See, for example, the special edition of *Science in Context* (2011) on 'Lay Participation in the History of Scientific Observation', Secord (1994) and Silvertown (2009).
2 See for example the OED's #WordsWhereYouAre Twitter campaign ('Shakespeare's World Talk #OED', Ongoing), and integration with the Shakespeare's World project (Durkin, 2017).
3 Sample projects are listed in exercises at https://bitly.com/BL_105 (Ridge, 2018).
4 For example, Rose Holley's extensive publications, the 'Meta' publications about the Zooniverse project (https://www.zooniverse.org/about/publications) and individual books and reports Crowdsourcing Consortium (2015), Simon (2010) and (United States Government, n.d.).
5 This is based on my doctoral research (2015).
6 The categories used here are designed to provide an overview of task types for people planning crowdsourcing projects, rather than formalise a typology. The most useful typology will depend on the context in which it is being used. In 2011, I devised 'activity types' related to crowdsourcing games in museums, and in 2012 Dunn and Hedges devised a typology for academic humanities crowdsourcing based on asset type, process type, task type, and output type (Dunn & Hedges, 2013; Ridge, 2011a). See also (Ridge, 2015).
7 http://buildinginspector.nypl.org/
8 http://blogs.ucl.ac.uk/transcribe-bentham/
9 Causer and Terras report that the requirement to mark-up the text in *Project Bentham* appears to be an added 'aggravation' (2014). See also (Causer & Wallace, 2012; Reside, 2014).
10 http://forum.oldweather.org/
11 https://trove.nla.gov.au/newspaper/
12 http://menus.nypl.org/
13 http://playbills.libcrowds.com/
14 https://www.flickr.com/commons/
15 Archived at https://web.archive.org/web/sitemap/steve.museum
16 http://www.bl.uk/georeferencer/ (Fleet, Kowal, & Přidal, 2012)
17 https://livesofthefirstworldwar.org/
18 https://contribute.europeana.eu/migration
19 https://sounds.bl.uk/Sound-Maps/UK-Soundmap
20 http://letters1916.maynoothuniversity.ie/
21 Also described as 'suites' in (Ridge, 2011a).
22 For exceptions to this, see National Archives of Australia (n.d.), von Ahn & Dabbish (2008) and WieWasWie Project informatie (n.d.).
23 In a telling example, the first post on an *Old Weather* thread called 'Signs of OW addiction' said one of the 'Top Ten' signs of addiction might be that 'You spend more time on the forum than you do transcribing' (Forum posters, 2010).
24 Figures are available from https://www.zooniverse.org/ and http://trove.nla.gov.au/system/stats?env=prod#corrNewspapers.
25 The Europeana Impact Playbook provides some useful headings for planning to report impact on various factors (Verwayen, Fallon, Schellenberg, & Kyrou, 2017).
26 The time required will vary according to your specific goals, material, volunteers, etc., but as a rough guide, I may spend up to an hour and a half each week on an active project.
27 http://www.fossilfinder.org/
28 Each platform produces differently formatted outputs – text transcribed via FromThePage will look different to that transcribed via the Zooniverse Project Builder. Technical resources to convert JSON and XML-formats might be required.
29 See also Fugelstad et al. (2012).
30 Ancestry's World Archives Project https://web.archive.org/web/20150905125517/http://landing.ancestry.com/wap/learnmore.aspx
31 *Children of the Lodz Ghetto Research Project* https://web.archive.org/web/20180614032124/https://www.ushmm.org/online/lodzchildren/

32 *Building Inspector* http://buildinginspector.nypl.org/

33 *DIY History* https://diyhistory.lib.uiowa.edu/

34 This is not always as easy as it sounds, as enthusiasm can get ahead of resources (Ridge, 2014).

35 See also Preist et al. (2014) on the 'normalising' effect of displaying participant activity.

36 See also Paas, Renkl, & Sweller (2003) and Van Merriënboer, Kirschner, and Kester (2003).

37 I expand on the application of these heuristics in (Ridge, 2015).

38 Motivation seems to reduce the impact of task size, in that some large, complex tasks (such as those in the *Dickens Journals Online* text correction project or *Children of the Lodz Ghetto*) can still attract participants if the motivation and/or challenge is strong enough. The combination of task size and motivation could be called the task 'weight', but further research is needed to test this model. See also (Ridge, 2015).

39 The research compared macrotask and microtask versions of the same overall task. It also found that microtasks took more time combined than the equivalent macrotask (Cheng, Teevan, Iqbal, & Bernstein, 2015).

40 For a visual representation of this see (Brohan, 2012).

41 As the field of human computation develops, systems should increasingly be able to support participants with feedback specifically tailored to their performance of a task.

42 For more on tutorial design see Bedford (2014) and Paas et al (2003). Research on the techniques game designers use for including skills tests and tutorials may be relevant for projects that wish to teach specific skills or knowledge to participants undertaking tasks. See Mayer & Moreno (2003) and Ridge (2011b).

43 This was difficult back in 2011 (as discussed in (Ridge, 2011a)) but advances in human computation should make it easier. See also: Grayson (2016).

44 There is a significant body of literature on this subject. A useful place to start is von Ahn & Dabbish (2008).

45 For example, (Brohan, 2014).

46 For example, the authors whose affiliation is listed as 'Planet Hunter' in (Schmitt et al., 2014).

47 E.g. when *In the Spotlight* launched, participants requested the ability to tag playbills with specific topics.

48 The project collected letters, diaries and items related to Brighton and Hove.

49 Face-to-face events might also help reach those not online. One First World War project heard from a potential contributor 'aged 89 and nearly blind' who had asked neighbour to email the project after hearing about it on the radio (Dillon-Scott, 2011).

50 Forums were particularly important for early Zooniverse projects, but they have moved to 'Talk' pages that are more closely integrated with task interfaces. Publications listed at https://www.zooniverse.org/about/publications provide more information.

51 E.g. transcribers in the *Smithsonian Transcription Center* can leave notes for other transcribers and reviewers on specific pages or post questions on social media. https://transcription.si.edu/

52 Discussed further in (Ridge, 2015).

53 https://transkribus.eu/Transkribus/

54 See also research on 'social machines', in which people and computers are part of a larger integrated system (Smart, Simperl, & Shadbolt, 2014).

55 This does not mean that projects should only offer 'easy' microtasks, as the relationship between challenge and enjoyment is complex, but they may allow for a broader range of participants and thereby create more opportunities for deeper engagement.

References

Alam, S. L., & Campbell, J. (2017). Temporal motivations of volunteers to participate in cultural crowdsourcing work. *Information Systems Research*. https://doi.org/10.1287/isre.2017.0719

Bedford, A. (2014, February 16). Instructional Overlays and Coach Marks for Mobile Apps. Retrieved 12 September 2014, from Nielsen Norman Group website: http://www.nngroup.com/articles/mobile-instructional-overlay/

Berglund Prytz, Y. (2013, June 24). The Oxford Community Collection Model. Retrieved 22 October 2018, from RunCoCo website: http://blogs.it.ox.ac.uk/runcoco/2013/06/24/the-oxford-community-collection-model/

Bernstein, S. (2014). Crowdsourcing in Brooklyn. In M. Ridge (Ed.), *Crowdsourcing Our Cultural Heritage*. Retrieved from http://www.ashgate.com/isbn/9781472410221

Bitgood, S. (2010). *An attention-value model of museum visitors* (pp. 1–29). Retrieved from Center for the Advancement of Informal Science Education website: http://caise.insci.org/uploads/docs/VSA_Bitgood.pdf

Bonney, R., Ballard, H., Jordan, R., McCallie, E., Phillips, T., Shirk, J., & Wilderman, C. C. (2009). *Public Participation in Scientific Research: Defining the Field and Assessing Its Potential for Informal Science Education. A CAISE Inquiry Group Report* (pp. 1–58). Retrieved from Center for Advancement of Informal Science Education (CAISE) website: http://caise.insci.org/uploads/docs/PPSR%20report%20FINAL.pdf

Brohan, P. (2012, July 23). One million, Six Hundred Thousand New Observations. Retrieved 30 October 2012, from Old Weather Blog website: http://blog.oldweather.org/2012/07/23/one-million-six-hundred-thousand-new-observations/

Brohan, P. (2014, August 18). In Search of Lost Weather. Retrieved 5 September 2014, from Old Weather Blog website: http://blog.oldweather.org/2014/08/18/in-search-of-lost-weather/

Brumfield, B. W. (2012a, March 5). Quality Control for Crowdsourced Transcription. Retrieved 9 October 2013, from Collaborative Manuscript Transcription website: http://manuscripttranscription.blogspot.co.uk/2012/03/quality-control-for-crowdsourced.html

Brumfield, B. W. (2012b, March 17). Crowdsourcing at IMLS WebWise 2012. Retrieved 8 September 2014, from Collaborative Manuscript Transcription website: http://manuscripttranscription.blogspot.com.au/2012/03/crowdsourcing-at-imls-webwise-2012.html

Budiu, R. (2014, March 2). Login Walls Stop Users in Their Tracks. Retrieved 7 March 2014, from Nielsen Norman Group website: http://www.nngroup.com/articles/login-walls/

Causer, T., & Terras, M. (2014). 'Many Hands Make Light Work. Many Hands Together Make Merry Work': Transcribe Bentham and Crowdsourcing Manuscript Collections. In M. Ridge (Ed.), *Crowdsourcing Our Cultural Heritage*. Retrieved from http://www.ashgate.com/isbn/9781472410221

Causer, T., & Wallace, V. (2012). Building a volunteer community: Results and findings from Transcribe Bentham. *Digital Humanities Quarterly*, *6*(2). Retrieved from http://www.digitalhumanities.org/dhq/vol/6/2/000125/000125.html

Cheng, J., Teevan, J., Iqbal, S. T., & Bernstein, M. S. (2015, April). *Break It Down: A Comparison of Macro- and Microtasks.* 4061–4064. https://doi.org/10.1145/2702123.2702146

Clary, E. G., Snyder, M., Ridge, R. D., Copeland, J., Stukas, A. A., Haugen, J., & Miene, P. (1998). Understanding and assessing the motivations of volunteers: A functional approach. *Journal of Personality and Social Psychology*, *74*(6), 1516–30.

Collings, R. (2014, May 5). The art of Computer Image Recognition. Retrieved 25 May 2014, from The Public Catalogue Foundation website: http://www.thepcf.org.uk/what_we_do/48/reference/862

Collings, R. (2015, February 1). The Art of Computer Recognition. Retrieved 22 October 2018, from Art UK website: https://artuk.org/about/blog/the-art-of-computer-recognition

Crowdsourcing Consortium. (2015). *Engaging the Public: Best Practices for Crowdsourcing Across the Disciplines.* Retrieved from http://crowdconsortium.org/

Crowley, E. J., & Zisserman, A. (2016). *The Art of Detection.* Presented at the Workshop on Computer Vision for Art Analysis, ECCV. Retrieved from https://www.robots.ox.ac.uk/~vgg/publications/2016/Crowley16/crowley16.pdf

Csikszentmihalyi, M., & Hermanson, K. (1995). Intrinsic Motivation in Museums: Why Does One Want to Learn? In J. Falk & L. D. Dierking (Eds.), *Public Institutions for Personal Learning: Establishing a Research Agenda* (pp. 66–77). Washington D.C.: American Association of Museums.

Dafis, L. L., Hughes, L. M., & James, R. (2014). What's Welsh for 'Crowdsourcing'? Citizen Science and Community Engagement at the National Library of Wales. In M. Ridge (Ed.), *Crowdsourcing Our Cultural Heritage*. Retrieved from http://www.ashgate.com/isbn/9781472410221

Das Gupta, V., Rooney, N., & Schreibman, S. (n.d.). Notes from the Transcription Desk: Modes of Engagement between the Community and the Resource of the Letters of 1916. *Digital Humanities 2016: Conference Abstracts.* Presented at the Digital Humanities 2016, Kraków. Retrieved from http://dh2016.adho.org/abstracts/228

De Benetti, T. (2011, June 16). The Secrets of Digitalkoot: Lessons Learned Crowdsourcing Data Entry to 50,000 People (for free). Retrieved 9 January 2012, from Microtask website: http://blog.microtask.com/2011/06/the-secrets-of-digitalkoot-lessons-learned-crowdsourcing-data-entry-to-50000-people-for-free/

de Boer, V., Hildebrand, M., Aroyo, L., De Leenheer, P., Dijkshoorn, C., Tesfa, B., & Schreiber, G. (2012). Nichesourcing: Harnessing the power of crowds of experts. *Proceedings of the 18th International Conference on Knowledge Engineering and Knowledge Management, EKAW 2012*, 16–20. Retrieved from http://dx.doi.org/10.1007/978-3-642-33876-2_3

DH2016 Expert Workshop. (2016, July 12). DH2016 Crowdsourcing Workshop Session Overview. Retrieved 5 October 2018, from DH2016 Expert Workshop: Beyond The Basics: What Next For Crowdsourcing? website: https://docs.google.com/document/d/1sTII8P67mOFKWxCaAKd8SeF56PzKcklxG7KDfCRUF-8/edit?usp=drive_open&ouid=0&usp=embed_facebook

Dillon-Scott, P. (2011, March 31). How Europeana, Crowdsourcing & Wiki Principles Are Preserving European History. Retrieved 15 February 2015, from The Sociable website: http://sociable.co/business/how-europeana-crowdsourcing-wiki-principles-are-preserving-european-history/

DiMeo, M. (2014, February 3). First Monday Library Chat: University of Iowa's DIY History. Retrieved 7 September 2014, from The Recipes Project website: http://recipes.hypotheses.org/3216

Dunn, S., & Hedges, M. (2012). *Crowd-Sourcing Scoping Study: Engaging the Crowd with Humanities Research* (p. 56). Retrieved from King's College website: http://www.humanitiescrowds.org

Dunn, S., & Hedges, M. (2013). Crowd-sourcing as a component of humanities research infrastructures. *International Journal of Humanities and Arts Computing, 7*(1–2), 147–169. https://doi.org/10.3366/ijhac.2013.0086

Durkin, P. (2017, September 28). Release Notes: A Big Antedating for White Lie—and Introducing Shakespeare's World. Retrieved 29 September 2017, from Oxford English Dictionary website: http://public.oed.com/the-oed-today/recent-updates-to-the-oed/september-2017-update/release-notes-white-lie-and-shakespeares-world/

Eccles, K., & Greg, A. (2014). Your Paintings Tagger: Crowdsourcing Descriptive Metadata for a National Virtual Collection. In M. Ridge (Ed.), *Crowdsourcing Our Cultural Heritage*. Retrieved from http://www.ashgate.com/isbn/9781472410221

Edwards, D., & Graham, M. (2006). Museum volunteers and heritage sectors. *Australian Journal on Volunteering, 11*(1), 19–27.

European Citizen Science Association. (2015). *10 Principles of Citizen Science.* Retrieved from https://ecsa.citizen-science.net/sites/default/files/ecsa_ten_principles_of_citizen_science.pdf

Eveleigh, A., Jennett, C., Blandford, A., Brohan, P., & Cox, A. L. (2014). Designing for dabblers and deterring drop-outs in citizen science. 2985–2994. https://doi.org/10.1145/2556288.2557262

Eveleigh, A., Jennett, C., Lynn, S., & Cox, A. L. (2013). I want to be a captain! I want to be a captain!: Gamification in the old weather citizen science project. *Proceedings of the First International Conference on Gameful Design, Research, and Applications*, 79–82. Retrieved from http://dl.acm.org/citation.cfm?id=2583019

Ferriter, M., Rosenfeld, C., Boomer, D., Burgess, C., Leachman, S., Leachman, V., ... Shuler, M. E. (2016). We learn together: Crowdsourcing as practice and method in the Smithsonian Transcription Center. *Collections, 12*(2), 207–225. https://doi.org/10.1177/155019061601200213

Fleet, C., Kowal, K., & Přidal, P. (2012). Georeferencer: Crowdsourced georeferencing for map library collections. *D-Lib Magazine, 18*(11/12). https://doi.org/10.1045/november2012-fleet

Forum posters. (2010, present). Signs of OW addiction ... Retrieved 11 April 2014, from Old Weather Forum » Shore Leave » Dockside Cafe website: http://forum.oldweather.org/index.php?topic=1432.0

Fugelstad, P., Dwyer, P., Filson Moses, J., Kim, J. S., Mannino, C. A., Terveen, L., & Snyder, M. (2012). What Makes Users Rate (Share, Tag, Edit...)? Predicting Patterns of Participation in Online Communities. *Proceedings of the ACM 2012 Conference on Computer Supported Cooperative Work*, 969–978. Retrieved from http://dl.acm.org/citation.cfm?id=2145349

Gilliver, P. (2012, October 4). 'Your Dictionary Needs You': A Brief History of the OED's Appeals to the Public. Retrieved from Oxford English Dictionary website: https://public.oed.com/history/history-of-the-appeals/

Goldstein, D. (1994). 'Yours for science': The Smithsonian Institution's correspondents and the shape of scientific community in nineteenth-century America. *Isis, 85*(4), 573–599.

Grayson, R. (2016). A life in the trenches? The use of operation war diary and crowdsourcing methods to provide an understanding of the British army's day-to-day life on the western front. *British Journal for Military History, 2*(2). Retrieved from http://bjmh.org.uk/index.php/bjmh/article/view/96

Hess, W. (2010, February 16). Onboarding: Designing Welcoming First Experiences. Retrieved 29 July 2014, from UX Magazine website: http://uxmag.com/articles/onboarding-designing-welcoming-first-experiences

Holley, R. (2009). *Many Hands Make Light Work: Public Collaborative OCR Text Correction in Australian Historic Newspapers* (No. March). Canberra: National Library of Australia.

Holley, R. (2010). Crowdsourcing: How and why should libraries do it? *D-Lib Magazine, 16*(3/4). https://doi.org/10.1045/march2010-holley

Holmes, K. (2003). Volunteers in the heritage sector: A neglected audience? *International Journal of Heritage Studies, 9*(4), 341–355. https://doi.org/10.1080/1352725022000155072

Kittur, A., Nickerson, J. V., Bernstein, M., Gerber, E., Shaw, A., Zimmerman, J., ... Horton, J. (2013). The future of crowd work. *Proceedings of the 2013 Conference on Computer Supported Cooperative Work*, 1301–1318. Retrieved from http://dl.acm.org/citation.cfm?id=2441923

Lambert, S., Winter, M., & Blume, P. (2014, March 26). Getting to Where We Are Now. Retrieved 4 March 2015, from 10most.org.uk website: http://10most.org.uk/content/getting-where-we-are-now

Lascarides, M., & Vershbow, B. (2014). What's on the Menu?: Crowdsourcing at the New York Public Library. In M. Ridge (Ed.), *Crowdsourcing Our Cultural Heritage*. Retrieved from http://www.ashgate.com/isbn/9781472410221

Latimer, J. (2009, February 25). Letter in the Attic: Lessons Learnt from the Project. Retrieved 17 April 2014, from My Brighton and Hove website: http://www.mybrightonandhove.org.uk/page/letterintheatticlessons?path=0p116p1543p

Lazy Registration Design Pattern. (n.d.). Retrieved 9 December 2018, from Http://ui-patterns.com/patterns/LazyRegistration website: http://ui-patterns.com/patterns/LazyRegistration

Crowdsourcing in cultural heritage

Leon, S. M. (2014). Build, Analyse and Generalise: Community Transcription of the Papers of the War Department and the Development of Scripto. In M. Ridge (Ed.), *Crowdsourcing Our Cultural Heritage*. Retrieved from http://www.ashgate.com/isbn/9781472410221

Mayer, R. E., & Moreno, R. (2003). Nine ways to reduce cognitive load in multimedia learning. *Educational Psychologist, 38*(1), 43–52.

McGonigal, J. (n.d.). *Gaming the Future of Museums*. Retrieved from http://www.slideshare.net/avantgame/gaming-the-future-of-museums-a-lecture-by-jane-mcgonigal-presentation#text-version

Mills, E. (2017, December). The Flitch of Bacon: An Unexpected Journey Through the Collections of the British Library. Retrieved 17 August 2018, from British Library Digital Scholarship blog website: http://blogs.bl.uk/digital-scholarship/2017/12/the-flitch-of-bacon-an-unexpected-journey-through-the-collections-of-the-british-library.html

Mitra, T., & Gilbert, E. (2014). *The Language that Gets People to Give: Phrases that Predict Success on Kickstarter*. Retrieved from http://comp.social.gatech.edu/papers/cscw14.crowdfunding.mitra.pdf

Mugar, G., Østerlund, C., Hassman, K. D., Crowston, K., & Jackson, C. B. (2014). *Planet Hunters and Seafloor Explorers: Legitimate Peripheral Participation Through Practice Proxies in Online Citizen Science*. Retrieved from http://crowston.syr.edu/sites/crowston.syr.edu/files/paper_revised%20copy%20to%20post.pdf

Mugar, G., Østerlund, C., Jackson, C. B., & Crowston, K. (2015). Being Present in Online Communities: Learning in Citizen Science. *Proceedings of the 7th International Conference on Communities and Technologies*, 129–138. https://doi.org/10.1145/2768545.2768555

Museums, Libraries and Archives Council. (2008). Generic Learning Outcomes. Retrieved 8 September 2014, from Inspiring Learning website: http://www.inspiringlearningforall.gov.uk/toolstemplates/genericlearning/

National Archives of Australia. (n.d.). ArcHIVE – homepage. Retrieved 18 June 2014, from ArcHIVE website: http://transcribe.naa.gov.au/

Nielsen, J. (1995). 10 Usability Heuristics for User Interface Design. Retrieved 29 April 2014, from http://www.nngroup.com/articles/ten-usability-heuristics/

Nov, O., Arazy, O., & Anderson, D. (2011). Technology-Mediated Citizen Science Participation: A Motivational Model. *Proceedings of the AAAI International Conference on Weblogs and Social Media*. Presented at the Barcelona, Spain. Barcelona, Spain.

Oomen, J., Gligorov, R., & Hildebrand, M. (2014). Waisda?: Making Videos Findable through Crowdsourced Annotations. In M. Ridge (Ed.), *Crowdsourcing Our Cultural Heritage*. Retrieved from http://www.ashgate.com/isbn/9781472410221

Paas, F., Renkl, A., & Sweller, J. (2003). Cognitive load theory and instructional design: Recent developments. *Educational Psychologist, 38*(1), 1–4. https://doi.org/10.1207/S15326985EP3801_1

Part I: Building a Great Project. (n.d.). Retrieved 9 December 2018, from Zooniverse Help website: https://help.zooniverse.org/best-practices/1-great-project/

Preist, C., Massung, E., & Coyle, D. (2014). Competing or aiming to be average?: Normification as a means of engaging digital volunteers. *Proceedings of the 17th ACM Conference on Computer Supported Cooperative Work & Social Computing*, 1222–1233. https://doi.org/10.1145/2531602.2531615

Raddick, M. J., Bracey, G., Gay, P. L., Lintott, C. J., Murray, P., Schawinski, K., … Vandenberg, J. (2010). Galaxy Zoo: Exploring the motivations of citizen science volunteers. *Astronomy Education Review, 9*(1), 18.

Raimond, Y., Smethurst, M., & Ferne, T. (2014, September 15). What We Learnt by Crowdsourcing the World Service Archive. Retrieved 15 September 2014, from BBC R&D website: http://www.bbc.co.uk/rd/blog/2014/08/data-generated-by-the-world-service-archive-experiment-draft

Reside, D. (2014). *Crowdsourcing Performing Arts History with NYPL's ENSEMBLE*. Presented at the Digital Humanities 2014. Retrieved from http://dharchive.org/paper/DH2014/Paper-131.xml

Ridge, M. (2011a). Playing with Difficult Objects – Game Designs to Improve Museum Collections. In J. Trant & D. Bearman (Eds.), *Museums and the Web 2011: Proceedings*. Retrieved from http://www.museumsandtheweb.com/mw2011/papers/playing_with_difficult_objects_game_designs_to

Ridge, M. (2011b). *Playing with difficult objects: Game designs for crowdsourcing museum metadata* (MSc Dissertation, City University London). Retrieved from http://www.miaridge.com/my-msc-dissertation-crowdsourcing-games-for-museums/

Ridge, M. (2013). From tagging to theorizing: Deepening engagement with cultural heritage through crowdsourcing. *Curator: The Museum Journal, 56*(4).

Ridge, M. (2014, November). *Citizen History and Its Discontents*. Presented at the IHR Digital History Seminar, Institute for Historical Research, London. Retrieved from https://hcommons.org/deposits/item/hc:17907/

Ridge, M. (2015). *Making digital history: The impact of digitality on public participation and scholarly practices in historical research* (Ph.D., Open University). Retrieved from http://oro.open.ac.uk/45519/

Ridge, M. (2018). *British Library Digital Scholarship Course 105: Exercises for Crowdsourcing in Libraries, Museums and Cultural Heritage Institutions.* Retrieved from https://docs.google.com/document/d/1tx-qULCDhNdH0JyUR qXERoPFzWuCreXAsiwHlUKVa9w/

Rotman, D., Preece, J., Hammock, J., Procita, K., Hansen, D., Parr, C., … Jacobs, D. (2012). Dynamic changes in motivation in collaborative citizen-science projects. *Proceedings of the ACM 2012 Conference on Computer Supported Cooperative Work*, 217–226. https://doi.org/10.1145/2145204.2145238

Sample Ward, A. (2011, May 18). Crowdsourcing vs Community-sourcing: What's the Difference and the Opportunity? Retrieved 6 January 2013, from Amy Sample Ward's Version of NPTech website: http://amysampleward.org/2011/05/18/crowdsourcing-vs-community-sourcing-whats-the-difference-and-the-opportunity/

Schmitt, J. R., Wang, J., Fischer, D. A., Jek, K. J., Moriarty, J. C., Boyajian, T. S., … Socolovsky, M. (2014). Planet hunters. VI. An independent characterization of KOI-351 and several long period planet candidates from the Kepler Archival Data. *The Astronomical Journal*, *148*(2), 28. https://doi.org/10.1088/0004-6256/148/2/28

Secord, A. (1994). Corresponding interests: Artisans and gentlemen in nineteenth-century natural history. *The British Journal for the History of Science*, *27*(04), 383–408. https://doi.org/10.1017/S0007087400032416

Shakespeare's World Talk #OED. (Ongoing). Retrieved 21 April 2019, from https://www.zooniverse.org/projects/zooniverse/shakespeares-world/talk/239

Sharma, P., & Hannafin, M. J. (2007). Scaffolding in technology-enhanced learning environments. *Interactive Learning Environments*, *15*(1), 27–46. https://doi.org/10.1080/10494820600996972

Shirky, C. (2011). *Cognitive Surplus: Creativity and Generosity in a Connected Age.* London, U.K.: Penguin.

Silvertown, J. (2009). A new dawn for citizen science. *Trends in Ecology & Evolution*, *24*(9), 467–71. https://doi.org/10.1016/j.tree.2009.03.017

Simmons, B. (2015, August 24). Measuring Success in Citizen Science Projects, Part 2: Results. Retrieved 28 August 2015, from Zooniverse website: https://blog.zooniverse.org/2015/08/24/measuring-success-in-citizen-science-projects-part-2-results/

Simon, N. K. (2010). *The Participatory Museum.* Retrieved from http://www.participatorymuseum.org/chapter4/

Smart, P. R., Simperl, E., & Shadbolt, N. (2014). A Taxonomic Framework for Social Machines. In D. Miorandi, V. Maltese, M. Rovatsos, A. Nijholt, & J. Stewart (Eds.), *Social Collective Intelligence: Combining the Powers of Humans and Machines to Build a Smarter Society.* Retrieved from http://eprints.soton.ac.uk/362359/

Smithsonian Institution Archives. (2012, March 21). Meteorology. Retrieved 25 November 2017, from Smithsonian Institution Archives website: https://siarchives.si.edu/history/featured-topics/henry/meteorology

Springer, M., Dulabahn, B., Michel, P., Natanson, B., Reser, D., Woodward, D., & Zinkham, H. (2008). *For the Common Good: The Library of Congress Flickr Pilot Project* (pp. 1–55). Retrieved from Library of Congress website: http://www.loc.gov/rr/print/flickr_report_final.pdf

Stebbins, R. A. (1997). Casual leisure: A conceptual statement. *Leisure Studies*, *16*(1), 17–25. https://doi.org/10.1080/026143697375485

The Culture and Sport Evidence (CASE) programme. (2011). *Evidence of What Works: Evaluated Projects to Drive Up Engagement* (No. January; p. 19). Retrieved from Culture and Sport Evidence (CASE) programme website: http://www.culture.gov.uk/images/research/evidence_of_what_works.pdf

Trant, J. (2009). *Tagging, Folksonomy and Art Museums: Results of steve.museum's Research* (p. 197). Retrieved from Archives & Museum Informatics website: https://web.archive.org/web/20100210192354/http://conference.archimuse.com/files/trantSteveResearchReport2008.pdf

United States Government. (n.d.). Federal Crowdsourcing and Citizen Science Toolkit. Retrieved 9 December 2018, from CitizenScience.gov website: https://www.citizenscience.gov/toolkit/

Van Merriënboer, J. J. G., Kirschner, P. A., & Kester, L. (2003). Taking the load off a learner's mind: Instructional design for complex learning. *Educational Psychologist*, *38*(1), 5–13.

Vander Wal, T. (2007, February 2). Folksonomy. Retrieved 8 December 2018, from Vanderwal.net website: http://vanderwal.net/folksonomy.html

Veldhuizen, B., & Keinan-Schoonbaert, A. (2015, February 11). MicroPasts: Crowdsourcing Cultural Heritage Research. Retrieved 8 December 2018, from Sketchfab Blog website: https://blog.sketchfab.com/micropasts-crowdsourcing-cultural-heritage-research/

Verwayen, H., Fallon, J., Schellenberg, J., & Kyrou, P. (2017). *Impact Playbook for Museums, Libraries and Archives.* Europeana Foundation.

Vetter, J. (2011). Introduction: Lay participation in the history of scientific observation. *Science in Context*, *24*(02), 127–141. https://doi.org/10.1017/S0269889711000032

von Ahn, L., & Dabbish, L. (2008). Designing games with a purpose. *Communications of the ACM*, *51*(8), 57. https://doi.org/10.1145/1378704.1378719

Crowdsourcing in cultural heritage

Wenger, E. (2010). Communities of Practice and Social Learning Systems: The Career of a Concept. In *Social Learning Systems and communities of practice*. Springer Verlag and the Open University.

Whitenton, K. (2013, December 22). Minimize Cognitive Load to Maximize Usability. Retrieved 12 September 2014, from Nielsen Norman Group website: http://www.nngroup.com/articles/minimize-cognitive-load/

WieWasWie Project informatie. (n.d.). Retrieved 1 August 2014, from VeleHanden website: http://velehanden.nl/projecten/bekijk/details/project/wiewaswie_bvr

Willett, K. (n.d.). New Paper: Galaxy Zoo and Machine Learning. Retrieved 31 March 2015, from Galaxy Zoo website: http://blog.galaxyzoo.org/2015/03/31/new-paper-galaxy-zoo-and-machine-learning/

Wood, D., Bruner, J. S., & Ross, G. (1976). The role of tutoring in problem solving. *Journal of Child Psychology and Psychiatry, and Allied Disciplines, 17*(2), 89–100.

23

E-LEARNING IN THE DIGITAL HUMANITIES

Leveraging the Internet for scholarship, teaching and learning

Rebecca A. Croxton

23.1 E-Learning in the digital humanities:
Leveraging the Internet for scholarship, teaching, and learning

With near ubiquitous Internet access and the explosion of information available digitally, the time is ripe for a convergence between the digital humanities and e-Learning. E-Learning typically refers to a course, program or degree delivered completely online" (eLearningNC). Throughout this chapter and e-Learning scholarship at large, the term "e-Learning" is often used interchangeably with the terms "online learning" and "distance learning," though distance learning is a broader term that encompasses the education of a student who is not physically present in a brick and mortar school. The e-Learning context affords new opportunities for scholars, teachers, and learners to contribute to the digital humanities conversation in a facilitated environment in which "students and faculty alike are *making things* as they study and per- form research, generating not just texts (in the form of analysis, commentary, narration, critique) but also images, interactions, cross-media corpora, software, and platforms" (Burdick, Drucker, Lunenfeld, Presner, & Schnapp, 2012, p. 10). The digital classroom, which aligns nicely with the subjects encompassed by the digital humanities, is one that affords teaching faculty opportunities to not only leverage the Internet in a way that allows universities to reach a broader audience of learners, but does so in an environment that promotes the modeling of digital humanist thought and behavior in teaching, learning, and scholarship. The "suite of expressive forms" available to the digital humanities is additive and has expanded beyond print and orality and now "encompasses the use of sound, motion, graphics, animation, screen capture, video, audio, and the appropriations and remixing of code that underlies game engines" (Burdick et al., 2012, p. 11). The continuously widening array of ways to express oneself and communicate is particularly well suited for an active, engaging, and authentic online learning experience. While there are some, like Guerlac (2011), who feel that Learning is best suited to "right answer" disciplines such as basic mathem- atics, foreign languages, business at the introductory level, engineering, and computer science, as well as skills training" (p. 110), with thoughtful course design and pedagogy, teaching the digital humanities in the e-Learning context can provide an unexpectedly rich and satisfying teaching and learning experience that may even, perhaps, supersede that which can be achieved in the traditional face-to-face classroom.

Online education can be a great equalizer, allowing students who are confronted with barriers in achieving a campus-based education an opportunity to earn a college degree in a convenient context. Rather than running of the risk of being left behind, institutions around the world are racing to provide distance education opportunities in all subjects, including the humanities. However, there remains much skepticism about the quality of instruction and the educational experience that students receive. Can an online education be "just as good" as a face-to-face education? How can students develop the professional identity of a digital humanist in the e-Learning context? To address these critical issues, this chapter provides a survey of research and best practices relating to online pedagogies and professional identity development that are grounded in educational theory.

23.2 Rise in e-Learning

Online learning as an educational medium for all disciplines in higher education, including the humanities and digital humanities, must not be ignored. Those who bury their heads in the sand and resist teaching and learning in this context run the risk of becoming irrelevant. In the United States alone, distance education enrollments increased annually from 2002 to 2016, with over 6.3 million students enrolled in at least one distance course in Fall 2016. This figure represents 31.6% of all students enrolled in U.S. degree-granting higher education institutions (Seaman, Allen, & Seaman, 2018, p. 3). This continual rise in e-Learning enrollment comes at a time when overall enrollments in U.S. higher education programs have experienced a six-year steady decline (National Student Clearinghouse, 2017). Online courses are often touted as a medium by which nontraditional students or those who have temporal or proximal limitations can earn a college degree without traveling to campus (Bacon, Bowen, Guthrie, Lack, & Long, 2012; Chow & Croxton, 2017; Guerlac, 2011; Lee & Gupta, 2012). While this is the case for many, just over half (52.8%) of all U.S. students enrolled in at least one distance course in Fall 2016 were also enrolled in an on-campus course (Seaman et al., 2018), thereby suggesting that convenience or course availability may be a determining factor for many students to enroll in an online course over proximity. As online course offerings continue to increase and enrollment continues to rise, university administrators, faculty, and students must ensure that the learning that occurs in online courses is as good as, if not better, than the learning achieved in face-to-face courses.

23.3 Skepticism about e-Learning

Skepticism abounds about the quality of an online education. University presidents across the United States recognize that in order to stay competitive and meet the demands of their students, they must offer online learning opportunities (Allen & Seaman, 2013; Chow & Croxton, 2017; Gaytan, 2009). Survey findings by Allen & Seaman (2013) indicated that 69% of chief academic leaders in the United States said online learning is critical to their long-term strategy. At the same time, a Pew Research Center study of U.S. college presidents revealed that only 51% said online courses provide the same value as face-to-face instruction (Parker, Lenhart, & Moore, 2011), while a separate study found that 26% of chief academic officers considered online learning outcomes to be inferior (Allen & Seaman, 2014).

Similarly, university faculty remain skeptical about the quality of online learning (Allen & Seaman, 2013; Chow & Croxton, 2017; Graham & Jones, 2011). While many faculty members acknowledge that distance education is more convenient, many also perceive that the quality is "just not the same as the richness of the personal class experience" (Graham & Jones, 2011, p. 219). In a survey study about faculty perceptions about online learning, Chow and Croxton (2017) noted that, on a 7-point scale, faculty remained skeptical that the quality of online learning was equal to face-to-face (M=3.1), though they felt that online learning was already (or soon would be) relevant in their field (M=4.9). As online learning opportunities increase, so does uncertainty among members of the public about the quality of online learning. In a Pew Research Center study conducted in the United States, only 29% of all respondents said online classes offer an equal value as face-to-face instruction and, perhaps even more remarkable, 57% of the participants who had taken an online course noted that this type of instruction did not provide an equal value of learning compared to face-to-face (Parker et al., 2011). Though many of these findings may be specific to the United States, the insights suggest that, regardless of country or locale, it is critical for course designers and instructors to continually remind themselves that online courses start off with a "strike against them" with respect to perceptions of lower quality, simply due to the medium of delivery.

Given the rise in online courses and skepticism about the quality of learning that occurs online, a pressing question is whether the online context can provide an environment that is conducive to rich, higher-order learning that equals or surpasses the learning that occurs in traditional classrooms. Findings in the empirical literature suggest that these perceptions of inferiority of online learning are mixed. While numerous studies suggest that learning outcomes in online courses equal or surpass that which occurs face-to-face, student satisfaction is often sacrificed in these online classrooms (Aykol & Garrison, 2011; Block, Udermann, Felix, Reineke, & Murray, 2008; Croxton, 2014). Findings from myriad other studies suggest the quality of online learning is inferior to the traditional classroom environment (Graham & Jones, 2011; Keramidas, 2012; Roby, Ashe, Singh, & Clark, 2013).

Apart from concerns about the quality of learning and teaching in online classrooms, an additional area which lends itself to skepticism is whether and/or how a professional identity can be developed for a learner who is enrolled in a fully online degree program. While online faculty work to support the identity development of emerging professionals through guided conversation, assignments, and activities (Puddephatt, Kelly, & Adorjan, 2006), what is sometimes overlooked is the professional socialization that provides opportunities for learning from and alongside a community of like-minded professionals (Colbeck, 2008; Croxton, 2016; McAlpine & Amundsen, 2009). In other words, can a student learn to be a digital humanist in an online context that does not require live interaction with others? Stets and Burke (2000) purport that social interactions within a community are a critical component of identity development. Scholars, teachers, and learners in the digital humanities must recognize that online learning is happening and will likely continue into the unforeseeable future.

23.4 Part I: Pedagogy grounded in theory

While there remains deep skepticism and valid concerns about the quality of learning that can be achieved online, these issues can be overcome if practical online teaching and learning strategies are grounded in sound pedagogy that promotes deep, rich learning and satisfaction, regardless of context. In the online learning literature, two key theories have continuously surfaced in discussions about how learning and cognition occur in the online context. Both social cognitive theory and social constructivist theory have proven useful when exploring the ways in which learning occurs in online courses. Concurrently, social identity theory and the communities of practice approach are useful for exploring how professional identities can be developed for online learners. In Part I of this chapter, these learning theories and their critical interpretations in the online context are presented. In Part II, practical applications of these learning theories are illustrated in two online course scenarios.

23.4.1 Social cognitive theory

Social cognitive theory has proven to be a useful lens for understanding how learning occurs in online courses. Social cognitive theory postulates that motivational processes influence both learning and performance through a triadic reciprocality in which personal factors, behaviors, and environmental influences interact with and affect each other (Bandura, 2001). According to social cognitive theory, knowledge is constructed when individuals engage in activities (e.g., readings, practice exercises, viewing videos), receive feedback from instructor or peers, and participate in other forms of interaction in social contexts (e.g., group discussions, online blog conversations, group projects). Two primary motivational processes of social cognitive theory, self-efficacy and self-regulation, have been found to directly impact student motivation in online courses and, consequently, positively affect student learning (Gunter, 2008; Hill, Song, & West, 2009;

E-learning in the digital humanities

LaRose & Whitten, 2000; Shih, 2008). First, self-efficacy, or one's perceived capabilities to learn or perform actions at designated levels (i.e., "I can be successful"), is an important component of learning motivation that must be attended to in any learning context, including online. Self-efficacy is a significant predictor of learning and achievement (Schunk, 1981). Efficacy cues derived during task engagement include performance outcomes (how well a person does on a task), outcome patterns (does a student do well consistently), attributions (do students attribute their success to studying), model similarity (observing peers perform a task well), persuader credibility (is the person providing the feedback trustworthy), and bodily symptoms (increased heart rate and sweating) (Schunk, Pintrich, & Meece, 2008). When positive efficacy cues are perceived, there exists a greater likelihood that increased motivation and, consequently, learning will occur.

A second primary motivational process that is important for understanding social cognitive theory in the online learning context is self-regulation. Self-regulation refers to the process by which learners systematically direct their thoughts, feelings, and actions toward the attainment of their goals (Zimmerman & Schunk, 2001). Essential to promoting self-regulating behavior is providing learners with choices about when and how to participate, which methods to use, outcomes, and social and physical setting (Schunk, 2012). Instructors can help promote the development of their students' self-regulatory behaviors through a variety of strategies such as asking students to keep a weekly journal of course progress and study habits, having them reflect, and then adjust their approach to the course accordingly (Wandler & Imbriale, 2017). Allowing online students the freedom and flexibility to self-regulate their behavior has proven successful in enhancing online learner motivation and, consequently, learning (Gunter, 2008; Shih, 2008; Young & Norgard, 2006).

23.4.2 *Social constructivist theory*

Social constructivist theory, the roots of which stem primarily from the work of Vygotsky, is another useful theoretical lens through which to view how learning occurs in online courses (Anderson & Dron, 2011). Central to this theory is the belief that knowledge is constructed through the interaction of interpersonal (social), cultural-historical, and individual factors (abilities) (Schunk, 2012). From a social constructivist perspective, an online course that provides opportunities for active engagement with others (peers and instructor) through discovery (or problem-based inquiry) is particularly conducive to learning (Anderson & Dron, 2011; Jonassen, 2001; Rovai, 2004). According to this theory, learning is promoted in a student-centered context in which students actively participate in and construct their own learning (Rovai, 2004). Schunk (2012) goes on to explains that active learning involves students in doing things, thinking about the things they are doing, and may include learning a variety of activities including holding active discussions, cooperative learning, debates, role playing, simulations, and problem-based learning.

Anderson's interaction equivalency theorem aligns nicely with both the social cognitive and social constructivist theories. In this theorem, Anderson (2003) suggests that when at least one form of interaction, whether student-student, student-instructor, or student-content, is present at a high level, meaningful learning can occur and a more satisfying experience will ensue. While course interactivity is a strong predictor of student satisfaction in online courses, findings from numerous studies suggest that social interactivity, especially between student and instructor, is a primary factor in satisfying student needs (Chejlyk, 2006; Croxton, 2014; Keeler, 2006: Kuo, Walker, Schroeder, & Belland, 2014). Student preferences for interaction, however, have been noted to vary depending upon the level of and type of learner (Croxton, 2016; Glassmeyer, Dibbs, & Jensen, 2011; Mahle, 2011; Park & Choi, 2009). For example, Espansa and Meneses (2010), in a survey study of 186 online graduate students, found a statistically significant relationship between instructor feedback received, student satisfaction, and final course grades. With respect to student-student interaction, Walker and Kelly (2007) found that undergraduate students enjoyed sharing their work with other students more than graduate students. Still other studies noted that student conversations via asynchronous online discussion boards are often a source of dissatisfaction for students. Some students find themselves impatient waiting for their classmates to engage in online conversations (Hill et al., 2009), while others feel conversations are forced and unnatural (Biesenbach-Lucas, 2003). These studies and myriad others suggest that when designing online courses, instructors must take care to provide rich and meaningful interactions with students, instructors, and content, while prioritizing student-instructor interactions (Liu, Magjuka, Bonk, & Lee, 2007; Offir, Belazel, & Barth, 2007; Sun, Tsai, Finger, Chen, & Yeh, 2008).

23.4.3 Social identity theory and communities of practice

As entire learning programs move online, it is becoming increasingly important for educators to consider not only how to help students develop the skills and knowledge necessary to become practicing members of their fields, but also how to promote the development of the professional identities required to become meaningful contributors to digital humanities fields. While online teaching faculty guide students through learning experiences that promote the skills development required for success in their future professions, increasingly important, though often not overtly addressed is the need for appropriate socialization into the profession (Colbeck, 2008; McAlpine & Amundsen, 2009; Puddephatt et al., 2006). Stets and Burke (2000), leaders in social identity research, explain that the process of identifying as a member of a particular group develops as an individual feels "at one" within a certain group. The concept of social identity, introduced by Tajfel (1972) and Turner (1975), describes aspects of an individual's self-concept based upon group memberships along with corresponding emotional, evaluative, and psychological factors. Building upon these concepts of social identity development, Lave (1996) argues that learning should occur in "communities of practice" in which people engage in interdependent activities for substantial periods of time. This engagement not only helps students acquire knowledge, but is key to identity development (Lave & Wenger, 1991). Together, social identity theory and the communities of practice approach suggest development of a professional identity must occur in a social context that allows new or emerging members to adopt the beliefs, values, perspectives, and behaviors that are common among group members (Croxton, 2014; Lave, 1996; Lave & Wenger, 1991; Stets & Burke, 2000). Building opportunities for social and professional identity development in online programs requires explicit thought on the program level. Students must have opportunities to interact in-depth with their faculty who are experts in and have practiced in the field, current working practitioners in the field, and students who are working together within these contexts of working and learning. These opportunities may be facilitated through learning cohorts, in-the-field learning experiences (e.g., projects or internships) with expert practitioners, and opportunities to work on class related exercises that simulate real world practice. A specific example of the application of these theoretical principles is provided below in Scenario 2: Fostering a Community of Practice in a Graduate Level Online Program.

23.4.4 Theoretical predictions regarding online learning quality and professional identity development

Both social cognitive and social constructivist theories provide useful frameworks for understanding how rich, higher-order learning occurs in an online context. According to these theories, when instructors take into consideration learners' prior experiences, provide socially interactive and supportive learning environments, and encourage participation in meaningful, authentic learning tasks, deep learning and cognition has a greater likelihood of occurring. Further, student-centered learning contexts that promote self-efficacy and allow students to self-regulate their learning by providing choices relating to what, where, when, and how to learn are more likely to produce an environment that promotes learning. When online course instructors apply the principles of these two theories in online course design and instruction, high quality learning that equals, or even exceeds, that which occurs in a face-to-face learning context is anticipated. Consistent with the principles of both social cognitive and social constructivist theories, course design and teaching, rather than delivery modality (online versus face-to-face), may play a primary role in influencing student learning. When online courses lack rich social interaction between students and/or student-instructor, active and socially engaged learning is not promoted, and students' prior experiences are not considered, the likelihood that student learning will be negatively impacted increases. Concurrently, as indicated in the social identify theory and communities of practice approach, online teaching faculty and course designers must build in opportunities for students to develop their professional identities by fostering relationships between students, faculty members, and practitioners in the field as students begin to take on the role of professionals through guided activities.

23.5 Part II: Putting theory into practice in digital humanities online classrooms

Using the theoretical foundations outlined above, two online teaching scenarios – one in an undergraduate level classroom and the other for a graduate level course in an online program are outlined below. These scenarios have been developed using online pedagogical best practices and are grounded in the educational theories described above. While these scenarios can easily be adapted for either an in-person or online course in the digital humanities, extra care must be taken in the online teaching and learning environment to ensure student-instructor interaction is prioritized.

23.5.1 Scenario one: Promoting motivation and active learning in an undergraduate level online course

23.5.1.1 Course context

Individual learning occurs in a myriad of settings, reaching far beyond today's traditional classroom. An increasingly popular learning environment is the virtual classroom in which students and teachers work asynchronously. Such a class is DH 281: Introduction to the Digital Humanities, a requirement for all students pursuing a major in the digital humanities in a public, higher education institution in the southeastern region United States. Accessible via the Canvas learning management system, this 3 credit, 15-week semester-long course provides students with an introduction to basic concepts and methods used in the digital humanities. There is one online instructor and 25 students, typically in their freshman or sophomore year. Ages range from 19-year-old recent high school graduates to middle-aged adults. Technology skill levels are diverse and range from those who are highly confident to others with minimal technology experience. Though live, face-to-face interaction is not part of this course, active online engagement with the (1) course content through readings, videos, and practice exercises, the (2) instructor through a homework and project submission/feedback process, and (3) peers via the course discussion board all help to ensure that the triadic reciprocity that is the hallmark of social cognitive theory is present.

The instructor serves as *facilitator*, a guide who communicates and shares instructional materials via the Internet including video tutorials, required readings, online discussions, personal journaling, and assigned projects. Course projects include writing a grant proposal, designing and delivering an audio/visual online presentation, and researching and creating a multimedia website related to a digital humanities topic of interest.

23.5.1.2 Audio/visual digital presentation assignment

To enhance student learning, many motivational processes are applied in this online classroom including modeling, reinforcement, shaping, and self-efficacy. Application of these processes in relation to the audio/visual online presentation is described below. This two-week assignment, presented in the later part of the semester, requires students to create and publish an online presentation using either Voice Thread or Prezi, two freely available online tools. This assignment may seem daunting to those who have never used these tools before. To assuage anxiety and enhance students' motivated learning, the instructor models use of the online tools by creating video tutorials to demonstrate how to use each tool to create sample presentations. In the tutorials, students watch the instructor's movements on the computer screen while listening to the instructor's audio narration. In the video, the instructor occasionally missteps, but with "think aloud" narration students can see and hear how the mistakes are corrected. Additionally, students are provided with models of student work from prior semesters – both high level and lower level (all "A" work) so students can realize that this assignment is manageable, regardless of incoming skill level.

By the half-way point of the course (approximately week 7 in a 15-week course), students have completed and received feedback and grades for all homework and project assignments submitted to date. Students have consistently been given positive reinforcement in the form of personalized, positive feedback, grades of A's or B's, and encouragement for each assignment. Grades are typically high because a mastery approach is utilized such that, if student work is not optimal when first submitted, corrective feedback is provided with an option to resubmit. Throughout the two-week duration of this assignment, prompt instructor responses are provided for all student inquiries and encouragement is given in all communications. Based upon feedback from prior course evaluations, students find personal satisfaction in a job well done, good grades, and personalized positive feedback to be reinforcing, thus motivating them to learn and do well on future projects.

Shaping is an important motivational learning process utilized throughout the course. To assess incoming student knowledge about technology, each student was asked to complete a brief survey before the first day of class. Since technical proficiency varies from novice to proficient, the instructor creates and includes video tutorials demonstrating the use of technology for each assignment and provides exemplars of student work samples so students can visualize the desired outcomes for each unit. Based upon prior teaching experiences with this course, the instructor identified several reinforcements that include prompt, positive, assignment-specific feedback, opportunities to receive good grades, and the pride of completing a final product that can shared with prospective employers or used in their future classrooms. Written instruction is broken into small, easy-to-manage, sequential steps that students can follow while working on their projects. Since this is a two-week assignment, the instructor utilizes a student check-in process whereby students share their progress and questions part way through the assignment period, thus allowing the instructor to provide reinforcement and corrective feedback before the due date.

Building, maintaining, and attending to student self-efficacy is a key motivational learning process used in teaching this course. At the onset of the course, many students expressed concern about their abilities to manage course requirements. As they progress through the semester, students' self-efficacy typically improves as they create projects of which they are proud while also receiving instructor praise and favorable grades. To further build self-efficacy, student work samples are provided (both high and lower level – all "A" work). Viewing other students' work may help strengthen self-efficacy as students perceive that they can do as well or better than shown in the samples. Further, instructor modeling through video tutorials may help build self-efficacy as students realize that assignments are manageable. Students can select their topics, are encouraged to be creative, and are given a choice of which presentation program to use. Allowing students choice may promote self-efficacy as they select material that is familiar or of interest and a technology tool they feel is manageable. Persuasive encouragement is given to all students across all assignments.

In review, instructors play a critical role in motivating students to learn. By helping to promote self-efficacy through modeling desired behavior, reinforcing student performance, shaping responses to the desired outcomes, and strengthening students' confidence that they can be successful, instructors will create a rich learning environment in which students are motivated to learn and are able to achieve their desired outcomes.

E-learning in the digital humanities

23.5.1.3 Multimedia website assignment

The final course assignment requires students to research a digital humanities topic of interest and create a multimedia website. For this assignment, the instructor helps to promote both self-regulatory behavior and self-efficacy by implementing and modeling goal setting strategies in order to ease student anxiety and enhance student motivation. Research suggests that goals that are proximal, specific, and moderately difficult raise self-efficacy which can, in turn, positively enhance motivation (Locke & Latham, 2002; Nussbaum & Kardash, 2005; Schunk, 1995). Schunk (1995) further explains that positive role models can influence goal setting and the self-efficacy to achieve them. Thus, the instructor models setting specific, short-term, yet appropriately challenging goals by sharing a sample goal plan (Figure 23.1). Since goal progress feedback has been found to play a positive role in raising self-efficacy (Schunk & Schwartz, 1993), students are asked to create their own goals/timeline which includes two ungraded submissions of work for instructor feedback. Along with goal setting, the instructor illustrates what each checkpoint in the plan looks like by providing work samples that correspond to the goals.

Attributions can also have significant effects on achievement, beliefs, behaviors, and emotions (Schunk et al., 2008). In a study working with children on arithmetic skills, Schunk (1982) found that periodically providing children with verbal feedback linking their prior achievements with effort enhanced their motivation, self-efficacy, and skill acquisition. For this course assignment, feedback is provided incrementally at two points during the assignment period and upon completion of the assignment. The staged feedback acknowledges the amount of effort put forth as it relates to the quality and quantity of progress. With this feedback, students will be able to attribute their success to date (or lack of) to the amount of effort expended and make effort adjustments before the assignment is submitted, thereby demonstrating both their self-efficacy and self-regulatory processes. Final project feedback will not only include statements about the quality of the website but will also address student effort and any positive statements of ability if merited.

The value students place on specific tasks also plays a role in their motivation. Eccles and Wigfield (1995) define four components of achievement task value: attainment value, intrinsic value, utility value, and cost belief. In presenting the assignment, the instructor will help students find value in this project by addressing these components. First, students will be reminded that it is important to do well on this project (*attainment value*), as it is required to pass the course. Second, the instructor hopes to pique *intrinsic interest* by allowing students to be creative and have some fun, critical elements of the self-regulatory process of social cognitive theory. Third, the instructor will address the utility of assignment (*utility value*). By creating a webpage

> **Sample Plan of Goals and Timetable**
> - Day 1 – Assignment given
> - Day 3 – Mock up complete
> - Day 4 – Submit for instructor feedback
> - Day 6 – Online structure complete / begin adding content
> - Day 8 – Submit for instructor feedback
> - Day 10 – add links, photos, calendar
> - Day 12 – Share with classmate for review
> - Day 14 – Share with instructor

Figure 23.1 Sample Goal Plan

which relates to skills needed in their future profession, students will not only know how to create interactive, multimedia websites, but will have a nice piece to share with prospective employers. Finally, *cost belief* will be addressed. Though the final product might look as though it took a great deal of work, the instructor will assure the students that putting together a multimedia website need not take a great many hours, using personal experiences as an example (2 hours - structure & layout, 2 hours – content development, 1 hour –editing). While this conversation of value and cost may seem, at first glance, extraneous to the conversation, they are very much intertwined with both the self-regulatory and self-efficacy processes discussed above. In other words, students have the freedom to self-regulate their behavior by designing their own project of interest, setting their own goals and timelines, and adjusting their work based upon progress and feedback. Further, students will become more self-efficacious as they receive positive feedback and attributions at the short-term progress checkpoints and review the instructor's sample work as an attainable model.

Finally, students' outcome expectations also play a role in motivation. Bandura (1982) explains that students with both high self-efficacy and high-outcome expectations are more likely to have high cognitive engagement in a task. This may then lead to successful achievement and enhance motivation. Throughout the series of homework assignments in this course, the instructor has employed a mastery system whereby if students do not master an activity on the first try, they may keep working through guided instruction until mastery is achieved. Therefore, final grades on assigned projects tend to be high as students develop mastery. Because all students can master the tasks, students have high outcome expectations (good grades) in this class. In turn, this helps students to feel self-efficacious as they realize they "can" achieve.

In summary, developing homework assignments needs to be much more than simply putting together an assignment and hoping students will successfully fulfill the requirements. By implementing carefully structured and modeled goal setting strategies, building in opportunities for attributional feedback, helping students realize the value of assignments, and developing a mastery system in which all students can expect to be successful if they put forth the required effort, homework and project assignments become meaningful activities that enhance, rather than diminish motivation for learning.

23.5.2 Scenario two: Fostering a community of practice in a graduate level online program

Connectedness, interactivity, collaboration, and authentic "real world" learning opportunities help to promote professional identity development (Croxton 2014; Espasa & Meneses, 2010; Liu et al., 2007; Mahle, 2011; Park & Choi, 2009). Though perceptions of community are often bound by geographic proximity, online communities can be developed and sustained through electronic media (Haythornthwaite, Kazmer, Robins, & Shoemaker, 2004; Reid, 1995; Smith, McLaughlin, & Osborne, 1997). Haythornthwaite et al. (2004) explain, "…when we view community as what activities people do together, rather than where or through what means they do them, we can see that community can exist liberated from geography, physical neighborhood, and campuses" (p. 36).

23.5.2.1 Synchronous communication

Communication in online courses can take many forms, including emails with peers and faculty, online discussion boards, and live online course meetings, to name just a few. While many boast the merits of asynchronous online learning to be "any time, any place," other studies, particularly related to graduate learning, have revealed that participation in live, synchronous lectures with other students promoted more community building than all other forms of communication (Croxton, 2016; Haythornthwaite & Bregman, 2004; Haythornthwaite et al. 2004). Haythornthwaite and Bregman (2004) explain, "The immediacy afforded by synchronous communication media, and the greater number of physical cues offered by synchronous video over audio over text each contribute to a greater sense of being there with others" (p. 139). In a study of graduate online learners, Croxton (2016) highlighted the positive feedback of students who participated in regular synchronous online sessions with their instructor and peers. One student noted,

> I was blown away with how well the courses were conducted. I enjoy using Blackboard Collaborate because it allows me to interact with instructors and students in real time instead of sending emails or relying on discussion forums. … I am glad that I have this opportunity to interact with my peers and feel that I interact just as well with them online as being in the classroom. (p. 137)

In this same study, another student explained,

> The way that [my] university does it is a lot better than other online classes I had because… people interact in the online class, whereas in the classes I took prior it was just me reading stuff and me interacting with the professor. So, I think you still get the same kind of face to face contact. (p. 137)

As such, faculty members who are considering ways by which to foster the development of professional identities for their learners might consider opportunities for live interactions within the learning community of students and instructor. So long as these sessions are recorded for those who are not able to attend the "live" sessions, there still remains the luxury of "any time, any place." If regular synchronous class sessions are not an option, another consideration is for faculty members to facilitate periodic, individual synchronous sessions with their students, either by video or phone conference. In the Croxton (2016) study, one interviewee noted,

> [My professor] requires students to have a phone/Collaborate meeting with her during the semester and it was such a wonderful opportunity to talk and get to know each other. It meant quite a bit to me that she took the time to get to know me as a person. (p. 134)

While there are many facets involved in building an online community of practice, opportunities for synchronous interactivity remain critical for professional identity development.

23.5.2.2 Learning cohorts

Another means by which online learning programs can help to foster professional identity development is through learning cohorts. Belonging to a learning community or cohort has been noted to enhance students' feelings of connectedness, satisfaction, and educational success (Armstrong & Sanson, 2011; Conrad 2005; Croxton, 2016; Engstrom, Santo, & Yost 2008; Maddix, 2010). Returning to the social identify theory, the learning cohort model can help to promote an individual's identification as a member of a group (Stets & Burke, 2000) by attending to the emotional, evaluative, and psychological factors that come with being part of a group (Tajfel, 1972; Turner, 1975). For the purposes of this chapter, a community is described as "a general sense of connection, belonging, and comfort that develops over time among members of a group who share purpose or commitment to a common goal" (Conrad, 2005, p. 2), while a cohort is defined as group of learners who complete an entire program as single unit (Lawrence, 2002). A cohort model that requires students to take courses together in a sequence helps participants form bonds with other as they move throughout their programs. Adding in professional practitioners, mentors, and consistent instructional faculty to the cohort further facilitates the development of professional identity as students learn from and alongside like-minded peers and professionals.

23.5.2.3 Authentic, experiential learning

Finally, authentic, experiential learning that occurs within a community of practice is an important component of identity development (Lave & Wenger, 1991). As such, online programs can help to foster such experiences by ensuring that students collaborate on guided activities and projects that are reflective of professional practice and require interactions with practitioners in the field. In doing so, online learners are afforded opportunities to learn from each other, their professors, and working professionals. Through these interdependent interactions, new and emerging members in a group will begin to adopt the "beliefs, values, perspectives, and behaviors" of the group (Croxton, 2014; Lave, 1996; Lave & Wenger, 1991; Stets & Burke, 2000). To stimulate and maintain interest, learning activities should also be developed to promote learner self-efficacy and self-regulatory behavior by addressing student competence, control, creativity, collaboration, and caring.

When possible, it is recommended that students are allowed the freedom to select topics that are of personal interest. With a sense of control over a topic and anticipation of meaningful engagement, relevance of the assignment may become apparent to the student while also allowing them to self-regulate their behavior. It is anticipated that students will care about learning the material presented as it directly relates to their success not only in the class but in their future professional practice. A sense of control over a meaningful task may, in turn, enhance interest as Harackiewicz, Barron, Tauer, Carter, and Elliot (2000) explain, "… the long term development of interest seems to be better by the use of meaningful tasks and student involvement in active learning." Students should be afforded opportunities to work collaboratively. A hallmark of the social constructivist perspective on learning is that it is an inherently social activity (Hickey, 1997). Therefore, opportunities for meaningful engagement and social collaboration may further enhance interest. Finally, through active engagement in completing a group assignment and preparing deliverables, students will begin to develop a sense of interest and competency as they master and share required concepts. Competency plays an important role in developing interest, as researchers explain, "Students who believe they are competent enjoy tasks much more…" (Boggiano, Main, & Katz, 1988; Gottfried, 1985, 1990).

One assignment which was explicitly developed to use a community of practice approach for graduate level students in the digital humanities is the Organizational Analysis. In this assignment, students work in groups of 5 or 6 and carry out a guided analysis of an organization that employs digital humanists and/or uses digital humanities methods or practices in their work. Students must have the sites for the organizational assessments approved by the instructor in advance of contacting the organization of interest. This project is designed to be a community engaged service-learning opportunity for students. Engaging in authentic, "real life" practice within organizations is an essential element of developing professional identities. Through this assignment, professional identity development is fostered not only from interactions with instructors and peers, but with professionals practicing in the field. Additionally, as a service to the collaborating organizations, students are required to share findings and recommendations (via a written report and digital presentation) with them. These findings may have a real impact upon the future of these organizations.

Working in teams, especially on this type of project, is an efficient way to accomplish a lot of work. Since students are enrolled in a 100% online program, it is critical that they are mindful of the diversity and geographic distribution of their teammates. Some instructor guidance and modeling in advance of the assignment may be helpful to help facilitate this group work. For example, equipping students with links and tutorials to common communication and collaborative tools such as online video conferencing systems (e.g, WebEX, Google Hangout, Blackboard Collaborate), online scheduling tools (e.g., Doodle), and use of shared drives (e.g., Google or Drop Box) may help facilitate meaningful interactions and assuage the frustrations and angst that often come with group projects.

Throughout the project, the instructor will serve an active role as facilitator. It is recommended that the instructor ask a representative from each group to submit weekly status reports via email, thereby ensuring

E-learning in the digital humanities

a high level of student-instructor feedback, an essential element for student learning and satisfaction as outlined in Anderson's interaction equivalency theorem (2003). This practice not only helps hold groups accountable but also allows alerts the instructor if a group is encountering roadblocks or challenges with group dynamics before the final project is due. To alleviate the potential for students to be overwhelmed with the expectations, it is also recommended that the instructor carefully outline assignment details,[1] provide an exemplary sample, a template for the final deliverable,[2] and detailed scoring rubric.[3] By providing these resources, students can then focus on the desired activities and learning experiences while knowing exactly what is expected.

Conclusion

Online learning is happening and universities and their educational programs must adapt or run the risk of being left behind. The deep, higher order thinking that educators strive to facilitate for their students requires active, social engagement with rich content and sound pedagogy, regardless of the teaching medium. Thus, the question should not be whether online learning is "just as good" as the traditional face-to-face classroom. Rather, educators must step away from their traditional teaching methods for a moment and start anew, considering ways by which they can leverage the power of the Internet to their students' advantage. By infusing sound pedagogical principles that are grounded in social cognitive and social constructivist theories and which allow students develop their professional identifies within communities of practice, the online teaching and learning environment can be one that is rich, promotes higher order thinking, and allows students to learn in a context that is not only convenient, but aligns nicely with careers in the digital humanities.

Notes

1 Organization Assessment Assignment Details: https://tinyurl.com/OrgAssessSlides
2 Organizational Assessment Template: https://tinyurl.com/croxton-dighumanities-template
3 Organizational Assessment Assignment Scoring Rubric: http://tinyurl.com/crox-paper-rubric

References

Allen, I. E., & Seaman, J. (2013). *Changing course: Ten years of tracking online education in the United States.* Retrieved from http://www.onlinelearningsurvey.com/reports/changingcourse.pdf

Allen, I. E., & Seaman, J. (2014). *Grade change: Tracking online education in the United States.* Retrieved from https://www.onlinelearningsurvey.com/reports/gradechange.pdf

Anderson, T. (2003). Getting the mix right again: An updated and theoretical rationale for interaction. *The International Review of Research in Open and Distance Learning, 4*(2). Retrieved from http://www.irrodl.org/index.php/irrodl/article/view/149/230

Anderson, T, & Dron. J. (2011). Three generations of distance education pedagogy. *International Review of Research in Open and Distance Learning, 12*(3), 80–97.

Armstrong, S., & Sanson, M. (2011). From confusion to confidence: Transitioning to law school. *Queensland University of Technology Law & Justice Journal, 12*(1):21–44.

Aykol, Z., & Garrison, D. R. (2011). Understanding cognitive presence in an online and blended community of inquiry: Assessing outcomes and processes for deep approaches to learning. *British Journal of Educational Technology, 42,* 233–250. doi:10.1111/j.1467-8535.2009.01029.x

Bacon, L. S., Bowen, W. G., Guthrie, K. M., Lack, K. A., & Long, M. P. (2012). *Barriers to adoption of online learning systems in U.S. higher education.* New York: ITHAKA. Retrieved from https://sr.ithaka.org

Bandura, A. (1982). Self-efficacy mechanism in human agency. *American Psychologist, 37,* 122–147.

Bandura, A. (2001). Social cognitive theory: An agentic perspective. *Annual Review of Psychology, 52,* 1–26.

Biesenbach-Lucas, S. (2003). Asynchronous discussion groups in teacher training classes: Perceptions of native and non-native students. *Journal of Asynchronous Learning Networks, 7*(3). 24–46.

Block, A., Udermann, B., Felix, M., Reineke, D., & Murray, S. R. (2008). Achievement and satisfaction in an online versus a traditional health and wellness course. *Journal of Online Learning & Teaching, 4*(1), 57–66.

Boggiano, A. K., Main, D. S., & Katz, P. A. (1988). Children's preference for challenge: The role of perceived competence and control. *Journal of Personality and Social Psychologist, 54*, 134–141.

Burdick, A., Drucker, J., Lunenfeld, P., Presner, T., & Schnapp, J. (2012). *Digital humanities.* Cambridge, MA: MIT Press.

Chow, A. S., & Croxton, R. A. (2017). Designing a responsive e-learning infrastructure: Systemic change in higher education. *American Journal of Distance Education, 31*(1), 20–42.

Chejlyk, S. (2006). *The effects of online course format and three components of student perceived interactions on overall course satisfaction* (Doctoral dissertation). Available from ProQuest Dissertations & Theses database. (UMI No. 3213421)

Colbeck, C. L. (2008). Professional identity development theory and doctoral education. *New Directions for Teaching and Learning, 113*, 9–16.

Conrad, C. (2005). Building and maintaining community in cohort-based online learning. *Journal of Distance Education, 20*(1), 1–20.

Croxton, R. A. (2014). The role of interactivity in student satisfaction and persistence in online learning. *MERLOT Journal of Online Teaching and Learning, 10,* 314–324.

Croxton, R. A. (2016). Professional identity development among graduate library and information studies online learners: A mixed methods study. *Community & Junior College Libraries,* 1–17.

Eccles, J. S., & Wigfield, A. (1995). In the mind of the actor: The structure of adolescents' achievement task values and expectancy-related beliefs. *Personality and Social Psychology Bulletin, 21*, 215–225.

eLearningNC. (2018). *What is eLearning?* Retrieved from http://www.elearningnc.gov

Engstrom, M. E., Santo, S. A., & Yost, R. M. (2008). Knowledge building in an online cohort. *Quarterly Review of Distance Education, 9*(2), 151–167.

Espasa, A., & Meneses, J. (2010). Analyzing feedback processes in an online teaching and learning environment: An exploratory study. *Higher Education, 59*(3), 277–292. doi:10.1007/s10734-009-9247-4

Gaytan, J. (2009). Analyzing online education through the lens of institutional theory and practice: The need for research-based and validated frameworks for planning, designing, delivering, and assessing online instruction. *Delta Pi Epsilon Journal, 51*(2), 62–75.

Glassmeyer, D. M., Dibbs, R. A., & Jensen, R. T. (2011). Determining utility of formative assessment through virtual community: Perspectives of online graduate students. *Quarterly Review of Distance Education, 12*(1), 23–35.

Gottfried, A. E. (1985). Academic intrinsic motivation in elementary and junior high school students. *Journal of Educational Psychology, 77,* 631–645.

Gottfried, A. E. (1990). Academic intrinsic motivation in young elementary school children. *Journal of Educational Psychology, 82,* 525–538.

Graham, C. M., & Jones, N. (2011). Cognitive dissonance theory and distance education: Faculty perceptions on the efficacy of and resistance to distance education. *International Journal of Business, Humanities and Technology, 1*(2), 212–227.

Guerlac, S. (2011). Humanities 2.0: E-learning in the digital world. *Representations, 116*, 102–127.

Gunter, G. A. (2008). The effects of the impact of instructional immediacy on cognition and learning in online classes. *International Journal of Social Sciences, 2*(3), 196–202.

Harackiewicz, J. M., Barron, K. E., Tauer, J. M., Carter, S., & Elliot, A. J. (2000). Short-term and long-term consequences of achievement goals: Predicting interest and performance over time. *Journal of Educational Psychology, 92,* 316–330.

Haythornthwaite, C., & Bregman, A. (2004). Affordances of persistent conversation: Promoting communities that work. In C. Haythornthwaite & M. M. Kazmer (Eds.), *Learning, culture and community in online education: Research and practice* (pp. 129–143). New York, NY: Peter Lang.

Haythornthwaite, C., Kazmer, M. M., Robins, J. & Shoemaker, S. (2004). J. Robins, & S. Shoemaker. (2004). Community development among distance learners: Temporal and technological dimension. In C. Haythorthwaite & M. M. Kazmer, *Learning, culture and community in online education: Research and practice* (pp. 35–57). New York, NY: Peter Lang.

Hickey, D. (1997). Motivation and contemporary socioconstrutivist instructional perspectives. *Educational Psychologist, 32,* 175–193.

Hill, J. R., Song, L., & West, R. E. (2009). Social learning theory and web-based learning environments: A review of research and discussion of implications. *American Journal of Distance Education, 23*(2), 88–103.

Jonassen, D. H. (2000). Transforming learning with technology: Beyond modernism and postmodernism or whoever controls the technology creates the reality. *Educational Technology, 40*(2), 21–25.

Keeler, L. C. (2006). *Student satisfaction and types of interaction in distance education courses* (Doctoral dissertation). Available from ProQuest Dissertations & Theses database. (UMI No. 3233345)

Keramidas, C. G. (2012). Are undergraduate students ready for online learning?: A comparison of online and face-to-face sections of a course. *Rural Special Education Quarterly, 31*(4), 25–32.

E-learning in the digital humanities

Kuo, Y.-C., Walker, A. E., Schroder, K. E. E., & Belland, B. R. (2014). Interaction, Internet self-efficacy, and self-regulated learning as predictors of student satisfaction in online education courses. *The Internet and Higher Education, 20*, 35–50. doi:10.1016/j.iheduc.2013.10.001

LaRose, R., & Whitten, P. (2000). Re-thinking instructional immediacy for web courses: A social cognitive exploration. *Communication Education, 49*(4), 320–338.

Lave, J. (1996). Teaching, as learning, in practice. *Mind, Culture, and Activity 3*(3), 149–64.

Lave, J., & Wenger, E. (1991). *Situated learning: Legitimate peripheral participation.* Cambridge, MA: Cambridge University Press.

Lawrence, R. (2002). A small circle of friends: Cohort groups as learning communities. *New Directions for Adult & Continuing Education, 95*, 83–92.

Lee, S. A., & Gupta, R. K. (2012). College distance education courses: Evaluating benefits and costs from institutional, faculty, and students' perspectives. *Education, 130*(4), 616–631.

Liu, X., Magjuka, R. J., Bonk, C. J., & Lee, S.-H. (2007). Does sense of community matter? An examination of participants' perceptions of building learning communities in online courses. *Quarterly Review of Distance Education, 8*(1), 9–24.

Locke, E. A., & Latham, G. P. (2002). Building a practically useful theory of goal setting and task motivation: A 35-year odyssey. *American Psychologist, 57,* 705–717.

Maddix, M. A. (2010). Online learning communities: The heart of online learning. *Common Ground Journal, 7*(2), 10–15.

Mahle, M. (2011). Effects of interactivity on student achievement and motivation in distance education. *Quarterly Review of Distance Education, 12*(3), 207–215.

McAlpine, L., & Amundsen, C. (2009). Identity and agency: Pleasures and collegiality among the challenges of the doctoral journey. *Studies in Continuing Education, 31*(2), 109–25. doi:10.1080/01580370902927378.

National Student Clearinghouse. (2017). *Current term enrollment - Fall 2017.* National Student Clearinghouse Research Center. Retrieved from https://nscresearchcenter.org

Nussbaum, E. M., & Kardash, C. M. (2005). The effects of goal instructions and text on the generation of counterarguments during writing. *Journal of Educational Psychology, 97*, 159.

Offir, B., Belazel, R., & Barth, I. (2007). Introverts, extroverts, and achievement in a distance learning environment. *American Journal of Distance Education, 21*(1), 3–19. doi:10.1080/08923640701298613

Park, J.-H., & Choi, H. J. (2009). Factors influencing adult learners' decision to drop out or persist in online learning. *Educational Technology & Society, 12*(4), 207–217.

Parker, K., Lenhart, A., & Moore, K. (2011). *The digital revolution and higher education: College presidents, public differ on value of online learning.* Washington, DC: Pew Research Center Social & Demographic Trends. Retrieved from http://www.pewsocialtrends.org/2011/08/28/the-digital-revolution-and-higher-education

Puddephatt, A. J., Kelly, B. W., & Adorjan, M. (2006). Unveiling the cloak of competence: Cultivating authenticity in graduate sociology. *The American Sociologist, 37*(3), 84–98.

Reid, E. (1995). Virtual worlds: Culture and imagination. In S. G. Jones (Ed.), *Computer-mediated communication and community* (pp. 164–183). Thousand Oaks, CA: Sage.

Roby, T., Ashe, S., Singh, N., & Clark, C. (2013). Shaping the online experience: How administrators can influence student and instructor perceptions through policy and practice. *Internet and Higher Education, 17*, 29–37.

Rovai, A. P. (2004). A constructivist approach to online college learning. *Internet and Higher Education, 7*, 79–93.

Schunk, D. H. (1981). Modeling and attributional effects on children's achievement: A self-efficacy analysis. *Journal of Educational Psychology, 95*, 426–442.

Schunk, D. H. (1982). Effects of effort attributional feedback on children's perceived self-efficacy and achievement. *Journal Educational Psychology, 74*, 548–556

Schunk, D. H. (1995). Self-efficacy and education and instruction. In J. E. Maddux (Ed.), *Self-efficacy, adaptation, and adjustment: Theory, research, and application* (pp. 281–303). New York: Plenum Press.

Schunk, D. H. (2012). *Learning theories: An educational perspective* (6th ed). Boston, MA: Pearson.

Schunk, D. H. Pintrich, P. R., & Meece, J. L. (2008). *Motivation in education: Theory, research, and applications* (3rd ed.). Upper Saddle River, NJ: Pearson.

Schunk, D. H., & Swartz, C. W. (1993). Goals and progress feedback: Effects on self-efficacy and writing achievement. *Contemporary Educational Psychology, 18*, 337–354.

Seaman, J. E., Allen, I. E., & Seaman, J. (2018). *Grade increase: Tracking distance education in the United States.* Babson Park, MA: Babson Survey Research Group. Retrieved from https://www.onlinelearningsurvey.com/highered.html

Shih, H. P. (2008). Using a cognition–motivation–control view to assess the adoption intention for web-based learning. *Computers & Education, 50*, 327–337.

Smith, C. B., McLaughlin, M. L., & Osborne, K. K. (1997). Conduct control on Usenet. *Journal of Computer-Mediated Communication, 2*(4), n.p. doi:10.1111/j.1083-6101.1997.tb00197.x.

Stets, J. E., & Burke, P. J. (2000). Identity theory and social identity theory. *Social Psychology Quarterly*, *63*(3), 224–237.

Sun, P.-C., Tsai, R. J., Finger, G., Chen, Y.-Y., & Yeh, D. (2008). What drives a successful e-learning? An empirical investigation of the critical factors influencing learner satisfaction. *Computers & Education*, *50*(4), 1183–1202. doi:10.1016/j.compedu.2006.11.007

Tajfel, H. (1972). La categorisation sociale. In S. Moscovici (Ed.), *Introduction a la Psychologie Sociale* (pp. 272–302). Pans: Larousse.

Turner, J. C. (1975). Social comparison and social identity: Some prospects for intergroup behaviour. *European Journal of Social Psychology*, *5*, 5–34.

Walker, C. E., & Kelly, E. (2007). Online instruction: Student satisfaction, kudos, and pet peeves. *Quarterly Review of Distance Education*, *8*(4), 309–319.

Wandler, J., & Imbriale, W. (2017). Promoting undergraduate student self-regulation in online learning enviroments. *Online Learning*, *21*(2), 1–16. doi: 10.24059/olj.v21i2.881

Young, A., & Norgard, C. (2006). Assessing the quality of online courses from a students' perspective. *Internet and Higher Education*, *9*, 107–115.

Zimmerman, B. J., & Schunk, D. H. (Eds.) (2001). *Self-regulated learning and academic achievement: Theoretical perspectives* (2nd ed.) Mahway, NJ: Erlbaum.

24

EYE TRACKING FOR THE EVALUATION OF DIGITAL TOOLS AND ENVIRONMENTS

New avenues for research and practice

Dinara Saparova

24.1 Introduction

Digital tools for humanities research are defined as "software developed for the creation, interpretation, or sharing and communication of digital humanities resources and collections" (Nguen & Shilton, 2008:59). These tools serve many purposes—they help scholars work with texts (e.g., digitize documents and use archives); analyze texts (e.g., conduct computational analysis, study metadata, perform text mining); create other tools (e.g., games, applications, collections, databases); assist with methodological aspects of their work (e.g., help with field work, ethnographic research, user research); and support traditional scholarly activities (e.g., reading, studying historic documents, writing) (Given & Willson, 2018). Due to the social nature of digital humanities research, tools or their features that support communication, collaboration and information sharing are a must (Carter, 2013). Available for free or on subscription or paid only basis, digital tools differ in complexity and completeness – some are as simple that can be readily used without any special knowledge, others are complex and require a certain set of skills; some are fully developed and some appear to be under some stage of development. Digital tools for humanities provide access to scholarly content in different modalities (e.g., texts, images, video and audio or combinations of thereof) and can be available as a stand-alone technology or through a shared Internet-enabled resource hub of research applications and communication tools, known as Virtual Research Environments (de La Flor, Jirotka, Luff, Pybus, & Kirkham, 2010).

Advances in the development of information technology have also resulted in the development of a broad spectrum of digital tools for humanities research. The fact that these tools are rapidly created and improved and redesigned on a regular basis contributes to situations of too many choices. Large variability in designs and functionality of digital tools and their availability for digital humanities scholarship, however, does not always result in their high utilization (Gibbs & Owens, 2012; Warwick, Terras, & Nyhan, 2012). During the 2005 Summit on Digital Tools at the University of Virginia, it was reported that only about six percent of humanist scholars used more complex digital tools in their scholarship while the majority of scholars preferred to use general purpose information technology (Summit on Digital Tools for the Humanities, 2005). It is very likely that the use of digital tools in humanities research has improved over the years; nevertheless, noticeably low and slow adoption rates of digital infrastructures intended for research purposes in this domain remain to be an issue. This status quo, therefore, calls for more research in search of reasons underlying successful adoption and use of new technology as well as strategies for improving the processes of technology design and development.

24.1.1 *Adoption and use of digital humanities tools and environments*

Other than the fact that researchers may simply be unaware of the existence of certain digital humanities tools, or they may be hard to access, there are other reasons why scholars may be reluctant to use a digital tool. For example, "e-humanists" may be hesitant to adopt and/or use a digital tool if they have difficulty understanding its purpose (Warwick, Terras, Huntington, & Pappa, 2008). In some cases, unclear name of the tool can contribute even more confusion to understanding its purpose, make the user not trust the resource or unwilling to give it a try (Warwick et al., 2008). In other cases, humanities academic users are less likely to adopt a digital tool if additional time and training is required to learn how to use it (Given & Willson, 2018). Among the most significant reason for low and slow digital tool adoption is the mismatch between user needs, preferences and expectations of the system and its actual design and functionality (Juola, 2008). This mismatch may manifest itself on different levels, including interface design features, functionality, quality of content, etc.

As with any technology, interfaces of digital humanities tools and environments are expected to be easy and intuitive to use. If, however, users experience discomfort with unfamiliar interface or perceive it as difficult to use and navigate, they may regard it as untrustworthy, neglect it and go back to more familiar resources. Up to this date, many digital tool developers seem to believe that certain features are essential in system's design. One of such presumed functionalities is advanced search, which in reality happens to be underused because digital humanists tend to avoid performing complex precise keyword searches and instead browse through the content and select information pieces or citations that are relevant to their searches (Warwick et al., 2012). Another example of the mismatch between user needs and system design is when digital tools and environments is the lack of functionality allowing users to perform qualitative and quantitative analyses of the content within the same tool (Steiner et al., 2014). Further, the need to annotate while interacting with the material is crucial for researchers in humanities; without this functionality digital collections become impractical, as they do not provide enough support to interact and engage with the content (de La Flor et al., 2010). More, digital humanities scholars appreciate flexibility of digital tools when it comes to choosing the format of outcomes presentation and ways of sharing the results (Trace & Karadkar, 2017). Lastly, e-humanists give preference to tools that can be integrated with other technology and environments over stand-alone, single purpose tools (Given & Willson, 2018).

One big category of issues with the design and functionality of digital tools and environments in humanities research that often gets overlooked is the lack of compatibility with the principles of universal design and accessibility (Williams, 2012). Universal design provides users with options to navigate and use digital technology in multiple ways, in accordance with specific user needs, preferences and learning styles (Cordell & Gomis, 2015). However, due to the complexity of existing artifact collections and user characteristics, a One-size-fits-all approach to the design of digital humanities technology is, therefore, considered unfortunate due to the complexity of available artifact collections and user characteristics (e.g., novice vs expert users) (Steiner et al., 2014). Accessibility, as the word implies, provides access to technology for users with different physiological needs and capabilities. In the absence of features and functionality that provide and support accessibility of digital tools and environments, most valuable digital resources become unusable by a large audience of people who are deaf or hard of hearing, blind, have low vision, or have difficulty distinguishing particular colours (Williams, 2012). Both principles – universal design and accessibility – contribute to a larger concept of universal usability, which conveys the short and clear message, that information and communication technology (ICT) should be usable by all.

Vanderheiden (2000) suggested two major reasons why universal usability has been gaining interest of designers and developers of ICT. Firstly, there is the rise of mobile computing, which demands that products like information communication systems are usable in various environments (e.g., low vs high speed Internet connection), circumstances (e.g., low vs high income users) and devices (e.g., small vs high resolution displays). Secondly, government regulations (e.g., the Telecommunication Act, the Rehabilitation

Evaluation of digital tools

Act, etc.), mandate that manufacturers of telecommunication products and services make them accessible by people with a wide range of disabilities and age-related limitations. He grouped government guidelines and regulations into the following five basic components of universal usability:

1. Ensuring that all information presented by or through the device can be perceived (even if all sensory channels are not available to the individual).
2. Ensuring that the device is operable by the user (even if they are operating under constraints).
3. Facilitating the ability of the individual to navigate through the information and controls (even if they are operating with constraints).
4. Facilitating their ability to understand the content.
5. If it is not possible to achieve the above four objectives directly, the goal is to make the product compatible with the common tools that users may have with them in order to maximally achieve the above four objectives.

Low and slow adoption rates of digital tools and environments in digital humanities research coupled with their inefficient use demand some action. One way to understand the underlying reasons is to ask current and potential users of this technology. Engaging users in the process of tool development and evaluation is a proven method of conducting needs assessment so necessary for design decisions. Early and continuous user studies could be a sure way to validate intended designs of digital tools and environments against the actual needs and expectations of the intended audience.

24.1.2 User studies in digital humanities

As in other disciplines, many problems with the adoption and use of digital tools and environments in humanities research arise when developers presume first-hand knowledge of features and functionality instead of being guided in their design of technology of technology by the actual user needs, (Warwick et al., 2012). Proponents of such an approach are of the opinion that users in digital humanities do not know what they want from the tools and it does not do any good to engage them during early phases of product development cycle (Kemman & Kleppe, 2014). The outcome of such an approach, however, are tools and environments that are unusable by the target audience due, for instance, to high levels of system complexity or failure to provide support in daily research activities (e.g., annotating, analyzing, sharing, etc.). The opposing approach advocated by user experience researchers as a more efficient way to building technology is rooted in the principles of user-centered design. This ensures that considerations of user needs and preferences, various user characteristics, environments, tasks and workflows, are included. One of the main strengths of this approach is the fact that user needs and preferences associated with the use of technology are taken into consideration long before the final product is fully developed. The principles of user–centered design thus promote design of products and technology that users should find effective, efficient, satisfactory, and easy to learn or, in other words, usable (emphasis mine) in their daily activities. Validation of product characteristics against user requirements typically occurs during usability studies, which allow for timely identification of problems with product design or functionality ahead of the investment of too much work and human and financial resources.

In digital humanities, user involvement in usability work aimed at improving user experience with technology is, unfortunately, greatly underrepresented. Despite the positive and beneficial impact of usability on system success, interface work remains marginal rather than central in digital humanities (Smith et al., 2008). A decade ago, a survey of tool developers for humanities research revealed that only one third of them ran usability studies (Schreibman & Hanlon, 2010). It is desirable to believe that over the years the situation with usability evaluations of digital tools and environments for the field of digital humanities has greatly improved, yet, up to this day research reporting on this line of work remains rare (Gibbs &

Owens, 2012; Thoden, Stiller, Bulatovic, Meiners, & Boukhelifa, 2017; Warwick et al., 2012). In search of reasons for the scarcity of usability research in digital humanities, some suggest that evaluations of digital tools primarily focus on their functional requirements rather than user experience, which eliminates the need for usability studies in principle (Tracy, 2016). Others note that the problem is not with the shortage of usability studies per se but the lack of follow through when it comes to implementation of usability findings (Thoden et al., 2017).

To demonstrate the issues with the dearth of published usability research in digital humanities, I conducted a literature search on this topic from the last ten years (2008–2018). The search was conducted in Google Scholar. The choice of the database was intentional for a number of reasons: first, Google Scholar is free and easy does not require training to use; second, it is known to provide access to practically all digitally available research (Falagas, Pitsouni, Malietzis, & Pappas, 2008); third, it catalogues between 2 and 100 million records of both academic and grey literature, which makes it a useful database for systematic reviews (Haddaway, Collins, Coughlin, & Kirk, 2015). The literature search focused on finding studies reporting on usability evaluations of digital tools and environments specifically intended for use in digital humanities research (e.g., text analysis tools such as Omeka, Many Eyes, Voyant) as opposed to digital tools and environments of more general purpose also used by humanists (e.g., digital libraries, collections, general communication tools such as Skype, data bases such as JSTOR or MLA, tools for online storage of data such as Dropbox or Google Drive, etc.) during the last ten years. The searches, conducted in Google Scholar, therefore, included the combination of terms "usability", "evaluations", "methods", "digital humanities", "digital tools", and "digital environments". Table 24.1 includes examples of studies reporting on usability evaluations of digital tools and environments in the field of digital humanities over the last ten years. It is also worth noting that some of the studies included in the review clearly stated their intention to evaluate usability of digital tools while others avoided using the term 'usability' yet still reported on user experiences when interacting with the systems under evaluation.

Although brief, this overview covers a large variety of usability methods that are being used for evaluating digital tools and environments. Such a variety of usability evaluation methods is deemed appropriate though since it allows to account for various user characteristics (e.g., novice vs expert) as well as characteristics of digital tools (e.g., stationary vs mobile) and working environments (e.g., office vs field). For the purpose of convenience, usability evaluation methods can be subdivided into different categories. One way to classify them is to divide them into empirical and analytic (Rosson & Carroll, 2002). Empirical methods allow for the collection of information about the usability of a system by observing and/or interviewing actual users, while analytic methods rely on feedback from usability experts who try to put themselves in the position of actual users. Analytic methods are typically employed during the early phases in the development process because they are less labor intensive. Empirical methods, on the contrary, are used later in the development process and are more demanding, as they require involvement of real users as well as usability experts to interpret their feedback afterwards. Another classification of usability methods puts them into three groups (Lazar, Feng, & Hochheiser, 2017): empirical methods that focus on understanding user experiences with the product under evaluation; inspection methods that involve the expertise of usability professionals to analyze features of a given product; and inquiry methods that aim to obtain user opinions and requirements based on observations and interviews. One more way to look at usability evaluation methods is to divide them into user-oriented, system-oriented, and systematic (Saracevic, 2000). A user-oriented evaluation approach focuses on psychological and cognitive characteristics of the user and how these influence the use of the system; system-oriented evaluation approach zooms in on the technological characteristics of the system; systematic approach addresses a combination of the previous two.

As seen from the review of the literature (Table 24.1), empirical, user-centered usability evaluation methods and approaches receive a greater emphasis in digital humanities research. Interviews (e.g., contextual, think-aloud) and discussions with users were found to be the dominant usability evaluation methods in almost every study. There is no doubt that these methods allow for a convenient (e.g., can

Evaluation of digital tools

Table 24.1 Examples of studies reporting the evaluations of digital tools and environments

#	Authors	Purpose of the study	Usability methods
1.	Thoden et al. (2017)	Evaluation of existing tools and services as well as their integration into a digital workflow within the CENDARI and DARIAH infrastructure projects for the arts and humanities	Heuristic evaluation, think aloud
2.	Heuwing et al. (2016)	Design and evaluation of tools providing interactive analysis of historical texts	Contextual interviews, design workshops and evaluation of prototypes
3.	Tracy (2016)	Pattern uses and usability issues of an open-source DH publishing platform for media-rich projects, Scalar, as well as user experiences with the use of the system	Survey, interviews, content analysis
4.	Wusteman (2017)	Usability testing of a prototype version of the Letters of 1916 Digital Edition	Think-aloud interviews, scenario-based tasks
5.	Green (2014)	Analysis of the use of MONK text mining research software	Web analytics, user interviews
6.	Kemman, Scagliola, de Jong & Ordelman (2014)	Evaluation of a research tool exploring Oral History Today collections by providing overview and zooming facilities as well as supporting exploration strategies	User interviews
7.	Steiner et al. (2014)	Evaluation of the virtual research environment CULTURA that provides innovative functions to support research and exploration of digital heritage collections through various digital tools	Questionnaires (the System Usability Scale, the technology acceptance model), discussions, interaction logs
8.	Burghardt (2012)	Evaluating the usability of annotation tools	Heuristic walkthrough
9.	de la Flor et al. (2010)	Evaluating a prototype of the Virtual Research Environment for the Study of Documents and Manuscripts used for displaying and annotating images as well as for collaborative pointing and sharing	Prototype evaluation through reflective feedback and actual use, user observations
10.	Gibbs & Owens (2012)	Revealing user expectations of digital tools for text mining and visualization in history	Open-ended survey and a virtual panel discussion
11.	Warwick et al. (2009)	Study of user reactions to the use of digital recording pens and notebooks during archaeological excavations	A diary study, fieldwork observations

be administered face to face and/or remotely, verbally or in writing) and informative way of obtaining information about how the system is used and which features are favored or disliked. This feedback, however, should be approached critically as self-reported measurements such as think-aloud protocols or questionnaires can produce biased or even wrong inaccurate data that are not predictive of the actual user behavior (Schiessl, Duda, Thölke, & Fischer, 2003). In addition, during think-aloud interviews users may experience what is known as Hawthorn effect, i.e., when users perform at much higher levels due to their being observed and studied as experiment participants. To obtain valid results, it is considered a good practice to counterbalance subjective and objective measurements by applying several usability evaluation methods. When it comes to analytic, inspection methods, such as heuristic evaluations and cognitive walkthroughs, they may be more useful for making decisions about the design of the tool under development as opposed to helping to understand if the tool is usable (Goldberg & Wichansky, 2003).

As a method that can provide additional value during usability evaluations of digital tools and environments for the field of digital humanities eye tracking is relatively new. None of the studies included in the review reported the use of this methodology. The application of eye tracking is extremely efficient in revealing user preferences for or resistance against certain features and functionality during digital tools development and evaluation. First, eye tracking can provide more thorough insights into user interactions with interface and other design elements, e.g., user's attention distribution and eye grabbing properties. Second, eye tracking can help deepen the findings from other usability evaluation methods by offering explanations of certain user behaviors with technology. Researchers may find this methodology particularly useful because eye tracking is based on obtaining objective psychophysiological metrics during their interaction with digital technology in most unobtrusive ways.

24.1.3 Eye tracking: The basics

Eye tracking, as the term suggests, is used for tracking and recording an individual's eye movement. It is an informative methodology that offers insight into people's visual and cognitive processes during information processing, be it reading, visual search or natural scene perception. Historically eye tracking started in psychology for studying eye movements during reading. As personal computers began to gain popularity in the 1980s, so did the attempts of researchers to incorporate eye tracking into the field of Human-Computer Interaction. Later, with the invention of Internet and Web 2.0, researchers tried to apply eye tracking to address questions of usability. Eye tracking methodology is rooted in the eye-mind hypothesis (Just & Carpenter, 1980), which suggests that visual and cognitive processes are interrelated, i.e., visual activity of users can be considered a direct reflection of processes occupying their cognitive domain. During information processing the two basic components of eye movements are saccades and fixations (Rayner, 2009). During fixations, the eye remains fairly still, and new information is acquired from the visual array. Saccades, on the other hand, are fast ballistic movements of the eye that occur between fixations, during which no new information is acquired. The number and duration of fixations along with saccade length and direction, gaze rate and duration, blink rate and duration, changes in pupillary activity, and scan paths duration and length represent the most common eye metrics indicative of human cognitive activity.

When deciding on whether to use eye tracking for usability evaluation purposes, one must take into consideration both the strengths and weaknesses of this approach. Among the major strengths of eye tracking methodology are the following:

- Eye tracking can be used at any stage of the usability testing cycle with low, medium and high-fidelity prototypes of interfaces (Bergstrom & Schall, 2014).
- Eye tracking studies can provide reliable results from a relatively small number of participants (e.g., 6-30) (Goldberg & Wichansky, 2003).

Evaluation of digital tools

- Modern eye tracking systems, although different in types and applications, are easy to operate, with quick and easy setup and eye calibration (Jacob & Karn, 2003).
- Eye tracking technology can be wearable or remote, which allows for data collection in naturalistic environments (e.g., walking, shopping, driving) and/or laboratory settings (Goldberg & Wichansky, 2003). The leading hardware vendors in this industry are Tobii (https://tobii.com), SMI (SensoMotoric Instruments) (https://www.smivision.com/) and EyeLink (https://www.sr-research.com/).
- Eye tracking metrics can provide valuable insight into usability problems revealed through the application of traditional usability evaluation methods (Ehmke & Wilson, 2007; Wang et al., 2018).
- Eye tracking software offers a variety of data outputs that are visually attractive and intuitive to understand (e.g., heat maps, gaze plots, areas of interest) (Bergstrom & Schall, 2014).

The weaknesses when employing the eye tracking approach mainly come down to either technical or methodological. Technical issues may include the following:

- Loss of tracking or calibration on an eye tracking system during data collection (Goldberg & Wichansky, 2003).
- Wearable eye tracking technology, in particular, head-mounted eye trackers, may cause user discomfort during the experiments and restrict their naturalistic behavior (Jacob & Karn, 2003).
- Glasses and contact lenses worn by the experiment participants are frequently problematic to effective eye tracking to the point that either additional work like minimizing head motion and frequently inspecting camera setup is required or it is recommended to altogether avoid recruiting participants with eye wear (Goldberg & Wichansky, 2003; Poole & Ball, 2005).

Among methodological issues of employing eye tracking methodology are the following:

- Labor-intensive and prone to errors data extraction of metrics that are not automatically exported by the eye tracking software
- Labor intensive data analysis (Jacob & Karn, 2003).
- Difficulties with data interpretation, for example, dual meaning of some of the eye movement metrics (e.g., higher number of fixations within a particular area can suggest a greater interest in it or higher workload indicative of more intense information processing) (Jacob & Karn, 2003).

24.1.4 Possible applications of eye tracking in digital humanities

In this section I discuss how the field of digital humanities can benefit from the application of eye tracking methodology during the design and development of digital tools and environments. I start with an overview of eye tracking for usability evaluations of ICT and then propose how it could be used to expand our understanding of 1) why digital humanities users give preference to certain tools over others; and 2) design considerations for the design of digital tools and environments that ensure conformance to the principles of accessibility and universal design.

24.1.4.1 Eye tracking for usability

The International Organization for Standardization defines usability as the extent to which a user can fulfill a task using a tool effectively, efficiently, and with satisfaction (ISO: 1998). When interacting with certain tools, user' cognitive processes (e.g., attention distribution) are affected by the amount of cognitive load imposed by either demands of the task itself (i.e., intrinsic cognitive load), individual user characteristics (i.e., germane cognitive load) or design and functionality of the system (i.e., extraneous cognitive load). These three types of cognitive load are central concepts of cognitive load theory proposed by John Sweller in the late 1980s, which was originally concerned with the development of instructional methods and materials that take into account the limitations of learner's cognitive processing capacity. A recurring usability goal is to reduce memory load for users (Van Nimwegen et al., 2006). From the three types of cognitive load experienced by users during information tasks, it is the extraneous cognitive load that represents particular interest for human-computer interactions and usability research. The main reason for such interest is the fact that extraneous cognitive load can be deliberately manipulated through the design appearances of a system by eliminating unnecessary features that distract user attention when completing a task. The most common techniques include having users focus on recognition rather than recall, chunking content, optimizing response time, and avoiding visual clutter and interface complexity.

Since cognitive processes find reflection in eye movement (e.g., the eye-mind hypothesis by Just & Carpenter (1980)), it is certain eye movement characteristics that infer the amounts of cognitive load experienced by users during their interactions with technology as well as other cognitive demands associated with task performance. Readings of certain eye certain movements are, therefore, a useful way for understanding how design and functionality of information systems affect user cognitive processes and subsequently user experiences and perceptions of usability of these systems. For instance, higher number of fixations within a particular area can indicate a greater interest in it and signify that this area is more noticeable or more important to the viewers (Jacob & Karn, 2003). Alternatively, higher number of fixations, also known as longer gaze, may suggest difficulties experienced by the user while viewing the area of interest and indicate user attempts to better understand or clarify the information piece (Jacob & Karn, 2003). Pupil size has been found to correlate with mental workload on the tasks: the harder the task at hand, the larger the pupil tends to dilate (Recarte, Pérez, Conchillo, & Nunes, 2008). Blink rates as well could be considered as the correlates of mental workload: blink rate increases in situations of high mental workload but decreases in situations of high visual demands (Recarte et al., 2008). Ehmke & Wilson (2007) took their research even further when they proposed correlations between the appearance of a specific eye tracking pattern and a usability problem. As such she found that overloaded, ineffective information presentation is associated with a lot of short fixations within a single area followed by longer saccades and regressions; unclear functionality of elements (e.g., text elements appear clickable but in fact are not) is associated with longer fixations on misleading elements; unclear grouping that contradicts mental models of information users is associated with higher number of fixations overall but low number of fixations on areas of unclear groupings, etc. This information can provide designers with knowledge critical for understanding how to design usable tools and systems that do not overload users.

In an attempt to justify the application of eye tracking for conducting usability evaluations, several studies explored the relationships between eye tracking and traditional usability testing methods (Schiessl et al., 2003; Wang et al., 2018). The general conclusion from these studies is that eye tracking metrics should not be solely relied on for the interpretation of evidence from usability studies. Instead, eye tracking metrics are most helpful when they are used in combination with other measurements of usability obtained from more traditional approaches such as task completion time, think aloud, expert evaluations, user interviews, observations, surveys, etc. In addition, it is considered good practice to supplement quantitative outputs of eye tracking metrics with their qualitative interpretations. For instance, video play back of eye movements can provide insights into the patterns of attending to various features and areas of the interface.

Applications of eye tracking for usability evaluations of products and technology are currently many. Examples include e-voting systems (Realpe-Muñoz et al., 2018), restaurant menus (Kim, Tang, Meusel, & Gupta: 2018), online learning environments (Majooni, Akhavan, & Offenhuber, 2018), maps (Göbel, Kiefer, Giannopoulos, Duchowski, & Raubal, 2018) and many others. In digital humanities research, the applications of eye tracking for evaluating the usability of digital infrastructures are few. One study I found utilized eye tracking for evaluating the use of a collapsible facets panel in a search interface of a digital library (PoliMedia) for the minutes of the Dutch parliament, linked to the media coverage of the debates. Two representations of facets were evaluated – one where the facet panel is collapsible and the other where the panel is visible. To analyze search efficiency and distribution of attention, the researchers relied on the total number of fixations and total viewing duration overall in the system and per specific areas of interest as well as user satisfaction. Despite the fact that the findings from both eye tracking and user satisfaction metrics did not produce significant results, the authors concluded that eye tracking methodology could be a beneficial way to evaluate and understand user interactions with technology. It is our hope that by providing awareness of new methodologies available for evaluating usability of systems and technology, more eye tracking studies will be taking take place in digital humanities research.

24.1.4.2 Eye tracking for evaluating digital tools' perceived complexity

In their seminal work, Jacob & Karn (2003) provided valuable insights on the application of eye tracking for human-computer interaction and usability research and proposed a number of directions for future studies. One particularly interesting suggestion is this: "When users search for a tool, menu item, icon, etc. in a typical human-computer interface, they often do not have a good representation of the target. Most of the literature on visual search starts with the participant knowing the specific target. We need more basic research in visual search when the target is not known completely. A more realistic search task is looking for the tool that will help me do a specific task, having not yet seen a tool" (p. 587). This suggestion can open a new research avenue in digital humanities of applying eye tracking methodology. Coupled with other methods of inquiry, eye tracking could be useful in providing answers as to why only certain tools in digital humanities research instantaneously attract user attention (for reasons other than tool's primary purpose) and later become adopted and used.

Users are known to form an impression of a web-based resource within 50 msec of a page's presentation (Lindgaard, Fernandes, Dudek, & Brown, 2006). During this short time, users also make up their minds as to whether they are going to continue to use this resource. Even though this time is too short to perform a conscious critical evaluation of the resource, it is enough to understand if the resource is 'right' or 'wrong' (Warwick et al., 2012). Prompt decisions regarding favoring or disliking the information resource based on perceptions of the look and feel emphasize the important role interface design plays in making impressions on the users. Interfaces that look unfamiliar or too difficult to use (i.e., too complex) create unfavorable impressions on potential users and result in their decisions to abandon the resource. This knowledge implies that digital resources, especially the novel ones, need to make a positive impression on the potential users at first sight; this knowledge also suggests that initial impression of complexity is an important factor in tool adoptability and use.

Complexity of a web resource is a difficult concept to define as it depends on several factors. Typically, complexity increases with the number of elements on the page (Harper, Michailidou, & Stevens, 2009), perceived unfamiliarity (Forsythe, Mulhern, & Sawey, 2008) and preexisting expectations and even the age of users (Donderi, 2006). While forming the impressions of complexity, users experience a range of emotions. These emotions carry both dimensions: valence (i.e., positive and negative) and arousal (i.e., resting to excited) (Goldberg, 2012). Scales and surveys or physiological methods can measure these dimensions; however, the former are not efficient in capturing the fleeting feelings and the latter suffer from validity issues (Hazlett & Benedek: 2007). A more suitable method for capturing user feelings may involve studying patterns of eye movement, blinks and pupil changes (de Lemos, Sadeghnia, Ólafsdóttir, & Jensen, 2008). An example of such a study is Goldberg (2012) who investigated the relationship between perceived web page complexity and emotional valence through the application of subjective ratings, facial analysis and eye tracking. He found that eye tracking and emotional valence measures were related to conscious subjective judgments of complexity thus concluding that eye tracking was a valid method for evaluating interfaces for perceived complexity.

It has also been found that there is a positive correlation between users' perceptions of visual complexity and aesthetic appearance of a web page, i.e., less complex pages were perceived as more visually appealing and vice versa (Michailidou, Harper, & Bechhofer, 2008). Studies that try to determine user perceptions of the aesthetic qualities of web-based technology emphasize visual clarity and visual richness as the two most important aesthetic dimensions (Lavie & Tractinsky, 2004). Design elements that shape these dimensions to a significant degree are text/background colour combinations (Hall & Hanna, 2004), font type and size (Bernard, Liao, & Mills, 2001) and headers, menus, search boxes and logos (Yesilada, Jay, Stevens, & Harper, 2008).Visually pleasing interfaces have also been found to be more trustworthy (Robins & Holmes, 2008). Djamasbi and colleagues (2010) conducted an eye tracking study where they examined how features of social presence (e.g., images of faces) contributed to visual appeal of web pages and consequently user trust. Analysis of heat maps representing the accumulation and duration of fixations helped explain that users found pages with images of faces more visually appealing, more trustworthy and more helpful in retrieving and processing the needed information over the pages with images of logos.

Findings like this indicate that aesthetics and visual appeal can be good predictors of trust, which is an important criterion in the selection of websites and digital tools and environments. However, in trying to provide aesthetic appearance of technology, it is critical to remember that visual appeal is not the only requirement for its successful use – utility and functionality are also expected (Tractinsky, 2004). In addition, the right balance between design elements that support visually pleasing interfaces should be observed in order to avoid excessive cognitive load these features may impose on the user. In situations where a wide range of digital tools and environments available to humanities researchers contributes to intense competition for retaining the interest of old older users and especially gaining the interest of new ones, it is important to pay special attention to good system design overall and especially, good design of interfaces, which act as the first point of encounter between the user and the tool. Testing the benefits as well as potential weaknesses of proposed designs by employing various methodological approaches is therefore crucial. A large set of tools and methodologies can be used to understand the nature of these encounters and eye tracking could be particularly useful.

24.1.4.3 Eye tracking, digital tools and environments, and accessibility

It was estimated that there are were 285 million visually impaired people in the world, with 39 million blind and 246 million having low vision (Pascolini & Mariotti, 2012). In fact, there are as many as three times more partially sighted people than people who are functionally or fully blind (Newell & Gregor, 1997). People with partial vision usually experience issues with visual acuity, contrast sensitivity, field of vision and color perception (Jacko & Sears, 1998). Another widespread partial vision condition is the age-related macular degeneration (AMD), which is associated with a loss of acuity in the central visual field. This condition affects millions of Americans and is the leading cause of visual impairments for individuals 55 years and older (American Macular Degeneration Foundation, 2002). It is estimated that by the year 2030, in the United States alone, approximately 70 million people will be over the age of 65 (Jacko et al., 2000), which suggests that at least half of them are likely to experience decreasing quality of vision due to AMD. People with vision limitations make a distinct category of users who, in order to efficiently interact with the Internet and technology, require alterations of traditional user interfaces. When developing user interfaces, researchers continue to explore alternatives such as audio and/or tactile presentations (i.e., haptic interfaces) of textual information for fully blind users (Power & Jürgensen, 2010). Users with partial visual impairments, however, require a very different set of alternatives – they heavily rely on features like compatibility of content with screen readers, availability of tags on graphics, color schemes that take into consideration users with color blindness,

Evaluation of digital tools

ability to magnify content and manipulate contrast, etc. Despite federal attempts to make ICT accessible for people with a wide range of disabilities, up to this day, these well sought after and needed enhancements are still largely lacking, which suggests that visually impaired users remain inefficient users of technological advances (Jaeger, 2012).

Eye tracking could be a useful tool for evaluating accessibility of technology by empowering developers in their knowledge of principles of accessible design. Dr. Julie Jacko and her research collaborators conducted a series of experiments investigating how users with visual impairments suffering from age-related macular degeneration (AMD), interact with technology (Jacko et al., 2001; Jacko et al., 2000). Their studies demonstrated that eye movement analysis could be an excellent methodological tool for understanding the peculiarities of search and selection strategies by low vision computer users compared to fully sighted participants. Researchers gathered eye tracking metrics (e.g., scan time, spatial density, and number of fixations) during a continuous matching task while manipulating the size of icons (9.2 mm, 14.6 mm, 23.2 mm, 36.8 mm and 58.3 mm), their number (two, three, four, five and six icons) and the background color (fully saturated black, blue, green, red and white). The findings from the experiments suggested that AMD users required less time to process information on the screen when the background was colored in black, blue or white than green and red; when the icon size increased; and when the number of icons displayed on the screen increased as well. Specifically, the icon identification time was the shortest for icon size of 36.8 mm but there were no changes in performance when the icon size was 58.3 mm and even a decrease in performance when the AMD users were simultaneously presented with five to six icons.

The general conclusion from this line of research is that users with AMD significantly differ from fully sighted users in their interactions with ICT; therefore, it is a big limitation in the design of technology not to provide users with limited visual capabilities an opportunity to become more efficient users of technology. When it comes to design and functionality of the majority of digital humanities technology, conformity to the principles of accessibility, or, to be exact, the lack of thereof, still remains an issue (Williams, 2012). Limitations in the design of these tools that do not allow to meet the needs of people with various impairments significantly narrow the pool of potential users and adopters of such technology. It is therefore with hope that eye tracking methodology along with other evaluation methodologies can provide useful take-aways for the accessible design of digital tools and environments.

24.1.4.4 Eye tracking, digital tools and environments, and universal design

Technology compliance with the principles of universal design provides its users an opportunity to utilize technology on the move, instead of in a stationary setting, and access it from a variety of mobile hand-held devices (e.g., smartphones, tablets, personal digital assistants). As a way of promoting universal design of digital tools and environments in humanities research, an opportunity to present information in different formats on multiple devices needs to be taken into consideration as well (Zundert, 2012); however, not all tools can benefit from this approach. This claim is supported by several reasons. First, the number of active mobile devices keeps growing (e.g., by the year 2017, 2,890 million smartphones were reported worldwide) (statista, 'Smartphones worldwide installed base from 2008 to 2017 (in millions),' 2017); second, there is a significant overlap between making an information resource accessible from a mobile device and for people with disabilities (Williams, 2012); third, there is a growing need to use digital tools in naturalistic work environments (de La Flor et al., 2010; Warwick et al., 2009). The fourth and unofficial reason is that for most scholars their projects and research activities become an essential part of their daily lives that occupy a significant amount of their professional and personal time. As a result, they may need a quick reference with research material in order to confirm or refute spontaneous ideas and serendipitous discoveries could be a necessity.

24.1.4.5 Universal design and mobile eye tracking

The type of eye tracking that is most suitable for evaluations of mobile applications and technology is mobile eye tracking; i.e. collecting data by means of wearable or portable eye tracking equipment. This is becoming a popular trend in eye tracking research, which solicits the move away from the laboratory setting to more natural mobile environments, both indoors and outdoors (Bulling & Gellersen, 2010). Advances in wearable eye tracking equipment such as unobtrusive video-based systems that are fully integrable into an ordinary glasses frame (e.g., Tobii glasses) make it feasible to collect data on the move, in naturalistic contexts. Examples of ethnographic research from realistic settings supported by mobile eye tracking methodology include studies from aviation, automotive industry, consumer research, marketing and advertising and many others.

From the published studies on the use of mobile devices in digital humanities, one study that stands out is the investigation of handheld personal digital assistants (PDAs)' use during archaeological excavations (Warwick et al., 2009). In their understanding of how mobile devices were used in the field, the authors relied on diary studies. Dairy studies are a form of observation when participants are asked to keep detailed record of their work over a short period of time (S. Carter & Mankoff, 2005). In this study, the participants were asked to document what they were doing, how they were using the technology and what problems they were experiencing during these activities. While diary studies are a useful and informative method of obtaining information from first-hand sources, it certainly has limitations. For instance, this method is based on obtaining subjective reporting of individual perceptions and interpretations; it may be considered time consuming as it requires participants to spend additional time to document their reflections; and user reflections and documentation of experiences happens post-factum, which may alter the memories of the actual events. In search of other methods and approaches suitable for understanding user experiences with mobile applications and technology in situ, mobile eye tracking could be a potential solution.

During the applications of mobile eye tracking, it is important to consider the limitations of both mobile devices and mobile eye tracking equipment. Limitations of mobile technology are usually caused by issues with connectivity (i.e., the strength of the signal), limited screen size, reduced display resolution, limited processing capabilities and power, and difficulties with data entry (i.e., data entry requires a certain level of proficiency) (Zhang & Adipat, 2005). Limitations of mobile eye tracking equipment result from the fact that they consider varying distances between the interface and the user; therefore, they are less precise due to issues with overall eye tracking accuracy, calibration quality, and calibration drift during operation (Bulling & Gellersen, 2010). In addition, a valid concern with mobile video-based eye trackers remains to be a considerable processing power, which allows only for two to four hours of operating time (Bulling & Gellersen, 2010). To address these concerns, evaluations of mobile applications through mobile eye tracking is usually supplemented with eye movement data obtained from stationary/remote eye tracking systems. Cheng (2011) proposed a framework for eye tracking-based usability evaluation of mobile devices rooted in the combination of eye movement data obtained from stationary and portable eye trackers as well as performance metrics. In particular, the study proposed that eye movement data obtained from a remote eye tracker is more suitable for quantitative analysis and interpretations (e.g., fixation duration time, fixation count) while eye movement data obtained from a portable eye tracker is better intended for qualitative analysis (e.g., observations of user's eye movement processes and hand-eye coordination processes). To validate the findings from eye tracking methods, performance evaluation metrics (e.g., task completion time and error count) could also be used. Such combined approaches allow for comprehensive evaluations that improve the accuracy and reliability of the findings.

Recently, a new comprehensive model for evaluating mobile applications for their usability, People At the Center of Mobile Application Development (PACMAD), has been proposed (Harrison, Flood, & Duce, 2013). One feature that distinguishes this model from other existing usability models is the inclusion of cognitive load as an important attribute of mobile usability evaluation. One rationale for adding

Evaluation of digital tools

cognitive load as a usability attribute is that cognitive load imposed by the design of technology can be adjusted. Another rationale for considering cognitive load when evaluating usability of mobile devices is the assumption that the use of mobile technology never happens in isolation, i.e., along with the use of mobile devices, users typically attend to other tasks as well, like walking or driving (Salvucci, 2001; Schidbach & Rukzio, 2010). Attending to another task while using a mobile application typically results in divided attention: attention devoted to the use of mobile application and attention devoted to performing the second task. In ideal scenarios, when cognitive load imposed by interactions with a mobile application is low due to good usability characteristics, more cognitive capacity is allocated to performing the second task. Alternatively, if users experience high cognitive load caused by issues with usability of a mobile application, they are likely to struggle to perform the second task as well. Salvucci (2001) studied the effects of in-car phone interface use on driver performance. He found that the full-manual interface had large significant effect on driver performance; specifically, it took the drivers almost two seconds longer to complete a dialing task. The voice interface, on the other hand, had no significant effect on driving at all. In addition, the speed-manual interface required the least time to dial a number while the full-voice interface required the most time.

24.1.4.6 Universal design and expertise levels

Technology conformance to the principles of universal design, therefore, should also warrant equal experiences for users with various experience and expertise levels. Lately, numerous digital humanities tools and environments are being reportedly used by the general population and students for purposes like learning or personal curiosity (Carter, 2013). This presumes that such digital environments need to be designed with considerations for users of all backgrounds and expertise levels. Eye tracking could be a useful tool for revealing the differences in user behaviors that find reflection in certain eye movement characteristics. For instance, in visual domain experts tend to demonstrate more fixations on task-relevant areas and fewer fixations on task-redundant areas; they also have longer saccades and shorter times to first fixate relevant information (Gegenfurtner, Lehtinen, & Säljö, 2011). Such eye movement patterns are the result of information behavior supported by sufficient domain knowledge or expertise that allows the optimization of the amount of processed information by making users overlook task-irrelevant facts and actively focus on task-relevant information. When it comes to novices, it is safe to assume that their eye movement characteristics during performance on information tasks in visual domain are the opposite of experts. Due to lack of prior knowledge, it takes them longer to first fixate on relevant information, they have shorter saccades as they tend to read most of the textual content and they cannot immediately differentiate between relevant and irrelevant content, which results in equal distribution of fixations on task-relevant and task-redundant areas.

Mental effort due to lack of expertise is associated with high intrinsic cognitive load linked to the difficulty of material and germane cognitive load linked to the cognitive processing of the material. If, in situations of already high intrinsic and germane cognitive load, extraneous cognitive load is also high, user satisfaction with the system use and quality of learning is likely to suffer. Saparova & Nolan (2016) reported on the differences in cognitive load among medical students who used three different information resources for learning. In this study medical students were considered novices in the medical domain, and the measurements of experienced cognitive load were based on eye movement characteristics. The authors found that when medical students used information resources intended for experts, they experienced higher cognitive load that received manifestation in higher fixation counts, longer fixation duration and longer total visit duration within the resource. The findings suggested that when novices use information resources intended for experts, they find themselves under the threats of cognitive overload, which gets manifestation in their eye movement characteristics. Therefore, eye tracking could be a useful methodology for unraveling those differences.

Organization and presentation of content supported by certain design elements has been found to play an important role in facilitating information acquisition. Well-defined structures were shown to be more suitable for learners with low prior knowledge, because such structures help these learners clearly see the hierarchical relationships of knowledge organization that they are lacking (Potelle & Rouet, 2003). Another widely acknowledged approach to promoting universal design of digital infrastructures when it comes to users with various expertise levels is the multi-layered interface design (Shneiderman: 2003). This approach has been among the most prominent ways to address the differences in user characteristics. The essence of this approach is to provide users with control over the sets of features available to them at any moment. Similar to methods that lead learners through a number of levels or milestone to obtain a set of new skills, multi-layered interface design allows users to activate layers of interface one by one in order to reduce complexity and increase the convenience of using the technology in more personalized, individual ways.

Conclusion

The literature search reported in this chapter showed the scarcity of publications on the topics of evaluations of digital tools and environments on different stages of their development in the field of digital humanities. Published evaluation results are still few, and most report on the use of other, more traditional usability testing methods. This chapter offers a detailed overview into how research and scholarship in digital humanities can benefit from eye tracking methodology during design and evaluation of digital tools and environments. It is hoped that awareness of this relatively novel field for the digital humanities can spark new interest and suggest new directions during development and evaluation of information infrastructures. The undeniable strengths of eye tracking methodology are in providing access to individuals' psychophysiological reactions in often unobtrusive and convenient ways. Access to such reactions allows for understanding of the underlying processes behind certain user actions and reactions. In addition, eye tracking adds insights and deeper meaning into the evaluation results obtained from more traditional methods.

Interpretation of results from eye tracking studies, however, should be performed with a lot of precision and caution since many factors associated with the application of eye tracking methodology can contribute to the skewed results. It is, therefore, recommended to avoid using eye tracking as a single methodology and always supplement its application with other methods. A special interest of this chapter included the discussion of possible applications of eye tracking beyond traditional usability evaluations of technology. The two directions included discussions on how eye tracking could be useful for evaluating digital technology for accessibility and universal design. References and examples from studies outside digital humanities provided informational references into how these goals could be achieved. Universal usability of digital tools and environments can, therefore, become a new, important direction of future research in designing technology suitable for individuals with various individual characteristics.

References

American Macular Degeneration Foundation. (2002).

Bergstrom, J. R., & Schall, A. J. (2014). *Eye tracking in user experience design*. Morgan Kaufmann, Waltham, MA, USA.

Bernard, M., Liao, C. H., & Mills, M. (2001). The effects of font type and size on the legibility and reading time of online text by older adults. In *CHI'01 extended abstracts on human factors in computing systems*, 175–176. ACM, New York, NY, USA.

Bulling, A., & Gellersen, H. (2010). Toward mobile eye-based human-computer interaction. *IEEE Pervasice Computing*, 4. 8–12.

Burghardt, M. (2012). Usability recommendations for annotation tools. In *Proceedings of the 6th Linguistic Annotation Workshop*, 104–112. Jeju, Republic of Korea: Association for Computational Linguistics.

Carter, B. (2013). *Digital humanities: Current perspectives, practices, and research*. (B. W. Carter, Ed.). Emerald Group, Bingley, UK.

Carter, S., & Mankoff, J. (2005). When participants do the capturing: the role of media in diary studies. In *Proceedings of the SIGCHI Conference on Human Factors in Computing Systems*, 899–908, ACM.

Evaluation of digital tools

Cheng, S. (2011). The research framework of eye-tracking based mobile device usability evaluation. In *Proceedings of the 1st International Workshop on Pervasive Eye Tracking & Mobile Eye-Based Interaction*, 21–26. Beijing, China: ACM.

Cordell, S. A., & Gomis, M. (2015). Looks matter: The impact of visual and inclusive design on usability, accessibility, and online learning. In *Proceedings of ACRL*, 489–496, Portland, Oregon, USA.

de La Flor, G., Jirotka, M., Luff, P., Pybus, J., & Kirkham, R. (2010). Transforming scholarly practice: Embedding technological interventions to support the collaborative analysis of ancient texts. *Computer Supported Cooperative Work*, 19(3–4), 309–334.

de Lemos, J., Sadeghnia, G. R., Ólafsdóttir, Í., & Jensen, O. (2008). Measuring emotions using eye tracking. In A. Spink, M. Ballintijn, N. Bogers, F. Grieco, L. Loijens, L. Noldus, … P. Zimmerman (Eds.), *Proceedings of the 6th International Conference on Methods and Techniques in Behavioral Research "Measuring Behavior 2008"*, 226, Maastricht, The Netherlands: Noldus Information Technology.

Djamasbi, S., Siegel, M., & Tullis, T. (2010). Efficiency, trust, and visual appeal: Usability testing through eye tracking. In *Proceedings of the 43rd Hawaii International Conference on System Sciences*, 1–10.

Donderi, D. C. (2006). Visual complexity: a review. *Psychological Bulletin*, 132(1), 73.

Ehmke, C., & Wilson, S. (2007). Identifying web usability problems from eye-tracking data. In *Proceedings of the 21st British HCI Group Annual Conference on People and Computers: HCI… but not as we know it* - Volume 1, 119–128, British Computer Society.

Falagas, M. E., Pitsouni, E. I., Malietzis, G. A., & Pappas, G. (2008). Comparison of PubMed, Scopus, Web of Science, and Google Scholar: strengths and weaknesses. *The FASEB Journal*, 22(2), 338–342.

Forsythe, A., Mulhern, G., & Sawey, M. (2008). Confounds in pictorial sets: The role of complexity and familiarity in basic-level picture processing. *Behavior Research Methods*, 40(1), 116–129.

Gegenfurtner, A., Lehtinen, E., & Säljö, R. (2011). Expertise differences in the comprehension of visualizations: A meta-analysis of eye-tracking research in professional domains. *Educational Psychology Review*, 23, 523–552.

Gibbs, F., & Owens, T. (2012). Building better digital humanities tools. *DH Quarterly*, 6(2).

Given, L., & Willson, R. (2018). Information technology and the humanities scholar: Documenting digital research practices. *JASIS&T*, 69(6), 807–819.

Göbel, F., Kiefer, P., Giannopoulos, I., Duchowski, A. T., & Raubal, M. (2018). Improving map reading with gaze-adaptive legends. In *Proceedings of the 2018 ACM Symposium on Eye Tracking Research & Applications - ETRA '18*, 1–9. Warsaw, Poland: ACM.

Goldberg, H. J., & Wichansky, A. M. (2003). Eye tracking in usability evaluation: A practitioner's guide. In J. Hyönä, R. Radach, & H. Deubel (Eds.), *The Mind's Eyes: Cognitive and Applied Aspects of Eye Movements*, 493–516. Elsevier Science, Oxford.

Goldberg, J. H. (2012). Relating Perceived Web Page Complexity to Emotional Valence and Eye Movement Metrics Impression of Complexity. In *Proceedings of the Human Factors and Ergonomics Society 56th Annual Meeting*, 501–505.

Green, H. E. (2014). Under the workbench: An analysis of the use and preservation of MONK text mining research software. *Literary and Linguistic Computing*, 29(1), 23–40.

Haddaway, N. R., Collins, A. M., Coughlin, D., & Kirk, S. (2015). The role of Google Scholar in evidence reviews and its applicability to grey literature searching. *PLOS One*, 10(9).

Hall, R. H., & Hanna, P. (2004). The impact of web page text-background colour combinations on readability, retention, aesthetics and behavioural intention. *Behaviour & Information Technology*, 23(3), 183–195.

Harper, S., Michailidou, E., & Stevens, R. (2009). Toward a definition of visual complexity as an implicit measure of cognitive load. *ACM Transactions on Applied Perception*, 6(2), 1–18.

Harrison, R., Flood, D., & Duce, D. (2013). Usability of mobile applications: literature review and rationale for a new usability model. *Journal of Interaction Science*, 1(1), 1–16.

Hazlett, R. L., & Benedek, J. (2007). Measuring emotional valence to understand the user's experience of software. *International Journal of Human-Computer Studies*, 65(4), 306–314.

Heuwing, B., Mandl, T., & Womser-hacker, C. (2016). Methods for user-centered design and evaluation of text analysis tools in a digital history project. In *Proceedings of the 79th ASIS&T Annual Meeting: Creating Knowledge, Enhancing Lives through Information & Technology*. American Society for Information Science.

ISO. (1998). ISO 9241-11 Ergonomic requirements for office workers with visual display terminals (VDTs) – Part 11: Guidance on usability.

Jacko, J. A., Barr, A. B., Chu, J. Y. M., Scott, I. U., Rosa, R. H., & Pappas, J. C. C. (2000). Macular degeneration and visual search: what we can learn from eye movement analysis. In *Proceedings of the Human Factors and Ergonomics Society Annual Meeting*, 116–119. Sage CA: Los Angeles, CA: SAGE Publications.

Jacko, J. A., Scott, I. U., Barreto, A. B., Bautsch, H. S., Chu, J. Y. M., & Fain, W. B. (2001). Iconic visual search strategies: a comparison of computer users with AMD versus computer users with normal vision. In M. J. Smith & G. Salvendy (Eds.), *Systems, Social and Internalization Design Aspects of Human-Computer Interaction*, 423–427. Lawrence Erlbaum Associates, Publishers.

Jacko, J. A., & Sears, A. (1998). Designing interfaces for an overlooked user group: Considering the visual profiles of partially sighted users. In *Proceedings of the 3rd International ACM conference on Assistive Technologies*, 75–77. ACM.

Jacob, R. J. K., & Karn, K. S. (2003). Eye tracking in human—computer interaction and usability research: Ready to deliver the promises. In Hyöna, Radach & Deubel (Eds.), *The Mind's Eye: Cognitive and Applied Aspects of Eye Movement Research*, 573–605. Oxford, England: Elsevier Science BV.

Jaeger, P. T. (2012). *Disability and the internet: Confronting a digital divide*. Boulder, CO: Lynne Rienner Publishers.

Juola, P. (2008). Killer applications in digital humanities. *Literary and Linguistic Computing*, 23(1), 73–83.

Just, M. A., & Carpenter, P. A. (1980). A theory of reading: From eye fixations to comprehension. *Psychological Review*, 87(4), 329–354.

Kemman, M., & Kleppe, M. (2014). Too many varied user requirements for digital humanities projects. In *The 3rd CLARIN ERIC Annual Conference*, 2–5.

Kemman, M., Scagliola, S., de Jong, F., & Ordelman, R. (2014). Talking with scholars: Developing a research environment for oral history collections. In Ł. Bolikowski, V. Casarosa, P. Goodale, N. Housson, P. Manghi, & J. Schirrwagen (Eds.), *Theory and Practice of Digital Libraries - TPDL 2013 Selected Workshops*, vol. 416, 97–201. Springer International Publishing.

Kim, E., Tang, L., Meusel, C., & Gupta, M. (2018). Optimization of menu-labeling formats to drive healthy dining: An eye tracking study. *International Journal of Hospitality Management*, 70(March), 37–48.

Lavie, T., & Tractinsky, N. (2004). Assessing dimensions of perceived visual aesthetics of web sites. *International Journal of Human-Computer Interaction*, 60(3), 269–298.

Lazar, J., Feng, J. H., & Hochheiser, H. (2017). *Research methods in human-computer interaction*. Morgan Kaufman.

Lindgaard, G., Fernandes, G., Dudek, C., & Brown, J. (2006). Attention web designers: You have 50 milliseconds to make a good first impression! *Behaviour & Information Technology*, 25(2), 115–126.

Majooni, A., Akhavan, A., & Offenhuber, D. (2018). An Eye-tracking study on usability and efficiency of blackboard platform. In *Proceedings of the International Conference on Applied Human Factors and Ergonomics*. Springer.

Michailidou, E., Harper, S., & Bechhofer, S. (2008). Visual complexity and aesthetic perception of web pages. In *Proceedings of the 26th annual ACM international conference on design and communication*, 215–224. Lisbon, Portugal: ACM.

Newell, A. F., & Gregor, P. (1997). Chapter 35 - Human computer interfaces for people with disabilities. In *Handbook of Human-Computer Interaction*, 2nd ed., 813–824. Amsterdam: North-Holland.

Nguen, L., & Shilton, K. (2008). Tools for humanists. In D. Zorich (Ed.), *A Survey of Digital Humanities Centers in the United States*. Washington, D.C.: Council on Library and Information Resources.

Pascolini, D., & Mariotti, S. P. (2012). Global estimates of visual impairment: 2010. *British Journal of Ophtalmology*, 96, 614–619.

Poole, A., & Ball, L. J. (2005). Eye tracking in human-computer interaction and usability research: Current status and future prospects. In C. Ghaoui (Ed.), *Encyclopedia of Human-Computer Interaction*. Pennsylvania: Idea Group, Inc.

Potelle, H., & Rouet, J. F. (2003). Effects of content representation and readers' prior knowledge on the comprehension of hypertext. *International Journal of Human-Computer Studies*, 58(3), 327–345.

Power, C., & Jürgensen, H. (2010). Accessible presentation of information for people with visual disabilities. *Universal Access in the Information Society*, 9(2), 97–119.

Rayner, K. (2009). Eye movements and attention in reading, scene perception, and visual search. *Quarterly Journal of Experimental Psychology*, 62(8), 1457–1506.

Realpe-Muñoz, P., Collazos, C. A., Hurtabo, J., Granollers, T., Muñoz-Arteaga, J., & Velasco-Medina, J. (2018). Eye tracking-based behavioral study of users using e-voting systems. *Computer Standards & Interfaces*, 55(January), 182–195.

Recarte, M. A., Pérez, E., Conchillo, A., & Nunes, L. M. (2008). Mental workload and visual impairment: differences between pupil, blink, and subjective rating. *The Spanish Journal of Psychology*, 11(2), 374–85.

Robins, D., & Holmes, J. (2008). Aesthetics and credibility in web site design. *Information Processing & Management*, 44, 386–399.

Rosson, M. B., & Carroll, J. M. (2002). *Usability engineering: scenario-based development of human-computer interaction*. Morgan Kaufman.

Salvucci, D. D. (2001). Predicting the effects of in-car interface use on driver performance: an integrated model approach. *International Journal of Human-Computer Studies*, 55, 85–107.

Saparova, D., & Nolan, N. S. (2016). Evaluating the appropriateness of electronic information resources for learning. *Journal of the Medical Library Association*, 104(1).

Saracevic, T. (2000). Digital library evaluation: Toward an evolution of concepts. *Library Trends*, 49(3), 350–369.

Schidbach, S., & Rukzio, E. (2010). Investigating selection and reading performance on a mobile phone while walking. In *Proceedings of the 12th International Conference on Human Computer Interaction with Mobile Devices and Services*, 93–102.

Evaluation of digital tools

Schiessl, M., Duda, S., Thölke, A., & Fischer, R. (2003). Eye tracking and its application in usability and media research. *MMI-Interaktiv Journal*, 6, 41–50.

Schreibman, S., & Hanlon, A. M. (2010). Determining value for digital humanities tools: Report on a survey of tool developers. *Digital Humanities Quarterly*, 4(2).

Shneiderman, B. (2003). Promoting universal usability with multi-layer interface design. In *ACM SIGCAPH Computers and the Physically Handicapped*, 1–8. Vancouver, British Columbia, Canada.

Smith, M. N., Brown, S., Mandell, L., King, K., Lindermann, M., Krefting, R., & Wong, A. S. (2008). Feminist critical inquiry, knowledge building, digital humanities. In *Digital Humanities 2008*, 35–37. University of Oulu.

statista, "Smartphones worldwide installed base from 2008 to 2017 (in millions)." (2017). Retrieved from https://www.statista.com/statistics/371889/smartphone-worldwide-installed-base/

Steiner, C. M., Agosti, M., Sweetnam, M. S., Hillemann, E. C., Orio, N., Ponchia, C., … Conlan, O. (2014). Evaluating a digital humanities research environment: the CULTURA approach. *International Journal on Digital Libraries*, 15(1), 53–70.

Summit on Digital Tools for the Humanities. (2005).

Thoden, K., Stiller, J., Bulatovic, N., Meiners, H., & Boukhelifa, N. (2017). User-centered design practices in digital humanities – Experiences from DARIAH and CENDARI. *ABI Technik*, 37(1), 2–11.

Trace, C. B., & Karadkar, U. P. (2017). Information management in the humanities: Scholarly processes, tools, and the construction of personal collections. *JASIS&T*, 68, 491–507.

Tractinsky, N. (2004). Toward the study of aesthetics in information technology. In *Proceedings of the 25th international Conference on Information Systems*, 11–20.

Tracy, D. G. (2016). Assessing digital humanities tools: Use of Scalar at a research university. *Libraries and the Academy*, 16(1), 163–189.

Van Nimwegen, C., Van Oostendorp, H., Burgos, D., Koper, R., Nimwegen, C. Van, & Oostendorp, H. Van. (2006). Does an interface with less assistance provoke more thoughtful behavior? In *ICLS '06: Proceedings of the 7th international conference on Learning Sciences*, 785–791. International Society of the Learning Sciences.

Vanderheiden, G. (2000). Fundamental principles and priority setting for universal usability. *Proceedings on the 2000 Conference on Universal Usability* - CUU '00, 32–37.

Wang, J., Antonenko, P., Celepkolu, M., Jimenez, Y., Fieldman, E., & Fieldman, A. (2018). Exploring relationships between eye tracking and traditional usability testing data. *International Journal of Human-Computer Interaction*, 1–12.

Warwick, C., Fisher, C., Terras, M., Baker, M., Clarke, A., Fulford, M., … Rains, M. (2009). iTrench: a study of user reaction to the use of information technology in field archaeology. *Literary and Linguistic Computing*, 24(2), 211–223.

Warwick, C., Terras, M., Huntington, P., & Pappa, N. (2008). 'If you build it will they come? The LAIRAH study: quantifying the use of online resources in the arts and humanities through statistical analysis of user log data. *Literary and Linguistic Computing*, 23(1), 85–102.

Warwick, C., Terras, M., & Nyhan, J. (2012). *Digital humanities in practice.* (C. Warwick, M. Terras, & J. Nyhan, Eds.). London: Facet Publishing.

Williams, G. H. (2012). Disability, universal design, and the digital humanities. In *Debates in the Digital Humanities*, 202–212.

Wusteman, J. (2017). Usability testing of the Letters of 1916 Digital Edition. *Library Hi Tech*, 35(1), 120–143.

Yesilada, Y., Jay, C., Stevens, R., & Harper, S. (2008). Validating the use and role of visual elements of web pages in navigation with an eye-tracking study. In *Proceedings of the 17th international conference on World Wide Web*, 11–20. ACM.

Zhang, D., & Adipat, B. (2005). Challenges, methodologies, and issues in the sability testing of mobile applications. *International Journal of Human-Computer Interaction*, 18(3), 293–308.

Zundert, J. v. (2012). If you build it, will we come? Large scale digital infrastructures as a dead end for digital humanities. *Historical Social Research*, 37(3), 165–186.

25

WHAT ETHICS CAN OFFER THE DIGITAL HUMANITIES AND WHAT THE DIGITAL HUMANITIES CAN OFFER ETHICS

Nicholas Proferes

25.1 Introduction

Most digital-humanities scholars would likely agree that work in the discipline should be ethical. After all, who is going to defend *unethical* work? But there are numerous challenges moving from a fuzzy feel good buzzword to the brass-tacks of operationalizing ethics as part of one's practice. How should we navigate the gap between what we feel is morally correct and what institutional policies might require? How do we weigh particular values such as privacy, against other values that we might care about, such as sharing research and knowledge? And will our ethical frameworks always provide a clear-cut set of answers to the moral quandaries we might encounter?

This chapter explores the gray space ethical issues in the digital humanities frequently occupy. First, the chapter describes two models of how ethics is operationalized in the academy, ethics as *compliance* and ethics as *contemplation*. It traces some of the history of how we have arrived at ethics as compliance as a prevailing model. Next, this chapter argues that as novel application of information communication technologies (ICTs) and digital methods to humanities focused work surfaces new moral quandaries, digital humanities scholars cannot simply rely on ethics as compliance to guide their work. Dilemmas about the ethics of data collection, data use, and sharing both research outputs and the underlying data are creating challenges that necessitate ethics as contemplation; that is, moral reasoning that includes both a descriptive and normative component.

The chapter suggests that digital humanists, as part of their work, should consider engaging what Brey (2000, 2010) describes as *disclosive ethics*. Disclosive ethics helps identify morally opaque facets of practices that use digital technologies and surface values that are in tension. Disclosive ethics provides a toolkit useful when answers to moral dilemmas are not readily available in rules or guidebooks. Disclosive ethical analysis can help researchers interrogate their practices of data collection, data use, and data sharing that undergird digital humanities projects. It offers a way to develop best-practices rather than rely on policies that may have been written for research as it was done in a predigital age.

Rather than simply offering a prescriptive model of what certain ethical approaches can do for digital humanists, this chapter concludes by suggesting that the digital humanities offers a tremendous space from which to offer its own insights to conversations around ethics. The unique arrangement of interdisciplinarity, technologically-driven methods, partnerships that often span multiple parts of the university, and humanist ideals, brings with it the opportunity to explore and examine ethical questions that are new and novel in their configuration. It provides a chance for those working in the digital humanities to explore what our moral commitments are as researchers, and to foster dialogue among academics and the public.

25.2 What's the point of ethics?

Why should researchers care about ethics? What does attention to ethics help us achieve? The answer to this, in academia, is two-fold. Ethics, in one (ideal) sense, is about using our capacities for reason and judgment to achieve "the good life" vis-à-vis moral actions and/or personal character. This is what this chapter will refer to as ethics as *contemplation*. However, ethics as it is operationalized in the academy today is often about making certain that specific kinds of institutional rules are followed. This is what this chapter will refer to as *ethics as compliance*. A brief explanation of each follows.

Traditionally, ethics are about the systems of principles that we use to guide us in making moral evaluations. Sometimes, these moral frameworks are applied at the level of individual action. For example, a consequentialist framework will suggest that the "right" moral action is determined by the consequences of an action. Utilitarianism (a form of consequentialism) will suggest the moral action is the one that promotes the most "good" in its consequences or outcomes (for more on utilitarianism see: [de Lazari-Radek & Singer, 2017; Lyons & Lyons, 1965; Mill, 1895; Sen & Williams, 1982; Sinnott-Armstrong, 2003]). A deontological framework will suggest that actions cannot be justified by their consequences, that moral judgment should be based on the nature of the act itself, and that there are certain actions that are always morally forbidden. Depending on the particular deontological framework, what is morally forbidden may be based on what our duties are (for more on deontology, see: [Akrich, 1992; Alexander & Moore, 2007; Louden, 1996]). For example, we may have a duty not to use others as means to ends, but rather, always treat others as ends in themselves. And, rather than focusing on the consequences or intrinsic nature of a specific act, there are other moral frameworks that focus on the kinds of persons we ought to be. As part of the *Nicomachean Ethics and Politics*, Aristotle asked, "What is the highest good for human beings?" The answer, Aristotle suggests, is about the maximization of our faculties as human begins. We must contemplate, learn, and strive towards excellence in character. This version of ethics is known as virtue ethics (for more on virtue ethics, see: [Crisp & Slote, 1997; Hursthouse & Pettigrove, 2018; Swanton, 2003; Vallor, 2016]).

Across these different philosophical frameworks (and many others), ethics and moral evaluation is about considering and contemplation, using our capacities for reason and judgment to critically examine our actions and our character. However, in the academy today, the term "ethics" is also sometimes used as a shorthand for *compliance*. When individuals talk about having to submit paperwork to an Institutional Review Board, it is sometimes couched as doing the ethics portion of the project (as though ethics is a form that's filled out once and then forgotten). This version of ethics is ultimately more about mitigating risk (and liability), and ensuring compliance with laws which were passed to make sure researchers do not violate certain baseline rules regarding the treatment of others.

These laws and policies with which researchers must comply are still based on mixes of different philosophical frameworks. For example, in U.S. institutions, research does not have to present zero risk to research subjects, but rather, that risk must be properly disclosed, mitigated, and the ultimate benefits of the research must outweigh the risk. This logic is clearly tied to the utilitarian principle of maximizing benefit. Consent of the research is almost always a requirement for work that presents any substantial risk to the subject. This fits into certain deontological models of treating people as ends in themselves rather than means.

While some may read a dismissive tone in this account of ethics as compliance, this is not to say it isn't important; ethics as compliance has its place, it can help ensure that consent is respected, that persons in precarious positions who might be subject to burdensome requests are treated fairly, and that researchers have met some basic minimum thresholds for responsible conduct. However, as research ethics has become more about paperwork that shows conformity with policies and guidelines, considering and contemplation are sometimes put on the backburner. Yet, both versions of ethics are critically important. Ethics as contemplation suggests an ongoing practice of inwards reflection about our own actions and about what is right and just. Ethics as compliance is a kind of outward check, ensuring that we have not fallen out of line in our own thinking with the agreed upon standards of the society we live in. Ethics as compliance is a ground floor. Ethics as contemplation is an ideal we should continuously aspire towards.

Researchers working in all disciplines need both forms. However, as part of our academic upbringing, the amount of attention we have been trained to give varies. Because the digital humanities are an interdisciplinary space, this can lead to conflicts in terms of what researchers may think is necessary in a given situation. The next section of this chapter outlines some of the histories of research ethics as part of the antecedent disciplines that now make-up parts of the digital humanities.

25.3 Research ethics (A brief history)

Research ethics in the academy often focuses on collection, use, and potential sharing of human subjects data. In the United States, all institutions involved in research with human subjects that also receive federal funds are required to have an Institutional Review Board (IRB). Researchers who collect human subjects data without having gone through institutional review may be breaking the law and can jeopardize the university's ability to receive federal funds. As a result, U.S. universities typically pay close attention to guidelines about what does and does not constitute ethical research. While this chapter focuses much of its attention on ethics as compliance as it pertains to policies and laws that apply in the United States, researchers working in other contexts may have their own relative policies and laws to consider. For example, researchers receiving funding from the European Union are required to comply with relevant national, EU and international legislation, for example, the *Charter of Fundamental Rights of the European Union* and the *European Convention on Human Rights* (see [European Commission, 2019] for more).

The United States' *National Research Act* passed in 1974 created the *National Commission for the Protection of Human Subjects of Biomedical and Behavioral Research*. One of the charges to the Commission was to "identify the basic ethical principles that should underlie the conduct of biomedical and behavioral research involving human subjects and to develop guidelines which should be followed to assure that such research is conducted in accordance with those principles" (Department of Health, 2014). The commission produced a report, known as *The Belmont Report*, which summarizes the basic ethical principles identified by the Commission. Building on earlier global guidelines such as the *Nuremberg Code* and *The Declaration of Helsinki*, *The Belmont Report* lays out three guiding values for researchers: respect for persons, beneficence, and justice.

These principles (and their suggested operationalization) are derived from a mix of ethics frameworks rather than a singular analytical framework. *Respect for persons* is typically operationalized as protecting the autonomy of all people, treating them with courtesy and respect, and typically requiring their informed consent. This position draws heavily on deontological frameworks regarding the duties of researchers and not treating individuals as means to ends. *Beneficence* is typically operationalized as the weighing of risks against reward and making sure that risks to research subjects are minimized as much as possible. This is a position of balance that considers outcomes, fitting neatly into certain kinds of utilitarian logic. Lastly, *justice* is typically operationalized as making sure that the selection of research subjects is done in a fair and equitable manner, that research subjects aren't being exploited, and that there is a fair distribution of benefits for participation. Philosophical traditions of care ethics and justice as fairness both undergird this (Hoffmann & Jonas, 2016).

The *Belmont Report's* emphasis on respect for persons, beneficence, and justice comes from a disturbing global and U.S. history of researchers abusing human research subjects. During the horrors of World War Two, German physicians conducted medical experiments on concentration camp prisoners without their consent, killing or permanently injuring many (see, among others: [Caplan, 2012; Utley, 1992; Vollmann & Winau, 1996]). During the forty-year period between 1932 and 1972 the U.S. Public Health Service conducted the Tuskegee Syphilis experiments. In these experiments, black men were in some cases infected with the disease without any semblance of consent. Even though penicillin because available as a cure in the 1950s, the study continued until 1972 with many participants being denied appropriate medical treatment. In some cases, when subjects were diagnosed as having syphilis by other physicians, researchers actually *intervened* to prevent treatment. Many subjects died of the disease during the course of the study (Mandal, Acharya, & Parija, 2011). Painful medical experiments have also been conducted on prison inmates who have been unable to meaningful opt-out (Hornblum, 2013). These incidents are among dozens of other abuses of research subjects over the course of the past century (for more on this see, among others: [Hornblum, Newman, & Dober, 2013; Lederer & Davis, 1995; Mabrey, 2005; Stein, 2010; Washington, 2006; Whitaker, 2001]).

In the United States, the *Belmont Report* has served as a prominent guide for years. It has been further refined in its implementation through the adoption of the Federal "Common Rule" (Department of Health and Human Services, 2018), a federal policy regarding human subjects protection that applies to 17 federal agencies and offices, many of whom offer grants for which grantees must also comply. These research guidelines were also written in relationship to data collection, use, and sharing practices as they existed at an earlier point in time, and often in relation to practices in biomedical research. The ability to observe research subjects at a distance, to intervene without revealing one's self as a researcher, and to collect and share large swathes of data in seconds was far more curtailed than it is today. As a result, today's models of compliance often govern practices not as common to the digital humanities. Research and research methodologies that fall outside of this scope often do not come under the scrutiny of ethics review boards. For example, in the United States, the use of publicly available data from social media platforms may not meet the threshold criteria of "research involving human subjects," and thus, an IRB may exempt these kinds of studies from ongoing compliance review and may waive informed consent practices. As a result of this categorization, most researchers who collect this kind of content do not get consent from users. However, projects using publicly available data from social media sites do not lack ethical dimensions. They just fall out of the purview of the *compliance* side of ethics.

The humanities have often been exempted from certain kinds of institutional ethics oversight because the projects are often not considered to be involving human subjects data. Yet, there is no shortage of ethical issues that have cropped up in the field that require deep contemplation and reflection (Stenmark et al., 2010). To give just one example, historians often build archives select, preserve, and make available primary sources that document the activities of institutions, communities, and individuals. However, some archives, such as many Native American, First Nation, and Aboriginal community archives held at universities, house materials which were collected without the community's original consent. There is pressing ethical question about what obligations and duties stewards of these collections have, and whether or not to continue to make that content accessible if asked not to. Fundamentally, the question here is about respect for persons and justice. Recently, a group of nineteen Native American and non-Native American archivists, librarians, museum curators, historians, anthropologists, and representatives from fifteen Native American, First Nation, and Aboriginal communities met to discuss these kinds of questions. Ultimately, this group developed a set of ethically informed best professional practices for culturally responsive care and use of archival material held by non-tribal organizations. This set of practices has since been adopted and endorsed by the Society of American Archivists (Underhill, 2006). This was not simply a matter of making sure the actions fit within the ethics compliance checkboxes, but rather a matter of arriving at informed decisions and practices through contemplative ethics.

Thankfully, many (but certainly not all) programs of humanist study have prepared students in moral reasoning as part of their education and training. However, this is not necessarily true for all the fields that contribute and participate in the digital humanities. The field of computer science, which the digital humanities frequently integrates methodologies, research designs, and processes from, does not have the same length of experience in engagement with ethics, either as compliance or as contemplative practice. This is not to say that computer scientists don't think about ethics. Many certainly do. However, as a field, computer science does not have the same length of experience in engaging this as part of curricula, and at times, has struggled with the integration of ethics training as part of pedagogy (for more on early pushes to integrate ethics training more robustly in computer science training, see: [Miller, 1988]).

Research in computer science has frequently been considered exempt from ethics as compliance for many of the same reasons as work in the traditional humanities: it is often not considered to involve human subjects or human subjects data. Yet, computer scientists who build technologies have the chance to have a tremendous impact on the lives of individuals, as the design of technologies bears "directly and systematically on the realization, or suppression, of particular configurations of social, ethical, and political values" (Flanagan, Howe, & Nissenbaum, 2005). For example, while some may argue that search engine algorithms are inherently unbiased, work by scholars such as Goldman (2005); Introna and Nissenbaum (2000); Kay, Matuszek, and Munson (2015); Noble (2018); and Zimmer (2009) has challenged this assumption, demonstrating various ways in which search engines results negatively impact different communities. This can include search results that reinforce gendered stereotypes, highly sexualized search results for racial search terms, and results that reinforce racist ideologies, among many other morally-laden problems.

Part of the challenge facing the digital humanities in relation to ethics comes from antecedent disciplines, such as the humanities and computer science, having conflicting histories with and approaches to training researchers to confront ethical dimensions of their work. Adding to the complication, the meshing of different approaches to research can result in entirely new ethical questions. These novel problems may require more than ethics as compliance. They require ethics as contemplation.

25.4 The challenge of ethics in DH

The digital humanities raise a host of ethical and moral questions. For reasons of space, this chapter will focus on particular parts of the research process where these crop up: data collection, data use, and data sharing. Each of these areas is deserving of far deeper attention than can possibly be given in this chapter. Instead, this chapter will instead briefly highlight outstanding moral questions and suggest why they call for a heightened practice of ethics as contemplation.

25.4.1 Data collection

Building data collections in the digital humanities typically involves the digitization of existing physical materials or aggregation and processing of "born digital" content (such as through web-archiving) (de Klerk & Serrao, 2018). There are several moral questions that individuals involved with data collection might face. For example, can data collection cause privacy concerns? What should a researcher do if the originating material suddenly becomes unavailable? And what should a researcher do if asked to remove content from a collection? Each of these questions is explored further below.

Broadly defined, privacy is the "right to be let alone" (Warren & Brandeis, 1890). In the case of digitization, it is possible that if a collection contains artifacts such as personal letters, and the individual who wrote them is living, or persons mentioned in the letters are living, that the digitalization could bring with it privacy concerns. While physical materials may have still been accessible within the context of the archive, digitization can make that content subsequentially more discoverable, easier to copy, and easier to transmit. This can bring with it a loss of what some privacy scholars have called "privacy via obscurity" (Zimmer & Hoffmann, 2011). And while it may seem as though aggregating "born digital content," such as social media posts that are already available on the web, might not carry with it the possibility of privacy violations, that is not necessarily the case. For example, while many Twitter users are likely aware that the platform is "public," a study by Fiesler and Proferes (2018) found that Twitter users were broadly unaware of the fact that researchers use their data, and a study by Proferes (2017) found many users were unaware of the fact that (at the time of the study) the Library of Congress archived tweets. Further, while some users may realize content is "public" they may still unintentionally post sensitive information, such as GPS information, as a result of default settings they are unaware of.

For projects that archive born-digital content, there is the question of what to do when the original work disappears. One's ethical obligations could depend on whether or not the author intended to delete the content. Imagine a project that leverages archives of social media posts. Users may choose to delete their original posts because they later regret posting the content, because it could contain embarrassing or sensitive data, or because they just want to exercise control over their data (Wang et al., 2011). Researchers may feel they have ethical obligations to respect the decisions made by users and delete that content from their own archives. In fact, researchers could be breaking some social media companies' Terms of Service depending on whether or not they circulate previously deleted data (Addady, 2016). At the same time, there are important histories that can be lost if the researchers decides to delete the information. In studying the crisis response on Twitter in relation to #JeSuisCharlie, researcher Ed Summers found, "1.1 million tweets out of the 13.9 million tweet dataset have been deleted" (Summers, 2015). Losing ten percent of the data could be a significant blow to those trying to understand the event. Here, careful reflection on the ethical values of the project are important. Researchers must ask what the forms of harm are that could come from removing the content from the collection versus the forms of harm resulting from an incomplete account, and, depending on the choice made, how can the researcher best mitigate these potential harms.

Aggregation itself also has ethical import. For example, let's imagine an archive of Facebook posts that we describe as examples of social media posts from individuals that we have identified, because of the sentiment in their word choice, as having depression. What are the ethical implications of aggregating such a collection and labeling it as such? Even though such a collection may not count as "human subjects data" under the model of ethics as *compliance*, there are ethical stakes in play. Researchers carry a tremendous power in their ability to classify and label, and these actions carry potential consequences for the data subjects they represent.

Researchers should also consider to what degree threats to privacy and autonomy created by data collection are or are not evenly distributed, and whether the potential harms are fair for groups that have already been historically overburdened. For example, Christen (2011) writes, "While digital technologies allow for items to be repatriated quickly, circulated widely, and annotated endlessly, these same technologies pose challenges to some indigenous communities who wish to add their expert voices to public collections and also maintain some traditional cultural protocols for the viewing, circulation, and reproduction of some materials" (p. 185). Digital humanities scholars will benefit from examining codes of ethics outside of their own disciplines as part of their ethics practice. For example, in this circumstance, the Society for American Archivists have developed protocols for "engaging in culturally responsive care of Native American archival material and in providing culturally appropriate service to communities" (Punzalan, as quoted in Agarwal, 2018) which can help researchers in their contemplative efforts.

Finally, there is an important question about what the researchers' obligations are if an individual whose information is contained in such a collection contacts the researcher and asks the have the content removed. The researcher may not have any obligations under the strict model of *ethics as compliance*, but that does not necessarily absolve them from contemplating their other ethical duties and obligations. For example, they may consider whether or not there is a greater benefit to the whole of society if individuals are allowed to have about themselves removed entirely, or to have them embargoed for some period of time. They might consider what kinds of duties they have, whether or not they are treating individuals as a means to end, or treating individuals as ends in themselves.

Nicholas Proferes

25.4.2 Data use

Although data may have been collected in an ethical manner, that does not mean that all subsequent uses of a particular dataset will be ethical. For example, a study by Wang and Kosinski (2017) used training data collected from publicly available dating profiles to develop an algorithm meant to detect someone's sexual orientation based on a photograph. But LGBTQ advocacy groups and privacy organizations called into question the ethics of such a project because of its "clear lack of representation, racial bias and reducing the sexuality spectrum to a binary" (Mezzofiore, 2017). It is important for researchers to contemplate the intentions creators have for content in relation to how the data is being used in a particular project. This is not to say researchers cannot use data in ways users didn't imagine, but rather, researchers need to actively consider the moral dimensions of doing so.

There are also important questions researchers must consider in relation to the ownership of content. Universities often care about protecting themselves from liability should someone attempt to sue for infringing uses of intellectual materials, and so intellectual property laws can tend to drive conversations about property rights and ethics towards a compliance-side approach. However, digital humanities projects can add new wrinkles that call for revisiting the philosophical tradition undergirding why we protect intellectual property.

Intellectual property rights typically help protect "creations of the mind," that is, inventions, literary and artistic works, symbols, names, images, and designs. Creators are given a certain set of rights regarding how their creations may be used. In order to bestow these rights, we use legal frameworks to compensate creators for their efforts and protect their creations, and give the creators controls on who can make copies, distribute, perform, adapt of a particular creation of the mind. There are three main philosophical foundations that underpin our concepts of intellectual property. In the Anglo-American tradition, three approaches dominate: labor theory, utilitarian theory, and personality theory.

The labor theory of property traces its origins to the 17th century philosopher John Locke. Under this framework, individuals are conceived of as having a natural right of self-ownership, and thus, own the products of their labor. In this view, individuals are provided property rights for the products that result from their labor, their "blood and sweat." If we produce books through our labor, we have a natural right to own what we produce.

The idea behind utilitarian approaches is that the goal of society should be to preserve what is sometimes referred to as the "natural incentive" to labor found in nature, that is, when people get hungry they have to work to find food. This situation created a natural feedback loop between subsistence and labor. Many utilitarian thinkers believe we need to grant property rights in order to preserve this loop (labor meaningfully and get rewarded) in order to ensure that a sufficient amount of goods and services are produced to benefit the entire society. The reasoning is that, if people do not have an incentive to produce (such as the incentive to gain property rights), then they will not produce, and society will suffer as a result. Property rights are thus granted to encourage creators and inventors to bring forth their artistic works and inventions into the marketplace.

Personality theory is loosely rooted in the continental philosophical tradition, as represented by the work of Hegel. On this account, intellectual works are said to be an expression and extension of the creator's personality, and, as a result, the creator should have the right to dictate how his or her works are used. This view is found more readily in continental European traditions. Intellectual property is an expression of the creator's personality, thus she should have the ability to dictate how her works are used.

At the same time, the authors' rights to their creation are balanced against public rights of fair-use. In the U.S., fair-use exceptions are granted for work for criticism, for the purposes of news reporting, for the purposes of teaching, scholarship, or research. However, making the determination if something is a fair use or not gets complicated. Courts typically look at four factors, the purpose and character of the use, the nature of the copyrighted work, the amount and substantiality of piece used compared to work as a whole and the effect of use on potential market for or value of the work.

An important ethical consideration as part of any digital humanities project is the extent to which the authors' rights are being appropriately balanced against the fair-use rights of the researchers. While it may be tempting to claim everything we do is fair-use, researchers should contemplate whether the philosophical goals of intellectual property rights are being met. Namely, to what extent is the creator being expropriated from their labor, to what extent would this aggregation or digitization prevent the author from bringing additional intellectual goods that would benefit society to the marketplace of ideas, and to what extent does a project violate the integrity of a particular work, potentially confounding the authors' moral rights.

25.4.3 Data sharing

Part of the reason that digital humanities projects are often so exciting is because of the possibilities they offer for sharing collections of data and research outputs. Yet, there are many ethical dimensions to data sharing that need to be considered. Choosing whether to share raw datasets, where to publish, and whether to share outputs with specific communities are all choices with ethical dimensions.

Some fields, such as social psychology, have been struggling with a so-called crisis of replicability (Earp & Trafimow, 2015). This crisis has been precipitated by the realization within the academic community that the findings from many studies have been difficult, and in some cases, impossible to replicate. This throws into question the theory that stems from these studies and raises the possibility that the knowledge produced by this work is on, at best, a shaky foundation. Sharing raw datasets is one way of helping address this problem. It allows findings to more easily be peer-reviewed and double-checked. While not all digital humanities projects strive towards the goal of scientific reproducibility, data-sharing as a practice may be situationally important, as it upholds ethical commitments the researcher may have towards to progress of knowledge and human flourishing.

In practice, the brass-tacks of data sharing is often governed under ethics as compliance. For example, human subjects data often cannot be shared without consent from users. However, even when dealing with content that's not "human subjects data," there can be ethical dimensions at play that call for more than just compliance. Ethical contemplation regarding data sharing should also consider the potential for harm. Such a situation occurred to the *Documenting the Now* project, which chronicles and archives the social media responses around significant social events. The project had amassed a collection of tweets, collected during the community responses to the police shooting of Michael Brown Jr. in Ferguson, Missouri. Shortly after announcing they had collected this data, the project team received a request to share the content from a data-mining company. When they pulled up the firm's website, "they read that its clients included the Department of Defense and, ominously, 'the intelligence community'" (Caplan-Bricker, 2018). The researchers on the team contemplated the implications of sharing the data, ultimately deciding against it. The question was inherently ethical in nature, but not one clearly covered under the model of ethics as compliance.

Research publications are another important consideration. Anyone who works in academia has likely heard of the so called serials crisis: the cost of journal subscriptions has been increasing exponentially, putting a dire strain on library budgets (McGuigan, 2004). Consolidation in the publisher market, commercial publishers taking over journals previously housed by scholarly societies, and increasing commercial profits have all contributed to this situation. In response to this crisis, some universities have begun to encourage "faculty members to make their research freely available through open access journals and to resign from publications that keep articles behind paywalls" (Sample, 2012). Digital humanities scholars considering publication venues for their projects may find it important to consider such contextual factors when making their decisions. They may benefit from asking whether it is ethically permissible for research results from public universities and potentially funded through public dollars to be pay-walled off.

In addition to considerations about publishing venue, for researchers who are working with collections of data about people, an important consideration is sharing research outputs with those individuals and communities themselves. Sharing outputs with research subjects can be a fruitful way to share knowledge in a more equitable manner and can help build and maintain relationships. But, this is not to say that researchers *must* always share outputs, particularly if it creates the possibility that the researchers themselves could face harm as a result. For example, researchers Suomela, Chee, Berendt, and Rockwell (2019) built a collection of content from groups dedicated to online harassment that they describe as "toxic material." Embracing a care ethics approach, the team actively contemplated whether or not it was in their interests to share research outputs with this community, ultimately deciding to post a subset of their data to a publicly available data repository, but not necessarily take the full work to the community. They explained, "We did this because we believe in openness as a general principle and in attempting to develop dialogue with people who may have views that are different from our own" (p. 17). Deciding that sharing some data, but not all data, with this community appeared a way to partially satisfy a competing set of values.

25.5 Disclosive ethics

When we look at the breadth of ethical questions associated with work in the digital humanities, it may seem surprising how few of them are governed by *ethics as compliance*, a predominant mode of ethics in the academy. Instead, we may realize the need to use our capacities for ethics as contemplation to work through many of these dilemmas. While there are existing philosophical frameworks that can suggest how we ought to behave in a given situation once we properly understand a particular problem, projects in the digital humanities projects can evade easy solutions precisely because they are novel. Complicating matters even more, digital humanities projects may rely on the use of tools and technologies which may have embedded values in themselves, which may also need to be interrogated. Thus, while the chapter has already made an argument in favor of the expanded practice of moral contemplation in relation to digital humanities projects, it now suggests a multi-stage process to help guide that contemplation based on the work of Philip Brey (2000, 2010).

Brey argues for the importance of a practice he identifies as "disclosive ethics." He posits that many practices in relation to computer technology are already widely recognized in society as morally controversial. For example, systems that violate intellectual property in an unjust manner can be considered morally controversial. Brey argues practices such as these are "morally transparent" because "the practice is known and it is roughly understood what moral values are at stake in relation to it." (2010, p. 51). However, in many novel uses of technology, the moral issues that are involved "may not be sufficiently recognized" (2010, p. 51). This is because the practices themselves are new, or because "they are well-known but not recognized as morally charged because they have a false appearance of moral neutrality" (2010, p. 51). Brey refers to these as *morally opaque*, meaning that it is not generally understood that the practice raises ethical questions or what these questions may be.

Disclosive ethics is a methodology that can help identify morally opaque practices, and once properly identified, help the researcher reflect on these features from a moral perspective. The method is descriptive rather than normative. Once the morally opaque features of a practice have been identified, then the researcher moves on to the application of normative frameworks, such as utilitarianism, deonotology, virtue ethics, etc.

Brey's vision of disclosive ethics as a method requires three levels of analysis: the disclosure level, the theoretical level, and the application level. At the disclosure level, morally opaque practices or features of a technical system are considered from a values-driven perspective. For example, stemming from the suggestions of the *Belmont Report*, a researcher may choose to think about their project from the perspective of respect for persons, beneficence, and justice. It is critical for the researcher to identify a plurality of values

What ethics can offer the DH

to consider, and this is often best done in consultation with a wide variety of other people, including, if possible, "ethicists, computer scientists and social scientists" (Brey, 2010, p. 53). The researcher should then describe how their project promotes or demotes the relevant value in relation to different stakeholders. Stakeholders may include not just persons whose data appears in the archive, but also should include relevant communities that may be impacted by the project; researchers and partners on the projects, potentially including librarians, professional staff, and student workers; and institutional actors such as the local ethics review boards. The researcher should also detail the exact means by which these values are realized, carefully considering any technological mechanisms by which this happens. As Brey points out, in the first stage, "very little moral theory is introduced into the analysis, and only a coarse definition of the value in question is used that can be refined later" (2010, p. 52).

The second level of analysis is the theoretical level. At this level, the researcher must ask if existing moral theory has "adequately theorized these values." For example, Brey writes, "Privacy… is now recognized by many computer ethicists as requiring more attention than it has previously received in moral theory. In part, this is due to reconceptualizations of the private and public sphere, brought about by the use of computer technology, which has resulted in inadequacies in existing moral theory about privacy" (2010, p. 52). Here, the researcher should also identify any conflicts between the values and between stakeholders. In digital humanities projects, researchers are likely to encounter conflicts. For example, in the *Documenting the Now* example, there was a conflict between the value of sharing knowledge (through data) and the potential harms that could come to individuals whose data was being collected. In the online harassment community study, the researchers identified a conflict between the potential for harm to the researchers themselves and the value of sharing research outputs with a studied community. At this point in the process, the researcher's job is not to solve the problem, but merely to describe the tensions and gaps as thoroughly as possible.

Lastly, in the application level, moral theory is applied to analyses. For example, Brey writes, "the question of what actions governments should take in helping citizens have access to computers may be answered by applying Rawls's principles of justice" (p. 52). It is in the application level is where the competing values are actually balanced against each other in relationship to normative moral theory. Balancing values is not easy and requires careful reasoning, deliberation, and where possible, working through questions with others. As such, a critical component of this process is to document the reasoning itself. This is particularly important because, in the event of a dearth of existing work to guide the researcher, the researcher's decisions and thought-processes may be critical to other researchers who may someday face similar questions. Documenting these decisions creates a kind of ethics provenance and can be used to ultimately develop best practices within a particular research area.

Conclusion

Rather than simply offering a prescriptive model of how digital humanists can benefit from the use of disclosive ethics, this chapter concludes by suggesting that the digital humanities offers a tremendous space from which to offer its own insights to conversations around ethics. Despite the challenges of doing ethics in relation to digital humanities project, it is the interdisciplinary of the field that carries the incredible potential making contributions to accepted ethical practice. The application of disclosive ethics requires "considerable knowledge of the technological aspects of the system or practice that is studied and may also require expertise in social science for the analysis of the way in which the functioning of systems is dependent on human actions, rules and institutions" (2010, p. 53). Digital humanists have the expert knowledge and position within the academy to posit new, ethically driven approaches to doing research in a still inchoate space.

The unique arrangement of interdisciplinarity, technologically-driven methods, partnerships that often span multiple parts of the university, and humanist ideals, brings with it the opportunity to explore and examine ethical questions that are new and novel in their configuration. In their work, digital humanists can explore what our moral commitments ought to be as researchers, and to foster dialogue among our fellow academics and the public. Ethics, as part of humanist investigation, should be about not just compliance, but reflection, using our capacities for reason about our actions and the impacts that they may have on others, and attempting to act with moral wisdom. Digital humanists can support moving research beyond the ground floor of ethics as compliance, bringing with them a unique vision of the good life.

References

Addady, M. (2016). Twitter Just Shut Down a Website Archiving Users' Deleted Tweets. *Fortune*. Retrieved April 29, 2019, from Fortune website: http://fortune.com/2016/07/11/deleted-tweets/

Agarwal, K. (2018). A Way Forward. *American Historical Association*. Retrieved April 29, 2019, from Historians.org website: https://www.historians.org/publications-and-directories/perspectives-on-history/october-2018/a-way-forward-the-society-of-american-archivists-endorses-protocols-for-native-american-materials

Akrich, M. (1992). *The de-scription of technical objects* (W. Bijker & J. Law, Eds.). Cambridge, MA: MIT Press.

Alexander, L., & Moore, M. (2007). Deontological Ethics. *The Stanford Encyclopedia of Philosophy* (Winter 2016 Edition), Edward N. Zalta (Ed.), Retrieved from https://stanford.library.sydney.edu.au/archives/win2015/entries/ethics-deontological/

Brey, P. (2000). Disclosive computer ethics. *ACM SIGCAS Computers and Society, 30*(4), 10–16.

Brey, P. (2010). Values in technology and disclosive computer ethics. In L. Floridi (Ed.), *The Cambridge Handbook of Information and Computer Ethics* (pp. 41–58), Cambridge, United Kingdom: Cambridge University Press. https://doi.org/10.1017/CBO9780511845239.004

Caplan, A. L. (2012). *When medicine went mad: Bioethics and the Holocaust.* Springer Science & Business Media.

Caplan-Bricker, N. (2018, December). Preservation Acts. *Harper's Magazine*. Retrieved from https://harpers.org/archive/2018/12/preservation-acts-archiving-twitter-social-media-movements/

Christen, K. (2011). Opening Archives: Respectful Repatriation. *The American Archivist, 74*(1), 185–210. https://doi.org/10.17723/aarc.74.1.4233nv6nv6428521

Crisp, R., & Slote, M. (1997). *Virtue ethics* (Vol. 10). Oxford readings in Philosophy.

de Klerk, T., & Serrao, J. (2018). Ethics in Archives: Decisions in Digital Archiving. *North Carolina State University Libraries*. Retrieved April 24, 2019, from NC State University Libraries website: https://www.lib.ncsu.edu/news/special-collections/ethics-in-archives%3A-decisions-in-digital-archiving

de Lazari-Radek, K., & Singer, P. (2017). *Utilitarianism: A very short introduction.* Oxford University Press.

Department of Health and Human Services. (2018). Subpart A of 45 CFR Part 46: Basic HHS Policy for Protection of Human Subjects [Text]. Retrieved April 23, 2019, from HHS.gov website: https://www.hhs.gov/ohrp/sites/default/files/revised-common-rule-reg-text-unofficial-2018-requirements.pdf

Department of Health, Education, and Welfare. (2014). The Belmont Report. Ethical principles and guidelines for the protection of human subjects of research. *The Journal of the American College of Dentists, 81*(3), 4.

Earp, B. D., & Trafimow, D. (2015). Replication, falsification, and the crisis of confidence in social psychology. *Frontiers in Psychology, 6*, 621.

European Commission. (2019). Science with and for Society—Research and Innovation. Retrieved from http://ec.europa.eu/research/swafs/index.cfm?pg=policy&lib=ethics

Fiesler, C., & Proferes, N. (2018). "Participant" perceptions of Twitter research ethics. *Social Media+ Society, 4*(1).

Flanagan, M., Howe, D., & Nissenbaum, H. (2005). Values at play: Design tradeoffs in socially-oriented game design. *Conference on Human Factors in Computing Systems*, 751–760.

Goldman, E. (2005). Search engine bias and the demise of search engine utopianism. *Yale JL & Tech., 8*, 188.

Hoffmann, A. L., & Jonas, A. (2016). Recasting justice for Internet and online industry research ethics. *Internet Research Ethics for the Social Age: New Cases and Challenges*. M. Zimmer and K. Kinder-Kuranda *(Eds.), Bern, Switzerland: Peter Lang*.

Hornblum, A. M. (2013). *Acres of skin: Human experiments at Holmesburg prison.* Routledge.

Hornblum, A. M., Newman, J. L., & Dober, G. J. (2013). *Against their will: The secret history of medical experimentation on children in cold war America.* Macmillan.

Hursthouse, R., & Pettigrove, G. (2018). Virtue ethics. In E. N. Zalta (Ed.), *The Stanford Encyclopedia of Philosophy* (Winter 2018). Retrieved from https://plato.stanford.edu/archives/win2018/entries/ethics-virtue/

Introna, L., & Nissenbaum, H. (2000). Shaping the web: Why the politics of sEngines matters. *The Information Society, 16*(3), 169–185.

Kay, M., Matuszek, C., & Munson, S. A. (2015). Unequal representation and gender stereotypes in image search results for occupations. *Proceedings of the 33rd Annual ACM Conference on Human Factors in Computing Systems*, 3819–3828. ACM.

Lederer, S., & Davis, A. B. (1995). Subjected to science: human experimentation in America before the Second World War. *History: Reviews of New Books, 24*(1), 13–13.

Louden, R. B. (1996). Toward a genealogy of 'deontology'. *Journal of the History of Philosophy, 34*(4), 571–592

Lyons, L., & Lyons, D. (1965). *Forms and limits of utilitarianism.* Oxford: Clarendon Press.

Mabrey, V. (2005). A Dark Chapter In Medical History. *CBS News.* Retrieved April 23, 2019, from https://www.cbsnews.com/news/a-dark-chapter-in-medical-history-09-02-2005/

Mandal, J., Acharya, S., & Parija, S. C. (2011). Ethics in human research. *Tropical Parasitology, 1*(1), 2–3. https://doi.org/10.4103/2229-5070.

McGuigan, G. S. (2004). Publishing perils in academe: The serials crisis and the economics of the academic journal publishing industry. *Journal of Business & Finance Librarianship, 10*(1), 13–26.

Mezzofiore, G. (2017). Everything that's wrong with that study which used AI to "identify sexual orientation." *Mashable.* Retrieved May 1, 2019, from Mashable website: https://mashable.com/2017/09/11/artificial-intelligence-ai-lgbtq-gay-straight/

Mill, J. S. (1895). *Utilitarianism.* Longmans, Green and Company, London, England.

Miller, K. (1988). Integrating computer ethics into the computer science curriculum. *Computer Science Education, 1*(1), 37–52. https://doi.org/10.1080/0899340880010104

Noble, S. U. (2018). *Algorithms of oppression: How search engines reinforce racism.* NYU Press.

Proferes, N. (2017). Information flow solipsism in an exploratory study of beliefs About Twitter. *Social Media + Society, 3*(1). https://doi.org/10.1177/2056305117698493

Sample, I. (2012, April 24). Harvard University says it can't afford journal publishers' prices. *The Guardian.* Retrieved from http://www.theguardian.com/science/2012/apr/24/harvard-university-journal-publishers-prices

Sen, A., & Williams, B. (1982). *Utilitarianism and beyond.* Cambridge University Press.

Sinnott-Armstrong, W. (2003). *Consequentialism. The Stanford Encyclopedia of Philosophy* (Winter 2015 Edition), Edward N. Zalta (ed.) Retrieved from https://stanford.library.sydney.edu.au/archives/win2015/entries/consequentialism/

Stein, R. (2010). U.S. apologizes for newly revealed syphilis experiments done in Guatemala. *Washington Post.* Retrieved from http://www.washingtonpost.com/wp-dyn/content/article/2010/10/01/AR2010100104457.html

Stenmark, C. K., Antes, A. L., Martin, L. E., Bagdasarov, Z., Johnson, J. F., Devenport, L. D., & Mumford, M. D. (2010). Ethics in the humanities: Findings from focus groups. *Journal of Academic Ethics, 8*(4), 285–300. https://doi.org/10.1007/s10805-010-9120-1

Summers, E. (2015). Tweets and Deletes. *Medium.* Retrieved April 29, 2019, from On Archivy website: https://medium.com/on-archivy/tweets-and-deletes-727ed74f84ed

Suomela, T., Chee, F., Berendt, B., & Rockwell, G. (2019). Applying an ethics of care to internet research: Gamergate and digital humanities. *Digital Studies/Le Champ Numérique, 9*(1), 4. https://doi.org/10.16995/dscn.302

Swanton, C. (2003). *Virtue ethics: A pluralistic view.* Clarendon Press, Oxford, United Kingdom.

Underhill, K. J. (2006). Protocols for Native American archival materials. *RBM: A Journal of Rare Books, Manuscripts, and Cultural Heritage, 7*(2), 134–145.

Utley, G. J. A. E. R. (1992). *The Nazi doctors and the Nuremberg Code: Human rights in human experimentation: human rights in human experimentation.* Oxford University Press, USA.

Vallor, S. (2016). *Technology and the virtues: A philosophical guide to a future worth wanting.* Oxford University Press.

Vollmann, J., & Winau, R. (1996). Informed consent in human experimentation before the Nuremberg code. *Bmj, 313*(7070), 1445–1447.

Wang, Yang, Norcie, G., Komanduri, S., Acquisti, A., Leon, P. G., & Cranor, L. F. (2011). "I Regretted the Minute I Pressed Share": A qualitative study of regrets on Facebook. *Proceedings of the Seventh Symposium on Usable Privacy and Security*, 10:1–10:16. https://doi.org/10.1145/2078827.2078841

Wang, Yilun, & Kosinski, M. (2017). Deep neural networks are more accurate than humans at detecting sexual orientation from facial images. *Journal of Personality and Social Psychology, 114*(2), 246.

Warren, S., & Brandeis, L. (1890). The right to privacy. *Harvard Law Review, 4*, 193–200.

Washington, H. A. (2006). *Medical apartheid: The dark history of medical experimentation on Black Americans from colonial times to the present.* Doubleday Books.

Whitaker, R. (2001). *Mad in America: Bad science, bad medicine, and the enduring mistreatment of the mentally ill.* Basic Books, New York.

Zimmer, M. (2009). Web search studies: Multidisciplinary perspectives on web search engines. In *International Handbook of Internet Research* (pp. 507–521). Springer.

Zimmer, M., & Hoffmann, A. (2011). *Privacy, context, and oversharing: Reputational challenges in a Web 2.0 world* (H. Masum & M. Tovey, Eds.). Cambridge, MA: MIT Press.

26

INTELLECTUAL PROPERTY GUIDELINES FOR THE DIGITAL HUMANITIES

Kenneth Haggerty

26.1 Intellectual property terms and concepts

As the world has become more globalized, creative activity often extends across national borders. Consequently, the World Intellectual Property Organization (WIPO) was created in 1967 and has since become part of the United Nations system, in order "to lead the development of a balanced and effective international intellectual property (IP) system that enables innovation and creativity for the benefit of all" (Inside WIPO, n.d.). Yet, despite the existence of an international organization to help form intellectual property treaties and conventions, not all copyright laws are the same and creators need to be aware of the existing copyright laws in the country where they are attempting to publish. WIPO defines intellectual property as "creations of the mind, such as inventions; literary and artistic works; designs; and symbols, names and images used in commerce" (WIPO: What is Intellectual Property, n.d.). Individuals in the digital humanities have responsibilities that range from creating digitized resources to preserving valuable copyrighted materials. Thus, it is invaluable that individuals in the digital humanities have a deep understanding of intellectual property to recognize their rights as creators and reusers of content. There are three primary types of intellectual property: copyright, patents, and trademarks. Given that practitioners in the digital humanities are the creators of new content as well as the reusers of existing materials, in this chapter I will focus solely on copyright. Patents refer to inventions and trademarks refer to brand names, which are typically not applicable in the digital humanities.

26.1.1 Copyright

Although copyright has changed significantly over the past three centuries, the purpose of copyright remains the same as in 1710 when the Statute of Anne was passed by the Parliament in Great Britain. Copyright is a legal right granted to the creators of works of authorship. According to Article 1, Section 8 of the U.S. Constitution, the intention of copyright law in the United States is to promote the advancement of knowledge by "securing for limited Times to Authors and Inventors the exclusive Right to their respective Writings and Discoveries" (U.S. Const. art. I, § 8.). In Europe, copyright law is for the most part standardized between nations of the European Union and is based on the copyright directives that are

Intellectual property guidelines

meant to unify copyright laws and policies. According to WIPO (2016), the following economic rights are protected:

- reproduction of the work in various forms, such as printed publications or sound recordings;
- distribution of copies of the work;
- public performance of the work;
- broadcasting or other communication of the work to the public;
- translation of the work into other languages; and
- adaptation of the work, such as turning a novel into a screenplay.

In addition, the following moral rights are protected:

- the right to claim authorship of a work (sometimes called the right of paternity or the right of attribution);
- the right to object to any distortion or modification of a work, or other derogatory action in relation to a work, which would be prejudicial to the author's honor or reputation (sometimes called the right of integrity).

These rights are similar to rights granted to authors in the United States, which include the exclusive right to reproduce their copyrighted work, prepare derivative works, distribute copies to the public, perform their copyrighted work, display the copyrighted work publicly and for sound recordings, and perform their work "by means of a digital audio transmission" (17 U.S.C. § 106). However, there are limitations on the creator's exclusive rights, most notably fair use/fair dealing.

26.1.2 Fair use/fair dealing

Section 107 of the United States Code states that "fair use of a copyrighted work for designated purposes such as "criticism, comment, news report, teaching (including multiple copies for classroom use), scholarship, or research, is not an infringement of copyright" (17 U.S.C. § 107). The Copyright Act of 1976 defines four factors used to determine whether the use of a copyrighted work is fair use:

1. The purpose and character of the use, including whether such use is of commercial nature or is for nonprofit educational purpose;
2. The nature of the copyrighted work;
3. The amount and substantiality of the portion used in relation to the copyrighted work as a whole; and
4. The effect of the use upon the potential market for, or value of, the copyrighted work (17 U.S.C. § 107).

While the four factors were originally defined in the United States by the Copyright Act of 1976, several Supreme Court cases have impacted how the factors are prioritized. In *Harper & Row Publishers v. The Nation Enterprises,* emphasis was given to the effect of use upon the market. After *TIME* magazine secured permission to publish the presidential memoirs of President Gerald Ford, *The Nation* magazine released an unauthorized version before *TIME*'s print date. The Supreme Court weighed each of the four factors and ruled that although *The Nation* published an insubstantial amount of the memoirs, it copied the "heart" of the work and the release had a negative effect on *TIME*'s market gain. Thus, the Supreme Court ruled that *The Nation* was guilty of copyright infringement. Despite all four factors being considered when making their decision, the Supreme Court asserted that the effect on the market "is undoubtedly the single most important element of fair use" (*Harper & Row Publishers v. The Nation Enterprises*, 1985, p. 566).

Although *Harper & Row Publishers v. The Nation Enterprises* established that the effect on the market was the most important factor, a series of cases have supported the idea that transformation is an acceptable practice when using copyrighted materials. In *Campbell v. Acuff-Rose Music, Inc.*, the rap group 2 Live Crew produced a commercial parody of the song "Oh, Pretty Woman" by Roy Orbison. Although 2 Live Crew's song used practically identical background music to the original song, the Supreme Court ruled in favor of fair use because of the transformative nature of the lyrics and the fact that the song was considered a parody of the original work (*Campbell v. Acuff-Rose Music, Inc.*, 1994). According to Supreme Court Justice Souter:

The goal of copyright, to promote science and the arts, is generally furthered by the creation of transformative works. Such works thus lie at the heart of the fair use doctrine's guarantee of breathing space within the confines of copyright, see, *e.g., Sony. supra,* at 478–480 (Blackmun, J., dissenting), and the more transformative the new work, the less will be the significance of other factors, like commercialism, that may weigh against a finding of fair use (*Campbell v. Acuff-Rose Music, Inc.*, 1994, p. 579).

The Supreme Court's decision continues to have an impact on fair use cases, displaying the significance of "transformativeness" in deciding if a fair use claim is valid (Aufderheide and Jaszi, 2011, p. 84). Thus, fair use is a viable option for creators to build upon the works of others as long as the use falls within the modern framework and interpretation of the four factors.

On a global scale, fair use is typically referred to as fair dealing. However, while similar in concept, the way fair dealing is measured is not dependent on four factors. For example, in Canada fair dealing is decided through a six-factor analysis that was created after the case of *CCH Canadian Ltd. v. Law Society of Upper Canada* (2004). These factors include purpose, character, amount, alternatives, nature, and the effect of the dealing on the work (*CCH Canadian Ltd. v. Law Society of Upper Canada,* 2004). According to Giuseppina D'Agostino (2008), "Fair dealing in Canada has been criticized as weak and overly restrictive, applying only to works used for a closed list of purposes," but after *CCH* in 2004, fair dealing became a user's right and more of an acceptable practice for creators (p. 309). In the United Kingdom, fair dealing has remained for the most part unchanged since the *UK Copyright, Designs and Patents Act 1988.* To determine fair dealing in the UK, less emphasis is placed on factors. Instead, how the original work is used is the primary determinate on whether fair dealing is acceptable. For example, if the use of the work falls under the category of "research and private study", "criticism, review and news reporting," or "caricature, parody or pastiche," then fair dealing would be acceptable (UK Copyright, Designs and Patents Act, 1988, c. 48 Pt. 1 Ch. 11 ss. 29-20). In Europe, permitted copying comes in the form of limitations defined in Copyright Direction Article 5, which include parodies, library use and non-commercial research and study. The directives adopted in Europe defining the types of non-permitted use of copyrighted materials is more straightforward than fair use, but they do not allow for as much flexibility for creative ventures that are often accepted in the U.S (Boyle, 2015, p. 10). Hence, despite there being uses of copyrighted materials without permission that are accepted internationally such as for research and private study, copyright policies regarding use can vary from country to country.

26.1.3 Fair use/fair dealing in the digital humanities

Many of the actions by practitioners in the digital humanities can be considered fair use/fair dealing on a global scale. For example, the purpose of many digitization projects is for preservation, which is a generally acceptable practice. Also, practitioners in the digital humanities typically copy resources for non-profit educational purposes, which make the use more likely to be fair than if resources were copied for commercial purposes. In addition, many of the items copied by digital humanities practitioners are facts, which make use more likely to be fair. Yet fair use or fair dealing always carries a certain amount of risk due to

Intellectual property guidelines

the subjective nature of deciding what constitutes legally using copyrighted materials without permission. Thus, if there is any doubt, the best practice is to check and see if resources are in the public domain or seek permission to reuse copyrighted materials.

26.1.4 *The public domain*

A work that does not have copyright due to expired protection, being ineligible for protection, or being donated to the public are in the public domain. Most works in the public domain were previously copyrighted works that lost protection due to expiration. As an act of the Parliament of Great Britain, the Statute of Anne (1710) declared that authors "have the sole liberty of printing and reprinting such book and books for the term of fourteen years, to commence from the day of the first publishing the same and no longer" (8 Anne, c.19, 1710). Despite the declaration of a limited copyright term, publishers in Great Britain continued to assume that copyright protection was unlimited. In *Millar v. Taylor* (1769), the King's Bench decided that works did not enter the public domain despite reaching the end of a fourteen-year term. However, in 1774 the House of Lords overruled the case in *Donaldson v. Beckett* (1774) by stating their support for the Statute of Anne. The Statute of Anne was the source of the declared duration for the first limited term of the Copyright Act of 1790 in the United States as well as an optional renewal term of 14 years before a work entered the public domain. However, since the Copyright Act of 1831, Congress has constantly extended copyright protection, placing a limitation on the number of works that enter the public domain. After the Sonny Bono Copyright Term Extension Act (1998) was passed in the United States, a copyrighted work does not enter the public domain for 70 years after the death of the creator and 95 years from publication or 120 years from when the work is first created, if the work is of corporate authorship . This has caused millions of works that would have originally lost copyright protection to remain out of the public domain causing a shortage of public domain works.

The shrinking public domain is an international occurrence due to a worldwide increase in copyright duration. The Berne Convention for the Protection of Literary and Artistic Works was created in 1886 for the purpose of globalizing minimum copyright principles among all nations. The Berne Convention defines minimum copyright provisions including the basic copyright principles, the minimum standards of protection, and certain limitations and exceptions of use. Within the minimum standards of protection, "the general rule is that protection must be granted until the expiration of the 50th year after the author's death" (WIPO Summary of Berne Convention, 2018). Thus, every nation that joins the Berne Convention agrees to abide by the minimum standards including expanding the duration of copyright protection granted to authors and corporations. Since the original Convention in 1886, over 190 nations have joined and share minimum duration copyright standards.

In the United States, the Supreme Court case *Eldred v. Ashcroft* had a major effect on the length of time it takes for a copyrighted work to fall into the public domain. A frequent re-publisher of public domain works, Eric Eldred filed a lawsuit against the Attorney General of the United States claiming that the Copyright Term Extension Act was unconstitutional. However, the Supreme Court decided that despite constant extensions of copyright protection since 1831, Congress "acted within its authority and did not transgress constitutional limitations" when it passed the 1998 Copyright Term Extension Act (*Eldred v. Ashcroft*, 2003, p. 187). Congress's decision to extend copyright protection in 1998 caused an unknown number of works to remain under copyright protection and was strongly opposed by scholars, filmmakers, artists, and dissenting Supreme Court Judge Justice Breyer. Breyer stated that the "primary legal effect" of the extension was to "grant the extended term not to authors, but their heirs, estates, or corporate successors" (*Eldred v. Ashcroft*, 2003, p. 243).

In addition to copyright protection being extended, the case of *Golan v. Holder* (2012) granted copyright protection to foreign works that had previously been in public domain. The Supreme Court case examined the constitutionality of the Uruguay Round Agreements Act (URAA) of 1994, which required that the United States abide by the requirements of the Berne Convention of 1988. Thus, foreign works that previously did not hold copyright in the United States were granted protection. Consequently, works that had copyright protection in their country of origin, but were previously in the public domain in the United States, were granted protection under the URAA (565 U.S. __ 2012). This case demonstrates not only that it is possible for works to lose public domain status but also that copyright laws are internationally connected through treaties, conventions, and organizations.

One issue that has become more common due to the extension of copyright protection on a global scale is the increasing number of orphan works, which are materials in which the copyright status of a material is not known. The extension of copyright protection and the removed requirement of a copyright notice has caused an increase in the number of orphan works. Archives all over the world hold content in which the owner of many of their materials is unknown, which presents challenges for making the content available to the public. Currently how orphan works are curated and accessed in an archive often depends on how much risk an archive is willing to take. Some archives do not make content available unless the materials are in the public domain or the archive has the permission of the copyright owner. Other archives do make their orphan works accessible, but only after conducting a due diligence search to find the owner. The United States Congress introduced orphan works bills in 2006 and 2008 that called for decreased infringement penalties, support for creators who attempt to locate orphan works owners, and protection for libraries and archives (United States Copyright Office, 2015, p. 12). However, those bills did not pass and as of 2019, no other orphan works legislation has passed through Congress.

In the U.S., there are certain types of works that enter the public domain from the moment of creation. According to Section 105 of the United States Code, copyright protection for works created by the federal government "is not available," "but the United States Government is not precluded from receiving and holding copyrights transferred to it by assignment, bequest, or otherwise" (17 U.S.C. § 105). Thus, presidential speeches, public records, and materials from United States court cases are in the public domain, and can be copied by the public. However, what is considered to be in the public domain can vary by country, and in many countries, government works are protected and not freely available for reuse (House Report No. 94-1476, 1976).

Digitizing content in the public domain can help bring new life to older, valuable resources. As creators of new content, practitioners in the digital humanities can take steps to increase the number of works available for free use. Although the extension of copyright duration has limited the number of works that have fallen into the public domain over the past two decades on an international level, a new tool has recently been developed to allow creators to donate their works into the public domain. The CC0 tool created by Creative Commons allows creators to place their works "as completely as possible in the public domain, so that others may freely build upon, enhance and reuse the works for any purposes without restriction under copyright or database law" (About CC0, n.d.).

26.1.5 Creative Commons

In 2001, Creative Commons was founded to provide digital licenses to creators who wish to specifically designate how their works can be used by the public (Creative Commons History, n.d.). The organization was a response to the constant extension of copyright protection as well as several Supreme Court decisions, including *Eldred v. Ashcroft* and *Golan v. Holder*. The licenses allow creators to state whether other people need to acknowledge them when using their work, whether the work can be transformed through remix, or if the work can be used for commercial purposes.

Every Creative Commons license, except the CC0 license, requires creators to acknowledge the original author when reusing a copyrighted work. Each license without the ND designation allows creators

Intellectual property guidelines

Table 26.1 Creative Commons License Types

License	Need to Acknowledge	Remix?	Commercial Use?
CC0	**No**	**Yes**	**Yes**
Attribution CC BY	**Yes**	**Yes**	**Yes**
Attribution CC BY-SA	**Yes**	**Yes**	**Yes**
Attribution-NoDerivs CC BY-ND	**Yes**	**No**	**Yes**
Attribution-NonCommercial CC BY-NC	**Yes**	**Yes**	**No**
Attribution-NonCommercial-ShareAlike CC BY-NC-SA	**Yes**	**Yes**	**No**
Attribution-NonCommercial-NoDerivs CC BY-NC-ND	**Yes**	**No**	**No**

to remix original copyrighted materials to create derivative works, and every license without the NC designation allows for reuse of copyrighted works for commercial purposes. The SA designation stands for Share-alike, which means if someone decided to remix, transform, or build upon a work, it must be distributed under the same license as the original (Creative Commons Licensing Types, n.d.) (Table 26.1). Creative Commons licenses have provided an opportunity for creative works to be shared and built upon, yet it is important to remember to acknowledge the original creator unless the work is in the public domain.

In the digital humanities, the focus of many projects is digitizing content and making materials open to the public. Open Educational Resources continue to increase on a global scale due to how the Internet has changed the access to information. The philosophy of Open Educational Resources is for academics to "create, share and allow their teaching resources not only to be re-used, but also to be amended, improved and transformed" (Warwick, Terras, & Nyhan, 2012, p. 167). For individuals in the humanities, projects are becoming bigger and more complex, thus collaboration and sharing is necessary for projects to be successful. Since the purpose of Creative Commons is to allow creators to share their works, many Open Educational Resources carry a Creative Commons license. Many organizations that digitize and make educational resources freely available, such as the Internet Archive and the Digital Public Library of America, have thousands of Creative Commons resources that are free to download and use for the public.

26.1.6 Seeking permission

The safest option to use a copyrighted work is to get consent. Consent means getting permission from the copyright owner to use a work in a way that would normally constitute infringement. Getting consent can be as easy as asking the owner to sign a document and being able to use the work at no cost. However, getting permission can also be a daunting process especially when the owner is difficult to track down. If a creator is unsure of the copyright status of a work or is not confident that reusing a work is considered fair use in the court of law, then the best option is to seek permission from the owner despite challenges and expenses. However, since the requirement for a copyright notice is no longer needed for copyright protection, uncovering the copyright status of a work is not always routine. Also, the increase in copyright duration may mean that the original copyright owner may not own the rights to a work due to transfers of ownership or even the death of the original author. Fortunately, the Internet has made it easier to locate copyright owners and get permission because of tools such as renewal and transfer searches available through the Copyright Office website. The Copyright Clearance Center allows the public to gain automatic permission to use copyrighted materials from all over the world. Through the pay-per-use option on the website users can specify a permission type, such as a work as part of a course material, photocopying for academic or general use, or republishing or displaying content. The user then must enter the details of use, such as who will republish the content and the lifetime unit quantity of the new product. Although the Copyright Clearance Center presents a viable option to gain permission, it also represents a method of control that owners have over their works. It can be easy to exceed permission especially in the digital age, in which new types of technology are constantly transforming how we use copyrighted materials.

Undertaking a full investigation on the copyright status of a work is known as conducting due diligence. Due diligence often is applied to the work performed during a business transaction. For example, Ian Cockburn, a Web Editor, Manager Advertising & Marketing at PIPERS - Global, a patent attorney firm, defines due diligence as "an evaluation, performed by investors or their agents, into the details of a potential investment or purchase, where the evaluation involves a verification of all the material facts relevant to the investment or purchase" (Cockburn, n.d.). However, due diligence can also be applied to the work performed in the digital humanities when attempting to discover the copyright status of an orphan work. In all cases of conducting a due diligence search, it is important to trace copyright ownership back to the original author and review all transferred rights from previous transactions. According to WIPO (2004):

Part of the due diligence process should include tracing the chain of title of existing copyright rights. The licensing party (i.e., the party granting rights, the "licensor") may have acquired the subject copyright rights from a third party, in which case further assignment of such rights may require review of the prior transfers to confirm that all relevant rights were conveyed and that there are no breaks in the chain of title. Where the licensing party is not the sole author of a copyright work, it may be proper, depending on local law, to confirm as well that the licensing party has secured rights from all co-authors (p. 5).

Copyright has become more divisible, meaning that owners can keep portions of their exclusive rights and sell others (17 U.S.C. § 201). For example, a license may allow the licensee to reproduce a copyrighted work, but the copyright owner may retain the right to distribute copies. The divisibility of copyrights and the common practice of transferring ownership makes conducting a thorough due diligence search more important than ever before.

Once an owner of intellectual property has been tracked down, permission is typically granted in the form of a license. Some licenses are short, such as a one-page permission letter, while other licenses come in the form of lengthy contracts. Although licenses are a necessary tool for creators to maintain copyright over their works, contracts can be more beneficial for corporations in order to obtain copyright from the original creators and are often "notoriously one-sided, sometimes to the point of absurdity" (Patry, 2011, p. 29). For example, a publishing corporation acquiring copyright over a book created by an individual author.

26.1.7 Archival donor agreements

Many digital humanities projects involve accessing and digitizing materials from archives. According to Arjun Sabharwal (2015), "Digital humanities presents an emerging interdisciplinary framework for integrating digital technologies and engaging archives in humanities research and teaching" (p. 20). Although archives often own the copyright to a large portion of their holdings, many archives develop their collections through donations. Building a collection often depends on the agreement between donors and the archive. Although agreements have not always been well documented, in recent years a deed of gift has become common practice between the archive and the donor (McKay, 2015, p. 181).

The deed of gift serves as an official document for when archival materials are physically transferred to an archive. A deed of gift usually allows donors to choose whether they would like to transfer copyright ownership to the archive or have a "license authorizing reuse" (McKay, 2015, p. 180). Deed of gifts usually consists of a transfer of ownership, a declaration of the current copyright ownership and control, the terms of the transfer (exclusive rights, perpetuity, etc.), and the signatures of the donor and the individual

Intellectual property guidelines

accepting the items on behalf of the archive (McKay, 2015, p. 228). For example, the Deed of Gift at the Dartmouth College library contains donor information, a description of the gift, dates, donor acquisition information, intellectual property interests and conveyance, a statement concerning future gifts, signatures, and terms and conditions (Dartmouth Deed of Gift, n.d.). In some cases, donors may attempt to maintain complete control over how their collections are maintained and made accessible to the public, yet the Society of American Archivists recommends that a clause is added stating that archives can make copies and "preserve materials by reformatting" (McKay, 2015, p. 182). Furthermore, the Society of American Archivists recommends archives encourage donors to hand over all intellectual property rights to the archive to advance accessibility and preservation of the materials.

26.1.8 *Digital rights management*

Technology has constantly transformed copyright both in terms of how owners protect their works and how creators copy, use and transform existing works. As stated in *Sony Corp of America v. Universal City Studios* (1984):

> From its beginning, the law of copyright has developed in response to significant changes in technology. Indeed it was the invention of a new form of copying equipment—the printing press—that gave rise to the original need for copyright protection. Repeatedly, as new developments have occurred in this county, it has been Congress that has fashioned the new rules that new technology made necessary. (*Sony Corp of America v. Universal Studios* 464 U.S. 430, 431 (1984))

Since technology has made it easier to copy, use, and put works into new digital mediums, issues of ownership and control have developed over the last two decades. While technology could appear as a threat to copyright owners since it is now easier to copy protected materials such as books, images and audiovisual works, technology also provides the ability for individuals to restore, remix and preserve works. The new tools available could potentially bring new life to works in the public domain. For example, Project Gutenberg has digitized thousands of items in the public domain that are free to use by the public. The rapid development of digitization technologies and the Internet have caused changes in copyright legislation all over the world.

In 1996, the World Intellectual Property Organization adopted a copyright treaty that listed obligations concerning technological measures and rights management information (WIPO Copyright Treaty, 1996). In 1998, the United States Congress passed the Digital Millennium Copyright Act (DMCA) implementing the treaty into U.S. law in order to criminalize the development of technologies aimed to gain access to preventative measures protecting copyright works. According to the Executive Summary by the United States Copyright Office,

> The Digital Millennium Copyright Act of 1998 (DMCA) was the foundation of an effort by Congress to implement United States treaty obligations and to move the nation's copyright law into the digital age. But as Congress recognized, the only thing that remains constant is change. The enactment of the DMCA was only the beginning of an ongoing evaluation by Congress on the relationship between technological change and U.S. copyright law.

The Act is also meant to reduce liability from unknowing online service providers (OSP) if the OSPs take down infringing material, and when notified, inform the infringer with a take-down notice in writing. If an OSP has specific knowledge of an infringement taking place, it can be held responsible (Digital

Millennium Copyright Act. Pub L. No. 105-304. 112 Stat. 2860. (1998)). The European Community also implemented the treaty through a series of directives protecting software, databases and restricting technologies meant to by-pass protective measures.

26.1.9 Digitization projects

Many projects in the digital humanities involve making copyrighted materials accessible online. Yet, with so much content being housed in archives all over the world, digitizing and building online collections has many challenges and can be time consuming. In one study, Jean Dryden, Professor of Continuing Studies at the University of Toronto, investigated the online holdings of 96 repositories, 66 survey responses and 18 interviews to understand the process of how archives select what to host online. The study also analyzed the degree to which the archives gain permission from copyright owners to add their materials online (Dryden, 2014, p. 67). During the interviews, many archivists articulated frustrations with current copyright laws, stating that copyright protection was too long and clearing content should be easier. According to the study findings, archives typically play it safe when making decisions about what materials to put online, such as only adding works in which there are no copyright complications present (i.e. items in the public domain). However, Dryden identified a trend of many archives taking a riskier approach to make items available online. Dryden (2014) states that eight of the archivists interviewed "follow a risk-assessment approach that looks at broad factors such as date span of the materials, how well-known rights holders are, commercial value of the materials, likelihood of a challenge, and so on rather than an item-by-item copyright review" (p. 81). Dryden argues that this trend must continue in archives, because discovering the copyright status of every item is impossible and eventually the number of public domain works will "run out" (p. 82). Thus, in an age where there is an expectation for items to be digitally available, archives need to use risk assessment tools, such as best practice documents to make their collections accessible online.

Additional studies have examined the extent to which archives attempt to obtain copyright permissions, and the success rate of those efforts. A 2010 study by Dharma Akmon, director of the National Archive of Data on Arts & Culture at the University of Michigan, examined the motivation of copyright owners to place their research papers online in the Jon Cohen AIDS Research Collection. According to her findings, the main challenge was that many copyright holders did not respond to archival request. Akmon states that over thirty percent of archival requests to obtain permission from copyright holders to place material online were met with a non-response (p. 62). However, the study also observed that when copyright holders do respond, they are often willing to give permission. Individual rights holders granting permission to make their materials accessible is supported by Dryden's study, which found that 67% of right holders were "pleased that the document is being used" (Dryden, 2014, p. 79). However, commercial copyright holders, are less likely to grant permission (Akmon, 2010, p. 62). Akron states that, "repositories might only be able to display a small portion of collections with many corporate third-party rights holders. In addition, corporate and government copyright holders are the least likely to respond to permission request" (p. 62).

In another study, archivists at the Southern Historical Collection and the Carolina Digital Library at the University of North Carolina documented their investigation of the copyright status of the Thomas E. Watson manuscript collection. Although the archive gained permission from the Watson family to place the collection online, it also contained some third-party materials. Thus, under the "strict interpretation of copyright law," the archivists needed to identify all copyright owners within the collection to establish the copyright status of each item (Dickson, 2010, p. 627). The team spent over 450 hours conducting a copyright investigation and spent approximately $8000 U.S. dollars to attempt to track down the copyright status of all objects in the Watson collection. After establishing the copyright status on as many items as possible, the archivists conducted a fair use analysis. Although the archive decided that there was some risk to

Intellectual property guidelines

place the Watson papers online, after consulting with legal counsel the archive decided that the level of risk was "an acceptable one", especially considering the archive's liberal take-down policy, in which "challenged items can be removed quickly" (Dickson, 2010, p. 636).

26.1.10 *Preservation and access in archives and libraries*

The struggle between the willingness of copyright holders to control ownership and the ability of creators to access and preserve owned works will continue to shape modern copyright laws. Technology in the digital age has provided new tools for archives to preserve materials and place collections online but also a fear from copyright holders that their copyrights may be infringed upon. According to Peter Hirtle (2015),

> The digital age presents new opportunities but also seemingly new threats. Digital reproduction and distribution can provide unparalleled access to our rich archival holdings. Yet at the same time, the visibility that digital access provides may increase the risk that a copyright owner could complain about archival practices (p. 2).

In the United States the 1976 Copyright Act added Section 108 that incorporates an exception for non-profit libraries to make copies for certain purposes such as preservation and nonprofit research. Section 108 was expanded under the Copyright Term Extension Act in 1998 to include subsection (h) that allows libraries and archives "to reproduce, distribute, display, or perform" copies of works that are in the last 20 years of copyright protection for purposes of "preservation, scholarship, and research" (17 U.S.C. §108 (h)(1)). In Europe, several directives allow for libraries and archives to make copies of copyrighted materials for education and preservation purposes. For example, the Information Society directive in 2001 allows member states who implement the directive to allow copying "made by publicly accessible libraries, educational establishments or museums, or by archives, which are not for direct or indirect economic or commercial advantage" (Ligue des Bibliothèques Européennes de Recherche (LIBER), 2016, p. 3). Another directive that affects libraries' actions and policies in Europe is the Database directive, which provides protection to databases (LIBER, 2016, p. 3). Although some directives may have a positive effect on library and archives, European nations are not required to implement the directives and there are still changes that need to be made to European Union copyright laws to benefit libraries and archives.

Preservation is typically the first priority among archivists, and can be enacted without making the materials accessible to the public. Yet by further removing copyright restrictions on an international level, archives would be able to invest time and resources in their collections and display items as a means of promoting materials that are culturally significant. However, until there are significant changes to international copyright laws, archivists and other digital humanities practitioners must continue to make tough decisions concerning fair use, seeking permission, and licensing copyrighted content.

26.2 Intellectual property for the digital humanities in practice

Digital humanities is a very broad area that encompasses many different fields. Therefore, the actions of digital humanities practitioners are difficult to define. Yet, in any context, digital humanities practitioners work with digital objects, be they born-digital content or physical materials to be digitized. Thus, the first step in a digital humanities project is to identify the content and the copyright status of all materials in a collection. If the content is in the public domain or has a Creative Commons license that allows for free use, then the materials are open to be copied. However, if the materials are copyright protected then the user has two options: claim fair use/fair dealing or ask for permission. Fair use/fair dealing is not internationally consistent and what constitutes fair use can vary on a number of factors so users of copyrighted content must conduct a fair use analysis to decide whether they are legally copying content. The safest option is to ask permission to use copyrighted content. It is possible that the owner of the copyrighted content will give permission for all materials to be used, especially if the content is going to be used primarily for research and preservation purposes. However, asking permission can often entail negotiating rights for access and paying licensing fees.

Perhaps one of the most common projects in the digital humanities is the development of digital archives. Applying the context in previous paragraph to a digital archives project shows that there are multiple facets that a project leader must consider both as someone who is acquiring copyrighted materials as well as providing access to digitized content. For example, if a project leader wants to create a digital collection of archival footage, he or she must consider the copyright status of the footage they are acquiring and the copyright policies to be enforced upon future users of the content, such as documentary filmmakers. First, the project leader must identify the copyright status of the content. If it is an older work (pre-1923), then it could be in the public domain, in which no further considerations need to be made. However, if the content is owned by a third party then the project leader must decide on whether to claim fair use in order to curate the work or gain permission from the owner. Gaining permission usually requires a formal transfer of ownership through contracts, which can require legal counsel. Once the project leader has accessed or owns the work, he or she then must decide how available it will be to the public. Many digital humanities project are open access, meaning they are online and free for the public to use. However, opening up digital collections to the public presents new questions about how the content will be used such as whether high resolution content will be available for purchase.

26.3 Intellectual property summary of best practices

Intellectual property is complex, yet as both the creators of new content and the copyright holders of digital collections, individuals in the digital humanities can play a role in educating creators on copyright issues. According to Aprille C. McKay (2015), the chair of Society of American Archivists' Intellectual Property Working Group, "the copyright regime in the United States is already unduly complicated and paralyzes creators such as documentary filmmakers, journalists, and historians who want to incorporate archival images or texts into their new works" (p. 177). Thus, archivists must "strive for clarity and transparency and to reduce the complexity of their work whenever possible" (p. 177). This is especially true in academic environments, in which technology has led to an intellectual property gap among students and faculty. According to Julia E. Rodriguez, Katie Greer, and Barbara Shipman (2014), "Copyright outreach often has been more reactive than proactive, particularly when addressing students' use of music or faculty members' use of copyrighted materials in their teaching" (p. 487). Individuals in the digital humanities can change this by taking a proactive role in addressing the intellectual property needs of the academic community. For example, digital humanities practitioners should feel free to share their experiences with fair use/fair dealing. In addition, using works in the public domain is important from a historical perspective, because it allows older works to live on, while at the same time, allows a new generation of creators to transform public domain works to represent modern culture. Thus, digital humanities practitioners should educate other creators on the potential of public domain content and do everything possible to provide open access to these works when it is economically feasible.

In addition to being educators, digital humanities practitioners should also make sure to record the copyright status of all curated items and develop a detailed copyright policy for collections. As more content becomes digital and openly accessible, it is vital to keep track of the owner and copyright status of all

Intellectual property guidelines

materials in digital collections. Changes in technology will always affect how users access and copy information, yet with a detailed copyright policy, practitioners in the digital humanities can be better prepared for potential complications and lawsuits. Through a process discovering the copyright status of content, preserving materials, defining intellectual property policies and promoting open resources, individuals in the digital humanities can advance access to educational resources.

References

17 U.S.C. §105 (1976).

17 U.S.C. §106 (1976).

17 U.S.C. §107 (1976).

17 U.S.C. §108 (1976).

17 U.S.C. §201 (1976).

17 U.S.C. §302(a)(c) (1976).

Akmon, D. (2010). "Only with Your Permission: How Rights Holders Respond (or Don't Respond) to Requests to Display Archival Materials Online." *Archival Science 10*(1), 45–64.

Aufderheide, P & Jaszi, P. (2011). *Reclaiming Fair Use: How to Put the Balance Back in Copyright*. Chicago, IL: The University of Chicago Press.

The Berne Convention Implementation Act, Pub. L. No. 100-568, 102 Stat 2853 (1988).

Boyle, J. (2015). (When) Is Copyright Reform Possible? Lessons from the Hargreaves Review. Retrieved from http://www.thepublicdomain.org/wp-content/uploads/2015/02/Is-Copyright-Reform-Possible1.pdf

Campbell v. Acuff-Rose Music, Inc. 510 U.S. 569, 579 (1994).

CCH Canadian Ltd. v. Law Society of Upper Canada. 1 SCR 339. (2004).

Cockburn, I. (n.d.) IP Due Diligence – A Necessity, Not a Luxury. WIPO Documents. Retrieved from https://www.wipo.int/sme/en/documents/ip_due_diligence_fulltext.html.

Creative Commons. (n.d.). About CC0 — "No Rights Reserved." *Creative Commons*. Retrieved from https://creativecommons.org/share-your-work/public-domain/cc0/.

Creative Commons. (n.d.). History. *Creative Commons*. Retrieved from https://creativecommons.org/about/history/.

Creative Commons. (n.d.) Licensing Types. *Creative Commons*. Retrieved from https://creativecommons.org/share-your-work/licensing-types-examples/.

Dartmouth College Library. (n.d.) Deed of Gift. Retrieved from https://www.dartmouth.edu/~library/rauner/docs/pdf/Deed.pdf.

D'Agostino, G. (2008). "Healing Fair Dealing? A Comparative Copyright Analysis of Canada's Fair Dealing to U.K. Fair Dealing and U.S. Fair Use." *McGill Law Journal* 53, 309–63.

Dickson, A. (2010). "Due Diligence, Futile Effort: Copyright and the Digitization of the Thomas Watson Papers." *The American Archivist 73*(2), 626–36.

Digital Millennium Copyright Act. Pub L. No. 105-304. 112 Stat. 2860 (1998).

Donaldson v. Beckett. HL 22 (1774).

Dryden J. (2014). "The Role of Copyright in Selection for Digitization." *The American Archivist* 77(1), 64–95.

Eldred et al., v. Ashcroft, Attorney General, 537 U.S. 186, 187, 243 (2003).

Golan v. Holder, 132 S. Ct 873, 875 (2012).

Harper & Row v. The Nation Enterprises, 471 U.S. 539, 544, 566 (1985).

Hirtle, P. (2015) Introduction. *Rights in the Digital Era*. Chicago, IL: Society of American Archivists.

Copyright Law Revision. House Report No. 94-1476 (1976).

Ligue des Bibliothèques Européennes de Recherche (LIBER). (2016). *Limitations and Exceptions in EU Copyright Law for Libraries, Educational and Research Establishments: A Basic Guide*. Retrieved from https://libereurope.eu/wp-content/uploads/2016/10/A-Basic-Guide-to-Limitations-and-Exceptions-in-EU-Copyright-Law-for-Libraries-Educational-and-Research-FINAL-ONLINE.pdf.

McKay, A. (2015) Module 7: Managing Rights and Permissions. *Rights in the Digital Era*. Chicago, IL: Society of American Archivists.

Millar v. Taylor. 4 Burr. 2303, 98 ER 201 (1769).

Orphan Works Act, H.R.5439. 109th Cong. (2006).

Orphan Works Act, H.R. 5889. 110th Cong. (2008).

Patry, W. (2011). *How to Fix Copyright*. Oxford, UK: Oxford University Press.

Rodriguez, J., Greer, K. & Shipman, B. (2014). "Copyright and You: Copyright Instruction for College Students in the Digital Age." *The Journal of Academic Librarianship* 40, 486–491.

Sabharwal A. (2015). *Digital Curation in the Digital Humanities: Preserving and Promoting Archival and Special Collections.* Amsterdam, The Netherlands: Chandos Publishing.

Sonny Bono Copyright Term Extension Act, 17 U.S.C. §108, 203(a)(2), 301(c), 302, 303, 304(c)(2) (1998).

Sony Corp of America v. Universal Studios 464 U.S. 430, 431 (1984).

Statute of Anne. 8 Ann. c. 21 (1710).

UK Copyright, Designs and Patents Act. (1988). c. 48 Pt. 1 Ch. 11 ss. 29-20.

United States Copyright Office. (2015). *Orphan Works and Mass Digitization: A Report of the Register of Copyrights.* Retrieved from http://www.copyright.gov/orphan/reports/orphan-works2015.pdf

U.S. Const. art. I, § 8.

Warwick, C, M. Terras, & J. Nyhan (2012). *Digital Humanities in Practice.* London: Facet Publishing.

World Intellectual Property Organization (WIPO). Inside WIPO. Retrieved from http://www.wipo.int/about-wipo/en/.

World Intellectual Property Organization (WIPO). (2018). Summary of the Berne Convention for the Protection of Literary and Artistic Works (1886). Retrieved from http://www.wipo.int/treaties/en/ip/berne/summary_berne.html

World Intellectual Property Organization (WIPO). What is Intellectual Property? Retrieved from http://www.wipo.int/about-ip/en/.

World Intellectual Property Organization (WIPO). WIPO Copyright Treaty. Retrieved from https://www.wipo.int/treaties/en/text.jsp?file_id=295166#P136_19843.

World Intellectual Property Organization (WIPO). (2016). *Understanding Copyright and Related Rights.* Geneva: WIPO. Retrieved from https://www.wipo.int/edocs/pubdocs/en/wipo_pub_909_2016.pdf.

World Intellectual Property Organization (WIPO). (2004). *WIPO Guide on the Licensing of Copyright and Related Rights.* Retrieved from https://www.wipo.int/edocs/pubdocs/en/copyright/897/wipo_pub_897.pdf.

27

PRACTICING GOODWILL ETHICS WITHIN DIGITAL RESEARCH METHODS

Brit Kelley

27.1 Practicing goodwill ethics within digital research methods

The Cambridge Analytica scandal started with the broadcast of an undercover interview with the company's then CEO, Mr. Nix, where he allegedly boasted about his work with Donald Trump's presidential campaign, and other work the firm had done to discredit politicians online (Watkins & Jordan, 2018). While Cambridge Analytica initially disregarded this interview, complaining both that it was entrapment and that it did not reflect the company's mission, whistle-blower, Christopher Wylie told *The Observer* that Cambridge Analytica illegally obtained and used the data of 50 million users to send them pro-Trump material in an effort to sway the 2016 US presidential election (Cadwalladr & Graham-Harrison, 2018). As whistle-blower Christopher Wylie told *The Observer*: "We exploited Facebook to harvest millions of people's profiles. And built models to exploit what we knew about them and target their inner demons. That was the basis the entire company was built on" (quoted in Cadwalladr & Graham-Harrison, 2018). Since then, it has been revealed that the quiz Cambridge Analytica used to do this, called This is Your Digital Life, was originally developed by an academic at Cambridge University, psychology professor Dr Aleksandr Kogan, who contracted with the company to create a data scraping application and mass survey to help him model how and why people do what they do on Facebook.

Dr Kogan and Cambridge University immediately came under fire for the data breach, and the misuse of this data. Dr Kogan has claimed that he was made into a scapegoat, while Cambridge Analytica and Facebook initially denied any responsibility, pinning the blame largely on Kogan and his team. Since March of 2018, however, it has been further revealed that the This is Your Digital Life app was created by Kogan in a contract between his company Global Science Research or GSR and Cambridge Analytica, and that he had received grant money from the Russian government to research the emotions of Facebook users (Cadwalladr & Graham-Harrison, 2018). While all parties in the scandal are currently under investigation, it is not yet clear what the results of these investigations will be, nor, indeed, what larger institutions, both academic and corporate, will be required to do to protect users' personal information.

Above all, what the Cambridge Analytica event has demonstrated is that the affordances of internet technology have outstripped many traditional views on what constitutes the public versus private spheres, data ownership rights, and the boundaries between "just talking" and official publication or public distribution. This event has demonstrated, as Rebecca MacKinnon (2012) so sagely put it: "In the twenty-first century, many of the most acute political and geopolitical struggles will involve access to and control of information" (p. xxii). Dr Kogan certainly took advantage of the ever-diminishing control we each have over our own content in online spaces. This event raises key questions for those of us doing research within the digital humanities, chief among them being: What might the unforeseen consequences of our research be? As the Cambridge Analytica event taught us, even a project that might seem relatively harmless on the surface—participants of a social networking site *choosing* to complete a survey—can have massive negative implications not only when it comes to personal information, but even for the larger geopolitical context. Therefore, it is our duty as researchers in the digital humanities, our "covenant," as Brydon-Miller (2009) puts it, to develop and maintain ethical online spaces and practices.

As internet technologies and practices continue to change, it has become increasingly difficult, even for experienced researchers, to know how best to achieve effective *and* ethical research online. In this chapter, I will present one approach to achieving ethical research practices—goodwill ethics. Goodwill ethics means committing to an ongoing process of research design from a disposition of empathy, as well as a willingness to negotiate with potential participants. These goodwill ethics are best achieved through four major principles: respect, reciprocity, transparency, and, crucially, vulnerability (Kelley, 2016). We show respect by openly and carefully representing ourselves, as complex as that prospect is. And we show respect by representing participants in ways they might represent themselves. We enact reciprocity not only by providing balanced accounts of the communities we study, but also by accepting and fulfilling some roles these communities might ask of us (Powell & Takayoshi, 2003). We are transparent when we state our positions, values, institutional affiliations, and methods, and are willing to negotiate the latter. And, finally, we can best achieve all three by doing vulnerability.

I will return below to what I mean by these values, especially "doing vulnerability," but first I will address how these values have come to take shape for me as a researcher and writer. I will begin by briefly reviewing the history of ethical clearance in the United States and European Union. I will then discuss the current case-based and flexible approach to ethics, introducing key figures in the debate. Next, I will briefly discuss how this theoretical background has continued to inform my own work with online fanfiction writers. Finally, based upon my own experience, and the work of key scholars, I will present sets of questions that researchers can consider as they design approaches to text collection, observation, consent, data protection, and reporting on their findings. Ultimately, my goal is to help researchers approach ethics as an ongoing process.

27.2 From the Nuremberg Code to the Belmont Report: A brief history of research ethics

When it comes to research ethics, the best place to start is the Nuremberg Code. Written in the wake of the Nuremberg trials in 1947, which prosecuted War Crimes, including illegal and deeply unethical medical experimentation that was perpetrated by Nazis during World War II, the key components of the code are: 1) the necessity of voluntary and informed consent; and 2) the reduction of risk to "physical and mental suffering and injury." This code was initially geared towards biomedical research, but it has come to be applied across research contexts. Despite the Nuremberg Code, however, studies of dubious value and research design continued to take place, such as the infamous Tuskegee Syphilis Study. Taking place between 1932 and 1972, physicians and scientists studied a total of 600 African American men, 399 of which had syphilis, and 201 of which did not (CDC, 2015). These researchers allowed many study participants to suffer and die from syphilis, even after a cure was discovered in 1945 (CDC, 2015).

What's more, work in fields such as psychology began to demonstrate that even non-medical research could have highly negative and long-term effects on subjects. One famous example is the Milgram "Obedience Study," conducted at Yale University initially in 1961. The experiment asked participants to act as judges to a series of questions to be answered by what participants assumed to be another study volunteer. When a person answered a question incorrectly, participants were told to administer an electric shock. The study showed that most people continued to administer electric shocks, regardless of hearing screaming from the other side of the screen. No participants were physically hurt during the experiment, but researchers did lead participants to believe that they had seriously injured and even killed other people, because of their blind acceptance of authority. Many participants suffered severe psychological distress for

Achieving ethical research practices

years in the wake of this study. Yet another infamous study was the Stanford Prison Experiment in 1971, which asked a group of graduate students to set up a makeshift prison on Stanford's campus, with some playing the role of prisoners and others the role of prison guard. The experiment was abandoned after six days because of the degree of cruelty the appointed prison guards showed to the appointed prisoners. Again, participants suffered psychological distress in the wake of the experiment[1].

In response to these kinds of studies, and extending the early work of the Nuremberg Code, the Belmont Report was prepared by the United States Department of Health, Education, and Welfare in 1979. Ultimately, it expanded and further codified definitions of "harm," legality in research, and, most importantly, how to consider and achieve informed consent. The three central tenets of the Belmont Report are respect for persons, beneficence, and justice. Respect for persons is defined as incorporating "at least two ethical convictions: first, that individuals should be treated as autonomous agents, and second, that persons with diminished autonomy are entitled to protection." Beneficence is defined as following "two general rules": "(1) do not harm and (2) maximize possible benefits and minimize possible harms." And finally, justice is conceived of as providing equal opportunities for people or communities to participate in a study, as well as for researchers to carefully consider the benefits and burdens their studies may carry with them for participating communities.

The Belmont Report and Nuremberg Code have been interpreted in different ways over time, but typically, in the United Kingdom and the United States, they have been codified into a system of ethical clearance applications, which must be approved by a committee of university officials, usually professors across a range of departments. Typically, the process for ethical approval at any academic institution will progress according to the following pattern.

This typical pattern (See Figure 27.1) is used to help researchers make clear decisions on their next steps. Often, once a researcher works through this flow chart, they will decide that they are ready to move forward with further methods design and even ethical clearance. This will often require researchers to create a statement of research, including the questions and goals of the research, as well as a clear statement of all individual methods to be used. In addition, researchers are often asked to write up sample questions they might use in interviews and surveys, as well as to prepare sample recruitment materials. In the United States, researchers at any academic institution are then required to complete ethics training through an online course before they can even begin an application. In the United Kingdom, the requirement for previous training varies, but often the application process is the same: a researcher will fill out an application based upon the assessed risk level of their research. If the researcher is working with QUILTBAG+[2] youth (people under 16 years of age), for example, then they will need to complete a full application, in which they will be required to gain both parental and participant consent. If the researcher, however, is conducting a large-scale survey online, and they will not be gathering any personal information, then often they will be able to complete a shortened or "expedited" application. For an example of what this process looks like the United Kingdom, I have included a link to the ethics office at King's College London: https://internal.kcl.ac.uk/innovation/research/ethics/do-i-require/ethical-clearance.aspx. For information about what this process might and can look like in the United States, I have also included a link to the Human Subjects Protection Office at the University of Louisville: http://louisville.edu/research/humansubjects/lifecycle/before-you-begin. For more links to a range of ethical standards from academia, journalism, and industry, see Deller (2018).

The key question, according to McKee and Porter (2009) in this process is: Am I doing research with humans? If one wishes to conduct face-to-face research with another human (or humans) through interviews, tests, observations, etc., then the answer to this question is clear: Yes – I am doing research with humans. However, as many scholars have pointed out (McKee & Porter, 2009; Whiteman, 2012; Markham & Buchanan, 2012; Kozinets, 2015; Kara, 2018), research into online spaces complicates the answer to this question. Because so much of our experience of the internet is mediated through print text or images (whether moving or still), it can be particularly difficult to decide whether the focus is the *text* or the people behind the text. What's more, even if the focus is the text, as many fan scholars have pointed out

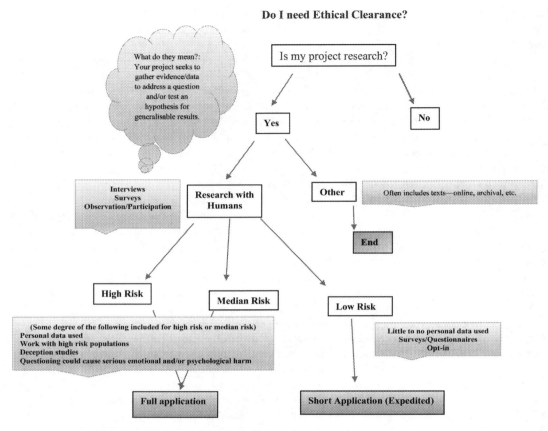

Figure 27.1 Typical risk factor judgment for ethical clearance

(Busse & Hellekson, 2012; Jones, 2016; Kelley, 2016; Deller, 2018), that does not necessarily mean that all texts can be and should be treated equally. Some texts, as fan scholar Bethan Jones (2016) has wisely put it, are posted to online fan websites as "private [acts] in a public space" and, therefore, cannot be saved, analysed, and reported on in the same ways as texts posted online by major commercial presses, such as *The New York Times*, academic presses such as Routledge, or even articles published online via *Transformative Works and Cultures* (an open-access academic journal focusing on fan studies). I will discuss in more depth below how to approach different kinds of texts that we might find online, but for now, it is enough to understand that the answer to this question is not as straightforward as it might at first appear.

Finally, this process is not only central in helping researchers decide what they can and cannot do in a research study, but also whether and how they should gain consent from their participants[3]. Often, consent is gained in one of three ways: for interviews, observations, etc., consent is either gained by 1) a printed, signed form discussed by participant and researcher, or 2) conducted orally between researcher and participant; for other types of research, particularly questionnaires or surveys, consent is 3) garnered when the participant chooses to fully complete and submit the survey or questionnaire form. In any case, all three forms of consent require some degree of information about the project: its focus, its goal, its eventual audience, and, of course, contact information for the researcher and their advisor(s). However, as scholars Thomas Newkirk (1996) and Heidi McKee (2008) have pointed out, the official consent form can sometimes be misleading, and even "seduce" participants, as Newkirk (1996) puts it, into saying more than they otherwise would. It is important, therefore, to take the process represented above, and the template consent forms that might be provided by the institution, as a *starting place* to research methods design, rather than the end of ethical considerations. As Whiteman (2012) has argued, research methods must *always* be an ongoing process. In an effort to demonstrate what this ongoing process might look like, in the following section I will critically discuss the methods I used when I began my research into online fanfiction during my doctoral programme. Using this as a starting place, I will then discuss how these methods have shifted and changed in the six years since.

27.3 Brit the fanwriter v. Dr Kelley the fan researcher

27.3.1 Developing goodwill and vulnerability in my own research ethics

Within the current climate, the ever-shifting affordances and practices online present numerous challenges even to the most experienced researchers. When I first started my research into online fanwriting in early 2012, there was even less guidance on how to treat texts posted openly and publicly (in other words, not protected by passwords) on the internet. As I will come to discuss in this section, my development of ethical research guidelines, what I came, eventually, to call goodwill ethics, began with a major split between my fan self—Brit the Harry Potter fan—and my academic self—Brit Kelley the PhD student. While at first, the split seemed both insurmountable and potentially irrelevant, it turned out to be crucial to my development of ethical research methods.

While I say that my journey to develop ethical research methods started in 2012, in many ways, it started much earlier. In one respect, it started with my discovery of Harry Potter as a fifteen-year-old seeking friends at my new school. At the time, I was desperate for belonging, so when Zoë, another new student, asked me if I wanted to go to a movie called *Harry Potter and the Sorcerer's Stone,* I said yes, even though I was very uncertain whether I would like the film. However, very unexpectedly, the whimsy and the drama and the larger-than-life score completely captivated me. By the end of the first Quidditch scene, I was hooked. What had seemed to me, at the time, as a concession towards friendship soon became a veritable obsession for the franchise. In fact, only a few years after this event, during my final year of university, I discovered fanfiction for the very first time. After a few months of spending long nights reading fanfiction online, rather than focusing on my assigned homework, I started writing my own story. Doing so not only helped me to continue my excitement for the *Harry Potter* series, nor only did it provide me with an effective procrastination mechanism, but, more importantly, it helped me to rediscover my love of writing. This rediscovery would eventually lead me to an entirely new direction on my career path—form Linguistics to Rhetoric and Composition, and then again to Digital Humanities. Put simply, discovering fanfiction was a transformative experience for me.

But why share any of this? Why does any of this matter if we are trying to better understand ethical research methods? It matters because these kinds of emotionally-charged, human moments are a central part of the practices and interactions in online spaces, particularly within more niche communities. Moreover, it serves as a useful reminder that, as Jones (2016) has argued, many members of online communities view their online postings as private acts. Within this context, then, it is useful to remember our own experiences within online spaces, so that we can better consider how to treat the spaces we study with respect. Finally, I share my own somewhat embarrassing experience with fandom here, because it raises a whole host of complications within the research process that so often get obscured by institutional ethical clearance requirements and consent forms, namely: 1) what leads researchers to their sites of study in the first place; and 2) the complexity of human decisions, especially when it comes to the people who agree to participate in research studies. In short, my own story is used here not for the sake of confession, but as a reminder that the human component of research is key to doing effective *and* ethical research online—or goodwill ethics.

Before I go into more depth about these goodwill ethics, I'd like to briefly explain what fanfiction is. Fanfiction is a literacy practice where fans take their favourite characters, settings, and plot points, and use these to write new stories of their own. As I recounted above, I discovered fanfiction during my last year at university. Years later, as I was just starting my PhD program in rhetoric and composition, it became increasingly clear to me that there was something unique and powerful happening in online fanfiction communities that I should share with academia. My first step was to return to my fanfiction website of choice, attempting the mindset of an outsider. Early in my research, I saw *Sycophant Hex* as an archive of texts, rather than, say, a community where fans share their writing. Part of this decision came from the welcome page on the website itself: "Sycophant Hex is a site for quality Harry Potter fanfiction, and we are delighted to provide this service to you free of charge." Moreover, it was clear from that same welcome page that there was a complex set of rules at the site, as it warned: "We want you, the readers and members of the site, to enjoy what we have to offer here....All we ask in return is that you respect J.K. Rowling, this site, and your fellow fans." I searched for at least one fanwriter whom I could track beyond their work at this one website. It took about two days before I found a story by the well-liked and relatively prolific fanwriter, chivalric.

I discovered her through a short story that she had posted, "Divorce." It is a story about major *Harry Potter* characters, Severus Snape (who is the Hogwarts Potions Master, and in his late 30s in the original series) and Hermione Granger (who is a Hogwarts student, one of Harry's closest friends, and in her teen years in the books). In this story, Hermione has been forcibly married to Severus in the wake of Harry Potter's defeat of Voldemort. The Ministry of Magic, so it would appear, was eager to join couples who would produce what they considered to be "strong magical stock." Several years later, however, the Ministry of Magic passes a new law that forcibly dissolves all Marriage Law unions. This story focuses on Hermione and Severus' reactions to the rescinded law. This story has top ratings (it has achieved a five-star rating, the highest possible at this particular website[4]) within the *Sycophant Hex* community, and can be found within the Ashwinder archive, which is geared towards "SS/HG shipper fics," or stories that deal with a romantic and/or sexual relationship between Severus and Hermione.

As I read, I learned from chivalric's author notes and reader reviews that she was well-liked and active in the fanfiction community. Her profile included when she became a member, September of 2007, as well as the number of stories she had posted, 21. As I continued to read through these stories, I learned through author's notes that chivalric is a woman, and that she is highly active on another fanfiction website, *The Petulant Poetess*. When I sought her profile at *The Petulant Poetess,* I learned a great deal more about her. I learned her real name, Sam C. Leonhard, as well as how active she is across multiple sites, including the personal blogging website, *Live Journal*, which I also explored. In her profile at *Live Journal*, I learned that Sam is a mother, that she is bilingual, and that she had published two original novels on Amazon, *Tainted Blood* and *Tainted Soul*.

The crucial point here is that I was able to find a great deal of information about chivalric within only a few days of discovering her work, despite having no specialist knowledge in computer programming, data scraping, etc. In addition, because none of her works (or profiles) were password protected, I felt that I could use them completely freely without seeking her consent. This aligned comfortably with what I had been taught by the professor overseeing this project that semester. At the time, I had a huge and growing file of screen captures of the website, chivalric's profile, stories, and author's notes, as well as many reader reviews during this period. It simply did not occur to me at the time that what I was doing might be intrusive.

When I first discovered this website, *Sycophant Hex*, I was a fan participant, and it was through hours and hours of reading that I learned about the community and began to feel both comfortable enough and empowered enough to write. Because of that, perhaps, when I re-entered the space, I felt like it was *mine*—and, as mine, I was free to share it however and with whomever I pleased. In addition, I was coming from a very text-focused field, so the public availability of these texts, and their print form, made them

Achieving ethical research practices

seem like any other text we might explore in the humanities. For example, if we are not required to gain consent from authors of published texts, such as Toni Morrison, even when those texts appear online, as they might in the form of news articles or editorials, then why should we need consent from the author of a fanfiction text that has not been password-protected? Given this background, and my position as fan and researcher, I did not pause to consider that my methods of text collection could be problematic—at least, not until I was informed by a friend and colleague that some fans were uncomfortable with researchers. This moment marked a major shift in my approach to fanfiction research. I reflected on how I might feel if one of my colleagues published an in-depth textual analysis of my fanfiction, or if a scholar in digital humanities were to report, somehow, on my *Live Journal* entries from high school. Knowing full well that I would be extremely embarrassed, I realised just how problematic my approach had been. I realised that I was researching *people* online, and not simply their texts. This realisation led me to feel extremely vulnerable, both as someone who has long used the internet to post creative work and personal experiences, *and* as a researcher new to academia.

This vulnerability, however, was essential, as it led me to consider my own stake in the research. I needed to reflect on what my actual position was, and what I stood to gain. As an academic, I have a huge responsibility to fellow fans—to listen to them and protect their identities. The academy is a formidable institution, and while some may argue that the small networks that read academic articles are unlikely to cross paths with those who write fanfiction, it is not the case that academic use of fanfiction sites is harmless. For example, in the "Theory of Ficgate" case, where, in 2014, a class on fanfiction was run at UC Berkeley which required students to not only read fanfiction but to leave comments on authors' works, some students left not only unrelated, but in some cases, hurtful comments (Waldorph, 2014; Fanlore, 2016). The harm to Waldorph and other fanwriters was not the goal of the course, but was a result, nonetheless. This harm could have been mitigated by course leaders (who were, admittedly, undergraduate students—see Van Tooke, 2015) asking fans for consent to both use and respond to their work in a classroom setting.

In addition, I have a responsibility to academia—to do critical research into spaces that can help us to better understand how and why people learn and do what they do online. While it is true that the academy is a powerful institution, it is also true that academia plays a crucial role in intervening in problematic practices of other powerful institutions, as well as providing carefully researched critique of cultural phenomena. What's more, it is important to remember that while academia can often seem (and perhaps sometimes is) a massive publishing machine, it is still subject to attacks on academic freedom. This freedom to openly study and critique must be maintained, at least insofar as it does not cause undue harm to those studied. Acknowledging and *doing* vulnerability is the way to achieve these dual purposes.

Ultimately, if I wanted to do important and responsible academic work, I needed to engage both with my vulnerability and with my sense of goodwill towards my fellow fans. After all, fanfiction is *writing*, and writing is already a vulnerable practice. In his new book, *Embarrassment: The emotional underlife of learning,* Thomas Newkirk (2017) addresses how learning more generally, but certainly learning how to write, is a bumpy process often beset with embarrassment, shame, and anxiety. As David Riche (2017) has argued, however, this vulnerability is part of what makes writing so powerful: "My existence as a rhetorical being necessitates my existence as a vulnerable being, someone whose life is contingent, perpetually exposed, and always subject to the effects of language (among countless other factors)" (Riche, 2017). In other words, vulnerability is the capacity to both affect and be affected by something. Considering the very vulnerability of writing overall, it becomes much easier to understand why Jones (2016) would argue that, for fans, posting a fanfiction story is similar to "A woman talking about an abortion with a friend in a café" that it is "a private act in a public space."

Importantly, then, while we cannot simply use whatever is not password protected online, by the same token, not everything that an individual person might post in a privately-public (Lange, 2007) manner is hands off[5]. Academics should have the freedom to engage critically with cultural texts, including online fan texts. But I would also point out that, unlike authors of traditionally published works (that is, works published through academic or commercial presses), fan writers are often highly vulnerable. Online fan spaces were created as safe zones for reading and writing that was otherwise unsanctioned. Because of this, fans developed certain rules of engagement in order to both support and protect each other. Busse and Hellekson (2012) have argued that "many fans find unacceptable the notion that their works may be freely perused by outsiders. Fan publications…are perceived as existing in a closed, private space even though they may be publicly available" (p.39). This perception has a long history in fan communities that have been extremely stigmatized (Jenkins 1992; Bacon-Smith 1992). Historically, fans have seen themselves as resistant to dominant forms of consumption, and this status is fiercely protected and defended in fan circles.

As we've already seen from Jones (2016) and Busse and Hellekson (2012), many fans tend to feel very uncomfortable with the prospect of having their work read and shared by community outsiders, and it is certainly important to bear this in mind. However, as Busse and Hellekson (2012) have discussed, if the scholarly focus is largely on a close reading of a text, then the discursive features matter, and, therefore, authors should receive credit for their work (p. 49). While it is true that many, perhaps most, fans expect that their writing will circulate only among fellow fans, I would argue (as does Whiteman, 2012) that either requiring each author's consent to discuss a story or speaking of stories only in the aggregate is not only largely untenable but potentially disruptive, and, what's more, not necessarily in the best interest of either scholarship or fandom. A goodwill approach to fan scholarship should take the time to consider and negotiate fans' privacy concerns and make research findings fully available to fans. Furthermore, goodwill requires what bell hooks would call a "loving critique": taking the time to analyse, engage with, and question fan texts just as fans do with popular culture texts. As I've already begun to argue, approaching this kind of context from a disposition of goodwill does not mean not studying fans, but it *does* mean being willing to negotiate ethics on a case-by-case basis. It means, ultimately, being willing to *do vulnerability.*

Vulnerability is a tricky term here. According to the *Oxford English Dictionary Online* (hereafter *OED*), the word "vulnerable" comes from the Latin *vulnerabilis* or "wounding." It has generally meant being open to attack. But *vulnerabilis* comes from the Latin verb *vulnerare* or "to wound," so earlier, now obsolete uses from the 17th century have included "the power to wound." I'd like to recover this double meaning here, as I began to do above when I discussed Riche's (2017) work. When I use the term "vulnerable" in my work, I am admitting that my academic position gives me the power to wound, which then requires that I be willing to accept being wounded myself. Of course, "vulnerability" often carries with it the connotations of being weak, inept, and, perhaps, overly emotional. These connotations, while troubling, are unavoidable. In fact, I argue that these connotations can be helpful in my structuring of "vulnerability" as they highlight the emotional and embodied elements of experience, which are crucial to academic work. I argue that it is possible—à la Micciche (2007)—to *do* vulnerability, to turn vulnerability into a calculated, rhetorical move or device that may undermine the potentially violent appropriation of communities by academe. If I do vulnerability, then I must open myself up, truly, to critique by fans, in order to mediate and/or rid myself of the unnecessary wounding my work could do.

In my own research methods, I decided on the following sets of values and practices as a way to be transparent with my fan participants about my research goals, to show these participants respect for the gift of their time, stories, and interviews, to acknowledge the vulnerability of their positions as fanwriters in the first place, and, certainly, to open the door to reciprocity—to fulfilling some roles that these participants might ask of me as we go through the research process together.

- I need to remember that my perspective of what using online fanfiction websites is like is *not* the same as all other fans' experiences. I need to continue considering what other fans expect of who is using a space and how it should be used. This could eventually mean that I will need to receive consent for every story I quote and analyse in my research outputs.
- I need to keep in mind that because story reviews and forum discussion comments are more like private conversations, I need to gain consent in order to use and quote these conversations in my research.

Achieving ethical research practices

- I need to remember that consent must *always* be an ongoing process. (For example, I am still in touch with participants from my earliest study, and I consult them before I present any new materials of their online fandom at new conferences, in new publications, or in the classroom). Participants must always have the option to opt out.
- I need to be willing to redact previous research if I receive a complaint from a participant.
- I need to be open to fulfilling requests that participants might have for me, such as reviewing their stories or books in good faith or acting as a beta reader (editor) for future work.
- I need to be open about my fan and academic position to fans, academics, and aca-fans alike.
- I need to engage in an ongoing process of self-reflection, which means continuing to ask questions such as: Is my research focus truly helpful within academia? Have I really considered all of the ethical issues at hand? Have I lost sight of the fans in my zeal to share what I have found? Have I done my best to represent the fans in the way that they would likely represent themselves? Etc.

These are the main goodwill practices I have developed so far in my research. But I do want to reiterate that, in order to fully *do vulnerability*, I must always be willing to revisit and redesign these practices as I continue my research, especially when that research moves into new sites and communities. I would also like to remind readers that I came to these practices over six years of research and engagement with my online fan participants. But this process is not finished for me, and, hopefully, will never be fully settled, since, as Whiteman (2012) urges us, we must always treat "ethics as, and in, process" (p. 9). In addition, it is important to note that many of these principles require the researcher to go above and beyond requirements set for them by ethics committees. However, while this approach requires more attention from the researcher, because they are most familiar with their site(s) and community(ies) of research, overall, these values are in keeping with the spirit of the Belmont Report (discussed above); they are extensions of the founding principles of respect, beneficence, and justice—not divergences from these. Finally, I should note that these practices are just one example of a possible, ethical approach to online research. In the next section, I will discuss in more depth the processes one might use to help them design ethical methods appropriate to their own specific questions, foci, and contexts.

27.4 Visualising ethical design of digital research methods

The ethical practices presented in the last section were one example of what a goodwill ethics approach might look like—in that case, work with online fanfiction writers. In this section, I will present the process one can go through to achieve their own set of ethical practices in their own contexts of research online. Because uses of digital and online technologies are various, this discussion will necessarily be general. Nonetheless, it should help both new and experienced researchers to make more confident decisions about what ethical research can and should look like for them. For our purposes here, let's skip the first typical question in the ethical clearance process: Is my project research?

Instead, we can begin with a question much more focused on methodological design: How can I best go about seeking answers to my question? Starting here positions us as people who are truly curious and open to the answers we might find. In the figure that follows, I model the ongoing reflexive and recursive process that good research should be. By "recursive," I mean that research can never follow fully linear steps. Some actions will be taken only once, while others will be taken multiple times throughout the research process. By "reflexive," I mean that researchers should always undertake careful and critical reflection about their questions, assumptions, and methods throughout the entire process of planning a project, collecting data, analysing that data, and reporting on that data.

The figure above is an especially useful representation of the recursive process of research method design. Research moves forward, much as wheels do. However, in the process of moving forward, each spoke is always returned to. What's more, each spoke—each element of the design—is connected to every other

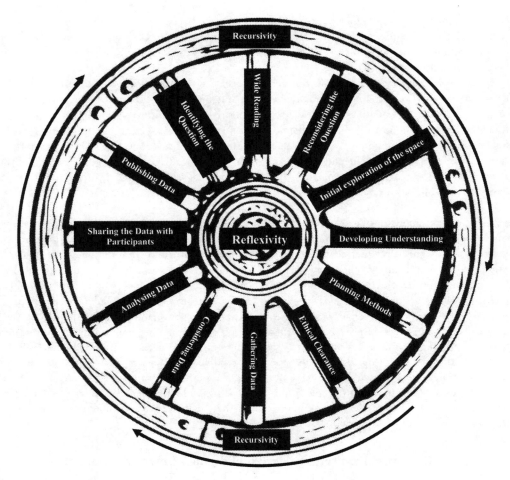

Figure 27.2 How can I best seek answers to my questions?

element. Should one spoke break, the entire wheel might break as well, rendering the wheel useless until it is repaired. Similarly, if a researcher approaches the research process as a linear set of steps, and fails to start the process with a disposition of goodwill and vulnerability, it could "break the wheel," as it were, and halt the forward progress of the research.

Figure 27.2 above is heavily influenced by the work of McKee and Porter (2009), Markham and Buchanan (2012) (of the Association of Internet Researchers), and Whiteman (2012), particularly when it comes to: 1) remembering that internet research *always* deals with people in some way, and 2) always treating research ethics as a process. The following values are reflected in Figure 27.2, and should be taken as key values to ethical research design.

- Research into any online space/community requires the researcher to take the time to understand how that space operates, and to ask: What do the users imagine the space is for? Who do they imagine use the space? What does that mean for how I will research this space? In other words, online research always requires an "ethnographic perspective" (see Heath and Street, 2008).

Achieving ethical research practices

- Most research online (unless it is focused solely on web articles or images published by commercial or academic presses meant for public consumption and distribution) deals with *people*, so the researcher *must* consider the ethical clearance process, even if, ultimately, gaining consent is untenable or even disruptive to the space.
- Any research, whether it is qualitative or quantitative, should always be a recursive and reflexive process. Responsible researchers must always interrogate their assumptions, premises, questions, goals, and methods.
- Studies of the contemporary internet can and should consider the use of big data analytics and/or social network analysis. However, just because the data is "big," and even if the researcher can assume that the data is likely to be fully anonymised and represented only in the aggregate, the researcher still has a responsibility to consider the *people* behind this data. Responsible researchers must always be careful to fully consider how they collect their data, and the potential partnerships they might form in order to do so[6].
- Finally, it is crucial that researchers remember that what they write to share their findings is not and can/could never be a transparent representation of the results. The written document is *always* a construction that is shaped by/shaping dominant ideologies and systems of power relations.

I argue that doing all of this well requires that researchers remember and honour the highly vulnerable positions that research can put participants in. Ultimately, this means being willing to negotiate with participants where necessary (and possible) and being willing to *not* research certain spaces or use certain methods if these could potentially cause undue harm to the human beings behind the data.

A key element of the process represented above, and certainly of the human-centred values underlying this process, is the decision of whether and how to gain participant consent. McKee and Porter (2009) presented a figure in an effort to help researchers judge when they should gain consent before using certain content in any stage of their research, arguing that the more private and sensitive the information, the more ethically necessary it becomes for the researcher to gain informed consent. McKee and Porter's (2009) approach is a helpful guide to considering informed consent. But I would add, here, that not all content that seems public (non-password protected) or non-sensitive (like a general *Harry Potter* fanfiction story, for example) is necessarily viewed as "public" or "non-sensitive" by the poster. It could very well be, as we see in many social networking and social media spaces that the content posted is, as Patricia Lange (2007) has put it, "publicly private"—that is, technically publicly available, but meant for a small network of people.

Furthermore, it is not always tenable to gain consent. What's more, the process of gaining informed consent could potentially disrupt the kinds of interactions that might happen in a particular online space—as Whiteman (2012) has argued, in response to McKee and Porter (2009): "The sensitivity or vulnerability of researched activity cannot just be defined from an external perspective, however. Scholars have also recognised the fact that 'the topics and activities defined as sensitive vary widely across cultures and situations' (Dickson-Swift et al. 2008, 3) and that the 'definition of a "sensitive" research topic is dependent on both context and cultural norms and values' (McCosker et al. 2001, no page nos.)" (p. 64). Whiteman (2012) goes on to argue, in keeping with her view that we cannot and should not have a blanket approach to research ethics, that the decision to seek consent requires that researchers become familiar with the way the site of study operates—that they may need to negotiate the presumed privacy and sensitivity with website users.

To take a very different example from the online fanfiction sites that have been discussed so far, consider a study that wishes to see the shifts in discourses on gender and sexuality in relation to the #MeToo and the subsequent #TimesUp movements on Twitter. Not only is Twitter a massive and massively open space, making it literally impossible to gain consent to use all tweets related to a certain hashtag, it might also disrupt the consciousness-raising and the "personal is political" feminist foundation of much of the movement to even attempt to gain consent. Given such an example, researchers are reminded that the process of informed consent, and the figure above, are to be taken as starting places in ongoing methodological design, and not as a one-size-fits-all approach.

Conclusion: Practicing goodwill and doing vulnerability in methodological design

I began this chapter discussing the Cambridge Analytica incident both because it is the largest recent scandal to remind us that data is never neutral, and because it raises important questions regarding ethical research methods for academia and industry alike in this age of "datafication and dataveillance" (van Dijck, 2014) and "platform capitalism" (Srnicek, 2017). Within this context, data has become "the new oil" (Parkins, 2017), and companies have learned that the only way to survive is to collect, process, and sell the truly massive amounts of data that users provide, both knowingly and unknowingly. Dr Kogan, Facebook, Cambridge Analytica, and allegedly the Russian government all saw the potential value of this data, without considering the very real, very material consequences of not only gathering and analysing but operationalising this data. This is a context, then, of mass vulnerability for many, and, therefore, massive responsibility for those working within institutions of power, as most researchers do.

In this chapter, I have responded to this context by showing how a researcher might best approach methodological design in a sustainably ethical way by considering both goodwill and vulnerability. As can be seen with the development of the Nuremberg Code and, subsequently, the Belmont Report, our past has taught us that "for the greater good" is not only impossible to define, but, what's more, not nearly enough to justify any research project. The ends do not justify the means. And while it is true that research using digital methods, at least the kinds that we have been discussing in this book, are not medical in nature, like those that led to the Doctor Trials at Nuremberg or to the eventual conclusion of the Tuskegee Syphilis Study, they can possibly have the power to negatively affect just as many if not more people, as the Cambridge Analytica scandal has demonstrated.

In discussing my own experiences of research into online fanfiction communities, I demonstrated both that mistakes in ethical decisions are frequent and inevitable, and that these mistakes can be mediated and ameliorated. When I began my research as a PhD student, I was unaware of how fans felt about researchers, and I initially had little guidance to help me consider larger ethical concerns of research in online spaces. And while I did not, at first, make the right ethical decisions about my research, upon learning about the concerns of my methods, I immediately sought to rectify them. This is the beauty of treating ethics as an ongoing process—it allows researchers to modify their methods in the wake of new information, technologies, and contexts.

Ultimately, practicing goodwill in digital research methods requires two things: first, that a researcher treat ethical method design as a recursive and reflexive *process*; and second, that the researcher *do* vulnerability. In the first case, a researcher must consistently check their questions, assumptions, goals, and approaches to the research, keeping in mind that they may need to make major changes, and/or return to previous actions multiple times throughout the research. In the second case, the researcher must always keep in mind that their work could cause grave harm, and that they should consistently revisit how they can mitigate this potential harm. Doing so often requires that a researcher be open to possible reciprocity—that is, they must be open to the possibility that participants may want to partner in the research or gain something specific from the research or researcher. Finally, this is best done through a dedication to transparency—about the research goals, methods, and audiences for the research. Total transparency demonstrates respect for the people that one researches, whether these people are the direct focus or not. Ethical research is sustainable research, and it cannot be achieved without a disposition of goodwill.

Achieving ethical research practices

Notes

1 It has recently been suggested by Jon Ronson (2015) that the details of the Stanford Prison Experiment were either exaggerated or misrepresented by the principal investigator, Philip Zimbardo. While this is entirely possible, the Stanford Prison Experiment is still taught in many introductory psychology courses, so I include it here.

2 QUILTBAG+ refers to a community of people who identify as "queer/questioning, undecided, intersex, lesbian, trans★, bisexual/pansexual, asexual/allied, gay/genderqueer, and other identities". I use this acronym versus LGBTQIA+ because I think it covers a wider range of potential identities.

3 It should be noted that some researchers will use the term "respondents" instead of "participants." When I am discussing interviews or surveys, I too will often use this term. Other researchers will choose to use "subjects" when referring to the people they study. I believe this term is too alienating to be helpful in designing ethical and sustainable research methods for work with human beings. I prefer the term participants, ultimately, because it highlights not only respect for these human beings, but also the possibility that researchers will collaborate with those they research (and vice versa). This is a perspective I have taken from feminist research methods and action research—see, especially Powell & Takayoshi, 2003; and Brydon-Miller, 2008, 2009.

4 At *Sycophant Hex*, registered site users (those who have joined the site using a penname and password) can leave ratings on stories. These ratings exist on a scale of 1 to 5 stars (similar to an Amazon review), with 5 stars being the highest rating. In addition to these ratings, fans can leave comments for the authors.

5 As we come to see here, fans have been and remain vulnerable to powerful institutions, especially producers of their favourite content (and their lawyers—see especially Jenkins, 2006). The best way to address this vulnerability, then, is to refer back to the Belmont Report's value of beneficence, which states: "(1) do not harm and (2) maximize possible benefits and minimize possible harms." Acting beneficently (and with goodwill) means that a researcher will make judgments about what they can report on in conjunction with fans, but also in relation to what needs to be critiqued about those communities, especially when those communities act in racist, sexist, and homophobic ways.

6 For more on big data and ethics, see: boyd & Crawford, 2012; Tractenberg, et al., 2014; Mittelstadt & Floridi, 2016; and Leurs, 2017.

References

Bacon-Smith, C. (1992). *Enterprising women: Television fandom and the creation of popular myth*. Philadelphia, PA: University of Pennsylvania Press.

boyd, d. & Crawford, K. (2012). Critical questions for big data. *Information, Communication, & Society*, 15(5): 662–679. https://doi.org/10.1080/1369118X.2012.678878.

Brydon-Miller, M. (2009). Covenantal ethics and action research: Exploring a common foundation for social research. In D.M. Mertens & P.E. Ginsberg (Eds.) *The handbook of social research ethics* (243–258). London: Sage Publications.

Brydon-Miller, M. (2008). Ethics and action research: Deepening our commitment to principles of social justice and redefining systems of democratic practice. In R. Reason & H. Bradbury (Eds.) *The SAGE Handbook of action research* (199–210).

Busse, K., & Hellekson, K. (2012). Identity, ethics, and fan privacy. In K. Larsen & L. Zubernis (Eds.) *Fan culture: Theory/practice* (38–56). Newcastle: Cambridge Scholars Publishing.

Cadwalladr, C. & Graham-Harrison, E. (2018, May 17). Revealed: 50 million Facebook profiles harvested for Cambridge Analytica in major data breach. *The Guardian*. Retrieved from: https://www.theguardian.com/news/2018/mar/17/cambridge-analytica-facebook-influence-us-election.

CDC Centers for Disease Control and Prevention. (2015, Dec. 14). Tuskegee study, 1932–1972. *U.S. Public Health Service syphilis study at Tuskegee*. Retrieved from: https://www.cdc.gov/tuskegee/index.html.

chivalric. (2012, 16 Jan.) Divorce. *Sycophant Hex*. Retrieved from: http://ashwinder.sycophanthex.com/viewstory.php?sid=25499.

Deller, R. (2018). Ethics in fan studies research. In P. Booth (Ed.) *A companion to media fandom and fan studies* (123–139).

Department of Health, Education, and Welfare. (1979). *The Belmont Report*. (DHEW Publication No. L. 93-348). Washington, DC: U.S. Government Printing Office. Retrieved from: https://www.hhs.gov/ohrp/regulations-and-policy/belmont-report/read-the-belmont-report/index.html.

Fanlore. (2016, 14 Dec.). So your fic is required reading: Hahahanope. *Fanlore.org*. Retrieved from: https://fanlore.org/wiki/So_Your_Fic_is_Required_Reading:_Hahahanope.

Heath, S. B., & Street, B.V. (2008). *On ethnography: Approaches to language and literacy research*. New York: Teachers College Press.

Jenkins, H. (2006). *Convergence culture: Where old and new media collide*. New York: New York University Press.

Jenkins, H. (1992). *Textual poachers: Television fans and participatory culture*. London: Routledge.

Jones, B. (2016, March 25). "The ethical hearse": Privacy, identity and fandom online. *The Learned Fangirl*. Retrieved from: http://thelearnedfangirl.com/2016/03/the-ethical-hearse-privacy-identity-and-fandom-online/.

Kara, H. (2018). *Research ethics in the real world*. Bristol, U.K.: Policy Press.

Kelley, B. (2016). Toward a goodwill ethics of online research methods. *Transformative Works and Cultures*, 22. https://doi.org/10.3983/twc.2016.0891.

Kozinets, R.V. (2015). *Netnography: Redefined* (2nd ed.). London: Sage. doi:978-1-4462-8574-9

Lange, P. G. (2007): Publicly private and privately public: Social network on YouTube. *Journal of Computer-Mediated Communication* 13(1): 361–380. *https://doi.org/10.1111/j.1083-6101.2007.00400.x*.

Leurs, K. (2017). Feminist data studies: Using digital methods for ethical, reflexive and situated socio-cultural research. *Feminist Review* 115: 130–154. DOI 0141-7789/17.

MacKinnon, R. (2012) *Consent of the networked: The worldwide struggle for internet freedom*. New York: Basic Books.

Markham, A. & Buchanan, E. (2012). Ethical decision-making and internet research: Recommendations from the AoIR working committee. *Aoir.org*. Retrieved from: https://aoir.org/reports/ethics2.pdf

McKee, H. (2008). Ethical and legal issues for writing researchers in an age of media convergence. *Computers and Composition*, 25: 104–122. https://doi.org/10.1016/j.compcom.2007.09.007

McKee, H., & Porter, J. (2009). *The ethics of internet research: A rhetorical, case-based process*. New York: Peter Lang.

Micciche, L. (2007). *Doing emotion: Rhetoric, writing, teaching*. Portsmouth, NH: Boynton/Cook.

Mittelstadt, B. D. & Floridi, L. (2016). The ethics of big data: Current and foreseeable issues in biomedical contexts. *Science and Engineering Ethics*. 22: 303–341. https://doi.10.1007/s11948-015-9652-2.

Newkirk, T. (2017). *Embarrassment: And the emotional underlife of learning*. Portsmouth, NH: Heinemann.

(1996). Seduction and betrayal in qualitative research. In G. E. Kirsch & P. Mortensen (Eds.) *Ethics and representation in qualitative studies of literacy*. Urbana, IL: NCTE.

Parkins, D. (2017, 6 May). The world's most valuable resource is no longer oil, but data. *The economist*. Retrieved from: https://www.economist.com/leaders/2017/05/06/the-worlds-most-valuable-resource-is-no-longer-oil-but-data.

Powell, K. M., & Takayoshi, P. (2003). Accepting roles created for us: The ethics of reciprocity. *College Comp. & Comm.* 54 (3): 394–422. DOI: 10.2307/3594171.

Riche, D. (2017). Toward a theory and pedagogy of rhetorical vulnerability. *LICS*, 5(2), 84–102. Retrieved from: http://licsjournal.org/OJS/index.php/LiCS/article/view/171/222.

Ronson, J. (2015). *So you've been publicly shamed*. London: Picador.

Srnicek, N. (2017). *Platform capitalism*. Cambridge, UK: Polity.

Tractenberg, R.E., et al. (2015). Using ethical reasoning to amplify the reach and resonance of professional codes of conduct in training big data scientists. *Science and Engineering Ethics*. 21: 1485–1507. https://DOI.10.1007/s11948-014-9613-1.

van Dijck, J. (2014). Datafication, dataism and dataveillance: Big data between scientific paradigm and ideology. *Surveillance & Society* 12(2): 197–208. http://www.surveillance-and-society.org.

Van Tooke, R.P. (2015, 13 Feb.). Students explore erotica in fan fiction DeCal at UC Berkeley. *The Daily Californian*. Retrieved from: http://www.dailycal.org/2015/02/13/students-explore-erotica-fan-fiction-decal-uc-berkeley/.

Waldorph. (2014, 22 Feb.) So your fic is required reading: Hahahanope. *Tumblr*.

Watkins, E. & Jordan, C. (2018, March 21). Cambridge Analytica suspends CEO Alexander Nix after undercover recordings air. *CNN Politics*. Retrieved from: https://edition.cnn.com/2018/03/20/politics/alexander-nix-cambridge-analytica/index.html.

Whiteman, N. (2012). *Undoing ethics: Rethinking practice in online research*. New York: Springer.

INDEX

Italicized and **bold** pages refer to figures and tables respectively, and page numbers followed by "n" refer to notes.

Academia.edu 249
Academia Sinica Center for Digital Cultures 193
academic identities 239–240
academic literature 198
access, archives and libraries 437
accessibility 263–264, 278, 400, 409
achievement task 391
ActiveCollab project management tool 165
active learning 389–392
actor-oriented networks 101
actors 117–118
administrators *vs.* educators 17–22
Adult and Continuing Education Centre at UCC 16
aesthetics 49–50, 54, 408
Africa 40
age-related macular degeneration (AMD) 408, 409
Agile DSDM® 162–163, 166
Aidemark, J. 125
Akmon, Dharma 436
Alam, S. L. 368
Albers, A. 23, 25; Line Involvement VI (artwork) *27*; Red Meander II (artwork) *24*; tactile model (artwork) *24, 27*
Albers, J. 23, 25; Homages to the Square (artwork) *21*
alignment of syllabi 345
Allen, I. E. 385
All My Humming Birds Have Alibis (Ernst) 58n16
Almanach de la Librairie 118
Almanach Royal 118
altruistic motivations 368; *see also* motivations
Amazon 365
Amazon Web Services 161
ambiguity 55, 113, 313
American Historical Society 121n1

Amsterdam School of the Arts 34
analysis: of data 244, 252–255, 270; data management 132–134; document 288; encoding and 283–289; point pattern *226*; project 288–289
analytical approach 66–67
analytical skills 16, 33
analytical viewing *321–327, 324–327*
Anarchive 50
ancien régime 112
Ancient Greek 263–264, 266–267, 269–272, 315
Anderson, L. 58n16
Anderson, S. 318
Anderson, T. 387, 395
Andeweg, A. 357
Andrew R. Mellon Foundation 313
Andrews, T. 276
Anna Pavlova 39
annotations 36–38, 309, 322–323, 329–330
Annotation Studio **193**
anonymity 84–85
AntConc 280, 282
Anthologize 360
AntiGate: Amplitude Version 56
APIs 42, 112, 118
Applegate, M. 198
Application Lifecycle Management (ALM) 166
approaches: to learning and teaching 16; multi-sited ethnography in migration research 78–81; statistical 224–227; time-based 96
aptitude *see* digital aptitude
ArcGIS (software) **193**, 224, 255
Archer, D. 264
archival donor agreements 434–435
archives, preservation and access in 437
Aristotle 417
arithmetic skills 391
Armstrong, J. 14, 18, 23

Index

Art & Architecture Thesaurus 96
Art as Therapy (De Botton and Armstrong) 14
artfair 71–72
articulation 41–42, 162–163, 167–168
artificial intelligence 32, 103, 262, 268
Artintact 50
artistic research 46–57; aesthetics 49–50; artistry 51–52; critical thinking 55–56; digital shadows 51–52; genealogy 48–49; individual virtuosity 52–53; powers 53–55; remediations 49–50; *see also* research
artistry 51–52
Artist's Interactive CD-ROMagazine 50
art museum *see* Glucksman Gallery at UCC
arts-based research techniques 63–64
Asana (web-based management applications) 199
Asia 40
assignments 315–319; audio digital presentation 389–390; multimedia website 391–392; Scalar-based design 319; stages 324–330; visual digital presentation 389–390
Association for Computers and the Humanities 192
Association for Project Management 359
Association of Computing in the Humanities and the Association of Literary and Linguistic Computing Joint International Conference (ACH/ALLC) 346
Association of Digital Humanities Organizations (ADHO) 190, 192, 194–197, **196**, 199–200, 332, 340
Association of Internet Researchers 84
Atlantic Europe in the Metal Ages (Koch) 165
Atlas 249
Atlas linguistique de Gascogne 225
Atlas of Early Printing 111
Atlas of the Rhode Island Book Trade 111
attainment value 391; *see also* values
attributions 387, 391–392
audio digital presentation assignment 389–390
auditory 25
Australasia 40
Australia 111
Australian Common Reader database 111
authentic learning 394–395; *see also* learning

backward design 353, 354–356
Bacon, F. 155
Bahde, A. 197
Baird, S. F. 364
Bakhtin, M. 101
Bandura, A. 392
Barber, K. 80
Bar Code Hotel (Hoberman) 59n26
Barron, K. E. 394
Barthes, R. 277
Basch, L. 80
Bates, M. J. 144
Battershill, C. 332–333
Battistoni, G. 23, 25
Bauman, S. 280, 289n5

Bauman, Z. 158, 239
Bawden, D. 141
Bay-Cheng, S. 48
Bédier, J. 277
Bel, J. 38
The Belmont Report 418, 419, 424
Bench, H. 32–33, 35, 38–39, 41–42, 48
beneficence 418
Benveniste, E. 265
Berendt, B. 424
Berens, K. I. 297
Berne Convention for the Protection of Literary and Artistic Works 431, 432
Berners-Lee, T. 278–279
Berry, D. M. 59n25, 287
Between Meaning and Machine (Ribes and Bowker) 127
Beyond Women's Words— feminisms and the practices of oral history in the twentyfirst century (Srigley) 303
Bianco, J. 295
Bibframe 114–115
bibliographic data models 112–117; *see also* data
Bibliographie du genre Romanesque française, 1751–1800 (Martin, Mylne and Frautschi) 110, 116
Biblos 18 database 110; *see also* data
BiBO 114–115
Biesta, G. 141
big ideas 355, 357–358, 361
Big Tent 142
Billy Budd, Sailor (Melville) 290n28
Billy Waters: The London Fiddler 51
Bj 581 299
Black Cultural Archives (BCA) 303
Black Women Big Data project 297
Black Women's Movement 303
Blanc, B. 79
Blanc, S. 79
Blanc-Szanton, C. 80
Blas, Z. 59n25
Bleeker, M. 32–33
(BLOCK)CHAIN OF LOVE 58n17
blogging 343, **343**
Bod, R. 158
Bodard, G. 281–282
Bodleian Library 121
Bonds, L. 332
Book of Genesis 92
books 112–117
Borgman, C. 128
born-digital content 420–421
Boschetti, F. 266
Boulez, P. 58n21
boundary objects 159
Bowers, F. 277
Bowers, J. 56
Bowker, G. C. 127, 195
Bowling Green State University **336**, **346**
Boyd, D. 71

456

Index

Boyles, C. 360
Bradley, J. 165
Bregman, A. 392–393
Brey, Philip 424–425
bricolage 361
bridge problem *see* Königsberg bridge problem
Brigham Young University (BYU) **336**, **346**
British Library 146, 366–367, 376
The British Museum is Falling Down (Lodge) 1
British Psychological Society 84
Brooklyn Museum 367
Brown, Michael, Jr. 423
Brown, N. M. 297
Broye, L. 50
Brumfield, B. 374
Bryant, J. 277
bubbles 67–69, *68*, 71–72
Buchanan, S. 139
BugsCEP (fossil insect database) 206
build, laboratory 164–166
Building Inspector 366–367
Burgess, M. 256
Burke, P. J. 386, 388
Burrows, J. F. 276
Burrows, S. 111, 116, 121
Busa, R. 303–304
Bush, V. 125
Butler, J. 298
Byrne, R. 18; 'Colour Threshold #3'
    (installation art) *27*

Calvert, T. 58n7
Campbell, J. 267, 368
Campbell v. Acuff-Rose Music, Inc. 430
Campus, P. 50
campus-based education 384; *see also* e-Learning
Canada 111, 143, 199, 335, **336**
Candea, M. 79, 87
Caplan, D. 48
care ethics approach 424
Carleton University **336**, **346**
Carter, S. 394
Cartesian mapping 215; *see also* mapping
cartography 203–205, 210, 215, 219, 230; *see also* digital
    cartography; manual cartographies
case studies: digital research and data 250–256;
    Scalar (online platform) 319–330
Castells, M. 80
Caswell, M. 138–140, 143
CataRT (software) 53
Caton, A. P. 163, 165–166, 169n14
CCH Canadian Ltd. v. Law Society of Upper Canada 430
CDROMs 50
CEA Critic 332
Center for Digital Liberal Arts (CDLA) 309, 318
Centre for Computing and the Humanities 159
Centre for e-Research 159

Centre for the Integration of Research, Teaching and
    Learning (CIRTL) 13, 16
Century Black Drama 297
CERL 118
CERN 157
Cervantes 313, *316*, 317, *318*, 323–324
challenges: complexities 29; mapping 210; in online
    teaching 14, 17–22; paradigm 121; project 375;
    societal 211; software development 38; work 54
Charter of Fundamental Rights of the European Union
    418
Chee, F. 424
choreographer-led research 32
*A Choreographer's Score: Fase, Rosas danst Rosas, Elena's
    Aria, Bartók* (de Keersmaeker and Cveji¿) 34
Choreographic Language Agent (project) 34
choreographic objects 33–35, 39
*Choreographic Objects: Traces and Artifacts of Physical
    Intelligence* (project) 33
Chow, A. S. 385
Christ 264
Christen, K. 421
chronophotography 216n2
chronotope 204
CIDOC-CRM 96, 103–104, 173, 179–182, *181*, 187
CIRTL *see* Centre for the Integration of Research,
    Teaching and Learning (CIRTL)
citations 330; analysis 195; data management and 257–258
CJ-Junkman (Feingold) 50
CLARIN 253, 256
Clary, E. G. 368, 371
Clayton, P. 145
Clement, T. 144, **336**, **340**, 341, 346–347
Cockburn, I. 434
cognitive load 405–406, 411
co-instruction 337–338
collaboration: co-production of scholarship 191–194;
    course design 358–361; data management 130–132;
    project-based 192
collaborative advantage 191
Collaborative Research in the Digital Humanities (McCarty
    and Deegan) 358–359
colleagues and clients 131
collections-based research (CBR) 311, 312, 313
College English Association 332
collegiality 345
Collingwood, R. G. 158
colours *71*, 71–73
'Colour Threshold #3' (installation art) *27*, 27–28
Common Language Resources and Technology
    Infrastructure(CLARIN) 242
common practice-based patterns 104–106
communications: among research communities
    253, 255–256; communities and 246–248, *247*,
    256–257; data management 130–132; digital
    research and data 256–257; lack of 267; roles *249*;
    see also synchronous communication

Index

communities: communication and 246–248, *247*, 256–257; digital research and data 256–257; engagement 375–376; of practice 241, 388, 392–395

community-based research practices 257–258

Community Collection Model 367

community-sourcing 365

competency 394

complete spatial randomness (CSR) 224–225

compliance *see* ethics

Comptes faits 119

computational methods 195, 271

computational models 269–270; *see also* model/modelling

computational skills 138; *see also* skills

computational studies 265–266

computer-aided design 36

computer mapping 221; *see also* mapping

computer science research, ethics and 419–420

computer-supported cooperative work (CSCW) 190, 194, 197–198, 365

conceptual frameworks 364–365

conceptual model/modelling 103–104, 173, 179; *see also* model/modelling

conceptual work 156–157

confidentiality of data 84–85; *see also* data

Conkey, M. W. 299

connectedness 345, 392

consent 433–434

Consortium of European Social Science Data Archives (CESSDA) 242

contemporary migrants 80

content management system (CMS) 192

contraption 54

Cook, T. 143, 302

co-production of scholarship 191–194

copyright 423, 428–439; fair use 422–423, 429–431; goal of 430; public domain 431–432; *see also* intellectual property

Copyright Act of 1790 431

Copyright Act of 1831 431

Copyright Act of 1976 429, 437

Copyright Clearance Center 433–434

Copyright Direction Article 5 430

Copyright Term Extension Act 431, 437

Cordell, R. 332

corpus 334–337, **336**, 343–345

Corpus Inscriptionum Latinarum 282

Corpus of Historical American English 264

cost belief 391–392

Cotter, M. 18

course/module link **336**, **340**, 353–361; backward design 354–356; bricolage 361; collaboration 358–361; context 389; material 313–315; methodology 356–357; Moore's Law 353; planning 311; project and 338–339; scaffolding 313–315; schedule 312

Cramer, L. 298

Cramming More Components onto Integrated Circuits (Moore) 353

Crane, G. 289, 289n1

Crawford, C. D. 197

Creative Commons 432–433, **433**

creativity 27–28

crisis of replicability 423

Critical Commons 311, 314–315, 318–319, **320–321**, 324, *326–327*, 327

Critical Heritage Studies (CHS) 295–304

critical theory 49

critical thinking 55–56, 59n25

Cronin, J. G. R. 16

crowdfunding 68, *68*

crowdsourcing 130, 363–377; community engagement 375–376; conceptual frameworks 364–365; in cultural heritage 363–364, 366–368, 376; data re-use 370–371; developing 372–373; documentation 374; future 376; launching 375; managing organisational impact 370; onboarding 373; participant discussion 375; participant recruitment 371; people contribution to 368; planning 369, 370–371, 376; quality control 374; reality check 372; recognition 374; research frameworks 364–365; rewards 374; running 375; source collections 370; success 369; task design 373–374; testing 372–373; turning into reality 368–369; tutorials 374; validation 374; verification systems 374

Croxall, B. **336**, 337–338, **338–340**, 339, **346**, 346–347

Croxton, R. A. 385, 393

CSS 339

'Cube' (Forrest) 26, *26*

Cueing System *34*

cultural heritage 363–364, 366–368, 376; *see also* digital cultural heritage

Cummings, J. 280

Cunin, D. 50

Cunningham, M. 49

Cunningham, P. 331, 334–335, 339, 342

curation *see* digital curation

Curran, M. 116

Currier, B. 360

Cvejic, B. 34–35

cyber-ethnography 77

D'Agostino, Giuseppina 430

dance *see* digital dance

Dance in Transit (project) 35

dance research 31; *see also* research

Daniel, B. K. 357

Daniels, J. 278

DariahTeach 239

Darnton, R. 109, 121n1

Darwin Correspondence Project 263

data: access 255; acquisition 222–223; analysis 244, 252–255, 270, 364; annotation 270; bibliographic models 112–117; citation 253, 255, 257–258; collection 64–66, 224; confidentiality of 84–85;

Index

data management and 222–224; data sources and 111–112; incomplete 119; inconsistent 119; layers 219; modelling 179–182; obtaining 252, 254; open 54, 112, 133, 255, 278; palaeoenvironmental 216n3; poor-quality 119; post-processing 371; processing *251*, 364; quality 223–224; re-use 370–371; types 197–198, 222–223, *251*, 252, 254; visualisation 227–233, *251*; *see also* digital research and data

data collection, ethics and 420–421

data management 125–135, 242–243, 248–250, 252–255; analysis 132–134; citation and 257–258; collaboration 130–132; communication 130–132; data and 222–224; described 128; digital curation 128; recommendations for professionals 134–135; research 128–130

data sharing, ethics and 423–424

data use, ethics and 422–423

Davies, M. 264

Davies, S. 33–34

DCC Curation Lifecycle Model 128, *129*

Debates in the Digital Humanities 2, 332–333

De Botton, A. 14, 18, 23

de Cervantes, M. 314, 316

de Cessolis, J. 121

decision-making 127, 132, 282, 287, 302, 334

The Declaration of Helsinki 418

Declerck, T. 264

deed of gifts 434–435

Deegan, M. 358–359

de Fermat, P. 359

de Jauregui, J. 313

de Keersmaeker, A. T. 34–35

deLahunta, S. 33, 48–49

Delauney triangles *232*

Delitsch, J. 95

democratisation 300

Denmark 230

de Sade, M. 113

design: backward 353, 354–356; laboratory 162–164; language 310; *see also* research

Design of Controlled Vocabularies (Svenonious) 127

Deutsches Textarchiv 264

Dewey Decimal Classification 175

Dewey Decimal System 96

Diamond Light Source synchrotron 157

dictionaries and word-net 102–103

Dietrich, C. 309

digital aptitude 31–42; choreographic objects 33–35; digital dance 31–33; mapping touring 38–42; Movement on the Move (project) 33, 35

digital archival content 198

Digital Atlas of the Roman Empire (DARE) 212

digital cartography 215; *see also* cartography

digital cultural heritage 295–304; digital heritage as bridge 300–301; gender and digital humanities 296–298; gender and heritage 298–300; methodologies 301–304

digital curation 128

digital dance 31–33; defined 32; evolution 32

digital ethnography 77

digital geographies 203–206

Digital Ghost Hunt (Hall) 169n22

Digital Hand (animation) 51

digital historical bibliometric research 109–121; actors 117–118; bibliographic data models 112–117; books 112–117; data and data sources 111–112; incomplete data 119; inconsistent data 119; Linked Open Data 120–121; machine learning 119–120; networks 117–118; optical character recognition (OCR) 119–120; poor-quality data 119; publishing and presenting 120; readers 117–118; taxonomic description 112–117; types 110–111; *see also* research

Digital Humanities Data Curation (website) 357

Digital Humanities in the Library (Hartsell-Gundy) 138

Digital humanities knowledge: Reflections on the introductory graduate syllabus (Selisker) 333

Digital Humanities Pedagogy: Practices, Principles and Politics (Hirsch, B. D.) 332–333

Digital Humanities Quarterly 332

digital labs 191–192; *see also* laboratory

Digital Liberal Arts Lab 313, *314*, 324

digitally mediated social relations 62–74; activating 71–73; analytical approach 66–67; arts-based research techniques 63–64; data collection 64–66; hand-drawn network maps 63–64, 67–73; quality 63–64

digital materials, interdisciplinary approaches to 137–149

Digital Millennium Copyright Act of 1998 (DMCA) 435–436

digital monograph collections 198

digital research and data 239–259; academic identities 239–240; case studies 250–256; communication 256–257; communities 256–257; community-based research practices 257–258; methodology 243–244; research communities 240–242; scholarly practices 242–243; self-identity 256–257; *see also* data

Digital Research Infrastructure for Arts and Humanities (DARIAH) 242, 256, 259n1, 334

digital research methods 190–191

digital rights management 435–436

digital shadows 51–52

digital sociality 62–63

digital tools and environment 399–412; adoption and use of 400–401; interfaces of 400; one-size-fits-all approach to 400; perceived complexity 407–408; usability evaluations 401–404, **403**

digitization 38, 49, 121, 126, 162, 263, 370; copyright 436–437; data collections 224, 420–421; data types 254; democratisation of heritage 300; Photographic Collection 174

dilemmas in online teaching 17–22

disclosive ethics 416, 424–425; *see also* ethics

Distributed Proofreaders 372

Distributive Open Collaborative Course 296

DIY History 370

Django Python software 160

document analysis 288
documentation 288, 312, 374
Documenting Performance: The Context and Processes of Digital Curation and Archiving (Sant) 35
Documenting the Now project 423, 425
Donaldson v. Becket 431
Double Skin/Double Mind (Scholten) 34
Downing, J. 360
Dropbox Business 255
Dropping the Digital (Sayers) 356
Drucker, J. 298
Dryden, Jean 436
due diligence 434
Duguet, A.-M. 50
Duits, R. 180
Dunham's Data (project) 35
Dunn, S. 287

Early English Books Online (EEBO) 119, 121, 263
Early Modern Letters Online (EMLO) 112, 118
East Prussia 93
Eccles, J. S. 391
Edelstein, D. 118
editing 275–289, 330
Edwards, E. 115
Edwards, P. N. 198
e-humanists 400
Eide, Ø. 92
Eighteenth-Century Collections Online (ECCO) 115, 119
Eine kleine Nachtmusik 56
ekphrasis 315–317, *316–318*, 319, **320**, 321–324, 329
ELAN 249, 258
Eldred, Eric 431
Eldred v. Ashcroft 431, 432
e-Learning 384–395; defined 384; pedagogy 386–389; putting theory into practice 389–395; quality 388–389; rise in 385; skepticism 385–386; *see also* learning
Electronics 353
Eliot, T. S. 289
Elkins, J. 15–16
Elleström, L. 92
Elliot, A. J. 394
Elswit, K. 33, 35, 38–39, 41–42, 48
Embodied AudioVisual Interaction (EAVI) 53
embodiment 18–19, 22
Emerson, R. W. 277
emotion 26–28, 264
encoding and analysis 283–289
EndNote 249, 255
Engagement in the real space (study) 18
England 65, 199
English texts 283–289
environment *see* digital tools and environment
environmental humanists 254–256
EpiDoc 280–283

EpiDoc Front End Services (EFES) 282
epistemic virtues 289n3
eResearch 159, 161; *see also* research
Ernst, M. 58n16
error checking 288
e-Science Data Management Model *129*
Escobar, A. 77
Espasa, A. 387
ESRI 224
Eternal Resonance Machine 56
ethical reality check 372
ethical values 421; *see also* values
ethics 416–425; challenge 420–424; as compliance 417–418; computer science research 419–420; concept 417–418; as contemplation 417, 418; data collection 420–421; data sharing 423–424; data use 422–423; disclosive 416, 424–425; frameworks 418; humanities and 419; overview 416; virtue 417
Euler, L. 94
Eulerian circuits 94
Europe 40, 155, 206, 244, 334
Europeana 179, 197, 367
European Citizen Science Association 372
European Commission 242
European Convention on Human Rights 418
European Holocaust Research Infrastructure (EHRI) 242, 259n6
European Organization for Nuclear Research 193
evaluation: assessment and 145; computational models 269–270; expectations in 269; paradigms 269–270; reflective 16
Evans, L. 239
expectations 7, 56, 163, 166, 241, 269, 272, 310, 354, 357, 359, 372, 375, 392, 395, 400–401, 407
experiential learning 332, 394–395; *see also* learning
Exploratory programming in digital humanities pedagogy and research (Montfort) 333
eXtensible Markup Language (XML) 96–97, 99, 102, 105, 178, 182, 184, 186–188, 276, 278–280, 282, 285, 287, 289, 357
extrinsic motivations 368; *see also* motivations
eye tracking 404–412; accessibility 409; perceived web page complexity 407–408; universal design 409–412; usability/usability evaluation 405–407

F1/F2 space 222, 225, *226*
FaBiO 114–115
Facebook 62, 66, 72, 87–88, 101, 246, 249, 262, 421
face-to-face: classroom 384; communications 253, 259; contact 241, 275; instruction 385; interactions 86, 246, 257, 389; interviews 77, 244; learning context 388; online teaching 13–14, 19–20; research 443; transition to online facilitation 17
facilitator 389; *see also* instructors
Fagerjord, A. 59n25, 287
fair-use/fair dealing 422–423, 429–431
Falzon, M. 79

FamilySearch Indexing 372
feasibility check 372
Federal "Common Rule" 419
Fedora Commons repository 178, 186
Fedora Content Model Architecture 178
Feingold, K. 50
feminist digital humanities 295–304
Feminist Game Studies 298
feminist objectivity 144
Feminist Technology Studies 297
FemTechNet 296
Ferraro, G. 169n14
Ferriter, M. 368, 377
Fiebrink, R. 53
fieldworks and sites 79
Fiesler, C. 421
film clips 329
Findlay, M. 23, 27
Firth, J. R. 266
fixation 406
Flanders, J. 279–281
flexibility in online learning 22–23
Flickr Commons 365–367
Foakes, R. A. 283, *284*
Foka, A. 160
following the people 79–81
Folsom, R. 357
font 330
formatting 330
formulating interpretation 66–67, 69
Forrest, R. 18; 'Cube' 26, *26*; 'Hive' 21, *21*
Forsythe, W. 33, 48–49
The Forsythe Company (TFC) 37
Fortune, S. 54
Fossil Finder 371
Fraistat, N. 279
France 110, 115, 120
Frankenstein 287
Frautschi, R. 110, 116
FRBRoo 114–115, 179
Freak Show 58n16
French Book Trade in Enlightenment Europe (FBTEE) 109–112, 115–117, 119–120
Frermann, L. 269, 271
FromThePage 365
Fujihata, M. 50
Fujimura, J. H. 159, 162, 167
Functional Requirements of Bibliographic Records (FRBR) *113*, 113–115
Fundacion Juan March 131–133
Furet, F. 109, 116, 121n1
fuzzy (search algorithms) 102

Galaxy Zoo 368
galleries, libraries, archives, and museums (GLAM) 114, 128, 138, 157, 162, 179–180, 365, 367–368, 376
Gallica 116

The Game and Playe of the Chesse (de Cessolis) 121
game theory 359
Garin, E. 156
Garner, M. 357
gazetteers 203, 212–213, 223, 231
Geeraerts, D. 225
gender: archaeology 299; digital humanities and 296–298; heritage and 298–300
genealogy 48–49
General Data Protection Regulation (GDPR) 255
geographical modelling of linguistic data 220–222
geographic information system (GIS) 111, 203, 205, 214, 218–233; applications 224–233; data and data management 222–224; geographical modelling of linguistic data 220–222; mapping 360; methods 224–233
Geography of the London Ballad Trade, 1500–1700 111
Geonames 232
Georeferencer 367
George Mason University 192, 360
Georgia GOOSE *228*
Georgian Papers Programme (GPP) 169n23
geovisualization 203–216; concept 204; GIS and 204; Mekhane team 211–212; place-making processes 210; as research tool 205; *see also* socio-ecological landscapes; visualisations
Gephi **193**
German Federal Archive 193
German Federal Ministry of Education and Research 48
Gesture Recognition Toolkit (Gillian and Nicolls) 53
Getty Thesaurus of Geographic Names 96
Gieryn, T. 168n5
Gillian, N. 53
Gilliland-Swetland, A. 128
Gillis, S. 132
GitHub **193**
Glanllynnau *208*
Glissant, E. 59n25
Global Historical Bibliometrics project 110
Gluck, S. B. 303
Glucksman Gallery at UCC 13–16, 18–19, 25
Goatley, W. 54–55
Godart, F. 64
Golan v. Holder 431–432
Gold, M. 356
Goldberg, J. H. 407
Golden Age of Spanish Literature and Film 313
Gombrich, E. 174
Gooday, G. 156
Google 38, 191
Google API (programmers' interface) 220
Google Books 116, 249, 264, 267
Google Books Ngram Corpus 264, 266
Google maps 220
Google Scholar 347, 349n1, 402
Google Sheet *317*
GOOSE 225, *228*

Index

Gorman, G. E. 145
Gould, P. 218, 233
graceful exit 376
graduate course **336**, **340**, 343, 344
graduate level online program 392–395
graduate syllabi 340–343
Graham, S. 333, **336**, 337, 340, **340**, 343, **344**, **346**
Grant, I. 51–52
graphics processing units (GPUs) 161
Great Britain 15, 66, 111, 138, 147, 157, 161, 174
Greco, E. 34
Greece 204
Green, O. 56
Greer, Katie 438
Greetham, D. 277
Greg, W. W. 277
Greschke, M. 79, 83
Grieve, J. 225
Griffin, G. 357
Groves, R. 33
Grusin, R. 46
Grzinic, M. 50
Guardian 190
Guerlac, S. 384
guest speakers 337–338
Guez, E. 50
Guillen, F. 313, 328–329

Hackney, S. E. 331, 334–335, 339, 342
Hahn, U. 264
Hall, E. 169n22
Hall, J. 303
Hallett, R.E. 80
Hamilton, W. L. 266
hand-drawn network maps 63–64, *65*, 67–73; bubbles 67–69, *68*; colours *71*, 71–73; hashtags 69–71; shapes 67–69, *68*; symbols *69*, 69–71
handmaidens of historians 143
Hannerz, U. 79
Hansa network 100
'Happy Valley Band' (HVB) 56
Harackiewicz, J. M. 394
Harland, T. 357
Harlem Shadows (McKay) 341–342
Harper & Row Publishers v. The Nation Enterprises 429–430
Hartsell-Gundy, A. 138
Harvey, A. 59n25
Harvey, R. 128
Harwood, G. 54, 58n8, 58n24
hashtags 69–71
Hathi Trust 116
HathiTrust Digital Library 121
HathiTrust Research Centre 121
Hauck, J. 139
Haviland, W. A. 81
Hawkins, A. R. 332
Hawthorn effect 404

Hay, D. *36*, 36–37
Haythornthwaite, C. 392–393
Hearing voices in an 18th century coutrtroom: Sound, space and experience at the Old Bailey (Hitchcock) 58n22
Hellrich, J. 264
Hemming, J. 359
Hendrix, J. 52
Henkel, M. 240, 256
Henry, J. 363–364
Henslowe, P. 283
heritage 300; *see also* cultural heritage
Hewson, C. 86
Hicks, M. 160
hierarchies 139–140
Higher Education Authority (Ireland) 16
Higher Education Research Methodology (Daniel and Harland) 357
high performance computing (HPC) 161
Hijacking Listening Machines for Performative Research (Bowers and Green) 56
Hine, C. 77
Hirsch, B. D. 332, 337
Hirst, P. 141
Hirtle, P. 437
historians, handmaidens of 143
historical texts 261–272; bridging gap between disciplines 267–271; complications of 263; interdisciplinary pitfalls 265–267; semantics 261–265
History Harvest 375
History of Art at UCC 15
Hitchcock, T. 58n22
'Hive' (Forrest) 21, *21*
Hoberman, P. 59n26
Hochschule Mainz – University of Applied Sciences 48
Homages to the Square (Albers) *21*
homo faber 156
homo sapiens 156
Hoover, D. 289n5
Housman, A. E. 278
How not to teach digital humanities (Cordell) 332
How to Get Grant Money in the Humanities and Social Sciences (Folsom) 357
HTML 286, 339
Humanist 2
humanistic expertise 270–271
humanities computing 169n10
HumlabX 160
Humphrey, C. 128, *129*, 130
Huxham, C. 191
hypermediacy 7

IconClass 175
iconography 173–174
ideas *see* big ideas
identity: academic 239–240; professional 386, 388–389, 393–394; social 388; *see also* self-identity
IFLA-LRM 104

Index

image upload 322
Imagining the DH Undergraduate: Special Issue in Undergraduate Education in DH (Murphy and Smith) 332
Impalpability (Fujihata) 50
Improvisation Technologies: A Tool for the Analytic Dance Eye (Forsythe) 33
in-class labs 311–312, 319, **320–321**
inclusion in online learning 22–23
incomplete data 119; *see also* data
inconsistent data 119; *see also* data
Index Thomisticus 59n27
India 40
individual virtuosity 52–53
Industrial Memories 302
information and communication technologies (ICT) 190–191, 400; in humanities scholarship **193**; infrastructure and 192–194; use in data analysis 197
information literacy 310, *315*
information management 128; *see also* data management
Information Object 180
informed consent 84–86
infrastructure: defined 193; indicators 194; information communication technologies (ICT) and 192–194; inversion 195; laboratory 159–161; limits of 194; potential 199–200
Inscriptiones Graecae 282
"Inside-Out" Spike Island (exhibition) 17
Instagram 62
Institutional Review Board (IRB) 417, 418, 419
instruction 339–340
instructors **336**, **338**, **340**, **345**, 345–347, 359–360, 387, 394
integrated course learning goals *315*
The Intellectual Foundation of Information Organization (Svenonious) 127
intellectual property 422–423; archival donor agreements 434–435; best practices 438–439; Creative Commons 432–433, **433**; defined 428; digital humanities and 428, 437–438; digital rights management 435–436; digitization projects 436–437; fair use 422–423, 429–431; guidelines 428–439; labor theory 422; personality theory 422; public domain 431–432; rights 422–423; seeking permission 433–434; terms and concepts 428–437; utilitarian theory 422
intellectual skills 53
interaction: equivalency theorem 387, 395; face-to-face 86, 246, 257, 389; symbols as facilitators of 69–71
interdisciplinarity 137–149; *see also* libraries
interdisciplinary gaps 267
interdisciplinary pitfalls 265–267
interface-based skill 51
International Federation of Library Associations and Institutions 132
International Organization for Standardization 405
Internet Archive 311
Internet Mediated Research (IMR) 83
Internet Service Providers (ISP) 55

Interom (Muntadas) 50
interoperability 177–179, 186–188, 205
interpretation *see* formulating interpretation
interviews 83–86, 244; access 85–86; informed consent 85–86; offline 86–87; trust 86
In the Spotlight (project) 366, 371, 376, 378n47
intrinsic motivations 368; *see also* motivations
intrinsic value 391; *see also* values
introductory course 337
Invisible Airs 54–55
Ionad Bairre 16
iPython 197
IRCAM 53
Ireland 302, 335, **336**
Isaksen, L. 122n31
isoglosses 229
Italian Gals in London (community) 87, 88n1
Italiani a Londra (community) 88n1
Italians 76, 82–83, 85–88
Italians of London (community) 86
Italy *213*
Ivy League institution 192

Jacko, Julie 409
James, W. 275
Jane Austen's Fiction Manuscripts 280
JavaScript 160, 276
Jenett, F. 48
Jenkins, R. 240
Jennings Gallery 16–17
Jenset, G. B. 261, 265, 267, 270
Jeremijenko, N. 59n26
Jockers, M. 142
Johnson, D. 286
Johnson, M. 218
Johnson, S. 109, 278
Jonson, B. 155
Jorgensen, J. 297
'Josef and Anni Albers: Voyage Inside a Blind Experience' (exhibition) 14, 18
JSON 276
JSTOR 249
Jupyter Notebook **193**
justice 418
Justine (de Sade) 113
'Just What the Doctor Ordered: Arts & Creative Expressions by Medical Graduates' Jennings Gallery (2017) 17

Kant, D. 56
Karlsruhe 116, 119
Kawulich, B. 357
KDL 16n15, 159, *161*, 163–164, 166, *167*, 169n13, 169n22–23, 169n26, 169n29
Keating, J. J. 17
Keats Library 286
Kehrein, R. 230

Index

Kelly, E. 387
Kemman, M. 243
Kern, D. 37
kernel density 224, 233
Ketzan, E. 197
Kickstarter 67, 70
Kim, E. 197
King's Digital Lab 131, 135n1, 155–168
Kirk, D. 356
Kirk, J. 218
Kizart, W. 52
Klein, J. T. 140, 149
Klein, U. 156
Knorr-Cetina, K. 158–159
Knott, C. 112
knowledge management 125; *see also* data management
knowledge organization 127–128
Knuuttila, T. 92
Koch, J. T. 165
Kolivras, K. N. 230
Königsberg bridge problem 93–94, *93–95*, 105
Kosinski, M. 422
Kralemann, B. 92
Kress Foundation 174
Kretzschmar, W. A., Jr. 218, 229, 233
Krohn, J. 205
Krohn, K. 205
Kuhn, T. S. 240
Kulturwissenschaftliche Bibliothek Warburg 173–174
Kuntzel, T. 50
laboratory 155–168; build 164–166; design 162–164; infrastructure 159–161; maintain 166–167; monitor 167–168; sociology 157–159; studies 157; *see also* digital labs; King's Digital Lab; STEM laboratories
labor theory of intellectual property 422
Labov, W. 221, *222*
Lachmann, K. 277
Lakoff, G. 218
Lameli, A. 230
language study *see* geographic information system (GIS)
Lansdale, M. 126
Lapata, M. 269, 271
Large Hadron Collider 157, 193
Lascarides, M. 370
LaTeX 249
LatinISE 264
Latour, B. 157
Lattmann, C. 92
Lave, J. 388
lazy registration 372
Leach, J. 33
Leaflet Library 230
learning: active 389–392; activity 310–312; authentic 394–395; cohorts 393; components 240; experiential 332, 394–395; machine 55, 119–120, 163, 297; *see also* virtual learning
Leeson, L. H. 59n26

Legrady, G. 50
Lehigh University **336, 346**
le jeune 118
Letter in the Attic 375
Letters 1916–1923 (project) 367
Levenshtein distance 224–225, *227*
lexical polysemy 262
lexical semantics 262
lexical semantics change 269–270
LGBTQ+ 300
Librairie générale française 113
librarians 342–343
libraries 137–149, 342–343; hierarchies 139–140; importance of user studies in 145–148; information studies 144–145; interdisciplinarity 140–143; preservation and access in 437; values-based methods 144–145
Library and Information History (Burrows) 121
Library and Information Science program 341
Library Digitization project 191
Library of Congress (LOC) 113–114, 116–117, 182, 185, 421
Licklider, J. C. R. 1–2
Line Involvement VI (Albers) *27*
Linguistic Atlas Eastern States data 220
Linguistic Atlas Project 223–224
linguistic data 220–222; *see also* data
linguistic landscapes 209–211
linguistic maps 220
linguistic thematic *229*
LinkedIn 246
Linked Open Data (LOD) 114, 120–121, 212, 257, 282–283
Linker (software) 58n24
Linode 161
liquid modernity 158
Listening in on the conversations: An overview of digital humanities pedagogy (Bonds) 332
literacy *see* information literacy
A Literary Atlas of Europe 111
Literary Data Processing Centre (CAAL) 304
Liu, A. 55, 295, 349n3
Liu, V. 55–56
Lives of the First World War (project) 367
Live Wire (Dangling String) (Jeremijenko) 59n26
Livingstone, S. 156
Livre de Poche 113
Livre et Société (Mornet and Furet) 116
Lodge, D. 1
London 66, 76, 82, 87
London Link (community) 88n1
longue durée 156
Los Angeles 313–314
The Loss of Small Detail (Forsythe) 48
Lowenthal, D. 299
Luebbering, C. R. 230
Lugli, L. 163–164

Index

MacDonald, S. 302
machine learning 55, 119–120, 163, 297
machine listening 56
MAchine-Readable Cataloguing (MARC) 115, 119
macrotasks 366–367
MADS RDF 114–115
Mahoney, S. 357
maintaining laboratory 166–167
managing organisational impact 370
Man Computer Symbiosis (Licklider) 1
manual cartographies 203–206; *see also* cartography
Mao, Y. 283
Mapes, K. **336**, **338–340**, **344**, **346**
MapInfo® Pro (software) 224
map/mapping: Cartesian 215; computer 221; creating 92; geographic information system (GIS) 360; Google 220; hand-drawn network 63–64, *65*, 67–73; linguistic landscapes 209–211, 220; networks and 103; socio-ecological landscapes 203–215; touring 38–42; vector 220
Mapping Colonial Americas Publishing 111
Mapping Multilingualism project 209–211
Mapping Print, Charting Enlightenment (grant) 110
Mapping the Lakes: A Literary GIS 111
Mapping Touring (project) 35, 38–42
Map Visualisation map 39–40, *40*
Marchand, P. 115
Marcus, G. 77–78, 80–81
markup and transcription 288
The Martian (Ketzan & Schöch) 197
Martin, A. 110, 116
Martin, G. 115
masculine paradigms 296
Massey, D. 80
Massive Online Online Course (MOOC) 296
Material for the Spine: A Movement Study (Paxton) 34
MAXQDA 255
Maxwell, J. C. 156, 275
Maynooth University **336**, **346**
Maynor, A. 192
McCarthy, M. 16
McCarty, W. 142, 358–359
McGann, J. 105, 277
McGillivray, B. 261, 265, 267, 270–271
McGonigal, J. 368
McGregor, W. 34
McKay, Aprille C. 438
McKay, C. 341
McKenzie, D. F. 277
McKerrow, R. B. 277
McLuhan, M. 5
McMahon, J. P. 16
McMullan, G. 164
McPherson, T. 58n9, 295
McTighe, J. 354–355
mechanical arts 155
mechanical task 366

Mechanical Turk 365
media import 309–311, 322
Media Platform Synochronoptic 50
MEDIATE Project 109–112, 117, 119–120
Mekhane (online database) 204, *211*, 211–214, *213*, *215*
Melville, H. 290n28
Melville Electronic Library 280, 290n28
Melville's Marginalia Online (MMO) 284–286
Memoirs of Libraries (Edwards) 115
Meneses, J. 387
metacognition 319
metacognitive approaches to learning and teaching 16
Metadata Authority Description Schema (MADS) 182–186
Metadata Encoding and Transmission Standard (METS) 178–179, 184–186
Metadata Object Description Schema (MODS) 184–186
metatasks 366–367
Michigan State University (MSU) **336**, **346**
Micropasts 367
Microsoft Azure 161
Microsoft Office 249
microtasks 366–367, 373, 378n55
micro-volunteering 365
Middle East 40
migration research *see* multi-sited ethnography in migration research
militarism 359
Millar v. Taylor 431
Mills, E. 376
Milton, J. 286
Mirza, R. 360
Moby-Dick (Shakespeare) 286
model/modelling: conceptual 103–104; data 179–182; defined 91; with networks 91–95; pragmatic view of 92; serializing 182–185; *see also* networks
MODS 114–115
monitoring laboratory 167–168
Montfort, N. 333
Montoya, A. 110–111
Moore, G. E. 125, 353
Moore's Law 353
morally opaque 424
moral values 424
Moreno, J. L. 95
Mornet, D. 110, 116
MoSCoW 163, 166
Motion Bank (project) 36–37, 42, 48–49
motivations 368, 389–392
Movement on the Move (project) 33, 35, 38, 42
"Moving Images" 315, 324–330
"Moving Pictures" 317–319, 329
MPEG Streamclip 325, *325–326*
multi-dimensional scaling (MDS) 225, *227*
multimedia 329–330; website assignment 391–392
multi-sensory experiences 23–28

Index

multi-sited ethnography in migration research 76–88; approaches 78–81; defined 78–79; in digital 81–82; interviews 83–86; offline interviews 86–87; online forum analysis 83–85; online participant observation 83–85; participant observation 86–87; research design 82–83

Muntadas, A. 50

Murphy, E. C. 332

Murphy, J. S. 277

Murphy, M. 16

Murphy, S. 16

Murthy, D. 77, 81

Museum of Design in Plastics 367

Mylne, V. 110, 116

mySql 120, 173, 175–177, 179, 183

Nakaya, F. 50

Named Entity Recognition (NER) 282

Narayanan, Y. 299

National Academy for the Integration of Research Teaching and Learning (NAIRTL) 16–17

National Commission for the Protection of Human Subjects of Biomedical and Behavioral Research 418

National Endowment for the Humanities Start Up Grant 341

National Library of Australia 366

National Research Act 418

negotiation 3–4, 6, 8, 78, 87, 166, 168, 278, 359

neoliberalism 359

Nerbonne, J. 225

Nersessian, N. J. 106

Netherlands 111, 119, 335, **336**

network-based research 96, 101

networked publics 71

networks 95–96, 117–118; actor-oriented 101; defined 95; fixation 100; manipulation 100; maps and 103; neural 104; sociality 62; in textual studies 101–102; in use 100–101; visualisations 96, 99–100; *see also* model/modelling

neural networks 104

New Companion to Digital Humanities 333

New England 133

Newton, I. 191

New York Public Library 366

The New York Times 190

New Zealand 111

New Zealand Law & Literature/Law & Visual Media Database 110

Nezvanova, N. 58n18

nichesourcing 365

Nicolls, S. 53

Niculescu, M. 52

Nielsen, J. 373

Nine(9) (software) 58n24

Nineteenth Century Newspapers (BNCN) 146–147

NLP 280

Noël, G. 163

Nolan, N. S. 411

non-credentialed 138

non-representational theory 47

non-traditional learning communities 17

Norrland 209

Norse World project 230, *231*

North America 334

Norton, D. 51

Notes from Nature 373

No Time to Fly (Hay) 36–37

Novum Organum (Bacon) 155

Nowviskie, B. 138

Nuremberg Code 418

Nurmikko-Fuller, T. 121

NVivo 83, 249, 252, 258

Nyhan, J. 303

Object Based Learning Approaches (OBL) 15

objectivity *see* feminist objectivity

Occidental College 309, 313

offline interviews 86–87; *see also* interviews

"Oh, Pretty Woman" (song) 430

Old Testament 176

Old Weather 366, 373, 377n23

olfactory 25–26

Olga (software) 38

Oliver, G. 128

Oliver, J. 59n25

Omeka 193, **193**, 255, 355

onboarding 373

One Flat Thing, reproduced (Forsythe) 33, *34*, 49

One Week One Tool program 360, 361n1, 361n3

Ong, T. 169n14

online courses 385; *see also* e-Learning

online education *see* e-Learning

online forum analysis 83–85

online learning 22–23; *see also* e-Learning

online participant observation 83–85

online service providers (OSP) 435–436

online teaching 13–14

open data 54, 112, 133, 255, 278

Open Educational Resources 433

OpenLayers 212

Open Online Communities (OOCs) 130

open science 255

Open Sound Control (OSC) 51

Optical Character Recognition (OCR) 102, 119–120, 255, 376

Oral Site 38

Orbison, Roy 430

ORBIS project 103

Oregon State University 197

organizational assessments 394

organizations 126–127, 191, 193, 264, 297, 357, 394

Orlando 297

O'Shea, J. 31

Otth, J. 50

Owens, T. 356
Oxford English Dictionary (OED) 198, 364

page titles 330
palaeoenvironmental data 216n3; *see also* data
Palazzi, M. 49
Palmer, C. L. 242
Pálsson, G. 205
Panofsky, E. 174
paradigms: challenges 121; evaluation 269–270; masculine 296; research 240–241
Paradise Lost (Milton) 286
participants: discussion 375; observation 86–87; recruitment 371
Pascal, B. 359
Patai, D. 303
Pausanias 204
Paxton, S. 34
pedagogy 331–349; alignment of syllabi 345; background 332–334; corpus 334–337, **336**, 343–345; e-Learning 386–389; graduate syllabi 340–343; teaching and research 345–347, **346**; undergraduate syllabi 337–340; *see also* e-Learning
Pederson, L. 218
Peirce, C. S. 275
Pelagios 282–283
Pelati, G. 86
people, following the 79–81
performative idiom 47
Periegesis (project) 212
Periegesis Hellados (Description of Greece) (Pausanias) 204
PeriodO 212
Perrone, V. 269, 271
Perseus Digital Library 263
personality theory of intellectual property 422
perspective 13–29; arts in education pedagogies at UCC 15–18; Glucksman Gallery at UCC 13–15; online teaching 17–22
Pettegree, A. 110
Pew Research Center 385
Philippines 120
physical objects 23–25
physical puppetry 52; *see also* puppetry
Pickering, A. 155, 157
Piecemaker (web-based application) 37
Pierazzo, E. 275, 278, 289n2, 357
Piez, W. 289n5
Pinterest 66
Pirmann, C. M. 242
Pitney Bowes 224
Pitts, F. R. 95
Planet eStream 37
planning: communications 371; crowdsourcing projects 369; data re-use 370–371; graceful exit 376; participant recruitment 371; workflows 370–371
'Please Touch: Tactile Encounters' (exhibition) 14, 18
Pleiades 212

poem *96–97, 97, 98*
Poeter, D. 125
point pattern analysis *226*
Pollard, A. W. 277
polysemy 262
poor-quality data 119
Posner, M. 198–199, **336**, 337, **338–340**, 339–340, 342, 344, **346**, 346–347, 350n17
post-processing 288
Potomac river 112
powers, artistic research 53–55
PRAAT 250
Praat 249
practical reality check 372
practical skills 359; *see also* skills
practice-as-research 32
practice turn 47
pragmatism 290n23
Pratt Institute **336, 346**
preservation, archives and libraries 437
Preservation & Art - Media Archaeology Lab (PAMAL) 50
PREservation Metadata: Implementation Strategies (PREMIS) 185–186
Prezi 390
Price Lab for Digital Humanities 191–192
Principal Research Software Engineer 164–165
print cartography 205; *see also* cartography
Prisley, S. P. 230
privacy 420–421; *see also* ethics
Product Quote (PQ) 163–164, 166
Proferes, N. 421
professional enhancement 17
professional identity 386, 388–389, 393–394
professionalization 340–342
professional values 143
Programming with Humanists: Reflections on raising an army of hacker-scholars in the digital humanities (Ramsay) 333
project: analysis 288; challenge 375; course design 338–339; management 198–199, 359–360; planning 288; role 340–342; success 368–369; work days *339*; *see also specific project*
project-based collaboration 192
Project Gutenberg 116
Project Management Institute 198–199, 359
Project Zero 16–17
property rights *see* intellectual property
public domain 431–432; *see also* copyright; intellectual property
public work 343, **344**
Puckette, M. 53
Puppet Motel (Anderson) 58n16
puppetry 51–52
Pybossa 365
Pythagoras' theorem 94
Python (software) 224, 276, 280, 282, 284

Index

QGIS (software) 224, 255
qualitative studies 265–266
quality: assurance 166; control 374; digitally mediated social relations 63–64; e-Learning 388–389
Quan-Haase, A. 199
quarter of 220–221, *221*
quarter till 220
quarter to 220
Quaternary period 216n5
Queen Elizabeth I 155

Rabanus, S. 230
Radboud University 110
raison d'etre 156
Ramsay, S. 333, 356
Ranganathan, S. R. 145
Raspberry Pi 54–55
readers 117–118
reading experience database (RED) 111
Reading Faces 315–317
reality check 372
reassembling parts 323
recognition 374
Re-De-Reverberation 56
Red Meander II (Albers) *24*
Reflectance Transformation Imaging (RTI) 281
reflecting interpretation 66
Reiniger, L. 51
religious iconography 175
remediations, artistic research 49–50
Republic of Letters (project) 103
RERO 116
research 82–83, 364; area *245*; choreographer-led 32; communities 240–242, 245, *246*, 252–254; conducting 248–250; data management 128–130; ethical 450; ethnographic 78–79; facility 157; findings 196–198; frameworks 42, 364–365; infrastructures 253, 256; life cycle 357; methods 160, 195–197, 243–244; multi-layered 81; paradigms 240–241; questions 268; social identity 388; steps 82–83; sustaining 132; teaching and 345–347, **346**; topics 197
research data management (RDM) 128–130, 166
ResearchGate 257
Research Software Analyst (RSA) 162, 164
Research Sprints 360
Resource Description Framework (RDF) 104, 121, 178
respect for persons 418
respondents 245
rewards 374
Ribes, D. 127
Rickert, R. T. 283, *284*
Ricks, C. 277–278
rights: digital 435–436; fair use 422–423; intellectual property 422–423
right to be let alone 420
Risam, R. 298, 347
Robinson, L. 140

Rockwell, G. 424
Rodda, M. A. 270
Rodriguez, Julia E. 438
Rogers, R. 77, 81
Roma JS application 280
Ross, S. 301, 332–333
Rotman, D. 375
Rouffineau, G. 50
Route Visualisation 40–41, *41*
Rowan, A. 15
Royal Society Corpus 264
Roy Rosenzweig Center for History and New Media 360, 361n1–2
RStudio 197, 250
Ruhleder, K. 194–196, 198–200
RunCoCo 367
Russia 40
Rutner, J. 243
Ryan, T. 17

Sabharwal, Arjun 434
Sade-Beck, L. 87
Saldaña, J. 195
Sampson, G. 267
Sant, T. 35, 39
Saparova, D. 411
Saxl, F. 174
Sayers, J. 356
Scalar (online platform) 309–330, 341; annotation 328; assignment 315–319; case study 319–330; course scaffolding 313–315; documentation of collective process 312; learning activity 310–312; media 327–328, 329; planning a term 310–312; usage 310
Scalar-based assignment design 319
Scalar-partner Critical Commons 311
Scandinavia 40
Schiller, N. G. 79–80
Schiphorst, T. 58n7
Schlechtmusik 56
Schöch, C. 197
Schofield, T. 356
scholarly practices 242–243
scholarship: co-production of 191–194; humanities **193**
Scholarship of Teaching and Learning (SoTL) 14
Scholten, P. C. 34
Schonfeld, R. C. 243
School of Pharmacy 17
Schreibman, S. **336, 340**, 342, **346**, 346–347
Schrooten, M. 84
Schunk, D. H. 387, 391
Schwarz, D. 53
Science and Technology Studies (STS) 157, 167
Scrivener 249
Seaman, J. 385
seeking permission 433–434
Séguy, J. 225
self-concept 388

Index

self-designation 240
self-efficacy 386–392, 394
self-identify 132, 240, 252, 254, 258
self-identity 240, 254, 256–257
Self Meant to Govern (stage performance) 48
self-reflection 47, 449
self-regulation 386–387
Selisker, S. 333, 337
semantics 261–265; change 261–262, 266, 269–271; gap 367; historical research 264–265; inaccessibility of 263–264
SemCor 269
sense of control 394
Serendip-o-matic 360, 361n2
serialization 178, 182–185, 187
Service Level Agreement (SLA) 166
ShadowEngine (Grant) 51–52
shadow puppetry 51–52
Shadows, Touch and Digital Puppeteering (Grant) 51
Shakespeare, W. 285–286, 316–317, *318*, 323
Shakespeare in the Royal Collections (McMullan) 164, *165*
shallow diversity 59n30
Shambrarian 149n1
shapes 67–69, *68*
shaping 390
SHARP-L 2
Shaw, N. Z. 49
Shelley-Godwin Archive 287
Shipman, Barbara 438
Shocket, A. M. **336**, 341, 344, **346**, 347
Short, H. 142, 165
Shotton, D. 114
Sibler, P. 230
Siemens, L. 199
Siemens, R. 142, 277
Silverman, D. 83
Singh, A. **336**, 337, **340**, 341–344, **344**, **346**, 347, 350n17
Siobhan Davies Replay 33–34
sites and fieldworks 79
skepticism 385–386
Sketch Engine 264
skills: analytical 16, 33, 313–314; arithmetic 391; computational 138; development 42, 388; encoding 282; gaps 47; information literacy 310; intellectual 53; knowledge and 8; labour and 35; librarians 139; practical 359; project management 200, 359; puppetry 51; shortages 178, 191; supplementary 354; technical 52–53, 316; training and 3
Skype 85, 87
Slack (web-based management applications) 199
Slippery Traces (Legrady) 50
Slob, D. 357
Smid, A. 50
Smith, S. R. 332
Smithies, J. 160
Smithsonian Transcription Center 373, 375–376, 378n51
Snow, M. 50

social capital 64
social cognitive theory 386–387
social constructivist theory 386, 387–388
social identity 386, 388, 393
social psychology 423
social relations *see* digitally mediated social relations
Social Studies of Science (Fujimura) 162
Société typographique de Neuchâtel (STN) 110
Society of American Archivists 419, 435, 438
socio-ecological landscapes 203–216; digital geographies 203–206; manual cartographies 203–206; Mekhane (online database) *211*, 211–214, *213*, *215*; Strategic Environmental Archaeology Database (SEAD) 206–209, *207*; visualizations for geospatial analysis 214–215
sociolinguists 252–253
sociology, laboratory 157–159
Software Development Lifecycle (SDLC) 166, *167*
Sonny Bono Copyright Term Extension Act 431
Sony Corp of America v. Universal Studios 435
Sorting out the Digital Humanities (Svensson) 333
Sorting Things (Star and Bowker) 127
SoTL *see* Scholarship of Teaching and Learning (SoTL)
source collections 370
South America 40
space of flows 80
SPAN 320 313, *318*, **320–321**, 324
Spanish language development *315*
SPARKLE project 240
SPARQL 121, 257
spatial referencing 222–223
spatial turn 218
Spector, J. D. 299
Speculum Mentis (Collingwood) 158
Speelman, D. 225
Spider 255
Spiro, L. 331, 334–335, 343–345, 349n1
SPSS 249–250
SQL 223
Srigley, K. 303
standards 193
Stanford Literary Lab 268
Star, S. L. 127, 159, 194–196, 198–200
statistical approaches 224–227
Statute of Anne 431
Steen, G. 218
Stein, B. 58n16
STEM laboratories 157, 160; *see also* laboratory
Stets, J. E. 386, 388
storytelling 18
Stoyanova, S. 281–282
Strategic Environmental Archaeology Database (SEAD) 204, 206–209, *207–208*, 214, *214*
student-centered learning 388
Studio for Electro-Instrumental Music (STEIM) 52, 58n18
study 343–345
style 330

Index

stylistic consistency 330
Subotnick, M. 58n16
subtleties 113
Sula, C. A. 331, 334–335, **336**, 339, **340**, 341–343, **344**, **346**, 346–347
Summit on Digital Tools at the University of Virginia (2005) 399
Suomela, T. 424
supplementary skills 354
survey 243–250
sustaining research 132; *see also* research
Svenonious, E. 127
Svensson, P. 142, 333
Sweden 209, *210*, 230
Sweller, John 406
syllabi/syllabus 337–343, 345
Symbolic Object 180
symbols *69*, 69–71, 73
synchronous communication 392–393; *see also* communications
Synchronous Objects for One Flat Thing, reproduced (website) 33, 49
syphilis 419
systematic approach 270

Tableau Public 35
Taborn, K. F. 339
tactile model (Albers) *24*, *27*
TaDiRAH 334
Taglioni, M. 52
Tag! You're It (game) 367
Tajfel, H. 388
Talmy, L. 267
Tanner, S. 145
Tanselle, G. T. 277, 288–289
targeted crowdsourcing 365; *see also* crowdsourcing
task *see* achievement task
Tauer, J. M. 394
Taylor, C. 240
teaching *see* active learning; e-Learning; online teaching
Teaching Research Methods in the Social Sciences (Garner, Wagner and Kawulich) 357
technical skills 52–53, 316
technological change 353, 358, 435
technology *see* wearable technologies
Teffeau, L. C. 242
TEI-XML 162, 280
The Tempest (Shakespeare) 285
10 Most Wanted (project) 367
Ten Principles of Citizen Science 372
tensions in online teaching 17–22
Terras, M. 332, 335, 339, 344
testing, crowdsourcing 372–373
Text Encoding Initiative (TEI) 96–97, *97–99*, 99, 105, 165, 182, 276, 279–280, 283–287, 289n5, 290n28, 344
texts 330; English 283–289; historical 261–272; markup 322; mining 297

textual editing 275–289; for digital publication 275; encoding and analysis 283–289; EpiDoc 280–283
Thesaurus Linguae Graecae corpus 266
Thistlethwaite, P. 278
3D scanning 213
ti 249
Till, E. 360
TIME 429
time-based approaches 96
timeless time 80
time-space compression 80
title 330
tools and environment *see* digital tools and environment
Törmä, T. 38
trading zones 142
Transcribe Bentham 366
transcription 288, 366
transition from amateur to intermediate 328–329
Transkribus (project) 376
transmigrants 80
Transmission in Motion: The Technologizing of Dance (Bleeker) 32–33
Transparency in Learning and Teaching (TILT) 355
tree(s) 96–99
tree-based model 96
Trello (web-based management applications) 199
Très Grande Infrastructure de Recherche (TGIR) 254
Trinity Laban 37
Trismegistos 212
Trojan Horse markup 292n61
Troubles with Sex, Theory and History (Grzinic and Smid) 50
Trove 366, 369, 373, 376
trust 18, 86
Tsatsou, P. 81
Turn All Things (Liu) 55
Turner, J. C. 388
Tuskegee Syphilis experiments 419
tutorials 374
Twitter 62, 66, 69–70, 246, 249, 255, 262, 347, 421
2 Live Crew 430

ubiquity 55, 310
UCREL Semantic Analysis System 264
UK Copyright, Designs and Patents Act 1988 430
UK RED 111
UK Soundmap (project) 367
Umeå, Sweden *210*
Umeå University 160
un-boundedness 87
undergraduate course **336**, **338**, **340**, 343, **344**; *see also* course/module link
undergraduate syllabi 337–340
Understanding by Design 354
Understanding Media (McLuhan) 5
UNESCO 304n1–2
unexpected finding 197–198

Uniform Resource Identifiers (URIs) 212
United States 15, 40, 102, 133, 138, 157, 192, 199, 335, **336**, 360, 385, 389
universal design: digital tools and environment 400, 409; expertise levels 411–412; eye tracking 409–412; mobile eye tracking 410–411
Universal Short Title Catalogue (USTC) 109–110, 112, 116
Universiteit Leiden **336**
Universiteit Twente (public research university) 133
University College Cork (UCC) 13–14, 17–18; Adult and Continuing Education Centre 16; Centre for the Integration of Research, Teaching and Learning (CIRTL) 13; Glucksman Gallery (art museum) 13–15; History of Art 15; Jennings Gallery 16–17; metacognitive approaches to learning and teaching 16; Project Zero 16; visual thinking strategies 16
University of California (UCLA) 121, 191, 314, **336**, **346**
University of Illinois at Urbana-Champaign 355
University of Kansas Libraries 360, 361n4
University of Minnesota Libraries 360, 361n4
University of Nevada Las Vegas 355
University of Pennsylvania 191–192
University of Southern California 313–314
University of Texas **336**
Unsworth, J. 57n4, 243
urbanization 360
Uruguay Round Agreements Act (URAA) 432
usability/usability evaluation 373; digital tools 401–404, **403**; eye tracking 405–407
Using Digital Humanities in the Classroom (Battershill and Ross) 332–333
utilitarianism 417; theory of intellectual property 422
utility value 391

Vakkari, P. 140
validation 97, 374
values 345; alternative 358; cultural norms and 451; ethical 421, 450–451; expression 29; intangible cultural 49; library 148; moral 424; professional 143; *see also specific values*
The Values of French 166
van Dalen-Oskam, K. 289n5
Vanderheiden, G. 400
Vangen, S. 191
Van Zundert, J. 199
vector maps 220
Venable, L. 58n11
verification systems 374
Vershbow, B. 370
Vieira, M 169n14
Viennese Danse Macabre Corpus 264
Vierthaler, P. **336**, 337–338, **338–340**, 339, 344, **346**, 347
Viking warrior 299
Vimeo 38
Viral Texts Project 102
virtual ethnography 77

Virtual International Authority File (VIAF) 118
virtual learning 23–28
virtual reality 32
virtue ethics 417
visual cues 64–67, *67–69, 71*, 73
visual digital presentation assignment 389–390
visualisations 99–100; data 227–233, *251*; geospatial analysis 214–215
Visual Practices Across the University (Elkins) 15–16
visual thinking 16, 99–100
Voice Thread 390
Voronoi polygons 224, 232, *232*
Voyager Company 50
Voyant 280, 282, 286

Wagner, C. 357
Waisda? 367
Waisvisz, M. 58n18
Waldron, M. 16
Walker, C. E. 387
Walker, D. M. 82
Walking Harlem (Taborn) 339
Wang, Yilun 422
Warburg, A. 173–174
Warburg Iconographic Database 174–177, *176–177*
Warburg Institute in London 173–188; data model 179–182; Iconographic Database 174–177, *176–177*; iconography and 173–174; interoperability 177–179; serializing the model 182–185
Warburg Institute Photographic Collection 183
Warwick, C. 148–149
Watchorn, K. 18
Waterford Memories Project 302
Watson, Thomas E. 436–437
wearable technologies 32
Weber, A. 36, *36*
web log analysis 146
Weingart, S. 297, 335, 344, 346
Weiser, M. 53, 58n23
Wekinator (software) 53
Welsh Newspapers Online (WNO) 146
Wenger, E. 240
Wenger-Trayner, B. 241, 257
Wenger-Trayner, E. 241, 257
Wernimont, J. 297
Whatley, S. 33
What's on the Menu (project) 366, 370, 373
White, H. C. 64
White, R. 39, 218, 233
Whitelaw, M. 356
Whitley, E. **336**, 337, **340**, 341–343, 344, **346**, 347, 350n17
Wigfield, A. 391
Wiggins, G. 354–355
Wikimedia 372
Wikimedia Commons 193
Wikimedia Foundation 193

Index

Wikipedia 364
William Blake Archive 144
William Forsythe: Improvisation Technologies. A Tool for the Analytical Eye (Ziegler) 49
Wilson, R. 300
Wireless Fidelity (Goatley) 54–55
Witcomb, A. 298
Wittel, A. 62–63
Wittkower, R. 174
'Women Sing the Blues' (exhibition) 303
Women's Words: The Feminist Practice of Oral History (Gluck and Patai) 303
Women Writers project 281, 297
Woolgar, S. 157
word-net and dictionaries 102–103
Wordnets 102–103
WordPress 355
workflows 126, 128, 130, 164, 205, 242–243, 276, 278, 281, 287, 288, 297, 312, 369–371, 401
WorldCat 116, 119

World Intellectual Property Organization (WIPO) 428, 435
World Service Archive 367
World War Two 418
Worm Community System (WCS) 194, 199
Worthey, G. 142
WYSIWYG editor 316

XML *see* eXtensible Markup Language (XML)
XSLT 276, 285–286

YoHa (project) 54
Yokokoji, M. 54
YouTube 36, 37, 311

Zaenen, A. 264
Ziegler, C. 49
ZKM/Center for Art and Media 33
Zooniverse Project Builder 365, 368–370, 372
Zorich, D. 198
Zotero **193**, 194